W9-CCC-938

The Cross-Platform Prep Course

Welcome to the Cross-Platform Prep Course Edition! McGraw-Hill Education's multi-platform course gives you a variety of tools to raise your scores and get in to the school of your choice. Whether you're studying at home, the library, or on-the-go, you can find practice content in the format you need—print, online, or mobile.

Print Book

This print book gives you the tools you need to ace the test. In its pages you'll find smart test-taking strategies, in-depth reviews of key topics, and ample practice questions and tests. See the Welcome section of your book for a step-by-step guide to its features.

Online Platform

The Cross-Platform Prep Course's online platform gives you additional study and practice content that you can access *anytime, anywhere*. You can create a personalized study plan based on your test date that sets daily goals to keep you on track. Integrated lessons provide important review of key topics. Practice questions, exams, and flashcards give you the practice you need to build test-taking confidence. The game center is filled with challenging games that allow you to practice your new skills in a fun and engaging way. You can interact with other test-takers in the discussion section and gain valuable peer support.

Getting Started

To get started, open your account on the online platform:

Go to www.xplatform.mhprofessional.com

↓

Enter your access code, which you can find on the inside back cover of your book

↓

Provide your name and e-mail address to open your account and create a password

↓

Click "Start Studying" to enter the platform

It's as simple as that. You're ready to start studying online.

Your Personalized Study Plan

First, select your test date on the calendar, and you're on your way to creating your personalized study plan. Your study plan will help you stay organized and on track and will guide you through the course in the most efficient way. It is tailored to *your* schedule and features daily tasks that are broken down into manageable goals. You can adjust your end date at any time and your daily tasks will be reorganized into an updated plan.

Choose Your Test Date For GRE 2016 Prep by McGraw-Hill Education

We need you to tell us about your study schedule before you get started. Select the date of your exam or the date you wish to complete the course by. We will adjust our plan to fit your timeframe. You can change this date anytime from the Study Plan section.

03/25/2016

Mar ▾ | 2016 ▾
Su Mo Tu We Th Fr Sa
28 29 1 2 3 4 5
6 7 8 9 10 11 12
13 14 15 16 17 18 19
20 21 22 23 24 25 26
27 28 29 30 31 1 2
3 4 5 6 7 8 9

Continue

You can track your progress in real time on the Study Plan Dashboard. The Today's Knowledge Goal progress bar gives you up-to-the minute feedback on your daily goal. Fulfilling this is the most efficient way to work through the entire course. You can get an instant view of where you stand in the entire course with the Study Plan Progress bar.

> *If you need to exit the program before completing a task, you can return to the Study Plan Dashboard at any time. Just click the Study Task icon and you can automatically pick up where you left off.*

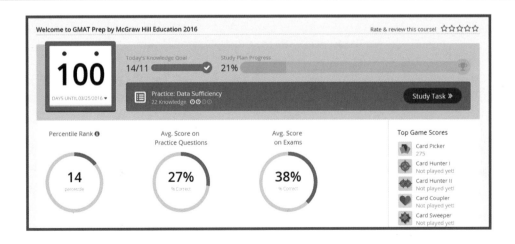

Practice Tests

One of the first tasks in your personalized study plan is to take the Diagnostic Test. At the end of the test, a detailed evaluation of your strengths and weaknesses shows the areas where you need to focus most. You can review your practice test results either by the question category to see broad trends or question-by-question for a more in-depth look.

The full-length tests are designed to simulate the real thing. Try to simulate actual testing conditions and be sure you set aside enough time to complete the full-length test. You'll learn to pace yourself so that you can get the best possible score on test day.

Full Length Test 1						Reset Test
	Question Review Category Scores					Review All
	# ▾	✓ ⬍	Preview (Click to toggle full preview)	Time ⬍	Difficulty ⬍	
38% Correct	246	✓	Direction : For the following question, select the best of the answer choices given. There are few things worse for a new parent...	0 min 13 sec	Unrated	Review
	247	✗	Direction : For the following question, select the best of the answer choices given. Charlie's Chainsaw Company has reason to be...	0 min 31 sec	Unrated	Review
	248	✗	Direction : For the following question, select the best of the answer choices given. A dog enthusiast took home two puppies from...	0 min 9 sec	Unrated	Review
Questions Taken 93 of 93	249	✓	Direction : For the following question, select the best of the answer choices given. Paleontologists hypothesize that modern bi...	0 min 12 sec	Unrated	Review
Avg. Answer Time 0 min 19 sec	250	✓	Direction : For the following question, select the best of the answer choices given. Bob and Linda are tired of the freezing co...	0 min 19 sec	Unrated	Review
Avg. Correct Answer Time 0 min 23 sec	251	✗	Direction : For the following question, select the best of the answer choices given. Although many people would not believe it, ...	0 min 13 sec	Unrated	Review
Avg. Incorrect Answer Time 0 min 16 sec	252	✓	Direction : The following question present a sentence, part of which or all of which is underlined. Beneath the sentence, you will find five w...	0 min 26 sec	Unrated	Review
	253	✓	Direction : The following question present a sentence, part of which or all of which is underlined. Beneath the sentence, you will find five w...	0 min 37 sec	Unrated	Review
	254	✓	Direction :The following question present a sentence, part of which or all of which is underlined. Beneath the sentence, you will find five wa...	0 min 19 sec	Unrated	Review

Lessons

The lessons in the online platform are divided into manageable pieces that let you build knowledge and confidence in a progressive way. They cover the full range of topics that appear on your test.

After you complete a lesson, mark your confidence level. (You must indicate a confidence level in order to count your progress and move on to the next task.) You can also filter the lessons by confidence levels to see the areas you have mastered and those that you might need to revisit.

> *Use the bookmark feature to easily refer back to a concept or leave a note to remember your thoughts or questions about a particular topic.*

Practice Questions

All of the practice questions are based on real-life exams and simulate the test-taking experience. The Review Answer gives you immediate feedback on your answer. Each question includes a rationale that explains why the correct answer is right and the others are wrong. To explore any topic further, you can find detailed explanations by clicking the "Help me learn about this topic" link.

You can go to the Practice Dashboard to find an overview of your performance in the different categories and sub-categories.

Practice

Practice	🖥 Dashboard	👆 Confidence Levels	✏ Notes	🔖 Bookmarks

Dashboard   Reset All Questions

77% Correct

Questions Taken
159 of 491

Avg. Answer Time
2 min 52 sec

Avg. Correct Answer Time
2 min 20 sec

Avg. Incorrect Answer Time
3 min 6 sec

Avg. Session Duration
18 min 41 sec

Question Categories

Category Name	Completion	% Correct	
Quantitative-Problem Solving	94 of 297	72%	»
Arithmetic	75 of 75	84%	
Elementary Algebra	35 of 189	60%	
Geometry	0 of 49	--	
Quantitative-Data Sufficiency	49 of 49	81%	
Arithmetic	6 of 6	75%	
Elementary Algebra	30 of 30	86%	
Geometry	13 of 13	82%	
Verbal	0 of 129	--	
Reading Comprehension	0 of 46	--	
Critical Reasoning	0 of 64	--	
Sentence Correction	0 of 19	--	

Dashboard

Visit the dashboard to see personalized information on your progress and performance. The Percentile Rank icon shows your position relative to all the other students enrolled in the course. You can also find information on your average scores in practice questions and exams.

A detailed overview of your strengths and weaknesses shows your proficiency in a category based on your answers and difficulty of the questions. By viewing your strengths and weaknesses, you can focus your study on your weaker spots.

Percentile Rank ⓘ	Avg. Score on Practice Questions	Avg. Score on Exams
14 percentile	**28%** % Correct	**38%** % Correct

Strengths & Weaknesses ⓘ

Quantitative-Data Sufficiency   Beginner

Data Sufficiency - Arithmetic	Beginner
Data Sufficiency - Elementary Algebra	Beginner
Data Sufficiency - Geometry	N/A

Quantitative-Problem Solving   Beginner

Problem Solving - Arithmetic	Beginner
Problem Solving - Elementary Algebra	N/A
Problem Solving - Geometry	Beginner

Verbal   Beginner

Flashcards

Hundreds of flashcards are perfect for learning key terms quickly, and the interactive format gives you immediate feedback. You can filter the cards by category and confidence level for a more organized approach. Or, you can shuffle them up for a challenge.

Flashcards: Category Quantitative Reasoning : Algebra   Study   Community Sets   My Sets

Card Sets: GMAT Prep by McGraw Hill Education 2016 (257) ▼   Filter: Quantitative Reasoning : Algebra   ▼   Subfilter: All   ▼

◄ ►   C ✕

5 of 12

$$x^2 + 2xy + y^2$$

Did you get it right?

| No | Kinda | Yes |

Another way to customize the flashcards is to create your own sets. You can keep these private or share or them with the public. Subscribe to Community Sets to access sets from other students preparing for the same exam.

Flashcards   Study   Community Sets   My Sets

Create Set

Title
Math review

Description

Topic – Select one of our topics from the dropdown or add your own
Math equations   ▼

Access
● Public
○ Private

Create Set   Cancel

Game Center

Play a game in the Game Center to test your knowledge of key concepts in a challenging but fun environment. Up the difficulty level and complete the games quickly to build the highest score. Be sure to check the leaderboard to see who's on top.

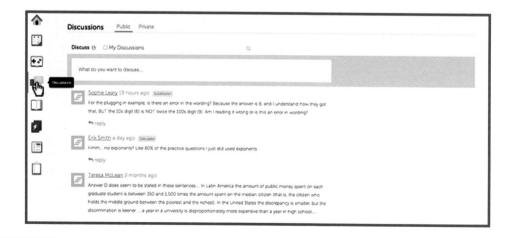

Social Community

Interact with other students who are preparing for your test. Start a discussion, reply to a post, or even upload files to share. You can search the archives for common topics or start your own private discussion with friends.

Mobile App

The companion mobile app lets you toggle between the online platform and your mobile device without missing a beat. Whether you access the course online or on your smartphone or tablet, you'll pick up exactly where you left off.

Go to the iTunes or Google Play stores and search "BenchPrep Companion" to download the companion iOS or Android app. Enter your e-mail address and the same password you created for the online platform to open your account.

Now, let's get started!

5 STEPS TO A 5™

AP Chemistry

2018

ELITE STUDENT EDITION

5 STEPS TO A 5™

AP Chemistry

2018

John T. Moore, EdD
Richard H. Langley, PhD

Mc Graw Hill Education

New York   Chicago   San Francisco   Athens   London   Madrid
Mexico City   Milan   New Delhi   Singapore   Sydney   Toronto

Copyright © 2017 by McGraw-Hill Education. All rights reserved. Printed in the United States of America. Except as permitted under the United States Copyright Act of 1976, no part of this publication may be reproduced or distributed in any form or by any means, or stored in a database or retrieval system, without the prior written permission of the publisher.

1 2 3 4 5 6 7 8 9   LHS   22 21 20 19 18 17 (Cross-Platform Prep Course only)
1 2 3 4 5 6 7 8 9   LHS   22 21 20 19 18 17 (Elite Student Edition)

ISBN   978-1-259-91125-5 (Cross-Platform Prep Course only)
MHID   1-259-91125-X

e-ISBN   978-1-260-00992-7 (e-book Cross-Platform Prep Course alone)
e-MHID   1-260-00992-0

ISBN   978-1-259-86402-5 (Elite Student Edition)
MHID   1-259-86402-2

e-ISBN   978-1-259-86403-2 (e-book Elite Student Edition)
e-MHID   1-259-86403-0

McGraw-Hill Education, the McGraw-Hill Education logo, *5 Steps to a 5*, and related trade dress are trademarks or registered trademarks of McGraw-Hill Education and/or its affiliates in the United States and other countries and may not be used without written permission. All other trademarks are the property of their respective owners. McGraw-Hill Education is not associated with any product or vendor mentioned in this book.

AP, Advanced Placement Program, and *College Board* are registered trademarks of the College Board, which was not involved in the production of, and does not endorse, this product.

The series editor was Grace Freedson, and the project editor was Del Franz.
Series design by Jane Tenenbaum.

McGraw-Hill Education products are available at special quantity discounts to use as premiums and sales promotions or for use in corporate training programs. To contact a representative, please visit the Contact Us pages at www.mhprofessional.com.

JOHN MOORE grew up in the foothills of western North Carolina. He attended the University of North Carolina–Asheville, where he received his bachelor's degree in chemistry. He earned his master's degree in chemistry from Furman University in Greenville, South Carolina. After a stint in the United States Army he decided to try his hand at teaching. In 1971 he joined the faculty of Stephen F. Austin State University in Nacogdoches, Texas, where he still teaches chemistry. In 1985 he started back to school part-time, and in 1991 received his doctorate in education from Texas A&M University. In 2003 his first book, *Chemistry for Dummies*, was published.

RICHARD LANGLEY grew up in southwestern Ohio. He attended Miami University in Oxford, Ohio, where he earned bachelor's degrees in chemistry and mineralogy and a master's degree in chemistry. He next went to the University of Nebraska in Lincoln, where he received his doctorate in chemistry. He took a postdoctoral position at Arizona State University in Tempe, Arizona, then became a visiting assistant professor at the University of Wisconsin–River Falls. He has taught at Stephen F. Austin State University in Nacogdoches, Texas, since 1982.

The authors are coauthors of *Chemistry for the Utterly Confused*, *Biochemistry for Dummies*, and *Organic Chemistry II for Dummies*.

Both authors are graders for the free-response portion of the AP Chemistry exam. In fact, between them, they have over twenty-five years of AP grading experience and estimate that together they have graded over 125,000 exams.

CONTENTS

STEP 5 # Build Your Test-Taking Confidence

ELITE
STUDENT
EDITION

5 Minutes to a 5

Appendixes

PREFACE

Welcome to the AP Chemistry Five-Step Program. The fact that you are reading this preface suggests that you will be taking the AP exam in chemistry. The AP Chemistry exam is constantly evolving and so this guide has evolved. We have updated the book to match the new AP Chemistry exam. The new exam has an emphasis on sets—a series of questions that refer to the same given information, along with changes in the free-response portion.

The AP Chemistry exam certainly isn't easy, but the rewards are worth it—college credit and the satisfaction of a job well done. You will have to work and study hard to do well, but we will, through this book, help you to master the material and get ready for the exam.

Both of us have many years of experience in teaching introductory general chemistry at the university level. John Moore is the author of *Chemistry for Dummies*, and he and Richard "Doc" Langley have also written *Chemistry for the Utterly Confused*, a guide for college/high school students. Each of us has certain skills and experiences that will be of special help in presenting the material in this book. Richard has also taught high school science, and John has years of experience teaching chemistry to both public school teachers and students. Both of us have been graders for the AP Exam chemistry free-response questions for years and have firsthand knowledge of how the exam is graded and scored. We have tried not only to make the material understandable but also to present the problems in the format of the AP Chemistry exam. By faithfully working the problems you will increase your familiarity with the exam format, so that when the time comes to take the exam there will be no surprises.

Use this book in addition to your regular chemistry text. We have outlined three different study programs to prepare you for the exam. If you choose the yearlong program, use it as you are taking your AP Chemistry course. It will provide additional problems in the AP format. If you choose one of the other two programs, use it with your chemistry textbook also; but you may need to lean a little more on this review book. Either way, if you put in the time and effort, you will do well.

Now it's time to start. Read the Introduction: The Five-Step Program; Chapter 1, What You Need to Know About the AP Chemistry Exam; and Chapter 2, How to Plan Your Time. Then take the Diagnostic Exam in Chapter 3. Your score will show how well you understand the material right now and point out weak areas that may need a little extra attention. Use the review exams at the end of the chapters to check your comprehension. Also, pay attention to the free-response questions. That is where you can really shine, and they are worth almost as much as the multiple-choice part. Use the Rapid Reviews to brush up on the important points in the chapters. Just before taking the exam, review the section on avoiding "stupid" mistakes at the back of this book. Keep this book handy—it is going to be your friend for the next few weeks or months.

Good luck: but remember that luck favors the prepared mind.

ACKNOWLEDGMENTS

The authors would like to thank Grace Freedson, who believed in our abilities and gave us this project. Many thanks also to Del Franz, whose editing polished up the manuscript and helped its readability. Thanks to our colleagues at the AP Chemistry readings for their helpful suggestions.

INTRODUCTION: THE FIVE-STEP PROGRAM

The Basics

Not too long ago, you enrolled in AP Chemistry. A curiosity about chemistry, encouragement from a respected teacher, or the simple fact that it was a requirement may have been your motivation. No matter what the reason, you find yourself flipping through a book that promises to help you culminate this experience with the highest of honors, a 5 in AP Chemistry. Yes, it is possible to achieve this honor without this book. There are many excellent teachers of AP Chemistry out there who teach, coax, and otherwise prepare their students into a 5 every year. However, for the majority of students preparing for the exam, the benefits of buying this book far outweigh its cost.

The key to doing well on the Advanced Placement (AP) Chemistry exam is to outline a method of attack and not to deviate from this method. We will work with you to make sure you take the best path towards the test. You will need to focus on each step, and this book will serve as a tool to guide your steps. But do not forget—no tool is useful if you do not use it.

Organization of the Book

This book conducts you through the five steps necessary to prepare yourself for success on the exam. These steps will provide you with the skills and strategies vital to the exam, and the practice that will lead you towards the perfect 5.

First, we start by introducing the basic five-step plan used in this book. Then in Chapter 1, we will give you some background information about the AP Chemistry exam. Next, in Chapter 2, we present three different approaches to preparing for the exam. In Chapter 3, we give you an opportunity to evaluate your knowledge with a Diagnostic Exam. The results of this exam will allow you to customize your study. In Chapter 4, we offer you a multitude of tips and suggestions about the different types of questions on the AP Chemistry exam. Many times good test-taking practices can help raise your score.

Since the volume of the material to be mastered can be intimidating, Chapters 5 to 19 present a comprehensive review of the material that you will cover in an AP Chemistry course. This is review material, but since not all of this material appears in every AP Chemistry class, it will also help to fill in the gaps in your chemistry knowledge. You can use it in conjunction with your textbook if you are currently taking AP Chemistry, or you can use it as a review of the concepts you covered. At the end of each chapter, you will find both a multiple-choice and free-response exam for you to test yourself. The answers and explanations are included. This will also help you identify any topics that might require additional study.

After these content chapters, there are two complete chemistry practice exams, including multiple-choice and free-response questions. The answers and explanations are included. These exams will allow you to test your skills. The multiple-choice questions will provide you with practice on questions similar to those asked on past AP exams. These are not the exact questions, but ones that will focus you on the key AP Chemistry topics. There are also examples of free-response questions; there are fewer of these, since they take much longer to answer. After you take an exam, you should review each question. Ask yourself, why was this question present? Why do I need to know this? Make sure you check your answers against the explanations. If necessary, use the index to locate a particular topic and reread the review material. We suggest that you take the first exam, identify those areas that need additional study, and review the appropriate material. Then take the second exam and use the results to guide your additional study.

Finally, in the appendixes you will find additional resources to aid your preparation. These include:

- A tip sheet on how to avoid "stupid" mistakes and careless errors
- Common conversions
- How to balance redox equations
- A list of common ions
- A bibliography
- A number of useful websites
- A glossary of terms related to AP Chemistry
- A table of half-reactions for use while answering free-response questions
- A table of equations and abbreviations for use while answering free-response questions
- A periodic table for use when answering any exam questions

The Five-Step Program

Step 1: Set Up Your Study Program

In Step 1, you will read a brief overview of the AP Chemistry exams, including an outline of the topics. You will also follow a process to help determine which of the following preparation programs is right for you:

- Full school year: September through May.
- One semester: January through May.
- Six weeks: Basic training for the exam.

Step 2: Determine Your Test Readiness

Step 2 provides you with a diagnostic exam to assess your current level of understanding. This exam will let you know about your current level of preparedness and on which areas you should focus your study.

- Take the diagnostic exam slowly and analyze each question. Do not worry about how many questions you get right. Hopefully this exam will boost your confidence.
- Review the answers and explanations following the exam, so that you see what you do and do not yet fully understand.

Step 3: Develop Strategies for Success

Step 3 provides strategies that will help you do your best on the exam. These strategies cover both the multiple-choice and free-response sections of the exam. Some of these tips are based upon experience in writing questions, and others have been gleaned from our years of experience reading (grading) the AP Chemistry exams.

- Learn how to read and analyze multiple-choice questions.
- Learn how to answer multiple-choice questions.
- Learn how to plan and write answers to the free-response questions.

Step 4: Review the Knowledge You Need to Score High

Step 4 encompasses the majority of this book. In this step, you will learn or review the material you need to know for the test. Your results on the diagnostic exam will let you know on which material you should concentrate your study. Concentrating on some material does not mean you can ignore the other material. You should review all the material, even what you already know.

There is a lot of material here, enough to summarize a yearlong experience in AP Chemistry and highlight the, well, highlights. Some AP courses will have covered more material than yours, some will have covered less; but the bottom line is that if you thoroughly review this material, you will have studied all that is on the exam, and you will have significantly increased your chances of scoring well. This edition gives new emphasis to some areas of chemistry to bring your review more in line with the revised AP Chemistry exam format. For example, there is more discussion of reactions and the laboratory experience. Each chapter contains a short exam to monitor your understanding of the current chapter.

Step 5: Build Your Test-Taking Confidence

In Step 5, you will complete your preparation by testing yourself on practice exams. This section contains *two* complete chemistry exams, solutions, and sometimes more important, advice on how to avoid the common mistakes. In this edition, the free-response exams have been updated to more accurately reflect the content tested on the AP exams. Be aware that these practice exams are *not* reproduced questions from actual AP Chemistry exams, but they mirror both the material tested by AP and the way in which it is tested.

The Graphics Used in This Book

To emphasize particular skills and strategies, we use several icons throughout this book. An icon in the margin will alert you to pay particular attention to the accompanying text. We use these four icons:

This icon highlights a very important concept or fact that you should not pass over.

This icon calls your attention to a strategy that you may want to try.

This icon indicates a tip that you might find useful.

This icon points to material that is not directly tested on the AP Chemistry exam but may be required by your teacher in high school and certainly by your college teacher. Although you won't find this specific content on the AP exam, knowing it will improve your understanding of chemistry, helping you to better grasp the material that is directly tested on the exam.

Boldfaced words indicate terms that are included in the glossary at the end of this book.

STEP 1

Set Up Your Study Program

What You Need to Know About the AP Chemistry Exam

IN THIS CHAPTER

Summary: Learn what topics are on the test, how the ETS scores the test, and basic test-taking information.

Key Ideas

✪ Most colleges will award credit for a score of 4 or 5.
✪ Multiple-choice questions account for half of your final score.
✪ Points are not deducted for incorrect answers to multiple-choice questions. You should try to eliminate incorrect answer choices and then guess; there is no penalty for guessing.
✪ Free-response questions account for half of your final score.
✪ There is a conversion of your composite score on the two test sections to a score on the 1-to-5 scale.

Background of the Advanced Placement Program

The College Board began the Advanced Placement program in 1955 to construct standard achievement exams that would allow highly motivated high school students the opportunity to receive advanced placement as first-year students in colleges and universities in the United States. Today, there are 34 courses and exams with more than 2 million students from every state in the nation and from foreign countries taking the annual exams in May.

The AP programs are for high school students who wish to take college-level courses. In our case, the AP Chemistry course and exam involve high school students in college-level chemistry studies.

Who Writes the AP Chemistry Exam?

A group of college and high school chemistry instructors known as the AP Development Committee creates the AP Chemistry exam. The committee's job is to ensure that the annual AP Chemistry exam reflects what is taught in college-level chemistry classes at high schools.

This committee writes a large number of multiple-choice questions, which are pre-tested and evaluated for clarity, appropriateness, and range of possible answers.

The free-response essay questions that make up Section II go through a similar process of creation, modification, pre-testing, and final refinement, so that the questions cover the necessary areas of material and are at an appropriate level of difficulty and clarity. The committee also makes a great effort to construct a free-response exam that will allow for clear and equitable grading by the AP readers.

It is important to remember that the AP Chemistry exam undergoes a thorough evaluation after the yearly administration of the exam. This way, the College Board can use the results to make course suggestions and to plan future tests.

The AP Grades and Who Receives Them

Once you have taken the exam and it has been scored, your test will be graded with one of five numbers by the College Board:

- A 5 indicates that you are extremely well qualified.
- A 4 indicates that you are well qualified.
- A 3 indicates that you are adequately qualified.
- A 2 indicates that you are possibly qualified.
- A 1 indicates that you are not qualified to receive college credit.

A grade report, consisting of a grade of 1 to 5, will be sent to you in July. You will also indicate the college to which you want your AP score sent at the time of the exam. The report that the college receives contains your score for every AP exam you took that year and the grades you received in prior years, except for any that you request withheld. In addition, your scores will be sent to your high school.

Reasons for Taking the AP Chemistry Exam

Why put yourself through a year of intensive study, pressure, stress, and preparation? Only you can answer that question. Following are some of the reasons that students have indicated to us for taking the AP exam:

- Because colleges look favorably on the applications of students who elect to enroll in AP courses
- To receive college credit or advanced standing at their colleges or universities
- To compare themselves with other students across the nation
- For personal satisfaction
- Because they love the subject
- So that their families will be proud of them

There are other reasons, but no matter what they are, the primary reason for your enrolling in the AP Chemistry course and taking the exam in May is to feel good about yourself and the challenges that you have met.

While there may be some idealistic motivators, let's face it: most students take the exam because they are seeking college credit. This means you are closer to graduation before you even start attending classes. Even if you do not score high enough to earn college credit, the fact that you elected to enroll in AP courses tells admission committees that you are a high achiever and serious about your education.

Questions Frequently Asked About the AP Chemistry Exam

What Is Going to Appear on the Exam?

This is an excellent question. The College Board, having consulted with those who teach chemistry, develops a curriculum that covers material that college professors expect to cover in their first-year classes. Based upon this outline of topics, the multiple-choice exams are written such that those topics are covered in proportion to their importance to the expected chemistry understanding of the student. Confused? Suppose that faculty consultants agree that environmental issues are important to the chemistry curriculum, maybe to the tune of 10 percent. If 10 percent of the curriculum in an AP Chemistry course is devoted to environmental issues, you can expect roughly 10 percent of the multiple-choice exam to address environmental issues. Remember this is just a guide and each year the exam differs slightly in the percentages.

How Is the Advanced Placement Chemistry Exam Organized?

Table 1.1 summarizes the format of the AP Chemistry exam.

Table 1.1

SECTION	NUMBER OF QUESTIONS	TIME LIMIT
I. Multiple-Choice Questions	60	90 minutes
II. Free-Response Questions		105 minutes
Long Questions	3	20–25 minutes per question
Short Questions	4	3–10 minutes per question

The exam is a two-part exam designed to take about three hours. The first section has 60 multiple-choice questions. You will have 90 minutes to complete this section.

The second part of the exam is the free-response section. You will begin this section after you have completed and turned in your multiple-choice scan sheet. There will be a break before you begin the second section. The length of this break will vary from school to school. You will not be able to go back to the multiple-choice questions later.

You will receive a test booklet for the free-response section of the test. You will have 105 minutes to answer seven questions. These questions may cover any of the material in the AP Chemistry course. The free-response section consists of two parts. In both parts, you may use a calculator. There will probably be two lab questions—one an experimental design question and the other question an analysis of data or observations. There will be two questions involving representations of molecules—one involving a conversion between different types of representations, and the other requiring an analysis or creation of an atomic or molecular view explaining a representation. Finally, there will be a quantitative question involving reasoning to solve a problem.

Who Grades My AP Chemistry Exam?

Every June a group of chemistry teachers gathers for a week to assign grades to your hard work. Each of these "Faculty Consultants" spends a day or so in training on a question. Each reader becomes an expert on that question, and because each exam book is anonymous, this process provides a very consistent and unbiased scoring of that question. During a typical day of grading, there is a selection of a random sample of each reader's scores for cross-checking by other experienced "Table Leaders" to ensure that the graders maintain a level of consistency throughout the day and the week. Statistical analysis of each reader's scores on a given question assure that they are not giving scores that are significantly higher or lower than the mean scores given by other readers of that question. All these measures assure consistency and fairness for your benefit.

Will My Exam Remain Anonymous?

Absolutely. Even if your high school teacher happens to read your booklet, there is virtually no way he or she will know it is you. To the reader, each student is a number, and to the computer, each student is a bar code.

What About That Permission Box on the Back?

The College Board uses some exams to help train high school teachers so that they can help the next generation of chemistry students to avoid common mistakes. If you check this box, you simply give permission to use your exam in this way. Even if you give permission, no one will ever know it is your exam.

How Is My Multiple-Choice Exam Scored?

You will place your answers to the multiple-choice questions on a scan sheet. The scan sheet is computer graded. The computer counts the number of correct responses. There is no penalty for incorrect answers or for leaving an answer blank.

How Is My Free-Response Exam Scored?

You are required to answer seven free-response questions. The point totals will vary, but there is an adjustment of the points to match the assigned weighting of the question. For example, question #1 may be on a scale of 10 points, while question #2 may be on a scale of 7 points, and question #3 on a scale of 5 points. Since these questions are to count equally, a multiplier will be used to adjust the points to the same overall value.

So How Is My Final Grade Determined and What Does It Mean?

Your total composite score for the exam is found by adding the value from the multiple-choice section to the score from the free-response section and rounding that sum to the nearest whole number.

Keep in mind that the total composite scores needed to earn a 5, 4, 3, 2, or 1 change each year. A committee of AP, College Board, and Educational Testing Service (ETS) directors, experts, and statisticians determines these cutoffs. The same exam that is given to the AP Chemistry high school students is given to college students. The various college professors report how the college students fared on the exam. This provides information for the chief faculty consultant on where to draw the lines for a 5, 4, 3, 2, or 1 score. A score of 5 on this AP exam is set to represent the average score received by the college students who scored an A on the exam. A score of 3 or 4 is the equivalent of a college grade B, and so on.

How Do I Register and How Much Does It Cost?

If you are enrolled in AP Chemistry in your high school, your teacher is going to provide all of these details. You do not have to enroll in the AP course to register for and complete the AP exam. When in doubt, the best source of information is the College Board's website: www.collegeboard.org.

Students who demonstrate financial need may receive a refund to help offset the cost of testing. There are also several optional fees that are necessary if you want your scores rushed to you, or if you wish, to receive multiple grade reports.

What Should I Do the Night Before the Exam?

Last-minute cramming of massive amounts of material will not help you. It takes time for your brain to organize material. There is some value to a last-minute review of material. This may involve looking over the Rapid Review portions of a few (not all) chapters, or looking through the Glossary. The night before the test should include a light review, and various relaxing activities. **A full night's sleep is one of the best preparations for the test**.

What Should I Bring to the Exam?

Here are some suggestions:

- Several pencils and an eraser that does not leave smudges.
- Black- or blue-colored pens for use on the free-response section.
- A watch so that you can monitor your time. You never know if the exam room will, or will not, have a clock on the wall. Make sure you turn off the beep that goes off on the hour.
- A calculator that you have used during your preparation for the exam. Do not bring a new or unfamiliar calculator.
- Your school code.
- Your photo identification and social security number.
- Tissues.
- Your quiet confidence that you are prepared and ready to rock and roll.

What Should I NOT Bring to the Exam?

It's probably a good idea to leave the following items at home:

- A smartphone, cellphone, or any other electronic communication device.
- Books, a dictionary, study notes, flash cards, highlighting pens, correction fluid, a ruler, or any other office supplies.
- Portable music of any kind.
- Clothing with any chemistry on it.
- Panic or fear. It's natural to be nervous, but you can comfort yourself that you have used this book and that there is no room for fear on your exam.

You should:

- Allow plenty of time to get to the test site.
- Wear comfortable clothing.
- Eat a light breakfast and/or lunch.
- Remind yourself that you are well prepared and that the test is an enjoyable challenge and a chance to share your knowledge.
- Be proud of yourself!
- Review the tip sheet on avoiding "stupid" mistakes at the back of this book.

Once test day comes, there is nothing further you can do. Do not worry about what you could have done differently. It is out of your hands, and your only job is to answer as many questions correctly as you possibly can. The calmer you are, the better your chances of doing well.

How to Plan Your Time

IN THIS CHAPTER

Summary: The right preparation plan for you depends on your study habits and the amount of time you have before the test.

Key Idea

✪ Choose the study plan that's right for you.

Three Approaches to Preparing for the AP Chemistry Exam

You are the best judge of your study habits. You should make a realistic decision about what will work best for you. Good intentions and wishes will not prepare you for the exam. Decide what works best for you. Do not feel that you must follow one of these schedules exactly; you can fine-tune any one of them to your own needs. Do not make the mistake of forcing yourself to follow someone else's method. Look at the following descriptions, and see which best describes you. This will help you pick a prep mode.

You're a full-year prep student if:

1. You are the kind of person who likes to plan for everything very far in advance.

2. You arrive very early for appointments.

3. You like detailed planning and everything in its place.

4. You feel that you must be thoroughly prepared.

5. You hate surprises.

If you fit this profile, consider **Plan A**.

You're a one-semester prep student if:

1. You are always on time for appointments.

2. You are willing to plan ahead to feel comfortable in stressful situations, but are OK with skipping some details.

3. You feel more comfortable when you know what to expect, but a surprise or two is good.

If you fit this profile, consider **Plan B.**

You're a six-week prep student if:

1. You get to appointments at the last second.

2. You work best under pressure and tight deadlines.

3. You feel very confident with the skills and background you learned in your AP Chemistry class.

4. You decided late in the year to take the exam.

5. You like surprises.

If you fit this profile, consider **Plan C.**

Look now at Table 2.1 and the following calendars for plans A, B, and C. Choose the plan that will best suit your particular learning style and timeline. For best results, choose a plan and stick with it.

Table 2.1   General Outline of Three Different Study Plans

Month	PLAN A (Full School Year)	PLAN B (One Semester)	PLAN C (Six Weeks)
September–October	Introduction to material and Chapter 5	Introduction to material	Introduction to material and Chapters 1–4
November	Chapters 6–7		
December	Chapters 8–9		
January	Chapters 10–11	Chapters 5–7	
February	Chapters 12–13	Chapters 8–10	
March	Chapters 14–16	Chapters 11–14	
April	Chapters 17–19; Practice Exam 1	Chapters 15–19; Practice Exam 1	Skim Chapters 5–14; all Rapid Reviews; Practice Exam 1
May	Review everything; Practice Exam 2	Review everything; Practice Exam 2	Skim Chapters 15–19; Practice Exam 2

Calendar for Each Plan

Plan A: You Have a Full School Year to Prepare

The main reason for you to use this book is as a preparation for the AP Chemistry exam. However, this book can fill other roles. It can broaden your study of chemistry, help your analytical skills, and enhance your scientific- writing abilities. These will aid you in a college course in chemistry. Use this plan to organize your study during the coming school year.

SEPTEMBER–OCTOBER (Check off the activities as you complete them.)
— Determine the student mode (A, B, or C) that applies to you.
— Carefully read Chapters 1–4 of this book. You should highlight material that applies specifically to you.
— Take the Diagnostic Exam.
— Pay close attention to your walk-through of the Diagnostic Exam.
— Look at the AP and other websites.
— Skim the review chapters in Step 4 of this book. (Reviewing the topics covered in this section will be part of your yearlong preparation.)
— Buy a few color highlighters.
— Look through the entire book. You need to get some idea of the layout, and break it in. Highlight important points.
— Have a clear picture of your school's AP Chemistry curriculum.
— Use this book as a supplement to your classroom experience.

NOVEMBER (The first 10 weeks have elapsed.)
— Read and study Chapter 5, Basics.
— Read and study Chapter 6, Reactions and Periodicity.
— Read and study Chapter 7, Stoichiometry.

DECEMBER
— Read and study Chapter 8, Gases.
— Read and study Chapter 9, Thermodynamics.
— Review Chapters 5–7.

JANUARY (20 weeks have elapsed.)
— Read and study Chapter 10, Spectroscopy, Light, and Electrons.
— Read and study Chapter 11, Bonding.
— Review Chapters 5–10.

FEBRUARY
— Read and study Chapter 12, Solids, Liquids, and Intermolecular Forces.
— Read and study Chapter 13, Solutions and Colligative Properties.
— Review Chapters 5–11.
— Evaluate your weaknesses and refer to the appropriate chapters. You may wish to retake part of the Diagnostic Exam.

MARCH (30 weeks have now elapsed.)
— Read and study Chapter 14, Kinetics.
— Read and study Chapter 15, Equilibrium.
— Read and study Chapter 16, Electrochemistry.
— Review Chapters 5–13.

APRIL
— Take Practice Exam 1 in the first week of April.
— Evaluate your strengths and weaknesses. Review the appropriate chapters to correct any weaknesses.
— Read and study Chapter 17, Nuclear Chemistry.
— Read and study Chapter 18, Organic Chemistry.
— Read and study Chapter 19, Experimental Investigations.
— Review Chapters 5–16.

MAY (first 2 weeks) (THIS IS IT!)
— Review Chapters 5–19—all the material!
— Take Practice Exam 2.
— Score your exam.
— Review the tip sheet on avoiding "stupid" mistakes at the back of this book.
— Get a good night's sleep before the exam. Fall asleep knowing you are well prepared.

GOOD LUCK ON THE TEST!

Plan B: You Have One Semester to Prepare

This approach uses the assumption that you have completed at least one semester of AP Chemistry. This calendar begins in mid-year and prepares you for the mid-May exam.

JANUARY–FEBRUARY
— Read Chapters 1–4 in this book.
— Pay careful attention to the Diagnostic Exam.
— Pay close attention to your walk-through of the Diagnostic Exam.
— Read and study Chapter 5, Basics.
— Read and study Chapter 6, Reactions and Periodicity.
— Read and study Chapter 7, Stoichiometry.
— Read and study Chapter 8, Gases.
— Read and study Chapter 9, Thermodynamics.
— Evaluate your strengths and weaknesses.
— Re-study appropriate chapters to correct your weaknesses.

MARCH (10 weeks to go.)
— Read and study Chapter 10, Spectroscopy and Electrons.
— Review Chapters 5–7.
— Read and study Chapter 11, Bonding.
— Read and study Chapter 12, Solids, Liquids, and Intermolecular Forces.
— Review Chapters 8–10.
— Read and study Chapter 13, Solutions and Colligative Properties.
— Read and study Chapter 14, Kinetics.

APRIL
— Take Practice Exam 1 in the first week of April.
— Evaluate your strengths and weaknesses.
— Study appropriate chapters to correct your weaknesses.
— Read and study Chapter 15, Equilibrium.
— Review Chapters 5–10.
— Read and study Chapter 16, Electrochemistry.
— Read and study Chapter 17, Nuclear Chemistry.
— Review Chapters 11–14.
— Read and study Chapter 18, Organic Chemistry.
— Read and study Chapter 19, Experimental Investigations.

MAY (first 2 weeks) (THIS IS IT!)
— Review Chapters 5–19—all the material!
— Take Practice Exam 2.
— Score your exam.
— Review the tip sheet on avoiding "stupid" mistakes at the back of this book.
— Get a good night's sleep before the exam. Fall asleep knowing you are well prepared.

GOOD LUCK ON THE TEST!

Plan C: You Have Six Weeks to Prepare

This approach is for students who have already studied most of the material that may be on the exam. The best use of this book for you is as a specific guide towards the AP Chemistry exam. There are time constraints to this approach, as the exam is only a short time away. This is not the best time to try to learn new material.

APRIL 1–15
— Skim Chapters 1–4.
— Go over Chapter 5.
— Skim Chapters 6–9.
— Carefully go over the Rapid Review sections of Chapters 5–9.
— Complete Practice Exam 1.
— Score the exam and analyze your mistakes.
— Skim and highlight the Glossary.

APRIL 15–MAY 1
— Skim Chapters 10–14.
— Carefully go over the Rapid Review sections of Chapters 10–14.
— Carefully go over the Rapid Review sections of Chapters 5–9 again.
— Continue to skim and highlight the Glossary.

MAY (first 2 weeks) (THIS IS IT!)
— Skim Chapters 15–19.
— Carefully go over the Rapid Reviews for Chapters 15–19.
— Complete Practice Exam 2.
— Score the exam and analyze your mistakes.
— Review the tip sheet on avoiding "stupid" mistakes at the back of this book.
— Get a good night's sleep before the exam. Fall asleep knowing that you are well prepared.

GOOD LUCK ON THE TEST!

STEP **2**

Determine Your Test Readiness

CHAPTER **3** Take a Diagnostic Exam

CHAPTER 3

Take a Diagnostic Exam

IN THIS CHAPTER

Summary: The diagnostic exam is for your benefit. It will let you know where you need to spend the majority of your study time. Do not make the mistake of studying only those parts you missed; you should always review all topics. It may be to your advantage to take the diagnostic exam again just before you begin your final review for the exam. This exam has only multiple-choice questions. It will give you an idea of where you stand with your chemistry preparation. The questions have been written to approximate the coverage of material that you will see on the AP exam and are similar to the review questions that you will see at the end of each chapter. However, there will be a few questions on content that will not be directly tested on the AP exam; these questions refer to basic chemistry knowledge that your teacher will expect you to know and that you will need to know before taking the AP Chemistry Exam. Once you are done with the exam, check your work against the given answers, which also indicate where you can find the corresponding material in the book. We also provide you with a way to convert your score to a rough AP score.

Key Ideas

✪ Answer questions that approximate the coverage of topics on the real exam.
✪ Check your work against the given answers.
✪ Determine your areas of strength and weakness.
✪ Highlight the pages that you must give special attention to.

Getting Started: The Diagnostic Exam

The following problems refer to different chapters in the book. The important thing is not whether you get the correct answer, but whether you have difficulty with one or more questions from a chapter. If so, then review the material in that chapter. You may use a calculator and periodic table. For each question, circle the letter of your choice.

Chapter 5

1. In most of its compounds, this element exists as a monatomic cation.

   (A) F
   (B) S
   (C) N
   (D) Ca

2. Which of the following groups has the species correctly listed in order of decreasing radius?

   (A) Cu^{2+}, Cu^+, Cu
   (B) V, V^{2+}, V^{3+}
   (C) F^-, Br^-, I^-
   (D) B, Be, Li

3. Which of the following elements has the lowest electronegativity?

   (A) F
   (B) I
   (C) Ba
   (D) Al

4. Which of the following represents the correct formula for hexaamminecobalt(III) nitrate?

   (A) $[Co(NH_3)_6](NO_3)_3$
   (B) $[Co(NH_3)_6](NO_2)_3$
   (C) $Am_6Co(NO_3)_3$
   (D) $(NH_3)_6Co_3(NO_3)$

5. Which of the following represents the correct formula for hexaamminechromium(III) chloride?

   (A) $[Cr(NH_3)_6](ClO_3)_3$
   (B) $(NH_3)_6Cr_3Cl$
   (C) Am_6CrCl_3
   (D) $[Cr(NH_3)_6]Cl_3$

6. The discovery that atoms have small, dense nuclei is credited to which of the following?

   (A) Einstein
   (B) Dalton
   (C) Bohr
   (D) Rutherford

Chapter 6

7. ___ $Mn(OH)_2(s)$ + ___ $H_3AsO_4(aq) \rightarrow$ ___ $Mn_3(AsO_4)_2(s)$ + ___ $H_2O(l)$

   After the above chemical equation is balanced, the lowest whole-number coefficient for water is:

   (A) 6
   (B) 2
   (C) 12
   (D) 3

8. Which of the following best represents the net ionic equation for the reaction of calcium hydroxide with an aqueous sodium carbonate solution to form a precipitate?

   (A) $Ca^{2+} + Na_2CO_3 \rightarrow CaCO_3 + 2\,Na^+$
   (B) $2\,Ca(OH) + Na_2CO_3 \rightarrow Ca_2CO_3 + 2\,NaOH$
   (C) $Ca(OH)_2 + CO_3^{2-} \rightarrow CaCO_3 + 2\,OH^-$
   (D) $Ca^{2+} + CO_3^{2-} \rightarrow CaCO_3$

9. A student mixes 50.0 mL of 0.10 M $Fe(NO_3)_2$ solution with 50.0 mL of 0.10 M KOH. A green precipitate forms, and the concentration of the hydroxide ion becomes very small. Which of the following correctly places the concentrations of the remaining ions in order of decreasing concentration?

   (A) $[Fe^{2+}] > [NO_3^-] > [K^+]$
   (B) $[Fe^{2+}] > [K^+] > [NO_3^-]$
   (C) $[NO_3^-] > [K^+] > [Fe^{2+}]$
   (D) $[K^+] > [Fe^{2+}] > [NO_3^-]$

10. Solutions containing this ion give a reddish-brown precipitate upon standing.

    (A) Cu^{2+}
    (B) CO_3^{2-}
    (C) Fe^{3+}
    (D) Al^{3+}

Chapter 7

11. $14 H^+(aq) + 6 Fe^{2+}(aq) + Cr_2O_7^{2-}(aq) \rightarrow$ $2 Cr^{3+}(aq) + 6 Fe^{3+}(aq) + 7 H_2O(l)$

The above reaction is used in the titration of an iron solution. What is the concentration of the iron solution if it took 45.20 mL of 0.1000 M $Cr_2O_7^{2-}$ solution to titrate 75.00 mL of an acidified iron solution?

(A) 0.1000 M
(B) 0.4520 M
(C) 0.3616 M
(D) 0.7232 M

12. Manganese, Mn, forms a number of oxides. A particular oxide is 49.5% by mass Mn. What is the simplest formula for this oxide?

(A) MnO
(B) Mn_2O_3
(C) Mn_2O_7
(D) MnO_2

13. $2 KMnO_4(aq) + 5 H_2C_2O_4(aq) + 3 H_2SO_4(aq) \rightarrow$ $K_2SO_4(aq) + 2 MnSO_4(aq) + 10 CO_2(g) +$ $8 H_2O(l)$

How many moles of $MnSO_4$ are produced when 2.0 mol of $KMnO_4$, 2.5 mol of $H_2C_2O_4$, and 3.0 mol of H_2SO_4 are mixed?

(A) 1.0 mol
(B) 3.5 mol
(C) 2.0 mol
(D) 2.5 mol

14. ____ $KClO_3 \rightarrow$ ____ $KCl +$ ____ O_2

After the above equation is balanced, how many moles of O_2 can be produced from 1.0 mol of $KClO_3$?

(A) 1.5 mol
(B) 3.0 mol
(C) 1.0 mol
(D) 3.0 mol

Chapter 8

15. $Ba(s) + 2 H_2O(l) \rightarrow Ba(OH)_2(aq) + H_2(g)$

Barium reacts with water according to the above reaction. What volume of hydrogen gas, at standard temperature and pressure, is produced from 0.400 mol of barium?

(A) 8.96 L
(B) 5.60 L
(C) 4.48 L
(D) 3.36 L

16. A sample of chlorine gas is placed in a container at constant pressure. The sample is heated until the absolute temperature is doubled. This will also double which of the following?

(A) potential energy
(B) moles
(C) density
(D) volume

17. A balloon contains 2.0 g of hydrogen gas. A second balloon contains 4.0 g of helium gas. Both balloons are at the same temperature and pressure. Which of the following statements is true?

(A) The number of hydrogen molecules is less than the number of helium atoms in each balloon.
(B) The density of the helium in its balloon is less than the density of the hydrogen in its balloon.
(C) The volume of the hydrogen balloon is less than that of the helium balloon.
(D) The average kinetic energy of the molecules/atoms in each balloon is the same.

18. The volume and pressure of a real gas are NOT the same as those calculated from the ideal gas equation, because the ideal gas equation does NOT take into account:

(A) the volume of the molecules and the attraction between the molecules.
(B) the volume of the molecules and the mass of the molecules.
(C) the attraction between the molecules and the mass of the molecules.
(D) the volume of the molecules and variations in the absolute temperature.

19. Aluminum metal reacts with gaseous HCl to produce aluminum chloride and hydrogen gas. What volume of hydrogen gas, at STP, is produced when 13.5 g of aluminum is mixed with an excess of HCl?

 (A) 22.4 L
 (B) 33.6 L
 (C) 11.2 L
 (D) 16.8 L

20. A sample containing the gases carbon dioxide, carbon monoxide, and water vapor was analyzed and found to contain 4.5 mol of carbon dioxide, 4.0 mol of carbon monoxide, and 1.5 mol of water vapor. The mixture had a total pressure of 1.2 atm. What was the partial pressure of the carbon monoxide?

 (A) 0.48 atm
 (B) 0.18 atm
 (C) 5.4 atm
 (D) 0.54 atm

21. An ideal gas sample weighing 0.548 g at 100°C and 0.993 atm has a volume of 0.237 L. Determine the molar mass of the gas.

 (A) 71.3 g/mol
 (B) 143 g/mol
 (C) 19.1 g/mol
 (D) 0.0140 g/mol

22. If a sample of He effuses at a rate of 30 mol per hour at 45°C, which of the gases below will effuse at approximately one-half the rate under the same conditions?

 (A) CH_4
 (B) O_3
 (C) N_2
 (D) H_2

23. The average kinetic energy of nitrogen molecules changes by what factor when the temperature is increased from 30°C to 60°C?

 (A) (333 − 303)
 (B) 2
 (C) 1/2
 (D) $\sqrt{303-333}$

Chapter 9

24. Which of the following is the required energy to produce a gaseous cation from a gaseous atom in the ground state?

 (A) free energy
 (B) lattice energy
 (C) kinetic energy
 (D) ionization energy

25. The average _____ is the same for any ideal gas at a given temperature.

 (A) free energy
 (B) lattice energy
 (C) kinetic energy
 (D) ionization energy

26. Which of the following is the maximum energy available for useful work from a spontaneous reaction?

 (A) free energy
 (B) lattice energy
 (C) kinetic energy
 (D) ionization energy

27. The energy required to completely separate the ions from a solid is which of the following?

 (A) free energy
 (B) lattice energy
 (C) kinetic energy
 (D) ionization energy

28. Oxidation of ClF by F_2 yields ClF_3, an important fluorinating agent formerly used to produce the uranium compounds in nuclear fuels:

$$ClF(g) + F_2(g) \rightarrow 2\ ClF_3(l)$$

Use the following thermochemical equations to calculate $\Delta H°_{rxn}$ for the production of ClF_3:

 1. $2\ ClF(g) + O_2(g)$ $\Delta H° = 167.5$ kJ
    $\rightarrow Cl_2O(g) + OF_2(g)$

 2. $2\ F_2(g) + O_2(g)$ $\Delta H° = -43.5$ kJ
    $\rightarrow 2\ OF_2(g)$

 3. $2\ ClF_3(l) + 2\ O_2(g)$ $\Delta H° = 394.1$ kJ
    $\rightarrow Cl_2O(g) + 3\ OF_2(g)$

 (A) +270.2 kJ
 (B) −135.1 kJ
 (C) 0.0 kJ
 (D) −270.2 kJ

29. Choose the reaction expected to have the greatest increase in entropy.

   (A) $N_2(g) + O_2(g) \rightarrow 2\ NO(g)$
   (B) $CO_2(g) \rightarrow CO_2(s)$
   (C) $2\ XeO_3(s) \rightarrow 2\ Xe(g) + 3\ O_2(g)$
   (D) $2\ K(s) + F_2(g) \rightarrow 2\ KF(s)$

30. A certain reaction is nonspontaneous under standard conditions but becomes spontaneous at lower temperatures. What conclusions may be drawn under standard conditions?

   (A) $\Delta H > 0$, $\Delta S > 0$, and $\Delta G > 0$
   (B) $\Delta H < 0$, $\Delta S < 0$, and $\Delta G = 0$
   (C) $\Delta H < 0$, $\Delta S > 0$, and $\Delta G > 0$
   (D) $\Delta H < 0$, $\Delta S < 0$, and $\Delta G > 0$

Chapter 10

31. Which of the following groups contains only atoms that are paramagnetic in their ground state?

   (A) Be, O, and N
   (B) Mg, He, and Rb
   (C) K, C, and Fe
   (D) Br, Sb, and Kr

32. Which of the following could be the electron configuration of a transition metal ion?

   (A) $1s^2 1p^6 2s^2 2p^3$
   (B) $1s^2 2s^2 2p^6 3s^2 3p^6 4s^2 3d^{10} 4p^5$
   (C) $1s^2 2s^2 2p^6 3s^2 3p^6 3d^3$
   (D) $1s^2 2s^2 2p^5$

33. Which of the following is the configuration of a noble gas?

   (A) $1s^2 1p^6 2s^2 2p^3$
   (B) $1s^2 2s^2 2p^6 3s^2 3p^6 4s^2 3d^{10} 4p^6$
   (C) $1s^2 2s^2 2p^6 3s^2 3p^6 3d^3$
   (D) $1s^2 2s^2 2p^5$

34. Which of the following is the electron configuration of a halogen?

   (A) $1s^2 1p^6 2s^2 2p^3$
   (B) $1s^2 2s^2 2p^6 3s^2 3p^6 4s^2 3d^{10} 4p^6$
   (C) $1s^2 2s^2 2p^6 3s^2 3p^6 3d^3$
   (D) $1s^2 2s^2 2p^5$

35. Which of the following is an impossible electron configuration?

   (A) $1s^2 1p^6 2s^2 2p^3$
   (B) $1s^2 2s^2 2p^6 3s^2 3p^6 4s^2 3d^{10} 4p^6$
   (C) $1s^2 2s^2 2p^6 3s^2 3p^6 3d^3$
   (D) $1s^2 2s^2 2p^5$

36. This explains why the exact position of an electron is not known.

   (A) Pauli exclusion principle
   (B) Electron shielding
   (C) Hund's rule
   (D) Heisenberg uncertainty principle

37. This is why nitrogen atoms, in their ground state, are paramagnetic.

   (A) Pauli exclusion principle
   (B) Electron shielding
   (C) Hund's rule
   (D) Heisenberg uncertainty principle

38. This means that an atomic orbital can hold no more than two electrons.

   (A) Pauli exclusion principle
   (B) Electron shielding
   (C) Hund's rule
   (D) Heisenberg uncertainty principle

39. Which of the following explains why the 4s orbital fills before the 3d?

   (A) Pauli exclusion principle
   (B) Electron shielding
   (C) Hund's rule
   (D) Heisenberg uncertainty principle

40. Magnesium reacts with element X to form an ionic compound. If the ground-state electron configuration of X is $1s^2 2s^2 2p^3$, what is the simplest formula for this compound?

   (A) MgX_2
   (B) Mg_2X_3
   (C) Mg_3X_2
   (D) MgX

Chapter 11

41. VSEPR predicts that an IF_5 molecule will have which of the following shapes?

(A) tetrahedral
(B) trigonal bipyramidal
(C) square pyramid
(D) trigonal planar

42. Which of the following does NOT have one or more π bonds?

(A) SO_2
(B) SF_6
(C) O_2
(D) SO_3

43. Which of the following is nonpolar?

(A) IF_5
(B) BrF_3
(C) CF_4
(D) SF_4

44. The only substance listed below that contains ionic, σ, and π bonds is:

(A) Na_3N
(B) NO_2
(C) $NaNO_3$
(D) NH_3

45. Which molecule or ion in the following list has the greatest number of unshared electron pairs around the central atom?

(A) SO_2
(B) CO_3^{2-}
(C) XeF_2
(D) CF_4

46. What types of hybridization of carbon are in the compound acetic acid, CH_3COOH?

(A) sp^3, sp^2, and sp
(B) sp^3 only
(C) sp^3 and sp^2
(D) sp^2 and sp

Chapter 12

47. Which of the following is the best description of the structure of graphite?

(A) composed of atoms held together by delocalized electrons
(B) composed of molecules held together by intermolecular dipole-dipole interactions
(C) composed of positive and negative ions held together by electrostatic attractions
(D) composed of macromolecules held together by strong bonds

48. Which of the following best describes Ca(s)?

(A) composed of atoms held together by delocalized electrons
(B) composed of molecules held together by intermolecular dipole-dipole interactions
(C) composed of positive and negative ions held together by electrostatic attractions
(D) composed of macromolecules held together by strong bonds

49. Which of the following categories best describes $CaCO_3(s)$?

(A) composed of atoms held together by delocalized electrons
(B) composed of molecules held together by intermolecular dipole-dipole interactions
(C) composed of positive and negative ions held together by electrostatic attractions
(D) composed of macromolecules held together by strong bonds

50. Which of the following is applicable to $SO_2(s)$?

(A) composed of atoms held together by delocalized electrons
(B) composed of molecules held together by intermolecular dipole-dipole interactions
(C) composed of positive and negative ions held together by electrostatic attractions
(D) composed of macromolecules held together by strong bonds

51. The critical point on a phase diagram represents:

(A) the highest temperature and pressure where a substance can sublime

(B) the highest temperature and pressure where the substance may exist as discrete solid and gas phases

(C) the temperature and pressure where the substance exists in equilibrium as solid, liquid, and gas phases

(D) the highest temperature and pressure where the substance may exist as discrete liquid and gas phases

52. This explains why copper is ductile.

(A) London dispersion forces

(B) covalent bonding

(C) hydrogen bonding

(D) metallic bonding

53. This is why acetic acid, CH_3COOH, molecules exist as dimers in the gaseous phase.

(A) London dispersion forces

(B) covalent bonding

(C) hydrogen bonding

(D) metallic bonding

54. For the following, pick the answer that most likely represents their relative solubilities in water.

(A) $CH_3CH_2CH_2OH < HOCH_2CH_2OH$
    $< CH_3CH_2CH_2CH_3$

(B) $CH_3CH_2CH_2CH_3 < HOCH_2CH_2OH$
    $< CH_3CH_2CH_2OH$

(C) $CH_3CH_2CH_2CH_3 < CH_3CH_2CH_2OH$
    $< HOCH_2CH_2OH$

(D) $CH_3CH_2CH_2OH < CH_3CH_2CH_2CH_3$
    $< HOCH_2CH_2OH$

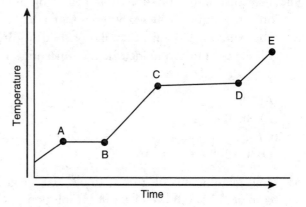

55. The above diagram represents the heating curve for a pure crystalline substance. The solid is the only phase present up to point:

(A) C

(B) B

(C) E

(D) A

56. For all one-component phase diagrams, choose the correct statement from the following list.

(A) The line separating the gas from the liquid phase may have a positive or negative slope.

(B) The line separating the solid from the liquid phase may have a positive or negative slope.

(C) The line separating the solid from the liquid phase has a positive slope.

(D) The temperature at the triple point is the same as at the freezing point.

Chapter 13

57. A solution is prepared by dissolving 0.500 mol of NaCl in 500.0 g of water. Which of the following would be the best procedure to determine the molarity of the solution?

(A) Measure the volume of the solution.

(B) Titrate the solution with standard silver nitrate solution.

(C) Determine the freezing point of the solution.

(D) Determine the osmotic pressure of the solution.

58. A chemist needs 800.0 mL of a 0.50 M bromide ion, Br^-, solution. She has 800.0 mL of a 0.20 M KBr solution. How many moles of solid $MgBr_2$ will she need to add to increase the concentration to the desired value?

(A) 0.24
(B) 0.50
(C) 0.30
(D) 0.12

59. How many grams of HNO_3 (molecular weight 63.0) are in 500.0 mL of a 5.00 M solution?

(A) 31.5 g
(B) 63.0 g
(C) 5.00 g
(D) 158 g

60. If a solution of ethyl ether, $(C_2H_5)_2O$, in ethanol, C_2H_5OH, is treated as an ideal solution, what is the mole fraction of ethyl ether in the vapor over an equimolar solution of these two liquids? The vapor pressure of ethyl ether is 480 mm Hg at 20°C, and the vapor pressure of ethanol is 50 mm Hg at this temperature.

(A) 0.50
(B) 0.76
(C) 0.91
(D) 0.27

Chapter 14

61. Step 1: $2 NO_2(g) \rightarrow N_2(g) + 2 O_2(g)$

Step 2: $2 CO(g) + O_2(g) \rightarrow 2 CO_2(g)$

Step 3: $N_2(g) + O_2(g) \rightarrow 2 NO(g)$

The above represents a proposed mechanism for the reaction of NO_2 with CO. What are the overall products of the reaction?

(A) NO and CO_2
(B) O_2 and CO_2
(C) N_2 and NO
(D) NO only

62. The difference in energy between the transition state and the reactants is:

(A) the kinetic energy
(B) the activation energy
(C) the free energy
(D) the reaction energy

63. The table below gives the initial concentrations and rates for three experiments.

EXPERIMENT	INITIAL $[ClO_2]$ (mol L^{-1})	INITIAL $[OH^-]$ (mol L^{-1})	INITIAL RATE OF FORMATION OF ClO_2 (mol $L^{-1} s^{-1}$)
1	0.100	0.100	2.30×10^5
2	0.200	0.100	9.20×10^5
3	0.200	0.200	1.84×10^6

The reaction is $2ClO_2(aq) + 2OH^-(aq) \rightarrow ClO_2^-(aq) + ClO_3^-(aq) + H_2O(l)$. What is the rate law for this reaction?

(A) Rate = $k[ClO_2]^2[OH^-]^2$
(B) Rate = $k[ClO_2]$
(C) Rate = $k[ClO_2]^2[OH^-]$
(D) Rate = $k[OH^-]^2$

Chapter 15

64. Which of the following CANNOT behave as both a Brønsted base and a Brønsted acid?

(A) HCO_3^-
(B) HPO_4^{2-}
(C) HSO_4^-
(D) CO_3^{2-}

65.

Acid	K_a, acid dissociation constant
H_3PO_4	7.2×10^{-3}
$H_2PO_4^-$	6.3×10^{-8}
HPO_4^{2-}	4.2×10^{-13}

Using the information from the preceding table, which of the following is the best choice for preparing a pH = 8.5 buffer?

(A) $K_2HPO_4 + K_3PO_4$
(B) $K_2HPO_4 + KH_2PO_4$
(C) K_3PO_4
(D) K_2HPO_4

66. What is the ionization constant, K_a, for a weak monoprotic acid if a 0.5 molar solution has a pH of 5.0?

(A) 3×10^{-4}
(B) 2×10^{-10}
(C) 7×10^{-8}
(D) 1×10^{-6}

67. Assuming all concentrations are 1 M, which of the following is the most acidic solution (lowest pH)?

(A) KBr (potassium bromide) and HBr (hydrobromic acid)
(B) $H_2C_2O_4$ (oxalic acid) and KHC_2O_4 (potassium hydrogen oxalate)
(C) NH_3 (ammonia) and NH_4NO_3 (ammonium nitrate)
(D) $(CH_3)_2NH$ (dimethylamine) and $HC_2H_3O_2$ (acetic acid)

68. Assuming all concentrations are equal, which of the following solutions has pH nearest 7?

(A) KBr (potassium bromide) and HBr (hydrobromic acid)
(B) $H_2C_2O_4$ (oxalic acid) and KHC_2O_4 (potassium hydrogen oxalate)
(C) NH_3 (ammonia) and NH_4NO_3 (ammonium nitrate)
(D) $(CH_3)_2NH$ (dimethylamine) and $HC_2H_3O_2$ (acetic acid)

69. Which of the following yields a buffer with a pH > 7 upon mixing equal volumes of 1 M solutions?

(A) KBr (potassium bromide) and HBr (hydrobromic acid)
(B) $H_2C_2O_4$ (oxalic acid) and KHC_2O_4 (potassium hydrogen oxalate)
(C) NH_3 (ammonia) and NH_4NO_3 (ammonium nitrate)
(D) $(CH_3)_2NH$ (dimethylamine) and $HC_2H_3O_2$ (acetic acid)

70. Which of the following will give a buffer with a pH < 7 when equal volumes of 1 M solutions of each of the components are mixed?

(A) KBr (potassium bromide) and HBr (hydrobromic acid)
(B) $H_2C_2O_4$ (oxalic acid) and KHC_2O_4 (potassium hydrogen oxalate)
(C) NH_3 (ammonia) and NH_4NO_3 (ammonium nitrate)
(D) $(CH_3)_2NH$ (dimethylamine) and $HC_2H_3O_2$ (acetic acid)

71. Determine the $OH^-(aq)$ concentration in 0.0010 M pyridine (C_5H_5N) solution. (The K_b for pyridine is 9×10^{-9}.)

(A) $5 \times 10^{-1}\ M$
(B) $1 \times 10^{-3}\ M$
(C) $3 \times 10^{-6}\ M$
(D) $9 \times 10^{-9}\ M$

72. $SnS(s) + 2H^+(aq) \rightleftharpoons Sn^{2+}(aq) + H_2S(aq)$

The successive acid dissociation constants for H_2S are 9.5×10^{-8} (K_{a1}) and 1×10^{-19} (K_{a2}). The K_{sp}, the solubility product constant, for SnS equals 1.0×10^{-25}. What is the equilibrium constant for the above reaction?

(A) $9.5 \times 10^{-8}/1.0 \times 10^{-25}$
(B) $9.5 \times 10^{-27}/1.0 \times 10^{-25}$
(C) $1.0 \times 10^{-25}/9.5 \times 10^{-27}$
(D) $1 \times 10^{-19}/1.0 \times 10^{-25}$

73. $N_2O_4(g) \rightleftharpoons 2NO_2(g)$ endothermic

An equilibrium mixture of the compounds is placed in a sealed container at 150°C. Which of the following changes may increase the amount of the product?

(A) raising the temperature of the container
(B) increasing the volume of the container and raising the temperature of the container
(C) adding 1 mole of Ar(g) to the container
(D) adding 1 mole of Ar(g) to the container and raising the temperature of the container

74. The K_{sp} for LaF_3 is 2×10^{-9}. What is the molar solubility of this compound in water?

(A) $2 \times 10^{-9}/27$
(B) $\sqrt[4]{2 \times 10^{-19}}$
(C) $\sqrt[2]{2 \times 10^{-19}}$
(D) $\sqrt[4]{2 \times 10^{-9}/27}$

75. The K_{sp} for $Mn(OH)_2$ is 1.6×10^{-13}. What is the molar solubility of this compound in water?

(A) $\sqrt[3]{4.0 \times 10^{-14}}$
(B) 1.6×10^{-13}
(C) $\sqrt[3]{4.0 \times 10^{-13}}$
(D) $\sqrt[2]{4.0 \times 10^{-14}}$

76. $FeS(s) + 2\,H^+(aq) \rightleftharpoons Fe^{2+}(aq) + H_2S(aq)$

What is the equilibrium constant for the above reaction? The successive acid dissociation constants for H_2S are 9.5×10^{-8} (K_{a1}) and 1×10^{-19} (K_{a2}). The K_{sp}, the solubility product constant, for FeS equals 5.0×10^{-18}.

(A) $9.5 \times 10^{-27}/5.0 \times 10^{-18}$
(B) $5.0 \times 10^{-18}/9.5 \times 10^{-27}$
(C) $5.0 \times 10^{-18}/9.5 \times 10^{-8}$
(D) $9.5 \times 10^{-8}/5.0 \times 10^{-18}$

77. The K_{sp} for $Cr(OH)_3$ is 1.6×10^{-30}. What is the molar solubility of this compound in water?

(A) $\sqrt[4]{1.6 \times 10^{-30}}$

(B) $\sqrt[4]{1.6 \times 10^{-30}/27}$

(C) 1.6×10^{-30}
(D) $1.6 \times 10^{-30}/27$

Chapter 16

78. $I^-(aq) + H^+(aq) + MnO_4^-(aq) \rightarrow Mn^{2+}(aq) + H_2O(l) + I_2(s)$

What is the coefficient of H^+ when the above reaction is balanced?

(A) 12
(B) 32
(C) 16
(D) 8

79. How many moles of Au will deposit on the cathode when 0.60 Faradays of electricity is passed through a 1.0 M solution of Au^{3+}?

(A) 0.60 mol
(B) 0.30 mol
(C) 0.40 mol
(D) 0.20 mol

80. $Sn^{2+}(aq) + 2\,Fe^{3+}(aq) \rightarrow Sn^{4+}(aq) + 2\,Fe^{2+}(aq)$

The reaction shown above was used in an electrolytic cell. The voltage measured for the cell was not equal to the calculated E° for the cell. Which of the following could explain this discrepancy?

(A) Both of the solutions were at 25°C instead of 0°C.
(B) The anode and cathode were different sizes.
(C) The anion in the anode compartment was chloride instead of nitrate, as in the cathode compartment.
(D) One or more of the ion concentrations was not 1 M.

Questions 81–82 refer to the following half-reaction in an electrolytic cell:

$2\,SO_4^{2-}(aq) + 10\,H^+(aq) + 8\,e^- \rightarrow S_2O_3^{2-}(aq) + 5\,H_2O(l)$

81. Choose the correct statement from the following list.

(A) The sulfur is oxidized.
(B) This is the cathode reaction.
(C) The oxidation state of sulfur does not change.
(D) The H^+ serves as a catalyst.

82. If a current of 0.60 amperes is passed through the electrolytic cell for 0.75 h, how should you calculate the grams of $S_2O_3^{2-}(aq)$ formed?

(A) (0.60) (0.75) (3,600) (112)/(96,500) (8)
(B) (0.60) (0.75) (3,600) (112)/(96,500) (10)
(C) (0.60) (0.75) (60) (32)/(96,500) (8)
(D) (0.60) (0.75) (3,600) (112)/(10)

83. $2\,BrO_3^-(aq) + 12\,H^+(aq) + 10\,e^- \rightarrow Br_2(aq) + 6\,H_2O(l)$

If a current of 5.0 A is passed through the electrolytic cell for 0.50 h, how should you calculate the number of grams of Br_2 that will form?

(A) (5.0) (0.50) (3,600) (159.8)/(10)
(B) (5.0) (0.50) (3,600) (159.8)/(96,500) (10)
(C) (5.0) (0.50) (60) (159.8)/(96,500) (10)
(D) (5.0) (0.50) (3,600) (79.9)/(96,500) (10)

84. $2\,IO_3^-(aq) + 6\,H_2O(l) + 10\,e^- \rightarrow I_2(s) + 12\,OH^-(aq)$

Using the above reaction, if a current of 7.50 A is passed through the electrolytic cell for 0.45 h, how should you calculate the grams of I_2 that will form?

(A) (7.50) (0.45) (3,600) (253.8)/(10)
(B) (7.50) (0.45) (3,600) (126.9)/(96,500) (10)
(C) (7.50) (0.45) (60) (253.8)/(96,500) (10)
(D) (7.50) (0.45) (3,600) (253.8)/(96,500) (10)

Chapter 17

85. When $^{226}_{88}Ra$ decays, it emits two α particles, then a β particle, followed by an α particle. The resulting nucleus is:

(A) $^{212}_{83}Bi$
(B) $^{222}_{86}Rn$
(C) $^{214}_{82}Pb$
(D) $^{214}_{83}Bi$

86. Which of the following lists the types of radiation in the correct order of increasing penetrating power?

(A) α, γ, β
(B) β, α, γ
(C) α, β, γ
(D) β, γ, α

87. What is the missing product in the following nuclear reaction?

$$^{236}_{92}U \rightarrow 4\,^1_0n + \,^{136}_{53}I + \_\_\_$$

(A) $^{90}_{39}Y$
(B) $^{96}_{38}Sr$
(C) $^{96}_{39}Y$
(D) $^{98}_{40}Zr$

88. If 75% of a sample of pure ^3_1H decays in 24.6 yr, what is the half-life of ^3_1H?

(A) 24.6 yr
(B) 18.4 yr
(C) 12.3 yr
(D) 6.15 yr

Chapter 18

89. Alkenes are hydrocarbons with the general formula C_nH_{2n}. If a 1.40 g sample of any alkene is combusted in excess oxygen, how many moles of water will form?

(A) 0.2
(B) 0.1
(C) 1.5
(D) 0.7

90. What type of compound is shown?

$$\overset{\displaystyle O}{\underset{\displaystyle \|}{H-C-CH_2-CH_3}}$$

(A) an alcohol
(B) an aldehyde
(C) a ketone
(D) an ester

Chapter 19

Questions on this chapter are incorporated into the chapters concerning the specific experiments.

› Answers and Explanations

Chapter 5

1. **D**—The others (nonmetals) form anions.

2. **B**—Decreasing radii is related to increasing charges, or for going up a column (with equal charges), or moving toward the right in a period of the periodic table. This explanation will not be sufficient for the free-response portion of the test, where it is necessary to address such factors as the effective nuclear charge.

3. **C**—The element that is farthest away from F on the periodic table.

4. **A**—Hexaammine = $(NH_3)_6$; cobalt(III) = Co^{3+}; and nitrate = NO_3^-.

5. **D**—Hexaammine = $(NH_3)_6$; chromium(III) = Cr^{3+}; chloride = Cl^-

6. **D**—Rutherford, and students, determined this by bombarding gold foil with alpha particles and detecting the deflection of some of the particles.

Chapter 6

7. **A**—The balanced chemical equation is:

    $3\ Mn(OH)_2(s) + 2\ H_3AsO_4(aq) \rightarrow$
    $Mn_3(AsO_4)_2(s) + 6\ H_2O(l)$

8. **D**—$Ca(OH)_2$, NaOH, and Na_2CO_3 are strong electrolytes (strong bases or soluble salts) and should be separated. You should know all the strong bases and that sodium compounds are soluble. Cancel all spectator ions (Na^+ and OH^-).

9. **C**—The hydroxide is low because it combined with some of the iron, so Fe^{2+} will be low. There is no other ion that the hydroxide ion could combine with to form a precipitate. The nitrate is double the potassium because there are two moles of nitrate per mole of iron(II) nitrate instead of one ion per mole, as in potassium hydroxide.

10. **C**—Copper is blue, not red, and carbonate and aluminum are colorless. Iron slowly hydrolyzes (reacts with water) to form solid $Fe(OH)_3$ (rust).

Chapter 7

11. **C**—$(0.1000\ mol\ Cr_2O_7^{2-}/1{,}000\ mL)(45.20\ mL)$ $(6\ mol\ Fe^{2+}/1\ mol\ Cr_2O_7^{2-})(1/75.00\ mL)$ $(1{,}000\ mL/L)$

12. **C**—Either calculate the percent Mn in each oxide: (A) 77.4%; (B) 69.6%; (C) 49.5%; (D) 63.2%, or determine the empirical formula from the percent manganese and the percent oxygen (= 100.0 − 49.5).

13. **A**—$H_2C_2O_4$ is the limiting reagent as the amount is less than the stoichiometric ratio indicates. The calculation is $(2.5\ mol\ H_2C_2O_4)\left(\dfrac{2\ mol\ MnSO_4}{5\ mol\ H_2C_2O_4}\right)$.

14. **A**—The coefficients in the balanced equation are 2, 2, and 3. Therefore, $(1.0\ mol\ KClO_3)\ (3\ mol\ O_2/$ $2\ mol\ KClO_3) = 1.5\ mol$.

Chapter 8

15. **A**—$(0.400\ mol\ Ba)(1\ mol\ H_2/1\ mol\ Ba)$ $(22.4\ L/mol)$. Note that the 22.4 L/mol only works at STP.

16. **D**—This is an application of Charles's law, which relates volume to temperature. There is a direct relationship between volume and the absolute temperature. Doubling either volume or temperature, with moles and pressure remaining constant, doubles the other.

17. **D**—The average kinetic energy of a gas depends upon the temperature. Since the temperature of the two gases is the same, the average kinetic energy of the gases is the same. The moles are the same, so the number of particles and the volumes must be the same. Density is mass over volume, and since the balloons have the same volume, the one with more mass will have the higher density.

18. **A**—These are the basic differences between ideal and real gases.

19. **D**—It is necessary to first write the balanced chemical equation:

    $2\ Al(s) + 6\ HCl(g) \rightarrow 2\ AlCl_3(s) + 3\ H_2(g)$

    $(13.5\ g\ Al)(1\ mol\ Al/27.0\ g\ Al)(3\ mol\ H_2/$ $2\ mol\ Al)(22.4\ L/mol\ H_2)$

20. **A**—The mole fraction of CO times the total pressure yields the partial pressure. The mole fraction of CO is the moles of CO (4.0) divided by the total moles (10.0).

21. **A**—$n = PV/RT = (0.993 \text{ atm})(0.237 \text{ L})/$
$(0.0821 \text{ L atm/K mol})(373 \text{ K})$
$= 7.69 \times 10^{-3} \text{ mol}$

molar mass = $0.548 \text{ g}/7.69 \times 10^{-3} \text{ mol}$
$= 71.3 \text{ g/mol}$

This example illustrates the importance of rounding in calculations where no calculator is available. The answers are not close together; therefore, a rough calculation will lead to the correct answer. Also, you should notice the answer D is impossible for any substance.

22. **A**—For the rate to be one-half, the molar mass of the other gas must be the square of the molar mass of helium ($4^2 = 16$).

23. **A**—The average kinetic energy of the molecules depends on the temperature. The correct answer involves a temperature difference (333 K − 303 K). Do not forget that ALL gas law calculations require Kelvin temperatures.

Chapter 9

24. **D**—This is the definition of the ionization energy.

25. **C**—This is a basic postulate of kinetic molecular theory.

26. **A**—This is one of the properties of free energy.

27. **B**—This is the definition of the lattice energy.

28. **B**—This is an application of Hess's law.

½[2 ClF(g) + O₂(g)
→ Cl₂O(g) + OF₂(g)]   ½(167.5 kJ)

½[2 F₂(g) + O₂(g)
→ 2 OF₂(g)]   ½(−43.5 kJ)

½[Cl₂O(g) + 3 OF₂(g)
→ 2 ClF₃(l) + 2 O₂(g)]   −½(394.1 kJ)

ClF(g) + F₂(g) → ClF₃(l)   −135.1 kJ

As always, rounding and estimating will save time.

29. **C**—The one with the greatest increase in the moles of gas.

30. **D**—Nonspontaneous means $\Delta G > 0$. For a reaction to become spontaneous at lower temperature ($\Delta G < 0$) means $\Delta H < 0$ and $\Delta S < 0$.

Chapter 10

31. **C**—Atoms with completely filled shells or subshells are not paramagnetic; they are diamagnetic. From the choices in this problem, these are Be, Mg, He, Kr, and Zn; therefore, any answer containing one of these cannot be the correct choice. It is not necessary to work through a possible solution until encountering a diamagnetic species. Also, it might be helpful to look on the periodic table.

32. **C**—Transition metal ions are, in general, s^0 and p^0 or p^6 with the possibility of having one or more electrons in the d orbitals. C could be Cr^{3+}.

33. **B**—The noble gases, except helium, are ns^2np^6. In this case, $n = 4$, and the gas is krypton.

34. **D**—Halogens are ns^2np^5. In this case, $n = 2$, and the halogen is F.

35. **A**—The 1p orbital does not exist.

36. **D**—This is a statement of the uncertainty principle.

37. **C**—According to Hund's rule, the nitrogen 2p electrons enter the 2p orbitals individually (with spins parallel).

38. **A**—The Pauli exclusion principle states this limitation for all orbitals.

39. **B**—The d orbitals are less effectively shielded than the s orbitals. Due to this difference, the s orbitals have lower energy.

40. **C**—Mg becomes Mg^{2+}. The element is N, which can become N^{3-}.

Chapter 11

41. **C**—The iodine has five bonding pairs and one lone pair.

42. **B**—This is the only one with only single bonds. The other molecules have double or triple bonds. All double and triple bonds are a combination of σ and π bonds.

43. **C**—Use VSEPR; only the tetrahedral CF_4 is nonpolar. The other materials form a square pyramidal (IF_5), T-shaped (BrF_3), and irregular tetrahedral (SF_4), and, therefore, are polar.

44. **C**—The only ionic bonds are present in the sodium compounds (eliminating B and D). The nitride ion has no internal bonding (eliminating A), but the nitrate ion has both σ and π bonds.

45. **C**—Draw the Lewis structures. The number of unshared pairs: (A) 1; (B) 0; (C) 3; (D) 0.

46. **C**—Draw the Lewis structure; the carbon on the left in the formula is sp^3, and the other is sp^2.

Chapter 12

47. **D**—Both graphite and diamond are covalent network solids.

48. **A**—Calcium is a metal, and answer A applies to metallic bonding.

49. **C**—Calcium carbonate is an ionic compound.

50. **B**—Sulfur dioxide consists of polar molecules.

51. **D**—This is the definition of the critical point.

52. **D**—This is a consequence of metallic bonding as the atoms can easily move past each other without breaking any bonds.

53. **C**—The carbonyl, C=O, and —OH groups are capable of participating in hydrogen bonds.

54. **C**—The more —OH groups, the more hydrogen bonding, and the more soluble in water (where hydrogen bonding also occurs).

55. **D**—The solid begins to melt at A and finishes melting at B.

56. **B**—The gas-liquid line always has a positive slope, which eliminates A. Answer B negates C; therefore, both cannot be correct. The triple point is not the same as the freezing point.

Chapter 13

57. **A**—Molarity is moles per liter, and the moles are already known; therefore, only the volume is necessary to complete the determination.

58. **D**—(0.800 L)(0.50 mol Br^-/L) = 0.40 mol needed.

    (0.800 L)(0.20 mol Br^-/L) = 0.16 mol present.

    [(0.40 − 0.16) mol Br^- to be added]
    (1 mol $MgBr_2$/2 mol Br^-)

59. **D**—(0.5000 L)(5.00 mol/L)(63.0 g/mol) = 158 g. As always, estimate the answer by rounding the values.

60. **C**—Equimolar gives a mole fraction of 0.5. 0.5 × 480 mm Hg + 0.5 × 50 mm Hg = 265 mm Hg (total vapor pressure) mole fraction ethyl ether = (0.5 × 480 mm Hg)/265 mm Hg.

Chapter 14

61. **A**—Add the equations and cancel anything that appears on both sides of the reaction arrows.

62. **B**—This is the definition of the activation energy.

63. **C**—The table shows second order in chlorine dioxide (comparing experiments 1 and 2), because doubling the ClO_2 concentration quadruples (2^2) the rate. The reaction is first order in the hydroxide ion (comparing experiments 2 and 3), because doubling the OH^- concentration doubles (2^1) the rate. When making this determination, make sure there is only one concentration changing; i.e., do not compare experiments 1 and 3.

Chapter 15

64. **D**—To be an acid, the species must have an H^+ to donate, and to be a base, the species must be able to accept an H^+. The carbonate ion has no H^+ to donate to be an acid.

65. **B**—Start with the acid with a pK_a as near 8.5 ($K = 10^{-8.5}$) as possible ($H_2PO_4^-$). To go to a higher pH, add the acid (conjugate base) with the smaller K_a (higher pK_a).

66. **B**—This is an approximation. At pH = 5, $[H^+]$ = 10^{-5} M; therefore, $K_a = (10^{-5})^2/0.5$.

67. **A**—HBr is a strong acid, and with equal concentrations and no base present, it will give the lowest pH.

68. **D**—The weak acid and weak base give a nearly neutral solution, as they will tend to neutralize each other.

69. **C**—Only B and C are buffers. B is acidic (pH < 7) and C is basic (pH > 7).

70. B—Only B and C are buffers. B is acidic (pH < 7) and C is basic (pH > 7).

71. C—$[OH^-] = (0.0010 \times 9 \times 10^{-9})^{1/2} = (9 \times 10^{-12})^{1/2}$

Estimate—the square root of 10^{-12} will be 10^{-6}.

72. C—$K = K_{sp}/K_{a1}K_{a2}$

In this case, the key is setting up the calculation but not doing the calculation.

73. B—Adding Ar yields no change, as it is not part of the equilibrium. Increasing the temperature of an endothermic equilibrium will increase the amount of product.

74. D—$K_{sp} = [La^{3+}][F^-]^3 = [x][3x]^3 = 27x^4$. Solve for x. It is only necessary to set up the problem. This requires a knowledge of what the equilibrium is $(LaF_3(s) \rightleftharpoons La^{3+}(aq) + 3\ F^-(aq))$ and how to write the equilibrium expression $(K_{sp} = [La^{3+}][F^-]^3)$.

75. A—The equilibrium constant expression for the dissolving of manganese(II) hydroxide is:
$$K_{sp} = [Mn^{2+}][OH^-]^2 = 1.6 \times 10^{-13}$$
If s is used to indicate the molar solubility, the equilibrium expression becomes:
$$K_{sp} = (s)(2s)^2 = 4s^3 = 1.6 \times 10^{-13}$$
This rearranges to: $\quad s = \sqrt[3]{K/4}$

76. B—$K = K_{sp}/K_{a1}K_{a2} = 5.0 \times 10^{-18}/(9.5 \times 10^{-8})$ (1×10^{-19})

77. B—$K_{sp} = [Cr^{3+}][OH^-]^3 = [x][3x]^3 = 27x^4 = 1.6 \times 10^{-30}$. Solve for x.

Chapter 16

78. C—The balanced equation is:
$$10\ I^-(aq) + 16\ H^+(aq) + 2\ MnO_4^-(aq)$$
$$\rightarrow 2\ Mn^{2+}(aq) + 8\ H_2O(l) + 5\ I_2(s)$$

79. D—It is only necessary to know the mole ratio for the reaction $(Au^{3+}(aq) + 3\ e^- \rightarrow Au(s))$, which gives $(0.60\ F)(1\ mol\ Au/3\ F) = 0.20$ moles.

80. D—The cell must be nonstandard. This could be due to variations in temperature (not 25°C) or concentrations (1 M) that are not standard.

81. B—A reduction is shown. Reductions take place at the cathode.

82. A—Use dimensional analysis:
$(0.60\ coul/s)(0.75\ h)(3,600\ s/h)(112\ g\ S_2O_3^{2-}/$ $mol\ S_2O_3^{2-})/(96,500\ coul/F)(8\ F/mol\ S_2O_3^{2-})$

83. B—Recall that 5.0 amp is 5.0 C/s. The calculation would be:
$$\left(\frac{5.0\ C}{s}\right)\left(\frac{3,600\ s}{h}\right)(0.50\ h)\left(\frac{1\ F}{96,500\ C}\right) \times$$
$$\left(\frac{1\ mol\ Br_2}{10\ F}\right)\left(\frac{159.8\ g\ Br_2}{1\ mol\ Br_2}\right)$$

84. D—Dimensional analysis:
$(7.50\ coul/s)(0.45\ h)(3,600\ s/h)(253.8\ g\ I_2/mol\ I_2)/$ $(96,500\ coul/F)(10\ F)$

Chapter 17

85. D—The mass of an alpha particle is 4 and the mass of a beta particle is negligible. The mass number (superscript) should be $226 - (4 + 4 + 0 + 4) = 214$. The charge on an alpha particle is +2 and the charge on the beta particle is −1; therefore, the atomic number (subscript) should be $88 - (2 + 2 - 1 + 2) = 83$.

86. C—Alpha particles are the least penetrating, and gamma rays are the most penetrating.

87. C—Mass difference = $236 - 4(1) - 136 = 96$.

Atomic number difference = $92 - 4(0) - 53 = 39$.

88. C—After one half-life, 50% would remain. After another half-life this would be reduced by 1/2 to 25%. The total amount decayed is 75%. Thus, 24.6 years must be two half-lives of 12.3 years each.

Chapter 18

89. B—The general formula simplifies to CH_2, which has a molar mass of 14 g/mol. This leads to (1.40 g) (1 mol/14 g).

90. B.

Chapter 19

Questions on this chapter are incorporated into the chapters concerning the specific experiments.

Scoring and Interpretation

Now that you have finished and scored the diagnostic exam, it is time for you to learn what it all means. First, note any area where you had difficulty. This should not be limited to unfamiliar material. You should do this even if you got the correct answer. Determine where this material is covered in the book. Plan to spend additional time on the chapter in question. There is material you may not recognize because you have not gotten that far in class.

There are no free-response questions on this diagnostic exam; such questions are not useful at this point. There will be examples of free-response questions later in this book. We will use the multiple-choice questions to provide an estimate of your preparation. This is a simplified approach based on these questions. Do not try to do more than use these results as a general guide.

Raw Score (number right)	Approximate AP Score
55–91	5
41–54	4
30–40	3
18–29	2
0–17	1

If you did better than you expected—great! Be careful not to become overconfident. Much more will need to be done before you take the AP Chemistry exam.

If you did not do as well as you would have liked, don't panic. There is plenty of time for you to prepare for the exam. This is a guide to allow you to know which path you need to follow.

No matter what your results were, you are about to begin your 5 steps to a 5.

Good Luck!

STEP **3**

Develop Strategies for Success

CHAPTER 4

How to Approach
Each Question Type

IN THIS CHAPTER

Summary: Use these question-answering strategies to raise your AP score.

Key Ideas

Multiple-Choice Questions

✪ Read the question carefully.
✪ Try to answer the question yourself before reading the answer choices.
✪ Drawing a picture can help.
✪ Don't spend too much time on any one question.
✪ In-depth calculations are not necessary; approximate the answer by rounding.

Free-Response Questions

✪ Write clearly and legibly.
✪ Be consistent from one part of your answer to another.
✪ Draw a graph if one is required.
✪ If the question can be answered with one word or number, don't write more.
✪ If a question asks "how," tell "why" as well.

Multiple-Choice Questions

Because you are a seasoned student accustomed to the educational testing machine, you have surely participated in more standardized tests than you care to count. You probably know some students who always seem to ace the multiple-choice questions, and some students who would rather set themselves on fire than sit for another round of "bubble trouble." We hope that, with a little background and a few tips, you might improve your scores on this important component of the AP Chemistry exam.

First, the background. Every multiple-choice question has three important parts:

1. The **stem** is the basis for the actual question. Sometimes this comes in the form of a fill-in-the-blank statement, rather than a question.

   Example: The mass number of an atom is the sum of the atomic number and _____.

   Example: What two factors lead to real gases deviating from the predictions of Kinetic Molecular Theory?

2. The **correct answer option**. Obviously, this is the one selection that best completes the statement or responds to the question in the stem. Because you have purchased this book, you will select this option many, many times.

3. **Distracter options**. Just as it sounds, these are the incorrect answers intended to distract anyone who decided not to purchase this book. You can locate this person in the exam room by searching for the individual who is repeatedly smacking his or her forehead on the desktop.

Students who do well on multiple-choice exams are so well prepared that they can easily find the correct answer, but other students do well because they are perceptive enough to identify and avoid the distracters. Much research has been done on how best to study for, and complete, multiple-choice questions. You can find some of this research by using your favorite Internet search engine, but here are a few tips that many chemistry students find useful.

1. *Let's be careful out there.* You must carefully read the question. This sounds obvious, but you would be surprised how tricky those test developers can be. For example, rushing past, and failing to see, the use of a negative, can throw a student.

   Example: Which of the following is *not* true of the halogens?
   a. They are nonmetals.
   b. They form monatomic anions with a −1 charge.
   c. In their standard states they may exist as solids, liquids, or gases.
   d. All may adopt positive oxidation states.
   e. They are next to the noble gases on the periodic table.

   A student who is going too fast, and ignores the negative *not*, might select option (a), because it is true and it was the first option that the student saw.

   You should be very careful about the wording. It is easy to skip over small words like "not," "least," or "most." You must make sure you are answering the correct question. Many students make this type of mistake—do not add your name to the list.

2. *See the answer, be the answer.* Many people find success when they carefully read the question and, before looking at the alternatives, visualize the correct answer. This allows the person to narrow the search for the correct option and identify the distracters. Of course, this visualization tip is most useful for students who have used this book to thoroughly review the chemistry content.

Example: When Robert Boyle investigated gases, he found the relationship between pressure and volume to be _____.

Before you even look at the options, you should know what the answer is. Find that option, and then quickly confirm to yourself that the others are indeed wrong.

3. *Never say never.* Words like "never" and "always" are absolute qualifiers. If these words are in one of the choices, it is rarely the correct choice.

Example: Which of the following is true about a real gas?
a. There are never any interactions between the particles.
b. The particles present always have negligible volumes.

If you can think of any situation where the statements in (a) and (b) are untrue, then you have discovered distracters and can eliminate these as valid choices.

4. *Easy is as easy does.* It's exam day and you're all geared up to set this very difficult test on its ear. Question number one looks like a no-brainer. Of course! The answer is 7, choice (c). Rather than smiling at the satisfaction that you knew the answer, you doubt yourself. Could it be that easy? Sometimes they *are* just that easy.

5. *Sometimes, a blind squirrel finds an acorn.* Should you guess? Try to eliminate one or more answers before you guess. Then pick what you think is the best answer. You are not penalized for guessing, so don't leave an answer blank.

6. *Draw it, nail it.* Many questions are easy to answer if you do a quick sketch in the margins of your test book. Hey, you paid for that test book; you might as well use it.

Example: The rate of the reverse reaction will be slower than the rate of the forward reaction if the relative energies of the reactants and products are:

	Reactant	*Product*
a.	High	Equal to the reactants
b.	Low	Equal to the reactants
c.	High	Higher than the reactants
d.	Low	Higher than the reactants
e.	High	Lower than the reactants

These types of question are particularly difficult, because the answer requires two ingredients. The graph that you sketch in the margin will speak for itself.

7. *Come back, Lassie, come back!* Pace yourself. If you do not immediately know the answer to a question—skip it. You can come back to it later. You have approximately 90 seconds per question. You can get a good grade on the test even if you do not finish all the questions. If you spend too much time on a question you may get it correct; however, if you go on you might get several questions correct in the same amount of time. The more questions you read, the more likely you are to find the ones for which you know the answers. You can help yourself on this timing by practice.

Times are given for the various tests in this book; if you try to adhere strictly to these times, you will learn how to pace yourself automatically.

8. *Timing is everything, kid.* You have about 90 seconds for each of the 60 questions. Keep an eye on your watch as you pass the halfway point. If you are running out of time and you have a few questions left, skim them for the easy (and quick) ones so that the rest of your scarce time can be devoted to those that need a little extra reading or thought.

9. *Think!* But do not try to outthink the test. The multiple-choice questions are straightforward—do not over-analyze them. If you find yourself doing this, pick the simplest answer. If you know the answer to a "difficult" question—give yourself credit for preparing well; do not think that it is too easy and that you missed something. There are easy questions and difficult questions on the exam.

10. *Change is good?* You should change answers only as a last resort. You can mark your test so you can come back to a questionable problem later. When you come back to a problem, make sure you have a definite reason for changing the answer.

Other things to keep in mind:
- Take the extra half of a second required to fill in the bubbles clearly.
- Don't smudge anything with sloppy erasures. If your eraser is smudgy, ask the proctor for another.
- Absolutely, positively, check that you are bubbling the same line on the answer sheet as the question you are answering. I suggest that every time you turn the page you double-check that you are still lined up correctly.

Free-Response Questions

You will have 105 minutes to complete Section II, the free-response part of the AP Chemistry exam. There will be a total of seven free-response questions (FRQs) of two different types. Three questions will be of the long type. Plan on spending a maximum of 20–25 minutes per question on these three. You will be given some information (the question stem), and then you will have several questions to answer related to that stem. These questions will be, for the most part, unrelated to each other. You might have a lab question, an equilibrium constant question, and so on. But all of these questions will be related to the original stem. The other type of free-response question will be the short type. There will be four of these. Plan on allowing 3–10 minutes per question.

There are a number of kinds of questions that are fair game in the free-response section (Section II). One category is quantitative. You might be asked to analyze a graph or a set of data, and answer questions associated with this data. In many cases you will be required to perform appropriate calculations.

Another category of questions will be ones that refer to a laboratory setting/experiment. These lab questions tend to fall into two types: analysis of observations/data or the design of experiments. In the first type you might be given a set of data, for instance, kinetics data, and then be required to determine the order of reaction and/or the rate constant using that set of data. In the second type you might be asked to design a laboratory procedure given a set of equipment/reagents to accomplish a certain task, such as separation of certain metal ions in a mixture. You must use the equipment given, but you do not have to use all of the equipment.

The third category of questions on the exam involves questions related to representations of atoms or molecules. These representations might include such things as Lewis structures, ball-and-stick models, or space-filling models. You might be asked to take one and convert it to another or to choose a particular representation that is the most useful in describing certain observations.

Your score on the free-response questions amounts to one-half of your grade and, as long-time readers of essays, we assure you that there is no other way to score highly than to know your stuff. While you can guess on a multiple-choice question and have a 1/5 chance of getting the correct answer, there is no room for guessing in this section. There are, however, some tips that you can use to enhance your FRQ scores.

1. *Easy to read—easy to grade.* Organize your responses around the separate parts of the question and clearly label each part of your response. In other words, do not hide your answer; make it easy to find and easy to read. It helps you and it helps the reader to see where you are going. Trust me: helping the reader can never hurt. Which leads me to a related tip . . . Write in English, not Sanskrit! Even the most levelheaded and unbiased reader has trouble keeping his or her patience while struggling with bad handwriting. (We have actually seen readers waste almost 10 minutes using the Rosetta stone to decipher a paragraph of text that was obviously written by a time-traveling student from the Egyptian Empire.)

2. *Consistently wrong can be good.* The free-response questions are written in several parts. If you are looking at an eight-part question, it can be scary. However, these questions are graded so that you can salvage several points even if you do not correctly answer the first part. The key thing for you to know is that you must be consistent, even if it is consistently wrong. For example, you may be asked to draw a graph showing a phase diagram. Following sections may ask you to label the triple point, critical point, normal boiling point, and vapor pressure—each determined by the appearance of your graph. So let's say you draw your graph, but you label it incorrectly. Obviously, you are not going to receive that point. However, if you proceed by labeling the other points correctly in your *incorrect* quantity, you would be surprised how forgiving the grading rubric can be.

3. *Have the last laugh with a well-drawn graph.* There are some points that require an explanation (i.e., "Describe how . . ."). Not all free-response questions require a graph, but a garbled paragraph of explanation can be saved with a perfect graph that tells the reader you know the answer to the question. This does not work in reverse . . .

4. *If I say draw, you had better draw.* There are what readers call "graphing points," and these cannot be earned with a well-written paragraph. For example, if you are asked to draw a Lewis structure, certain points will be awarded for the picture, and only the picture. A delightfully written and entirely accurate paragraph of text will not earn the graphing points. You also need to label graphs clearly. You might think that a downward-sloping line is obviously a decrease, but some of those graphing points will not be awarded if lines and points are not clearly, and accurately, identified.

5. *Give the answer, not a dissertation.* There are some parts of a question where you are asked to simply "identify" something. This type of question requires a quick piece of analysis that can literally be answered in one word or number. That point will be given if you provide that one word or number whether it is the only word you write, or the fortieth. For example, you may be given a table that shows how a reaction rate varies with concentration. Suppose the correct rate is 2. The point is given if you say "2," "two," and maybe even "ii." If you write a novel concluding with the word "two," you will get the point, but you have wasted precious time. This brings me to . . .

6. *Welcome to the magic kingdom.* If you surround the right answer to a question with a paragraph of chemical wrongness, you will usually get the point, so long as you say the magic word. The only exception is a direct contradiction of the right answer. For example, suppose that when asked to "identify" the maximum concentration, you spend a paragraph describing how the temperature may change the solubility and the gases are more soluble under increased pressure, and then say the answer is two. You get the point! You said the "two" and "two" was the magic word. However, if you say that the answer is two, but that it is also four, but on Mondays, it is six, you have contradicted yourself and the point will not be given.

7. *"How" really means "how" and "why."* Questions that ask how one variable is affected by another—and these questions are legion—require an explanation, even if the question doesn't seem to specifically ask how *and* why. For example, you might be asked to explain how effective nuclear charge affects the atomic radius. If you say that the "atomic radius decreases," you may have received only one of two possible points. If you say that this is "because effective nuclear charge has increased," you can earn the second point.

8. *Read the question carefully.* The free-response questions tend to be long (multipart) questions. If you do not fully understand one part of the question, you should go on to the next part. The parts tend to be stand-alone. If you make a mistake in one part, you will not be penalized for the same mistake a second time.

9. *Budget your time carefully.* Spend 1–2 minutes reading the question and mentally outlining your response. You should then spend the next 3–5 minutes outlining your response. Finally, you should spend about 15 minutes answering the question. A common mistake is to overdo the answer. The question is worth a limited number of points. If your answer is twice as long, you will not get more points. You will lose time you could spend on the remainder of the test. Make sure your answers go directly to the point. There should be no deviations or extraneous material in your answer.

10. *Make sure you spend some time on each section.* Grading of the free-response questions normally involves a maximum of one to three points for each part. You will receive only a set maximum number of points. Make sure you make an attempt to answer each part. You cannot compensate for leaving one part blank by doubling the length of the answer to another part.

    You should make sure the grader is able to find the answer to each part. This will help to ensure that you get all the points you deserve. There will be at least a full page for your answer. There will also be questions with multiple pages available for the answer. You are not expected to use all of these pages. In some cases, the extra pages are there simply because of the physical length of the test. The booklet has a certain number of pages.

11. *Outlines are very useful.* They not only organize your answer, but they also can point to parts of the question you may need to reread. Your outline does not need to be detailed: just a few keywords to organize your thoughts. As you make the outline, refer back to the question; this will take care of any loose ends. You do not want to miss any important points. You can use your outline to write a well-organized answer to the question. The grader is not marking on how well you wrote your answer, but a well-written response makes it easier for the grader to understand your answer and to give you all the points you deserve.

12. *Grading depends on what you get right in your answer.* If you say something that is wrong, it is not counted against you. Always try to say something. This will give you a chance for some partial credit. Do not try too hard and negate something you have already said. The grader needs to know what you mean; if you say something and negate it later, there will be doubt.

13. *Do not try to outthink the test.* There will always be an answer. For example, in the reaction question, "no reaction" will not be a choice. If you find yourself doing this, pick the simplest answer. If you know the answer to a "difficult" question—give yourself credit for preparing well; do not think that it is too easy, and that you missed something. There are easy questions and difficult questions on the exam.

    Questions concerning experiments will be incorporated into both the multiple-choice and free-response questions. This means that you will need to have a better understanding of the experiments in order to discuss not only the experiment itself, but also the underlying chemical concepts.

14. *Be familiar with all the suggested experiments.* It may be that you did not perform a certain experiment, so carefully review any that are unfamiliar in Chapter 19. Discuss these experiments with your teacher.

15. *Be familiar with the equipment.* Not only be familiar with the name of the equipment used in the experiment, but how it is used properly. For example, the correct use of a buret involves reading of the liquid meniscus.

16. *Be familiar with the basic measurements required for the experiments.* For example, in a calorimetry experiment you do not *measure* the change in temperature, you *calculate* it. You measure the initial and final temperatures.

17. *Be familiar with the basic calculations involved in each experiment.* Review the appropriate equations given on the AP exam. Know which ones may be useful in each experiment. Also, become familiar with simple calculations that might be used in each experiment. These include calculations of moles from grams, temperature conversions, and so on.

18. *Other things to keep in mind:*

    - Begin every free-response question with a reading period. Use this time well to jot down some quick notes to yourself, so that when you actually begin to respond, you will have a nice start.
    - The questions are written in logical order. If you find yourself explaining part **C** before responding to part **B**, back up and work through the logical progression of topics.
    - Abbreviations are your friends. You can save time by using commonly accepted abbreviations for chemical variables and graphical curves. With practice, you will get more adept at their use. There are a number of abbreviations present in the additional information supplied with the test. If you use any other abbreviations, make sure you define them.

STEP 4

Review the Knowledge You Need to Score High

CHAPTER 5

Basics

IN THIS CHAPTER

Summary: This chapter on basic chemical principles should serve as a review if you have had a pre-AP chemistry course in school. We assume (and we all know about assumptions) that you know about such things as the scientific method, elements, compounds, and mixtures. We may mention elementary chemistry topics like this, but we will not spend a lot of time discussing them. When you are using this book, have your textbook handy. If we mention a topic and it doesn't sound familiar, go to your textbook and review it in depth. We will be covering topics that are on the AP exam. There is a lot of good information in your text that is not covered on the AP exam, so if you want more, read your text.

Keywords and Equations

This section of each chapter will contain the mathematical equations and constants that are supplied to you on the AP exam. We have tried to use, as much as possible, the exact format that is used on the test.

T = temperature	n = number of moles	m = mass	P = pressure
V = volume	D = density	v = velocity	M = molar mass
KE = kinetic energy	t = time (seconds)		

Boltzmann's constant, $k = 1.38 \times 10^{-23} \, \text{J K}^{-1}$
electron charge, $e = -1.602 \times 10^{-19}$ coulomb
1 electron volt per atom = 96.5 kJ mol^{-1}

$$D = \frac{m}{V} \qquad K = {}^{\circ}C + 273$$

Avogadro's number = $6.022 \times 10^{23} \, \text{mol}^{-1}$

Units and Measurements

Almost all calculations in chemistry involve both a number and a unit. One without the other is useless. Every time you complete a calculation, be sure that your units have canceled and that the desired unit is written with the number.
Always show your units!

Units

The system of units used in chemistry is the SI system (Système International), which is related to the metric system. There are base units for length, mass, etc. and decimal prefixes that modify the base unit. Since most of us do not tend to think in these units, it is important to be able to convert back and forth from the English system to the SI system. These three conversions are useful ones, although knowing the others might allow you to simplify your calculations:

mass: 1 pound = 0.4536 kg (453.6 g)
volume: 1 quart = 0.9464 dm^3 (0.9464 L)
length: 1 inch = 2.54 cm (exact)

As shown above, the SI unit for volume is the cubic meter (m^3), but most chemists use the liter (L, which is equal to 1 cubic decimeter (dm^3)) or milliliter (mL). The appendixes list the SI base units and prefixes, as well as some English–SI equivalents.

We in the United States are used to thinking of temperature in Fahrenheit, but most of the rest of the world measures temperature in Celsius. On the Celsius scale, water freezes at 0°C and boils at 100°C. Here are the equations needed to convert from Fahrenheit to Celsius and vice versa:

$$°C = \frac{5}{9}[°F - 32]$$

$$°F = \frac{9}{5}(°C) + 32$$

Many times, especially in working with gases, chemists use the Kelvin scale. Water freezes at 273.15 K and boils at 373.15 K. To convert from Celsius to Kelvin:

$$K = °C + 273.15$$

Absolute zero is 0 K and is the point at which all molecular motion ceases.

The density of a substance is commonly calculated in chemistry. The **density (D)** of an object is calculated by dividing the mass of the object by its volume. (Some authors will use a lowercase d to represent the density term; be prepared for either.) Since density is independent of the quantity of matter (a big piece of gold and a little piece have the same density), it can be used for identification purposes. The most common units for density in chemistry are g/cm^3 or g/mL.

Measurements

We deal with two types of numbers in chemistry—exact and measured. Exact values are just that—exact, by definition. There is no uncertainty associated with them. There are exactly 12 items in a dozen and 144 in a gross. Measured values, like the ones you deal with in the lab, have uncertainty associated with them because of the limitations of our measuring instruments. When those measured values are used in calculations, the answer must reflect that combined uncertainty by the number of significant figures that are reported in the final answer. The more significant figures reported, the greater the certainty in the answer.

The measurements used in calculations may contain varying numbers of significant figures, so carry as many as possible until the end and then round off the final answer. The least precise measurement will determine the significant figures reported in the final answer. Determine the number of significant figures in each *measured* value (not the exact ones) and then, depending on the mathematical operations involved, round off the final answer to the correct number of significant figures. Here are the rules for determining the number of significant figures in a measured value:

1. All non-zero digits (1, 2, 3, 4, etc.) are significant.
2. Zeroes between non-zero digits are significant.
3. Zeroes to the left of the first non-zero digit are not significant.
4. Zeroes to the right of the last non-zero digit are significant if there is a decimal point present, but not significant if there is no decimal point.

Rule 4 is a convention that many of us use, but some teachers or books may use alternative methods.

By these rules, 230,500. would contain 6 significant figures, but 230,500 would contain only 4.

Another way to determine the number of significant figures in a number is to express it in scientific (exponential) notation. The number of digits shown is the number of significant figures. For example, 2.305×10^{-5} would contain 4 significant figures. You may need to review exponential notation.

In determining the number of significant figures to be expressed in the final answer, the following rules apply:

1. For addition and subtraction problems, the answer should be rounded off to the same number of decimal places as the measurement with the fewest decimal places.
2. For multiplication and division problems, round off the answer to the same number of significant figures in the measurement with the fewest significant figures.

Remember: Carry as many numbers as possible throughout the calculation and only round off the final answer.

The use of an improper number of significant figures may lower your score on the AP exam.

Dimensional Analysis—the Factor Label Method

Dimensional analysis, sometimes called the factor label (unit conversion) method, is a method for setting up mathematical problems. Mathematical operations are conducted with the units associated with the numbers, and these units are canceled until only the unit of the desired answer is left. This results in a setup for the problem. Then the mathematical operations can efficiently be conducted and the final answer calculated and rounded off to the correct number of significant figures. For example, to determine the number of centimeters in 2.3 miles:

First, write down the initial data as a fraction:

$$\frac{2.3\,\text{mi}}{1}$$

Convert from miles to feet:

$$\frac{2.3\,\text{mi}}{1} \times \frac{5,280\,\text{ft}}{1\,\text{mi}}$$

Convert from feet to inches:

$$\frac{2.3\,\text{mi}}{1} \times \frac{5,280\,\text{ft}}{1\,\text{mi}} \times \frac{12\,\text{in}}{1\,\text{ft}}$$

Finally, convert from inches to centimeters:

$$\frac{2.3\,\text{mi}}{1} \times \frac{5,280\,\text{ft}}{1\,\text{mi}} \times \frac{12\,\text{in}}{1\,\text{ft}} \times \frac{2.54\,\text{cm}}{1\,\text{in}}$$

The answer will be rounded off to 2 significant figures based upon the 2.3 miles, since all the other numbers are exact:

$$\frac{2.3\,\text{mi}}{1} \times \frac{5,280\,\text{ft}}{1\,\text{mi}} \times \frac{12\,\text{in}}{1\,\text{ft}} \times \frac{2.54\,\text{cm}}{1\,\text{in}} = 3.7 \times 10^5\,\text{cm}$$

Sometimes on the AP exam, only setups will be given as possible answers. Write the correct setup to the problem and then see which one of the answers represents your answer.

Remember: The units must cancel!

Also: Make sure that the answer is legible and reasonable!

The States of Matter

Matter can exist in one of three states: solid, liquid, or gas. A **solid** has both a definite shape and a definite volume. At the molecular level, the particles that make up a solid are close together and many times are locked into a very regular framework called a crystal lattice. Molecular motion exists, but it is slight.

A **liquid** has a definite volume but no definite shape. It conforms to the container in which it is placed. The particles are moving much more than in the solid. There are usually clumps of particles moving relatively freely among other clumps.

A **gas** has neither definite shape nor volume. It expands to fill the container in which it is placed. The particles move rapidly with respect to each other and act basically independently of each other.

We will indicate the state of matter that a particular substance is in by a parenthetical s, l, or g. Thus, $H_2O(s)$ would represent solid water (ice), while $H_2O(g)$ would represent gaseous water (steam). For a more detailed discussion of solids, liquids, and gases see Chapters 8 and 12.

The Structure of the Atom

Historical Development

The first modern atomic theory was developed by John Dalton and first presented in 1808. Dalton used the term **atom** (first used by Democritus) to describe the tiny, indivisible particles of an element. Dalton also thought that atoms of an element are the same and atoms of different elements are different. In 1897, J. J. Thompson discovered the existence of the first subatomic particle, the **electron**, by using magnetic and electric fields. In 1909, Robert Millikan measured the charge on the electron in his oil drop experiment (electron charge $= -1.6022 \times 10^{-19}$ coulombs), and from that he calculated the mass of the electron.

Thompson developed an atomic model, the raisin pudding model, which described the atom as being a diffuse positively charged sphere with electrons scattered throughout.

Ernest Rutherford, in 1910, was investigating atomic structure by shooting positively charged alpha particles at a thin gold foil. Most of the particles passed through with no deflection, a few were slightly deflected, and every once in a while an alpha particle was deflected back towards the alpha source. Rutherford concluded from this scattering experiment that the atom was mostly empty space where the electrons were, and that there was a dense core of positive charge at the center of the atom that contained most of the atom's mass. He called that dense core the **nucleus**.

Subatomic Particles

Our modern theory of the atom describes it as an electrically neutral sphere with a tiny nucleus at the center, which holds the positively charged protons and the neutral neutrons. The negatively charged electrons move around the nucleus in complex paths, all of which compose the **electron cloud**. Table 5.1 summarizes the properties of the three fundamental subatomic particles:

Table 5.1 The Three Fundamental Subatomic Particles

NAME	SYMBOL	CHARGE	MASS (amu)	MASS (g)	LOCATION
proton	p^+	1+	1.007	1.673×10^{-24}	nucleus
neutron	n^0	0	1.009	1.675×10^{-24}	nucleus
electron	e^-	1−	5.486×10^{-4}	9.109×10^{-28}	outside nucleus

Many teachers and books omit the charges on the symbols for the proton and neutron.

The **amu (atomic mass unit)** is commonly used for the mass of subatomic particles and atoms. An amu is ½ the mass of a carbon-12 atom, which contains 6 protons and 6 neutrons (C-12).

Since the atom itself is neutral, the number of electrons must equal the number of protons. However, the number of neutrons in an atom may vary. Atoms of the same element (same number of protons) that have differing numbers of neutrons are called **isotopes**. A specific isotope of an element can be represented by the following symbolization:

$$_Z^A X$$

X represents the element symbol taken from the periodic table. Z is the **atomic number** of the element, the number of protons in the nucleus. A is the **mass number**, the sum of the protons and neutrons. By subtracting the atomic number (p) from the mass number (p + n), the number of neutrons may be determined. For example, $_{92}^{238}U$ (U-238) contains 92 protons, 92 electrons, and (238 − 92) 146 neutrons.

Electron Shells, Subshells, and Orbitals

According to the latest atomic model, the electrons in an atom are located in various energy levels or shells that are located at different distances from the nucleus. The lower the number of the shell, the closer to the nucleus the electrons are found. Within the shells, the electrons are grouped in **subshells** of slightly different energies. The number associated with the shell is equal to the number of subshells found at that energy level. For example, energy

Table 5.2 Summary of Atomic Shell, Subshells, and Orbitals for Shells 1–4

SHELL (ENERGY LEVEL)	SUBSHELL	NUMBER OF ORBITALS	ELECTRON CAPACITY
1	s	1	2 total
2	s	1	2
	p	3	6
			8 total
3	s	1	2
	p	3	6
	d	5	10
			18 total
4	s	1	2
	p	3	6
	d	5	10
	f	7	14
			32 total

level 2 (shell 2) has two subshells. The subshells are denoted by the symbols s, p, d, f, etc. and correspond to differently shaped volumes of space in which the probability of finding the electrons is high. The electrons in a particular subshell may be distributed among volumes of space of equal energies called **orbitals.** There is one orbital for an s subshell, three for a p, five for a d, seven for an f, etc. Only two electrons may occupy an orbital. Table 5.2 summarizes the shells, subshells, and orbitals in an atom. Chapter 10 on Spectroscopy, Light, and Electrons has a discussion of the origin of this system.

Energy-Level Diagrams

The information above can be shown in graph form as an energy-level diagram, as shown in Figure 5.1:

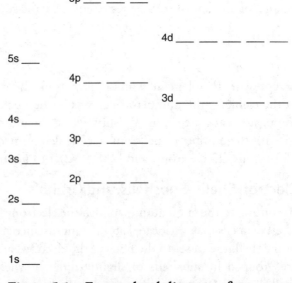

Figure 5.1   Energy-level diagram of an atom.

Be sure to fill the lowest energy levels first (**Aufbau principle**) when using the diagram in Figure 5.1. In filling orbitals having equal energy, electrons are added to the orbitals to half fill them all before any pairing occurs (**Hund's rule**). Sometimes it is difficult to remember the relative energy position of the orbitals. Notice that the 4s fills before the 3d. Figure 5.2 may help you remember the pattern in filling. Study the pattern and be able to reproduce it during the exam.

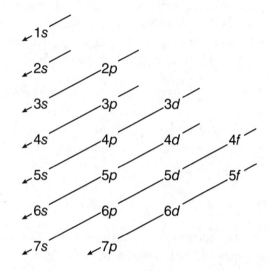

Figure 5.2   Orbital filling pattern.

Following these rules, the energy-level diagram for silicon (Z = 14) can be written as shown in Figure 5.3.

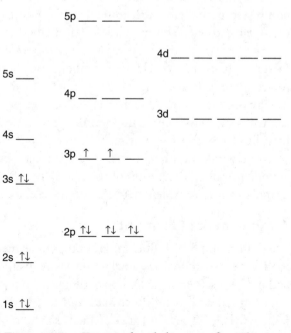

Figure 5.3   Energy-level diagram for silicon.

Although this filling pattern conveys a lot of information, it is bulky. A shorthand method for giving the same information has been developed—the electronic configuration.

Electronic Configurations

The **electronic configuration** is a condensed way of representing the pattern of electrons in an atom. Using the Aufbau build-up pattern that was used in writing the energy-level diagram, consecutively write the number of the shell (energy level), the type of orbital (s, p, d, etc.), and then the number of electrons in that orbital shown as a superscript. For example, $1s^2 2s^1$ would indicate that there are two electrons in the s-orbital in energy level (shell) 1, and one electron in the s-orbital in energy level 2. Looking at the energy-level diagram for silicon in Figure 5.3, the electronic configuration would be written as:

$$\text{silicon: } 1s^2 2s^2 2p^6 3s^2 3p^2$$

The sum of all the superscripts should be equal to the number of electrons in the atom (the atomic number, Z). Electronic configurations can also be written for cations and anions.

Periodic Table

If chemistry students had to learn the individual properties of the 100+ elements that are now known, it would be a monumental and frustrating task. Early scientists had to do just that. Then several scientists began to notice trends in the properties of the elements and began grouping them in various ways. In 1871, a Russian chemist, Dmitri Mendeleev, introduced the first modern periodic table. He arranged the elements in terms of increasing atomic mass. He then arranged columns so that elements that had similar properties were in the same column. Mendeleev was able to predict the existence and properties of elements that were then unknown. Later, when they were discovered, Mendeleev's predictions were remarkably accurate. Later the periodic table was rearranged to sequence the elements by increasing atomic number, not mass. The result is the modern periodic table shown in Figure 5.4.

This is not the periodic table supplied on the AP exam. The one in this book has family and period labels. Become familiar with these labels so that you can effectively use the unlabeled one. You may wish to add labels to the one supplied with the AP exam.

Each square on this table represents a different element and contains three bits of information. The first is the element symbol. You should become familiar with the symbols of the commonly used elements. Second, the square lists the atomic number of the element, usually centered above the element. This integer represents the number of protons in the element's nucleus. The atomic number will always be a whole number. Third, the square lists the element's mass, normally centered underneath the element symbol. This number is not a whole number, because it is the weighted average (taking into consideration abundance) of all the masses of the naturally occurring isotopes of that element. The mass number can never be less than the atomic number.

Arrangement of Elements

There are a number of different groupings of elements on the periodic table that may be utilized. One system involves putting the elements into three main groups—metals, nonmetals, and metalloids (semimetals). Look at Figure 5.4. Notice the heavy, stair-stepped line starting at boron (B) and going downward and to the right. The elements to the left of that line (except for H, Ge, and Sb) are classified as metals. **Metals** are normally solids (mercury being an exception), shiny, and good conductors of heat and electricity. They can be hammered

The periodic table

Key:

Atomic number
Symbol
Atomic weight (mean relative mass)

1	2		3	4	5	6	7	8	9	10	11	12	13	14	15	16	17	18
1 **H** 1.008																		2 **He** 4.002602(2)
3 **Li** 6.94	4 **Be** 9.012182(3)												5 **B** 10.81	6 **C** 12.011	7 **N** 14.007	8 **O** 15.999	9 **F** 18.9984032(5)	10 **Ne** 20.1797(6)
11 **Na** 22.98976928(2)	12 **Mg** 24.3050(6)												13 **Al** 26.9815386(2)	14 **Si** 28.085	15 **P** 30.973762(2)	16 **S** 32.06	17 **Cl** 35.45	18 **Ar** 39.948(1)
19 **K** 39.0983(1)	20 **Ca** 40.078(4)		21 **Sc** 44.955912(6)	22 **Ti** 47.867(1)	23 **V** 50.9415(1)	24 **Cr** 51.9961(6)	25 **Mn** 54.938045(5)	26 **Fe** 55.845(2)	27 **Co** 58.933195(5)	28 **Ni** 58.6934(4)	29 **Cu** 63.546(3)	30 **Zn** 65.38(2)	31 **Ga** 69.723(1)	32 **Ge** 72.63(1)	33 **As** 74.92160(2)	34 **Se** 78.96(3)	35 **Br** 79.904(1)	36 **Kr** 83.798(2)
37 **Rb** 85.4678(3)	38 **Sr** 87.62(1)		39 **Y** 88.90585(2)	40 **Zr** 91.224(2)	41 **Nb** 92.90638(2)	42 **Mo** 95.96(2)	43 **Tc** [97.91]	44 **Ru** 101.07(2)	45 **Rh** 102.90550(2)	46 **Pd** 106.42(1)	47 **Ag** 107.8682(2)	48 **Cd** 112.411(8)	49 **In** 114.818(3)	50 **Sn** 118.710(7)	51 **Sb** 121.760(1)	52 **Te** 127.60(3)	53 **I** 126.90447(3)	54 **Xe** 131.293(6)
55 **Cs** 132.9054519(2)	56 **Ba** 137.327(7)	57–70 *	71 **Lu** 174.9668(1)	72 **Hf** 178.49(2)	73 **Ta** 180.94788(2)	74 **W** 183.84(1)	75 **Re** 186.207(1)	76 **Os** 190.23(3)	77 **Ir** 192.217(3)	78 **Pt** 195.084(9)	79 **Au** 196.966569(4)	80 **Hg** 200.59(2)	81 **Tl** 204.38	82 **Pb** 207.2(1)	83 **Bi** 208.98040(1)	84 **Po** [209]	85 **At** [210]	86 **Rn** [222]
87 **Fr** [223.02]	88 **Ra** [226.03]	89–102 **	103 **Lr** [262.11]	104 **Rf** [265.12]	105 **Db** [268.13]	106 **Sg** [271.13]	107 **Bh** [270]	108 **Hs** [277.15]	109 **Mt** [276.15]	110 **Ds** [281.16]	111 **Rg** [280.16]	112 **Cn** [285.17]	113 **Nh** [284.18]	114 **Fl** [289.19]	115 **Mc** [288.19]	116 **Lv** [293]	117 **Ts** [294]	118 **Og** [294]

*lanthanoids	57 **La** 138.90547(7)	58 **Ce** 140.116(1)	59 **Pr** 140.90765(2)	60 **Nd** 144.242(3)	61 **Pm** [144.91]	62 **Sm** 150.36(2)	63 **Eu** 151.964(1)	64 **Gd** 157.25(3)	65 **Tb** 158.92535(2)	66 **Dy** 162.500(1)	67 **Ho** 164.93032(2)	68 **Er** 167.259(3)	69 **Tm** 168.93421(2)	70 **Yb** 173.054(5)
**actinoids	89 **Ac** [227.03]	90 **Th** 232.03806(2)	91 **Pa** 231.03588(2)	92 **U** 238.02891(3)	93 **Np** [237.05]	94 **Pu** [244.06]	95 **Am** [243.06]	96 **Cm** [247.07]	97 **Bk** [247.07]	98 **Cf** [251.08]	99 **Es** [252.08]	100 **Fm** [257.10]	101 **Md** [258.10]	102 **No** [259.10]

Figure 5.4 The periodic table.

into thin sheets (malleable) and extruded into wires (ductile). Chemically, metals tend to lose electrons in reactions, to form cations.

Elements bordering the stair-stepped line (B, Si, Ge, As, Sb, Te) are classified as metalloids. **Metalloids** have properties of both metals and nonmetals. Their unusual electrical properties make them valuable in the semiconductor and computer industry.

The rest of the elements, to the right of the metalloids, are called nonmetals. **Nonmetals** have properties that are often the opposite of metals. Some are gases, are poor conductors of heat and electricity, are neither malleable nor ductile, and tend to gain electrons in their chemical reactions to form anions.

Another way to group the elements on the periodic table is in terms of periods and groups (families). **Periods** are the horizontal rows, which have consecutive atomic numbers. The periods are numbered from 1 to 7. Elements in the same period do not have similar properties in terms of reactions.

The vertical rows on the periodic table are called **groups** or **families**. They may be labeled in one of two ways. An older and still widely used system is to label each group with a Roman numeral and a letter, A or B. The groups that are labeled with an A are called the main-group elements, while the B groups are called the **transition elements**. Two other horizontal groups, the **inner transition elements**, have been pulled out of the main body of the periodic table. The Roman numeral at the top of the main-group families indicates the number of **valence** (outermost shell) **electrons** in that element. **Valence electrons** are normally considered to be only the s and p electrons in the outermost energy level. The transition elements (B groups) are filling d-orbitals, while the inner transition elements are filling f-orbitals.

Four main-group families are given special names, which you should remember:

- IA group (Group 1)   alkali metals
- IIA group (Group 2)   alkaline earth metals
- VIIA group (Group 17)   halogens
- VIIIA group (Group 18)   noble gases

Another way to label the groups is to consecutively number the groups from left to right, 1–18. This method is newer than the other labeling method, and it has not gained wide use. Most teachers and chemists still prefer and use the older method.

Trends in Periodic Properties

Trends are useful on the multiple-choice portion of the AP exam, but simply stating a trend will **not** be sufficient on the free-response portion of the exam. You must give the reason behind the trend. For example, "higher on the periodic table" is a trend, but not a reason.

The overall attraction an electron experiences is due to the **effective nuclear charge**. This attraction is related to the positive nuclear charge interacting with the negative electrons. Electrons between the nucleus and the electron under consideration interfere with, or shield, that electron from the full nuclear charge. This shielding lessens the nuclear charge. Within a period, the shielding is nearly constant; however, the effective nuclear charge will increase with an increasing number of protons (atomic number). Within the same family or group, as the atomic number increases so does the shielding, resulting in a relatively constant effective nuclear charge.

The size of an atom is generally determined by the number of energy levels occupied by electrons. This means that as we move from top to bottom within a group, the size of the atom increases due to the increased number of shells containing electrons. As we move from left to right within a period (within the same valence shell), the atomic size decreases somewhat owing to the increased effective nuclear charge for the electrons. This increased attraction is related to the increasing number of protons within the nucleus. The size of a cation is smaller than the neutral atom, because in many cases an entire energy shell has been removed, while an anion is larger than the corresponding neutral atom since the nuclear attraction is being distributed over additional electrons. As the number of electrons changes so will the electron–electron repulsion. The greater the electron–electron repulsion, the larger the species becomes, and vice versa.

The **ionization energy (IE)** is the energy needed to completely remove an electron from an atom. It may be expressed in terms of 1 atom or a mole of atoms. Energy is required in this process in order to overcome the attraction of the nucleus for the electrons. There are two factors affecting the magnitude of the ionization energy. One is the size of the atom. The closer the electrons are to the nucleus, the more energy is needed to overcome the effective nuclear charge.

Therefore, ionization energy tends to decrease from top to bottom within a group, since the valence electrons (the first ones to be lost) are farther away from the nucleus.

The other factor is the magnitude of the effective nuclear charge. The greater the effective nuclear charge, the more energy is required to remove the electron. Since the effective nuclear charge increases from left to right within a period, the ionization energies will also increase from left to right. The increased effective nuclear charge results in the atom becoming slightly smaller, which also leads to a greater nuclear attraction for the electrons.

The ionization energy for the removal of a second electron is greater in all cases than the first, because the electron is being pulled away from a positively charged ion and the attraction is greater than from a neutral atom.

The **electron affinity (EA)** is the energy change that results from adding an electron to an atom or ion. The trends in electron affinity are not quite as regular as size or ionization energy. In general, electron affinity increases from left to right within a period (owing to the increased effective nuclear charge), and decreases from top to bottom within a group owing to increased atomic or ionic size. Noble gases are an exception—they have no EA.

Do not forget that the trends mentioned in this section may help you on the multiple-choice portion of the AP exam. However, it is the underlying reasons that you need for the free-response portion.

Oxidation Numbers

Oxidation numbers are bookkeeping numbers that allow chemists to do things like balance redox equations. Don't confuse oxidation numbers with the charge on an ion. Oxidation numbers are assigned to elements in their natural state or in compounds using the following rules:

- The oxidation number of an element in its elemental form (i.e., H_2, Au, Ag, N_2) is zero.
- The oxidation number of a monoatomic ion is equal to the charge on the ion. The oxidation number of Mg^{2+} is +2. Note that the charge is written with number first, then sign; for oxidation numbers it is sign, then number.
- The sum of all the oxidation numbers of all the elements in a neutral molecule is zero. The sum of all the oxidation numbers in a polyatomic ion is equal to the charge on the ion.
- The alkali metal ions have an oxidation number of +1 in all their compounds.
- The alkaline earth metals have an oxidation number of +2 in all their compounds.
- The oxidation number of hydrogen in compounds is +1, except it is −1 when combined with metals or boron in binary compounds.
- The oxidation number of halogens in their compounds is −1 except when combined with another halogen above them on the periodic table, or with oxygen.
- The oxidation number of oxygen is −2 in compounds, except for peroxides, in which it is −1.

Determine the oxidation number of sulfur in sulfuric acid, H_2SO_4. The sum of all the oxidation numbers must equal zero, since this is a neutral compound. The oxidation numbers of hydrogen (+1) and oxygen (−2) are known, so the oxidation number of sulfur can be determined:

$$2(+1) + ? + 4(-2) = 0$$
$$H_2SO_4$$

The oxidation number of sulfur in this compound must be +6.

Nomenclature Overview

This overview covers some of the rules for naming simple inorganic compounds. There are additional rules, and some exceptions to these rules. The first part of this overview discusses the rules for deriving a name from a chemical formula. In many cases, the formula may be determined from the name by reversing this process. The second part examines situations in which additional information is needed to generate a formula from the name of a compound. The transition metals present some additional problems; therefore, there is a section covering transition metal nomenclature and coordination compounds.

Binary Compounds

Binary compounds are compounds that consist of only two elements. Some binary compounds have special names, and these special names supersede any of the rules given below. H_2O is water, NH_3 is ammonia, and CH_4 is methane. All other binary compounds have a name with a suffix *ide*. Binary compounds may be subdivided into metal type, nonmetal type, and acid type.

(a) **Metal type** These binary compounds begin with metals. The metal is given first in the formula. In general, metals are the elements on the left-hand side of the periodic table, and the nonmetals are on the right-hand side. Hydrogen, a nonmetal, is an exception to this generalization.

First name the metal, then name the nonmetal with the suffix *ide*. Examples:

Formula	Name
Na_2O	sodium oxide
$MgCl_2$	magnesium chloride

The ammonium ion (NH_4^+) is often treated as a metal, and its compounds are named under this rule. Thus, NH_4Cl is named ammonium chloride.

(b) **Nonmetal type** These binary compounds have formulas that begin with a nonmetal. Prefixes are used to indicate the number of each atom present. No prefixes are used for hydrogen. Naming the compounds can best be explained using the following examples:

Formula	Name
CO	carbon monoxide
SO_3	sulfur trioxide
P_4O_{10}	tetraphosphorus decoxide

Carbon monoxide is one of the very few cases where the prefix *mono* is used. In general, you should not use *mono* in any other compound.

Some of the prefixes used to denote the numbers of atoms in a compound are listed below:

Number of atoms	Prefix
1	mono
2	di
3	tri
4	tetra
5	penta
6	hexa
7	hepta
8	octa
9	nona
10	deca

On many occasions the terminal *a* or *o* is dropped for oxides, so they read as pentoxide, heptoxide, or monoxide.

In normal nomenclature, the nonmetal prefixes are not used if a metal is present. One of the few exceptions to this is MnO_2, sometimes called manganese dioxide.

(c) **Acid type** These binary compounds have formulas that begin with hydrogen. If the compound is not in solution, the naming is similar to that of the metal type.

If the compound is dissolved in H_2O, indicated by (*aq*), the compound takes on the prefix *hydro* and the suffix *ic*. If the compound is not in solution, the state of matter should be shown as follows:

$$HCl(g), HF(l)$$

If the formula has no designation of phase or water, either name may be used. Examples for naming these compounds are:

Formula	Name
$HCl(g)$	hydrogen chloride
$H_2S(g)$	hydrogen sulfide
$HCl(aq)$	*hydro*chlor*ic* acid
$H_2S(aq)$	*hydro*sulfur*ic* acid
HCl	hydrogen chloride or *hydro*chlor*ic* acid
H_2S	hydrogen sulfide or *hydro*sulfur*ic* acid

HCN (hydrocyanic acid) is named using these rules. However, in this case, it does not matter if the phase or water is indicated.

Ternary Compounds

Ternary compounds are those containing three or more elements. If the first element in the formula is hydrogen, it is usually classified as an acid. If the formula contains oxygen in addition to the hydrogen, the compound is usually classified as an oxyacid. In general, if the first element in the formula is not hydrogen, the compound is classified as a salt.

Ternary acids are usually named with the suffixes *ic* or *ous*. The exceptions are the acids derived from ions with an *ide* suffix (see HCN in the preceding section). These acids undergo many reactions to form salts, compounds of a metal, and the ion of an acid. The ions from the acids H_2SO_4 and HNO_3 are SO_4^{2-}, NO_3^-. If an acid name has the suffix *ic*, the ion of this acid has a name with the suffix *ate*. If an acid name has the suffix *ous*, the ion has a name with the suffix *ite*. Salts have the same suffixes as the suffixes of the ions. The difference between the acid with a suffix *ic* and the acid with the suffix *ous* can many times be determined by visual inspection of the formula. The acid with the suffix *ous* usually has one fewer oxygen atom than the acid with the suffix *ic*. Examples:

Formula	Name of the acid	Formula	Name of the acid
H_2SO_4	sulfuric acid	HNO_3	nitric acid
H_2SO_3	sulfurous acid	HNO_2	nitrous acid

When the ternary compound is not an acid, the first element is usually a metal. In these cases, the name of the compound is simply the name of the metal followed by the name of the ion. The ammonium ion is treated as a metal in these cases.

The following are examples:

Acid formula	Acid name	Ion name	Salt formula	Salt name
H_2SO_4	sulfuric acid	sulfate ion	Na_2SO_4	sodium sulfate
H_2SO_3	sulfurous acid	sulfite ion	Na_2SO_3	sodium sulfite
HNO_3	nitric acid	nitrate ion	KNO_3	potassium nitrate
HNO_2	nitrous acid	nitrite ion	KNO_2	potassium nitrite
H_3PO_4	phosphoric acid	phosphate ion	$(NH_4)_3PO_4$	ammonium phosphate

Writing Formulas

To write the formula from the name of a binary compound containing only nonmetals, simply write the symbols for the separate atoms with the prefixes converted to subscripts.

In all compounds, the total charge must be zero. There are NO exceptions. Thus, to determine the formula in those cases where no prefixes are given, it is necessary to have some idea what the individual charges are. The species with the positive charge is listed and named first; this is followed by the species with the negative charge. Subscripts may be needed to make sure the sum of the charges (valances) will equal zero. Examples:

1. Magnesium oxide

$$Mg^{2+}O^{2-} = +2 - 2 = 0$$

This gives MgO.

2. Sodium oxide

$$Na^{1+}O^{2-} = +1 - 2 = -1; \text{ thus a subscript is needed}$$
$$Na_2^{2(1+)}O^{2-} = 2(+1) - 2 = 0$$

This gives Na_2O.

3. Aluminum oxide

$$Al^{3+}O^{2-} = +3 - 2 = +1; \text{ thus a subscript is needed}$$
$$Al_2^{2(3+)}O_3^{3(-2)} = 2(+3) + 3(-2) = 0$$

This gives Al_2O_3.

If a polyatomic ion must be increased to achieve zero charge, parentheses should be used. An example of this is shown as:

$$NH_4^+SO_4^{2-} = +1 - 2 = -1$$
$$(NH_4)_2^{2(1+)}SO_4^{2-} = 2(+1) - 2 = 0$$

This gives $(NH_4)_2SO_4$.

One way of predicting the values of the subscripts is to crisscross the valences. This is not a rule of nomenclature, but for practice purposes in this exercise it will be referred to as the crisscross rule. It works most of the time and therefore is worth considering. Example:

$Al^{3+}O^{2-}$ Crisscross the 2 from the oxygen charge to the aluminum and the 3 from the aluminum charge to the oxygen.

$Al_2^{3+}O_3^{2-}$

If the crisscross rule is applied, you should reduce the formula if possible. For example:

$Mn^{4+}O^{2-}$ crisscrosses to Mn_2O_4, which reduces to MnO_2.

If a formula is given, the crisscross rule can be reversed to give the valences:

$$Al_2O_3$$
$$Al_2^{3+}O_3^{2-}$$

As a first approximation, the valences of the representative elements can be predicted from their position on the periodic table. Hydrogen and the metals have positive charges beginning with +1 on the left and increasing by one as you proceed to the right on the periodic table (skipping the transition metals). Nonmetals begin with 0 in the rightmost column of the periodic table and decrease by 1 as you move to the left on the periodic table. Metalloids may be treated as metals or nonmetals. Examples are:

$$Na^+ \ Al^{3+} \ Pb^{4+} \ N^{3-} \ Se^{2-} \ I^-$$
$$Na^+ \ Mg^{2+} \ Al^{3+} \ Si^{4+} \ P^{3-} \ S^{2-} \ Cl^- \ Ar^0$$

Transition Metals

Many transition metals and the group of six elements centered around lead on the periodic table commonly have more than one valence. The valence of these metals in a compound must be known before the compound can be named. Modern nomenclature rules indicate the valence of one of these metals with a Roman numeral suffix (Stock notation). Older nomenclature rules used different suffixes to indicate the charge. Examples:

1. $FeCl_3$
   $Fe^{3+}Cl_3{}^{1-}$ (crisscross rule)

   The compound is named iron(III) chloride or ferric chloride.

2. $FeCl_2$

   If chloride is −1, two chloride ions are −2. Fe has a valence of +2, to give a total charge of zero. The name is iron(II) chloride or ferrous chloride.

3. MnO_2

   Mn^{4+} (found previously)
   The name would be manganese(IV) oxide, although it is often named manganese dioxide.

The Roman numeral suffix is part of the name of the metal. Thus iron(III) is one word.

Stock notation should be used for all metals that have a variable valence. This includes almost all the transition elements and the elements immediately around lead on the periodic table. Stock notation is often omitted for Zn, Cd, and Ag, as they do not have variable valences.

The valences of some common metals and acids are listed in the appendixes.

Coordination Compounds

Coordination compounds contain a complex. In general, a complex may be recognized because it is enclosed in square brackets [ ]. The square brackets are omitted when the actual structure of the complex is uncertain.

A complex is composed of a central atom, normally a metal, surrounded by atoms or groups of atoms called ligands. One way of forming a complex is illustrated below:

$$Ni^{2+} + 6 \ H_2O \rightarrow [Ni(H_2O)_6]^{2+}$$

In this reaction, the metal behaves as a Lewis acid and accepts a pair of electrons from the Lewis base (ligand). In this case, the ligand is water, with the oxygen atom donating one of its lone pairs to the nickel. The oxygen atom is called the donor atom. In this complex, there are six donor atoms.

A complex may be ionic or neutral. An ionic complex is called a complex ion. A neutral complex is a type of coordination compound. The only difference in naming coordination compounds or complex ions is that anionic complex ions have an *ate* suffix.

A coordination compound may contain more than one complex ion or material that is not part of the complex, but it must have an overall neutral charge. Examples of coordination compounds are: $[Pt(NH_3)_2Cl_2]$, $K_2[Mn(C_2O_4)_3]$, and $[Ni(H_2O)_6]SO_4$.

When writing formulas, the metal (central atom) is *always* listed first within the brackets. However, when writing names, the metal name is *always* given last. Any material not listed within the brackets is named separately.

Examples:

$[Ru(NH_3)_5(N_2)]Cl_2$	coordination compound
$[Ru(NH_3)_5(N_2)]^{2+}$	complex ion (cationic)
$[PtNH_3Cl_2(C_5H_5N)]$	coordination compound
$[IF_6]^-$	complex ion (anionic) (the name must end in -ate)
$K[IF_6]$	coordination compound (same -ate ending)

If everything in the formula is enclosed within one set of brackets, the entire name will be one word. If there is material outside the brackets, this outside material is named separately.

Just as with simpler compounds, cations are always named before anions. Thus, a cationic complex would be the first word in the name, and an anionic complex would be the last word in a name (with an *ate* ending).

Examples:

$[Ni(H_2O)_4Cl_2]$	tetraaquadichloronickel(II)
$[Co(NH_3)_6]Cl_3$	hexaamminecobalt(III) chloride
$K_2[PtCl_4]$	potassium tetrachloroplatinate(II)

When naming a complex, or when writing the formula for a complex, the ligands are listed alphabetically. Again, do not forget that metals are first in the formula and last in the name.

The names of anionic ligands always end in an *o*. Neutral ligands are basically unchanged. Two common exceptions in the case of neutral ligands are NH_3 = ammine (note the double *m*), and H_2O = aqua. Other common ligands and their names are listed in the appendixes.

Multiple identical ligands have prefixes added to designate the number of such ligands:

2	di-	5	penta-	8	octa-
3	tri-	6	hexa-	9	nona-
4	tetra-	7	hepta-	10	deca-

Examples:

$[Co(NH_3)_6]Cl_3$	hexaamminecobalt(III) chloride
$[Cr(NO)_4]$	tetranitrosylchromium(0)

If the ligand name contains a prefix or begins with a vowel (except ammine and aqua), alternative prefixes should be used:

2	bis-	5	pentakis-	8	octakis-
3	tris-	6	hexakis-	9	nonakis-
4	tetrakis-	7	heptakis-	10	decakis-

When using the alternative prefixes, it is common practice to enclose the name of the ligand within parentheses. Either type of prefix is added after the ligands have been alphabetized.

Examples:

$[Cr(en)_3]Cl_3$	Tris(ethylenediamine)chromium(III) chloride
$K_2[Ge(C_2O_4)_3]$	Potassium tris(oxalato)germanate

Anionic complexes always have names ending in *ate*. This will require a change in the name of the metal. Thus, aluminum would become aluminate, and zinc would become zincate. The only exceptions to this are some of the metals whose symbols are based on Latin or Greek names. These exceptions are:

Metal (Greek or Latin name)	Symbol	Anionic name
copper (cuprum)	Cu	cuprate
silver (argentum)	Ag	argentate
gold (aurum)	Au	aurate
iron (ferrum)	Fe	ferrate
tin (stannum)	Sn	stannate
lead (plumbum)	Pb	plumbate

Examples:

$K[Au(CN)_4]$ potassium tetracyanoaurate(III)

$(NH_4)_2[PbCl_6]$ ammonium hexachloroplumbate(IV)

If the metal ion may exist in more than one oxidation state, this oxidation state should be listed, in Roman numerals, *immediately* after the name of the metal ion. The Roman numeral is enclosed in parentheses and is considered part of the same word, and not a separate grouping. If the metal occurs in only one oxidation state, no such indicator is used. This notation is the Stock system discussed earlier.

Experiments

Experiments involving the basic material covered in this chapter have been placed in the in-depth chapters throughout the remainder of this book.

Common Mistakes to Avoid

Between the two of us, we have almost 60 years of teaching experience. We've seen a lot of student mistakes. We will try to steer you clear of the most common ones.

1. Always show your units in mathematical problems.
2. In the conversion from °F to °C, be sure to subtract 32 from the Fahrenheit temperature first, then multiply by 5/9.
3. In the conversion from °C to °F, be sure to multiply the Celsius temperature by 9/5, then add 32.
4. No degree sign is used for Kelvin.
5. Only consider measured values for significant figures.
6. When considering whether or not zeroes to the right of the last non-zero digit are significant, pay attention to whether or not there is a decimal point.
7. Round off only your final answer, not intermediate calculations.
8. In working problems, be sure that your units cancel.
9. If you are solving for cm, for example, be sure you end up with cm and not 1/cm.
10. Make sure your answer is a reasonable one.
11. Don't confuse the mass number (A) with the atomic number (Z).
12. When determining valence electrons, only the s and p electrons are considered.
13. Don't put more than 2 electrons in any individual orbital.

14. Always fill lowest energy levels first.
15. Half fill orbitals of equal energy before pairing up the electrons.
16. In writing the electronic configuration of an atom, make sure you use the correct filling order.
17. Don't confuse the periods with the groups on the periodic table.
18. Don't confuse ionization energy with electron affinity.
19. Don't confuse oxidation numbers with ionic charge.
20. In naming compounds, don't confuse metal and nonmetal type binary compounds. Prefixes are used only with nonmetal types.
21. Be careful when using the crisscross rule to reduce the subscripts to their lowest whole-number ratio.
22. Be sure to report the proper number of significant figures.
23. Simply knowing a periodic trend will allow you to pick the correct multiple-choice answer, but be prepared to explain the trend in free-response questions.

› Review Questions

Here are questions you can use to review the content of this chapter and practice for the AP Chemistry exam. First are 25 multiple-choice questions similar to what you will encounter in Section I of the AP Chemistry exam. Following those is a four-part free-response question like the ones in Section II of the exam. To make these questions an even more authentic practice for the actual exam, time yourself following the instructions provided.

Multiple-Choice Questions

Answer the following questions in 30 minutes. You may not use a calculator. You may use the periodic table and the equation sheet at the back of this book.

1. In most of its compounds, this element exists as a monatomic cation.

   (A) O
   (B) Cl
   (C) Na
   (D) N

2. This element may form a compound with the formula $CaXO_4$.

   (A) Se
   (B) Cl
   (C) P
   (D) Na

3. Which of the following elements may occur in the greatest number of different oxidation states?

   (A) C
   (B) F
   (C) O
   (D) Ca

4. Choose the group that does NOT contain isotopes of the same element.

		Number of protons	Number of neutrons
(A)	Atom I	18	18
	Atom II	18	19
(B)	Atom I	25	30
	Atom II	25	31
(C)	Atom I	37	42
	Atom II	37	41
(D)	Atom I	82	126
	Atom II	81	126

5. Which of the following groups has the species correctly listed in order of increasing radius?

   (A) Mg^{2+}, Ca^{2+}, Ba^{2+}
   (B) K^+, Na^+, Li^+
   (C) Br^-, Cl^-, F^-
   (D) Na, Mg, Al

6. Which of the following elements has the lowest electronegativity?

   (A) C
   (B) K
   (C) Al
   (D) I

7. Choose the ion with the largest ionic radius.

   (A) F^-
   (B) Al^{3+}
   (C) K^+
   (D) I^-

8. What is the name of the energy change when a gaseous atom, in the ground state, adds an electron?

   (A) ionization energy
   (B) sublimation energy
   (C) atomization energy
   (D) electron affinity

9. The following ionization energies are reported for element X. (All the values are in kJ/mol.)

   First Second Third Fourth Fifth
   500   4,560   6,910 9,540   13,400

   Based on the above information, the most likely identity of X is:

   (A) Mg
   (B) Cl
   (C) Al
   (D) Na

10. In general, as the atomic numbers increase within a period, the atomic radius:

    (A) decreases
    (B) increases
    (C) first decreases and then increases
    (D) does not change

11. Which of the following elements is a reactive gas?

    (A) chlorine
    (B) gold
    (C) sodium
    (D) radon

12. Which of the following elements is an unreactive metal?

    (A) chlorine
    (B) gold
    (C) sodium
    (D) radon

13. Which of the following represents the correct formula for potassium trisoxalatoferrate(III)?

    (A) $P_3[Fe(C_2O_4)_3]$
    (B) $K_3[Fe(C_2O_4)_3]$
    (C) $KFe_3(C_2O_4)_3$
    (D) $K_3[Fe_3(C_2O_4)_3]$

14. Which of the following substances will produce a colorless aqueous solution?

    (A) $Zn(NO_3)_2$
    (B) $CuSO_4$
    (C) $K_2Cr_2O_7$
    (D) $Co(NO_3)_2$

15. This element is a liquid at room temperature.

    (A) Hg
    (B) Th
    (C) Na
    (D) Cl

16. Which of the following elements is present in chlorophyll?

    (A) K
    (B) Ga
    (C) Al
    (D) Mg

17. What is the symbol for the element that forms a protective oxide coating?

    (A) K
    (B) Ga
    (C) Al
    (D) Mg

18. Which of the following elements is important in the semiconductor industry to improve the conductivity of germanium, Ge?

    (A) K
    (B) Ga
    (C) Al
    (D) Mg

19. Which of the following aqueous solutions is blue?

(A) $CuSO_4$
(B) $Cr_2(SO_4)_3$
(C) $NiSO_4$
(D) $ZnSO_4$

20. In order to separate two substances by fractional crystallization, the two substances must differ in which of the following?

(A) solubility
(B) specific gravity
(C) vapor pressure
(D) viscosity

21. In a flame test, copper compounds impart which of the following colors to a flame?

(A) red
(B) orange
(C) blue to green
(D) violet

22. What should you do if you spill sulfuric acid on the countertop?

(A) Neutralize the acid with vinegar.
(B) Sprinkle solid NaOH on the spill.
(C) Neutralize the acid with $NaHCO_3$ solution.
(D) Neutralize the acid with an Epsom salt ($MgSO_4$) solution.

23. Which of the following can be achieved by using a visible-light spectrophotometer?

(A) Run a flame test to determine if Na^+ or K^+ is in a solution.
(B) Find the concentration of a $KMnO_4$ solution.
(C) Detect the presence of isolated double bonds.
(D) Measure the strength of a covalent bond.

24. You have an aqueous solution of NaCl. The simplest method for the separation of NaCl from the solution is:

(A) evaporation of the solution to dryness
(B) centrifuging the solution
(C) filtration of the solution
(D) electrolysis of the solution

25. The determination that atoms have small, dense nuclei is attributed to:

(A) Rutherford
(B) Becquerel
(C) Einstein
(D) Dalton

Answers and Explanations for the Multiple-Choice Questions

1. **C**—All the other elements are nonmetals. Nonmetals usually form monatomic anions.

2. **A**—The element cannot be a metal (Na). A nonmetal that can have a +6 oxidation state is necessary. P has a maximum of +5. Cl may be +5 or +7. Se, in column 16, can easily be +6.

3. **A**—Based on their positions on the periodic table:

C	+4 to –4
F	–1 and 0 (element)
O	–2 to 0
Ca	+2 and 0

4. **D**—Isotopes MUST have the same number of protons. Different isotopes of an element have different numbers of neutrons.

5. **A**—All the others are in decreasing order. Ions in the same column and with the same charge increase in size when going down a column the same as atoms. Atoms in the same row increase in size toward the left side. This argument is not sufficient on the free-response portion of the exam.

6. **B**—In general, the element farthest from F on the periodic table will have the lowest electronegativity. There are exceptions, but you normally do not need to concern yourself with exceptions.

7. **D**—The very large iodine atom (near the bottom of the periodic table) gains an electron to make it even larger. This reasoning is not sufficient on the free-response portion of the exam.

8. **D**—The definition of electron affinity is the energy change when a ground-state gaseous atom adds an electron.

9. **D**—The more electrons removed, the higher the values should be. The large increase between the first and second ionization energies indicates a change in electron shell. The element, X, has only 1 valence electron. This is true for Na. For the other elements the numbers of valence electrons are: Mg – 2; Cl – 7; and Al – 3.

10. **A**—The increase in the number of protons in the nucleus has a greater attraction (greater effective nuclear charge) for the electrons being added in the same energy level. Thus, the electrons are pulled closer to the nucleus and the size slightly decreases. This thought process should be used on the free-response portion of the AP exam; however, simply remembering that radii decrease across a period is sufficient for most multiple-choice questions.

11. **A**—The only other gas is radon, and it is inert.

12. **B**—Sodium is a metal on the left side of the periodic table. Metals on the left side of the periodic table are very reactive. Radon is not a metal.

13. **B**—Ferrate(III) means Fe^{3+}, while trisoxalato means $(C_2O_4)_3^{6-}$; three potassium atoms are needed to balance the charge.

14. **A**—B is blue; C is orange; and D is pink to red.

15. **A**—Chlorine is a gas; all the others are solid metals.

16. **D**—Magnesium is present in chlorophyll.

17. **C**—Aluminum forms a protective oxide coating.

18. **B**—Gallium, adjacent to Ge on the periodic table, is one of the elements that will improve the conductivity of germanium.

19. **A**—B is purple; C is green; and D is colorless.

20. **A**—Fractional crystallization works because the less soluble material separates first.

21. **C**—A could be Li or Sr; B is Ca; and D is K.

22. **C**—Adding a weak base solution, such as $NaHCO_3$, which will not only neutralize the acid but will help to disperse the heat, is the best choice.

23. **B**—A solution containing a colored substance is necessary.

24. **A**—Separation of materials in solution is normally not simple; therefore, removal of the solvent through evaporation is the best choice.

25. **A**—Rutherford, and his students, demonstrated the existence of the nucleus.

Free-Response Question

Both authors have been AP free-response graders for years. Here is a free-response question for practice.

You have 10 minutes to do the following question. You may use a calculator and the tables in the back of the book.

Question 1

Use the periodic table and other information concerning bonding and electronic structure to explain the following observations.

(a) The radii of the iron cations are less than that of an iron atom, and Fe^{3+} is smaller than Fe^{2+}.

(b) When moving across the periodic table from Li to Be to B, the first ionization energy increases from Li to Be, then drops for B. The first ionization energy of B is greater than that of Li.

(c) The electron affinity of F is higher than the electron affinity of O.

(d) The following observations have been made about the lattice energy and ionic radii of the compounds listed below. Compare NaF to CaO, and then compare CaO to BaO. All of the solids adopt the same crystal structure.

Compound	Ionic radius of cation (pm)	Ionic radius of anion (pm)	Lattice energy (kJ/mole)
NaF	116	119	911
CaO	114	126	3,566
BaO	149	126	3,202

Answer and Explanation for the Free-Response Question

Notice that all the answers are very short. Do not try to fill all the space provided on the exam. You score points by saying specific things, not by the bulk of material. The graders look for certain keywords or phrases. The answers should not contain statements that contradict each other; otherwise, there may be a penalty. Contradictions most commonly occur when the student tries to say too much. On the AP exam, the different parts of the free-response questions tend to be more diverse than this one, as this question focuses on this chapter, whereas the AP free-response questions focus on the entire course.

(a) The observed trend of radii is $Fe > Fe^{2+} > Fe^{3+}$. There is an increase in the effective nuclear charge in this series. As electrons are removed, the repulsion between the remaining electrons decreases. The larger the effective nuclear charge, the greater the attraction of the electrons toward the nucleus and the smaller the atom or ion becomes.

Give yourself 1 point for "effective nuclear charge" and 1 point for the effective nuclear charge, and give yourself 1 point for the remainder of the discussion.

(b) When moving across a period on the periodic table, the value of the effective nuclear charge increases with atomic number. This causes a general increase from Li to Be to B. DO NOT use the argument that ionization energies increase to the right on the periodic table, unless you also discuss effective nuclear charge.

The even higher value of Be (greater than B) is due to the increased stability of the electron configuration of Be. Beryllium has a filled s-subshell. Filled subshells have an increased stability, and additional energy is required to pull an electron away.

This effective nuclear charge argument is worth 1 point. Give yourself 0 points if you say that the ionization energy increases to the right on the periodic table. This is an observation; it is not an explanation. Give yourself 1 more point for the filled subshell discussion.

(c) The effective nuclear charge in F is greater than the effective nuclear charge in O. This causes a greater attraction of the electrons. DO NOT use the argument that electron affinity increases to the right on the periodic table, unless you also discuss effective nuclear charge.

You get 1 point for this answer.

(d) Because all these solids adopt the same structure, the structure is irrelevant. The sizes of the anions are similar; thus, anion size arguments are not important. Two factors, other than structure and anion size, are important here. The two compounds with the highest lattice energies contain divalent ions (+2 or –2), while NaF contains univalent ions (+1 or –1). The higher the charge is, the greater the attraction between the ions is. The lattice energy increases as the attraction increases.

You get 1 point for correctly discussing the charges. The difference between the CaO and BaO values is because the larger the ion is, the lower the attraction is (greater separation). The lower attraction leads to a lower lattice energy. This size argument will get you 1 point.

Total your points. The maximum is 7.

› Rapid Review

Here is a brief review of the most important points in the chapter. If something sounds unfamiliar, study it in the chapter and your textbook.

- Know the metric measurement system and some metric/English conversions.
- Know how to convert from any one of the Fahrenheit/Celsius/Kelvin temperature scales to the other two.
- The density of a substance is mass per unit volume.
- Know how to determine the number of significant figures in a number, the rules for how many significant figures are to be shown in the final answer, and the round-off rules.
- Know how to set up problems using the factor label method.
- Know the differences between a solid, a liquid, and a gas at both the macroscopic and microscopic levels.
- Know what part Dalton, Thompson, Millikan, and Rutherford had in the development of the atomic model.
- Know the three basic subatomic particles—proton, neutron, and electron—their symbols, mass in amu, and their location.
- Isotopes are atoms of the same element that have differing numbers of neutrons.
- Electrons are located in major energy levels called shells. Shells are divided into subshells, and there are orbitals for each subshell.
- Know the electron capacity of each orbital (always 2).
- Be able to write both the energy-level diagram and the electronic configuration of an atom or ion by applying both the Aufbau build-up principle and Hund's rule.
- Know how the modern periodic table was developed, including the differences between Mendeleev's table and the current table.

- Periods are the horizontal rows on the periodic table; the elements have properties unlike the other members of the period.

- Groups or families are the vertical rows on the periodic table; the elements have similar properties.

- Know the properties of metals, nonmetals, and metalloids and which elements on the periodic table belong to each group.

- Valence electrons are outer-shell electrons.

- The IA family is known as the alkali metals; the IIAs are the alkaline earth metals; the VIIAs are the halogens; and the VIIIAs are the noble gases.

- Know why atoms get larger as we go from top to bottom in a group and slightly smaller as we move from left to right on the periodic table. Remember that on the free-response section, simply quoting a trend is not sufficient in answering the question. This is true for all trends.

- Ionization energy is the energy it takes to remove an electron from a gaseous atom or ion. It decreases from top to bottom and increases from left to right on the periodic table. Much the same trend is noted for electron affinity, the energy change that takes place when an electron is added to a gaseous atom or ion. The trends depend on the size of the atom or ion and its effective nuclear charge.

- Oxidation numbers are bookkeeping numbers. Know the rules for assigning oxidation numbers.

- Be able to name binary metal type and nonmetal type compounds, as well as ternary compounds, oxyacids, simple coordination compounds, etc.

CHAPTER 6

Reactions and Periodicity

IN THIS CHAPTER

Summary: Chemistry is the world of chemical reactions. Chemical reactions power our society, our environment, and our bodies. Some chemical species called **reactants** are converted into different substances called **products**. During this process, there are energy changes that take place. It takes energy to break old bonds. Energy is released when new bonds are formed. Does it take more energy to break the bonds than is released in the formation of the new bonds? If so, energy will have to be constantly supplied to convert the reactants into products. This type of reaction is said to be **endothermic**, absorbing energy. If more energy is released than is needed to break the old bonds, then the reaction is said to be **exothermic**, releasing energy. The chemical reactions that provide the energy for our world are exothermic reactions. In Chapter 9, Thermodynamics, you can read in more depth about the energy changes that occur during reactions.

Reactions occur because of collisions. One chemical species collides with another at the right place and transfers enough energy, and a chemical reaction occurs. Such reactions can be very fast or very slow. In Chapter 14 on Kinetics, you can study how reactions occur and the factors that affect the speed of reactions. But in this chapter we will review the balancing of chemical equations, discuss the general types of chemical reactions, and describe why these reactions occur.

Keywords and Equations

There are no keywords or equations listed on the AP exam that are specific to this chapter.

Reactions questions will always appear in the free-response section of the AP exam.

AP Exam Format

Beginning with the 2007 AP exam, the treatment of chemical reactions was changed from previous years. In the past, the free-response questions concerning chemical reactions simply involved the formulas of the reactants and products chosen from a series of reactions. You were not expected to write balanced chemical equations. However, under the current AP Chemistry exam format you no longer are able to choose from a list of reactions. You are expected to write a balanced chemical equation for every reaction given and answer one or more questions about each reaction. If the reaction occurs in aqueous solution, you will have to write the net ionic equation for the process. For the reactions question of the AP exam, you will be expected not only to balance the equation, but also to have an understanding of why the reaction occurs. The reactions and concepts described may also appear in other parts of the AP exam, such as the multiple-choice sections. Again, you will need to have an understanding of why a particular reaction occurs. As you study this chapter, pay particular attention to the explanations that accompany the reactions and equations. You will be expected to demonstrate your understanding on the AP exam.

General Aspects of Chemical Reactions and Equations

Balancing Chemical Equations

The authors hope that, because you are preparing to take the AP exam, you have already been exposed to the balancing of chemical equations. We will quickly review this topic and point out some specific aspects of balancing equations as the different types of chemical reactions are discussed.

A balanced chemical equation provides many types of information. It shows which chemical species are the reactants and which species are the products. It may also indicate in which state of matter the reactants and products exist. Special conditions of temperature, catalysts, etc. may be placed over or under the reaction arrow. And, very important, the coefficients (the integers in front of the chemical species) indicate the number of each reactant that is used and the number of each product that is formed. These coefficients may stand for individual atoms/molecules, or they may represent large numbers of them called moles (see Chapter 7, Stoichiometry, for a discussion of moles). The basic idea behind the balancing of equations is the **Law of Conservation of Matter**, which says that in ordinary chemical reactions matter is neither created nor destroyed. The number of each type of reactant atom has to equal the number of each type of product atom. This requires adjusting the reactant and product coefficients—balancing the equation. When finished, the coefficients should be in the lowest possible whole-number ratio.

Most equations are balanced by inspection. This means basically a trial-and-error, methodical approach to adjusting the coefficients. One procedure that works well is to balance the homonuclear (same nucleus) molecule last. Chemical species that fall into this category include the diatomic elements, which you should know: H_2, O_2, N_2, F_2, Cl_2, Br_2, and I_2. This is especially useful when balancing combustion reactions. If a problem states that oxygen gas was used, then knowing that oxygen exists as the diatomic element is absolutely necessary in balancing the equation correctly.

Periodic Relationships

The periodic table can give us many clues as to the type of reaction that is taking place. One general rule, covered in more detail in Chapter 11, Bonding, is that nonmetals react with other nonmetals to form covalent compounds, and that metals react with nonmetals to form ionic compounds. If the reaction that is producing the ionic compound is occurring in solution, you will be expected to write the net ionic equation for the reaction. Also, because of the wonderful arrangement of the periodic table, the members of a family or group (a vertical grouping) all react essentially in the same fashion. Many times, in reactions involving the loss of electrons (oxidation), as we proceed from top to bottom in a family the reaction rate (speed) increases. Conversely, in reactions involving the gain of electrons (reduction) the reaction rate increases as we move from the bottom of a family to the top. Recall also that the noble gases (VIIIA) undergo very few reactions. Other specific periodic aspects will be discussed in the various reaction sections.

General Properties of Aqueous Solutions

Many of the reactions that you will study occur in aqueous solution. Water is called the universal solvent, because it dissolves so many substances. It readily dissolves ionic compounds as well as polar covalent compounds, because of its polar nature. Ionic compounds that dissolve in water (dissociate) form **electrolyte** solutions, which conduct electrical current owing to the presence of ions. The ions can attract the polar water molecules and form a bound layer of water molecules around themselves. This process is called **solvation**. Refer to Chapter 13, Solutions and Colligative Properties, for an in-depth discussion of solvation.

Even though many ionic compounds dissolve in water, many others do not. If the attraction of the oppositely charged ions in the solid for each other is greater than the attraction of the polar water molecules for the ions, then the salt will not dissolve to an appreciable amount. If solutions containing ions such as these are mixed, precipitation will occur, because the strong attraction of the ions for each other overcomes the weaker attraction for the water molecules.

As mentioned before, certain covalent compounds, like alcohols, readily dissolve in water because they are polar. Since water is polar, and these covalent compounds are also polar, water will act as a solvent for them (general rule of solubility: "Like dissolves like"). Compounds like alcohols are **nonelectrolytes**—substances that do not conduct an electrical current when dissolved in water. However, certain covalent compounds, like acids, will **ionize** in water, that is, form ions:

$$HCl(aq) \rightarrow H^+(aq) + Cl^-(aq)$$

There are several ways of representing reactions that occur in water. Suppose, for example, that we were writing the equation to describe the mixing of a lead(II) nitrate solution with a sodium sulfate solution and showing the resulting formation of solid lead(II) sulfate. One type of equation that can be written is the **molecular equation**, in which both the reactants and products are shown in the undissociated form:

$$Pb(NO_3)_2(aq) + Na_2SO_4(aq) \rightarrow PbSO_4(s) + 2NaNO_3(aq)$$

Molecular equations are quite useful when doing reaction stoichiometry problems (see Chapter 7).

Showing the soluble reactants and products in the form of ions yields the **ionic equation** (sometimes called the total ionic equation):

$$Pb^{2+}(aq) + 2NO_3^-(aq) + 2Na^+(aq) + SO_4^{2-}(aq) \rightarrow PbSO_4(s) + 2Na^+(aq) + 2NO_3^-(aq)$$

Writing the equation in the ionic form shows clearly which species are really reacting and which are not. In the example above, Na^+ and NO_3^- appear on both sides of the equation. They do not react, but are simply there in order to maintain electrical neutrality of the solution. Ions like this, which are not actually involved in the chemical reaction taking place, are called **spectator ions**.

The **net ionic equation** is written by dropping out the spectator ions and showing only those chemical species that are involved in the chemical reaction:

$$Pb^{2+}(aq) + SO_4^{2-}(aq) \rightarrow PbSO_4(s)$$

This net ionic equation focuses only on the substances that are actually involved in the reaction. It indicates that an aqueous solution containing Pb^{2+} (any solution, not just $Pb(NO_3)_2(aq)$) will react with any solution containing the sulfate ion to form insoluble lead(II) sulfate. If this equation form is used, the spectator ions involved will not be known, but in most cases, this is not a particular problem, since the focus is really the general reaction, and not the specific one. You will be expected to write the balanced net ionic equation for many of the reactions on the test.

Precipitation Reactions

Precipitation reactions involve the formation of an insoluble compound, a **precipitate**, from the mixing of two soluble compounds. Precipitation reactions normally occur in aqueous solution. The example above that was used to illustrate molecular equations, ionic equations, etc., was a precipitation reaction. A solid, lead(II) sulfate, was formed from the mixing of the two aqueous solutions. In order to predict whether or not precipitation will occur if two solutions are mixed, you must:

1. Learn to write the correct chemical formulas from the names; on the AP exam, names are frequently given instead of formulas in the reaction section.

2. Be able to write the reactants and products in their ionic form, as in the ionic equation example above. Be sure, however, that you do not try to break apart molecular compounds such as most organic compounds, or insoluble species.

3. Know and be able to apply the following solubility rules by combining the cation of one reactant with the anion of the other in the correct formula ratio, and determining the solubility of the proposed product. Then do the same thing for the other anion/cation combination.

4. On the AP exam, you will be expected to explain why a substance is soluble/insoluble. Simply quoting the solubility rule is not sufficient.

Learn the following solubility rule:

All sodium, potassium, ammonium, and nitrate salts are soluble in water.

ENRICHMENT

Although not required for the AP exam, the following solubility rules are very useful:

- All salts containing acetate (CH_3COO^-), and perchlorates (ClO_4^-) are *soluble*.
- All chlorides (Cl^-), bromides (Br^-), and iodides (I^-) are *soluble*, except those of Cu^+, Ag^+, Pb^{2+}, and Hg_2^{2+}.
- All salts containing sulfate (SO_4^{2-}) are *soluble*, except those of Pb^{2+}, Ca^{2+}, Sr^{2+}, and Ba^{2+}.

Salts containing the following ions are normally **insoluble**:

- Most carbonates (CO_3^{2-}) and phosphates (PO_4^{3-}) are *insoluble*, except those of Group IA and the ammonium ion.
- Most sulfides (S^{2-}) are *insoluble*, except those of Group IA and IIA and the ammonium ion.
- Most hydroxides (OH^-) are *insoluble*, except those of Group IA, calcium, and barium.
- Most oxides (O^{2-}) are *insoluble*, except for those of Group IA, and Group IIA, which react with water to form the corresponding soluble hydroxides.

Let's see how one might apply these rules. Suppose a solution of lead(II) nitrate is mixed with a solution of sodium iodide. Predict what will happen.

Write the formulas:

$$Pb(NO_3)_2(aq) + NaI(aq) \rightarrow$$

Convert to the ionic form:

$$Pb^{2+}(aq) + 2NO_3^-(aq) + Na^+(aq) + I^-(aq) \rightarrow$$

Predict the possible products by combining the cation of one reactant with the anion of the other and vice versa:

$$PbI_2 + NaNO_3$$

Apply the solubility rules to the two possible products:

$PbI_2(s)$ *Insoluble*; therefore a precipitate will form.

$NaNO_3(aq)$ *Soluble*; no precipitate will form.

Complete the chemical equation and balance it:

$$Pb(NO_3)_2(aq) + 2NaI(aq) \rightarrow PbI_2(s) + 2NaNO_3(aq)$$

$$Pb^{2+}(aq) + 2I^-(aq) \rightarrow PbI_2(s)$$

If both possible products are soluble, then the reaction would be listed as NR (No Reaction). In the reaction question part of the AP exam, there will be a possible reaction for every part of the question. If at least one insoluble product is formed, the reaction is sometimes classified as a **double displacement (replacement) or metathesis reaction**.

Oxidation–Reduction Reactions

Oxidation–reduction reactions, commonly called **redox reactions**, are an extremely important category of reaction. Redox reactions include combustion, corrosion, respiration, photosynthesis, and the reactions involved in electrochemical cells (batteries). The driving force involved in redox reactions is the exchange of electrons from a more active species to a less active one. You can predict the relative activities from a table of activities or a half-reaction table. Chapter 16, Electrochemistry, goes into depth about electrochemistry and redox reactions.

The AP free-response booklet includes a table of half-reactions, which you may use for help during this part of the exam. A similar table can be found in the back of this book. Alternatively, you may wish to memorize the common oxidizing and reducing agents.

Redox is a term that stands for **red**uction and **ox**idation. **Reduction** is the gain of electrons, and **oxidation** is the loss of electrons. For example, suppose a piece of zinc metal is placed in a solution containing the blue Cu^{2+} cation. Very quickly, a reddish solid forms on the surface of the zinc metal. That substance is copper metal. As the copper metal is deposited, the blue color of the solution begins to fade. At the molecular level, the more active zinc metal is losing electrons to form the Zn^{2+} cation, and the Cu^{2+} ion is gaining electrons to form the less active copper metal. These two processes can be shown as:

$$Zn(s) \rightarrow Zn^{2+}(aq) + 2e^- \quad \text{(oxidation)}$$
$$Cu^{2+}(aq) + 2e^- \rightarrow Cu(s) \qquad \text{(reduction)}$$

The electrons that are being lost by the zinc metal are the same electrons that are being gained by the copper(II) ion. The zinc metal is being oxidized and the copper(II) ion is being reduced. Further discussions on why reactions such as these occur can be found in the section on single displacement reactions later in this chapter.

Something must cause the oxidation (taking the electrons), and that substance is called the **oxidizing agent** (the reactant being reduced). In the example above, the oxidizing agent is the Cu^{2+} ion. The reactant undergoing oxidation is called the **reducing agent** because it is furnishing the electrons that are being used in the reduction half-reaction. Zinc metal is the reducing agent above. The two half-reactions, oxidation and reduction, can be added together to give you the overall redox reaction. When doing this, the electrons must cancel—that is, there must be the same number of electrons lost as electrons gained:

$$Zn(s) + Cu^{2+}(aq) + 2e^- \rightarrow Zn^{2+}(aq) + 2e^- + Cu(s)$$

$$or \quad Zn(s) + Cu^{2+}(aq) \rightarrow Zn^{2+}(aq) + Cu(s)$$

In these redox reactions, there is a simultaneous loss and gain of electrons. In the oxidation reaction (commonly called a half-reaction) electrons are being lost, but in the reduction half-reaction those very same electrons are being gained. So, in redox reactions electrons are being exchanged as reactants are being converted into products. This electron exchange may be direct, as when copper metal plates out on a piece of zinc, or it may be indirect, as in an electrochemical cell (battery).

Another way to determine what is being oxidized and what is being reduced is by looking at the change in oxidation numbers of the reactant species. (See Chapter 5, Basics, for a discussion of oxidation numbers and how to calculate them.) On the AP exam, you may be asked to assign oxidation numbers and/or identify changes in terms of oxidation numbers. Oxidation is indicated by an increase in oxidation number. In the example above, the Zn metal went from an oxidation state of zero to +2. Reduction is indicated by a decrease in oxidation number. Cu^{2+} went from an oxidation state of +2 to zero. In order to figure out whether a particular reaction is a redox reaction, write the net ionic equation. Then determine the oxidation numbers of each element in the reaction. If one or more elements have changed oxidation number, it is a redox reaction.

There are several types of redox reaction that are given specific names. In the next few pages, we will examine some of these types of redox reaction.

Combination Reactions

Combination reactions are reactions in which two or more reactants (elements or compounds) combine to form one product. Although these reactions may be of a number of different types, some types are definitely redox reactions. These include reactions of metals with nonmetals to form ionic compounds, and the reaction of nonmetals with other nonmetals to form covalent compounds.

$$2K(s) + Cl_2(g) \rightarrow 2KCl(s)$$
$$2H_2(g) + O_2(g) \rightarrow 2H_2O(l)$$

In the first reaction, we have the combination of an active metal with an active nonmetal to form a stable ionic compound. The very active oxygen reacts with hydrogen to form the stable compound water. The hydrogen and potassium are undergoing oxidation, while the oxygen and chlorine are undergoing reduction.

Decomposition Reactions

Decomposition reactions are reactions in which a compound breaks down into two or more simpler substances. Although not all decomposition reactions are redox reactions, many are. For example, the thermal decomposition reactions, such as the common laboratory experiment of generating oxygen by heating potassium chlorate, are decomposition reactions:

$$2KClO_3(s) \xrightarrow{\Delta} 2KCl(s) + 3O_2(g)$$

In this reaction the chlorine is going from the less stable +5 oxidation state to the more stable −1 oxidation state. While this is occurring, oxygen is being oxidized from −2 to 0.

Another example is **electrolysis**, in which an electrical current is used to decompose a compound into its elements:

$$2H_2O(l) \xrightarrow{electricity} 2H_2(g) + O_2(g)$$

The spontaneous reaction would be the opposite one; therefore, we must supply energy (in the form of electricity) in order to force the nonspontaneous reaction to occur.

Single Displacement Reactions

Single displacement (replacement) reactions are reactions in which atoms of an element replace the atoms of another element in a compound. All of these single replacement reactions are redox reactions, since the element (in a zero oxidation state) becomes an ion. Most single displacement reactions can be categorized into one of three types of reaction:

- A metal displacing a metal ion from solution
- A metal displacing hydrogen gas (H_2) from an acid or from water
- One halogen replacing another halogen in a compound

Remember: It is an **element** displacing another atom from a compound. The displaced atom appears as an element on the product side of the equation.

Table 6.1   Activity Series of Metals in Aqueous Solution

Li(s)	→	Li^+(aq)	+	e^-	Most easily oxidized
K(s)	→	K^+(aq)	+	e^-	
Ba(s)	→	Ba^{2+}(aq)	+	$2\,e^-$	
Sr(s)	→	Sr^{2+}(aq)	+	$2\,e^-$	
Ca(s)	→	Ca^{2+}(aq)	+	$2\,e^-$	
Na(s)	→	Na^+(aq)	+	e^-	
Mg(s)	→	Mg^{2+}(aq)	+	$2\,e^-$	
Al(s)	→	Al^{3+}(aq)	+	$3\,e^-$	
Mn(s)	→	Mn^{2+}(aq)	+	$2\,e^-$	
Zn(s)	→	Zn^{2+}(aq)	+	$2\,e^-$	
Cr(s)	→	Cr^{2+}(aq)	+	$2\,e^-$	
Fe(s)	→	Fe^{2+}(aq)	+	$2\,e^-$	
Cd(s)	→	Cd^{2+}(aq)	+	$2\,e^-$	
Co(s)	→	Co^{2+}(aq)	+	$2\,e^-$	
V(s)	→	V^{3+}(aq)	+	$3\,e^-$	
Ni(s)	→	Ni^{2+}(aq)	+	$2\,e^-$	
Sn(s)	→	Sn^{2+}(aq)	+	$2\,e^-$	
Pb(s)	→	Pb^{2+}(aq)	+	$2\,e^-$	
H_2(g)	→	$2\,H^+$(aq)	+	$2\,e^-$	
Cu(s)	→	Cu^{2+}(aq)	+	$2\,e^-$	
Ag(s)	→	Ag^+(aq)	+	e^-	
Hg(l)	→	Hg^{2+}(aq)	+	$2\,e^-$	
Pd(s)	→	Pd^{2+}(aq)	+	$2\,e^-$	
Pt(s)	→	Pt^{2+}(aq)	+	$2\,e^-$	
Au(s)	→	Au^{3+}(aq)	+	$3\,e^-$	Least easily oxidized

Reactions will always appear in the free-response section of the AP Chemistry exam. This may not be true in the multiple-choice part.

For the first two types, a table of metals relating their ease of oxidation to each other is useful in being able to predict what displaces what. Table 6.1 shows the **activity series for metals**, which lists the metal and its oxidation in order of decreasing ease of oxidation. An alternative to the activity series is a table of half-cell potentials, as discussed in Chapter 16, Electrochemistry. In general, the more active the metal, the lower its potential.

Elements on this activity series can displace ions of metals *lower* than themselves on the list. If, for example, one placed a piece of tin metal into a solution containing $Cu(NO_3)_2$(aq), the Sn would replace the Cu^{2+} cation:

$$Sn(s) + Cu(NO_3)_2(aq) \rightarrow Sn(NO_3)_2(aq) + Cu(s)$$
$$Sn(s) + Cu^{2+}(aq) \rightarrow Sn^{2+}(aq) + Cu(s)$$

The second equation is the net ionic form that is often required on the AP exam.

If a piece of copper metal was placed in a solution of $Sn(NO_3)_2$(aq), there would be no reaction, since copper is lower than tin on the activity series. This table allows us to also predict that if sodium metal is placed in water, it will displace hydrogen, forming hydrogen gas:

$$2\,Na(s) + 2\,H_2O(l) \rightarrow 2\,NaOH(aq) + H_2(g)$$
$$2\,Na(s) + 2\,H_2O(l) \rightarrow 2\,Na^+(aq) + 2\,OH^-(aq) + H_2(g)$$

The Group IA and IIA elements on the activity table will displace hydrogen from water, but not the other metals shown. All the metals above hydrogen will react with acidic solutions to produce hydrogen gas:

$$Co(s) + 2\,HCl(aq) \rightarrow CoCl_2(aq) + H_2(g)$$
$$Co(s) + 2\,H^+(aq) \rightarrow Co^{2+}(aq) + H_2(g)$$

Halogen reactivity decreases as one goes from top to bottom in the periodic table, because of the decreasing electronegativity. Therefore, a separate activity series for the halogens can be developed:

$$F_2$$
$$Cl_2$$
$$Br_2$$
$$I_2$$

The above series indicates that if chlorine gas were dissolved in a KI(aq) solution, the elemental chlorine would displace the iodide ion:

$$Cl_2(aq) + 2\,KI(aq) \rightarrow 2\,KCl(aq) + I_2(s)$$
$$Cl_2(aq) + 2\,I^-(aq) \rightarrow 2\,Cl^-(aq) + I_2(s)$$

Combustion Reactions

Combustion reactions are redox reactions in which the chemical species rapidly combines with oxygen and usually emits heat and light. Reactions of this type are extremely important in our society as the sources of heat energy. Complete combustion of carbon yields carbon dioxide, and complete combustion of hydrogen yields water. The complete combustion of **hydrocarbons**, organic compounds containing only carbon and hydrogen, yields carbon dioxide and water:

$$2\,C_2H_6(g) + 7\,O_2(g) \rightarrow 4CO_2(g) + 6\,H_2O(g)$$

If the compound also contains oxygen, such as in alcohols, ethers, etc., the products are still carbon dioxide and water:

$$2\,CH_3OH(l) + 3\,O_2(g) \rightarrow 2CO_2(g) + 4\,H_2O(g)$$

If the compound contains sulfur, the complete combustion produces sulfur dioxide, SO_2:

$$2\,C_2H_6S(g) + 9\,O_2(g) \rightarrow 4\,CO_2(g) + 6\,H_2O(g) + 2\,SO_2(g)$$

If nitrogen is present, it will normally form the very stable nitrogen gas, N_2.

In all of these reactions, the driving force is the highly reactive oxygen forming a very stable compound(s). This is shown by the exothermic nature of the reaction.

In balancing any of these combustion reactions, it is helpful to balance the oxygen last.

Coordination Compounds

When a salt is dissolved in water, the metal ions, especially transition metal ions, form a complex ion with water molecules and/or other species. A **complex ion** is composed of a metal ion bonded to two or more molecules or ions called **ligands**. These are Lewis acid–base reactions. For example, suppose $Cr(NO_3)_3$ is dissolved in water. The Cr^{3+} cation attracts water molecules to form the complex ion $Cr(H_2O)_6^{3+}$. In this complex ion, water acts as the ligand. If ammonia is added to this solution, the ammonia can displace the water molecules from the complex:

$$[Cr(H_2O)_6]^{3+}(aq) + 6\ NH_3(aq) \leftrightarrows [Cr(NH_3)_6]^{3+}(aq) + 6\ H_2O(l)$$

In reactions involving coordination compounds, the metal acts as the Lewis acid (electron-pair acceptor), while the ligand acts as a Lewis base (electron-pair donor). In the reaction above, the ammonia ligand displaced the water ligand from the chromium complex because nitrogen is a better electron-pair donor (less electronegative) than oxygen.

The nitrogen in the ammonia and the oxygen in the water are the donor atoms. They are the atoms that actually donate the electrons to the Lewis acid. The **coordination number** is the number of donor atoms that surround the central atom. As seen above, the coordination number for Cr^{3+} is 6. Coordination numbers are usually 2, 4, or 6, but other values can be possible. Silver (Ag^+) commonly forms complexes with a coordination number of 2; zinc (Zn^{2+}), copper (Cu^{2+}), nickel (Ni^{2+}), and platinum (Pt^{2+}) commonly form complexes with a coordination number of 4; most other central ions have a coordination number of 6.

$$AgCl(s) + 2\ NH_3(aq) \rightarrow \left[Ag(NH_3)_2\right]^+(aq) + Cl^-(aq)$$
$$Zn(OH)_2(s) + 2\ OH^-(aq) \rightarrow \left[Zn(OH)_4\right]^{2-}(aq)$$
$$Fe^{3+}(aq) + 6\ CN^-(aq) \rightarrow \left[Fe(CN)_6\right]^{3-}(aq)$$

Acid–Base Reactions

Acids and bases are extremely common, as are the reactions between acids and bases. The driving force is often the hydronium ion reacting with the hydroxide ion to form water. Chapter 15 on Equilibrium describes the equilibrium reactions of acids and bases, as well as some information concerning acid–base titration. After you finish this section, you may want to review the acid–base part of the Equilibrium chapter.

Properties of Acids, Bases, and Salts

At the macroscopic level, acids taste sour, may be damaging to the skin, and react with bases to yield salts. Bases taste bitter, feel slippery, and react with acids to form salts.

At the microscopic level, **acids** are defined as proton (H^+) donors (Brønsted–Lowry theory) or electron-pair acceptors (Lewis theory). **Bases** are defined as proton (H^+) acceptors (Brønsted–Lowry theory) or electron-pair donors (Lewis theory). Consider the gas-phase reaction between hydrogen chloride and ammonia:

$$HCl(g) + :NH_3(g) \rightarrow HNH_3^+Cl^-(s)\ (\text{or}\ NH_4^+Cl^-(s))$$

HCl is the acid, because it is donating an H^+ and the H^+ will accept an electron pair from ammonia. Ammonia is the base, accepting the H^+ and furnishing an electron pair that the H^+ will bond with via coordinate covalent bonding. **Coordinate covalent bonds** are covalent bonds in which one of the atoms furnishes both of the electrons for the bond. After the bond is formed, it is identical to a covalent bond formed by donation of one electron by both of the bonding atoms.

Acids and bases may be **strong**, dissociating completely, or **weak**, partially dissociating and forming an equilibrium system.(See Chapter 15 for the details on weak acids and bases.) Strong acids include:

1. Hydrochloric, HCl

2. Hydrobromic, HBr

3. Hydroiodic, HI

4. Nitric, HNO_3

5. Chloric, $HClO_3$

6. Perchloric, $HClO_4$

7. Sulfuric, H_2SO_4

The strong acids above are all compounds that ionize completely in aqueous solution, yielding hydrogen ions and the anions from the acid.

Strong bases include:

1. Alkali metal (Group IA) hydroxides (LiOH, NaOH, KOH, RbOH, CsOH)

2. $Ca(OH)_2$, $Sr(OH)_2$, and $Ba(OH)_2$

The strong bases listed above are all compounds that dissociate completely, yielding the hydroxide ion (which is really the base, not the compound).

Unless told otherwise, assume that acids and bases not on the lists above are weak and will establish an equilibrium system when placed into water.

Some salts have acid–base properties. For example, ammonium chloride, NH_4Cl, when dissolved in water will dissociate and the ammonium ion will act as a weak acid, donating a proton. We will examine these acid–base properties in more detail in the next section.

Certain oxides can have acidic or basic properties. These properties often become evident when the oxides are dissolved in water. In most case, reactions of this type are not redox reactions.

Many oxides of metals that have a +1 or +2 charge are called basic oxides (basic anhydrides), because they will react with acids.

$$Fe_2O_3(s) + 6HCl(aq) \rightarrow 2FeCl_3(aq) + 3H_2O(l)$$
$$Fe_2O_3(s) + 6H^+(aq) \rightarrow 2Fe^{3+}(aq) + 3H_2O(l)$$

Many times they react with water to form a basic solution:

$$Na_2O(s) + H_2O(l) \rightarrow 2NaOH(aq)$$
$$Na_2O(s) + H_2O(l) \rightarrow 2Na^+(aq) + 2OH^-(aq)$$

Many nonmetal oxides are called acidic oxides (acidic anhydrides), because they react with water to form an acidic solution:

$$CO_2(g) + H_2O(l) \rightarrow H_2CO_3(aq)$$

$H_2CO_3(aq)$ is named carbonic acid and is the reason that most carbonated beverages are slightly acidic. It is also the reason that soft drinks have fizz, because carbonic acid will decompose to form carbon dioxide and water.

Acid–Base Reactions

In general, acids react with bases to form a salt and, usually, water. The salt will depend upon which acid and base are used:

$$HCl(aq) + NaOH(aq) \rightarrow H_2O(l) + NaCl(aq)$$
$$HNO_3(aq) + KOH(aq) \rightarrow H_2O(l) + KNO_3(aq)$$
$$HBr(aq) + NH_3(aq) \rightarrow NH_4Br(aq)$$

Reactions of this type are called **neutralization reactions**.

The first two neutralization equations are represented by the same net ionic equation:

$$H^+(aq) + OH^-(aq) \rightarrow H_2O(l)$$

In the third case, the net ionic equation is different:

$$H^+(aq) + NH_3(aq) \rightarrow NH_4^+(aq)$$

As mentioned previously, certain salts have acid–base properties. In general, salts containing cations of strong bases and anions of strong acids are neither acidic nor basic. They are neutral, reacting with neither acids nor bases. An example would be potassium nitrate, KNO_3. The potassium comes from the strong base KOH and the nitrate from the strong acid HNO_3.

Salts containing cations not of strong bases but with anions of strong acids behave as acidic salts. An example would be ammonium chloride, NH_4Cl.

$$2 NH_4Cl(aq) + Ba(OH)_2(aq) \rightarrow BaCl_2(aq) + 2 NH_3(aq) + 2 H_2O(l)$$
$$NH_4^+(aq) + OH^-(aq) \rightarrow NH_3(aq) + H_2O(l)$$

Cations of strong bases and anions not of strong acids are basic salts. An example would be sodium carbonate, Na_2CO_3. It reacts with an acid to form carbonic acid, which would then decompose to carbon dioxide and water:

$$2 HCl(aq) + Na_2CO_3(aq) \rightarrow 2 NaCl(aq) + H_2CO_3(aq)$$
$$\downarrow$$
$$CO2(g) + H2O(l)$$
$$2 H^+(aq) + CO_3^{2-} \rightarrow H_2CO_3(aq) \rightarrow CO_2(g) + H_2O(l)$$

The same type of reaction would be true for acid carbonates, such as sodium bicarbonate, $NaHCO_3$.

Another group of compounds that have acid–base properties are the hydrides of the alkali metals and of calcium, strontium, and barium. These hydrides will react with water to form the hydroxide ion and hydrogen gas:

$$NaH(s) + H_2O(l) \rightarrow NaOH(aq) + H_2(g)$$
$$NaH(s) + H_2O(l) \rightarrow Na^+(aq) + OH^-(aq) + H_2(g)$$

Note that in this case, water is behaving as H^+OH^-.

Acid–Base Titrations

A common laboratory application of acid–base reactions is a titration. A **titration** is a laboratory procedure in which a solution of known concentration is used to determine the concentration of an unknown solution. For strong acid/strong base titration systems, the net ionic equation is:

$$H^+(aq) + OH^-(aq) \rightarrow H_2O(l)$$

For example, suppose you wanted to determine the molarity of an HCl solution. You would pipet a known volume of the acid into a flask and add a couple of drops of a suitable acid–base indicator. An indicator that is commonly used is phenolphthalein, which is colorless in an acidic solution and pink in a basic solution. You would then fill a buret with a strong base solution (NaOH is commonly used) of known concentration. The buret allows you to add small amounts of the base solution to the acid solution in the flask. The course of the titration can also be followed by the use of a pH meter. Initially the pH of the solution will be low, since it is an acid solution. As the base is added and neutralization of the acid takes place, the pH will slowly rise. Small amounts of the base are added until one reaches the equivalence point. The **equivalence point** is that point in the titration where the number of moles of H^+ in the acid solution has been exactly neutralized with the same number of moles of OH^-:

$$\text{moles } H^+ = \text{moles } OH^- \quad \text{at the equivalence point}$$

For the titration of a strong acid with a strong base, the pH rapidly rises in the vicinity of the equivalence point. Then, as the tiniest amount of base is added in excess, the indicator turns pink. This is called the **endpoint** of the titration. In an accurate titration, the endpoint will be as close to the equivalence point as possible. For simple titrations that do not use a pH meter, it is assumed that the endpoint and the equivalence point are the same, so that:

$$\text{moles } H^+ = \text{moles } OH^- \quad \text{at the endpoint}$$

After the equivalence point has been passed, the pH is greater than 7 (basic solution) and begins to level out somewhat. Figure 6.1 shows the shape of the curve for this titration.

Reaction stoichiometry can then be used to solve for the molarity of the acid solution. See Chapter 7, Stoichiometry, for a discussion of solution stoichiometry.

An unknown base can be titrated with an acid solution of known concentration. One major difference is that the pH will be greater than 7 initially and will decrease as the titration proceeds. The other major difference is that the indicator will start pink, and the color will vanish at the endpoint.

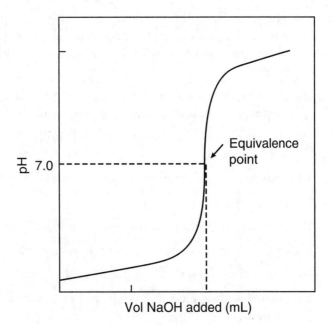

Figure 6.1 Titration of a strong acid with a strong base.

Experiments

Laboratory experiments involving reactions are usually concerned with both the reaction and the stoichiometry. You need some idea of the balanced chemical equation. In the case of an acid–base reaction, an acid reacts with a base. The acid supplies H^+ and the base accepts the H^+. If the acid is diprotic, such as H_2SO_4, it can donate two H^+.

The key to any reaction experiment is moles. The numbers of moles may be calculated from various measurements. A sample may be weighed on a balance to give the mass, and the moles calculated with the formula weight. Or the mass of a substance may be determined using a volume measurement combined with the density. The volume of a solution may be measured with a pipet, or calculated from the final and initial readings from a buret. This volume, along with the molarity, can be used to calculate the moles present. The volume, temperature, and pressure of a gas can be measured and used to calculate the moles of a gas. You must be extremely careful on the AP exam to distinguish between those values that you measure and those that you calculate.

The moles of any substance in a reaction may be converted to the moles of any other substance through a calculation using the balanced chemical equation. Other calculations are presented in Chapter 7, Stoichiometry.

Common Mistakes to Avoid

1. In balancing chemical equations **don't** change the subscripts in the chemical formula, just the coefficients.

2. Molecular compounds ionize, ionic compounds dissociate.

3. In writing ionic and net ionic equations, show the chemical species as they actually exist in solution (i.e., strong electrolytes as ions, etc.).

4. In writing ionic and net ionic equations, don't break apart covalently bonded compounds unless they are strong acids that are ionizing.

5. Know the solubility rules as guidelines, not explanations.

6. Oxidizing and reducing agents are reactants, not products.

7. The products of the complete combustion of a hydrocarbon are carbon dioxide and water. This is also true if oxygen is present as well; but if some other element, like sulfur, is present you will also have something else in addition to carbon dioxide and water.

8. If a substance that does not contain carbon, like elemental sulfur, undergoes complete combustion, no carbon dioxide can be formed.

9. If an alcohol like methanol, CH_3OH, is dissolved in water, no hydroxide ion, OH^-, will be formed.

10. Know the strong acids and bases.

11. HF is not a strong acid.

12. In titration calculations, you must consider the reaction stoichiometry.

13. Be sure to indicate the charges on ions correctly.

14. The common coordination numbers of complex ions are 2, 4, and 6.

15. Do not confuse measured values and calculated values.

❯ Review Questions

Here are questions you can use to review the content of this chapter and practice for the AP Chemistry exam. First are 16 multiple-choice questions similar to what you will encounter in Section I of the AP Chemistry exam. Following those is a short free-response question like ones in Section II of the exam. To make these review questions an even more authentic practice for the actual exam, time yourself following the instructions provided.

Multiple-Choice Questions

Answer the following questions in 20 minutes. You may not use a calculator. You may use the periodic table and the equation sheet at the back of this book.

1. $\_\_\_ Fe(OH)_2(s) + \_\_\_ H_3PO_4(aq) \rightarrow \_\_\_ Fe_3(PO_4)_2(s) + \_\_\_ H_2O(l)$

   After the above chemical equation is balanced, the lowest whole-number coefficient for water is:

   (A) 3
   (B) 1
   (C) 9
   (D) 6

2. This ion will generate gas bubbles upon the addition of hydrochloric acid.

   (A) Cu^{2+}
   (B) CO_3^{2-}
   (C) Fe^{3+}
   (D) Al^{3+}

3. Aqueous solutions of this ion are blue.

   (A) Cu^{2+}
   (B) CO_3^{2-}
   (C) Fe^{3+}
   (D) Al^{3+}

4. Which of the following best represents the balanced net ionic equation for the reaction of lead(II) carbonate with concentrated hydrochloric acid? In this reaction, all lead compounds are insoluble.

   (A) $Pb_2CO_3 + 2 H^+ + Cl^- \rightarrow Pb_2Cl + CO_2 + H_2O$
   (B) $PbCO_3 + 2 H^+ + 2 Cl^- \rightarrow PbCl_2 + CO_2 + H_2O$
   (C) $PbCO_3 + 2 H^+ \rightarrow Pb^{2+} + CO_2 + H_2O$
   (D) $PbCO_3 + 2 Cl^- \rightarrow PbCl_2 + CO_3^{2-}$

5. A sample of copper metal is reacted with concentrated nitric acid in the absence of air. After the reaction, which of these final products are present?

   (A) $CuNO_3$ and H_2O
   (B) $Cu(NO_3)_3$, NO, and H_2O
   (C) $Cu(NO_3)_2$, NO, and H_2O
   (D) $CuNO_3$, H_2O, and H_2

6. Which of the following is the correct net ionic equation for the reaction of acetic acid with potassium hydroxide?

   (A) $HC_2H_3O_2 + OH^- \rightarrow C_2H_3O_2^- + H_2O$
   (B) $HC_2H_3O_2 + K^+ \rightarrow KC_2H_3O_2 + H^+$
   (C) $HC_2H_3O_2 + KOH \rightarrow KC_2H_3O_2 + H_2O$
   (D) $H^+ + OH^- \rightarrow H_2O(l)$

7. Which of the following is the correct net ionic equation for the addition of aqueous ammonia to a precipitate of silver chloride?

   (A) $AgCl + 2 NH_3 \rightarrow [Ag(NH_3)_2]^+ + Cl^-$
   (B) $AgCl + 2 NH_4^+ \rightarrow [Ag(NH_4)_2]^{3+} + Cl^-$
   (C) $AgCl + NH_4^+ \rightarrow Ag^+ + NH_4Cl$
   (D) $AgCl + NH_3 \rightarrow Ag^+ + NH_3Cl$

8. Potassium metal will react with water to release a gas and form a potassium compound. Which of the following is true?

   (A) The final solution is basic.
   (B) The gas is oxygen.
   (C) The potassium compound precipitates.
   (D) The potassium compound will react with strong bases.

9. A sample is tested for the presence of the Hg_2^{2+} ion. This ion, along with others, may be precipitated with chloride ion. If Hg_2^{2+} is present in the chloride precipitate, a black color will form upon treatment with aqueous ammonia. The balanced net ionic equation for the formation of this black color is:

(A) $Hg_2Cl_2 + 2\ NH_3 + 2\ H_2O \rightarrow$
    $2\ Hg + 2\ NH_4^+ + 2\ Cl^- + 2\ OH^-$
(B) $Hg_2Cl_2 + 2\ NH_3 \rightarrow$
    $Hg + HgNH_2Cl + NH_4^+ + Cl^-$
(C) $Hg_2Cl_2 + 2\ NH_4^+ \rightarrow 2\ Hg + 2\ NH_4Cl$
(D) $Hg_2Cl_2 + NH_4^+ \rightarrow 2\ Hg + NH_4Cl + Cl^-$

10. How many moles of $Pb(NO_3)_2$ must be added to 0.10 L of a solution that is 1.0 M in $MgCl_2$ and 1.0 M in KCl to precipitate all of the chloride ion? The compound $PbCl_2$ precipitates.

(A) 1.0 mol
(B) 0.20 mol
(C) 0.50 mol
(D) 0.15 mol

11. When 50.0 mL of 1.0 M $AgNO_3$ is added to 50.0 mL of 0.50 M HCl, a precipitate of AgCl forms. After the reaction is complete, what is the concentration of silver ions in the solution?

(A) 0.50 M
(B) 0.0 M
(C) 1.0 M
(D) 0.25 M

12. A student mixes 50.0 mL of 0.10 M $Pb(NO_3)_2$ solution with 50.0 mL of 0.10 M KCl. A white precipitate forms, and the concentration of the chloride ion becomes very small. Which of the following correctly places the concentrations of the remaining ions in order of decreasing concentration?

(A) $[NO_3^-] > [Pb^{2+}] > [K^+]$
(B) $[NO_3^-] > [K^+] > [Pb^{2+}]$
(C) $[K^+] > [NO_3^-] > [Pb^{2+}]$
(D) $[Pb^{2+}] > [NO_3^-] > [K^+]$

13. A solution is prepared for qualitative analysis. The solution contains the following ions: Co^{2+}, Pb^{2+}, and Al^{3+}. Which of the following will cause no observable reaction?

(A) Dilute $NH_3(aq)$ is added.
(B) Dilute $K_2CrO_4(aq)$ is added.
(C) Dilute $HNO_3(aq)$ is added.
(D) Dilute $K_2S(aq)$ is added.

14. Chlorine gas is bubbled through a colorless solution and the solution turns reddish. Adding a little methylene chloride to the solution extracts the color into the methylene chloride layer. Which of the following ions may be present in the original solution?

(A) Cl^-
(B) I^-
(C) SO_4^{2-}
(D) Br^-

15. The addition of excess concentrated $NaOH(aq)$ to a 1.0 M $(NH_4)_2SO_4$ solution will result in which of the following observations?

(A) The solution becomes neutral.
(B) The formation of a brown precipitate takes place.
(C) Nothing happens because the two solutions are immiscible.
(D) The odor of ammonia will be detected.

16. ____$C_4H_{11}N(l)$ + ____$O_2(g) \rightarrow$ ____$CO_2(g)$ + ____$H_2O(l)$ + ____$N_2(g)$

When the above equation is balanced, the lowest whole number coefficient for CO_2 is:

(A) 4
(B) 16
(C) 27
(D) 22

Answers and Explanations for the Multiple-Choice Questions

1. **D**—The balanced equation is:

$$3\,Fe(OH)_2(s) + 2\,H_3PO_4(aq) \rightarrow$$
$$Fe_3(PO_4)_2(s) + 6\,H_2O\,(l)$$

2. **B**—Carbonates produce carbon dioxide gas in the presence of an acid. None of the other ions will react with hydrochloric acid to produce a gas.

3. **A**—Aqueous solutions of Cu^{2+} are normally blue. Iron ions give a variety of colors but are normally colorless, or nearly so, in the absence of complexing agents. The other ions are colorless.

4. **B**—Lead(II) carbonate is insoluble, so its formula should be written as $PbCO_3$. Hydrochloric acid is a strong acid so it should be written as separate H^+ and Cl^- ions. Lead(II) chloride, $PbCl_2$, is insoluble, and carbonic acid, H_2CO_3, quickly decomposes to CO_2 and H_2O. Also notice that A cannot be correct because the charges do not balance.

5. **C**—The balanced chemical equation is:

$3\,Cu(s) + 8\,HNO_3(aq) \rightarrow 3\,Cu(NO_3)_2(aq) + 2\,NO(g) + 4\,H_2O(l)$

The copper is below hydrogen on the activity series, so H_2 cannot form by this acid–metal reaction. Nitric acid causes oxidation, which will oxidize copper to Cu^{2+} giving $Cu(NO_3)_2$. Some of the nitric acid reduces to NO. An oxidation and a reduction must ALWAYS be together.

6. **A**—Acetic acid is a weak acid; as such, it should be written as $HC_2H_3O_2$. Potassium hydroxide is a strong base so it will separate into K^+ and OH^- ions. Any potassium compound that might form is soluble and will yield K^+ ions. The potassium ions are spectator ions and are left out of the net ionic equation.

7. **A**—Aqueous ammonia contains primarily NH_3, which eliminates choices B and C. NH_3Cl does not exist, which eliminates choice D. The reaction produces the silver-ammonia complex, $[Ag(NH_3)_2]^+$.

8. **A**—The reaction of potassium to produce a potassium compound is an oxidation; therefore, there must be a reduction, and the only species available for reduction is hydrogen. The reaction is:

$2\,K(s) + 2\,H_2O(l) \rightarrow 2\,KOH(aq) + H_2(g)$

KOH is a water-soluble strong base, which will not react with other strong bases.

9. **B**—The black color is due to the formation of metallic mercury. Aqueous ammonia contains primarily NH_3, which eliminates choices C and D. The total charges on each side of the reaction arrow must be equal, which eliminates choice A.

10. **D**—The magnesium chloride gives 0.20 moles of chloride ion, and the potassium chloride gives 0.10 moles of chloride ion. A total of 0.30 moles of chloride will react with 0.15 moles of lead, because two Cl^- require one Pb^{2+}.

11. **D**—The HCl is the limiting reagent. The HCl will react with one-half the silver to halve the concentration. The doubling of the volume halves the concentration a second time.

12. **B**—All the potassium and nitrate ions remain in solution, leaving $PbCl_2$ as the only possible precipitate. Equal volumes of equal concentrations give the same number of moles of reactants; however, two nitrate ions are produced per solute formula as opposed to only one potassium ion. Initially, the lead and potassium would be equal, but some of the lead is precipitated as $PbCl_2$.

13. **C**—Ammonia, as a base, will precipitate the metal hydroxides since the only soluble hydroxides are the strong bases. Chromate, sulfide, and chloride ions might precipitate one or more of the ions. Nitrates, from nitric acid, are soluble; therefore, this is the solution that is least likely to cause an observable change.

14. **D**—Chlorine causes oxidation. It is capable of oxidizing both B and D. Answer B gives I_2, which is brownish in water and purplish in methylene chloride. Bromine solutions are reddish in both.

15. **D**—Excess strong base will ensure the solution to be basic and not neutral. Both ammonium and sodium salts are soluble; therefore, no precipitate can form. One aqueous solution will mix with another aqueous solution. The following acid–base reaction occurs to release ammonia gas: $NH_4^+(aq) + OH^-(aq) \rightarrow NH_3(g) + H_2O(l)$.

16. **B**—$4\,C_4H_{11}N(l) + 27\,O_2(g) \rightarrow 16\,CO_2(g) + 22\,H_2O(l) + 2\,N_2(g)$

Free-Response Question

On the new AP exams, there will be both long-answer and short-answer free-response questions. The following is an example of a short-answer question.

You have 5 minutes to do the following question. You may use a calculator and the tables in the back of the book.

Question 1

A lead(II) nitrate, $Pb(NO_3)_2$, solution is mixed with an ammonium sulfate, $(NH_4)_2SO_4$, solution and a precipitate forms. What is the precipitate, and which ions, if any, are spectator ions in this reaction? Explain how you arrived at your answers.

Answer and Explanation for the Free-Response Question

There are four ions present. These ions are NH_4^+, SO_4^{2-}, Pb^{2+}, and NO_3^-. The starting materials are in solution; therefore, they are soluble. The compounds that might form in the reaction are NH_4NO_3 and $PbSO_4$. Since ammonium (and nitrate) salts are normally soluble, the precipitate must be $PbSO_4$. The spectator ions are the nitrate ions (NO_3^-) and the ammonium ions (NH_4^+), the ions not in the precipitate.

You get 1 point for correctly identifying the precipitate. You get an additional point for the identification of the spectator ions and 2 points for the explanation. There is a maximum of 4 points possible.

> Rapid Review

- Reaction questions will always appear in the free-response section of the AP exam. This may not be true in the multiple-choice part.

- Energy may be released in a reaction (exothermic) or absorbed (endothermic).

- Chemical equations are balanced by adding coefficients in front of the chemical species until the number of each type of atom is the same on both the right and left sides of the arrow.

- The coefficients in the balanced equation must be in the lowest whole-number ratio.

- Water is the universal solvent, dissolving a wide variety of both ionic and polar substances.

- Electrolytes are substances that conduct an electrical current when dissolved in water; nonelectrolytes do not.

- Most ions in solution attract and bind a layer of water molecules in a process called solvation.

- Some molecular compounds, like acids, ionize in water, forming ions.

- In the molecular equation, the reactants and products are shown in their undissociated/un-ionized form; the ionic equation shows the strong electrolytes in the form of ions; the net ionic equation drops out all spectator ions and shows only those species that are undergoing chemical change.

- Precipitation reactions form an insoluble compound, a precipitate, from the mixing of two soluble compounds.

- Learn and be able to apply the solubility rules.

- Redox reactions are reactions where oxidation and reduction take place simultaneously.

- Oxidation is the loss of electrons, and reduction is the gain of electrons.

- Combination reactions are usually redox reactions in which two or more reactants (elements or compounds) combine to form one product.

- Decomposition reactions are usually redox reactions in which a compound breaks down into two or more simpler substances.

- Single displacement reactions are redox reactions in which atoms of an element replace the atoms of another element in a compound.

- Know how to use the activity series to predict whether or not an element will displace another element.

- Combustion reactions are redox reactions in which the chemical species rapidly combine with diatomic oxygen gas, emitting heat and light. The products of the complete combustion of a hydrocarbon are carbon dioxide and water.

- Indicators are substances that exhibit different colors under acidic or basic conditions.

- Acids are proton donors (electron-pair acceptors).

- Bases are proton acceptors (electron-pair donors).

- Coordinate covalent bonds are covalent bonds in which one atom furnishes both of the electrons for the bond.

- Strong acids and bases completely ionize/dissociate, and weak acids and bases only partially ionize/dissociate.

- Know the strong acids and bases.

- Acids react with bases to form a salt and usually water in a neutralization reaction.

- Many hydrides react with water to form the hydroxide ion and hydrogen gas.

- A titration is a laboratory procedure for determining the concentration of an unknown solution using a solution of known concentration.

- The equivalence point of an acid–base titration is the point at which the moles of H^+ from the acid equals the moles of OH^- from the base. The endpoint is the point at which the indicator changes color, indicating the equivalence point.

- A complex ion is composed of a metal ion covalently bonded to two or more molecules or anions called ligands.

- The coordination number (usually 2, 4, or 6) is the number of donor atoms that can surround a metal ion in a complex.

CHAPTER 7

Stoichiometry

IN THIS CHAPTER

Summary: The previous chapter on chemical reactions discussed reactants and products in terms of individual atoms and molecules. But an industrial chemist is not interested in the number of molecules being produced; she or he is interested in kilograms or pounds or tons of products being formed per hour or day. How many kilograms of reactants will it take? How many kilograms of products will be formed? These are the questions of interest. A production chemist is interested primarily in the macroscopic world, not the microscopic one of atoms and molecules. Even a chemistry student working in the laboratory will not be weighing out individual atoms and molecules, but large numbers of them in grams. There must be a way to bridge the gap between the microscopic world of individual atoms and molecules, and the macroscopic world of grams and kilograms. There is—it is called the mole concept, and it is one of the central concepts in the world of chemistry.

Keywords and Equations

Avogadro's number $= 6.022 \times 10^{23} \, \text{mol}^{-1}$

Molarity, M = moles solute per liter solution

n = moles

m = mass

$$n = \frac{m}{M}$$

M = molar mass

Moles and Molar Mass

The **mole** (**mol**) is the amount of a substance that contains the same number of particles as atoms in exactly 12 grams of carbon-12. This number of particles (atoms or molecules or ions) per mole is called **Avogadro's number** and is numerically equal to 6.022×10^{23} particles. The mole is simply a term that represents a certain number of particles, like a dozen or a pair. That relates moles to the microscopic world, but what about the macroscopic world? The mole also represents a certain mass of a chemical substance. That mass is the substance's atomic or molecular mass expressed in grams. In Chapter 5, the Basics chapter, we described the atomic mass of an element in terms of atomic mass units (amu). This was the mass associated with an individual atom. Then we described how one could calculate the mass of a compound by simply adding together the masses, in amu, of the individual elements in the compound. This is still the case, but at the macroscopic level the unit of grams is used to represent the quantity of a mole. Thus, the following relationships apply:

$$6.022 \times 10^{23} \text{ particles} = 1 \text{ mol}$$

$$= \text{atomic (molecular, formula) mass in grams}$$

The mass in grams of one mole of a substance is the **molar mass**.

The relationship above gives a way of converting from grams to moles to particles, and vice versa. If you have any one of the three quantities, you can calculate the other two. This becomes extremely useful in working with chemical equations, as we will see later, because the coefficients in the balanced chemical equation are not only the number of individual atoms or molecules at the microscopic level, but also the number of moles at the macroscopic level.

How many moles are present in 1.20×10^{25} silver atoms?

Answer:

$$(1.20 \times 10^{25} \text{ Ag atoms}) \left(\frac{1 \text{ mol Ag atoms}}{6.022 \times 10^{23} \text{ Ag atoms}} \right) = 19.9 \text{ mol Ag}$$

Percent Composition and Empirical Formulas

If the formula of a compound is known, it is a fairly straightforward task to determine the percent composition of each element in the compound. For example, suppose you want to calculate the percentage of hydrogen and oxygen in water, H_2O. First calculate the molecular mass of water:

$$1 \text{ mol } H_2O = 2 \text{ mol } H + 1 \text{ mol } O$$

Substituting the masses involved:

$$1 \text{ mol } H_2O = 2 \ (1.0079 \text{ g/mol}) + 16.00 \text{ g/mol} = 18.0158 \text{ g/mol}$$

(intermediate calculation—don't worry about significant figures yet)

percentage hydrogen = [mass H/mass H_2O] × 100
= [2(1.0079 g/mol)/18.0158 g/mol] × 100
= 11.19% H

percentage oxygen = [mass O/mass H_2O] × 100
= [16.00 g/mol/18.0158 g/mol] × 100
= 88.81% O

As a good check, add the percentages together. They should equal 100% or be very close to it.

Determine the mass percent of each of the elements in $C_6H_{12}O_6$
Formula mass (FM) = 180.158 amu

Answer:

$$\%C = \frac{(6\,C\,atoms)(12.011\ amu/atom)}{(180.158\ amu)} \times 100\% = 40.002\%$$

$$\%H = \frac{(12\,H\,atoms)(1.008\ amu/atom)}{(180.158\ amu)} \times 100\% = 6.714\%$$

$$\%O = \frac{(6\,O\,atoms)(15.9994\ amu/atom)}{(180.158\ amu)} \times 100\% = 53.2846\%$$

$$\text{Total} = 100.001\%$$

The total is a check. It should be *very* close to 100%.

In the problems above, the percentage data was calculated from the chemical formula, but the empirical formula can be determined if the percent compositions of the various elements are known. The **empirical formula** tells us what elements are present in the compound and the simplest whole-number ratio of elements. The data may be in terms of percentage, or mass, or even moles. But the procedure is still the same: convert each to moles, divide each by the smallest number, then use an appropriate multiplier if needed. The empirical formula mass can then be calculated. If the actual molecular mass is known, dividing the molecular mass by the empirical formula mass gives an integer (rounded if needed) that is used to multiply each of the subscripts in the empirical formula. This gives the **molecular (actual) formula**, which tells which elements are in the compound and the actual number of each.

For example, a sample of a gas was analyzed and found to contain 2.34 g of nitrogen and 5.34 g of oxygen. The molar mass of the gas was determined to be about 90 g/mol. What are the empirical and molecular formulas of this gas?

Answer:

$$(2.34\ g\ N)\left(\frac{1\ mol\ N}{14.0\ g\ N}\right) = 0.167\ mol\ N \qquad \left(\frac{0.167}{0.167}\right) = 1\ N$$

$$(5.34\ g\ O)\left(\frac{1\ mol\ O}{16.0\ g\ O}\right) = 0.334\ mol\ O \qquad \left(\frac{0.334}{0.167}\right) = 2\ O$$

$$\therefore \text{Empirical Formula} = NO_2$$

The molecular formula may be determined by dividing the actual molar mass of the compound by the empirical molar mass. In this case, the empirical molar mass is 46 g/mol.

$$\text{Thus } \left(\frac{90\ g/mol}{46\ g/mol}\right) = 1.96 \text{ which, to one significant figure, is 2. Therefore, the molecular}$$

formula is twice the empirical formula—N_2O_4.

Be sure to use as many significant digits as possible in the molar masses. Failure to do so may give you erroneous ratio and empirical formulas.

Reaction Stoichiometry

As we have discussed previously, the balanced chemical equation not only indicates which chemical species are the reactants and the products, but also indicates the relative ratio of reactants and products. Consider the balanced equation of the Haber process for the production of ammonia:

$$N_2(g) + 3H_2(g) \rightarrow 2\,NH_3(g)$$

This balanced equation can be read as: *1 nitrogen molecule reacts with 3 hydrogen molecules to produce 2 ammonia molecules.* But as indicated previously, the coefficients can stand not only for the number of atoms or molecules (microscopic level), they can also stand for the number of *moles* of reactants or products. The equation can also be read as: *1 mol of nitrogen molecules reacts with 3 mol of hydrogen molecules to produce 2 mol of ammonia molecules.* And if the number of moles is known, the number of grams or molecules can be calculated. This is **stoichiometry**, the calculation of the amount (mass, moles, particles) of one substance in a chemical reaction through the use of another. The coefficients in a balanced chemical equation define the mathematical relationship between the reactants and products, and allow the conversion from moles of one chemical species in the reaction to another.

Consider the Haber process above. How many moles of ammonia could be produced from the reaction of 20.0 mol of nitrogen with excess hydrogen?

Before any stoichiometry calculation can be done, you must have a balanced chemical equation!

You are starting with moles of nitrogen and want moles of ammonia, so we'll convert from moles of nitrogen to moles of ammonia by using the ratio of moles of ammonia to moles of nitrogen as defined by the balanced chemical equation:

$$\frac{20.0 \text{ mol N}_2}{1} \times \frac{2 \text{ mol NH}_3}{1 \text{ mol N}_2} = 40.0 \text{ mol NH}_3$$

The ratio of 2 mol NH_3 to 1 mol N_2 is called the stoichiometric ratio and comes from the balanced chemical equation.

Suppose you also wanted to know how many moles of hydrogen it would take to fully react with the 20.0 mol of nitrogen. Just change the stoichiometric ratio:

$$\frac{20.0 \text{ mol N}_2}{1} \times \frac{3 \text{ mol H}_2}{1 \text{ mol N}_2} = 60.0 \text{ mol H}_2$$

Notice that this new stoichiometric ratio also came from the balanced chemical equation.

Suppose instead of moles you had grams and wanted an answer in grams. How many grams of ammonia could be produced from the reaction of 85.0 g of hydrogen gas with excess nitrogen?

In working problems that involve something other than moles, you will still need moles. And you will need the balanced chemical equation.

In this problem we will convert from grams of hydrogen to moles of hydrogen to moles of ammonia using the correct stoichiometric ratio, and finally to grams of ammonia. And we will need the molar mass of H_2 (2.0158 g/mol) and ammonia (17.0307 g/mol):

$$\frac{85.0 \text{ g H}_2}{1} \times \frac{1 \text{ mol H}_2}{2.0158 \text{ g}} \times \frac{2 \text{ mol NH}_3}{3 \text{ mol H}_2} \times \frac{17.0307 \text{ g}}{1 \text{ mol NH}_3} = 478.8 \text{ g NH}_3$$

Actually, you could have calculated the actual number of ammonia molecules produced if you had gone from moles of ammonia to molecules (using Avogadro's number):

$$\frac{85.0 \text{ g H}_2}{1} \times \frac{1 \text{ mol H}_2}{2.0158 \text{ g}} \times \frac{2 \text{ mol NH}_3}{3 \text{ mol H}_2} \times \frac{6.022 \times 10^{23} \text{ molecules NH}_3}{1 \text{ mol NH}_3}$$
$$= 1.693 \times 10^{25} \text{ molecules NH}_3$$

In another reaction, 40.0 g of Cl_2 and excess H_2 are combined. HCl will be produced. How many grams of HCl will form?

$$H_2(g) + Cl_2(g) \rightarrow 2\ HCl(g)$$

Answer: $(40.0\ g\ Cl_2)\left(\dfrac{1\ mol\ Cl_2}{70.906\ g\ Cl_2}\right)\left(\dfrac{2\ mol\ HCl}{1\ mol\ Cl_2}\right)\left(\dfrac{36.461\ g\ HCl}{1\ mol\ HCl}\right) = 41.1\ g\ HCl$

Limiting Reactants

In the examples above, one reactant was present in excess. One reactant was completely consumed, and some of the other reactant was left over. The reactant that is used up first is called the **limiting reactant** (L.R.). This reactant really determines the amount of product being formed. How is the limiting reactant determined? You can't assume it is the reactant in the smallest amount, since the reaction stoichiometry must be considered. There are generally two ways to determine which reactant is the limiting reactant:

1. Each reactant, in turn, is assumed to be the limiting reactant, and the amount of product that would be formed is calculated. The reactant that yields the *smallest* amount of product is the limiting reactant. The advantage of this method is that you get to practice your calculation skills; the disadvantage is that you have to do more calculations.
2. The moles of reactant per coefficient of that reactant in the balanced chemical equation is calculated. The reactant that has the smallest mole-to-coefficient ratio is the limiting reactant. This is the method that many use.

Let us consider the Haber reaction once more. Suppose that 50.0 g of nitrogen and 40.0 g of hydrogen were allowed to react. Calculate the number of grams of ammonia that could be formed.
First, write the balanced chemical equation:

$$N_2(g) + 3\ H_2(g) \rightarrow 2\ NH_3(g)$$

Next, convert the grams of each reactant to moles:

$$\frac{50.0\ g\ N_2}{1} \times \frac{1\ mol\ N_2}{28.014\ g\ N_2} = 1.7848\ mol\ N_2$$

$$\frac{40.0\ g\ H_2}{1} \times \frac{1\ mol\ H_2}{2.0158\ g\ H_2} = 19.8432\ mol\ H_2$$

Divide each by the coefficient in the balanced chemical equation. The smaller is the limiting reactant:

For N_2: 1.7848 mol N_2/1 = 1.7848 mol/coefficient *limiting reactant*
For H_2: 19.8432 mol H_2/3 = 6.6144 mol/coefficient

Finally, base the stoichiometry of the reaction on the limiting reactant:

$$\frac{50.0\ g\ N_2}{1} \times \frac{1\ mol\ N_2}{28.014\ g\ N_2} \times \frac{2\ mol\ NH_3}{1\ mol\ N_2} \times \frac{17.0307\ g}{1\ mol\ NH_3} = 60.8\ g\ NH_3$$

Any time the quantities of more than one reactant are given it is probably an L.R. problem.

Let's consider another case. To carry out the following reaction: $P_2O_5(s) + 3H_2O(l) \rightarrow 2H_3PO_4$ (aq) 125 g of P_2O_5 and 50.0 g of H_2O were supplied. How many grams of H_3PO_4 may be produced?

Answer:

1. Convert to moles:

$$\left(125 \text{ g } P_2O_5\right)\left(\frac{1 \text{ mol } P_2O_5}{142 \text{ g } P_2O_5}\right) = 0.880 \text{ mol } P_2O_5$$

$$\left(50.0 \text{ g } H_2O\right)\left(\frac{1 \text{ mol } H_2O}{18.0 \text{ g } H_2O}\right) = 2.78 \text{ mol } H_2O$$

2. Find the limiting reactant:

$$\frac{0.880 \text{ mol}}{1 \text{ mol}} = 0.880 \ P_2O_5$$

$$\frac{2.78 \text{ mol}}{3 \text{ mol}} = 0.927 \ H_2O$$

The 1 mol and the 3 mol come from the balanced chemical equation. The 0.880 is smaller, so this is the L.R.

3. Finish using the number of moles of the L.R.:

$$\left(0.880 \text{ mol } P_2O_5\right)\left(\frac{2 \text{ mol } H_3PO_4}{1 \text{ mol } P_2O_5}\right)\left(\frac{98.0 \text{ g } H_3PO_4}{1 \text{ mol } H_3PO_4}\right) = 172 \text{ g}$$

Percent Yield

In the preceding problems, the amount of product calculated based on the limiting-reactant concept is the maximum amount of product that could be formed from the given amount of reactants. This maximum amount of product formed is called the **theoretical yield**. However, rarely is the amount that is actually formed (the **actual yield**) the same as the theoretical yield. Normally it is less. There are many reasons for this, but the principal reason is that most reactions do not go to completion; they establish an equilibrium system (see Chapter 15, Equilibrium, for a discussion of chemical equilibrium). For whatever reason, not as much as expected is formed. The efficiency of the reaction can be judged by calculating the percent yield. The **percent yield** (**% yield**) is the actual yield divided by the theoretical yield, and the result is multiplied by 100% to generate percentage:

$$\% \text{ yield} = \frac{\text{actual yield}}{\text{theoretical yield}} \times 100\%$$

Consider the problem in which it was calculated that 60.8 g NH_3 could be formed. Suppose that reaction was carried out, and only 52.3 g NH_3 was formed. What is the percent yield?

$$\% \text{ yield} = \frac{52.3 \text{ g}}{60.8 \text{ g}} \times 100\% = 86.0\%$$

Let's consider another percent yield problem in which a 25.0-g sample of calcium oxide is heated with excess hydrogen chloride to produce water and 37.5 g of calcium chloride. What is the percent yield of calcium chloride?

$$CaO(s) + 2HCl(g) \rightarrow CaCl_2(aq) + H_2O(l)$$

Answer:

$$\left(25.0 \text{ g } CaO\right)\left(\frac{1 \text{ mol } CaO}{56.077 \text{ g } CaO}\right)\left(\frac{1 \text{ mol } CaCl_2}{1 \text{ mol } CaO}\right)\left(\frac{110.984 \text{ g } CaCl_2}{1 \text{ mol } CaCl_2}\right) = 49.478 \text{ g } CaCl_2$$

The theoretical yield is 49.5 g.

$$\frac{37.5 \text{ g CaCl}_2}{49.478 \text{ g CaCl}_2} \times 100\% = 75.8\%$$

Note: All the units except % must cancel. This includes canceling g $CaCl_2$ with g $CaCl_2$, not simply g.

Molarity and Solution Calculations

We discuss solutions further in Chapter 13, Solutions and Colligative Properties, but solution stoichiometry is so common on the AP exam that we will discuss it here briefly also. **Solutions** are homogeneous mixtures composed of a **solute** (substance present in smaller amount) and a **solvent** (substance present in larger amount). If sodium chloride is dissolved in water, the NaCl is the solute and the water the solvent.

One important aspect of solutions is their **concentration**, the amount of solute dissolved in the solvent. In Chapter 13 we will cover several concentration units, but for the purpose of stoichiometry, the only concentration unit we will use at this time is molarity. **Molarity** (M) is defined as the moles of solute per liter of solution:

$$M = \text{mol solute/L solution}$$

Let's start with a simple example of calculating molarity. A solution of NaCl contains 39.12 g of this compound in 100.0 mL of solution. Calculate the molarity of NaCl.

Answer:

$$\frac{(39.12 \text{ g NaCl}) \dfrac{[1 \text{ mol NaCl}]}{[58.45 \text{ g NaCl}]}}{(100.0 \text{ mL}) \dfrac{[1 \text{ L}]}{[1000 \text{ mL}]}} = 6.693 \ M \ \text{NaCl}$$

Knowing the volume of the solution and the molarity allows you to calculate the moles or grams of solute present.

Next, let's see how we can use molarity to calculate moles. How many moles of ammonium ions are in 0.100 L of a 0.20 M ammonium sulfate solution?

Answer:

$$\left[\frac{0.20 \text{ mol } (NH_4)_2SO_4}{L} \right] \left[\frac{2 \text{ mol } NH_4^+}{1 \text{ mol } (NH_4)_2SO_4} \right] (0.100 \text{ L}) = 0.040 \text{ mol } NH_4^+$$

Stoichiometry problems (including limiting-reactant problems) involving solutions can be worked in the same fashion as before, except that the volume and molarity of the solution must first be converted to moles.

If 35.00 mL of a 0.1500 M KOH solution is required to titrate 40.00 mL of a phosphoric acid solution, what is the concentration of the acid? The reaction is:

$$2KOH \text{ (aq)} + H_3PO_4 \text{ (aq)} \rightarrow K_2HPO_4 \text{ (aq)} + 2H_2O \text{ (l)}$$

Answer:

$$\frac{(35.00 \text{ mL}) \dfrac{(0.1500 \text{ mol KOH})(1 \text{ mol } H_3PO_4)}{(1{,}000 \text{ mL})(2 \text{ mol KOH})}}{(40.00 \text{ mL}) \dfrac{(1 \text{ L})}{(1{,}000 \text{ mL})}} = 0.06562 \ M \ \ H_3PO_4$$

Experiments

Stoichiometry experiments must involve moles. They nearly always use a balanced chemical equation. Measurements include initial and final masses, and initial and final volumes. Calculations may include the difference between the initial and final values. Using the formula mass and the mass in grams, moles may be calculated. Moles may also be calculated from the volume of a solution and its molarity.

Once the moles have been calculated (they are never measured), the experiment will be based on further calculations using these moles.

Common Mistakes to Avoid

1. Avogadro's number is 6.022×10^{23} (not 10^{-23}).
2. Be sure to know the difference between molecules and moles.
3. In empirical formula problems, be sure to get the lowest ratio of whole numbers.
4. In stoichiometry problems, be sure to use the *balanced chemical equation*.
5. The stoichiometric ratio comes from the *balanced chemical equation*.
6. When in doubt, convert to moles.
7. In limiting-reactant problems, don't consider just the number of grams or even moles to determine the limiting reactant—use the mol/coefficient ratio.
8. The limiting reactant is a reactant, a chemical species to the left of the reactant arrow.
9. *Use the balanced chemical equation.*
10. Percent yield is actual yield of a substance divided by the theoretical yield of the same substance multiplied by 100%.
11. Molarity is moles of *solute* per liter of *solution*, not solvent.
12. Be careful when using Avogadro's number—use it when you need or have the number of atoms, ions, or molecules.

〉 Review Questions

Use these questions to review the content of this chapter and practice for the AP Chemistry exam. First are 18 multiple-choice questions similar to what you will encounter in Section I of the AP Chemistry exam. Following those is a long free-response question like the ones in Section II of the exam. To make these questions an even more authentic practice for the actual exam, time yourself following the instructions provided.

Multiple-Choice Questions

Answer the following questions in 25 minutes. You may not use a calculator. You may use the periodic table and the equation sheet at the back of this book.

1. How many milliliters of 0.100 M H_2SO_4 are required to neutralize 50.0 mL of 0.200 M KOH?

(A) 25.0 mL
(B) 30.0 mL
(C) 20.0 mL
(D) 50.0 mL

2. A sample of oxalic acid, $H_2C_2O_4$, is titrated with standard sodium hydroxide, NaOH, solution. A total of 45.20 mL of 0.1200 M NaOH is required to neutralize completely 20.00 mL of the acid. What is the concentration of the acid?

(A) 0.2712 M
(B) 0.1200 M
(C) 0.1356 M
(D) 0.2400 M

3. A solution is prepared by mixing 50.0 mL of 0.20 M arsenic acid, H_3AsO_4, and 50.0 mL of 0.20 M sodium hydroxide, NaOH. Which anion is present in the highest concentration?

(A) $HAsO_4^{2-}$
(B) OH^-
(C) $H_2AsO_4^-$
(D) Na^+

4. $14\ H^+(aq)\ +\ 6\ Fe^{2+}(aq)\ +\ Cr_2O_7^{2-}(aq)\ \rightarrow$ $2\ Cr^{3+}(aq) + 6\ Fe^{3+}(aq) + 7\ H_2O(l)$

This reaction is used in the titration of an iron solution. What is the concentration of the iron solution if it takes 45.20 mL of 0.1000 M $Cr_2O_7^{2-}$ solution to titrate 50.00 mL of an acidified iron solution?

(A) 0.5424 M
(B) 0.1000 M
(C) 1.085 M
(D) 0.4520 M

5. Manganese, Mn, forms a number of oxides. A particular oxide is 63.2% Mn. What is the simplest formula for this oxide?

(A) MnO
(B) Mn_2O_3
(C) Mn_3O_4
(D) MnO_2

6. Vanadium forms a number of oxides. In which of the following oxides is the vanadium-to-oxygen mass ratio 2.39:1.00?

(A) VO
(B) V_2O_3
(C) V_3O_4
(D) VO_2

7. How many grams of nitrogen are in 25.0 g of $(NH_4)_2SO_4$?

(A) 5.30 g
(B) 1.30 g
(C) 0.190 g
(D) 2.65 g

8. Sodium sulfate forms a number of hydrates. A sample of a hydrate is heated until all the water is removed. What is the formula of the original hydrate if it loses 43% of its mass when heated?

(A) $Na_2SO_4 \cdot H_2O$
(B) $Na_2SO_4 \cdot 2H_2O$
(C) $Na_2SO_4 \cdot 6H_2O$
(D) $Na_2SO_4 \cdot 8H_2O$

9. $3\ Cu(s) + 8\ HNO_3(aq) \rightarrow 3\ Cu(NO_3)_2(aq)$ $+ 2\ NO(g) + 4\ H_2O(l)$

Copper metal reacts with nitric acid according to the above equation. A 0.30 mol sample of copper metal and 10.0 mL of 12 M nitric acid are mixed in a flask. How many moles of NO gas will form?

(A) 0.060 mol
(B) 0.030 mol
(C) 0.010 mol
(D) 0.20 mol

10. Gold(III) oxide, Au_2O_3, can be decomposed to gold metal, Au, plus oxygen gas, O_2. How many moles of oxygen gas will form when 221 g of solid gold(III) oxide is decomposed? The formula mass of gold(III) oxide is 442.

(A) 0.250 mol
(B) 0.500 mol
(C) 0.750 mol
(D) 1.00 mol

11. $\_C_4H_{11}N(l) + \_O_2(g) \rightarrow \_CO_2(g)$ $+ \_H_2O(l) + \_N_2(g)$

When the above equation is balanced, the lowest whole number coefficient for O_2 is:

(A) 4
(B) 16
(C) 22
(D) 27

12. $2\,KMnO_4(aq) + 5\,H_2C_2O_4(aq) + 3\,H_2SO_4(aq)$
$\rightarrow K_2SO_4(aq) + 2\,MnSO_4(aq) + 10\,CO_2(g)$
$+\,8\,H_2O(l)$

How many moles of $MnSO_4$ are produced when 1.0 mol of $KMnO_4$, 5.0 mol of $H_2C_2O_4$, and 3.0 mol of H_2SO_4 are mixed?

(A) 4.0 mol
(B) 5.0 mol
(C) 2.0 mol
(D) 1.0 mol

13. When the following equation is balanced, it is found that 1.00 mol of C_8H_{18} reacts with how many moles of O_2?

$\_\_C_8H_{18}(g) + \_\_O_2(g) \rightarrow \_\_CO_2(g) + \_\_H_2O(g)$

(A) 12.5 mol
(B) 10.0 mol
(C) 25.0 mol
(D) 37.5 mol

14. $Ca(s) + 2\,H_2O(l) \rightarrow Ca(OH)_2(aq) + H_2(g)$

Calcium reacts with water according to the above reaction. What volume of hydrogen gas, at standard temperature and pressure, is produced from 0.200 mol of calcium?

(A) 5.60 L
(B) 4.48 L
(C) 3.36 L
(D) 1.12 L

15. $2CrO_4^{2-}(aq) + 3SnO_2^{2-}(aq) + H_2O(l) \rightarrow$
$2\,CrO_2^{-}(aq) + 3\,SnO_3^{2-}(aq) + 2\,OH^{-}(aq)$

How many moles of OH^{-} form when 50.0 mL of 0.100 M CrO_4^{2-} is added to a flask containing 50.0 mL of 0.100 M SnO_2^{2-}?

(A) 0.100 mol
(B) 6.66×10^{-3} mol
(C) 3.33×10^{-3} mol
(D) 5.00×10^{-3} mol

16. A solution containing 0.20 mol of KBr and 0.20 mol of $MgBr_2$ in 2.0 liters of water is provided. How many moles of $Pb(NO_3)_2$ must be added to precipitate all the bromide as insoluble $PbBr_2$?

(A) 0.10 mol
(B) 0.50 mol
(C) 0.60 mol
(D) 0.30 mol

17. Cycloalkanes are hydrocarbons with the general formula C_nH_{2n}, where $n \geq 3$. If a 0.420 g sample of any alkene is combusted in excess oxygen, how many moles of water will form?

(A) 0.040
(B) 0.600
(C) 0.020
(D) 0.400

18. Manganese normally forms one of four oxides. The oxides are MnO, Mn_2O_3, MnO_2, and Mn_3O_4. Which of the four oxides has the highest percentage of oxygen? (Molar masses: O = 16.0 g mol^{-1}, Mn = 54.9 g mol^{-1}, MnO = 70.9 g mol^{-1}, Mn_2O_3 = 157.8 g mol^{-1}, MnO_2 = 86.9 g mol^{-1}, and Mn_3O_4 = 228.7 g mol^{-1}.)

(A) MnO_2
(B) Mn_3O_4
(C) Mn_2O_3
(D) MnO

Answers and Explanations for the Multiple-Choice Questions

1. D—The reaction is $H_2SO_4(aq) + 2\ KOH(aq) \rightarrow K_2SO_4(aq) + 2\ H_2O(l)$

$$(50.0\ \text{mL base}) \left(\frac{0.200\ \text{mol base}}{1,000\ \text{mL base}} \right) \left(\frac{1\ \text{mol acid}}{2\ \text{mol base}} \right) \left(\frac{1,000\ \text{mL acid}}{0.100\ \text{mol acid}} \right) = 50.0\ \text{mL}$$

2. C—The reaction is $H_2C_2O_4(aq) + 2\ NaOH(aq) \rightarrow Na_2C_2O_4(aq) + 2\ H_2O(l)$

$$(45.20\ \text{mL base}) \left(\frac{0.1200\ \text{mol base}}{1,000\ \text{mL base}} \right) \left(\frac{1\ \text{mol acid}}{2\ \text{mol base}} \right) \left(\frac{1}{20.00\ \text{mL}} \right) \left(\frac{1,000\ \text{mL}}{L} \right)$$
$$= 0.1356\ M\ \text{acid}$$

As always, round the values to get an estimate and pick the closest answer.

3. C—Moles acid = (50.0 mL) (0.20 mol acid/1,000 mL) = 0.0100 mol
Moles base = (50.0 mL) (0.20 mol base/1,000 mL) = 0.0100 mol

There is sufficient base to react completely with only one of the ionizable hydrogen ions from the acid. This leaves $H_2AsO_4^-$. Answer D cannot be correct because it is a cation.

4. A—

$$(45.20\ \text{mL}\ Cr_2O_7^{2-}) \left(\frac{0.1000\ \text{mol}\ Cr_2O_7^{2-}}{1,000\ \text{mL}\ Cr_2O_7^{2-}} \right) \left(\frac{6\ \text{mol}\ Fe^{2+}}{1\ \text{mol}\ Cr_2O_7^{2-}} \right) \left(\frac{1}{50.00\ \text{mL}} \right) \left(\frac{1,000\ \text{mL}}{L} \right)$$
$$= 0.5425\ M$$

This is a perfect example of where simplification is important. Change the above calculation to

$$(45.20\ \text{mL}\ \cancel{Cr_2O_7^{2-}}) \left(\frac{0.1000\ \text{mol}\ \cancel{Cr_2O_7^{2-}}}{1,000\ \text{mL}\ \cancel{Cr_2O_7^{2-}}} \right) \left(\frac{6\ \text{mol}\ Fe^{2+}}{1\ \text{mol}\ \cancel{Cr_2O_7^{2-}}} \right) \left(\frac{1}{50.00\ \cancel{\text{mL}}} \right) \left(\frac{1,000\ \cancel{\text{mL}}}{L} \right)$$
$$= 0.5425\ M$$

This becomes

$$(45.20) \left(\frac{0.1000}{1,\cancel{000}} \right) \left(\frac{6\ \text{mol}\ Fe^{2+}}{1} \right) \left(\frac{1}{50.00} \right) \left(\frac{1,\cancel{000}}{L} \right) = 0.5425\ M$$

Next round and simplify to

$$(\cancel{50}) \left(\frac{0.1000}{1} \right) \left(\frac{6\ \text{mol}\ Fe^{2+}}{1} \right) \left(\frac{1}{\cancel{50.00}} \right) \left(\frac{1}{L} \right) = 0.6\ M$$

Since the 45.20 was rounded up, the answer is slightly high; therefore, pick the closest answer that is lower.

5. D—63.2% Mn leaves 36.8% O (assuming 100 grams of sample) 63.2/54.94 = 1.15 mole Mn and 36.8/16.0 = 2.30 mole O

Thus, there is 1 Mn/2 O.

6. C—V: 2.39/50.94 = 0.0469 and for O:1.00/16.0 = 0.0625
0.0469/0.0469 = 1   0.0625/0.0469 = 1.33

Multiplying both by 3 gives 3 V and 4 O.

7. A—(25.0 g $(NH_4)_2SO_4$)(1 mol$(NH_4)_2SO_4$/132 g) =
(2 mol N/1 mol$(NH_4)_2SO_4$)(14.0 g N/1 mol N) = 5.30 g

8. **C**—[(6 mol H_2O)(18 g/mol H_2O)]/(250 g $Na_2SO_4 \cdot 6\ H_2O$) × 100% = 43%

9. **B**—Calculate the moles of acid to compare to the moles of Cu:

$$(10.0\ mL)(12\ mol/1{,}000\ mL) = 0.12\ mol$$

The acid is the limiting reactant, because 0.30 mol of copper requires 0.80 mol of acid. Use the limiting reactant to calculate the moles of NO formed:

$$(0.12\ mol\ acid)(2\ mol\ NO/8\ mol\ acid) = 0.030\ mol$$

10. **C**—The balanced chemical equation is:

$$2\ Au_2O_3 \rightarrow 4\ Au + 3\ O_2$$

$$(221\ g\ Au_2O_3)(1\ mol\ Au_2O_3/442\ g\ Au_2O_3)(3\ mol\ O_2/2\ mol\ Au_2O_3) = 0.750\ mol\ O_2$$

Note the 2:1 relationship between the formula mass and the mass of reactant.

11. **D**—The balanced equation is:

$$4\ C_4H_{11}N(l) + 27\ O_2(g) \rightarrow 16\ CO_2(g) + 22\ H_2O(l) + 2\ N_2(g)$$

12. **D**—The $KMnO_4$ is the limiting reagent. Each mole of $KMnO_4$ will produce a mole of $MnSO_4$.

13. **A**—The balanced equation is:

$$2\ C_8H_{18}(g) + 25\ O_2(g) \rightarrow 16\ CO_2(g) + 18\ H_2O(g)$$
$$(1.00\ mol\ C_8H_{18})(25\ mol\ O_2/2\ mol\ C_8H_{18}) = 12.5\ mol\ O_2$$

14. **B**—(0.200 mol Ca)(1 mol H_2/1 mol Ca)(22.4 L at STP/1 mol H_2) = 4.48 L

Be careful to only use 22.4 when at STP.

15. **C**—There are 5.00×10^{-3} mol of CrO_4^{2-} and an equal number of moles of SnO_2^{2-}. Thus, SnO_2^{2-} is the limiting reactant (larger coefficient in the balanced reaction).

$$(5.00 \times 10^{-3}\ mol\ SnO_2^{2-})(2\ mol\ OH^-/3\ mol\ SnO_2^{2-}) = 3.33 \times 10^{-3}\ mol\ OH^-$$

16. **D**—The volume of water is irrelevant. 0.20 mol of KBr will require 0.10 mol of $Pb(NO_3)_2$, and 0.20 mol of $MgBr_2$ will require 0.20 mol of $Pb(NO_3)_2$. Total the two yields.

17. **A**—One mole of a cycloalkane, C_nH_{2n}, will form n moles of water. It is possible to determine the value of n by dividing the mass of the cycloalkane by the empirical formula mass (CH_2 = 14 g/mol). This gives $\dfrac{0.560\ g}{14\ g/mol} = \dfrac{4\ (0.140)\ g}{14\ g/mol} = 0.040\ mol$

18. **A**—The general equation to determine the percent oxygen in the sample is: Percent oxygen $= \dfrac{(mass\ of\ oxygen)}{(mass\ of\ sample)} \times 100\%$

Free-Response Question

You have 15 minutes to answer the following question. You may use a calculator and the tables in the back of the book.

Question 1

The analysis of a sample of a monoprotic acid found that the sample contained 40.0% C and 6.71% H. The remainder of the sample was oxygen.

(a) Determine the empirical formula of the acid.

(b) A 0.2720 g sample of the acid, HA, was titrated with standard sodium hydroxide, NaOH, solution. Determine the molecular weight of the acid if the sample required 45.00 mL of 0.1000 M NaOH for the titration.

(c) A second sample was placed in a flask. The flask was placed in a hot water bath until the sample vaporized. It was found that 1.18 g of vapor occupied 300.0 mL at 100°C and 1.00 atmospheres. Determine the molecular weight of the acid.

(d) Using your answer from part **a**, determine the molecular formula for part **b** and for part **c**.

(e) Account for any differences in the molecular formulas determined in part **d**.

Answer and Explanation for the Free-Response Question

(a) The percent oxygen (53.3%) is determined by subtracting the carbon and the hydrogen from 100%. Assuming there are 100 grams of sample gives the grams of each element as being numerically equivalent to the percent. Dividing the grams by the molar mass of each element gives the moles of each.

For C: 40.0/12.01 = 3.33	Divide each	C = 1
For H: 6.71/1.008 = 6.66	of these by	H = 2
For O: 53.3/16.00 = 3.33	the smallest	O = 1
	(3.33)	

This gives the empirical formula: CH_2O.

You get 1 point for correctly determining any of the elements and 1 point for getting the complete empirical formula correct.

(b) Using HA to represent the monoprotic acid, the balanced equation for the titration reaction is:

$$HA(aq) + NaOH(aq) \rightarrow NaA(aq) + H_2O(l)$$

The moles of acid may then be calculated:

$$(45.00 \text{ mL NaOH})\left(\frac{0.1000 \text{ mol NaOH}}{1000 \text{ mL}}\right)\left(\frac{1 \text{ mol HA}}{1 \text{ mol NaOH}}\right) = 4.500 \times 10^{-3} \text{ mol HA}$$

The molecular mass is:

$$0.2720 \text{ g}/4.500 \times 10^{-3} \text{ mol} = 60.44 \text{ g/mol}$$

You get 1 point for the correct number of moles of HA (or NaOH) and 1 point for the correct final answer.

(c) There are several methods to solve this problem. One way is to use the ideal gas equation as done here. The equation and the value of R are in the exam booklet. First find the moles: $n = PV/RT$. Do not forget, you MUST change temperature to kelvin.

$$n = (1.00 \text{ atm})(300.0 \text{ mL})(1 \text{ L}/1{,}000 \text{ mL})/(0.0821 \text{ L atm/mol K})(373 \text{ K})$$

$$n = 9.80 \times 10^{-3} \text{ mol}$$

The molecular mass is $1.18 \text{ g}/9.80 \times 10^{-3} \text{ mol} = 120 \text{ g/mol}$

You get 1 point for getting any part of the calculation correct and 1 point for getting the correct final answer.

(d) The approximate formula mass from the empirical (CH_2O) formula is:

$$12 + 2(1) + 16 = 30 \text{ g/mol}$$

For part **b**: $(60.44 \text{ g/mol})/(30 \text{ g/mol}) = 2$

$$\text{Molecular formula} = 2 \times \text{Empirical formula} = C_2H_4O_2$$

For part **c**: (120 g/mol)/(30 g/mol) = 4

$$\text{Molecular formula} = 4 \times \text{Empirical formula} = C_4H_8O_4$$

You get 1 point for each correct molecular formula. If you got the wrong answer in part **a**, you can still get credit for one or both of the molecular formulas if you used the part **a** value correctly.

(e) The one formula is double the formula of the other. Thus, the smaller molecule dimerizes to produce the larger molecule.

You get 1 point if you "combined" two of the smaller molecules.

Total your points. There are 9 points possible.

〉Rapid Review

- The mole is the amount of substance that contains the same number of particles as exactly 12 g of carbon-12.

- Avogadro's number is the number of particles per mole, 6.022×10^{23} particles.

- A mole is also the formula (atomic, molecular) mass expressed in grams.

- If you have any one of the three—moles, grams, or particles—you can calculate the others.

- The empirical formula indicates which elements are present and the lowest whole-number ratio.

- The molecular formula tells which elements are present and the actual number of each.

- Be able to calculate the empirical formula from percent composition data or quantities from chemical analysis.

- Stoichiometry is the calculation of the amount of one substance in a chemical equation by using another one.

- *Always use the balanced chemical equation* in reaction stoichiometry problems.

- Be able to convert from moles of one substance to moles of another, using the stoichiometric ratio derived from the *balanced chemical equation.*

- In working problems that involve a quantity other than moles, sooner or later it will be necessary to convert to moles.

- The limiting reactant is the reactant that is used up first.

- Be able to calculate the limiting reactant by the use of the mol/coefficient ratio.

- Percent yield is the actual yield (how much was actually formed in the reaction) divided by the theoretical yield (the maximum possible amount of product formed) times 100%.

- A solution is a homogeneous mixture composed of a solute (species present in smaller amount) and a solvent (species present in larger amount).

- Molarity is the number of moles of solute per liter of solution. Don't confuse molarity, M or [ ], with moles, n or mol.

- Be able to work reaction stoichiometry problems using molarity.

- *Always use the balanced chemical equation* in reaction stoichiometry problems.

CHAPTER 8

Gases

IN THIS CHAPTER

Summary: Of the three states of matter—gases, liquids, and solids—gases are probably the best understood and have the best descriptive model. While studying gases in this chapter you will consider four main physical properties—volume, pressure, temperature, and amount—and their interrelationships. These relationships, commonly called gas laws, show up quite often on the AP exam, so you will spend quite a bit of time working problems in this chapter. But before we start looking at the gas laws, let's look at the Kinetic Molecular Theory of Gases, the extremely useful model that scientists use to represent the gaseous state.

Keywords and Equations

Gas constant, $R = 0.0821$ L atm mol^{-1} K^{-1}

$$\frac{r_1}{r_2} = \sqrt{\frac{M_2}{M_1}}$$

u_{rms} = root mean square speed
r = rate of effusion
STP = 0.000°C and 1.000 atm
$PV = nRT$

$$\left(P + \frac{n^2a}{V^2}\right)(V - nb) = nRT$$

$P_A = P_{total} \times X_A$, where $X_A = \dfrac{\text{moles A}}{\text{total moles}}$

$P_{total} = P_A + P_B + P_C + \dots$

$$\frac{P_1V_1}{T_1} = \frac{P_2V_2}{T_2}$$

$$u_{rms} = \sqrt{\frac{3kT}{m}} = \sqrt{\frac{3RT}{M}}$$

KE per molecule $= 1/2\ mv^2$

KE per mole $= \frac{3}{2}RT$

1 atm $=$ 760 mm Hg

$ =$ 760 torr

$$n = \frac{m}{M}$$

Kinetic Molecular Theory

KEY IDEA

The **Kinetic Molecular Theory** attempts to represent the properties of gases by modeling the gas particles themselves at the microscopic level. There are five main postulates of the Kinetic Molecular Theory:

1. Gases are composed of very small particles, either molecules or atoms.
2. The gas particles are tiny in comparison to the distances between them, so we assume that the volume of the gas particles themselves is negligible.
3. These gas particles are in constant motion, moving in straight lines in a random fashion and colliding with each other and the inside walls of the container. The collisions with the inside container walls comprise the pressure of the gas.
4. The gas particles are assumed to neither attract nor repel each other. They may collide with each other, but if they do, the collisions are assumed to be elastic. No kinetic energy is lost, only transferred from one gas molecule to another.
5. The *average* kinetic energy of the gas is proportional to the Kelvin temperature.

A gas that obeys these five postulates is an **ideal gas**. However, just as there are no ideal students, there are no ideal gases: only gases that approach ideal behavior. We know that real gas particles do occupy a certain finite volume, and we know that there are interactions between real gas particles. These factors cause real gases to deviate a little from the ideal behavior of the Kinetic Molecular Theory. But, a non-polar gas at a low pressure and high temperature would come pretty close to ideal behavior. Later in this chapter, we'll show how to modify our equations to account for non-ideal behavior.

Before we leave the Kinetic Molecular Theory (KMT) and start examining the gas law relationships, let's quantify a couple of the postulates of the KMT. Postulate 3 qualitatively describes the motion of the gas particles. The average velocity of the gas particles is called the **root mean square speed** and is given the symbol u_{rms}. This is a special type of average speed. It is the speed of a gas particle having the average kinetic energy of the gas particles. Mathematically it can be represented as:

$$u_{\text{rms}} = \sqrt{\frac{3kT}{m}} = \sqrt{\frac{3RT}{M}}$$

where R is the molar gas constant (we'll talk more about it in the section dealing with the ideal gas equation), T is the **Kelvin** temperature, and M is the molar mass of the gas. These root mean square speeds are very high. Hydrogen gas, H_2, at 20°C has a value of approximately 2,000 m/s.

Postulate 5 relates the average kinetic energy of the gas particles to the Kelvin temperature. Mathematically we can represent the average kinetic energy per molecule as:

$$KE \text{ per molecule} = 1/2 \; mv^2$$

where m is the mass of the molecule and v is its velocity.

The average kinetic energy per mol of gas is represented by:

$$KE \text{ per mol} = 3/2 \; RT$$

where R again is the ideal gas constant and T is the Kelvin temperature. This shows the direct relationship between the average kinetic energy of the gas particles and the Kelvin temperature.

Gas Law Relationships

The gas laws relate the physical properties of volume, pressure, temperature, and moles (amount) to each other. First we will examine the individual gas law relationships. You will need to know these relationships for the AP exam, but the use of the individual equation is not required. Then we will combine the relationships into a single equation that you will need to be able to apply. But first, we need to describe a few things concerning pressure.

Pressure

When we use the word **pressure**, we may be referring to the pressure of a gas inside a container or to atmospheric pressure, the pressure due to the weight of the atmosphere above us. These two different types of pressure are measured in slightly different ways. Atmospheric pressure is measured using a **barometer** (Figure 8.1).

An evacuated hollow tube sealed at one end is filled with mercury, and then the open end is immersed in a pool of mercury. Gravity will tend to pull the liquid level inside the tube down, while the weight of the atmospheric gases on the surface of the mercury pool will tend to force the liquid up into the tube. These two opposing forces will quickly balance each other, and the column of mercury inside the tube will stabilize. The height of the column of mercury above the surface of the mercury pool is called the atmospheric pressure. At sea level, the column averages 760 mm high. This pressure is also called 1 atmosphere (atm). Commonly, the unit torr is used for pressure, where 1 torr = 1 mm Hg, so that atmospheric pressure at sea level equals 760 torr. The SI unit of pressure is the pascal (Pa), so that 1 atm = 760 mm Hg = 760 torr = 101,325 Pa (101.325 kPa). In the United States pounds per square inch (psi) is sometimes used, so that 1 atm = 14.69 psi.

To measure the gas pressure inside a container, a **manometer** (Figure 8.2) is used. As in the barometer, the pressure of the gas is balanced against a column of mercury.

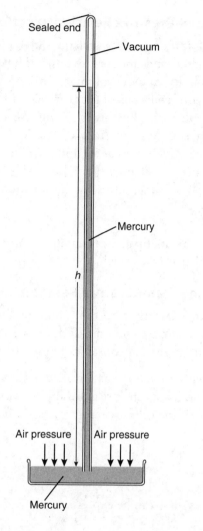

Figure 8.1   The mercury barometer.

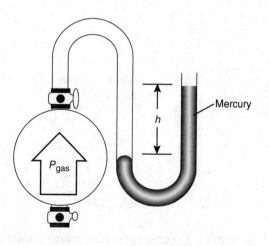

Figure 8.2   The manometer.

Volume–Pressure Relationship: Boyle's Law

Boyle's law describes the relationship between the volume and the pressure of a gas when the temperature and amount are constant. If you have a container like the one shown in Figure 8.3 and you decrease the volume of the container, the pressure of the gas increases because the number of collisions of gas particles with the container's inside walls increases.

Mathematically this is an inverse relationship, so the product of the pressure and volume is a constant: $PV = k_b$.

If you take a gas at an initial volume (V_1) and pressure (P_1) (amount and temperature constant) and change the volume (V_2) and pressure (P_2), you can relate the two sets of conditions to each other by the equation:

$$P_1V_1 = P_2V_2$$

In this mathematical statement of Boyle's law, if you know any three quantities, you can calculate the fourth.

Volume–Temperature Relationship: Charles's Law

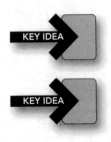

Charles's law describes the volume and temperature relationship of a gas when the pressure and amount are constant. If a sample of gas is heated, the volume must increase for the pressure to remain constant. This is shown in Figure 8.4.

Remember: In any gas law calculation, you must express the temperature in kelvin.

There is a direct relationship between the Kelvin temperature and the volume: as one increases, the other also increases. Mathematically, Charles's law can be represented as:

$$V/T = k_c$$

where k_c is a constant and the temperature is expressed in kelvin.

Again, if there is a change from one set of volume–temperature conditions to another, Charles's law can be expressed as:

$$V_1/T_1 = V_2/T_2$$

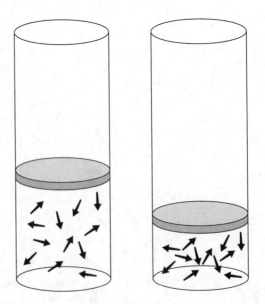

Figure 8.3   Volume–pressure relationship for gases. As the volume decreases, the number of collisions increases.

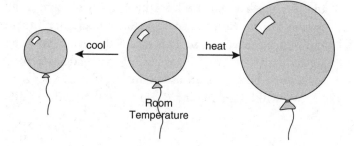

Figure 8.4   Volume–temperature relationship for gases.

Pressure–Temperature Relationship: Gay-Lussac's Law

Gay-Lussac's law describes the relationship between the pressure of a gas and its Kelvin temperature if the volume and amount are held constant. Figure 8.5 represents the process of heating a given amount of gas at a constant volume.

As the gas is heated, the particles move with greater kinetic energy, striking the inside walls of the container more often and with greater force. This causes the pressure of the gas to increase. The relationship between the Kelvin temperature and the pressure is a direct one:

$$P/T = k_g \quad \text{or} \quad P_1/T_1 = P_2/T_2$$

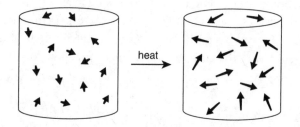

Figure 8.5   Pressure–temperature relationship for gases. As the temperature increases, the gas particles have greater kinetic energy (longer arrows) and collisions are more frequent and forceful.

Combined Gas Law

In the discussion of Boyle's, Charles's, and Gay-Lussac's laws we held two of the four variables constant, changed the third, and looked at its effect on the fourth variable. If we keep the number of moles of gas constant—that is, no gas can get in or out—then we can combine these three gas laws into one, the **combined gas law**, which can be expressed as:

$$(P_1 V_1)/T_1 = (P_2 V_2)/T_2$$

Again, remember: In any gas law calculation, you must express the temperature in kelvin.

In this equation, there are six unknowns; given any five, you should be able to solve for the sixth.

For example, suppose a 5.0-L bottle of gas with a pressure of 2.50 atm at 20°C is heated to 80°C. We can calculate the new pressure using the combined gas law. Before we start working mathematically, however, let's do some reasoning. The volume of the bottle hasn't changed, and neither has the number of moles of gas inside. Only the temperature and pressure have changed, so this is really a Gay-Lussac's law problem. From Gay-Lussac's law you know that if you increase the temperature, the pressure should increase if the amount and volume are constant. This means that when you calculate the new pressure, it should be greater than 2.50 atm; if it is less, you've made an error. Also, **remember that the temperatures must be expressed in kelvin**. 20°C = 293 K (K = °C + 273) and 80°C = 353 K.

We will be solving for P_2, so we will take the combined gas law and rearrange for P_2:

$$(T_2 P_1 V_1)/(T_1 V_2) = P_2$$

Substituting in the values:

$$(353 \text{ K})(2.50 \text{ atm})(5.0 \text{ L})/(293 \text{ K})(5.0 \text{ L}) = P_2$$

$$3.0 \text{ atm} = P_2$$

The new pressure is greater than the original pressure, making the answer a reasonable one. Note that all the units canceled except atm, which is the unit that you wanted.

Let's look at a situation in which two conditions change. Suppose a balloon has a volume at sea level of 10.0 L at 760.0 torr and 20°C (293 K). The balloon is released and rises to an altitude where the pressure is 450.0 torr and the temperature is −10°C (263 K). You want to calculate the new volume of the balloon. You know that you have to express the temperature in K in the calculations. It is perfectly fine to leave the pressures in torr. It really doesn't matter what pressure and volume units you use, as long as they are consistent in the problem. The pressure is decreasing, so that should cause the volume to increase (Boyle's law). The temperature is decreasing, so that should cause the volume to decrease (Charles's law). Here you have two competing factors, so it is difficult to predict the end result. You'll simply have to do the calculations and see.

Using the combined gas equation, solve for the new volume (V_2):

$$(P_1 V_1)/T_1 = (P_2 V_2)/T_2$$

$$(P_1 V_1 T_2)/(P_2 T_1) = V_2$$

Now substitute the known quantities into the equation. (You could substitute the knowns into the combined gas equation first, and then solve for the volume. Do it whichever way is easier for you.)

$$(760.0 \text{ torr})(10.0 \text{ L})(263 \text{ K})/(450.0 \text{ torr})(293 \text{ K}) = V_2$$

$$15.2 \text{ L} = V_2$$

Note that the units canceled, leaving the desired volume unit of liters. Overall, the volume did increase, so in this case the pressure decrease had a greater effect than the temperature decrease. This seems reasonable, looking at the numbers. There is a relatively small change in the Kelvin temperature (293 K versus 263 K) compared to a much larger change in the pressure (760.0 torr versus 450.0 torr).

Volume–Amount Relationship: Avogadro's Law

In all the gas law problems so far, the amount of gas has been constant. But, what if the amount changes? That is where Avogadro's law comes into play.

If a container is kept at constant pressure and temperature, and you increase the number of gas particles in that container, the volume will have to increase in order to keep the pressure constant. This means that there is a direct relationship between the volume and the number of moles of gas (n). This is **Avogadro's law** and mathematically it looks like this:

$$V/n = k_a \quad \text{or} \quad V_1/n_1 = V_2/n_2$$

We could work this into the combined gas law, but more commonly the amount of gas is related to the other physical properties through another relationship that Avogadro developed:

1 mol of any gas occupies 22.4 L at STP
[standard temperature and pressure of 0°C (273 K) and 1 atm]

The combined gas law and Avogadro's relationship can then be combined into the ideal gas equation, which incorporates the pressure, volume, temperature, and amount relationships of a gas.

Ideal Gas Equation

The **ideal gas equation** has the mathematical form of $PV = nRT$, where:

P = pressure of the gas in atm, torr, mm Hg, Pa, etc.
V = volume of the gas in L, mL, etc.
n = number of moles of gas
R = ideal gas constant: 0.0821 L·atm/K·mol
T = Kelvin temperature

This is the value for R if the volume is expressed in liters, the pressure in atmospheres, and the temperature in kelvin (naturally). You could calculate another ideal gas constant based on different units of pressure and volume, but the simplest thing to do is to use the 0.0821 and convert the given volume to liters and the pressure to atm. And remember that you **must express the temperature in kelvin**.

Let's see how we might use the ideal gas equation. Suppose you want to know what volume 20.0 g of hydrogen gas would occupy at 27°C and 0.950 atm. You have the pressure in atm, you can get the temperature in kelvin (27°C + 273 = 300.K), but you will need to convert the grams of hydrogen gas to moles of hydrogen gas before you can use the ideal gas equation. Also, remember that hydrogen gas is diatomic, H_2.

First, you'll convert the 20.0 g to moles:

$$(20.0 \text{ g/l}) \times (1 \text{ mol } H_2/2.016 \text{ g}) = 9.921 \text{ mol } H_2$$

(We're not worried about significant figures at this point, since this is an intermediate calculation.)

Now you can solve the ideal gas equation for the unknown quantity, the volume:

$$PV = nRT$$

$$V = nRT/P$$

Finally, plug in the numerical values for the different known quantities:

$$V = (9.921 \text{ mol})(0.0821 \text{ L atm/K mol}) (300.K)/0.950 \text{ atm}$$

$$V = 257 \text{ L}$$

Is the answer reasonable? You have almost 10 mol of gas. It would occupy about 224 L at STP (10 mol × 22.4 L/mol) by Avogadro's relationship. The pressure is slightly less than standard pressure of 1 atm, which would tend to increase the volume (Boyle's law), and temperature is greater than standard temperature of 0°C, which would also increase the volume (Charles's law). So you might expect a volume greater than 224 L, and that is exactly what you found.

Remember, the final thing you do when working any type of chemistry problem is answer this question: Is the answer reasonable?

Dalton's Law of Partial Pressures

Dalton's law says that in a mixture of gases (A + B + C . . .) the total pressure is simply the sum of the partial pressures (the pressures associated with each individual gas). Mathematically, Dalton's law looks like this:

$$P_{Total} = P_A + P_B + P_C + \cdots$$

Commonly Dalton's law is used in calculations involving the collection of a gas over water, as in the displacement of water by oxygen gas. In this situation, there is a gas mixture: O_2 and water vapor, $H_2O(g)$. The total pressure in this case is usually atmospheric pressure, and the partial pressure of the water vapor is determined by looking up the vapor pressure of water at the temperature of the water in a reference book. Simple subtraction generates the partial pressure of the oxygen.

If you know how many moles of each gas are in the mixture and the total pressure, you can calculate the partial pressure of each gas by multiplying the total pressure by the mole fraction of each gas:

$$P_A = (P_{Total})(X_A)$$

where X_A = mole fraction of gas A. The mole fraction of gas A would be equal to the moles of gas A divided by the total moles of gas in the mixture.

Graham's Law of Diffusion and Effusion

Graham's law defines the relationship of the speed of gas diffusion (mixing of gases due to their kinetic energy) or effusion (movement of a gas through a tiny opening) and the gases' molecular mass. The lighter the gas, the faster is its rate of effusion. Normally this is set up as the comparison of the effusion rates of two gases, and the specific mathematical relationship is:

$$\frac{r_1}{r_2} = \sqrt{\frac{M_2}{M_1}}$$

where r_1 and r_2 are the rates of effusion/diffusion of gases 1 and 2 respectively, and M_2 and M_1 are the molecular masses of gases 2 and 1 respectively. **Note that this is an inverse relationship**.

For example, suppose you wanted to calculate the ratio of effusion rates for hydrogen and nitrogen gases. Remember that both are diatomic, so the molecular mass of H_2 is 2.016 g/mol and the molecular mass of N_2 would be 28.02 g/mol. Substituting into the Graham's law equation:

$$\frac{r_{H_2}}{r_{N_2}} = \sqrt{\frac{M_{N_2}}{M_{H_2}}}$$

$$r_{H_2}/r_{N_2} = (28.02 \text{ g/mol}/2.016 \text{ g/mol})^{1/2} = (13.899)^{1/2} = 3.728$$

Hydrogen gas would effuse through a pinhole 3.728 times as fast as nitrogen gas. The answer is reasonable, since the lower the molecular mass, the faster the gas is moving. Sometimes we measure the effusion rates of a known gas and an unknown gas, and use Graham's law to calculate the molecular mass of the unknown gas.

Gas Stoichiometry

The gas law relationships can be used in reaction stoichiometry problems. For example, suppose you have a mixture of $KClO_3$ and $NaCl$, and you want to determine how many

grams of $KClO_3$ are present. You take the mixture and heat it. The $KClO_3$ decomposes according to the equation:

$$2\ KClO_3(s) \rightarrow 2\ KCl(s) + 3\ O_2(g)$$

The oxygen gas that is formed is collected by displacement of water. It occupies a volume of 542 mL at 27°C. The atmospheric pressure is 755.0 torr. The vapor pressure of water at 27°C is 26.7 torr.

First, you need to determine the pressure of just the oxygen gas. It was collected over water, so the total pressure of 755.0 torr is the sum of the partial pressures of the oxygen and the water vapor:

$$P_{Total} = P_{O_2} + P_{H_2O} \text{(Dalton's law)}$$

The partial pressure of water vapor at 27°C is 26.7 torr, so the partial pressure of the oxygen can be calculated by:

$$P_{O_2} = P_{Total} - P_{H_2O} = 755.0\ torr - 26.7\ torr = 728.3\ torr$$

At this point, you have 542 mL of oxygen gas at 728.3 torr and 300. K (27°C + 273). From this data, you can use the ideal gas equation to calculate the number of moles of oxygen gas produced:

$$PV = nRT$$
$$PV/RT = n$$

You will need to convert the pressure from torr to atm:

$$(728.3\ torr) \times (1\ atm/760.0\ torr) = 0.9583\ atm$$

and express the volume in liters: 542 mL = 0.542 L

Now you can substitute the quantities into the ideal gas equation:

$$(0.9583\ atm)(0.542\ L)/(0.0821\ L \cdot atm/K \cdot mol)(300.\ K) = n$$
$$0.02110\ mol\ O_2 = n$$

Now you can use the reaction stoichiometry to convert from moles O_2 to moles $KClO_3$ and then to grams $KClO_3$:

$$(0.02110\ mol\ O_2)\left(\frac{2\ mol\ KClO_3}{3\ mol\ O_2}\right)\left(\frac{122.55\ g\ KClO_3}{1\ mol\ KClO_3}\right) = 1.723\ g\ KClO_3$$

Non-Ideal Gases

We have been considering ideal gases, that is, gases that obey the postulates of the Kinetic Molecular Theory. But remember—a couple of those postulates were on shaky ground. The volume of the gas molecules was negligible, and there were no attractive forces between the gas particles. Many times approximations are fine and the ideal gas equation works well. But, it would be nice to have a more accurate model for doing extremely precise work or when a gas exhibits a relatively large attractive force. In 1873, Johannes van der Waals introduced a modification of the ideal gas equation that attempted to take into account the volume and attractive forces of real gases by introducing two constants—a and b—into the ideal gas equation. Van der Waals realized that the actual volume of the gas is less than the ideal gas because gas molecules have a finite volume. He also realized that the more moles of gas present, the greater the real volume. He compensated for the volume of the gas particles mathematically with:

$$\text{corrected volume} = V - nb$$

where n is the number of moles of gas and b is a different constant for each gas. The larger the gas particles, the more volume they occupy and the larger the b value.

The attraction of the gas particles for each other tends to lessen the pressure of the gas, because the attraction slightly reduces the force of gas particle collisions with the container walls. The amount of attraction depends on the concentration of gas particles and the magnitude of the particles' intermolecular force. The greater the intermolecular forces of the gas, the higher the attraction is, and the less the real pressure. Van der Waals compensated for the attractive force with:

$$\text{corrected pressure} = P + an^2/V^2$$

where a is a constant for individual gases. The greater the attractive force between the molecules, the larger the value of a. The n^2/V^2 term corrects for the concentration. Substituting these corrections into the ideal gas equation gives the **van der Waals equation**:

$$(P + an^2/V^2)(V - nb) = nRT$$

The larger, more concentrated, and stronger the intermolecular forces of the gas, the more deviation from the ideal gas equation one can expect and the more useful the van der Waals equation becomes.

Experiments

STRATEGY

Gas law experiments generally involve pressure, volume, and temperature measurements. In a few cases, other measurements such as mass and time are necessary. You should remember that ΔP, for example, is NOT a measurement; the initial and final pressure measurements are the actual measurements made in the laboratory. Another common error is the application of gas law type information and calculations for non-gaseous materials.

A common consideration is the presence of water vapor, $H_2O(g)$. Water generates a vapor pressure, which varies with the temperature. Dalton's law is used in these cases to adjust the pressure of a gas sample for the presence of water vapor. The total pressure (normally atmospheric pressure) is the pressure of the gas or gases being collected and the water vapor. When the pressure of an individual gas is needed, the vapor pressure of water is subtracted from the total pressure. Finding the vapor pressure of water requires measuring the temperature and using a table showing vapor pressure of water versus temperature.

In experiments on Graham's law, time is measured. The amount of time required for a sample to effuse is the measurement. The amount of material effusing divided by the time elapsed is the rate of effusion.

Most gas law experiments use either the combined gas law or the ideal gas equation. Moles of gas are a major factor in many of these experiments. The combined gas law can generate the moles of a gas by adjusting the volume to STP and using Avogadro's relationship of 22.4 L/mol at STP. The ideal gas equation gives moles from the relationship $n = PV/RT$.

> HINT: Make sure the conditions are STP before using 22.4 L/mol.

Two common gas law experiments are "Determination of Molar Mass by Vapor Density" and "Determination of the Molar Volume of a Gas." While it is possible to use the combined gas law (through 22.4 L/mol at STP) for either of these, the ideal gas equation is easier to use. The values for P, V, T, and n must be determined.

The temperature may be determined easily using a thermometer. The temperature measurement is normally in °C. The °C must then be converted to a Kelvin temperature (K = °C + 273).

Pressure is measured using a barometer. If water vapor is present, a correction is needed in the pressure to compensate for its presence. The vapor pressure of water is found in a table of vapor pressure versus temperature. Subtract the value found in this table from the measured pressure (Dalton's law). Values from tables are not considered to be measurements for an experiment. If you are going to use 0.0821 L atm/mol K for R, convert the pressure to atmospheres.

The value of V may be measured or calculated. A simple measurement of the volume of a container may be made, or a measurement of the volume of displaced water may be required. Calculating the volume requires knowing the number of moles of gas present. No matter how you get the volume, don't forget to convert it to liters when using $PV = nRT$ or STP.

The values of P, T, and V discussed above may be used, through the use of the ideal gas equation, to determine the number of moles present in a gaseous sample. Stoichiometry is the alternative method of determining the number of moles present. A quantity of a substance is converted to a gas. This conversion may be accomplished in a variety of ways. The most common stoichiometric methods are through volatilization or reaction. The volatilization method is the simplest. A weighed quantity (measure the mass) of a substance is converted to moles by using the molar mass (molecular weight). If a reaction is taking place, the quantity of one of the substances must be determined (normally with the mass and molar mass), and then, through the use of the mole-to-mole ratio, this value is converted to moles.

The values of P, T, and n may be used to determine the volume of a gas. If this volume is to be used with Avogadro's law of 22.4 L/mol, the combined gas law must be employed to adjust the volume to STP. This equation will use the measured values for P and T along with the calculated value of V. These values are combined with STP conditions (0°C [273.15 K] and 1.00 atm) to determine the molar volume of a gas.

Combining the value of n with the measured mass of a sample will allow you to calculate the molar mass of the gas.

Do not forget: Values found in tables and conversions from one unit to another are not experimental measurements.

Common Mistakes to Avoid

1. When using any of the gas laws, be sure you are dealing with gases, not liquids or solids. We've lost track of how many times we've seen people apply gas laws in situations in which no gases were involved.
2. In any of the gas laws, be sure to express the **temperature in kelvin**. Failure to do so is a quite common mistake.
3. Be sure, especially in stoichiometry problems involving gases, that you are calculating the volume, pressure, etc. of the correct gas. You can avoid this mistake by clearly labeling your quantities (*moles of O_2* instead of just *moles*).
4. Make sure your **answer is reasonable**. Analyze the problem; don't just write a number down from your calculator. Be sure to check your number of significant figures.
5. If you have a gas at a certain set of volume/temperature/pressure conditions and the conditions change, you will probably use the combined gas equation. If moles of gas are involved, the ideal gas equation will probably be useful.
6. Make sure your **units cancel**.
7. In using the combined gas equation, make sure you group all initial-condition quantities on one side of the equals sign and all final-condition quantities on the other side.
8. Be sure to use the correct molecular mass for those gases that exist as diatomic molecules—H_2, N_2, O_2, F_2, Cl_2, and Br_2 and I_2 vapors.
9. If the value 22.4 L/mol is to be used, make absolutely sure that it is applied to a **gas** at **STP**.

❭ Review Questions

Use these questions to review the content of this chapter and practice for the AP Chemistry exam. First are 16 multiple-choice questions similar to what you will encounter in Section I of the AP Chemistry exam. Following those is a long free-response question like the ones in Section II of the exam. To make these questions an even more authentic practice for the actual exam, time yourself following the instructions provided.

Multiple-Choice Questions

Answer the following questions in 20 minutes. You may not use a calculator. You may use the periodic table and the equation sheet at the back of this book.

1. A sample of argon gas is sealed in a container. The volume of the container is doubled. If the pressure remains constant, what happens to the absolute temperature?

   (A) It does not change.
   (B) It is halved.
   (C) It is doubled.
   (D) It is squared.

2. A sealed, rigid container is filled with three ideal gases: A, B, and C. The partial pressure of each gas is known. The temperature and volume of the system are known. What additional information is necessary to determine the masses of the gases in the container?

   (A) the average distance traveled between molecular collisions
   (B) the intermolecular forces
   (C) the molar masses of the gases
   (D) the total pressure

3. Two balloons are at the same temperature and pressure. One contains 14 g of nitrogen and the other contains 20.0 g of argon. Which of the following is true?

   (A) The density of the nitrogen sample is greater than the density of the argon sample.
   (B) The average speed of the nitrogen molecules is greater than the average speed of the argon molecules.
   (C) The average kinetic energy of the nitrogen molecules is greater than the average kinetic energy of the argon molecules.
   (D) The volume of the nitrogen container is less than the volume of the argon container.

4. An experiment to determine the molar mass of a gas begins by heating a solid to produce a gaseous product. The gas passes through a tube and displaces water in an inverted, water-filled bottle. Which of the following items may be determined after the experiment is completed?

   (A) vapor pressure of water
   (B) temperature of the displaced water
   (C) barometric pressure in the room
   (D) mass of the solid used

5. The true volume of a real gas is larger than that calculated from the ideal gas equation. This occurs because the ideal gas equation does not consider which of the following?

   (A) the attraction between the molecules
   (B) the shape of the molecules
   (C) the volume of the molecules
   (D) the mass of the molecules

6. Aluminum metal reacts with HCl to produce aluminum chloride and hydrogen gas. How many grams of aluminum metal must be added to an excess of HCl to produce 33.6 L of hydrogen gas, if the gas is at STP?

   (A) 18.0 g
   (B) 35.0 g
   (C) 27.0 g
   (D) 4.50 g

7. A reaction produces a gaseous mixture of carbon dioxide, carbon monoxide, and water vapor. After one reaction, the mixture was analyzed and found to contain 0.60 mol of carbon dioxide, 0.30 mol of carbon monoxide, and 0.10 mol of water vapor. If the total pressure of the mixture was 0.80 atm, what was the partial pressure of the carbon monoxide?

(A) 0.080 atm
(B) 0.34 atm
(C) 0.13 atm
(D) 0.24 atm

8. A sample of methane gas was collected over water at 35°C. The sample had a total pressure of 756 mm Hg. Determine the partial pressure of the methane gas in the sample. (The vapor pressure of water at 35°C is 41 mm Hg.)

(A) 760 mm Hg
(B) 41 mm Hg
(C) 715 mm Hg
(D) 797 mm Hg

9. A 1.15 mol sample of carbon monoxide gas has a temperature of 27°C and a pressure of 0.300 atm. If the temperature were lowered to 17°C, at constant volume, what would be the new pressure?

(A) 0.290 atm
(B) 0.519 atm
(C) 0.206 atm
(D) 0.338 atm

10. An ideal gas sample weighing 1.28 g at 127°C and 1.00 atm has a volume of 0.250 L. Determine the molar mass of the gas.

(A) 322 g/mol
(B) 168 g/mol
(C) 0.00621 g/mol
(D) 80.5 g/mol

11. Increasing the temperature of an ideal gas from 50°C to 75°C at constant volume will cause which of the following to increase for the gas?

(A) the average molecular mass of the gas
(B) the average distance between the molecules
(C) the average speed of the molecules
(D) the density of the gas

12. If a sample of CH_4 effuses at a rate of 9.0 mol per hour at 35°C, which of the gases below will effuse at approximately twice the rate under the same conditions?

(A) CO
(B) He
(C) O_2
(D) F_2

13. A steel tank containing argon gas has additional argon gas pumped into it at constant temperature. Which of the following is true for the gas in the tank?

(A) There is no change in the number of gas atoms.
(B) There is an increase in the volume of the gas.
(C) There is a decrease in the pressure exerted by the gas.
(D) The gas atoms travel with the same average speed.

14. Choose the gas that probably shows the greatest deviation from ideal gas behavior.

(A) He
(B) O_2
(C) SF_4
(D) SiH_4

15. Determine the formula for a gaseous silane (Si_nH_{2n+2}) if it has a density of 5.47 g per L at 0°C and 1.00 atm.

(A) SiH_4
(B) Si_2H_6
(C) Si_3H_8
(D) Si_4H_{10}

16. Which of the following best explains why a hot air balloon rises?

(A) The heating of the air causes the pressure inside the balloon to increase.
(B) The cool outside air pushes the balloon higher.
(C) The temperature difference between the inside and outside air causes convection currents.
(D) Hot air has a lower density than cold air.

Answers and Explanations for the Multiple-Choice Questions

1. **C**—This question relates to the combined gas law: $P_1V_1/T_1 = P_2V_2/T_2$. Since the pressure remains constant, the pressures may be removed from the combined gas law to produce Charles's law: $V_1/T_1 = V_2/T_2$. This equation may be rearranged to: $T_2 = V_2T_1/V_1$. The doubling of the volume means $V_2 = 2 V_1$. On substituting: $T_2 = 2V_1T_1/V_1$; giving $T_2 = 2T_1$. The identity of the gas is irrelevant in this problem.

2. **C**—This problem depends on the ideal gas equation: $PV = nRT$. R, V, and T are known, and by using the partial pressure for a gas, the number of moles of that gas may be determined. To convert from moles to mass, the molar mass of the gas is necessary.

3. **B**—Since T and P are known, and since the moles (n) can be determined from the masses given, this question could use the ideal gas equation. The number of moles of each gas is 0.50. Equal moles of gases, at the same T and P, have equal volumes, which eliminates answer choice D. Equal volume also means that the greater mass has the greater density, eliminating choice A. The average kinetic energy of a gas depends on the temperature. If the temperatures are the same, then the average kinetic energy is the same, eliminating C. Finally, at the same temperature, heavier gases travel slower than lighter gases. Nitrogen is lighter than argon, so it travels at a faster average speed, making B the correct answer. You may find this type of reasoning process beneficial on any question in which you do not immediately know the answer.

4. **A**—This experiment requires the ideal gas equation. The mass of the solid is needed (to convert to moles); this eliminates answer choice D. The volume, temperature, and pressure must also be measured during the experiment, eliminating choices B and C. The measured pressure is the total pressure. Eventually the total pressure must be converted to the partial pressure of the gas using Dalton's law. The total pressure is the sum of the pressure of the gas plus the vapor pressure of water. The vapor pressure of water can be looked up in a table when the calculations are performed (only the temperature is needed to find the vapor pressure in a table). Answer A is correct.

5. **C**—Real gases are different from ideal gases because of two basic factors (see the van der Waals equation): molecules have a volume, and molecules attract each other. The molecules' volume is subtracted from the observed volume for a real gas (giving a smaller volume), and the pressure has a term added to compensate for the attraction of the molecules (correcting for a smaller pressure). Since these are the only two directly related factors, answers B and D are eliminated. The question is asking about volume; thus, the answer is C.

6. **C**—A balanced chemical equation is necessary:

$$2\ Al(s) + 6\ HCl(aq) \rightarrow 2\ AlCl_3(aq) + 3\ H_2(g)$$

The reaction produced 33.6 L/22.4 L or 1.50 mol, at STP. To produce this quantity of hydrogen, (2 mol Al/3 mol H_2) × 1.50 mol H_2 = 1.00 mol of Al is needed. The atomic weight of Al is 27.0 g/mol; thus, 27.0 g of Al are required.

7. **D**—The partial pressure of any gas is equal to its mole fraction times the total pressure. The mole fraction of carbon monoxide is [0.30/(0.60 + 0.30 + 0.10)] = 0.30, and the partial pressure of CO is 0.30 × 0.80 atm = 0.24 atm.

8. **C**—Using Dalton's law ($P_{\text{Total}} = P_A + P_B + \ldots$), the partial pressure may be found by:

$$756\ \text{mm Hg} - 41\ \text{mm Hg} = 715\ \text{mm Hg}$$

9. **A**—You can begin by removing the volume (constant) from the combined gas law to produce Gay-Lussac's law = $P_1/T_1 = P_2/T_2$. This equation rearranges to $P_2 = P_1T_2/T_1 = 0.300$ atm × 290.0 K)/(300.0 K) = 0.290 atm. Estimation works well in the question as the "slight" temperature change should give a slight decrease in pressure. The moles are not important since they do not change. Some of the other answers result from common errors.

10. **B**—The molar mass may be obtained by dividing the grams by the number of moles (calculated from the ideal gas equation). Estimation works in this case as $n = PV/RT = (0.25)/(0.1 × 400)$. Do not forget to convert the temperature to kelvin.

11. **C**—Choice B requires an increase in volume, not allowed by the problem. Choice C requires

an increase in temperature. Choice A requires a change in the composition of the gas. Choice D requires a decrease in the volume.

12. **B**—Lighter gases effuse faster. The only gas among the choices that is lighter than methane is helium. To calculate the molar mass, you would begin with the molar mass of methane and divide by the rate difference squared.

13. **D**—A steel tank will have a constant volume, and the problem states that the temperature is constant. Adding gas to the tank will increase the number of moles of the gas and the pressure (forcing the argon atoms closer together). A constant temperature means there will be a constant average speed.

14. **C**—Deviations from ideal behavior depend on the size and the intermolecular forces between the molecules. The greatest deviation would be for a large polar molecule. Sulfur tetrafluoride is the largest molecule, and it is the only polar molecule listed.

15. **D**—The molar mass of gas must be determined. The simplest method to find the molar mass is: (5.47 g/L) × (22.4 L/mol) = 123 g/mol (simple factor label). The molar mass may also be determined by dividing the mass of the gas by the moles (using 22.4 L/mol for a gas at STP and using 1 L). If you did not recognize the conditions as STP, you could find the moles from the ideal gas equation. The correct answer is the gas with the molar mass closest to 123 g/mol.

16. **D**—The hot air balloon rises because it has a lower density than air. Less dense objects will float on more dense objects. In other words, "lighter" objects will float on "heavy" objects.

Free-Response Question

You have 20 minutes to do the following question. You may use a calculator and the tables in the back of the book.

Question 1

A sample containing 2/3 mol of potassium chlorate, $KClO_3$, is heated until it decomposes to potassium chloride, KCl, and oxygen gas, O_2. The oxygen is collected in an inverted bottle through the displacement of water. Answer the following questions using this information.

(a) Write a balanced chemical equation for the reaction.

(b) Calculate the number of moles of oxygen gas produced.

(c) The temperature and pressure of the sample are adjusted to STP. The volume of the sample is slightly greater than 22.4 liters. Explain.

(d) An excess of sulfur, S, is burned in one mole of oxygen, in the presence of a catalyst, to form gaseous sulfur trioxide, SO_3. Write a balanced chemical equation and calculate the number of moles of gas formed.

(e) After the sulfur had completely reacted, a sample of the residual water was removed from the bottle and found to be acidic. Explain.

Answer and Explanation for the Free-Response Question

(a) $2 \, KClO_3(s) \rightarrow 2 \, KCl(s) + 3 \, O_2(g)$

You get 1 point if you have the above equation.

(b) $(2/3 \, mol \, KClO_3)(3 \, mol \, O_2/2 \, moles \, KClO_3) = 1 \, mol \, O_2$

You get 1 point for the correct answer and 1 point for the work. You can get these points if you correctly use information from an incorrect equation in part **a**.

(c) At STP, the volume of 1 mol of O_2 should be 22.4 L. The volume is greater because oxygen was not the only gas in the sample. Water vapor was present. The presence of the additional gas leads to a larger volume.

You get 1 point for discussing STP and 22.4 L, and 1 point for discussing the presence of water vapor.

(d) The equation is:

$$2 \, S(s) + 3 \, O_2(g) \rightarrow 2 \, SO_3(g)$$

According to this equation:

$$(1 \, mol \, O_2)(2 \, mol \, SO_3/3 \, mol \, O_2) = 2/3 \, mol \, SO_3$$

You get 1 point for each of these solutions. You can get the 1 point if you used an incorrect number of moles of O_2 from an incorrectly balanced equation.

(e) A nonmetal oxide, such as sulfur trioxide, will dissolve in water to produce an acid. This will get you 1 point; you may wish to include the following equation:

$$SO_3(g) + H_2O(l) \rightarrow H_2SO_4(aq)$$

Total your points for the different parts. There are 8 points possible.

❯ Rapid Review

- Kinetic Molecular Theory—Gases are small particles of negligible volume moving in a random straight-line motion, colliding with the container walls (that is the gas pressure) and with each other. During these collisions, no energy is lost, but energy may be transferred from one particle to another; the Kelvin temperature is proportional to the average kinetic energy. There is assumed to be no attraction between the particles.

- Pressure—Know how a barometer operates and the different units used in atmospheric pressure.

- Boyle's law—The volume and pressure of a gas are inversely proportional if the temperature and amount are constant.

- Charles's law—The volume and temperature of a gas are directly proportional if the amount and pressure are constant.

- Gay-Lussac's law—The pressure and temperature of a gas are directly proportional if the amount and volume are constant.

- Combined gas law—Know how to use the combined gas equation: $P_1V_1/T_1 = P_2V_2/T_2$.

- Avogadro's law—The number of moles and volume of a gas are directly proportional if the pressure and temperature are constant. Remember that 1 mol of an ideal gas at STP (1 atm and 0°C) occupies a volume of 22.4 L. Remember that you should not use the 22.4 L unless the gas is at STP.

- Ideal gas equation—Know how to use the ideal gas equation: $PV = nRT$.

- Dalton's law—The sum of the partial pressures of the individual gases in a gas mixture is equal to the total pressure: $P_{Total} = P_A + P_B + P_c + \ldots$

- Graham's law—The lower the molecular mass of a gas, the faster it will effuse/diffuse. Know how to use Graham's law: $\dfrac{r_1}{r_2} = \sqrt{\dfrac{M_2}{M_1}}$.

- Gas stoichiometry—Know how to apply the gas laws to reaction stoichiometry problems.

- Non-ideal gases—Know how the van der Waals equation accounts for the non-ideal behavior of real gases.

- Tips—Make sure the **temperature is in kelvin**; gas laws are being applied to gases only; the **units cancel**; and the **answer is reasonable**.

- Gas laws are very useful for gases, but not for liquids and solids. Before applying a gas law, be sure you are dealing with a gas.

CHAPTER 9

Thermodynamics

IN THIS CHAPTER

Summary: Thermodynamics is the study of heat and its transformations. **Thermochemistry** is the part of thermodynamics that deals with changes in heat that take place during chemical processes. We will be describing energy changes in this chapter. Energy can be of two types: kinetic or potential. **Kinetic energy** is energy of motion, while **potential energy** is stored energy. Energy can be converted from one form to another but, unless a nuclear reaction occurs, energy cannot be created or destroyed (Law of Conservation of Energy). We will discuss energy exchanges between a system and the surroundings. The **system** is that part of the universe that we are studying. It may be a beaker or it may be Earth. The **surroundings** are the rest of the universe.

The most common units of energy used in the study of thermodynamics are the joule and the calorie. The **joule (J)** is defined as:

$$1 \text{ J} = 1 \text{ kg m}^2/\text{s}^2$$

The **calorie** was originally defined as the amount of energy needed to raise the temperature of 1 g of water 1°C. Now it is defined in terms of its relationship to the joule:

$$1 \text{ cal} = 4.184 \text{ J}$$

It is important to realize that this is not the same calorie that is commonly associated with food and diets. That is the nutritional Calorie, Cal, which is really a kilocalorie (1 Cal = 1,000 cal).

Keywords and Equations

$S°$ = standard entropy $H°$ = standard enthalpy
$G°$ = standard free energy q = heat
c = specific heat capacity C_p = molar heat capacity at constant pressure
$\Delta S° = \Sigma S°$ products $- \Sigma S°$ reactants

$\Delta H° = \Sigma \Delta H_f°$ products $- \Sigma \Delta H_f°$ reactants

$\Delta G° = \Sigma \Delta G_f°$ products $- \Sigma \Delta G_f°$ reactants

$\Delta G° = \Delta H° - T\Delta S°$

$\quad\quad = -RT \ln K = -2.303 \, RT \log K$

$\quad\quad = -n F E°$

$\Delta G = \Delta G° + RT \ln Q = \Delta G° + 2.303 \, RT \log Q$

$q = mc\Delta T$

$$C_p = \frac{\Delta H}{\Delta T}$$

Gas constant, $R = 8.31 \, \text{J mol}^{-1} \, \text{K}^{-1}$

Calorimetry

Calorimetry is the laboratory technique used to measure the heat released or absorbed during a chemical or physical change. The quantity of heat absorbed or released during a chemical or physical change is represented as q and is proportional to the change in temperature of the system being studied. This system has what is called a **heat capacity** (C_p), which is the quantity of heat needed to change the temperature 1 K. It has the form:

$$C_p = \text{heat capacity} = q/\Delta T$$

Heat capacity most commonly has units of J/K. The **specific heat capacity (or specific heat)** (**c**) is the quantity of heat needed to raise the temperature of 1 g of a substance 1 K:

$$c = q/(m \times \Delta T) \text{ or } q = cm\Delta T,$$

where m is the mass of the substance.

The specific heat capacity commonly has units of J/g · K. Because of the original definition of the calorie, the specific heat capacity of water is 4.184 J/g · K. If the specific heat capacity, the mass, and the change of temperature are all known, the amount of energy absorbed can easily be calculated.

Another related quantity is the **molar heat capacity** (C), the amount of heat needed to change the temperature of 1 mol of a substance by 1 K.

Calorimetry involves the use of a laboratory instrument called a calorimeter. Two types of calorimeter, a simple coffee-cup calorimeter and a more sophisticated bomb calorimeter, are shown in Figure 9.1, on the next page. In both, a process is carried out with known amounts of substances and the change in temperature is measured.

The coffee-cup calorimeter can be used to measure the heat changes in reactions or processes that are open to the atmosphere: q_p, constant-pressure reactions. These might be reactions that occur in open beakers and the like. This type of calorimeter is also commonly used to measure the specific heats of solids. A known mass of solid is heated to a certain temperature and then is added to the calorimeter containing a known mass of water at a known temperature. The final temperature is then measured allowing us to calculate the ΔT. We know that the heat lost by the solid (the system) is equal to the heat gained by the surroundings (the water and calorimeter, although for simple coffee-cup calorimetry the heat gained by the calorimeter is small and is ignored):

$$-q_{\text{solid}} = q_{\text{water}}$$

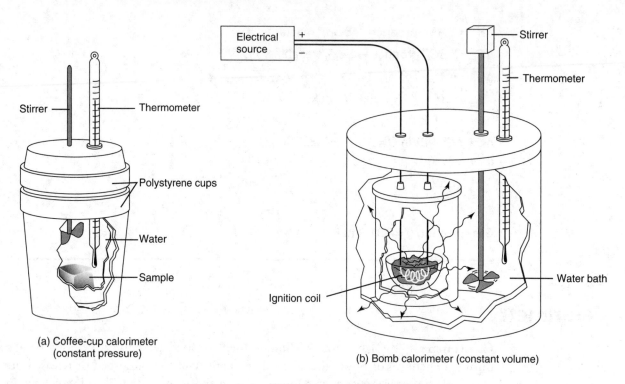

(a) Coffee-cup calorimeter
(constant pressure)

(b) Bomb calorimeter (constant volume)

Figure 9.1   Two types of calorimeters.

Substituting the mathematical relationship for q gives:

$$-(c_{solid} \times m_{solid} \times \Delta T_{solid}) = c_{water} \times m_{water} \times \Delta T_{water}$$

This equation can then be solved for the specific heat capacity of the solid.

The constant-volume bomb calorimeter is used to measure the energy changes that occur during combustion reactions. A weighed sample of the substance being investigated is placed in the calorimeter, and compressed oxygen is added. The sample is ignited by a hot wire, and the temperature change of the calorimeter and a known mass of water is measured. The heat capacity of the calorimeter/water system is sometimes known.

For example, a 1.5886 g sample of glucose ($C_6H_{12}O_6$) was ignited in a bomb calorimeter. The temperature increased by 3.682°C. The heat capacity of the calorimeter was 3.562 kJ/°C, and the calorimeter contained 1.000 kg of water. Find the molar heat of reaction (i.e., kJ/mole) for:

$$C_6H_{12}O_6(s) + 6\ O_2(g) \rightarrow 6\ CO_2(g) + 6\ O(l)$$

Answer:

$$\frac{(3.562\,kJ)}{(°C)}(3.682°C) = 13.12\,kJ$$

$$(1.000\ kg)\left(\frac{1,000\ g}{1\ kg}\right)\left(\frac{4.184\ J}{g°C}\right)\left(\frac{1\ kJ}{1,000\ J}\right)(3.682°C) = 15.40\ kJ$$

total heat = 13.12 kJ + 15.40 kJ = 28.52 kJ

Note: The temperature increased so the reaction was exothermic (−)

$$\rightarrow -28.52\ kJ$$

This is not molar (yet)

$$(1.5886\,\text{g})\frac{(1\,\text{mol})}{(180.16\,\text{g})} = 8.8177\times10^{-3}\,\text{mol}$$

Thus:

$$\frac{-28.52\,\text{kJ}}{8.8177\times10^{-3}\,\text{mol}} = -3,234\,\text{kJ/mol}$$

Laws of Thermodynamics

The **First Law of Thermodynamics** states that the total energy of the universe is constant. This is simply the Law of Conservation of Energy. This can be mathematically stated as:

$$\Delta E_{\text{universe}} = \Delta E_{\text{system}} + \Delta E_{\text{surroundings}} = 0$$

The Second Law of Thermodynamics involves a term called entropy. **Entropy (S)** is related to the disorder of a system. The **Second Law of Thermodynamics** states that all processes that occur spontaneously move in the direction of an increase in entropy of the universe (system + surroundings). Mathematically, this can be stated as:

$$\Delta S_{\text{universe}} = \Delta S_{\text{system}} + \Delta S_{\text{surroundings}} > 0 \qquad \text{for a spontaneous process}$$

For a reversible process $\Delta S_{\text{universe}} = 0$. The qualitative entropy change (increase or decrease of entropy) for a system can sometimes be determined using a few simple rules:

1. Entropy increases when the number of molecules increases during a reaction.
2. Entropy increases with an increase in temperature.
3. Entropy increases when a gas is formed from a liquid or solid.
4. Entropy increases when a liquid is formed from a solid.

Let us now look at some applications of these first two laws of thermodynamics.

Products Minus Reactants

Enthalpies

KEY IDEA

Many of the reactions that chemists study are reactions that occur at constant pressure. During the discussion of the coffee-cup calorimeter, the heat change at constant temperature was defined as q_p. Because this constant-pressure situation is so common in chemistry, a special thermodynamic term is used to describe this energy: enthalpy. The **enthalpy change**, ΔH, is equal to the heat gained or lost by the system under constant-pressure conditions. The following sign conventions apply:

If $\Delta H > 0$ the reaction is endothermic.

If $\Delta H < 0$ the reaction is exothermic.

If a reaction is involved, ΔH is sometimes called $\Delta H_{\text{reaction}}$. ΔH is often given in association with a particular reaction. For example, the enthalpy change associated with the formation of water from hydrogen and oxygen gases can be shown in this fashion:

$$2\,H_2(g) + O_2(g) \rightarrow 2\,H_2O(g) \qquad\qquad \Delta H = -483.6\,\text{kJ}$$

The negative sign indicates that this reaction is exothermic. This value of ΔH is for the production of 2 mol of water. If 4 mol were produced, ΔH would be twice -483.6 kJ. The techniques developed in working reaction stoichiometry problems (see Chapter 7, Stoichiometry) also apply here.

If the previous reaction for the formation of water were reversed, the sign of ΔH would be reversed. That would indicate that it would take 483.6 kJ of energy to decompose 2 mol of water. This would then become an endothermic process.

ΔH is dependent upon the state of matter. The enthalpy change would be different for the formation of liquid water instead of gaseous water.

ΔH can also indicate whether a reaction will be spontaneous. A negative (exothermic) value of ΔH is associated with a spontaneous reaction. However, in many reactions this is not the case. There is another factor to consider in predicting a reaction's spontaneity. We will cover this other factor a little later in this chapter.

Enthalpies of reaction can be measured using a calorimeter. However, they can also be calculated in other ways. **Hess's law** states that if a reaction occurs in a series of steps, then the enthalpy change for the overall reaction is simply the sum of the enthalpy changes of the individual steps. If, in adding the equations of the steps together, it is necessary to reverse one of the given reactions, then the sign of ΔH must also be reversed. Also, particular attention must be used if the reaction stoichiometry has to be adjusted. The value of an individual ΔH may need to be adjusted.

It doesn't matter whether the steps used are the actual steps in the mechanism of the reaction, because $\Delta H_{reaction}$ (ΔH_{rxn}) is a **state function**, a function that doesn't depend on the pathway, but only on the initial and final states.

Let's see how Hess's law can be applied, given the following information:

$C(s) + O_2(g) \rightarrow CO_2(g)$	$\Delta H = -393.5$ kJ
$H_2(g) + (1/2)O_2(g) \rightarrow H_2O(l)$	$\Delta H = -285.8$ kJ
$C_2H_2(g) + (5/2)O_2(g) \rightarrow 2\ CO_2(g) + H_2O(l)$	$\Delta H = -1{,}299.8$ kJ

Find the enthalpy change for:

$$2C(s) + H_2(g) \rightarrow C_2H_2(g)$$

Answer:

$2[C(s) + O_2(g) \rightarrow CO_2(g)]$	$2\ (-393.5$ kJ$)$
$H_2(g) + (1/2)\ O_2(g) \rightarrow H_2O(l)$	-285.8 kJ
$2\ CO_2(g) + H_2O(l) \rightarrow C_2H_2(g)\ _+ (5/2)\ O_2(g)$	$-(-1{,}299.8$ kJ$)$
$2C(s) + H_2(g) \rightarrow C_2H_2(g)$	227.0 kJ

Enthalpies of reaction can also be calculated from individual enthalpies of formation (or heats of formation), ΔH_f, for the reactants and products. Because the temperature, pressure, and state of the substance will cause these enthalpies to vary, it is common to use a standard state convention. For gases, the standard state is 1 atm pressure. For a substance in an aqueous solution, the standard state is 1 molar concentration. And, for a pure substance (compound or element), the standard state is the most stable form at 1 atm pressure and 25°C. A degree symbol to the right of the H indicates a standard state, $\Delta H°$. The **standard enthalpy of formation** of a substance ($\Delta H_f°$) is the change in enthalpy when 1 mol of the substance is formed from its elements when all substances are in their standard states. These values are then tabulated and can be used in determining $\Delta H°_{rxn}$.

$\Delta H_f°$ of an element in its standard state is zero.

$\Delta H_f°_{rxn}$ can be determined from the tabulated $\Delta H_f°$ of the individual reactants and products. It is the sum of the $\Delta H_f°$ of the products minus the sum of the $\Delta H_f°$ of the reactants:

$$\Delta H°_{rxn} = \Sigma\ \Delta H_f°\ \text{products} - \Sigma\ \Delta H_f°\ \text{reactants}$$

In using this equation be sure to consider the number of moles of each, because ΔH_f° for the individual compounds refers to the formation of 1 mol.

For example, let's use standard enthalpies of formation to calculate ΔH_{rxn} for:

$$6\ H_2O(g) + 4\ NO(g) \rightarrow 5\ O_2(g) + 4\ NH_3(g)$$

Answer:

$$\Delta H_{rxn} = \{5[\Delta H_f^\circ O_2(g)] + 4[\Delta H_f^\circ NH_3(g)]\}$$
$$- \{[6\Delta H_f^\circ H_2O(g)] + 4[\Delta H_f^\circ NO(g)]\}$$

Using tabulated standard enthalpies of formation gives:

$$\Delta H_{rxn} = [5(0.00\text{ kJ}) + 4(-46.19\text{ kJ})] - [6(-241.85\text{ kJ}) + 4(90.37)]$$
$$= 904.68\text{ kJ}$$

 People commonly forget to subtract *all* the reactants from the products.

The values of ΔH_f° will be given to you on the AP exam, or you will be asked to stop before putting the numbers into the problem.

An alternative means of estimating the heat of reaction is to take the sum of the average bond energies of the reactant molecules and subtract the sum of the average bond energies of the product molecules.

Entropies

In much the same way as ΔH° was determined, the **standard molar entropies** (S°) of elements and compounds can be tabulated. The standard molar entropy is the entropy associated with 1 mol of a substance in its standard state. Entropies are also tabulated, but unlike enthalpies, the entropies of elements are not zero. For a reaction, the standard entropy change is calculated in the same way as the enthalpies of reaction:

$$\Delta S^\circ = \Sigma\ S^\circ \text{ products} - \Sigma\ S^\circ \text{ reactants}$$

Calculate ΔS° for the following. If you do not have a table of S° values, just set up the problems.

Note: These are thermochemical equations, so fractions are allowed.

a. $H_2(g) + \frac{1}{2}\ O_2(g) \rightarrow H_2O(g)$

b. $H_2(g) + \frac{1}{2}\ O_2(g) \rightarrow H_2O(l)$

c. $CaCO_3(s) + H_2SO_4(l) \rightarrow CaSO_4(s) + H_2O(g) + CO_2(g)$

Answers:

a. H_2O H_2 O_2

    188.7 J/mol K − [131.0 + 1/2(205.0)]J/mol K

    = −44.8 J/mol K

b. H_2O H_2 O_2

    69.9 J/mol K − [131.0 + 1/2(205.0)]J/mol K

    = −163.6 J/mol K

c. CaSO₄   H₂O   CO₂   CaCO₃   H₂SO₄

[107 + 188.7 + 213.6] − [92.9 + 157] J/mol K

= 259 J/mol K

One of the goals of chemists is to be able to predict whether or not a reaction will be spontaneous. Some general guidelines for a spontaneous reaction have already been presented (negative ΔH and positive ΔS), but neither is a reliable predictor by itself. Temperature also plays a part. A thermodynamic factor that takes into account the entropy, enthalpy, and temperature of the reaction should be the best indicator of spontaneity. This factor is called the Gibbs free energy.

Gibbs Free Energy

The **Gibbs free energy** (**G**) is a thermodynamic function that combines the enthalpy, entropy, and temperature:

$$G = H - TS, \text{ where } T \text{ is the Kelvin temperature}$$

Like most thermodynamic functions, only the change in Gibbs free energy can be measured, so the relationship becomes:

$$\Delta G = \Delta H - T \Delta S$$

ΔG is the best indicator chemists have as to whether or not a reaction is spontaneous:

- If $\Delta G > 0$, the reaction is not spontaneous; energy must be supplied to cause the reaction to occur.
- If $\Delta G < 0$, the reaction is spontaneous.
- If $\Delta G = 0$, the reaction is at equilibrium.

If there is a ΔG associated with a reaction and that reaction is then reversed, the sign of ΔG changes.

Just like with the enthalpy and entropy, the standard Gibbs free energy change, $\Delta G°$, is calculated:

$$\Delta G° = \Sigma \Delta G_f° \text{ products} - \Sigma \Delta G_f° \text{ reactants}$$

$\Delta G_f°$ of an element in its standard state is zero.

$\Delta G°$ for a reaction may also be calculated by using the standard enthalpy and standard entropy of reaction:

$$\Delta G° = \Delta H°_{rxn} - T \Delta S°_{rxn}$$

Calculate $\Delta G°$ for:

(If you do not have a table of $\Delta G°$ values, just set up the problems.)

a. $2 \text{ NH}_4\text{Cl(s)} + \text{CaO(s)} \rightarrow \text{CaCl}_2\text{(s)} + \text{H}_2\text{O(l)} + 2 \text{ NH}_3\text{(g)}$

b. $\text{C}_2\text{H}_4\text{(g)} + \text{H}_2\text{O(g)} \rightarrow \text{C}_2\text{H}_5\text{OH(l)}$

c. $\text{Ca(s)} + 2 \text{ H}_2\text{SO}_4\text{(l)} \rightarrow \text{CaSO}_4\text{(s)} + \text{SO}_2\text{(g)} + 2 \text{ H}_2\text{O(l)}$

Answers:

a. CaCl₂(s)   H₂O(l)   NH₃(g)   NH₄Cl(s)   CaO(s)

−750.2   −237.2   −16.6   −203.9   −604.2 kJ/mol

$$[-750.2 + (-237.2) + 2(-16.6)] - [2(-203.9) + (-604.2)]$$

$$= -8.6 \text{ kJ/mole}$$

b. C$_2$H$_5$OH(l)　　　　　　　C$_2$H$_4$(g)　　　　　　　H$_2$O(g)

　　−174.18　　　　　　　　　68.12　　　　　　　　−228.6

　　$-174.18 - [68.12 + (-228.6)] = -13.7$ kJ/mol

c. CaSO$_4$(s)　　SO$_2$(g)　　　H$_2$O(l)　　　Ca(s)　　　H$_2$SO$_4$(l)

　　−1,320.3　　−300.4　　　−237.2　　　0.0　　　−689.9 kJ/mol

　　$[(-1,320.3) + (-300.4) + 2(-237.2)] - [(0.0) + 2(-689.9)]$

　　$= -715.3$ kJ/mol

Thermodynamics and Equilibrium

Thus far, we have considered only situations under standard conditions. But how do we cope with nonstandard conditions? The change in Gibbs free energy under nonstandard conditions is:

$$\Delta G = \Delta G° + RT \ln Q = \Delta G° + 2.303 \log Q$$

Q is the activity quotient, products over reactants. This equation allows the calculation of ΔG in those situations in which the concentrations or pressures are not 1.

Using the previous concept, calculate ΔG for the following at 500·K:

$$2 \text{ NO(g)} + \text{O}_2\text{(g)} \rightarrow 2 \text{ NO}_2\text{(g)}$$

$$\text{2.00 } M \quad \text{0.500 } M \quad \text{1.00 } M$$

$$\text{(Assume } \Delta G_f° = \Delta G_f^{500})$$

$$\Delta G_f° \quad (86.71 \quad 0.000 \quad 51.84) \text{ kJ/mol}$$

$$\Delta G_{rxn} = 2(51.84) - [2(86.71) + 0.000] = -69.74 \text{ kJ/mol}$$

$$\Delta G^{500} = \Delta G_{rxn} + RT \ln Q$$

$$Q = \frac{[\text{NO}_2]^2}{[\text{NO}]^2[\text{O}_2]}$$

$$= (-69.74 \text{ kJ}) (1,000 \text{ J/kJ}) + \left(8.314 \frac{\text{J}}{\text{mol K}}\right)(500. \text{ K}) \ln \frac{(1.00)^2}{(2.00)^2(0.500)}$$

$$= -7.262 \times 10^4 \text{ J/mol}$$

Note that Q, when at equilibrium, becomes K. This equation gives us a way to calculate the equilibrium constant, K, from a knowledge of the standard Gibbs free energy of the reaction and the temperature.

If the system is at equilibrium, then $\Delta G = 0$ and the equation above becomes:

$$\Delta G° = -RT \ln K = -2.303 \, RT \log K$$

For example, calculate $\Delta G°$ for:

$$2 \text{O}_3\text{(g)} \rightleftharpoons 3 \text{O}_2\text{(g)} \quad K_p = 4.17 \times 10^{14}$$

Note: ° = 298 K
Answer:

$$\Delta G° = -RT \ln K$$

$$= \frac{-(8.314\,\text{J})}{(\text{mol K})}(298\,\text{K})\ln 4.17 \times 10^{14}$$

$$= -8.34 \times 10^4\,\text{J/mol}$$

Experiments

The most common thermodynamic experiment is a calorimetry experiment. In this experiment, the heat of transition or heat of reaction is determined.

The experiment will require a balance to determine the mass of a sample and possibly a pipet to measure a volume, from which a mass may be calculated using the density. A calorimeter, usually a polystyrene (Styrofoam) cup, is needed to contain the reaction. Finally, a thermometer is required. Tables of heat capacities or specific heats may be provided.

Mass and possible volume measurements, along with the initial and final temperatures, are needed. Remember: you *measure* the initial and final temperature so you can *calculate* the change in temperature.

After the temperature change is calculated, there are several ways to proceed. If the calorimeter contains water, the heat may be calculated by multiplying the specific heat of water by the mass of water by the temperature change. The heat capacity of the calorimeter may be calculated by dividing the heat by the temperature change. If a reaction is carried out in the same calorimeter, the heat from that reaction is the difference between the heat with and without a reaction.

Do not forget, if the temperature increases, the process is exothermic and the heat has a negative sign. The opposite is true if the temperature drops.

Common Mistakes to Avoid

1. Be sure your units cancel giving you the unit desired in the final answer.
2. Check your significant figures.
3. Don't mix energy units, joules, and calories.
4. Watch your signs in all the thermodynamic calculations. They are extremely important.
5. Don't confuse enthalpy, ΔH, and entropy, ΔS.
6. Pay close attention to the state of matter for your reactants and products, and choose the corresponding value for use in your calculated entropies and enthalpies.
7. Remember: **products minus reactants**.
8. ΔH_f and ΔG_f are for 1 mol of substance. Use appropriate multipliers if needed.
9. ΔG_f and ΔH_f for an element in its standard state are zero.
10. All temperatures are in kelvin.
11. When using $\Delta G° = \Delta H°_{\text{rxn}} - T\,\Delta S°_{\text{rxn}}$, pay particular attention to your enthalpy and entropy units. Commonly, enthalpies will use kJ and entropies J.

› Review Questions

Use these questions to review the content of this chapter and practice for the AP Chemistry exam. First are 16 multiple-choice questions similar to what you will encounter in Section I of the AP Chemistry exam. Following those is a long free-response question like the ones in Section II of the exam. To make these questions an even more authentic practice for the actual exam, time yourself following the instructions provided.

Multiple-Choice Questions

Answer the following questions in 20 minutes. You may not use a calculator. You may use the periodic table and the equation sheet at the back of this book.

1. Which of the following is the minimum energy required to initiate a reaction?

   (A) free energy
   (B) lattice energy
   (C) kinetic energy
   (D) activation energy

2. What is the minimum energy required to force a nonspontaneous reaction to occur?

   (A) free energy
   (B) lattice energy
   (C) kinetic energy
   (D) activation energy

3. The average _____ is the same for any ideal gas at a given temperature.

   (A) free energy
   (B) lattice energy
   (C) kinetic energy
   (D) activation energy

4. What is the energy released when the gaseous ions combine to form an ionic solid?

   (A) free energy
   (B) lattice energy
   (C) kinetic energy
   (D) activation energy

5. Given the following information:

   $$C(s) + O_2(g) \rightarrow CO_2(g) \qquad \Delta H = -393.5 \text{ kJ}$$

   $$H_2(g) + (1/2) O_2(g) \rightarrow H_2O(l)$$
   $$\Delta H = -285.8 \text{ kJ}$$

   $$C_2H_2(g) + (5/2) O_2(g) \rightarrow 2 CO_2(g) + H_2O(l)$$
   $$\Delta H = -1{,}299.8 \text{ kJ}$$

   Find the enthalpy change for:

   $$2C(s) + H_2(g) \rightarrow C_2H_2(g)$$

   (A) 454.0 kJ
   (B) −227.0 kJ
   (C) 0.0 kJ
   (D) 227.0 kJ

6. A sample of gallium metal is sealed inside a well-insulated, rigid container. The temperature inside the container is at the melting point of gallium metal. What can be said about the energy and the entropy of the system after equilibrium has been established? Assume the insulation prevents any energy change with the surroundings.

   (A) The total energy increases. The total entropy will increase.
   (B) The total energy is constant. The total entropy is constant.
   (C) The total energy is constant. The total entropy will decrease.
   (D) The total energy is constant. The total entropy will increase.

7. When ammonium chloride dissolves in water, the temperature drops. Which of the following conclusions may be related to this?

(A) Ammonium chloride is more soluble in hot water.
(B) Ammonium chloride produces an ideal solution in water.
(C) The heat of solution for ammonium chloride is exothermic.
(D) Ammonium chloride has a low lattice energy.

8. Choose the reaction expected to have the greatest increase in entropy.

(A) $H_2O(g) \rightarrow H_2O(l)$
(B) $2\ KClO_3(s) \rightarrow 2\ KCl(s) + 3\ O_2(g)$
(C) $Ca(s) + H_2(g) \rightarrow CaH_2(s)$
(D) $N_2(g) + 3H_2(g) \rightarrow 2\ NH_3(g)$

9. Under standard conditions, calcium metal reacts readily with chlorine gas. What conclusions may be drawn from the fact?

(A) $K_{eq} < 1$ and $\Delta G° > 0$
(B) $K_{eq} > 1$ and $\Delta G° = 0$
(C) $K_{eq} < 1$ and $\Delta G° < 0$
(D) $K_{eq} > 1$ and $\Delta G° < 0$

10. Which of the following combinations is true when sodium chloride melts?

(A) $\Delta H > 0$ and $\Delta S > 0$
(B) $\Delta H = 0$ and $\Delta S > 0$
(C) $\Delta H > 0$ and $\Delta S < 0$
(D) $\Delta H < 0$ and $\Delta S < 0$

11. Which of the following reactions have a negative entropy change?

(A) $2\ C_2H_6(g) + 7\ O_2(g) \rightarrow 4\ CO_2(g) + 6\ H_2O(g)$
(B) $2\ NH_3(g) \rightarrow N_2(g) + 3\ H_2(g)$
(C) $CaCl_2(s) \rightarrow Ca(s) + Cl_2(g)$
(D) $2\ H_2(g) + O_2(g) \rightarrow 2\ H_2O(l)$

12. A certain reaction is nonspontaneous under standard conditions, but becomes spontaneous at higher temperatures. What conclusions may be drawn under standard conditions?

(A) $\Delta H < 0$, $\Delta S > 0$, and $\Delta G > 0$
(B) $\Delta H > 0$, $\Delta S < 0$, and $\Delta G > 0$
(C) $\Delta H > 0$, $\Delta S > 0$, and $\Delta G > 0$
(D) $\Delta H < 0$, $\Delta S < 0$, and $\Delta G > 0$

13. $2\ H_2(g) + O_2(g) \rightarrow 2\ H_2O(g)$

From the table below, determine the enthalpy change for the above reaction.

BOND	AVERAGE BOND ENERGY (kJ/mol)
H–H	436
O=O	499
H–O	464

(A) 0 kJ
(B) 485 kJ
(C) −485 kJ
(D) 464 kJ

14. Which of the following reactions would be accompanied by the greatest decrease in entropy?

(A) $N_2(g) + 3\ H_2(g) \rightarrow 2\ NH_3(g)$
(B) $C(s) + O_2(g) \rightarrow CO_2(g)$
(C) $2\ H_2(g) + O_2(g) \rightarrow 2\ H_2O(g)$
(D) $2\ Na(s) + Cl_2(g) \rightarrow 2\ NaCl(s)$

15. $CO(g) + 2\ H_2(g) \rightarrow CH_3OH(g)$ $\Delta H = -91kJ$

Determine ΔH for the above reaction if $CH_3OH(l)$ were formed in the above reaction instead of $CH_3OH(g)$. The ΔH of vaporization for CH_3OH is 37 kJ/mol.

(A) −128 kJ
(B) −54 kJ
(C) +128 kJ
(D) +54 kJ

16. A solution is prepared by dissolving solid ammonium nitrate, NH_4NO_3, in water. The initial temperature of the water was 25°C, but after the solid had dissolved, the temperature fell to 20°C. What conclusions may be made about ΔH and ΔS?

(A) $\Delta H < 0$ $\Delta S > 0$
(B) $\Delta H > 0$ $\Delta S > 0$
(C) $\Delta H > 0$ $\Delta S < 0$
(D) $\Delta H < 0$ $\Delta S < 0$

Answers and Explanations for the Multiple-Choice Questions

1. **D**—You may wish to review the Kinetics chapter if you have forgotten what the activation energy is.

2. **A**—The free energy is the minimum energy required for a nonspontaneous reaction and the maximum energy available for a spontaneous reaction.

3. **C**—This is a basic postulate of kinetic molecular theory.

4. **B**—This is the reverse of the lattice energy definition.

5. **D**

$$2[C(s) + O_2(g) \rightarrow CO_2(g)] \qquad 2(-393.5 \text{ kJ})$$

$$H_2(g) + (1/2)\, O_2(g) \rightarrow H_2O(l) \qquad -285.8 \text{ kJ}$$

$$2\, CO_2(g) + H_2O(l) \rightarrow C_2H_2(g) + (5/2)\, O_2(g)$$
$$-(-1{,}299.8 \text{ kJ})$$

$$2\, C(s) + H_2(g) \rightarrow C_2H_2(g) \qquad 227.0 \text{ kJ}$$

Simple rounding to the nearest 100 kJ gives 200 kJ.

6. **D**—The system is insulated and no work can be done on or by the system (rigid container); thus, the energy is constant. At the melting point, some of the gallium will spontaneously melt; changing a solid to a liquid increases the entropy.

7. **A**—The process is endothermic (the ammonium chloride is absorbing heat to cool the water). Endothermic processes are "helped" by higher temperatures. Answer C and possibly D would give an increase in temperature. There is insufficient information about answer B.

8. **B**—The reaction showing the greatest increase in the number of moles of gas will show the greatest entropy increase. If no gases are present, then the greatest increase in the number of moles of liquid would yield the greatest increase.

9. **D**—If the reaction occurs readily, it must be spontaneous. Spontaneous reactions require $\Delta G°$ < 0. A negative free energy leads to a large K (>1).

10. **A**—Heat is required to melt something ($\Delta H > 0$). A transformation from a solid to a liquid gives an increase in entropy ($\Delta S > 0$).

11. **D**—This equation has an overall decrease in the amount of gas (high entropy) present. The other answers produce more gas (increases entropy).

12. **C**—Nonspontaneous means that $\Delta G > 0$. Since the reaction becomes spontaneous, the sign must change. Recalling: $\Delta G = \Delta H - T\Delta S$. The sign change at higher temperature means that the entropy term (with $\Delta S > 0$) must become more negative than the enthalpy term ($\Delta H > 0$).

13. **C**—[2(436 kJ) + 499 kJ] – {2[2(464 kJ)]} = –485 kJ

14. **A**—The reaction that produces the most gas will have the greatest increase in entropy; the one losing the most gas would have the greatest decrease.

15. **A**—CO(g) + 2 H$_2$(g) → CH$_3$OH(g)
$$\Delta H = -91 \text{ kJ}$$

CH$_3$OH(g) → CH$_3$OH(l)
$$\Delta H = -37 \text{ kJ}$$

Total CO(g) + 2 H$_2$(g) → CH$_3$OH(l)
$$\Delta H = -128 \text{ kJ}$$

16. **B**—Dissolving almost always has $\Delta S > 0$. A decrease in temperature means the process has $\Delta H > 0$ (the system is absorbing energy from the surroundings).

Free-Response Question

You have 10 minutes to answer the following question. You may use a calculator and the tables in the back of the book.

Question 1

$$Xe(g) + 3F_2(g) \rightleftharpoons XeF_6(g)$$

Under standard conditions, the enthalpy change for the reaction going from left to right (forward reaction) is $\Delta H° = -294$ kJ.

(a) Is the value of $\Delta S°$, for the above reaction, positive or negative? Justify your conclusion.

(b) The above reaction is spontaneous under standard conditions. Predict what will happen to ΔG for this reaction as the temperature is increased. Justify your prediction.

(c) Will the value of K remain the same, increase, or decrease as the temperature increases? Justify your prediction.

(d) Show how the temperature at which the reaction changes from spontaneous to nonspontaneous can be predicted. What additional information is necessary?

Answer and Explanation for the Free-Response Question

(a) The value is negative. The decrease in the number of moles of gas during the reaction means there is a decrease in entropy.

Give yourself 1 point if you predicted this. Give yourself 1 point for discussing the number of moles of gas. You may get this point even if you did not get the first point.

(b) Recall $\Delta G = \Delta H - T\Delta S$ (this equation is given on the equation page of the AP exam).

The value of ΔG will increase (become less negative).

Give yourself 1 point for this answer if it is obvious that increasing means less negative.

In general, both ΔH and ΔS are relatively constant with respect to small temperature changes. As the temperature increases, the value of the entropy term, $T\Delta S$, becomes more negative. The negative sign in front of this term leads to a positive contribution. The value of ΔG will first become less negative (more positive), and eventually the value will be positive (no longer spontaneous).

Give yourself 1 point for the $\Delta G = \Delta H - T\Delta S$ argument even if you did not get the first point.

(c) Recall $\Delta G = -RT \ln K$ (this equation is given on the equation page of the AP exam).

The value of K will decrease.

You get 1 point for this answer.

As the value of ΔG increases (see part **b**), the value of K will decrease.

You get 1 point for using $\Delta G = -RT \ln K$ in your discussion.

If you got the justification for part **b** wrong, and you used the same argument here, you will not be penalized twice. You still get your point.

(d) Recall $\Delta G = \Delta H - T\Delta S$

Rearranging this equation to: $T = (\Delta G - \Delta H)/\Delta S$ will allow the temperature to be estimated.

This is worth 1 point. To do the calculation, the value of ΔS is necessary. Give yourself 1 point for this.

There are a total of 8 points possible. All of the mathematical relations presented in the answers are in the exam booklet.

Note that many students lose points on a question like this because their answers are too long. Keep your answers short and to the point, even if it appears that you have multiple pages available.

› Rapid Review

- Thermodynamics is the study of heat and its transformations.
- Kinetic energy is energy of motion, while potential energy is stored energy.
- The common units of energy are the joule, J, and the calorie, cal.
- A calorimeter is used to measure the heat released or absorbed during a chemical or physical change. Know how a calorimeter works.
- The specific heat capacity is the amount of heat needed to change the temperature of 1 gram of a substance by 1 K, while the molar heat capacity is the heat capacity per mole.
- The heat lost by the system in calorimetry is equal to the heat gained by the surroundings.
- The specific heat (c) of a solid can be calculated by: $-(c_{solid} \times m_{solid} \times \Delta T_{solid}) = c_{water} \times m_{water} \times \Delta T_{water}$ or by $g = cm\Delta T$.
- The First Law of Thermodynamics states that the total energy of the universe is constant. (Energy is neither created nor destroyed.)
- The Second Law of Thermodynamics states that all spontaneous processes move in a way that increases the entropy (disorder) of the universe.
- The enthalpy change, ΔH, is equal to the heat lost or gained by the system under constant pressure conditions.
- ΔH values are associated with a specific reaction. If that reaction is reversed, the sign of ΔH changes. If one has to use a multiplier on the reaction, it must also be applied to the ΔH value.
- The standard enthalpy of formation of a compound, ΔH_f°, is the enthalpy change when 1 mol of the substance is formed from its elements and all substances are in their standard states.
- The standard enthalpy of formation of an element in its standard state is zero.
- $\Delta H^\circ_{rxn} = \Sigma\, \Delta H_f^\circ$ products $- \Sigma\, \Delta H_f^\circ$ reactants. Know how to apply this equation.
- ΔH°_{rxn} is usually negative for a spontaneous reaction.
- $\Delta S^\circ = \Sigma\, S^\circ$ products $- \Sigma\, S^\circ$ reactants. Know how to apply this equation.
- ΔS° is usually positive for a spontaneous reaction.
- The Gibbs free energy is a thermodynamic quantity that relates the enthalpy and entropy, and is the best indicator for whether or not a reaction is spontaneous.
- If $\Delta G^\circ > 0$, the reaction is not spontaneous; if $\Delta G^\circ < 0$, the reaction is spontaneous; and if $\Delta G^\circ = 0$, the reaction is at equilibrium.
- $\Delta G^\circ = \Sigma\, \Delta G_f^\circ$ products $- \Sigma\, \Delta G_f^\circ$ reactants. Know how to apply this equation.
- $\Delta G^\circ = \Delta H^\circ_{rxn} - T\,\Delta S^\circ_{rxn}$. Know how to apply this equation.
- For a system not at equilibrium: $\Delta G = \Delta G^\circ + RT \ln Q = \Delta G^\circ + 2.303\, RT \log Q$. Know how to apply this equation.
- For a system at equilibrium: $\Delta G^\circ = -RT \ln K = -2.303\, RT \log K$. Know how to apply this equation to calculate equilibrium constants.

CHAPTER 10

Spectroscopy, Light, and Electrons

IN THIS CHAPTER

Summary: In developing the model of the atom, it was thought initially that all sub-atomic particles obeyed the laws of classical physics—that is, they were tiny bits of matter behaving like macroscopic pieces of matter. Later, however, it was discovered that this particle view of the atom could not explain many of the observations being made. About this time, the dual particle/wave model of matter began to gain favor. It was discovered that in many cases, especially when dealing with the behavior of electrons, describing some of their behavior in terms of waves explained the observations much better. Thus, the quantum mechanical model of the atom was born.

Keywords and Equations

Speed of light, $c = 3.0 \times 10^8 \text{ ms}^{-1}$

E = energy	v = frequency	λ = wavelength
p = momentum	v = velocity	n = principal quantum number

m = mass $E = hv$ $c = \lambda v$ $\lambda = \dfrac{h}{mv}$ $p = mv$

$$E_n = \frac{-2.178 \times 10^{-18}}{n^2} \text{ joule}$$

Planck's constant, $h = 6.63 \times 10^{-34}$ Js

The Nature of Light

Light is a part of the **electromagnetic spectrum**—radiant energy composed of gamma rays, X-rays, ultraviolet light, visible light, etc. Figure 10.1 shows the electromagnetic spectrum.

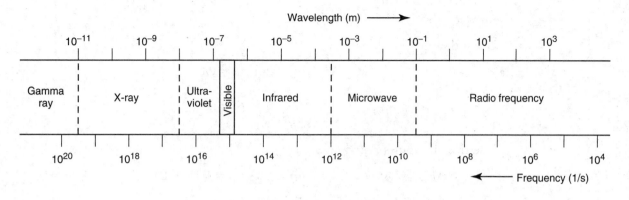

Figure 10.1   The electromagnetic spectrum.

The energy of the electromagnetic spectrum moves through space as waves that have three associated variables—frequency, wavelength, and amplitude. The **frequency, ν,** is the number of waves that pass a point per second. **Wavelength** (λ) is the distance between two identical points on a wave. **Amplitude** is the height of the wave and is related to the intensity (or brightness, for visible light) of the wave. Figure 10.2 shows the wavelength and amplitude of a wave.

The energy associated with a certain frequency of light is related by the equation:

$$E = h\nu \text{ where } h \text{ is Planck's constant} = 6.63 \times 10^{-34} \text{ Js}$$

In developing the quantum mechanical model of the atom, it was found that the electrons can have only certain distinct quantities of energy associated with them, and that in order for the atom to change its energy it has to absorb or emit a certain amount of energy. The energy that is emitted or absorbed is really the difference in the two energy states and can be calculated by:

$$\Delta E = h\nu$$

All electromagnetic radiation travels at about the same speed in a vacuum, 3.0×10^{8} m/s. This constant is called the **speed of light (c).** The product of the frequency and the wavelength is the speed of light:

$$c = \nu\lambda$$

Let's apply some of the relationships. What wavelength of radiation has photons of energy 7.83×10^{-19} J?

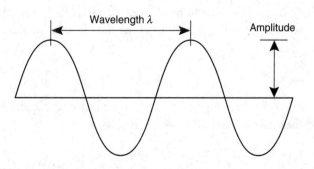

Figure 10.2   Wavelength and amplitude of a wave.

Answer:

Using the equations

$$\Delta E = h\nu \quad \text{and} \quad c = \nu\lambda$$

we get

$$\nu = \Delta E/h \quad \text{and} \quad \lambda = c/\nu$$

Inserting the appropriate values:

$$\nu = \Delta E/h = 7.83 \times 10^{-19}\ \text{J}/6.63 \times 10^{-34}\ \text{Js} = 1.18 \times 10^{15}\ \text{s}^{-1}$$

Then:

$$\lambda = c/\nu = (3.0 \times 10^{8}\ \text{m/s})/(1.18 \times 10^{15}\text{s}^{-1}) = 2.5 \times 10^{-7}\text{m}$$

This answer could have been calculated more quickly by combining the original two equations to give:

$$\lambda = hc/\Delta E$$

Wave Properties of Matter

The concept that matter possesses both particle and wave properties was first postulated by de Broglie in 1925. He introduced the equation $\lambda = h/m\nu$, which indicates a mass (m) moving with a certain velocity (v) would have a specific wavelength (λ) associated with it. (Note that this v is the velocity, not ν the frequency.) If the mass is very large (a locomotive), the associated wavelength is insignificant. However, if the mass is very small (an electron), the wavelength is measurable. The denominator may be replaced with the momentum of the particle ($p = m\nu$).

Atomic Spectra

Late in the 19th century, scientists discovered that when the vapor of an element was heated it gave off a **line spectrum**, a series of fine lines of colors, instead of a continuous spectrum like a rainbow. This was used in the developing quantum mechanical model as evidence that the energy of the electrons in an atom was **quantized**; that is, there could only be certain distinct energies (lines) associated with the atom. Niels Bohr developed the first modern atomic model for hydrogen using the concepts of quantized energies. The Bohr model postulated a **ground state** for the electrons in the atom, an energy state of lowest energy, and an **excited state**, an energy state of higher energy. In order for an electron to go from its ground state to an excited state, it must absorb a certain amount of energy. If the electron dropped back from that excited state to its ground state, that same amount of energy would be emitted. Bohr's model also allowed scientists to develop a method of calculating the energy associated with a particular energy level for the electron in the hydrogen atom:

$$E_n = \frac{-2.18 \times 10^{-18}}{n^2}\ \text{joule}$$

where n is the energy state. This equation can then be modified to calculate the energy difference between any two energy levels:

$$\Delta E = -2.18 \times 10^{-18}\ \text{J} \left(\frac{1}{n_{\text{final}}^2} - \frac{1}{n_{\text{initial}}^2} \right)$$

Atomic Orbitals

Bohr's model worked well for hydrogen, the simplest atom, but didn't work very well for any others. In the early 1900s, Schrödinger developed a more involved model and set of equations that better described atoms by using quantum mechanical concepts. His model introduced a mathematical description of the electron's motion called a **wave function** or **atomic orbital**. Squaring the wave function (orbital) gives the volume of space in which the probability of finding the electron is high. This is commonly referred to as the **electron cloud**.

Schrödinger's equation required the use of three **quantum numbers** to describe each electron within an atom, corresponding to the orbital size, shape, and orientation in space. It was also found that a quantum number concerning the spin of the electron was needed.

The first quantum number is the **principal quantum number (n)**. It describes the energy (related to size) of the orbital and relative distance from the nucleus. The allowed (by the mathematics of the Schrödinger equation) values are positive integers (1, 2, 3, 4, etc.). The smaller the value of n, the closer the orbital is to the nucleus. The number n is sometimes called the atom's **shell**.

The second quantum number is the **angular momentum quantum number (l)**. Its value is related to the principal quantum number and has allowed values of 0 up to $(n-1)$. For example, if $n = 3$, then the possible values of l would be 0, 1, and 2 $(3 - 1)$. This value of l defines the shape of the orbital:

- If $l = 0$, the orbital is called an s orbital and has a spherical shape with the nucleus at the center of the sphere. The greater the value of n, the larger the sphere.
- If $l = 1$, the orbital is called a p orbital and has two lobes of high electron density on either side of the nucleus. This makes for an hourglass or dumbbell shape.
- If $l = 2$, the orbital is a d orbital and can have variety of shapes.
- If $l = 3$, the orbital is an f orbital, with more complex shapes.

Figure 10.3, on the next page, shows the shapes of the s, p, and d orbitals. These are sometimes called **sublevels** or **subshells**.

The third quantum number is the **magnetic quantum number (m_l)**. It describes the orientation of the orbital around the nucleus. The possible values of m_l depend on the value of the angular momentum quantum number, l. The allowed values for m_l are $-l$ through zero to $+l$. For example, for $l = 2$ the possible values of m_l would be -2, -1, 0, $+1$, $+2$. This is why, for example, if $l = 1$ (a p orbital), then there are three p orbitals corresponding to m_l values of -1, 0, $+1$. This is also shown in Figure 10.3.

The fourth quantum number, the **spin quantum number (m_s)**, indicates the direction the electron is spinning. There are only two possible values for m_s, $+\frac{1}{2}$ and $-\frac{1}{2}$.

The quantum numbers for the six electrons in carbon would be:

QUANTUM NUMBER	FIRST ELECTRON	SECOND ELECTRON	THIRD ELECTRON	FOURTH ELECTRON	FIFTH ELECTRON	SIXTH ELECTRON
n	1	1	2	2	2	2
l	0	0	0	0	1	1
m_l	0	0	0	0	1	0
m_s	$+\frac{1}{2}$	$-\frac{1}{2}$	$+\frac{1}{2}$	$-\frac{1}{2}$	$+\frac{1}{2}$	$+\frac{1}{2}$

Therefore, the electron configuration of carbon is $1s^2 2s^2 2p^2$.

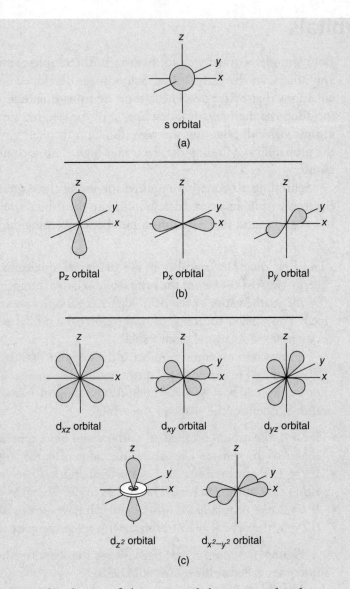

Figure 10.3 The shapes of the s, p, and d atomic orbitals.

Photoelectron (Photoemission) Spectroscopy (PES)

Photoelectron spectroscopy is one of a group of related techniques where high-energy photons remove an electron from an atom in a photoelectric effect process. The method relies on a measurement of the kinetic energy of the emitted electron. The kinetic energy is equal to the energy of the photon minus the binding energy of the electron. The binding energy is the energy holding the electron in the atom and can be rather difficult to measure.

X-ray photons can excite core electrons. For example, it is possible to focus on the 1s electrons of an oxygen atom. The binding energy is in part related to the effective nuclear charge experienced by the electron. In compounds, other atoms bonded to the atom of interest can influence the effective nuclear charge. Atoms donating electron density to the atom of interest decrease the effective nuclear charge, while electron-withdrawing atoms lead to an increase in the effective nuclear charge. An important factor in whether an atom donates or withdraws electron density is the relative electronegativity of the two atoms. This experimental method can be used to give information on which atoms are bonded to each other.

Experiments

No experimental questions related to this chapter have appeared on the AP exam in recent years.

Common Mistakes to Avoid

1. Be sure not to confuse wavelength and frequency.
2. The speed of light is 3.0×10^8 m/s. The exponent is positive.
3. The value of n is never zero.
4. The values of l and m_l include zero.
5. Do not confuse velocity (v) and frequency (ν).

› Review Questions

Use these questions to review the content of this chapter and practice for the AP Chemistry exam. First are 16 multiple-choice questions similar to what you will encounter in Section I of the AP Chemistry exam. Following those is a long free-response question like the ones in Section II of the exam. To make these questions an even more authentic practice for the actual exam, time yourself following the instructions provided.

Multiple-Choice Questions

Answer the following questions in 20 minutes. You may not use a calculator. You may use the periodic table and the equation sheet at the back of this book.

1. Which of the following represents the electron arrangement for the least reactive element?

    (A) 1s ↑ 2s ↑↓
    (B) 1s ↑↓ 2s ↑
    (C) [Kr] 5s ↑↓ 4d ↑↑ _ _ _
    (D) 1s ↑↓ 2s ↑↓ 2p ↑↓ ↑↓ ↑↓

2. Which of the following might refer to a transition element?

    (A) 1s ↑ 2s ↑↓
    (B) 1s ↑↓ 2s ↑
    (C) [Kr] 5s ↑↓ 4d ↑↑ _ _ _
    (D) 1s ↑↓ 2s ↑↓ 2p ↑↓ ↑↓ ↑↓

3. Which of the following electron arrangements refers to the most chemically reactive element?

    (A) 1s ↑ 2s ↑↓
    (B) 1s ↑↓ 2s ↑
    (C) [Kr] 5s ↑↓ 4d ↑↑ _ _ _
    (D) 1s ↑↓ 2s ↑↓ 2p ↑↓ ↑↓ ↑↓

4. Which of the following electron arrangements represents an atom in an excited state?

    (A) 1s ↑ 2s ↑↓
    (B) 1s ↑↓ 2s ↑
    (C) [Kr] 5s ↑↓ 4d ↑↑ _ _ _
    (D) 1s ↑↓ 2s ↑↓ 2p ↑↓ ↑↓ ↑↓

5. The ground-state configuration of Fe^{2+} is which of the following?

    (A) $1s^2 2s^2 2p^6 3s^2 3p^6 3d^5 4s^1$
    (B) $1s^2 2s^2 2p^6 3s^2 3p^6 3d^6$
    (C) $1s^2 2s^2 2p^6 3s^2 3p^6 3d^6 4s^2$
    (D) $1s^2 2s^2 2p^6 3s^2 3p^6 3d^8 4s^2$

6. Which of the following contain only atoms that are diamagnetic in their ground state?

    (A) Kr, Ca, and P
    (B) Ne, Be, and Zn
    (C) Ar, K, and Ba
    (D) He, Sr, and C

7. Which of the following is the electron configuration of a halogen?

(A) $1s^2 1p^6 2s^2 2p^3$
(B) $1s^2 2s^2 2p^6 3s^2 3p^6 4s^2 3d^{10} 4p^6 5s^2 4d^1$
(C) $1s^2 2s^2 2p^6 3s^2 3p^6 3d^3$
(D) $1s^2 2s^2 2p^5$

8. Which of the following is a possible configuration for a transition metal atom?

(A) $1s^2 1p^6 2s^2 2p^3$
(B) $1s^2 2s^2 2p^6 3s^2 3p^6 4s^2 3d^{10} 4p^6 5s^2 4d^1$
(C) $1s^2 2s^2 2p^6 3s^2 3p^6 3d^3$
(D) $1s^2 2s^2 2p^5$

9. Which of the following electron configurations is not possible?

(A) $1s^2 1p^6 2s^2 2p^3$
(B) $1s^2 2s^2 2p^6 3s^2 3p^6 4s^2 3d^{10} 4p^6 5s^2 4d^1$
(C) $1s^2 2s^2 2p^6 3s^2 3p^6 3d^3$
(D) $1s^2 2s^2 2p^5$

10. This is a possible configuration of a transition metal ion.

(A) $1s^2 1p^6 2s^2 2p^3$
(B) $1s^2 2s^2 2p^6 3s^2 3p^6 4s^2 3d^{10} 4p^6 5s^2 4d^1$
(C) $1s^2 2s^2 2p^6 3s^2 3p^6 3d^3$
(D) $1s^2 2s^2 2p^5$

11. Which idea relates to the fact that the exact position of an electron is not known?

(A) Pauli exclusion principle
(B) electron shielding
(C) Hund's rule
(D) Heisenberg uncertainty principle

12. Which of the following explains why oxygen atoms, in their ground state, are paramagnetic?

(A) Pauli exclusion principle
(B) electron shielding
(C) Hund's rule
(D) Heisenberg uncertainty principle

13. An atomic orbital can hold no more than two electrons; this is a consequence of which of the following?

(A) Pauli exclusion principle
(B) electron shielding
(C) Hund's rule
(D) Heisenberg uncertainty principle

14. Why does the 4s orbital fill before the 3d orbital starts to fill?

(A) Pauli exclusion principle
(B) electron shielding
(C) Hund's rule
(D) Heisenberg uncertainty principle

15. Calcium reacts with element X to form an ionic compound. If the ground-state electron configuration of X is $1s^2 2s^2 2p^4$, what is the simplest formula for this compound?

(A) CaX
(B) CaX_2
(C) Ca_4X_2
(D) Ca_2X_2

16. Which of the following best explains the diffraction of electrons?

(A) Pauli exclusion principle
(B) Hund's rule
(C) the wave properties of matter
(D) Heisenberg uncertainty principle

Answers and Explanations for the Multiple-Choice Questions

1. **D**—This configuration represents a noble gas (neon). The outer s and p orbitals are filled.

2. **C**—Transition elements have partially filled d orbitals. This configuration is for the metal zirconium, Zr.

3. **B**—The single electron in the s orbital indicates that this is the very reactive alkali metal lithium.

4. **A**—The 1s orbital is not filled. One indication of excited states is to have one or more inner orbitals unfilled.

5. **B**—The electron configuration for iron is $1s^2 2s^2 2p^6 3s^2 3p^6 3d^6 4s^2$. To produce an iron(II) ion, the two 4s electrons are removed first.

6. **B**—The elements that are normally diamagnetic are those in the same columns of the periodic table as Be, Zn, and He because all of the electrons are paired. All other columns are normally paramagnetic.

7. **D**—Halogens have a valence shell with $s^2 p^5$.

8. **B**—Transition metals have partially filled d orbitals (d^{1-10}), along with an s^1 or s^2.

9. **A**—The 1p orbital does not exist.

10. **C**—The outer s electrons are not present in most transition metal ions; however, d electrons may be present. C could be V^{2+}, Cr^{3+}, or Mn^{4+} (among other choices).

11. **D**—This is part of the Heisenberg uncertainty principle.

12. **C**—The four electrons in the oxygen 2p orbitals are arranged with one pair and two unpaired electrons with spins parallel. This makes the oxygen atom paramagnetic. This arrangement is due to Hund's rule.

13. **A**—The Pauli exclusion principle restricts the number of electrons that can occupy a single orbital.

14. **B**—The d orbitals are shielded more efficiently than the s orbitals. Thus, the less shielded d orbitals do not fill as readily as s orbitals with similar energy.

15. **A**—Calcium will form a +2 ion (Ca^{2+}), and X will need to gain two electrons to fill its outer shell and become a −2 ion (X^{2-}). The simplest formula for a compound containing a +2 ion and a −2 ion would be CaX. The other answers involve different charges or a formula that has not been simplified.

16. **C**—Diffraction is a wave phenomenon.

Free-Response Question

You have 15 minutes to answer the following question. You may use a calculator and the tables in the back of the book.

Question 1

(a) The bond energy of fluorine is 159 kJ mol^{-1}.

    i. Determine the energy, in J, of a photon of light needed to break an F–F bond.

    ii. Determine the frequency of this photon in s^{-1}.

    iii. Determine the wavelength of this photon in nanometers.

(b) Barium imparts a characteristic green color to a flame. The wavelength of this light is 551 nm. Determine the energy involved in kJ/mol.

Answer and Explanation for the Free-Response Question

(a) If you do not remember them, several of the equations given at the beginning of the exam are necessary. In addition, the values of Planck's constant, Avogadro's number, and the speed of light are necessary. These constants are also given on the exam.

    i. This is a simple conversion problem:

$$\left(\frac{159\,\text{kJ}}{\text{mol}}\right)\left(\frac{1\,\text{mol}}{6.022\times10^{23}}\right)\left(\frac{1{,}000\,\text{J}}{1\,\text{kJ}}\right) = 2.64\times10^{-19}\,\text{J}$$

Give yourself 1 point if you got this answer.

ii. This part requires the equation $\Delta E = h\nu$ (this equation is given on the equation page of the AP exam).

$$\nu = \frac{\Delta E}{h} = \frac{2.64 \times 10^{-19}\,\text{J}}{6.63 \times 10^{-34}\,\text{Js}} = 3.98 \times 10^{14}\,\text{s}^{-1}$$

Give yourself 1 point for this answer. If you got the wrong answer in the preceding part, but used it correctly here (in place of the 2.64×10^{-19} J), you still get 1 point.

iii. (a) The equation $c = \lambda\nu$ is needed. (This equation is given on the equation page of the AP exam.)

$$\lambda = \frac{c}{\nu} = \left(\frac{3.0 \times 10^{8}\,\text{m/s}}{3.98 \times 10^{14}\,\text{s}^{-1}}\right)\left(\frac{1\,\text{nm}}{10^{-9}\,\text{m}}\right) = 7.5 \times 10^{2}\,\text{nm}$$

Again, give yourself 1 point for the correct answer. If you correctly used a wrong answer from the preceding part, you still get 1 point.

(b) This can be done as a one-step or a two-step problem. The AP test booklet gives you the equations to solve this directly as a two-step problem. This method will be followed here. The two equations may be combined to produce an equation that will allow you to do the problem in one step.

Using $c = \lambda\nu$:

$$\nu = c/\lambda = \left(\frac{3.0 \times 10^{8}\,\text{m/s}}{551\,\text{nm}}\right)\left(\frac{1\,\text{nm}}{10^{-9}\,\text{m}}\right) = 5.4 \times 10^{14}\,\text{s}^{-1}$$

Using $\Delta E = h\nu$:

$$\Delta E = (6.63 \times 10^{-34}\,\text{Js})(5.4 \times 10^{14}\,\text{s}^{-1})(1\,\text{kJ}/1{,}000\,\text{J})(6.022 \times 10^{23}/\text{mol})$$
$$= 2.2 \times 10^{2}\,\text{kJ/mol}$$

Give yourself 1 point for each of these answers. If you did the problem as a one-step problem, give yourself 2 points if you got the final answer correct or 1 point if you left out any of the conversions.

The total for this question is 5 points, minus 1 point if any answer does not have the correct number of significant figures.

› Rapid Review

- Know the regions of the electromagnetic spectrum.
- The frequency, ν, is defined as the number of waves that pass a point per second.
- The wavelength, λ, is the distance between two identical points on a wave.
- The energy of light is related to the frequency by $E = h\nu$.
- The product of the frequency and wavelength of light is the speed of light: $c = \nu\lambda$.

- An orbital or wave function is a quantum mechanical, mathematical description of the electron.

- If all electrons in an atom are in their lowest possible energy level, then the atom is said to be in its ground state.

- If any electrons in an atom are in a higher energy state, then the atom is said to be in an excited state.

- The energy of an atom is quantized, existing in only certain distinct energy states.

- Quantum numbers are numbers used in Schrödinger's equation to describe the orbital size, shape, and orientation in space, and the spin of an electron.

- The principal quantum number, n, describes the size of the orbital. It must be a positive integer. It is sometimes referred to as the atom's shell.

- The angular momentum quantum number, l, defines the shape of the electron cloud. If $l = 0$, it is an s orbital; if $l = 1$, it is a p orbital; if $l = 2$, it is a d orbital; if $l = 3$, it is an f orbital, etc.

- The magnetic quantum number, m_l, describes the orientation of the orbital around the nucleus. It can be integer values ranging from $-l$ through 0 to $+l$.

- The spin quantum number, m_s, describes the spin of the electron and can only have values of $+\frac{1}{2}$ and $-\frac{1}{2}$.

- Be able to write the quantum numbers associated with the first 20 electrons.

CHAPTER > 11

Bonding

IN THIS CHAPTER

Summary: The difference between elements and compounds was discussed in the Basics chapter, and chemical reactions were discussed in the Reactions and Periodicity chapter. But what are the forces holding together a compound? What is the difference in bonding between table salt and sugar? What do these compounds look like in three-dimensional space?

Compounds have a certain fixed proportion of elements. The periodic table often can be used to predict the type of bonding that might exist between elements. The following general guidelines apply:

 KEY IDEA

metal + nonmetal → ionic bonds

nonmetal + nonmetal → covalent bonds

metal + metal → metallic bonding

We will discuss the first two types of bonding, ionic and covalent, in some depth. Metallic bonding is a topic that is very rarely encountered on the AP exam. Suffice it to say that metallic bonding is a bonding situation between metals in which the valence electrons are donated to a vast electron pool (sometimes called a "sea of electrons"), so that the valence electrons are free to move throughout the entire metallic solid.

The basic concept that drives bonding is related to the stability of the noble gas family (the group VIIIA or group 18 elements). Their extreme stability (lower energy state) is due to the fact that they have a filled valence shell, a full complement of eight valence electrons. (Helium is an exception. Its valence shell, the 1s, is filled with two electrons.) This is called the octet rule. During chemical reactions, atoms lose, gain, or share electrons in order to achieve a filled valence shell, to complete their octet. By completing their valence shell in this fashion, they become isoelectronic, having the same number and arrangement of electrons, as the closest noble gas.

There are numerous exceptions to the octet rule; for example, some atoms may have more than an octet.

Keywords and Equations

There are no keywords or equations on the AP exam specific to this chapter.

Lewis Electron-Dot Structures

The Lewis electron-dot symbol is a way of representing the element and its valence electrons. The chemical symbol is written, which represents the atom's nucleus and all inner-shell electrons. The valence, or outer-shell, electrons are represented as dots surrounding the atom's symbol. Take the valence electrons, distribute them as dots one at a time around the four sides of the symbol, and then pair them up until all the valence electrons are distributed. Figure 11.1 shows the Lewis symbol for several different elements.

The Lewis symbols will be used in the discussion of bonding, especially covalent bonding, and will form the basis of the discussion of molecular geometry.

$$\text{Na}\cdot \quad \cdot\text{Mg}\cdot \quad \cdot\overset{\cdot}{\underset{\cdot}{\text{C}}}\cdot \quad \cdot\overset{\cdot\cdot}{\text{N}}\cdot \quad :\overset{\cdot\cdot}{\underset{\cdot\cdot}{\text{F}}}:$$

Figure 11.1   Lewis electron-dot symbols for selected elements.

Ionic and Covalent Bonding

Ionic Bonding

Ionic bonding results from the transfer of electrons from a metal to a nonmetal with the formation of cations (positively charged ions) and anions (negatively charged ions). The attraction of the opposite charges forms the **ionic bond**. The metal loses electrons to form a cation (the positive charge results from having more protons than electrons), and the nonmetal becomes an anion by gaining electrons (it now has more electrons than protons). This is shown in Figure 11.2 for the reaction of sodium and chlorine to form sodium chloride.

The number of electrons to be lost by the metal and gained by the nonmetal is determined by the number of electrons lost or gained by the atom in order to achieve a full octet. There is a rule of thumb that an atom can gain or lose one or two and, on rare occasions, three electrons, but not more than that. Sodium has one valence electron in energy level 3.

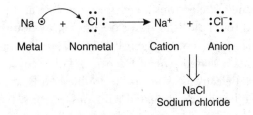

Figure 11.2   Formation of sodium chloride.

If it lost that one, the valence shell, now energy level 2, would be full (a more common way of showing this is with zero electrons). Chlorine, having seven valence electrons, needs to gain one more in order to complete its octet. So, an electron is transferred from sodium to chlorine, completing the octet for both.

If magnesium, with two valence electrons to be lost, reacts with chlorine (which needs one additional electron), then magnesium will donate one valence electron to each of *two* chlorine atoms, forming the ionic compound $MgCl_2$. Make sure the formula has the lowest whole-number ratio of elements.

If aluminum, with three valence electrons to be lost, reacts with oxygen, which needs two additional electrons to complete its octet, then the lowest common factor between 3 and 2 must be found—6. Two aluminum atoms would each lose 3 electrons (total of 6 electrons lost) to three oxygen atoms, which would each gain 2 electrons (total 6 electrons gained). The total number of electrons lost must equal the total number of electrons gained.

Another way of deriving the formula of the ionic compound is the **crisscross rule**. In this technique the cation and anion are written side by side. The numerical value of the superscript charge on the cation (without the sign) becomes the subscript on the nonmetal in the compound, and the superscript charge on the anion becomes the subscript on the metal in the compound. Figure 11.3 illustrates the crisscross rule for the reaction between aluminum and oxygen.

Figure 11.3 Using the crisscross rule.

If magnesium reacts with oxygen, then automatic application of the crisscross rule would lead to the formula Mg_2O_2, which is incorrect because the subscripts are not in the lowest whole-number ratio. For the same reason, lead(IV) oxide would have the formula PbO_2 and not Pb_2O_4. Make sure the formula has the lowest whole-number ratio of elements.

Ionic bonding may also involve polyatomic ions. The polyatomic ion(s) simply replace(s) one or both of the monoatomic ions.

Covalent Bonding

Consider two hydrogen atoms approaching each other. Both have only one electron, and each requires an additional electron to become isoelectronic with the nearest noble gas, He. One hydrogen atom could lose an electron; the other could gain that electron. One atom would have achieved its noble gas arrangement; but the other, the atom that lost its electron, has moved farther away from stability. The formation of the very stable H_2 cannot be explained by the loss and gain of electrons. In this situation, like that between any two nonmetals, electrons are shared, not lost and gained. No ions are formed. It is a covalent bond that holds the atoms together. **Covalent bonding** is the sharing of one or more *pairs* of electrons. The covalent bonds in a **molecule** often are represented by a dash, which represents a shared *pair* of electrons. These covalent bonds may be single bonds, one pair of shared electrons as in H–H; double bonds, two shared pairs of electrons, $H_2C{=}CH_2$; or triple bonds, three shared pairs of electrons, $N{\equiv}N$. The same driving force forms a covalent bond as an ionic bond—establishing a stable (lower energy) electron arrangement. In the case of the covalent bond, it is accomplished through sharing electrons.

In the hydrogen molecule, the electrons are shared equally. Each hydrogen nucleus has one proton equally attracting the bonding pair of electrons. A bond like this is called a **nonpolar covalent bond**. In cases where the two atoms involved in the covalent bond are not the same, the attraction is not equal, and the bonding electrons are pulled toward the atom with the greater attraction. The bond becomes a **polar covalent bond**, with the atom that has the greater attraction taking on a partial negative charge and the other atom a partial positive charge. Consider for example, HF(g). The fluorine has a greater attraction for the bonding pair of electrons (greater electronegativity) and so takes on a partial negative charge. Many times, instead of using a single line to indicate the covalent bond, an arrow is used with the arrowhead pointing toward the atom that has the greater attraction for the electron pair:

$$^{\delta+}H - F^{\delta-}$$

$$\longmapsto$$

The **electronegativity (EN)** is a measure of the attractive force that an atom exerts on a bonding pair of electrons. Electronegativity values are tabulated. In general, electronegativities increase from left to right on the periodic table, except for the noble gases, and decrease going from top to bottom. This means that fluorine has the highest electronegativity of any element. If the difference in the electronegativities of the two elements involved in the bond is great (>1.7), the bond is considered to be mostly ionic in nature. If the difference is slight (<0.4), it is mostly nonpolar covalent. Anything in between is polar covalent.

Many times the Lewis structure will be used to indicate the bonding pattern in a covalent compound. In Lewis formulas, the valence electrons that are not involved in bonding are shown as dots surrounding the element symbols, while a bonding pair of electrons is represented as a dash. There are several ways of deriving the Lewis structure, but here is one that works well for those compounds that obey the octet rule.

Draw the Lewis structural formula for CH_4O.

First, write a general framework for the molecule. In this case, the carbon must be bonded to the oxygen, because hydrogen can form only one bond. Hydrogen is *never* central. Remember: **Carbon forms four bonds.**

$$
\begin{array}{cccc}
 & H & & \\
H & C & O & H \\
 & H & &
\end{array}
$$

To determine where all the electrons are to be placed, apply the $N - A = S$ rule where:

N = sum of valence electrons needed for each atom. The two allowed values are two for hydrogen and eight for all other elements.
A = sum of all available valence electrons
S = # of electrons shared and $S/2$ = # bonds

For CH_4O, we would have:

	1 C		4 H		1 O	
N	8	+	4 (2) = 8	+	8	= 24
A	4	+	4(1) = 4	+	6	= 14

$S = N - A = 24 - 14 = 10$ $\qquad$ bonds $= S/2 = 10/2 = 5$

Place the electron pairs, as dashes, between the adjacent atoms in the framework and then distribute the remaining available electrons so that each atom has its full octet, eight electrons—bonding or nonbonding, shared or not—for every atom except hydrogen, which gets two. Figure 11.4 shows the Lewis structural formula of CH_4O.

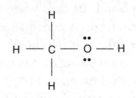

Figure 11.4   Lewis structure of CH_4O.

Lewis structures may also be written for polyatomic anions or cations. The $N - A = S$ rule can be used, but if the ion is an anion, extra electrons equal to the magnitude of the negative charge must be added to the electrons available. If the ion is a cation, electrons must be subtracted.

As we have mentioned previously, there are many exceptions to the octet rule. In these cases, the $N - A = S$ rule does not apply, as illustrated by the following example.

Draw the Lewis structure for XeF_4.

Answer:

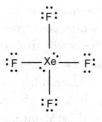

Each of the fluorines will have an additional three pairs of electrons. Only the four fluorine atoms have their octets.

This process will usually result in the correct Lewis structure. However, there will be cases when more than one structure may seem to be reasonable. One way to eliminate inappropriate structures is by using the formal charge.

There is a formal charge associated with each atom in a Lewis structure. To determine the formal charge for an atom, enter the number of electrons for each atom into the following relationship:

Formal charge = (number of valence electrons) – (number of nonbonding electrons + 1/2 number of bonding electrons)

A formal charge of zero for each atom in a molecule is a very common result for a favorable Lewis structure. In other cases, a favorable Lewis structure will follow these rules: The formal charges are:

1. Small numbers, preferably 0.
2. No like charges are adjacent to each other, but unlike charges are close together.
3. The more electronegative element(s), the lower the formal charge(s) will be.
4. The total of the formal charges equals the charge on the ion.

Now we will apply this formal-charge concept to the cyanate ion OCN^-. We chose this example because many students incorrectly write the formula as CNO^-, and then try to use this as the atomic arrangement in the Lewis structure. Based on the number of electrons needed, the carbon should be the central atom. We will work this example using both the incorrect atom arrangement and the correct atom arrangement. Notice that in both structures all atoms have a complete octet.

$$\left[\ddot{\text{O}}::\text{N}::\ddot{\text{C}}:\right]^{-} \quad \left[\ddot{\text{O}}::\text{C}::\ddot{\text{N}}:\right]^{-}$$

Number of valence electrons	6	5	4	6	4	5
– Number of nonbonding electrons	–4	–0	–4	–4	–0	–4
– 1/2 Number of bonding electrons	–2	–4	–2	–2	–4	–2
Formal charges	0	+1	–2	0	0	–1

The formal charges make the OCN arrangement the better choice.

Molecular Geometry—VSEPR

The shape of a molecule has quite a bit to do with its reactivity. This is especially true in biochemical processes, where slight changes in shape in three-dimensional space might make a certain molecule inactive or cause an adverse side effect. One way to predict the shape of molecules is the **VSEPR** (valence-shell electron-pair repulsion) **theory**. The basic idea behind this theory is that the valence electron pairs surrounding a central atom, whether involved in bonding or not, will try to move as far away from each other as possible to minimize the repulsion between the like charges. Two geometries can be determined; the *electron-group geometry,* in which all electron pairs surrounding a nucleus are considered, and *molecular geometry,* in which the nonbonding electrons become "invisible" and only the geometry of the atomic nuclei are considered. For the purposes of geometry, double and triple bonds count the same as single bonds. To determine the geometry:

> **KEY IDEA**

1. Write the Lewis electron-dot formula of the compound.
2. Determine the number of electron-pair groups surrounding the central atom(s). Remember that double and triple bonds are treated as a single group.
3. Determine the geometric shape that maximizes the distance between the electron groups. This is the geometry of the electron groups.
4. Mentally allow the nonbonding electrons to become invisible. They are still there and are still repelling the other electron pairs, but we don't "see" them. The molecular geometry is determined by the remaining arrangement of atoms (as determined by the bonding electron groups) around the central atom.

Figure 11.5, on the next page, shows the electron-group and molecular geometry for two to six electron pairs.

> **KEY IDEA**

For example, let's determine the electron-group and molecular geometry of carbon dioxide, CO_2, and water, H_2O. At first glance, one might imagine that the geometry of these two compounds would be similar, since both have a central atom with two groups attached. Let's see if that is true.

First, write the Lewis structure of each. Figure 11.6 shows the Lewis structures of these compounds.

Next, determine the electron-group geometry of each. For carbon dioxide, there are two electron groups around the carbon, so it would be linear. For water, there are four electron pairs around the oxygen—two bonding and two nonbonding electron pairs—so the electron-group geometry would be tetrahedral.

Finally, mentally allow the nonbonding electron pairs to become invisible and describe what is left in terms of the molecular geometry. For carbon dioxide, all groups are involved in bonding so the molecular geometry is also linear. However, water has two nonbonding

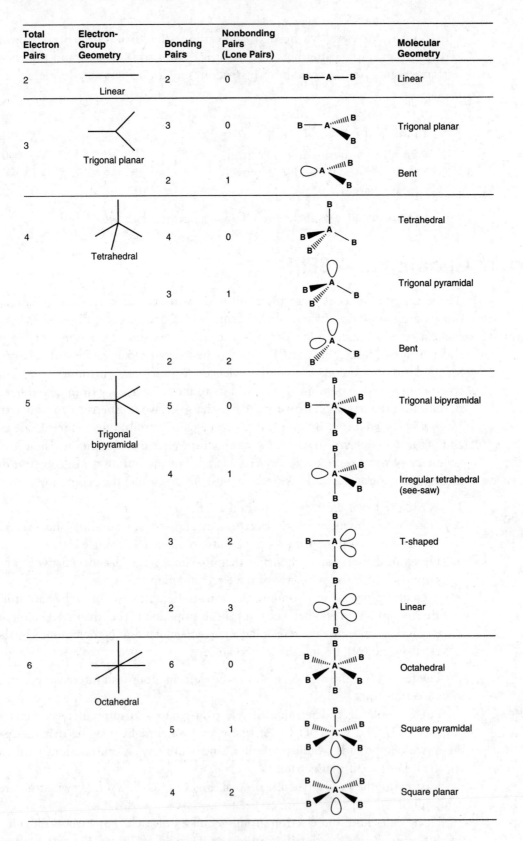

Total Electron Pairs	Electron-Group Geometry	Bonding Pairs	Nonbonding Pairs (Lone Pairs)		Molecular Geometry
2	Linear	2	0	B—A—B	Linear
3	Trigonal planar	3	0		Trigonal planar
		2	1		Bent
4	Tetrahedral	4	0		Tetrahedral
		3	1		Trigonal pyramidal
		2	2		Bent
5	Trigonal bipyramidal	5	0		Trigonal bipyramidal
		4	1		Irregular tetrahedral (see-saw)
		3	2		T-shaped
		2	3		Linear
6	Octahedral	6	0		Octahedral
		5	1		Square pyramidal
		4	2		Square planar

Figure 11.5 Electron-group and molecular geometry.

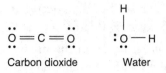

Figure 11.6 Lewis structures of carbon dioxide and water.

pairs of electrons so the remaining bonding electron pairs (and hydrogen nuclei) are in a bent arrangement.

This determination of the molecular geometry of carbon dioxide and water also accounts for the fact that carbon dioxide does not possess a dipole and water has one, even though both are composed of polar covalent bonds. Carbon dioxide, because of its linear shape, has partial negative charges at both ends and a partial charge in the middle. To possess a dipole, one end of the molecule must have a positive charge and the other a negative end. Water, because of its bent shape, satisfies this requirement. Carbon dioxide does not.

Valence Bond Theory

The VSEPR theory is only one way in which the molecular geometry of molecules may be determined. Another way involves the valence bond theory. The **valence bond theory** describes covalent bonding as the mixing of atomic orbitals to form a new kind of orbital, a hybrid orbital. **Hybrid orbitals** are atomic orbitals formed as a result of mixing the atomic orbitals of the atoms involved in the covalent bond. The number of hybrid orbitals formed is the same as the number of atomic orbitals mixed, and the type of hybrid orbital formed depends on the types of atomic orbital mixed. Figure 11.7 shows the hybrid orbitals resulting from the mixing of s, p, and d orbitals.

	Linear	Trigonal planar	Tetrahedral	Trigonal bipyramidal	Octahedral
Atomic orbitals mixed	one s	one s	one s	one s	one s
	one p	two p	three p	three p	three p
				one d	two d
Hybrid orbitals formed	two sp	three sp^2	four sp^3	five sp^3d	six sp^3d^2
Unhybridized orbitals remaining	two p	one p	none	four d	three d
Orientation					

Figure 11.7 Hybridization of s, p, and d orbitals.

sp hybridization results from the overlap of an s orbital with one p orbital. Two sp hybrid orbitals are formed with a bond angle of 180°. This is a linear orientation.

sp^2 hybridization results from the overlap of an s orbital with two p orbitals. Three sp^2 hybrid orbitals are formed with a trigonal planar orientation and a bond angle of 120°.

One place this type of bonding occurs is in the formation of the carbon-to-carbon double bond, as will be discussed later.

sp³ hybridization results from the mixing of one s orbital and three p orbitals, giving four sp³ hybrid orbitals with a tetrahedral geometric orientation. This sp³ hybridization is found in carbon when it forms four single bonds.

sp³d hybridization results from the blending of an s orbital, three p orbitals, and one d orbital. The result is five sp³d orbitals with a trigonal bipyramidal orientation. This type of bonding occurs in compounds like PCl_5. Note that this hybridization is an exception to the octet rule.

sp³d² hybridization occurs when one s, three p, and two d orbitals are mixed, giving an octahedral arrangement. SF_6 is an example. Again, this hybridization is an exception to the octet rule. If one starts with this structure and one of the bonding pairs becomes a lone pair, then a square pyramidal shape results, while two lone pairs give a square planar shape.

Figure 11.8 shows the hybridization that occurs in ethylene, $H_2C=CH_2$. Each carbon has undergone sp² hybridization. On each carbon, two of the hybrid orbitals have overlapped with an s orbital on a hydrogen atom, to form a carbon-to-hydrogen covalent bond. The third sp² hybrid orbital has overlapped with the sp² hybrid on the other carbon to form a carbon-to-carbon covalent bond. Note that the remaining p orbital on each carbon that has not undergone hybridization is also overlapping above and below a line joining the carbons. In ethylene, there are two types of bond. In **sigma (σ) bonds,** the overlap of the orbitals occurs on a line between the two atoms involved in the covalent bond. In ethylene, the C–H bonds and one of the C–C bonds are sigma bonds. In **pi (π) bonds,** the overlap of orbitals occurs above and below a line through the two nuclei of the atoms involved in the bond. A double bond always is composed of one sigma and one pi bond. A carbon-to-carbon triple bond results from the overlap of an sp hybrid orbital and two p orbitals on one carbon, with the same on the other carbon. In this situation, there will be one sigma bond (overlap of the sp hybrid orbitals) and two pi bonds (overlap of two sets of p orbitals).

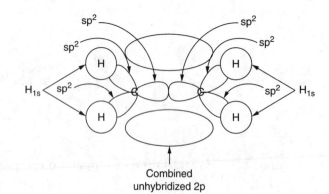
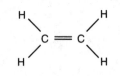

Figure 11.8   Hybridization in ethylene, $H_2C=CH_2$.

ENRICHMENT

Molecular Orbital Theory

Still another model to represent the bonding that takes place in covalent compounds is the molecular orbital theory. In the **molecular orbital (MO) theory** of covalent bonding, atomic orbitals (AOs) on the individual atoms combine to form orbitals that encompass the entire molecule. These are called molecular orbitals (MOs). These molecular orbitals have definite shapes and energies associated with them. When two atomic orbitals are added, two molecular orbitals are formed, one bonding and one antibonding. The bonding MO is of lower energy than the antibonding MO. In the molecular orbital model, the atomic orbitals are added together to form the molecular orbitals. Then the electrons are added to the molecular orbitals, following the rules used previously when filling orbitals: lowest-energy orbitals get filled first, maximum of two electrons per orbital, and half fill orbitals of equal energy before pairing electrons (see Chapter 5). When s atomic orbitals are added, one sigma bonding (σ) and one sigma antibonding (σ^*) molecular orbital are formed. Figure 11.9 shows the molecular orbital diagram for H_2.

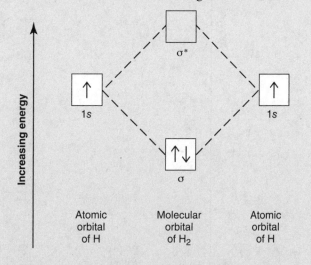

Figure 11.9   Molecular orbital diagram of H_2.

Note that the two electrons (one from each hydrogen) have both gone into the sigma bonding MO. The bonding situation can be calculated in the molecular orbital theory by calculating the MO bond order. The MO bond order is the number of electrons in bonding MOs minus the number of electrons in antibonding MOs, divided by 2. For H_2 in Figure 11.9 the bond order would be $(2 - 0)/2 = 1$. A stable bonding situation exists between two atoms when the bond order is greater than zero. The larger the bond order, the stronger the bond.

When two sets of p orbitals combine, one sigma bonding and one sigma antibonding MO are formed, along with two bonding pi MOs and two pi antibonding (π^*) MOs. Figure 11.10, on the next page, shows the MO diagram for O_2. For the sake of simplicity, the 1s orbitals of each oxygen and the MOs for these elections are not shown, just the valence-electron orbitals.

The bond order for O_2 would be $(10 - 6)/2 = 2$. (Don't forget to count the bonding and antibonding electrons at energy level 1.)

KEY IDEA

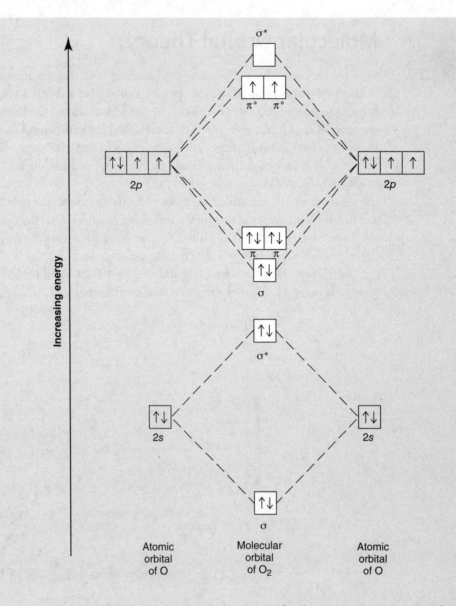

Figure 11.10   Molecular orbital diagram of valence-shell electrons of O_2.

Resonance

Sometimes when writing the Lewis structure of a compound, more than one possible structure is generated for a given molecule. The nitrate ion, NO_3^-, is a good example. Three possible Lewis structures can be written for this polyatomic anion, differing in which oxygen is double bonded to the nitrogen. None truly represents the actual structure of the nitrate ion; that would require an average of all three Lewis structures. **Resonance** theory is used to describe this situation. Resonance occurs when more than one Lewis structure can be written for a molecule. The individual structures are called resonance structures (or forms) and are written with a two-headed arrow ($\leftrightarrow$) between them. Figure 11.11 shows the three resonance forms of the nitrate ion.

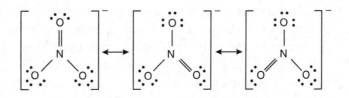

Figure 11.11   Resonance structures of the nitrate ion, NO_3^-.

Again, let us emphasize that the actual structure of the nitrate is not any of the three shown. Neither is it flipping back and forth among the three. It is an average of all three. All the bonds are the same, intermediate between single bonds and double bonds in strength and length.

Bond Length, Strength, and Magnetic Properties

The length and strength of a covalent bond is related to its bond order. The greater the bond order, the shorter and stronger the bond. Diatomic nitrogen, for example, has a short, extremely strong bond due to its nitrogen-to-nitrogen triple bond.

One of the advantages of the molecular orbital model is that it can predict some of the magnetic properties of molecules. If molecules are placed in a strong magnetic field, they exhibit one of two magnetic behaviors—attraction or repulsion. **Paramagnetism**, the attraction to a magnetic field, is due to the presence of unpaired electrons; **diamagnetism**, the slight repulsion from a magnetic field, is due to the presence of only paired electrons. Look at Figure 11.10, the MO diagram for diatomic oxygen. Note that it does have two unpaired electrons in the π_{2p}^* antibonding orbitals. Thus, one would predict, based on the MO model, that oxygen should be paramagnetic, and that is exactly what is observed in the laboratory.

Experiments

There have been no experimental questions concerning this material on recent AP Chemistry exams.

Common Mistakes to Avoid

1. Remember that metals + nonmetals form ionic bonds, while the reaction of two nonmetals forms a covalent bond.
2. The octet rule does not always work, but for the representative elements, it works the majority of the time.
3. Atoms that lose electrons form cations; atoms that gain electrons form anions.
4. In writing the formulas of ionic compounds, make sure the subscripts are in the lowest ratio of whole numbers.
5. When using the crisscross rule, be sure the subscripts are reduced to the lowest whole-number ratio.
6. When using the N – A = S rule in writing Lewis structures, be sure you add electrons to the A term for a polyatomic anion, and subtract electrons for a polyatomic cation.
7. In the N – A = S rule, only the *valence* electrons are counted.

8. In using the VSEPR theory, when going from the electron-group geometry to the molecular geometry, start with the electron-group geometry; make the nonbonding electrons mentally invisible; and then describe what is left.

9. When adding electrons to the molecular orbitals, remember: lowest energy first. On orbitals with equal energies, half fill and then pair up.

10. When writing Lewis structures of polyatomic ions, don't forget to show the charge.

11. When you draw resonance structures, you can move only electrons (bonds). Never move the atoms.

12. When answering questions, the stability of the noble-gas configurations is a result, not an explanation. Your answers will require an explanation, i.e., lower energy state.

› Review Questions

Use these questions to review the content of this chapter and practice for the AP Chemistry exam. First are 16 multiple-choice questions similar to what you will encounter in Section I of the AP Chemistry exam. Following those is a long free-response question like the ones in Section II of the exam. To make these questions an even more authentic practice for the actual exam, time yourself following the instructions provided.

Multiple-Choice Questions

Answer the following questions in 20 minutes. You may not use a calculator. You may use the periodic table and the equation sheet at the back of this book.

1. VSEPR predicts an SbF_5 molecule will be which of the following shapes?

   (A) tetrahedral
   (B) trigonal bipyramidal
   (C) square pyramid
   (D) trigonal planar

2. The shortest bond would be present in which of the following substances?

   (A) I_2
   (B) CO
   (C) CCl_4
   (D) O_2^{2-}

3. Which of the following does not have one or more π bonds?

   (A) H_2O
   (B) HNO_3
   (C) O_2
   (D) N_2

4. Which of the following is polar?

   (A) SF_4
   (B) XeF_4
   (C) CF_4
   (D) SbF_5

5. Resonance structures are necessary to describe the bonding in which of the following?

   (A) H_2O
   (B) ClF_3
   (C) HNO_3
   (D) CH_4

For questions 6 and 7, pick the best choice from the following:

   (A) ionic bonds
   (B) hybrid orbitals
   (C) resonance structures
   (D) van der Waals attractions

6. An explanation of the equivalent bond lengths of the nitrite ion is:

7. Most organic substances have low melting points. This may be because, in most cases, the intermolecular forces are:

8. Which of the following has more than one unshared pair of valence electrons on the central atom?

   (A) BrF_5
   (B) NF_3
   (C) IF_7
   (D) ClF_3

9. What is the expected hybridization of the central atom in a molecule of $TiCl_4$? This molecule is tetrahedral.

   (A) sp^3
   (B) sp^3d
   (C) sp
   (D) sp^2

10. The only substance listed below that contains ionic, σ, and π bonds is:

    (A) Na_2CO_3
    (B) $HClO_2$
    (C) H_2O
    (D) $NaCl$

11. The electron pairs point toward the corners of which geometrical shape for a molecule with sp^2 hybrid orbitals?

    (A) trigonal planar
    (B) octahedron
    (C) trigonal bipyramid
    (D) trigonal pyramid

12. Regular tetrahedral molecules or ions include which of the following?

    (A) SF_4
    (B) NH_4^+
    (C) XeF_4
    (D) ICl_4^-

13. Which molecule or ion in the following list has the greatest number of unshared electrons around the central atom?

    (A) CF_4
    (B) ClF_3
    (C) BF_3
    (D) NH_4^+

14. Which of the following molecules is the least polar?

    (A) PH_3
    (B) CH_4
    (C) H_2O
    (D) NO_2

15. Which of the following molecules is the most polar?

    (A) NH_3
    (B) N_2
    (C) CH_3I
    (D) BF_3

16. Which of the following processes involves breaking an ionic bond?

    (A) $H_2(g) + Cl_2(g) \rightarrow 2\ HCl(g)$
    (B) $2\ KBr(s) \rightarrow 2\ K(g) + Br_2(g)$
    (C) $Na(s) \rightarrow Na(g)$
    (D) $2\ C_2H_6(g) + 7\ O_2(g) \rightarrow 4\ CO_2(g) + 6\ H_2O(g)$

Answers and Explanations for the Multiple-Choice Questions

1. **B**—The Lewis (electron-dot) structure has five bonding pairs around the central Sb and no lone pairs. VSEPR predicts this number of pairs to give a trigonal bipyramidal structure.

2. **B**—All the bonds except in CO are single bonds. The CO bond is a triple bond. Triple bonds are shorter than double bonds, which are shorter than single bonds. Drawing Lewis structures might help you answer this question.

3. **A**—Answers B through D contain molecules or ions with double or triple bonds. Double and triple bonds contain π bonds. Water has only single (σ) bonds. If any of these are not obvious to you, draw a Lewis structure.

4. **A**—The VSEPR model predicts all the other molecules to be nonpolar.

5. **C**—All the other answers involve species containing only single bonds. Substances without double or triple bonds seldom need resonance structures.

6. **C**—Resonance causes bonds to have the same average length.

7. **D**—Many organic molecules are nonpolar. Nonpolar substances are held together by weak van der Waals attractions.

8. **D**—Lewis structures are required. You do not need to draw all of them. A and B have one unshared pair, while C does not have an unshared pair. D has two unshared pairs of electrons.

9. **A**—Tetrahedral molecules are normally sp^3 hybridized.

10. **A**—Only A and D are ionic. The chloride ion has no internal bonds, so σ and π bonds are not possible.

11. **A**—This hybridization requires a geometrical shape with three corners.

12. **B**—One or more Lewis structures may help you. A is an irregular tetrahedron (seesaw); C and D are square planar.

13. **B**—A has 0. B has 2. C and D have 0. You may need to draw one or more Lewis structures.

14. **B**—All the molecules are polar except B.

15. **A**—Drawing one or more Lewis structures may help you. Only A and C are polar. Only the ammonia has hydrogen bonding, which is very, very polar.

16. **B**—C is breaking metallic bonding. All the others involve covalently bonded molecules.

Free-Response Question

You have 15 minutes to answer the following question. You may use a calculator and the tables in the back of the book.

Question 1
Answer the following questions about structure and bonding.

(a) Which of the following tetrafluoride compounds is nonpolar? Use Lewis electron-dot structures to explain your conclusions.

$$SiF_4 \qquad SF_4 \qquad XeF_4$$

(b) Rank the following compounds in order of increasing melting point. Explain your answer. Lewis electron-dot structures may aid you.

$$SnF_2 \qquad SeF_2 \qquad KrF_2$$

(c) Use Lewis electron-dot structures to show why the carbon–oxygen bonds in the oxalate ion $(C_2O_4^{2-})$ are all equal.

(d) When PCl_5 is dissolved in a polar solvent, the solution conducts electricity. Explain why. Use an appropriate chemical equation to illustrate your answer.

Answer and Explanation for the Free-Response Question

(a) Silicon tetrafluoride is the only one of the three compounds that is not polar.

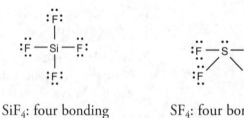

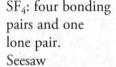

SiF₄: four bonding pairs and no lone pairs. Tetrahedral

SF₄: four bonding pairs and one lone pair. Seesaw

XeF₄: four bonding pairs and two lone pairs. Square planar

You get 1 point if you correctly predict only SiF_4 to be nonpolar. You get 1 additional point for each correct Lewis structure.

(b) The order is $KrF_2 < SeF_2 < SnF_2$.

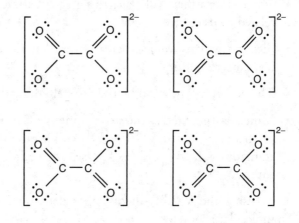

KrF$_2$: two bonding pairs and three nonbonding pairs

SeF$_2$: two bonding pairs and two nonbonding pairs

SnF$_2$: ionic

The Lewis structure indicates that KrF_2 is nonpolar. Thus, it only has very weak London dispersion forces between the molecules. SeF_2 is polar, and the molecules are attracted by dipole-dipole attractions, which are stronger than London. SnF_2 has the highest melting point, because of the presence of strong ionic bonds.

You get 1 point for the order and 1 point for the discussion.

(c) It is possible to draw the following resonance structures for the oxalate ion. The presence of resonance equalizes the bonds.

You get 1 point for any correct Lewis structure for $C_2O_4^{2-}$ and 1 point for showing or discussing resonance.

(d) PCl_5 must ionize. There are several acceptable equations, all of which must indicate the formation of ions. Here are two choices:

$$2\ PCl_5 \rightleftarrows PCl_4^+ + PCl_6^- \qquad \text{or} \qquad PCl_5 \rightleftarrows PCl_4^+ + Cl^-$$

You get 1 point for the explanation, and you get 1 point for either of the equations.

Total your points for the different parts. There are 10 points possible.

› Rapid Review

- Compounds are pure substances that have a fixed proportion of elements.

- Metals react with nonmetals to form ionic bonds, and nonmetals react with other nonmetals to form covalent bonds.

- The Lewis electron-dot structure is a way of representing an element and its valence electrons.

- Atoms tend to lose, gain, or share electrons to achieve the same electronic configuration as (become isoelectronic to) the nearest noble gas.

- Atoms are generally most stable when they have a complete octet (eight electrons).

- Ionic bonds result when a metal loses electrons to form cations and a nonmetal gains those electrons to form an anion.

- Ionic bonds can also result from the interaction of polyatomic ions.

- The attraction of the opposite charges (anions and cations) forms the ionic bond.

- The crisscross rule can help determine the formula of an ionic compound.

- In covalent bonding two atoms share one or more electron pairs.

- If the electrons are shared equally, the bond is a nonpolar covalent bond, but unequal sharing results in a polar covalent bond.

- The element that will have the greatest attraction for a bonding pair of electrons is related to its electronegativity.

- Electronegativity values increase from left to right on the periodic table and decrease from top to bottom.

- The $N - A = S$ rule can be used to help draw the Lewis structure of a molecule.

- Molecular geometry, the arrangement of atoms in three-dimensional space, can be predicted using the VSEPR theory. This theory says the electron pairs around a central atom will try to get as far as possible from each other to minimize the repulsive forces.

- In using the VSEPR theory, first determine the electron-group geometry, then the molecular geometry.

- The valence bond theory describes covalent bonding as the overlap of atomic orbitals to form a new kind of orbital, a hybrid orbital.

- The number of hybrid orbitals is the same as the number of atomic orbitals that were mixed together.

- There are a number of different types of hybrid orbital, such as sp, sp^2, and sp^3.

- In the valence bond theory, sigma bonds overlap on a line drawn between the two nuclei, while pi bonds result from the overlap of atomic orbitals above and below a line connecting the two atomic nuclei.

- A double or triple bond is always composed of one sigma bond and the rest pi bonds.

- In the molecular orbital (MO) theory of covalent bonding, atomic orbitals form molecular orbitals that encompass the entire molecule.

- The MO theory uses bonding and antibonding molecular orbitals.

- The bond order is (# electrons in bonding MOs – # electrons in anti-bonding MOs)/2.

- Resonance occurs when more than one Lewis structure can be written for a molecule. The actual structure of the molecule is an average of the Lewis resonance structures.

- The higher the bond order, the shorter and stronger the bond.

- Paramagnetism, the attraction of a molecule to a magnetic field, is due to the presence of unpaired electrons. Diamagnetism, the repulsion of a molecule from a magnetic field, is due to the presence of paired electrons.

CHAPTER 12

Solids, Liquids, and Intermolecular Forces

IN THIS CHAPTER

Summary: In the chapter on Gases, we discussed the gaseous state. In this chapter, we will discuss the liquid and solid states and the forces that exist between the particles—the intermolecular forces. A substance's state of matter depends on two factors: the average kinetic energy of the particles, and the intermolecular forces between the particles. The kinetic energy tends to move the particles away from each other. The temperature of the substance is a measure of the average kinetic energy of the molecules. As the temperature increases, the average kinetic energy increases and the particles tend to move farther apart. This is consistent with our experience of heating ice, for example, and watching it move from the solid state to the liquid state and finally to the gaseous state. For this to happen, the kinetic energy overcomes the forces between the particles, the intermolecular forces.

In the solid state, the kinetic energy of the particles cannot overcome the intermolecular forces; the particles are held close together by the intermolecular forces. As the temperature increases, the kinetic energy increases and begins to overcome the attractive intermolecular forces. The substance will eventually melt, going from the solid to the liquid state. As this melting takes place, the temperature remains constant even though energy is being added. The temperature at which the solid converts into the liquid state is called the **melting point (m.p.)** of the solid.

After all the solid has been converted into a liquid, the temperature again starts to rise as energy is added. The particles are still relatively close together, but possess enough kinetic energy to move with respect to each other. Finally, if enough energy is added, the particles start to break free of the intermolecular forces keeping them relatively close together and they escape the liquid as essentially independent gas particles. This process of going from the liquid state to the gaseous state is called boiling, and the temperature at which this occurs is called the **boiling point (b.p.)** of the liquid. Sometimes, however, a solid can go directly from the solid state to the gaseous state without ever having become a liquid. This process is called **sublimation.** Dry ice, solid carbon dioxide, readily sublimes.

These changes of state, called **phase changes**, are related to temperature, but sometimes pressure can influence the changes. We will see how these relationships can be diagrammed later in this chapter.

Keywords and Equations

No specific keywords or equations are listed on the AP exam for this topic.

Structures and Intermolecular Forces

Intermolecular forces are attractive or repulsive forces between molecules, caused by partial charges. The attractive forces are the ones that work to overcome the randomizing forces of kinetic energy. The structure and type of bonding of a particular substance have quite a bit to do with the type of interaction and the strength of that interaction. Before we start examining the different types of intermolecular forces, recall from the Bonding chapter that those molecules that have polar covalent bonding (unequal sharing of the bonding electron pair) may possess dipoles (having positive and negative ends due to charge separation within the molecule). Dipoles are often involved in intermolecular forces.

Ion–Dipole Intermolecular Forces

These forces are due to the attraction of an ion and one end of a polar molecule (dipole). This type of attraction is especially important in aqueous salt solutions, where the ion attracts water molecules and may form a hydrated ion, such as $Al(H_2O)_6^{3+}$. This is one of the strongest of the intermolecular forces.

It is also important to realize that this intermolecular force requires two different species—an ion and a polar molecule.

Dipole–Dipole Intermolecular Forces

These forces result from the attraction of the positive end of one dipole to the negative end of another dipole. For example, in gaseous hydrogen chloride, $HCl(g)$, the hydrogen end has a partial positive charge and the chlorine end has a partial negative charge, due to chlorine's higher electronegativity. Dipole–dipole attractions are especially important in polar liquids. They tend to be a rather strong force, although not as strong as ion–dipole attractions.

Hydrogen Bond Intermolecular Forces

Hydrogen bonding is a special type of dipole–dipole attraction in which a hydrogen atom is polar-covalently bonded to one of the following extremely electronegative elements: N, O, or F. These hydrogen bonds are extremely polar bonds by nature, so there is a great degree of charge separation within the molecule. Therefore, the attraction of the positively charged hydrogen of one molecule and the negatively charged N, O, or F of another molecule is extremely strong. These hydrogen bonds are, in general, stronger than the typical dipole–dipole interaction.

Hydrogen bonding explains why HF(aq) is a weak acid, while HCl(aq), HBr(aq), etc. are strong acids. The hydrogen bond between the hydrogen of one HF molecule and the fluorine of another "traps" the hydrogen, so it is much harder to break its bonds and free the hydrogen to be donated as an H^+. Hydrogen bonding also explains why water has such unusual properties— for example, its unusually high boiling point and the fact that its solid phase is less dense than its liquid phase. The hydrogen bonds tend to stabilize the water molecules and keep them from readily escaping into the gas phase. When water freezes, the hydrogen bonds are stabilized and lock the water molecules into a framework with a lot of open space. Therefore, ice floats in liquid water. Hydrogen bonding also holds the strands of DNA together.

Ion-Induced Dipole and Dipole-Induced Dipole Intermolecular Forces

These types of attraction occur when the charge on an ion or a dipole distorts the electron cloud of a nonpolar molecule and induces a temporary dipole in the nonpolar molecule. Like ion–dipole intermolecular forces, these also require two different species. They are fairly weak interactions.

London (Dispersion) Intermolecular Force

This intermolecular attraction occurs in all substances, but is significant only when the other types of intermolecular forces are absent. It arises from a momentary distortion of the electron cloud, with the creation of a very weak dipole. The weak dipole induces a dipole in another nonpolar molecule. This is an extremely weak interaction, but it is strong enough to allow us to liquefy nonpolar gases such as hydrogen, H_2, and nitrogen, N_2. If there were no intermolecular forces attracting these molecules, it would be impossible to liquefy them.

The Liquid State

At the microscopic level, liquid particles are in constant flux. They may exhibit short-range areas of order, but these do not last very long. Clumps of particles may form and then break apart. At the macroscopic level, a liquid has a specific volume but no fixed shape. Three other macroscopic properties deserve discussion: surface tension, viscosity, and capillary action. In the body of a liquid, the molecules are pulled in all different ways by the intermolecular forces between them. At the surface of the liquid, the molecules are only being pulled into the body of the liquid from the sides and below, not from above. The effect of this unequal attraction is that the liquid tries to minimize its surface area by forming a sphere. In a large pool of liquid, where this is not possible, the surface behaves as if it had a thin "skin" over it. It requires force to break the attractive forces at the surface. The amount of force required to break through this molecular layer at the surface is called the liquid's **surface tension**. The greater the intermolecular forces, the greater the surface tension. Polar liquids, especially those that undergo hydrogen bonding, have a much higher surface tension than nonpolar liquids.

Viscosity, the resistance of liquids to flow, is affected by intermolecular forces, temperature, and molecular shape. Liquids with strong intermolecular forces tend to have a higher viscosity than those with weak intermolecular forces. Again, polar liquids tend to have a higher viscosity than nonpolar liquids. As the temperature increases, the kinetic energy of the particles becomes greater, overcoming the intermolecular attractive forces. This causes a lower viscosity. Finally, the longer and more complex the molecules, the more contact the particles will have as they slip by each other, increasing the viscosity.

Capillary action is the spontaneous rising of a liquid through a narrow tube, against the force of gravity. It is caused by competition between the intermolecular forces in the liquid and those attractive forces between the liquid and the tube wall. The stronger the attraction between the liquid and the tube, the higher the level will be. Liquids that have weak attractions to the walls, like mercury in a glass tube, have a low capillary action. Liquids like water in a glass tube have strong attractions to the walls and will have a high capillary action.

As we have noted before, water, because of its stronger intermolecular forces (hydrogen bonding) has some very unusual properties. It will dissolve a great number of substances, both ionic and polar covalent, because of its polarity and ability to form hydrogen bonds. It is sometimes called the "universal solvent." It has a high **heat capacity**, the heat absorbed to cause the temperature to rise, and a high **heat of vaporization**, the heat needed to transform the liquid into a gas. Both of these thermal properties are due to the strong hydrogen bonding between the water molecules. Water has a high surface tension for the same reason. The fact that the solid form of water (ice) is less dense than liquid water is because water molecules in ice are held in a rigid, open, crystalline framework by the hydrogen bonds. As the ice starts melting, the crystal structure breaks and water molecules fill the holes in the structure, increasing the density. The density reaches a maximum at around 4°C; then the increasing kinetic energy of the particles causes the density to begin to decrease.

The Solid State

At the macroscopic level, a **solid** is defined as a substance that has both a definite volume and a definite shape. At the microscopic level, solids may be one of two types—amorphous or crystalline. **Amorphous solids** lack extensive ordering of the particles. There is a lack of regularity of the structure. There may be small regions of order separated by large areas of disordered particles. They resemble liquids more than solids in this characteristic. Amorphous solids have no distinct melting point. They simply get softer and softer as the temperature rises, leading to a decrease in viscosity. Glass, rubber, and charcoal are examples of amorphous solids.

Crystalline solids display a very regular ordering of the particles in a three-dimensional structure called the **crystal lattice**. In this crystal lattice there are repeating units called **unit cells**. Figure 12.1 shows the relationship of the unit cells to the crystal lattice.

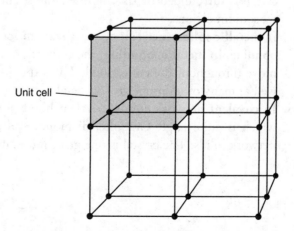

Unit cell

Figure 12.1   The crystal lattice for a simple cubic unit cell.

Several types of unit cells are found in solids. The cubic system is the most common type. Three types of unit cells are found in the cubic system:

1. The **simple cubic unit cell** has particles located at the corners of a simple cube.
2. The **body-centered unit cell** has particles located at the corners of the cube and in the center of the cube.
3. The **face-centered unit cell** has particles at the corners and one in the center of each face of the cube, but not in the center of the cube itself.

Figure 12.2 shows three types of cubic unit cells.

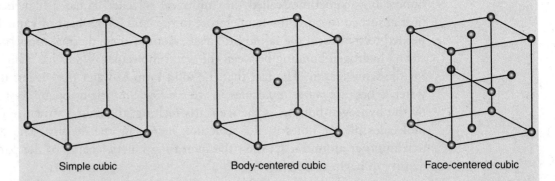

Simple cubic   Body-centered cubic   Face-centered cubic

Figure 12.2   The three types of unit cell of the cubic lattice.

Five types of crystalline solid are known:

1. In **atomic solids,** individual atoms are held in place by London forces. The noble gases are the only atomic solids known to form.
2. In **molecular solids,** lattices composed of molecules are held in place by London forces, dipole–dipole forces, and hydrogen bonding. Solid methane and water are examples of molecular solids.
3. In **ionic solids,** lattices composed of ions are held together by the attraction of the opposite charges of the ions. These crystalline solids tend to be strong, with high melting points because of the strength of the intermolecular forces. NaCl and other salts are examples of ionic solids. Figure 12.3 shows the lattice structure of NaCl. Each sodium cation is surrounded by six chloride anions, and each chloride anion is surrounded by six sodium cations.
4. In **metallic solids**, metal atoms occupying the crystal lattice are held together by metallic bonding. In **metallic bonding**, the electrons of the atoms are delocalized and are free to move throughout the entire solid. This explains electrical and thermal conductivity, as well as many other properties of metals.
5. In **covalent network solids**, covalent bonds join atoms together in the crystal lattice, which is quite large. Graphite, diamond, and silicon dioxide (SiO_2) are examples of network solids. The crystal is one giant molecule.

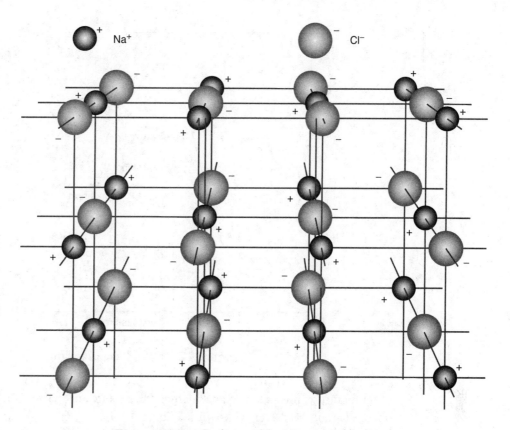

Figure 12.3   Sodium chloride crystal lattice.

Phase Diagrams

The equilibrium that exists between a liquid and its vapor is just one of several that can exist between states of matter. A **phase diagram** is a graph representing the relationship of a substance's states of matter to temperature and pressure. The diagram allows us to predict which state of matter a substance will assume at a certain combination of temperature and pressure. Figure 12.4, on the next page, shows a general form of the phase diagram.

Note that the diagram has three general areas corresponding to the three states of matter—solid, liquid, and gas. The line from A to C represents the solid's change in vapor pressure with changing temperature, for the sublimation equilibrium. The A-to-D line represents the variation in the melting point with varying pressure. The A-to-B line represents the variation of a liquid's vapor pressure with varying pressure. The B point shown on this phase diagram is called the **critical point** of the substance, the point beyond which the gas and liquid phases are indistinguishable from each other. At or beyond this critical point, no matter how much pressure is applied, the gas cannot be condensed into a liquid. Point A is the substance's **triple point**, the combination

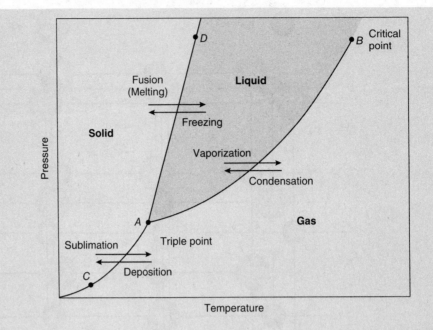

Figure 12.4   A phase diagram.

of temperature and pressure at which all three states of matter can exist together. The phase diagram for water is shown in Figure 12.5.

For each of the phase transitions, there is an associated enthalpy change or heat of transition. For example, there are heats of vaporization, fusion, sublimation, and so on.

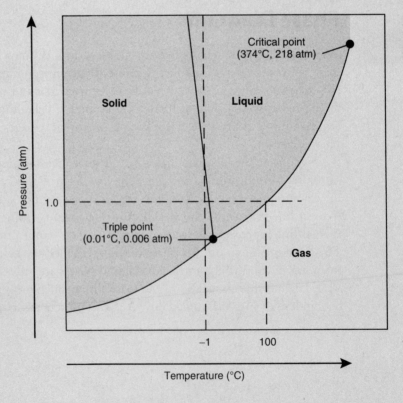

Figure 12.5   Phase diagram for H$_2$O.

Relationship of Intermolecular Forces to Phase Changes

The intermolecular forces can affect phase changes to a great degree. The stronger the intermolecular forces present in a liquid, the more kinetic energy must be added to convert it into a gas. Conversely, the stronger the intermolecular forces between the gas particles, the easier it will be to condense the gas into a liquid. In general, the weaker the intermolecular forces, the higher the vapor pressure. The same type of reasoning can be used about the other phase equilibria—in general, the stronger the intermolecular forces, the higher the heats of transition.

Example: Based on intermolecular forces, predict which will have the higher vapor pressure and higher boiling point, water or dimethyl ether, CH_3-O-CH_3.

Answer: Dimethyl ether will have the higher vapor pressure and the lower boiling point.

Explanation: Water is a polar substance with strong intermolecular hydrogen bonds. Dimethyl ether is a polar material with weaker intermolecular forces (dipole–dipole). It will take much more energy to vaporize water; thus, water has a lower vapor pressure and higher boiling point.

Experiments

The concept of intermolecular forces is important in the separation of the components of a mixture.

Common Mistakes to Avoid

1. Don't confuse the various types of intermolecular forces.
2. The melting point and the freezing point are identical.
3. Hydrogen bonding can occur only when a hydrogen atom is directly bonded to an N, O, or F atom.
4. When moving from point to point in a phase diagram, pay attention to which phase transitions the substance exhibits.
5. In looking at crystal lattice diagrams, be sure to count all the particles, in all three dimensions, that surround another particle.

› Review Questions

Use these questions to review the content of this chapter and practice for the AP Chemistry exam. Below are 14 multiple-choice questions similar to what you will encounter in Section I of the AP Chemistry exam. To make these questions an even more authentic practice for the actual exam, time yourself following the instructions provided.

Multiple-Choice Questions

Answer the following questions in 20 minutes. You may not use a calculator. You may use the periodic table and the equation sheet at the back of this book.

1. Which of the following best describes Fe(s)?

   (A) composed of macromolecules held together by strong bonds
   (B) composed of atoms held together by delocalized electrons
   (C) composed of positive and negative ions held together by electrostatic attractions
   (D) composed of molecules held together by intermolecular dipole–dipole interactions

2. The best description of the interactions in $KNO_3(s)$ is which of the following?

   (A) composed of macromolecules held together by strong bonds
   (B) composed of atoms held together by delocalized electrons
   (C) composed of positive and negative ions held together by electrostatic attractions
   (D) composed of molecules held together by intermolecular dipole–dipole interactions

3. Sand is primarily $SiO_2(s)$. Which of the following best describes the interactions inside a grain of sand?

   (A) composed of macromolecules held together by strong bonds
   (B) composed of atoms held together by delocalized electrons
   (C) composed of positive and negative ions held together by electrostatic attractions
   (D) composed of molecules held together by intermolecular dipole–dipole interactions

4. At sufficiently low temperatures, it is possible to form HCl(s). What best describes the interactions in this solid?

   (A) composed of macromolecules held together by strong bonds
   (B) composed of atoms held together by delocalized electrons
   (C) composed of positive and negative ions held together by electrostatic attractions
   (D) composed of molecules held together by intermolecular dipole–dipole interactions

5. Which of the following best describes diamond, C(s)?

   (A) an ionic solid
   (B) a metallic solid
   (C) a molecular solid containing polar molecules
   (D) a covalent network solid

6. What type of solid is solid sulfur dioxide, $SO_2(s)$?

   (A) an ionic solid
   (B) a metallic solid
   (C) a molecular solid containing polar molecules
   (D) a covalent network solid

7. The approximate boiling points for hydrogen compounds of some elements in the nitrogen family are $(SbH_3 - 15°C)$, $(AsH_3 - 62°C)$, $(PH_3 - 87°C)$, and $(NH_3 - 33°C)$. The best explanation for the fact that NH_3 does not follow the trend of the other hydrogen compounds is:

   (A) NH_3 is the only one to exhibit hydrogen bonding.
   (B) NH_3 is the only one that is water-soluble.
   (C) NH_3 is the only one that is nearly ideal in the gas phase.
   (D) NH_3 is the only one that is a base.

8. Why is it possible to solidify argon at a sufficiently low temperature?

   (A) London dispersion forces
   (B) covalent bonding
   (C) hydrogen bonding
   (D) metallic bonding

9. Which of the following best describes why diamond is so hard?

   (A) London dispersion forces
   (B) covalent bonding
   (C) hydrogen bonding
   (D) metallic bonding

10. A sample of a pure liquid is placed in an open container and heated to the boiling point. Which of the following may increase the boiling point of the liquid?

    (A) The moles of liquid are increased.
    (B) The size of the container is increased.
    (C) A vacuum is created over the liquid.
    (D) The container is sealed.

11. Which of the following best explains why 1-butanol, $CH_3CH_2CH_2CH_2OH$, has a higher surface tension than its isomer, diethyl ether, $CH_3CH_2OCH_2CH_3$?

   (A) the higher density of 1-butanol
   (B) the lower specific heat of 1-butanol
   (C) the lack of hydrogen bonding in 1-butanol
   (D) the presence of hydrogen bonding in 1-butanol

12. Pick the answer that most likely represents the substances' relative solubilities in water.

   (A) $CH_3CH_2CH_2CH_3$ < $CH_3CH_2CH_2OH$ < $HOCH_2CH_2OH$
   (B) $CH_3CH_2CH_2OH$ < $CH_3CH_2CH_2CH_3$ < $HOCH_2CH_2OH$
   (C) $CH_3CH_2CH_2CH_3$ < $HOCH_2CH_2OH$ < $CH_3CH_2CH_2OH$
   (D) $HOCH_2CH_2OH$ < $CH_3CH_2CH_2OH$ < $CH_3CH_2CH_2CH_3$

13. What is the energy change that accompanies the conversion of molecules in the gas phase to a liquid?

   (A) heat of condensation
   (B) heat of deposition
   (C) heat of sublimation
   (D) heat of fusion

14. Which of the following explains why the melting point of sodium chloride (NaCl 801°C) is lower than the melting point of calcium fluoride (CaF_2 1423°C)?

   (A) Sodium is more reactive than calcium is.
   (B) The chloride ion is smaller than the fluoride ion.
   (C) The charge on a sodium ion is less than the charge on a calcium ion.
   (D) The ratio of anions to cations is lower in sodium chloride.

Answers and Explanations for the Multiple-Choice Questions

1. **B**—This answer describes a metallic solid.

2. **C**—This answer describes an ionic solid.

3. **A**—This answer describes a covalent network solid.

4. **D**—This answers describes a solid consisting of discrete polar molecules. Even though HCl(aq) is a strong acid with ions in solution, there is no water here to lead to ionization.

5. **D**—Each of the carbon atoms is covalently bonded to four other carbon atoms.

6. **C**—Sulfur dioxide molecules are polar.

7. **A**—Hydrogen bonding occurs when hydrogen is directly bonded to F, O, and in this case N.

8. **A**—Argon is a noble gas; none of the other bonding choices is an option.

9. **B**—Diamond is a covalent network solid with a large number of strong covalent bonds between the carbon atoms.

10. **D**—The size of the container or the number of moles is irrelevant. Sealing the container will cause an increase in pressure that will increase the boiling point. A decrease in pressure will lower the boiling point.

11. **D**—The compound with the higher surface tension is the one with the stronger intermolecular force. The hydrogen bonding in 1-butanol is stronger than the dipole-dipole attractions in diethyl ether.

12. **A**—The sequence for these similar molecules is nonpolar, then one hydrogen bond, then two hydrogen bonds.

13. **A**—This change is condensation, so the energy is the heat of condensation.

14. **C**—The only applicable factor listed is the charge difference. The chloride ion is larger than the fluoride ion. The ion ratio is not important nor is the reactivity of the elements.

⟩ Rapid Review

- The state of matter in which a substance exists depends on the competition between the kinetic energy of the particles (proportional to temperature) and the strength of the intermolecular forces between the particles.

- The melting point is the temperature at which a substance goes from the solid to the liquid state and is the same as the freezing point.

- The boiling point is the temperature at which a substance goes from the liquid to the gaseous state. This takes place within the body of the liquid, unlike evaporation, which takes place only at the surface of the liquid.

- Sublimation is the conversion of a solid to a gas without ever having become a liquid. Deposition is the reverse process.

- Phase changes are changes of state.

- Intermolecular forces are the attractive or repulsive forces between atoms, molecules, or ions due to full or partial charges. Be careful not to confuse intermolecular forces with intramolecular forces, the forces within the molecule.

- Ion–dipole intermolecular forces occur between ions and polar molecules.

- Dipole–dipole intermolecular forces occur between polar molecules.

- Hydrogen bonds are intermolecular forces between dipoles in which there is a hydrogen atom attached to an N, O, or F atom.

- Ion-induced dipole intermolecular forces occur between an ion and a nonpolar molecule.

- London (dispersion) forces are intermolecular forces between nonpolar molecules.

- Liquids possess surface tension (liquids behaving as if they had a thin "skin" on their surface, due to unequal attraction of molecules at the surface of the liquid), viscosity (resistance to flow), and capillary action (flow up a small tube).

- Amorphous solids have very little structure in the solid state.

- Crystalline solids have a great deal of structure in the solid state.

- The crystal lattice of a crystalline solid is the regular ordering of the unit cells.

- Know the five types of crystalline solid: atomic, molecular, ionic, metallic, and network.

- Phase changes can be related to the strength of intermolecular forces.

CHAPTER 13

Solutions and Colligative Properties

IN THIS CHAPTER

Summary: A **solution** is a homogeneous mixture composed of a solvent and one or more solutes. The **solvent** is the substance that acts as the dissolving medium and is normally present in the greatest amount. Commonly the solvent is a liquid, but it doesn't have to be. Our atmosphere is a solution with nitrogen as the solvent; it is the gas present in the largest amount (79%). Many times, you will be dealing with a solution in which water is the solvent, an **aqueous solution**. The **solute** is the substance that the solvent dissolves and is normally present in the smaller amount. You may have more than one solute in a solution. For example, if you dissolved table salt (sodium chloride) and table sugar (sucrose) in water, you would have one solvent (water) and two solutes (sodium chloride and sucrose).

Some substances will dissolve in a particular solvent and others will not. There is a general rule in chemistry that states that "*like dissolves like.*" This general statement may serve as an answer in the multiple-choice questions, but does not serve as an explanation in the free-response questions. This simply means that polar substances (salts, alcohols, etc.) will dissolve in polar solvents such as water, and nonpolar solutes, such as iodine, will dissolve in nonpolar solvents such as carbon tetrachloride. The solubility of a particular solute is normally expressed in terms of grams solute per 100 mL of solvent (g/mL) at a specified temperature. The temperature must be specified because the solubility of a particular substance will vary with the temperature. Normally, the solubility of solids dissolving in liquids increases with increasing temperature, while the reverse is true for gases dissolving in liquids.

A solution in which one has dissolved the maximum amount of solute per given amount of solvent at a given temperature is called a **saturated solution**.

An **unsaturated solution** has less than the maximum amount of solute dissolved. Sometimes, if the temperature, purity of the solute and solvent, and other factors are just right, you might be able to dissolve more than the maximum amount of solute, resulting in a **supersaturated solution**. Supersaturated solutions are unstable, and sooner or later separation of the excess solute will occur, until a saturated solution and separated solute remain.

The formation of a solution depends on many factors, such as the nature of the solvent, the nature of the solute, the temperature, and the pressure. Some of these factors were addressed in the Reactions and Periodicity chapter. In general, the solubility of a solid or liquid will increase with temperature and be unaffected by pressure changes. The solubility of a gas will decrease with increasing temperature and will increase with increasing partial pressure of the gas (**Henry's law**).

Keywords and Equations

π = osmotic pressure

i = van't Hoff factor

K_f = molal freezing-point depression constant

K_b = molal boiling-point elevation constant

K_f for H_2O = 1.86 K kg mol^{-1}

K_b for H_2O = 0.512 K kg mol^{-1}

$\Delta T_f = iK_f$ molality

$\Delta T_b = iK_b$ molality

$\pi = iMRT$

molarity, M = moles solute per liter solution

molality, m = moles solute per kilogram solvent

Concentration Units

There are many ways of expressing the relative amounts of solute(s) and solvent in a solution. The terms *saturated*, *unsaturated*, and *supersaturated* give a qualitative measure, as do the terms *dilute* and *concentrated*. The term **dilute** refers to a solution that has a relatively small amount of solute in comparison to the amount of solvent. **Concentrated**, on the other hand, refers to a solution that has a relatively large amount of solute in comparison to the solvent. However, these terms are very subjective. If you dissolve 0.1 g of sucrose per liter of water, that solution would probably be considered dilute; 100 g of sucrose per liter would probably be considered concentrated. But, what about 25 g per liter—dilute or concentrated? In order to communicate effectively, chemists use quantitative ways of expressing the concentration of solutions. Several concentration units are useful, including percentage, molarity, and molality.

Percentage

One common way of expressing the relative amount of solute and solvent is through percentage, amount-per-hundred. Percentage can be expressed in three ways:

mass percent

mass/volume percent

volume/volume percent

Mass (Sometimes Called Weight) Percentage

The mass percentage of a solution is the mass of the solute divided by the mass of the solution, multiplied by 100% to get percentage. The mass is commonly measured in grams.

$$\text{mass \%} = (\text{grams of solute/grams solution}) \times 100\%$$

For example, a solution is prepared by dissolving 25.2 g of sodium chloride in 250.0 g of water. Calculate the mass percent of the solution.

Answer:

$$\text{mass \%} = \frac{(25.2 \text{ g solute})}{(25.2 + 250.0) \text{ g solution}} \times 100\% = 9.16\%$$

A common error is forgetting to add the solute and solvent masses together in the denominator.

When solutions of this type are prepared, the solute and solvent are weighed out separately and then mixed together to form a solution. The final volume of the solution is unknown.

Mass/Volume Percentage

The mass/volume percent of a solution is the mass of the solute divided by the volume of the solution, multiplied by 100% to yield percentage. The volume of the solution is generally expressed in milliliters.

$$\text{mass/volume \%} = (\text{grams solute/volume of solution}) \times 100\%$$

When mass/volume solutions are prepared, the grams of the solute are weighed out, dissolved, and diluted to the required volume.

For example, a solution is prepared by mixing 125.0 g of benzene with 250.0 g of toluene. The density of benzene is 0.8765 g/mL, and the density of toluene is 0.8669 g/mL. Determine the mass/volume percentage of the solution. Assume that the volumes are additive.

Answer:

First, determine the volume of the solution.

$$\begin{aligned}
\text{solution volume} &= (125.0 \text{ g benzene})(\text{mL}/0.8765 \text{ g benzene}) \\
&\quad + (250.0 \text{ g toluene})(\text{mL}/0.8669 \text{ g toluene}) \\
&= 431.0 \text{ mL}
\end{aligned}$$

Then

$$\text{mass \%} = \frac{(125.0 \text{ g benzene})}{431.0 \text{ mL solution}} \times 100\% = 29.00\%$$

Notice that it is not necessary to know the chemical formula of either constituent. A common error is forgetting to add the solute and solvent volumes together.

Volume/Volume Percentage

The third case is one in which both the solute and solvent are liquids. The volume percent of the solution is the volume of the solute divided by the volume of the solution, multiplied by 100% to generate the percentage.

$$\text{volume \%} = (\text{volume solute/volume solution}) \times 100\%$$

When volume percent solutions are prepared, the mL of the solute are diluted with solvent to the required volume.

For example, determine the volume percentage of carbon tetrachloride in a solution prepared by dissolving 100.0 mL of carbon tetrachloride and 100.0 mL of methylene chloride in 750.0 mL of chloroform. Assume the volumes are additive.

Answer:

$$\text{volume \%} = \frac{(100.0 \text{ mL carbon tetrachloride})}{(100.0 + 100.0 + 750.0) \text{ mL solution}} \times 100\% = 10.53\%$$

A common error is not to add all the volumes together to get the volume of the solution.

If the solute is ethyl alcohol and the solvent is water, then another concentration term is used, proof. The **proof** of an aqueous ethyl alcohol solution is twice the volume percent. A 45.0 volume % ethyl alcohol solution would be 90.0 proof.

Molarity

Percentage concentration is common in everyday life (3% hydrogen peroxide, 5% acetic acid, commonly called vinegar, etc.). The concentration unit most commonly used by chemists is molarity. **Molarity** (M) is the number of moles of solute per liter of solution.

$$M = \text{moles solute/liter solution}$$

In preparing a molar solution, the correct number of moles of solute (commonly converted to grams using the molar mass) is dissolved and diluted to the required volume.

Determine the molarity of sodium sulfate in a solution produced by dissolving 15.2 g of Na_2SO_4 in sufficient water to produce 750.0 mL of solution:

$$\text{molarity} = \frac{15.2 \text{ g } Na_2SO_4}{750.0 \text{ mL}} \times \frac{1 \text{ mol g } Na_2SO_4}{142 \text{ g } Na_2SO_4} \times \frac{1,000 \text{ mL}}{1L} = 0.143 \, M$$

The most common error is not being careful with the units. Grams must be converted to moles, and milliliters must be converted to liters.

Another way to prepare a molar solution is by dilution of a more concentrated solution to a more dilute one by adding solvent. The following equation can be used:

$$(M_{before})(V_{before}) = (M_{after})(V_{after})$$

In the preceding equation, *before* refers to before dilution and *after* refers to after dilution.

Let's see how to apply this relationship. Determine the final concentration when 500.0 mL of water is added to 400.0 mL of a 0.1111 M solution of HC1. Assume the volumes are additive.

$$M_{before} = 0.1111 \, M \qquad\qquad M_{after} = ?$$

$$V_{before} = 400.0 \text{ mL} \qquad\qquad V_{before} = (400.0 + 500.0) \text{ mL}$$

$$M_{after} = (M_{before})(V_{before})/(V_{after}) = (0.1111 \, M)(400.0 \text{ mL})/(900.0 \text{ mL})$$

$$= 0.04938 \, M$$

The most common error is forgetting to add the two volumes.

Molality

Sometimes the varying volumes of a solution's liquid component(s) due to changes in temperature present a problem. Many times volumes are not additive, but mass is additive. The chemist then resorts to defining concentration in terms of the molality. **Molality (m)** is defined as the moles of solute per kilogram of solvent.

$$m = \text{moles solute/kilograms solvent}$$

Notice that this equation uses kilograms of solvent, not solution. The other concentration units use mass or volume of the entire solution. Molal solutions use only the mass of the *solvent*. For dilute aqueous solutions, the molarity and the molality will be close to the same numerical value.

For example, ethylene glycol $(C_2H_6O_2)$ is used in antifreeze. Determine the molality of ethylene glycol in a solution prepared by adding 62.1 g of ethylene glycol to 100.0 g of water.

$$\text{molality} = \frac{62.1 \text{ g } C_2H_6O_2}{100.0 \text{ g } H_2O} \times \frac{1,000 \text{ g}}{1 \text{ kg}} \times \frac{1 \text{ mol } C_2H_6O_2}{62.1 \text{ g } C_2H_6O_2} = 10.0 \text{ } m \text{ } C_2H_6O_2$$

The most common error is to use the total grams in the denominator instead of just the grams of solvent.

Electrolytes and Nonelectrolytes

An **electrolyte** is a substance that, when dissolved in a solvent or melted, conducts an electrical current. A **nonelectrolyte** does not conduct a current when dissolved. The conduction of the electrical current is usually determined using a light bulb connected to a power source and two electrodes. The electrodes are placed in the aqueous solution or melt, and if a conducting medium is present, such as ions, the light bulb will light, indicating the substance is an electrolyte.

The ions that conduct the electrical current can result from a couple of sources. They may result from the dissociation of an ionically bonded substance (a salt). If sodium chloride (NaCl) is dissolved in water, it dissociates into the sodium cation (Na^+) and the chloride anion (Cl^-). But, certain covalently bonded substances may also produce ions if dissolved in water, a process called ionization. For example, acids, both inorganic and organic, will produce ions when dissolved in water. Some acids, such as hydrochloric acid (HCl), will essentially completely ionize. Others, such as acetic acid (CH_3COOH), will only partially ionize. They establish an equilibrium with the ions and the unionized species (see Chapter 15 for more on chemical equilibrium).

$$HCl(aq) \rightarrow H^+(aq) + Cl^-(aq) \qquad \text{100\% ionization}$$
$$CH_3COOH(aq) \rightleftharpoons H^+(aq) + CH_3COO^-(aq) \qquad \text{partial ionization}$$

Species such as HCl that completely ionize in water are called **strong electrolytes**, and those that only partially ionize are called **weak electrolytes**. Most soluble salts also fall into the strong electrolyte category.

Colligative Properties

Some of the properties of solutions depend on the chemical and physical nature of the individual solute. The blue color of a copper(II) sulfate solution and the sweetness of a sucrose solution are related to the properties of those solutes. However, some solution properties simply depend on the *number* of solute particles, not the type of solute. These properties are called **colligative properties** and include:

- vapor pressure lowering
- freezing-point depression
- boiling-point elevation
- osmotic pressure

Vapor Pressure Lowering

If a liquid is placed in a sealed container, molecules will evaporate from the surface of the liquid and eventually establish a gas phase over the liquid that is in equilibrium with the liquid phase. The pressure generated by this gas is the **vapor pressure** of the liquid. Vapor pressure is temperature dependent; the higher the temperature, the higher the vapor pressure. If the liquid is made a solvent by adding a nonvolatile solute, the vapor pressure of the resulting solution is always less than that of the pure liquid. The vapor pressure has been lowered by the addition of the solute; the amount of lowering is proportional to the number of solute particles added and is thus a colligative property.

Solute particles are evenly distributed throughout a solution, even at the surface. Thus, there are fewer solvent particles at the gas–liquid interface where evaporation takes place. Fewer solvent particles escape into the gas phase, and so the vapor pressure is lower. The higher the concentration of solute particles, the less solvent is at the interface and the lower the vapor pressure. This relationship is referred to as **Raoult's law**.

Freezing-Point Depression

The freezing point of a solution of a nonvolatile solute is always lower than the freezing point of the pure solvent. It is the number of solute particles that determines the amount of the lowering of the freezing point. The amount of lowering of the freezing point is proportional to the molality of the solute and is given by the equation

$$\Delta T_f = iK_f \text{ molality}$$

where ΔT_f is the number of degrees that the freezing point has been lowered (the difference in the freezing point of the pure solvent and the solution); K_f is the freezing-point depression constant (a constant of the individual solvent); the molality is the molality of the solute; and i is the van't Hoff factor—the ratio of the number of moles of particles released into solution per mole of solute dissolved. For a nonelectrolyte, such as sucrose, the van't Hoff factor would be 1. For an electrolyte, such as sodium chloride, you must take into consideration that if 1 mol of NaCl dissolves, 2 mol of particles would result (1 mol Na^+, 1 mol Cl^-). Therefore, the van't Hoff factor should be 2. However, because sometimes there is a pairing of ions in solution, the observed van't Hoff factor is slightly less (for example, it is 1.9 for a 0.05 m NaCl solution). The more dilute the solution, the closer the observed van't Hoff factor should be to the expected factor. If you can calculate the molality of the solution, you can also calculate the freezing point of the solution.

Let's learn to apply the preceding equation. Determine the freezing point of an aqueous solution containing 10.50 g of magnesium bromide in 200.0 g of water.

$$\Delta T = iK_f m = 3(1.86 \text{ K kg mol}^{-1}) \left[\frac{(10.50 \text{ g MgBr}_2)}{(200.0 \text{ g})} \frac{\frac{(1 \text{ mole MgBr}_2)}{184.113 \text{ g MgBr}_2}}{\left(\frac{1 \text{ kg}}{1,000 \text{ g}}\right)} \right]$$

$$= 1.59 \text{ K}$$

$$T_{fp} = (273.15 - 1.59) \text{ K} = 271.56 \text{ K} (= -1.59°\text{C})$$

The most common mistake is to forget to subtract the ΔT value from the normal freezing point.

The freezing-point depression technique is also commonly used to calculate the molar mass of a solute.

For example, a solution is prepared by dissolving 0.490 g of an unknown compound in 50.00 mL of water. The freezing point of the solution is –0.201°C. Assuming the compound is a nonelectrolyte, what is the molecular mass of the compound? Use 1.00 g/mL as the density of water.

$$m = \Delta T / K_f = 0.201 \text{ K}/(1.86 \text{ K kg mol}^{-1}) = 0.108 \text{ mol/kg}$$

$$50.00 \text{ mL } (1.00 \text{ g/mL}) (1 \text{ kg}/1,000 \text{ g}) = 0.0500 \text{ kg}$$

$$(0.108 \text{ mol/kg}) (0.0500 \text{ kg}) = 0.00540 \text{ mol}$$

$$0.490 \text{ g}/0.00540 \text{ mol} = 90.7 \text{ g/mol}$$

Many students make the mistake of stopping before they complete this problem.

Boiling-Point Elevation

Just as the freezing point of a solution of a nonvolatile solute is always lower than that of the pure solvent, the boiling point of a solution is always higher than the solvent's. Again, only the number of solute particles affects the boiling point. The mathematical relationship is similar to the one for the freezing-point depression above and is

$$\Delta T_b = iK_b \text{ molality}$$

where ΔT_b is the number of degrees the boiling point has been elevated (the difference between the boiling point of the pure solvent and the solution); K_b is the boiling-point elevation constant; the molality is the molality of the solute; and i is the van't Hoff factor. You can calculate a solution's boiling point if you know the molality of the solution. If you know the amount of the boiling-point elevation and the molality of the solution, you can calculate the value of the van't Hoff factor, i.

For example, determine the boiling point of a solution prepared by adding 15.00 g of NaCl to 250.0 g water. ($K_b = 0.512$ K kg mol^{-1})

$$\Delta T = iK_b m = 2(0.512 \text{ K kg mol}^{-1}) \left[\dfrac{(15.00 \text{ g NaCl}) \left(\dfrac{1 \text{ mole NaCl}}{58.44 \text{ g NaCl}} \right)}{(250.0 \text{ g}) \left(\dfrac{1 \text{ kg}}{1{,}000 \text{ g}} \right)} \right]$$

$$= 1.05 \text{ K}$$
$$T_{bp} = (373.15 + 1.05)\text{K} = 374.20 \text{ K} (= 101.05°\text{C})$$

A 1.00 molal aqueous solution of trichloroacetic acid (CCl_3COOH) is heated to the boiling point. The solution has a boiling point of 100.18°C.

Determine the van't Hoff factor for trichloroacetic acid (K_b for water = 0.512 K kg mol^{-1}).

$$\Delta T = (101.18 - 100.00) = 0.18°\text{C} = 0.18 \text{ K}$$

$$i = \Delta T/K_b m = 0.18 \text{ K}/(0.512 \text{ K kg mol}^{-1})(1.00 \text{ mol kg}^{-1}) = 0.35$$

A common mistake is the assumption that the van't Hoff factor must be a whole number. This is true only for strong electrolytes at very low concentrations.

Osmotic Pressure

If you were to place a solution and a pure solvent in the same container but separate them by a **semipermeable membrane** (which allows the passage of some molecules, but not all particles) you would observe that the level of the solvent side would decrease while the solution side would increase. This indicates that the solvent molecules are passing through the semipermeable membrane, a process called **osmosis**. Eventually the system would reach equilibrium, and the difference in levels would remain constant. The difference in the two levels is related to the **osmotic pressure**. In fact, one could exert a pressure on the solution side exceeding the osmotic pressure, and solvent molecules could be forced back through the semipermeable membrane into the solvent side. This process is called **reverse osmosis** and is the basis of the desalination of seawater for drinking purposes. These processes are shown in Figure 13.1.

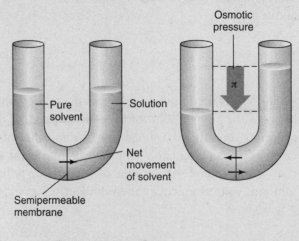

Figure 13.1   Osmotic pressure.

The osmotic pressure is a colligative property and mathematically can be represented as $\pi = (nRT/V)\, i$, where π is the osmotic pressure in atmospheres; n is the number of moles of solute; R is the ideal gas constant 0.0821 L · atm/K · mol; T is the Kelvin temperature; V is the volume of the solution; and i is the van't Hoff factor. Measurements of the osmotic pressure can be used to calculate the molar mass of a solute. This is especially useful in determining the molar mass of large molecules such as proteins.

For example, a solution prepared by dissolving 8.95 mg of a gene fragment in 35.0 mL of water has an osmotic pressure of 0.335 torr at 25.0°C. Assuming the fragment is a nonelectrolyte, determine the molar mass of the gene fragment.

Rearrange $\pi = (nRT/V)\, i$ to $n = \pi\, V/RT$ ($i = 1$ for a nonelectrolyte)

$$\frac{(0.335 \text{ torr})\,(35.0 \text{ mL})}{\left(0.0821\dfrac{\text{L atm}}{\text{mol K}}\right)(298.2 \text{ K})}\left(\frac{1 \text{ atm}}{760 \text{ torr}}\right)\left(\frac{1 \text{ L}}{1{,}000 \text{ mL}}\right) = 6.30\times10^{-7}\,\text{mol}$$

$$\frac{(8.95 \text{ mg})\,(0.001 \text{ g/mg})}{6.30\times10^{-7}\,\text{mol}} = 1.42\times10^{4}\,\text{g/mol}$$

Colloids

If you watch a glass of muddy water, you will see particles in the water settling out. This is a heterogeneous mixture where the particles are large (in excess of 1,000 nm), and it is called a **suspension**. In contrast, dissolving sodium chloride in water results in a true homogeneous **solution**, with solute particles less than 1 nm in diameter. True solutions do not settle out because of the very small particle size. But, there are mixtures whose solute diameters fall in between solutions and suspensions. These are called **colloids** and have solute particles in the range of 1 to 1,000 nm diameter. Table 13.1 shows some representative colloids.

Many times it is difficult to distinguish a colloid from a true solution. The most common method is to shine a light through the mixture under investigation. A light shone through a true solution is invisible, but a light shone through a colloid is visible because the light reflects off the larger colloid particles. This is called the **Tyndall effect**.

Table 13.1 Common Colloid Types

COLLOID TYPE	SUBSTANCE DISPERSED	DISPERSING MEDIUM	EXAMPLES
aerosol	solid	gas	smoke
aerosol	liquid	gas	fog
solid foam	gas	solid	marshmallow
foam	gas	liquid	whipped cream
emulsion	liquid	liquid	milk, mayonnaise
solid emulsion	liquid	solid	cheese, butter
sol	solid	liquid	paint, gelatin

Experiments

Experimental procedures for solutions involve concentration units. Keeping close track of the units may simplify the problem.

Concentration problems are concerned with the definitions of the various units. It is possible to calculate the mass and/or volume of the solvent and solute by taking the difference between the final and initial measurements. The density, if not given, is calculated, not measured. It is important to recognize the difference between the values that must be measured and those that can be calculated. Moles are also calculated, not measured.

Do not forget that nearly all the concentration units use the total for the solution in the denominator. For these units it is important to remember to combine the quantities for the solvent and all solutes present.

Common Mistakes to Avoid

1. In molarity problems, be sure to use liters of **solution**.
2. Make sure your units cancel, leaving you with the units desired in your final answer.
3. Round off your final numerical answers to the correct number of significant figures.
4. Remember, most molecular compounds—compounds containing only nonmetals—do not ionize in solution. Acids are the most common exceptions.

〉 Review Questions

Use these questions to review the content of this chapter and practice for the AP Chemistry exam. First are 14 multiple-choice questions similar to what you will encounter in Section I of the AP Chemistry exam. Following those are two long free-response questions like the ones in Section II of the exam. To make these questions an even more authentic practice for the actual exam, time yourself following the instructions provided.

Multiple-Choice Questions

Answer the following questions in 20 minutes. You may not use a calculator. You may use the periodic table and the equation sheet at the back of this book.

1. A solution is prepared by dissolving 1.25 g of an unknown substance in 100.0 mL of water. Which procedure from the following list could be used to determine whether the solute is an electrolyte?

(A) Measure the specific heat of the solution.
(B) Measure the volume of the solution.
(C) Measure the freezing point of the solution.
(D) Determine the specific heat of the solution.

2. What is the final K^+ concentration in a solution made by mixing 300.0 mL of 1.0 M KNO_3 and 700.0 mL of 2.0 M K_3PO_4?

(A) 4.5 M
(B) 5.0 M
(C) 3.0 M
(D) 2.0 M

3. Strontium sulfate, $SrSO_4$, will precipitate when a solution of sodium sulfate is added to a strontium nitrate solution. What will be the strontium ion, Sr^{2+}, concentration remaining after 30.0 mL of 0.10 M Na_2SO_4 solution are added to 70.0 mL of 0.20 M $Sr(NO_3)_2$ solution?

(A) 0.14 M
(B) 0.15 M
(C) 0.11 M
(D) 0.20 M

4. Which of the following is a strong electrolyte when it is mixed with water?

(A) HNO_2
(B) KNO_3
(C) C_2H_5OH
(D) CH_3COOH

5. A solution with a total chloride ion, Cl^-, concentration of 1.0 M is needed. Initially, the solution is 0.30 M in $MgCl_2$. How many moles of solid $CaCl_2$ must be added to 400 mL of the $MgCl_2$ solution to achieve the desired concentration of chloride ion?

(A) 0.10
(B) 0.080
(C) 0.20
(D) 0.15

6. Assuming the volumes are additive, what is the final $H^+(aq)$ concentration produced by adding 30.0 mL of 0.50 M HNO_3 to 70.0 mL of 1.00 M HCl?

(A) 0.75 M
(B) 1.50 M
(C) 1.25 M
(D) 0.85 M

7. To prepare 3.0 L of a 0.20 molar K_3PO_4 solution (molecular weight 212 g/mol), a student should follow which of the following procedures?

(A) The student should weigh 42 g of solute and add sufficient water to obtain a final volume of 3.0 L.
(B) The student should weigh 42 g of solute and add 3.0 Kg of water.
(C) The student should weigh 130 g of solute and add sufficient water to obtain a final volume of 3.0 L.
(D) The student should weigh 42 g of solute and add 3.0 L of water.

8. How many grams of $MgSO_4$ (molecular weight 120.4 g/mol) are in 100.0 mL of a 5.0 molar solution?

(A) 600 g
(B) 5.0 g
(C) 12 g
(D) 60.0 g

9. How many milliliters of concentrated nitric acid (16.0 molar HNO_3) are needed to prepare 0.500 L of 6.0 molar HNO_3?

(A) 0.19 mL
(B) 250 mL
(C) 375 mL
(D) 190 mL

10. A solution has 10 grams of urea in 100 grams of solution. Which item(s) from the following list are needed to calculate the molarity of this solution?

(A) the density of the solution and the molecular weight of urea
(B) the density of the solution and the molecular weight of urea
(C) the density of the solvent and the density of the solution
(D) the molecular weight of urea and the density of the solvent

11. Which of the following aqueous solutions would have the greatest conductivity?

(A) 0.2 M NaOH
(B) 0.2 M RbCl
(C) 0.2 M K_3PO_4
(D) 0.2 M HNO_2

12. How many milliliters of water must be added to 50.0 mL of 10.0 M HNO_3 to prepare 4.00 M HNO_3, assuming that the volumes of nitric acid and water are additive?

(A) 50.0 mL
(B) 125 mL
(C) 500 mL
(D) 75.0 mL

13. The best method to isolate pure $MgSO_4$ from an aqueous solution of $MgSO_4$ is to:

(A) evaporate the solution to dryness.
(B) titrate the solution.
(C) electrolyze the solution.
(D) use paper chromatography.

14. Pick the conditions that would yield the highest concentration of $N_2(g)$ in water.

(A) partial pressure of gas = 1.0 atm; temperature of water = 25°C
(B) partial pressure of gas = 0.50 atm; temperature of water = 55°C
(C) partial pressure of gas = 2.0 atm; temperature of water = 25°C
(D) partial pressure of gas = 2.0 atm; temperature of water = 85°C

Answers and Explanations for the Multiple-Choice Questions

1. C—If the solute is an electrolyte, the solution will conduct electricity and the van't Hoff factor, *i*, will be greater than 1. The choices do not include any conductivity measurements; therefore, the van't Hoff factor would need to be determined. This determination is done by measuring the osmotic pressure, the boiling-point elevation, or the freezing-point depression. The freezing-point depression may be found by measuring the freezing point of the solution.

2. A—The potassium ion contribution from the KNO_3 is:

(300.0 mL)(1.0 mol KNO_3/1,000 mL)(1 mol K^+/ 1 mol KNO_3) = 0.300 mol K^+

The potassium ion contribution from K_3PO_4 is:

(700.0 mL)(2.0 mol K_3PO_4/1,000 mL)(3 mol K^+/ 1 mol K_3PO_4) = 4.20 mol K^+

The total potassium is 4.50 mol in a total volume of 1.000 L. Thus, the potassium concentration is 4.50 *M*.

3. C—The reaction is:

$$Sr^{2+}(aq) + SO_4^{2-}(aq) \rightarrow SrSO_4(s)$$

The strontium nitrate solution contains:

(70.0 mL)(0.20 mol $Sr(NO_3)_2$/1,000 mL) × (1 mol Sr^{2+}/1 mol $Sr(NO_3)_2$) = 0.014 mol Sr^{2+}

The sodium sulfate solution contains:

(30.0 mL)(0.10 mol Na_2SO_4/1,000 mL)(1 mol SO_4^{2-}/1 mol Na_2SO_4) = 0.0030 mol SO_4^{2-}

The strontium and sulfate ions react in a 1:1 ratio, so 0.0030 mol of sulfate ion will combine with 0.0030 mol of strontium ion, leaving 0.011 mol of strontium in a total volume of 100.0 mL. The final strontium ion concentration is:

$$\left(\frac{0.011 \text{ mol } Sr^{2+}}{100.0 \text{ mL}} \right)\left(\frac{1 \text{ mL}}{0.001 \text{ L}} \right)$$

4. B—A (nitrous acid) and D (acetic acid) are weak acids. Weak acids and bases are weak electrolytes. C (ethanol) is a nonelectrolyte. Potassium nitrate (B) is a water-soluble ionic compound, which is normally a strong electrolyte.

5. B—The number of moles of chloride ion needed is:

(400 mL)(1.0 mol Cl^-/1,000 mL) = 0.40 mol Cl^-

The initial number of moles of chloride ion in the solution is:

(400 mL)(0.30 mol $MgCl_2$/1,000 mL)(2 mol Cl^-/ mol $MgCl_2$) = 0.24 mol Cl^-

The number of moles needed = [(0.40 − 0.24) mol Cl^-](1 mol $CaCl_2$/2 mol Cl^-) = 0.080 mol

6. D—Both of the acids are strong acids and yield 1 mol of H^+ each. Calculate the number of moles of H^+ produced by each of the acids. Divide the total number of moles by the final volume. (30.0 mL)(0.50 mol H^+/1,000 mL) + (70.0 mL) × (1.00 mol H^+/1,000 mL) = 0.085 mol H^+

$$\left(\frac{0.085 \text{ mol } H^+}{100.0 \text{ mL}} \right)\left(\frac{1 \text{ mL}}{0.001 \text{ L}} \right)$$

7. **C**—To produce a molar solution of any type, the final volume must be the desired volume. This eliminates answer D. B involves mass of water instead of volume. A calculation of the required mass will allow a decision between A and C.

$$(3.0 \text{ L})(0.20 \text{ mol K}_3\text{PO}_4/\text{L})(212 \text{ g K}_3\text{PO}_4/ 1 \text{ mol K}_3\text{PO}_4) = 130 \text{ g K}_3\text{PO}_4$$

8. **D**—$(5.0 \text{ mol MgSO}_4/1{,}000 \text{ mL})(100.0 \text{ mL}) \times (120.4 \text{ g MgSO}_4/\text{mol MgSO}_4) = 60.0 \text{ g MgSO}_4$

9. **D**—This is a dilution problem. $V_{\text{before}} = (M_{\text{after}})(V_{\text{after}})/(M_{\text{before}})$

$$(6.0 \text{ M HNO}_3)(0.500 \text{ L})(1{,}000 \text{ mL}/1 \text{ L})/ (16.0 \text{ M HNO}_3) = 190 \text{ mL}$$

10. **A**—To calculate the molarity, the moles of urea and the volume of the solution are necessary. The density of the solution and the mass of the solution give the volume of the solution (it may be necessary to convert to liters). The mass of urea and the molecular weight of urea give the moles of urea.

11. **C**—The strong electrolyte with the greatest concentration of ions is the best conductor. D is a weak electrolyte, not a strong electrolyte. The number of ions for the strong electrolytes may be found by simply counting the ions: A – 2, B – 2, C – 4. The best conductor has the greatest value when the molarity is multiplied by the number of ions.

12. **D**—This is a dilution problem. $V_{\text{after}} = (M_{\text{before}} V_{\text{before}})/(M_{\text{after}})$

$$(10.0 \text{ M HNO}_3 \times 50.0 \text{ mL})/(4.0 \text{ M HNO}_3) = 125 \text{ mL}$$

The final volume is 125 mL. Since the original volume was 50.0 mL, an additional 75.0 mL must be added.

13. **A**—Solutions cannot be separated by titrations or filtering. Electrolysis of the solution would produce hydrogen and oxygen gas. Chromatography might achieve a minimal separation.

14. **C**—The solubility of a gas is increased by increasing the partial pressure of the gas and by lowering the temperature.

Free-Response Questions

Question 1

You have 5 minutes to answer the following two-part question. You may use a calculator and the tables in the back of the book.

Five beakers each containing 100.0 mL of an aqueous solution are on a lab bench. The solutions are all at 25°C. Solution 1 contains 0.20 M KNO$_3$. Solution 2 contains 0.10 M BaCl$_2$. Solution 3 contains 0.15 M C$_2$H$_4$(OH)$_2$. Solution 4 contains 0.20 M (NH$_4$)$_2$SO$_4$. Solution 5 contains 0.25 M KMnO$_4$.

(a) Which solution has the lowest pH? Explain.

(b) Which solution would be the poorest conductor of electricity? Explain.

Question 2

You have 15 minutes to answer the following four-part question. You may use a calculator and the tables in the back of the book.

Five beakers are placed in a row on a countertop. Each beaker is half filled with a 0.20 M aqueous solution. The solutes, in order, are (1) potassium sulfate, K$_2$SO$_4$, (2) methyl alcohol, CH$_3$OH, (3) sodium carbonate, Na$_2$CO$_3$, (4) ammonium chromate, (NH$_4$)$_2$CrO$_4$, and (5) barium chloride, BaCl$_2$. The solutions are all at 25°C. Answer the following questions with respect to the five solutions listed above.

(a) Which solution will form a precipitate when ammonium chromate is added to it?

(b) Which solution is the most basic? Explain.

(c) Which solution would be the poorest conductor of electricity? Explain.

(d) Which solution is colored?

Answers and Explanations for the Free-Response Questions

Question 1

(a) Solution 4, because the ammonium ion is a weak acid

You get 1 point for picking solution 4 and 1 point for saying the ammonium ion (NH_4^+) is a weak acid, or that it undergoes hydrolysis.

(b) Solution 3, because the solute is a nonelectrolyte

Give yourself 1 point for picking solution 3 and 1 point for saying it is a nonelectrolyte or that it does not ionize.

Question 2

(a) The ammonium ion, from the ammonium chromate, will not form a precipitate since most ammonium compounds are water soluble. Therefore, the precipitate must contain the chromate ion combined with a cation from one of the solutions. Solution (2) is a nonelectrolyte; therefore, there are no cations present to combine with the chromate ion. The potassium and sodium ions, from solutions (1) and (3), give soluble salts like the ammonium ion. This only leaves solution (5), barium chloride, which will give a precipitate. The formula of the precipitate is $BaCrO_4$.

You get 1 point for picking the correct solution.

(b) Solution (3), sodium carbonate, is the most basic. Since the carbonate ion is the conjugate base of a weak acid, it will undergo significant hydrolysis to produce a basic solution.

You get 1 point for picking the correct solution and 1 point for the correct explanation.

(c) Methyl alcohol is a nonelectrolyte, so its solutions do not conduct electricity. The remaining solutions contain ionic salts, which in general are electrolytes in solution.

You get 1 point for picking the correct solution and 1 point for the correct formula for the explanation.

(d) Solution (4), ammonium chromate, is yellow. Most solutions containing a transition metal ion are colored.

You get 1 point for picking the correct solution.

Total your points for the different parts. There are 6 points possible.

❯ Rapid Review

- A solution is a homogeneous mixture composed of a solvent and one or more solutes. A solute is a substance that dissolves in the solvent and is normally present in smaller amount.

- The general rule of solubility is "like dissolves like." This means that polar solvents dissolve polar solutes and nonpolar solvents dissolve nonpolar solutes. Remember, however, that simply quoting this rule will not be sufficient as an explanation in the free-response section.

- A saturated solution is one in which the maximum amount of solute is dissolved for a given amount of solvent at a given temperature. Any solution with less than the maximum solute is called unsaturated. A solution with greater than maximum solute is supersaturated (an unstable state).

- For the chemist the most useful unit of concentration is molarity (M), which is the moles of solute per liter of solution. Know how to work molarity problems. Be careful not to confuse molarity, M or [ ], with moles, n or mol.

- Electrolytes conduct an electrical current when melted or dissolved in a solvent, whereas nonelectrolytes do not.

- A colloid is a mixture in which the solute particle size is intermediate between a true solution and a suspension. If a light is shone through a colloid, the light beam is visible. This is the Tyndall effect.

CHAPTER 14

Kinetics

IN THIS CHAPTER

Summary: Thermodynamics often can be used to predict whether a reaction will occur spontaneously, but it gives very little information about the speed at which a reaction occurs. **Kinetics** is the study of the speed of reactions and is largely an experimental science. Some general qualitative ideas about reaction speed may be developed, but accurate quantitative relationships require experimental data to be collected.

For a chemical reaction to occur, there must be a collision between the reactant particles. That collision is necessary to transfer kinetic energy, to break reactant chemical bonds and reform product ones. If the collision doesn't transfer enough energy, no reaction will occur. And the collision must take place with the proper orientation at the correct place on the molecule, the reactive site.

Five factors affect the rates of chemical reaction:
1. **Nature of the reactants**—Large, complex molecules tend to react more slowly than smaller ones because statistically there is a greater chance of collisions occurring somewhere else on the molecule, rather than at the reactive site.
2. **The temperature**—Temperature is a measure of the average kinetic energy of the molecules. The higher the temperature, the higher the kinetic energy and the greater the chance that enough energy will be transferred to cause the reaction. Also, the higher the temperature, the greater the number of collisions and the greater the chance of a collision at the reactive site.
3. **The concentration of reactants**—The higher the concentration of reactants, the greater the chance of collision and (normally) the greater the reaction rate. For gaseous reactants, the pressure is directly related to the concentration; the greater the pressure, the greater the reaction rate.

4. **Physical state of reactants**—When reactants are mixed in the same physical state, the reaction rates should be higher than if they are in different states, because there is a greater chance of collision. Also, gases and liquids tend to react faster than solids because of the increase in surface area. The more chance for collision, the faster the reaction rate.

5. **Catalysts**—A **catalyst** is a substance that speeds up the reaction rate and is (at least theoretically) recoverable at the end of the reaction in an unchanged form. Catalysts accomplish this by reducing the activation energy of the reaction. **Activation energy** is that minimum amount of energy that must be supplied to the reactants in order to initiate or start the reaction. Many times the activation energy is supplied by the kinetic energy of the reactants.

> KEY IDEA

Keywords and Equations

$\ln[A]_t - \ln[A]_0 = -kt$ (first order)

$\dfrac{1}{[A]_t} - \dfrac{1}{[A]_0} = kt$ (second order)

$t_{1/2} = \dfrac{\ln 2}{k} = \dfrac{0.693}{k}$

$\ln k = \dfrac{-E_a}{R}\left(\dfrac{1}{T}\right) + \ln A$

t = time (seconds)
E_a = activation energy
k = rate constant
A = frequency factor
Gas constant, $R = 8.314/\text{J mol}^{-1}\,\text{K}^{-1}$

Rates of Reaction

The rate (or speed) of reaction is related to the change in concentration of either a reactant or product with time. Consider the general reaction: $2A + B \rightarrow C + 3D$. As the reaction proceeds, the concentrations of reactants A and B will decrease and the concentrations of products C and D will increase. Thus, the rate can be expressed in the following ways:

$$\text{Rate} = -\frac{1}{2}\frac{\Delta[A]}{\Delta t} = -\frac{\Delta[B]}{\Delta t} = \frac{\Delta[C]}{\Delta t} = \frac{1}{3}\frac{\Delta[D]}{\Delta t}$$

The first two expressions involving the reactants are negative, because their concentrations will decrease with time. The square brackets represent moles per liter concentration (molarity).

The rate of reaction decreases during the course of the reaction. The rate that is calculated above can be expressed as the average rate of reaction over a given time frame or, more commonly, as the initial reaction rate—the rate of reaction at the instant the reactants are mixed.

The Rate Equation

The rate of reaction may depend upon reactant concentration, product concentration, and temperature. Cases in which the product concentration affects the rate of reaction are rare and are not covered on the AP exam. Therefore, we will not address those reactions. We will discuss temperature effects on the reaction later in this chapter. For the time being, let's just consider those cases in which the reactant concentration may affect the speed of reaction. For the general reaction: $a\,A + b\,B + \ldots \rightarrow c\,C + d\,D + \ldots$ where the lowercase letters are the coefficients in the balanced chemical equation; the uppercase letters stand for the reactant; and product chemical species and initial rates are used, the rate equation (rate law) is written:

$$\text{Rate} = k[A]^m[B]^n \ldots$$

In this expression, k is the **rate constant**—a constant for each chemical reaction at a given temperature. The exponents m and n, called the **orders of reaction**, indicate what effect a change in concentration of that reactant species will have on the reaction rate. Say, for example, $m = 1$ and $n = 2$. That means that if the concentration of reactant A is doubled, then the rate will also double ($[2]^1 = 2$), and if the concentration of reactant B is doubled, then the rate will increase fourfold ($[2]^2 = 4$). We say that it is first order with respect to A and second order with respect to B. If the concentration of a reactant is doubled and that has no effect on the rate of reaction, then the reaction is zero order with respect to that reactant ($[2]^0 = 1$). Many times the overall order of reaction is calculated; it is simply the sum of the individual coefficients, third order in this example. The rate equation would then be shown as:

$$\text{Rate} = k[A][B]^2 \text{ (If the exponent is 1, it is generally not shown.)}$$

It is important to realize that the rate law (the rate, the rate constant, and the orders of reaction) is determined experimentally. Do not use the balanced chemical equation to determine the rate law.

The rate of reaction may be measured in a variety of ways, including taking the slope of the concentration versus time plot for the reaction. Once the rate has been determined, the orders of reaction can be determined by conducting a series of reactions in which the reactant species concentrations are changed one at a time, and mathematically determining the effect on the reaction rate. Once the orders of reaction have been determined, it is easy to calculate the rate constant.

For example, consider the reaction:

$$2\,NO(g) + O_2(g) \rightarrow 2\,NO_2(g)$$

The following kinetics data were collected:

Experiment	Initial [NO]	Initial [O_2]	Rate of NO_2 formation (*M*/s)
1	0.01	0.01	0.05
2	0.02	0.01	0.20
3	0.01	0.02	0.10

There are a couple of ways to interpret the data to generate the rate equation. If the numbers involved are simple (as above and on most tests, including the AP exam), you can reason out the orders of reaction. You can see that in going from experiment 1 to experiment 2, the [NO] was doubled, ([O_2] held constant), and the rate increased fourfold. This means that the reaction is second order with respect to NO. Comparing experiments 1 and 3, you see that the [O_2] was doubled, ([NO] was held constant), and the rate doubled.

Therefore, the reaction is first order with respect to O_2 and the rate equation can be written as:

$$\text{Rate} = k[NO]^2[O_2]$$

The rate constant can be determined by substituting the values of the concentrations of NO and O_2 from any of the experiments into the rate equation above and solving for k.
Using experiment 1:

$$0.05\ M/s = k(0.01\ M)^2(0.01\ M)$$

$$k = (0.05\ M/s)(0.01\ M)^2(0.01\ M)$$

$$k = 5 \times 10^4/M^2s$$

Sometimes, because of the numbers' complexity, you must set up the equations mathematically. The ratio of the rate expressions of two experiments will be used in determining the reaction orders. The equations will be chosen so that the concentration of only one reactant has changed while the others remain constant. In the example above, the ratio of experiments 1 and 2 will be used to determine the effect of a change of the concentration of NO on the rate, and then experiments 1 and 3 will be used to determine the effect of O_2. Experiments 2 and 3 cannot be used, because both chemical species have changed concentration.

Remember: In choosing experiments to compare, choose two in which the concentration of only one reactant has changed while the others have remained constant.

 KEY IDEA

Comparing experiments 1 and 2:

$$\frac{0.05\ M/s = k[0.01]^m[0.01]^n}{0.20\ M/s = [0.02]^m[0.01]^n}$$

Canceling the rate constants and the $[0.01]^n$ and simplifying:

$$\frac{1}{4} = \left(\frac{1}{2}\right)^m$$

$$m = 2 \text{ (use logarithms to solve for } m)$$

Comparing experiments 1 and 3:

$$\frac{0.05\ M/s = k[0.01]^m[0.01]^n}{0.10\ M/s = [0.01]^m[0.02]^n}$$

Canceling the rate constants and the $[0.01]^n$ and simplifying:

$$\frac{1}{2} = \left(\frac{1}{2}\right)^n$$

$$n = 1$$

Writing the rate equation:

$$\text{Rate} = k[NO]^2[O_2]$$

Again, the rate constant k could be determined by choosing any of the three experiments, substituting the concentrations, rate, and orders into the rate expression, and then solving for k.

Integrated Rate Laws

Thus far, only cases in which instantaneous data are used in the rate expression have been shown. These expressions allow us to answer questions concerning the speed of the reaction at a particular moment, but not questions about how long it might take to use up a certain reactant, etc. If changes in the concentration of reactants or products over time are taken into account, as in the **integrated rate laws**, these questions can be answered. Consider the following reaction:

$$A \rightarrow B$$

Assuming that this reaction is first order, then the rate of reaction can be expressed as the change in concentration of reactant A with time:

$$\text{Rate} = -\frac{\Delta[A]}{\Delta t}$$

and also as the rate law:

$$\text{Rate} = k[A]$$

Setting these terms equal to each other gives:

$$-\frac{\Delta[A]}{\Delta t} = k[A]$$

and integrating over time gives:

$$\ln[A]_t - \ln[A]_0 = -kt$$

where ln is the natural logarithm, $[A]_0$ is the concentration of reactant A at time = 0, and $[A]_t$ is the concentration of reactant A at some time t.

If the reaction is second order in A, then the following equation can be derived using the same procedure:

$$\frac{1}{[A]_t} - \frac{1}{[A]_0} = kt$$

Consider the following problem: Hydrogen iodide, HI, decomposes through a second-order process to the elements. The rate constant is $2.40 \times 10^{-21}/M$ s at 25°C. How long will it take for the concentration of HI to drop from 0.200 M to 0.190 M at 25°C?

Answer:

1.10×10^{20} s. In this problem, $k = 2.40 \times 10^{-21}/M$ s, $[A]_0 = 0.200$ M, and $[A]_t = 0.190$ M. You can simply insert the values and solve for t, or you first can rearrange the equation to give $t = [1/[A]_t - 1/[A]_0]/k$. You will get the same answer in either case. If you get a negative answer, you interchanged $[A]_t$ and $[A]_0$. A common mistake is to use the first-order equation instead of the second-order equation. The problem will always give you the information needed to determine whether the first-order or second-order equation is required.

The order of reaction can be determined graphically through the use of the integrated rate law. If a plot of the ln[A] versus time yields a straight line, then the reaction is first order with respect to reactant A. If a plot of $\frac{1}{[A]}$ versus time yields a straight line, then the reaction is second order with respect to reactant A.

The reaction **half-life**, $t_{1/2}$, is the amount of time that it takes for a reactant concentration to decrease to one-half its initial concentration. For a first-order reaction, the half-life is a constant, independent of reactant concentration, and can be shown to have the following mathematical relationship:

$$t_{1/2} = \frac{\ln 2}{k} = \frac{0.693}{k}$$

For second-order reactions, the half-life does depend on the reactant concentration and can be calculated using the following formula:

$$t_{1/2} = \frac{1}{k[A]_0}$$

This means that as a second-order reaction proceeds, the half-life increases.

Radioactive decay is a first-order process, and the half-lives of the radioisotopes are well documented (see the chapter on Nuclear Chemistry for a discussion of half-lives with respect to nuclear reactions).

Consider the following problem: The rate constant for the radioactive decay of thorium-232 is 5.0×10^{-11}/year. Determine the half-life of thorium-232.

Answer: 1.4×10^{10} yr.

This is a radioactive decay process. Radioactive decay follows first-order kinetics. The solution to the problem simply requires the substitution of the k-value into the appropriate equation:

$$t_{1/2} = 0.693/k = 0.693/5.0 \times 10^{-11} \, yr^{-1} = 1.386 \times 10^{10} yr$$

which rounds (correct significant figures) to the answer reported.

Consider another case: Hydrogen iodide, HI, decomposes through a second-order process to the elements. The rate constant is $2.40 \times 10^{-21}/M$ s at 25°C. What is the half-life for this decomposition for a 0.200 M of HI at 25°C?

Answer: 2.08×10^{21} s.

The problem specifies that this is a second-order process. Thus, you must simply enter the appropriate values into the second-order half-life equation:

$$t_{1/2} = 1/k[A]_0 = 1/(2.40 \times 10^{-21}/M \, s)(0.200 \, M) = 2.08333 \times 10^{21} \text{ seconds}$$

which rounds to the answer reported.

If you are unsure about your work in either of these problems, just follow your units. You are asked for time, so your answer must have time units only and no other units.

Activation Energy

A change in the temperature at which a reaction is taking place affects the rate constant k. As the temperature increases, the value of the rate constant increases and the reaction is faster. The Swedish scientist Arrhenius derived a relationship in 1889 that related the rate constant and temperature. The Arrhenius equation has the form: $k = Ae^{-Ea/RT}$ where k is the rate constant, A is a term called the frequency factor that accounts for molecular orientation, e is the natural logarithm base, R is the universal gas constant 8.314 J mol K^{-1}, T is the Kelvin temperature, and E_a is the **activation energy**, the minimum amount of energy that is needed to initiate or start a chemical reaction.

The Arrhenius equation is most commonly used to calculate the activation energy of a reaction. One way this can be done is to plot the ln k versus $1/T$. This gives a straight line whose slope is $-E_a/R$. Knowing the value of R allows the calculation of the value of E_a.

Normally, high activation energies are associated with slow reactions. Anything that can be done to lower the activation energy of a reaction will tend to speed up the reaction.

Reaction Mechanisms

In the introduction to this chapter, we discussed how chemical reactions occurred. Recall that before a reaction can occur there must be a collision between one reactant with the proper orientation at the reactive site of another reactant that transfers enough energy to provide the activation energy. However, many reactions do not take place in quite this simple a way. Many reactions proceed from reactants to products through a sequence of reactions. This sequence of reactions is called the **reaction mechanism**. For example, consider the reaction

$$A + 2B \rightarrow E + F$$

Most likely, E and F are not formed from the simple collision of an A and two B molecules. This reaction might follow this reaction sequence:

$$A + B \rightarrow C$$

$$C + B \rightarrow D$$

$$D \rightarrow E + F$$

If you add together the three equations above, you will get the overall equation $A + 2B \rightarrow E + F$. C and D are called **reaction intermediates**, chemical species that are produced and consumed during the reaction, but that do not appear in the overall reaction.

Each individual reaction in the mechanism is called an **elementary step** or **elementary reaction**. Each reaction step has its own rate of reaction. One of the reaction steps is slower than the rest and is the **rate-determining step**. The rate-determining step limits how fast the overall reaction can occur. Therefore, the rate law of the rate-determining step is the rate law of the overall reaction.

The rate equation for an elementary step can be determined from the reaction stoichiometry, unlike the overall reaction. The reactant coefficients in the elementary step become the reaction orders in the rate equation for that elementary step.

Many times a study of the kinetics of a reaction gives clues to the reaction mechanism. For example, consider the following reaction:

$$NO_2(g) + CO(g) \rightarrow NO(g) + CO_2(g)$$

It has been determined experimentally that the rate law for this reaction is: Rate = $k[NO_2]^2$. This rate law indicates that the reaction does not occur with a simple collision between NO_2 and CO. A simple collision of this type would have a rate law of Rate = $k[NO_2][CO]$. The following mechanism has been proposed for this reaction:

$$NO_2(g) + NO_2(g) \rightarrow NO_3(g) + NO(g)$$

$$NO_3(g) + CO(g) \rightarrow NO_2(g) + CO_2(g)$$

Notice that if you add these two steps together, you get the overall reaction. The first step has been shown to be the slow step in the mechanism, the rate-determining step. If we write the rate law for this elementary step, it is: Rate = $k[NO_2]^2$, which is identical to the experimentally determined rate law for the overall reaction.

Also note that both of the steps in the mechanism are **bimolecular reactions**, reactions that involve the collision of two chemical species. In **unimolecular reactions**, a single chemical species decomposes or rearranges. Both bimolecular and unimolecular reactions are common, but the collision of three or more chemical species is quite rare. Therefore, in developing or assessing a mechanism, it is best to consider only unimolecular or bimolecular elementary steps.

Catalysts

A **catalyst** is a substance that speeds up the rate of reaction without being consumed in the reaction. A catalyst may take part in the reaction and even be changed during the reaction, but at the end of the reaction, it is at least theoretically recoverable in its original form. It will not produce more of the product, but it allows the reaction to proceed more quickly. In equilibrium reactions (see the chapter on Equilibrium), the catalyst speeds up both the forward and reverse reactions. Catalysts speed up the rates of reaction by providing a different mechanism that has a lower activation energy. The higher the activation energy of a reaction, the slower the reaction will proceed. Catalysts provide an alternative pathway that has a lower activation energy and thus will be faster. In general, there are two distinct types of catalyst.

Homogeneous Catalysts

Homogeneous catalysts are catalysts that are in the same phase or state of matter as the reactants. They provide an alternative reaction pathway (mechanism) with a lower activation energy.

The decomposition of hydrogen peroxide is a slow, one-step reaction, especially if the solution is kept cool and in a dark bottle:

$$2 \, H_2O_2 \rightarrow 2 \, H_2O + O_2$$

However, if ferric ion is added, the reaction speeds up tremendously. The proposed reaction sequence for this new reaction is:

$$2 \, Fe^{3+} + H_2O_2 \rightarrow 2 \, Fe^{2+} + O_2 + 2 \, H^+$$

$$2 \, Fe^{2+} + H_2O_2 + 2 \, H^+ \rightarrow 2 \, Fe^{3+} + 2 \, H_2O$$

Notice that in the reaction the catalyst, Fe^{3+}, was reduced to the ferrous ion, Fe^{2+}, in the first step of the mechanism, but in the second step it was oxidized back to the ferric ion. Overall, the catalyst remained unchanged. Notice also that although the catalyzed reaction is a two-step reaction, it is significantly faster than the original uncatalyzed one-step reaction.

Heterogeneous Catalysts

A **heterogeneous catalyst** is in a different phase or state of matter from the reactants. Most commonly, the catalyst is a solid and the reactants are liquids or gases. These catalysts lower the activation energy for the reaction by providing a surface for the reaction, and also by providing a better orientation of one reactant so its reactive site is more easily hit by the other reactant. Many times these heterogeneous catalysts are finely divided metals. The Haber process, by which nitrogen and hydrogen gases are converted into ammonia, depends upon an iron catalyst, while the hydrogenation of vegetable oil to margarine uses a nickel catalyst.

Experiments

Unlike other experiments, a means of measuring time is essential to all kinetics experiments. This may be done with a clock or a timer. The initial concentration of each reactant must be determined. Often this is done through a simple dilution of a stock solution.

The experimenter must then determine the concentration of one or more substances later, or record some measurable change in the solution. Unless there will be an attempt to measure the activation energy, the temperature should be kept constant. A thermometer is needed to confirm this.

"Clock" experiments are common kinetics experiments. They do not require a separate experiment to determine the concentration of a substance in the reaction mixture. In clock experiments, after a certain amount of time, the solution suddenly changes color. This occurs when one of the reactants has disappeared, and another reaction involving a color change can begin.

In other kinetics experiments, the volume or pressure of a gaseous product is monitored. Again, it is not necessary to analyze the reaction mixture. Color changes in a solution may be monitored with a spectrophotometer. Finally, as a last resort, a sample of the reaction mixture may be removed at intervals and analyzed.

The initial measurement and one or more later measurements are required. (Remember, you measure times; you calculate changes in time [Δt]). Glassware, for mixing and diluting solutions, and a thermometer are the equipment needed for a clock experiment. Other kinetics experiments will use additional equipment to measure volume, temperature, etc. Do not forget: In all cases, you measure a property and then calculate a change. You never measure a change.

Common Mistakes to Avoid

1. When working mathematical problems, be sure your units cancel to give you the desired unit in your answer.
2. Be sure to round your answer off to the correct number of significant figures.
3. In working rate law problems, be sure to use molarity for your concentration unit.
4. In writing integrated rate laws, be sure to include the negative sign with the change in *reactant* concentration, since it will be decreasing with time.
5. Remember that the rate law for an overall reaction must be derived from experimental data.
6. In mathematically determining the rate law, be sure to set up the ratio of two experiments such that the concentration of only one reactant has changed.
7. Remember that in most of these calculations the base e logarithm (ln) is used and not the base 10 logarithm (log).

› Review Questions

Use these questions to review the content of this chapter and practice for the AP Chemistry exam. First are 12 multiple-choice questions similar to what you will encounter in Section I of the AP Chemistry exam. Following those is a long free-response question like the ones in Section II of the exam. To make these questions an even more authentic practice for the actual exam, time yourself following the instructions provided.

Multiple-Choice Questions

Answer the following questions in 20 minutes. You may not use a calculator. You may use the periodic table and the equation sheet at the back of this book.

1. A reaction follows the rate law: Rate = $k[A]^2$. Which of the following plots will give a straight line?

   (A) $1/[A]$ versus 1/time
   (B) $[A]^2$ versus time
   (C) $1/[A]$ versus time
   (D) $\ln[A]$ versus time

2. For the following reaction: $NO_2(g) + CO(g) \rightarrow NO(g) + CO_2(g)$, the rate law is: Rate = $k[NO_2]^2$. If a small amount of gaseous carbon monoxide (CO) is added to a reaction mixture that was 0.10 molar in NO_2 and 0.20 molar in CO, which of the following statements is true?

   (A) Both k and the reaction rate remain the same.
   (B) Both k and the reaction rate increase.
   (C) Both k and the reaction rate decrease.
   (D) Only k increases, the reaction rate will remain the same.

3. The specific rate constant, k, for radioactive beryllium-11 is 0.049 s^{-1}. What mass of a 0.500 mg sample of beryllium-11 remains after 28 seconds?

   (A) 0.250 mg
   (B) 0.125 mg
   (C) 0.0625 mg
   (D) 0.375 mg

4. The slow rate of a particular chemical reaction might be attributed to which of the following?

   (A) a low activation energy
   (B) a high activation energy
   (C) the presence of a catalyst
   (D) the temperature is high

5. The steps below represent a proposed mechanism for the catalyzed oxidation of CO by O_3.

   Step 1: $NO_2(g) + CO(g) \rightarrow NO(g) + CO_2(g)$

   Step 2: $NO(g) + O_3(g) \rightarrow NO_2(g) + O_2(g)$

   What are the overall products of the catalyzed reaction?

   (A) CO_2 and O_2
   (B) NO and CO_2
   (C) NO_2 and O_2
   (D) NO and O_2

6. The decomposition of ammonia to the elements is a first-order reaction with a half-life of 200 s at a certain temperature. How long will it take the partial pressure of ammonia to decrease from 0.100 atm to 0.00625 atm?

   (A) 200 s
   (B) 400 s
   (C) 800 s
   (D) 1,000 s

7. The energy difference between the reactants and the transition state is:

   (A) the free energy
   (B) the heat of reaction
   (C) the activation energy
   (D) the kinetic energy

8. The purpose of striking a match against the side of a box to light the match is:
   (A) to supply the free energy for the reaction
   (B) to supply the activation energy for the reaction
   (C) to supply the heat of reaction
   (D) to supply the kinetic energy for the reaction

9. The following table gives the initial concentrations and rate for three experiments.

EXPERIMENT	INITIAL $[CO]$ $(mol\ L^{-1})$	INITIAL $[Cl_2]$ $(mol\ L^{-1})$	INITIAL RATE OF FORMATION OF $COCl_2$ $(mol\ L^{-1}$ $min^{-1})$
1	0.200	0.100	3.9×10^{-25}
2	0.100	0.200	3.9×10^{-25}
3	0.200	0.200	7.8×10^{-25}

The reaction is $CO(g) + Cl_2(g) \rightarrow COCl_2(g)$. What is the rate law for this reaction?

(A) Rate $= k[CO]$
(B) Rate $= k[CO]^2[Cl_2]$
(C) Rate $= k[CO][Cl_2]$
(D) Rate $= k[CO][Cl_2]^2$

10. The reaction $(CH_3)_3CBr(aq) + H_2O(l) \rightarrow (CH_3)_3COH(aq) + HBr(aq)$ follows the rate law: Rate $= k[(CH_3)_3CBr]$. What will be the effect of decreasing the concentration of $(CH_3)_3CBr$?

(A) The rate of the reaction will increase.
(B) More HBr will form.
(C) The rate of the reaction will decrease.
(D) The reaction will shift to the left.

11. When the concentration of $H^+(aq)$ is doubled for the reaction $H_2O_2(aq) + 2\ Fe^{2+}(aq) + 2\ H^+(aq) \rightarrow 2\ Fe^{3+}(aq) + 2\ H_2O(g)$, there is no change in the reaction rate. This indicates:

(A) the H^+ is a spectator ion.
(B) the rate-determining step does not involve H^+.
(C) the reaction mechanism does not involve H^+.
(D) the H^+ is a catalyst.

12. The following mechanism has been proposed for the reaction of $CHCl_3$ with Cl_2.

Step 1: $Cl_2(g) \rightarrow 2\ Cl(g)$ fast

Step 2: $Cl(g) + CHCl_3(g)$ $\rightarrow CCl_3(g) + HCl(g)$ slow

Step 3: $CCl_3(g) + Cl(g) \rightarrow CCl_4(g)$ fast

Which of the following rate laws is consistent with this mechanism?

(A) Rate $= k[Cl_2]$
(B) Rate $= k[CHCl_3][Cl_2]$
(C) Rate $= k[CHCl_3]$
(D) Rate $= k[CHCl_3][Cl_2]^{1/2}$

Answers and Explanations for the Multiple-Choice Questions

1. **C**—The "2" exponent means this is a second-order rate law. Second-order rate laws give a straight-line plot for $1/[A]$ versus t.

2. **A**—The value of k remains the same unless the temperature is changed or a catalyst is added. Only materials that appear in the rate law, in this case NO_2, will affect the rate. Adding NO_2 would increase the rate, and removing NO_2 would decrease the rate. CO has no effect on the rate.

3. **B**—The half-life is $0.693/k = 0.693/0.049\ s^{-1} = 14\ s$. The time given, 28 s, represents two half-lives. The first half-life uses one-half of the beryllium, and the second half-life uses one-half of the remaining material, so only one-fourth of the original material remains.

4. **B**—Slow reactions have high activation energies. High activation energies are often attributed to strong bonds within the reactant molecules. All the other choices give faster rates.

5. **A**—Add the two equations together:

$NO_2(g) + CO(g) + NO(g) + O_3(g) \rightarrow NO(g) + CO_2(g) + NO_2(g) + O_2(g)$

Then cancel identical species that appear on opposite sides:

$CO(g) + O_3(g) \rightarrow CO_2(g) + O_2(g)$

6. **C**—The value will be decreased by one-half for each half-life. Using the following table:

Half-lives	Remaining
0	0.100
1	0.0500
2	0.0250
3	0.0125
4	0.00625

Four half-lives = 4(200 s) = 800 s

7. **C**—This is the definition of the activation energy.

8. **B**—The friction supplies the energy needed to start the reaction. The energy needed to start the reaction is the activation energy.

9. **C**—Beginning with the generic rate law: Rate $= k[CO]^m[Cl_2]^n$, it is necessary to determine the values of m and n (the orders). Comparing Experiments 2 and 3, the rate doubles when the concentration of CO is doubled. This direct change means the reaction is first order with respect to CO. Comparing Experiments 1 and 3, the rate doubles when the concentration of Cl_2 is doubled. Again, this direct change means the reaction is first order. This gives: Rate $= k[CO]^1[Cl_2]^1 = k[CO][Cl_2]$.

10. **C**—The compound appears in the rate law, so a change in its concentration will change the rate. The reaction is first order in $(CH_3)_3CBr$, so the rate will change directly with the change in concentration of this reactant.

11. **B**—All substances involved, directly or indirectly, in the rate-determining step will change the rate when their concentrations are changed. The ion is required in the balanced chemical equation, so it cannot be a spectator ion, and it must appear in the mechanism. Catalysts will change the rate of a reaction. Since H^+ does not affect the rate, the reaction is zero order with respect to this ion.

12. **D**—The rate law depends on the slow step of the mechanism. The reactants in the slow step are Cl and $CHCl_3$ (one of each). The rate law is first order with respect to each of these. The Cl is half of the original reactant molecule Cl_2. This replaces the [Cl] in the rate law with $[Cl_2]^{1/2}$. Do not make the mistake of using the overall reaction to predict the rate law.

Free-Response Question

You have 15 minutes to answer the following long question. You may use a calculator and the tables in the back of the book.

Question 1

$$2\ ClO_2(aq) + 2\ OH^-(aq) \rightarrow ClO_3^-(aq) + ClO_2^-(aq) + H_2O(l)$$

A series of experiments were conducted to study the above reaction. The initial concentrations and rates are in the following table.

EXPERIMENT	INITIAL CONCENTRATIONS (mol/L)		INITIAL RATE OF FORMATION OF ClO_3^- (mol/L min)
	[OH⁻]	[ClO_2]	
1	0.030	0.020	0.166
2	0.060	0.020	0.331
3	0.030	0.040	0.661

(a) i. Determine the order of the reaction with respect to each reactant. Make sure you explain your reasoning.

    ii. Give the rate law for the reaction.

(b) Determine the value of the rate constant, making sure the units are included.

(c) Calculate the initial rate of disappearance of ClO_2 in experiment 1.

(d) The following is the proposed mechanism for this reaction:

Step 1: $ClO_2 + ClO_2 \rightarrow Cl_2O_4$

Step 2: $Cl_2O_4 + OH^- \rightarrow ClO_3^- + HClO_2$

Step 3: $HClO_2 + OH^- \rightarrow ClO_2^- + H_2O$

Which step is the rate-determining step? Show that this mechanism is consistent with both the rate law for the reaction and with the overall stoichiometry.

Answer and Explanation for the Free-Response Question

(a) i. This part of the problem begins with a generic rate equation: Rate = $k[ClO_2]^m[OH]^n$. The values of the exponents, the orders, must be determined. It does not matter which exponent is done first. If you want to begin with ClO_2, you must pick two experiments from the table where its concentration changes but the OH^- concentration does not change. These are experiments 1 and 3. Experiment 3 has twice the concentration of ClO_2 as experiment 1. This doubling of the ClO_2 concentration has quadrupled the rate. The relationship between the concentration ($\times 2$) and the rate ($\times 4 = \times 2^2$) indicates that the order for ClO_2 is 2 ($= m$). Using experiments 1 and 2 (only the OH^- concentration changes), we see that doubling the concentration simply doubles the rate. Thus, the order for OH^- is 1 ($= n$).
Give yourself 1 point for each order you got correct.

    ii. Inserting the orders into the generic rate law gives: Rate = $k[ClO_2]^2 [OH^-]^1$, which is usually simplified to: Rate = $k[ClO_2]^2[OH^-]$.
Give yourself 1 point if you got this equation correct.

(b) Any one of the three experiments may be used to calculate the rate constant. If the problem asked for an average rate constant, you would need to calculate a value for each of the experiments and then average the values.
The rate law should be rearranged to $k = $ Rate/$[ClO_2]^2[OH^-]$. Then the appropriate values are entered into the equation. Using experiment 1 as an example:

$$k = (0.166 \text{ mol/L min})/[(0.020 \ M)^2(0.030 \ M)]$$

$$= 1.3833 \times 10^4 \ M/M^3 \text{ min} = 1.4 \times 10^4/M^2 \text{ min}$$

The answer could also be reported as $1.4 \times 10^4 \ L^2/mol^2$ min. You should not forget that $M = $ mol/L.
Give yourself 1 point for the correct numerical value. Give yourself 1 point for the correct units. If you had the wrong rate law in part **a. ii**, and use it correctly in part **b**, you will still get the points.

(c) The coefficients from the equation say that for every mole of ClO_3^- that forms, 2 mol of ClO_2 reacted. Thus, the rate of ClO_2 is twice the rate of ClO_3^-. Do not forget that since ClO_3^- is forming, it has a positive rate, and since ClO_2 is reacting, it has a negative rate. Therefore:

Rearranging and inserting the rate from experiment 1 gives: $\Delta[\text{ClO}]/\Delta t =$ $-2(0.166 \text{ mol/L min})] = -8.332 \text{ mol/L min}$

Give yourself 2 points if you got the entire answer correct. You get only 1 point if the sign or units are missing.

(d) The rate-determining step must match the rate law. One approach is to determine the rate law for each step in the mechanism. This gives:

Step 1: Rate = $k[\text{ClO}_2]^2$
Step 2: Rate = $k[\text{Cl}_2\text{O}_4][\text{OH}^-] = k[\text{Cl}_2\text{O}]^2[\text{OH}^-]$
Step 3: Rate = $k[\text{HClO}_2][\text{OH}^-] = k[\text{ClO}_2][\text{OH}^-]^2$

For steps 2 and 3, it is necessary to replace the intermediates with reactants. Step 2 gives a rate law matching the one derived in part **a**.

Give yourself 1 point if you picked step 2, or if you picked a step with a rate law that matches a wrong answer for part **a**. Give yourself 1 more point if you explained the substitution of reactants for intermediates.

To see if the stoichiometry is correct, simply add the three steps together and cancel the intermediates (materials that appear on both sides of the reaction arrow).

Step 1: $\text{ClO}_2 + \text{ClO}_2 \rightarrow \text{Cl}_2\text{O}_4$
Step 2: $\text{Cl}_2\text{O}_4 + \text{OH}^- \rightarrow \text{ClO}_3^- + \text{HClO}_2$
Step 3: $\text{HClO}_2 + \text{OH}^- \rightarrow \text{ClO}_2^- + \text{H}_2\text{O}$
Total: $2\,\text{ClO}_2 + \text{Cl}_2\text{O}_4 + 2\,\text{OH}^- + \text{HClO}_2 \rightarrow$
$$\text{Cl}_2\text{O}_4 + \text{ClO}_3^- + \text{HClO}_2 + \text{ClO}_2^- + \text{H}_2\text{O}$$

After removing the intermediates (Cl_2O_4 and HClO_2):

$$2\,\text{ClO}_2 + 2\,\text{OH}^- \rightarrow \text{ClO}_3^- + \text{ClO}_2^- + \text{H}_2\text{O}$$

As this matches the original reaction equation, the mechanism fulfills the overall stoichiometry requirement.

Give yourself 1 point for summing the equations and proving the overall equation is consistent.

The total is 10 points for this question. Subtract 1 point if any answer has an incorrect number of significant figures.

› Rapid Review

- Kinetics is a study of the speed of a chemical reaction.
- The five factors that can affect the rates of chemical reaction are the nature of the reactants, the temperature, the concentration of the reactants, the physical state of the reactants, and the presence of a catalyst.
- The rate equation relates the speed of reaction to the concentration of reactants and has the form: Rate = $k[\text{A}]^m[\text{B}]^n$ . . . where k is the rate constant and m and n are the orders of reaction with respect to that specific reactant.
- The rate law must be determined from experimental data. Review how to determine the rate law from kinetics data.
- When mathematically comparing two experiments in the determination of the rate equation, be sure to choose two in which all reactant concentrations except one remain constant.
- Rate laws can be written in the integrated form.

- If a reaction is first order, it has the rate law of Rate $= k[A]$; $\ln [A]_t - \ln [A]_0 = -kt$; a plot of $\ln[A]$ versus time gives a straight line.

- If a reaction is second order, it has the form of Rate $= k[A]^2$; $\frac{1}{[A]_t} - \frac{1}{[A]_0} = kt$ (integrated rate law); a plot of $\frac{1}{[A]}$ versus time gives a straight line.

- The reaction half-life is the amount of time that it takes the reactant concentration to decrease to one-half its initial concentration.

- The half-life can be related to concentration and time by these two equations (first and second order, respectively): $t_{1/2} = \frac{\ln 2}{k} = \frac{0.693}{k}$ and $t_{1/2} = 1/k[A]_0$.

- The activation energy is the minimum amount of energy needed to initiate or start a chemical reaction.

- Many reactions proceed from reactants to products by a series of steps called elementary steps. All these steps together describe the reaction mechanism, the pathway by which the reaction occurs.

- The slowest step in a reaction mechanism is the rate-determining step. It determines the rate law.

- A catalyst is a substance that speeds up a reaction without being consumed in the reaction.

- A homogeneous catalyst is in the same phase as the reactants, whereas a heterogeneous catalyst is in a different phase from the reactants.

CHAPTER 15

Equilibrium

IN THIS CHAPTER

Summary: We've been discussing chemical reactions for several chapters. In the Kinetics chapter you saw how chemical reactions take place and some of the factors that affect the reactions' speed. In this chapter, we will discuss another aspect of chemical reactions: equilibrium.

A few chemical reactions proceed to completion, using up one or more of the reactants and then stopping. However, most reactions behave in a different way. Consider the general reaction:

$$aA + bB \rightarrow cC + dD$$

Reactants A and B are forming C and D. Then C and D start to react to form A and B:

$$cC + dD \rightarrow aA + bB$$

These two reactions proceed until the two rates of reaction become equal. That is, the speed of production of C and D in the first reaction is equal to the speed of production of A and B in the second reaction. Since these two reactions are occurring simultaneously in the same container, the amounts of A, B, C, and D become constant. A **chemical equilibrium** has been reached, in which two exactly opposite reactions are occurring at the same place, at the same time, and with the same rates of reaction. When a system reaches the equilibrium state, the reactions do not stop. A and B are still reacting to form C and D; C and D are still reacting to form A and B. But because the reactions proceed at the same rate, the amounts of each chemical species are constant. This state is sometimes called a **dynamic** equilibrium state to emphasize the fact that the reactions are still occurring—it is a dynamic, not a static state. An equilibrium state is indicated by a double arrow instead of a single arrow. For the reaction above it would be shown as:

$$aA + bB \rightleftharpoons cC + dD$$

It is important to remember that at equilibrium the concentrations of the chemical species are constant, not necessarily equal. There may be a lot of C and D and a little A and B, or vice versa. The concentrations are constant, unchanging, but not necessarily equal.

At any point during the preceding reaction, a relationship may be defined called the **reaction quotient,** Q. It has the following form:

$$Q = \frac{[C]^c[D]^d}{[A]^a[B]^b}$$

The reaction quotient is a fraction. In the numerator is the product of the chemical species on the right-hand side of the equilibrium arrow, each raised to the power of that species' coefficient in the balanced chemical equation. It is called the Q_c in this case, because molar concentrations are being used. If this was a gas-phase reaction, gas pressures could be used and it would become a Q_p.

Remember: products over reactants.

Keywords and Equations

Q = reaction quotient

$$Q = \frac{[C]^c[D]^d}{[A]^a[B]^b}, \text{ where } aA + bB \rightarrow cC + dD$$

Equilibrium Constants:
K = equilibrium constant
K_a (weak acid) K_b (weak base) K_w (water) K_p (gas pressure)
K_c (molar concentrations)

$$K_a = \frac{[H^+][A^-]}{[HA]} \qquad K_b = \frac{[OH^-][HB^+]}{[B]}$$

$K_w = [OH^-][H^+] = 1.0 \times 10^{-14} = K_a \times K_b$ at 25°C
pH = −log [H⁺], pOH = −log [OH⁻]
14 = pH + pOH

$$pH = pK_a + \log\frac{[A^-]}{[HA]}$$

$$pOH = pK_b + \log\frac{[HB^+]}{[B]}$$

$pK_a = -\log K_a$, $pK_b = -\log K_b$
$K_p = K_c(RT)^{\Delta n}$, where Δn = moles product gas − moles reactant gas
Gas constant, $R = 0.0821$ L atm mol⁻¹ K⁻¹

Equilibrium Expressions

The reactant quotient can be written at any point during the reaction, but the most useful point is when the reaction has reached equilibrium. At equilibrium, the reaction quotient becomes the **equilibrium constant**, K_c (or K_p if gas pressures are being used). Usually this equilibrium constant is expressed simply as a number without units, since it is a ratio of concentrations or pressures. In addition, the concentrations of solids or pure liquids (not in solution) that appear in the equilibrium expression are assumed to be 1, since their concentrations do not change.

Consider the Haber process for the production of ammonia:

$$N_2(g) + 3H_2(g) \rightleftharpoons 2NH_3(g)$$

The equilibrium constant expression would be written as:

$$K_c = \frac{[NH_3]^2}{[N_2][H_2]^3}$$

If the partial pressures of the gases were used, then K_p would be written in the following form:

$$K_p = \frac{P_{NH_3}^{\,2}}{P_{N_2} \times P_{H_2}^{\,3}}$$

There is a relationship between K_c and K_p: $K_p = K_c(RT)^{\Delta n}$, where R is the ideal gas constant (0.0821 L atm/mol K) and Δn is the change in the number of moles of gas in the reaction.

 Remember: Be sure that your value of R is consistent with the units chosen for the partial pressures of the gases.

For the following equilibrium $K_p = 1.90$: $C(s) = CO_2(g) \rightleftharpoons 2\,CO(g)$. Calculate K_c for this equilibrium at 25°C.

$$C(s) + CO_2(g) \rightleftharpoons 2CO(g) \quad K_p = 1.90$$

$$K_p = K_c(RT)^{\Delta n}$$

$$1.90 = K_c \frac{[(0.0826\ L\ atm)(298K)]^{(2-1)}}{[(mol\ K)]}$$

$$K_c = 0.0777$$

The numerical value of the equilibrium constant can give an indication of the extent of the reaction after equilibrium has been reached. If the value of K_c is large, that means the numerator is much larger than the denominator and the reaction has produced a relatively large amount of products (reaction lies far to the right). If K_c is small, then the numerator is much smaller than the denominator and not much product has been formed (reaction lies far to the left).

Le Châtelier's Principle

At a given temperature, a reaction will reach equilibrium with the production of a certain amount of product. If the equilibrium constant is small, that means that not much product will be formed. But is there anything that can be done to produce more? Yes, there is—through the application of **Le Châtelier's principle**. Le Châtelier, a French scientist, discovered that if a chemical system at equilibrium is stressed (disturbed) it will reestablish equilibrium by shifting the reactions involved. This means that the amounts of the reactants and products will change, but the final ratio will remain the same. The equilibrium may be stressed in a number of ways: changes in concentration, pressure, and temperature. Many times the use of a catalyst is mentioned. However, a catalyst will have no effect on the equilibrium amounts, because it affects both the forward and reverse reactions equally. It will, however, cause the reaction to reach equilibrium faster.

Changes in Concentration

If the equilibrium system is stressed by a change in concentration of one of the reactants or products, the equilibrium will react to remove that stress. If the concentration of a chemical species is decreased, the equilibrium will shift to produce more of it. In doing so, the concentration of chemical species on the other side of the reaction arrows will be decreased. If the concentration of a chemical species is increased, the equilibrium will shift to consume it, increasing the concentration of chemical species on the other side of the reaction arrows.

For example, again consider the Haber process:

$$N_2(g) + 3H_2(g) \rightleftharpoons 2NH_3(g)$$

If one increases the concentration of hydrogen gas, then the equilibrium shifts to the right to consume some of the added hydrogen. In doing so, the concentration of ammonia (NH_3) will increase and the concentration of nitrogen gas will decrease. On the other hand, if the concentration of nitrogen gas was decreased, the equilibrium would shift to the left to form more, the concentration of ammonia would decrease, and the concentration of hydrogen would increase.

Again, remember that the concentrations may change, but the value of K_c or K_p would remain the same.

Changes in Pressure

Changes in pressure are significant only if gases are involved. The pressure may be changed by changing the volume of the container or by changing the concentration of a gaseous species (although this is really a change in concentration and can be treated as a concentration effect, as above). If the container becomes smaller, the pressure increases because there is an increased number of collisions on the inside walls of the container. This stresses the equilibrium system, and it will shift to reduce the pressure. This can be accomplished by shifting the equilibrium toward the side of the equation that has the lesser number of moles of gas. If the container size is increased, the pressure decreases and the equilibrium will shift to the side containing more moles of gas to increase the pressure. If the number of moles of gas is the same on both sides, changing the pressure will not affect the equilibrium.

Once again, consider the Haber reaction:

$$N_2(g) + 3H_2(g) \rightleftharpoons 2NH_3(g)$$

Note that there are 4 mol of gas (1 of nitrogen and 3 of hydrogen) on the left side and 2 mol on the right. If the container is made smaller, the pressure will increase and the equilibrium will shift to the right because 4 mol would be converted to 2 mol. The concentrations of nitrogen and hydrogen gases would decrease, and the concentration of ammonia would increase.

Remember: Pressure effects are only important for gases.

Changes in Temperature

Changing the temperature changes the value of the equilibrium constant. It also changes the amount of heat in the system and can be treated as a concentration effect. To treat it this way, one must know which reaction, forward or reverse, is exothermic (releasing heat).

One last time, let's consider the Haber reaction:

$$N_2(g) + H_2(g) \rightleftharpoons 2NH_3(g)$$

The formation of ammonia is exothermic (liberating heat), so the reaction could be written as:

$$N_2(g) + 3H_2(g) \rightleftharpoons 2NH_3(g) + heat$$

If the temperature of the reaction mixture were increased, the amount of heat would be increased and the equilibrium would shift to the left to consume the added heat. In doing so, the concentration of nitrogen and hydrogen gases would increase and the concentration of ammonia gas would decrease. If you were in the business of selling ammonia, you would probably want to operate at a reduced temperature, in order to shift the reaction to the right.

Consider the following equilibrium (endothermic as written), and predict what changes, if any, would occur if the following stresses were applied after equilibrium was established.

$$CaCO_3(s) \rightleftharpoons CaO(s) + CO_2(g)$$

a. add CO_2
b. remove CO_2
c. add CaO
d. increase T
e. decrease V
f. add a catalyst

Answers:

a. Left—the equilibrium shifts to remove some of the excess CO_2.
b. Right—the equilibrium shifts to replace some of the CO_2.
c. No change—solids do not shift equilibria unless they are totally removed.
d. Right—endothermic reactions shift to the right when heated.
e. Left—a decrease in volume, or an increase in pressure, will shift the equilibrium toward the side with less gas.
f. No change—catalysts do not affect the position of an equilibrium.

Acid–Base Equilibrium

In the Reactions and Periodicity chapter, we introduced the concept of acids and bases. Recall that acids are proton (H^+) donors and bases are proton acceptors. Also, recall that acids and bases may be strong or weak. **Strong acids** completely dissociate in water; **weak acids** only partially dissociate. For example, consider two acids: HCl (strong) and CH_3COOH (weak). If each is added to water to form aqueous solutions, the following reactions take place:

$$HCl(aq) + H_2O(l) \rightarrow H_3O^+(aq) + Cl^-(aq)$$

$$CH_3COOH(aq) + H_2O(l) \rightleftharpoons H_3O^+(aq) + CH_3COO^-(aq)$$

The first reaction essentially goes to completion—there is no HCl left in solution. The second reaction is an equilibrium reaction—there are appreciable amounts of both reactants and products left in solution.

There are generally only two strong bases to consider: the hydroxide and the oxide ion (OH^- and O^{2-}, respectively). All other common bases are weak. **Weak bases**, like weak acids, also establish an equilibrium system, as in aqueous solutions of ammonia:

$$NH_3(aq) + H_2O(l) \rightleftharpoons OH^-(aq) + NH_4^+(aq)$$

In the Brønsted–Lowry acid–base theory, there is competition for an H^+. Consider the acid–base reaction between acetic acid, a weak acid, and ammonia, a weak base:

$$CH_3COOH(aq) + NH_3(aq) \rightleftharpoons CH_3COO^-(aq) + NH_4^+(aq)$$

Acetic acid donates a proton to ammonia in the forward (left-to-right) reaction of the equilibrium to form the acetate and ammonium ions. But in the reverse (right-to-left) reaction, the ammonium ion donates a proton to the acetate ion to form ammonia and acetic acid. The ammonium ion is acting as an acid, and the acetate ion as a base. Under the Brønsted–Lowry system, acetic acid (CH_3COOH) and the acetate ion (CH_3COO^-) are called a conjugate acid–base pair. **Conjugate acid–base pairs** differ by only a single H^+. Ammonia (NH_3) and the ammonium ion (NH_4^+) are also a conjugate acid–base pair. In this reaction, there is a competition for the H^+ between acetic acid and the ammonium ion. To predict on which side the equilibrium will lie, this general rule applies: *The equilibrium will favor the side in which the weaker acid and base are present.* Figure 15.1 shows the relative strengths of the conjugate acid–base pairs.

In Figure 15.1, you can see that acetic acid is a stronger acid than the ammonium ion and ammonia is a stronger base than the acetate ion. Therefore, the equilibrium will lie to the right.

The reasoning above allows us to find good qualitative answers, but in order to be able to do quantitative problems (how much is present, etc.), the extent of the dissociation of the weak acids and bases must be known. That is where a modification of the equilibrium constant is useful.

K_a—the Acid Dissociation Constant

Strong acids completely dissociate (ionize) in water. Weak acids partially dissociate and establish an equilibrium system. But as shown in Figure 15.1 there is a large range of weak acids based upon their ability to donate protons. Consider the general weak acid, HA, and its reaction when placed in water:

$$HA(aq) + H_2O(l) \rightleftharpoons H_3O^+(aq) + A^-(aq)$$

An equilibrium constant expression can be written for this system:

$$K_c = \frac{[H_3O^+][A^-]}{[HA]}$$

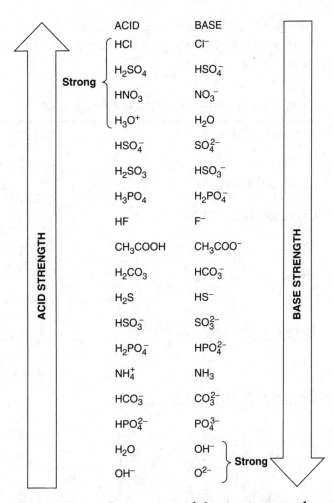

Figure 15.1   Conjugate acid–base pair strengths.

The [H_2O] is assumed to be a constant and is incorporated into the K_a value. It is not shown in the equilibrium constant expression.

Since this is the equilibrium constant associated with a weak acid dissociation, this particular K_c is most commonly called the **acid dissociation constant**, K_a. The K_a expression is then:

$$K_a = \frac{[H_3O^+][A^-]}{[HA]}$$

Many times the weak acid dissociation reaction will be shown in a shortened notation, omitting the water:

$$HA(aq) \rightleftharpoons H^+(aq) + A^-(aq) \qquad \text{with } K_a = \frac{[H^+][A^-]}{[HA]}$$

The greater the amount of dissociation is, the larger the value of K_a. Table 15.1, on the next page, shows the K_a values of some common weak acids.

Here are a couple of tips: For every H^+ formed, an A^- is formed, so the numerator of the K_a expression can be expressed as $[H^+]^2$ (or $[A^-]^2$, although it is rarely done this way). Also, the [HA] is the equilibrium molar concentration of the undissociated weak acid, not its initial concentration. The exact expression would then be $[HA] = M_{\text{initial}} - [H^+]$, where M_{initial} is the initial concentration of the weak acid. This is true because for every H^+ that is formed, an HA must have dissociated. However, many times if K_a is small, you can approximate the equilibrium concentration of the weak acid by its initial concentration, $[HA] = M_{initial}$.

Table 15.1 K_a Values for Selected Weak Acids

NAME (FORMULA)	LEWIS STRUCTURE	K_a
Iodic acid (HIO₃)	H—Ö—Ï=Ö ‖ :Ö:	1.6×10^{-1}
Chlorous acid (HClO₂)	H—Ö—Ċl=Ö	1.12×10^{-2}
Nitrous acid (HNO₂)	H—Ö—N̈=Ö	7.1×10^{-4}
Hydrofluoric acid (HF)	H—F̈:	6.8×10^{-4}
Benzoic acid (C₆H₅COOH)	⬡—C(=Ö)—Ö—H	6.3×10^{-5}
Acetic acid (CH₃COOH)	H—C(H)(H)—C(=Ö)—Ö—H	1.8×10^{-5}
Propanoic acid (CH₃CH₂COOH)	H—C(H)(H)—C(H)(H)—C(=Ö)—Ö—H	1.3×10^{-5}
Hypochlorous acid (HClO)	H—Ö—Ċl:	2.9×10^{-8}
Hypobromous acid (HBrO)	H—Ö—B̈r:	2.3×10^{-9}
Phenol (C₆H₅OH)	⬡—Ö—H	1.0×10^{-10}
Hypoiodous acid (HIO)	H—Ö—Ï:	2.3×10^{-11}

If the initial molarity and K_a of the weak acid are known, the $[H^+]$ (or $[A^-]$) can be calculated easily. And if the initial molarity and $[H^+]$ are known, K_a can be calculated.

For example, calculate the $[H^+]$ of a 0.300 M acetic acid solution.

$$K_a = 1.8 \times 10^{-5}$$
$$HC_2H_3O_2(aq) \rightleftharpoons H^+(aq) + C_2H_3O_2^-(aq)$$
$$0.300 - x \qquad x \qquad x$$
$$K_a = \frac{[H^+][C_2H_3O_2]}{[HC_2H_3O_2]} = 1.8 \times 10^{-5}$$
$$= \frac{(x)(x)}{0.300 - x} = 1.8 \times 10^{-5}$$
$$x = [H^+] = 2.3 \times 10^{-3} \; M$$

For **polyprotic acids**, acids that can donate more than one proton, the K_a for the first dissociation is much larger than the K_a for the second dissociation. If there is a third K_a, it is much smaller still. For most practical purposes, you can simply use the first K_a.

K_w—the Water Dissociation Constant

Before examining the equilibrium behavior of aqueous solutions of weak bases, let's look at the behavior of water itself. In the initial discussion of acid–base equilibrium above, we showed water acting both as an acid (proton donor when put with a base) and a base (proton acceptor when put with an acid). Water is **amphoteric**; it will act as either an acid or a base, depending on whether the other species is a base or acid. But in pure water the same amphoteric nature is noted. In pure water, a very small amount of proton transfer is taking place:

$$H_2O(l) + H_2O(l) \rightleftharpoons H_3O^+(aq) + OH^-(aq)$$

This is commonly written as:

$$H_2O(l) \rightleftharpoons H^+(aq) + OH^-(aq)$$

There is an equilibrium constant, called the **water dissociation constant**, K_w, which has the form:

$$K_w = [H^+][OH^-] = 1.0 \times 10^{-14} \text{ at } 25°C$$

Again, the concentration of water is a constant and is incorporated into K_w.

The numerical value of K_w of 1.0×10^{-14} is true for the product of the $[H^+]$ and $[OH^-]$ in pure water and for aqueous solutions of acids and bases.

In the discussion of weak acids, we indicated that the $[H^+] = [A^-]$. However, there are two sources of H^+ in the system: the weak acid and water. The amount of H^+ that is due to the water dissociation is very small and can be easily ignored.

pH

Because the concentration of the hydronium ion, H_3O^+, can vary tremendously in solutions of acids and bases, a scale to easily represent the acidity of a solution was developed. It is called the pH scale and is related to the $[H_3O^+]$:

$$pH = -\log [H_3O^+] \text{ or } -\log [H^+] \text{ using the shorthand notation}$$

Remember that in pure water $K_w = [H_3O^+][OH^-] = 1.0 \times 10^{-14}$. Since both the hydronium ion and hydroxide ions are formed in equal amounts, the K_w expression can be expressed as:

$$[H_3O^+]^2 = 1.0 \times 10^{-14}$$

Solving for $[H_3O^+]$ gives us $[H_3O^+] = 1.0 \times 10^{-7}$. If you then calculate the pH of pure water:

$$pH = -\log[H_3O^+] = -\log [1.0 \times 10^{-7}] = -(-7.00) = 7.00$$

The pH of pure water is 7.00. On the pH scale, this is called **neutral**. A solution whose $[H_3O^+]$ is greater than in pure water will have a pH less than 7.00 and is called **acidic**. A solution whose $[H_3O^+]$ is less than in pure water will have a pH greater than 7.00 and is called **basic**. Figure 15.2, on the next page, shows the pH scale and the pH values of some common substances.

The pOH of a solution can also be calculated. It is defined as $pOH = -\log[OH^-]$. The pH and the pOH are related:

$$pH + pOH = pK_w = 14.00 \text{ at } 25°C$$

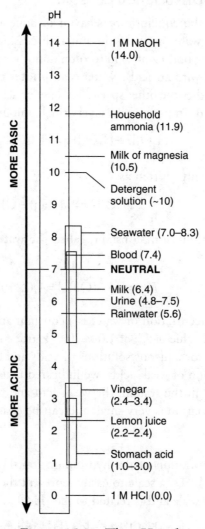

Figure 15.2   The pH scale.

In any of the problems above in which $[H^+]$ or $[OH^-]$ was calculated, you can now calculate the pH or pOH of the solution.

You can estimate the pH of a solution by looking at its $[H^+]$. For example, if a solution has an $[H^+] = 1 \times 10^{-5}$, its pH would be 5. This value was determined from the value of the exponent in the $[H^+]$.

K_b—the Base Dissociation Constant

Weak bases (B), when placed into water, also establish an equilibrium system much like weak acids:

$$B(aq) + H_2O(l) \rightleftharpoons HB^+(aq) + OH^-(aq)$$

The equilibrium constant expression is called the weak **base dissociation constant**, K_b, and has the form:

$$K_b = \frac{[HB^+][OH^-]}{[HB]}$$

The same reasoning that was used in dealing with weak acids is also true here: $[HB^+] = [OH^-]$; $[HB] \approx M_{initially}$; the numerator can be represented as $[OH^-]^2$; and knowing the initial molarity and K_b of the weak base, the $[OH^-]$ can easily be calculated. And if the initial molarity and $[OH^-]$ are known, K_b can be calculated.

For example, a 0.500 M solution of ammonia has a pH of 11.48. What is the K_b of ammonia?

$$pH = 11.48$$

$$[H^+] = 10^{-11.48}$$

$$[H^+] = 3.3 \times 10^{-12} M$$

$$K_w = [H^+][OH^-] = 1.0 \times 10^{-14}$$

$$[OH^-] = 3.0 \times 10^{-3} M$$

$$NH_3 + H_2O \rightleftharpoons NH_4^+ + OH^-$$

$$0.500 - x \qquad x \qquad x$$

$$K_b = \frac{[NH_4^+][OH^-]}{[NH_3]}$$

$$[OH^-] = [NH_4^+] = 3.0 \times 10^{-3} M$$

$$[NH_3] = 0.500 - 3.0 \times 10^{-3} = 0.497 M$$

$$K_b = \frac{(3.0 \times 10^{-3})^2}{(0.497)} = 1.8 \times 10^{-5}$$

The K_a and K_b of conjugate acid–base pairs are related through the K_w expression:

$$K_a \times K_b = K_w$$

This equation shows an inverse relationship between K_a and K_b for any conjugate acid–base pair.

This relationship may be used in problems such as: Determine the pH of a solution made by adding 0.400 mol of strontium acetate to sufficient water to produce 2.000 L of solution.

Solution:

The initial molarity is 0.400 mol/2.000 L = 0.200 M.

When a salt is added to water dissolution will occur:

$$Sr(C_2H_3O_2)_2 \rightarrow Sr^{2+}(aq) + 2C_2H_3O_2^-(aq)$$

The resultant solution, since strontium acetate is soluble, has 0.200 M Sr^{2+} and 0.400 M $C_2H_3O_2^-$.

Ions such as Sr^{2+}, which come from strong acids or strong bases, may be ignored in this type of problem. Ions such as $C_2H_3O_2^-$, from weak acids or bases, will undergo hydrolysis. The acetate ion is the conjugate *base* of acetic acid ($K_a = 1.8 \times 10^{-5}$). Since acetate is not a strong base this will be a K_b problem, and OH^- will be produced. The equilibrium is:

$$C_2H_3O_2^- + H_2O \rightleftharpoons OH^- + HC_2H_3O_2$$
$$0.400 - x \qquad\qquad +x \qquad +x$$

Determining K_b from K_a (using $K_w = K_a K_b = 1.0 \times 10^{-14}$) gives:

$$\frac{[x][x]}{0.400 - x} = K_b = 5.6 \times 10^{-10}$$

with $x = 1.5 \times 10^{-5} = [OH^-]$, and pH = 9.180

Acidic/Basic Properties of Salts

The behavior of a salt will depend upon the acid–base properties of the ions present in the salt. The ions may lead to solutions of the salt being acidic, basic, or neutral. The pH of a solution depends on hydrolysis, a generic term for a variety of reactions with water. Some ions will undergo hydrolysis, and this changes the pH.

The reaction of an acid and a base will produce a salt. The salt will contain the cation from the base and the anion from the acid. In principle, the cation of the base is the conjugate acid of the base, and the anion from the acid is the conjugate base of the acid. Thus, the salt contains a conjugate acid and a conjugate base. This is always true in principle. In some cases, one or the other of these ions is not a true conjugate base or a conjugate acid. Just because the ion is not a true conjugate acid or base does not mean that we cannot use the ion as if it were.

The conjugate base of any strong acid is so weak that it will not undergo any significant hydrolysis; the conjugate acid of any strong base is so weak that it, too, will not undergo any significant hydrolysis. Ions that do not undergo any significant hydrolysis will have no effect upon the pH of a solution and will leave the solution neutral. The presence of the following conjugate bases Cl^-, Br^-, I^-, NO_3^-, ClO_3^-, and ClO_4^- will leave the solution neutral. The cations from the strong bases, Li^+, Na^+, K^+, Rb^+, Cs^+ Ca^{2+}, Sr^{2+}, and Ba^{2+}, while not true conjugate acids, will also leave the solution neutral. Salts containing a combination of only these cations and anions are neutral.

The conjugate base from any weak acid is a strong base and will undergo hydrolysis in aqueous solution to produce a basic solution. If the conjugate base (anion) of a weak acid is in a salt with the conjugate of a strong base (cation), the solution will be basic, because only the anion will undergo any significant hydrolysis. Salts of this type are basic salts. All salts containing the cation of a strong base and the anion of a weak acid are basic salts.

The conjugate acid of a weak base is a strong acid, and it will undergo hydrolysis in an aqueous solution to make the solution acidic. If the conjugate acid (cation) of a weak base is in a salt with the conjugate base of a strong acid (anion), the solution will be acidic, because only the cation will undergo any significant hydrolysis. Salts of this type are acidic salts. All salts containing the cation of a weak base and the anion of a strong acid are acidic salts.

There is a fourth category, consisting of salts that contain the cation of a weak base with the anion of a weak acid. Prediction of the acid–base character of these salts is less obvious, because both ions undergo hydrolysis. The two equilibria not only alter the pH of the solution, but also interfere with each other. Predictions require a comparison of the K values for the two ions. The larger K value predominates. If the larger value is K_a, the solution is acidic. If the larger value is K_b, the solution is basic. In the rare case where the two values are equal, the solution would be neutral.

The following table summarizes this information:

CATION FROM	ANION FROM	SOLUTION
Strong Base	Strong Acid	Neutral
Strong Base	Weak Acid	Basic
Weak Base	Strong Acid	Acidic
Weak Base	Weak Acid	Must be determined by comparing K values

For example, suppose you are asked to determine if a solution of sodium carbonate, Na_2CO_3, is acidic, basic, or neutral. Sodium carbonate is the salt of a strong base (NaOH) and a weak acid (HCO_3^-). Salts of strong bases and weak acids are basic salts. As a basic salt, we know the final answer must be basic (pH above 7).

Buffers

Buffers are solutions that resist a change in pH when an acid or base is added to them. The most common type of buffer is a mixture of a weak acid and its conjugate base. The weak acid will neutralize any base added, and the weak base of the buffer will neutralize any acid added to the solution. The hydronium ion concentration of a buffer can be calculated using an equation derived from the K_a expression:

$$[H_3O^+] = K_a \times \frac{[HA]}{[A^-]}$$

Taking the negative log of both sides yields the **Henderson–Hasselbalch equation**, which can be used to calculate the pH of a buffer:

$$pH = pK_a + \log\frac{[A^-]}{[HA]}$$

The weak base K_b expression can also be used giving:

$$[OH^-] = K_b \times \frac{[B]}{[HB^+]} \quad \text{and} \quad pOH = pK_b + \log\frac{[HB^+]}{[B]}$$

These equations allow us to calculate the pH or pOH of the buffer solution knowing K of the weak acid or base and the concentrations of the conjugate weak acid and its conjugate base. Also, if the desired pH is known, along with K, the ratio of base to acid can be calculated. The more concentrated these species are, the more acid or base can be neutralized and the less the change in buffer pH. This is a measure of the **buffer capacity**, the ability to resist a change in pH.

Let's calculate the pH of a buffer. What is the pH of a solution containing 2.00 mol of ammonia and 3.00 mol of ammonium chloride in a volume of 1.00 L?

$$K_b = 1.81 \times 10^{-5}$$
$$NH_3 + H_2O \rightleftharpoons NH_4^+ + OH^-$$

There are two ways to solve this problem.

$$K_b = \frac{[NH_4^+][OH^-]}{[NH_3]} = \frac{(3.00+x)(x)}{(2.00-x)} = 1.81 \times 10^{-5}$$

Assume x is small:

$$1.81 \times 10^{-5} = \frac{3.00x}{2.00}$$
$$x = 1.21 \times 10^{-5}$$
$$pOH = 4.918$$
$$pH = 14.000 - 4.918 = 9.082$$

Alternative solution:

$$pOH = -\log 1.81 \times 10^{-5} + \log\frac{[NH_4^+]}{[NH_3]}$$
$$= 4.742 + \log\frac{3.00}{2.00}$$
$$= 4.918 \quad pH = 9.082$$

Titration Equilibria

An acid–base **titration** is a laboratory procedure commonly used to determine the concentration of an unknown solution. A base solution of known concentration is added to an acid solution of unknown concentration (or vice versa) until an acid–base **indicator** visually signals that the **endpoint** of the titration has been reached. The **equivalence point** is the point at which a stoichiometric amount of the base has been added to the acid. Both chemists and chemistry students hope that the equivalence point and the endpoint are close together.

If the acid being titrated is a weak acid, then there are equilibria which will be established and accounted for in the calculations. Typically, a plot of pH of the weak acid solution being titrated versus the volume of the strong base added (the **titrant**) starts at a low pH and gradually rises until close to the equivalence point, where the curve rises dramatically. After the equivalence point region, the curve returns to a gradual increase. This is shown in Figure 15.3.

In many cases, one may know the initial concentration of the weak acid, but may be interested in the pH changes during the titration. To study the changes one can divide the titration curve into four distinctive areas in which the pH is calculated

1. Calculating the initial pH of the weak acid solution is accomplished by treating it as a simple weak acid solution of known concentration and K_a.
2. As base is added, a mixture of weak acid and conjugate base is formed. This is a buffer solution and can be treated as one in the calculations. Determine the moles of acid consumed from the moles of titrant added—that will be the moles of conjugate base formed. Then calculate the molar concentration of weak acid and conjugate base, taking into consideration the volume of titrant added. Finally, apply your buffer equations.
3. At the equivalence point, all the weak acid has been converted to its conjugate base. The conjugate base will react with water, so treat it as a weak base solution and calculate the [OH$^-$] using K_b. Finally, calculate the pH of the solution.
4. After the equivalence point, you have primarily the excess strong base that will determine the pH.

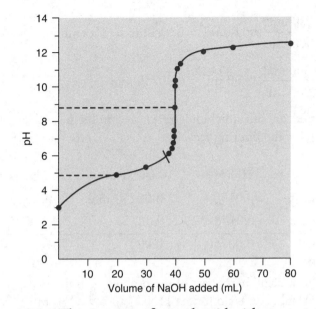

Figure 15.3   The titration of a weak acid with a strong base.

Let's consider a typical titration problem. A 100.0 mL sample of 0.150 M nitrous acid ($pK_a = 3.35$) was titrated with 0.300 M sodium hydroxide. Determine the pH of the solution after the following quantities of base have been added to the acid solution:

a. 0.00 mL
b. 25.00 mL
c. 49.50 mL
d. 50.00 mL
e. 55.00 mL
f. 75.00 mL

a. 0.00 mL. Since no base has been added, only HNO_2 is present. HNO_2 is a weak acid, so this can only be a K_a problem.

$$HNO_2 \rightleftharpoons H^+(aq) + NO_2^-$$
$$0.150 - x \qquad x \qquad x$$

$$K_a = 10^{-3.35} = 4.5 \times 10^{-4} = \frac{(x)(x)}{0.150 - x}$$

Quadratic needed: $x^2 + 4.47 \times 10^{-5}x - 6.70 \times 10^{-5} = 0$

(extra sig. figs.)

$$x = [H^+] = 8.0 \times 10^{-3}M \quad pH = 2.10$$

b. 25.00 mL. Since both an acid and a base are present (and they are not conjugates), this must be a stoichiometry problem. Stoichiometry requires a balanced chemical equation and moles.

$$HNO_2 + NaOH \rightarrow Na^+ + NO_2^- + H_2O$$

$Na^+ + NO_2^-$ could be written as $NaNO_2$, but the separated ions are more useful.

Acid: $\dfrac{0.150 \text{ mol}}{1{,}000 \text{ mL}} \cdot 100.00 \text{ mL} = 0.0150 \text{ mol}$ (This number will be used in all remaining steps.)

Base: $\dfrac{0.300 \text{ mol}}{1{,}000 \text{ mL}} \cdot 25.00 \text{ mL} = 0.00750 \text{ mol}$

Based on the stoichiometry of the problem, and on the moles of acid and base, NaOH is the limiting reagent.

	$HNO_2 +$	$NaOH \rightarrow$	$Na^+ +$	$NO_2^- + H_2O$
init.	0.0150	0.00750 mol	0	0
react.	-0.0148	-0.00750	$+0.00750$	$+0.00750$
final	0.00750	0.000	—	0.00750

The stoichiometry part of the problem is finished.

The solution is no longer HNO_2 and NaOH, but HNO_2 and NO_2^- (a conjugate acid–base pair).

Since a CA/CB pair is present, this is now a buffer problem, and the Henderson–Hasselbalch equation may be used.

$$pH + pK_a + \log (CB/CA) = 3.35 - \log (0.00750/0.00750) = 3.35$$

Note the simplification in the CB/CA concentrations. Both moles are divided by exactly the same volume (since they are in the same solution), so the identical volumes cancel.

$$\left[\dfrac{0.00750 \text{ mol base}}{0.12500 \text{ L solution}} \right]$$
$$\left[\dfrac{0.00750 \text{ mol acid}}{0.12500 \text{ L solution}} \right]$$

c. 49.50 mL. Since both an acid and a base are present (and they are not conjugates), this must be a stoichiometry problem again. Stoichiometry requires a balanced chemical equation and moles.

$$HNO_2 + NaOH \rightarrow Na^+ + NO_2^- + H_2O$$

Base: $\dfrac{0.300 \text{ mol}}{1000 \text{ mL}} \cdot 49.50 \text{ mL} = 0.0148 \text{ mole}$

Based on the stoichiometry of the problem, and on the moles of acid and base, NaOH is the limiting reagent.

	$HNO_2 +$	$NaOH \rightarrow$	$Na^+ +$	$NO_2^- + H_2O$
init.	0.0150	0.0148 mol	0	0
react.	-0.0148	-0.0148	$+0.0148$	$+0.0148$
final	0.0002	0.000	—	0.0148

The stoichiometry part of the problem is finished.

The solution is no longer HNO_2 and NaOH, but HNO_2 and NO_2^- (a conjugate acid–base pair).

Since a CA/CB pair is present, this is now a buffer problem, and the Henderson–Hasselbalch equation may be used.

$$pH = pK_a + \log(CB/CA) = 3.35 + \log(0.0148/0.0002) = 5.2$$

d. 50.00 mL. Since both an acid and a base are present (and they are not conjugates), this must be a stoichiometry problem. Stoichiometry requires a balanced chemical equation and moles.

$$HNO_2 + NaOH \rightarrow Na^+ + NO_2^- + H_2O$$

$$Base: \frac{0.300 \text{ mol}}{1,000 \text{ mL}} 50.00 \text{ mL} = 0.0150 \text{ mol}$$

Based on the stoichiometry of the problem, and on the moles of acid and base, both are limiting reagents.

	$HNO_2 +$	$NaOH \rightarrow$	$Na^+ +$	$NO_2^- + H_2O$
init.	0.0150	0.0150 mol	0	0
react.	−0.0150	−0.0150	+0.0150	+0.0150
final	0.0000	0.000	—	0.0150

$$[NO_2^-] = 0.0150 \text{ mol} / 0.150 \text{L} = 0.100 M$$

The stoichiometry part of the problem is finished.

The solution is no longer HNO_2 and $NaOH$, but an NO_2^- solution (a conjugate base of a weak acid).

Since the CB of a weak acid is present, this is a K_b problem.

$$pK_b = 14.000 - pK_a = 14.000 - 3.35 = 10.65$$

$$NO_2^- + H_2O \rightleftharpoons OH^- + HNO_2$$
$$0.100 - x \qquad x \qquad x$$

$$K_b = 10^{-10.65} = 2.24 \times 10^{-11} = \frac{(x)(x)}{0.100 - x} \quad (\text{neglect} -x)$$

$$x = [OH^-] = 1.50 \times 10^{-6} M \quad pOH = 5.82$$
$$pH = 14.00 - pOH^- = 14.00 - 5.82 = 8.18$$

e. 55.00 mL. Since both an acid and a base are present (and they are not conjugates), this must be a stoichiometry problem. Stoichiometry requires a balanced chemical equation and moles.

$$HNO_2 + NaOH \rightarrow Na^+ + NO_2^- + H_2O$$

$$Base: \frac{0.300 \text{ mol}}{1,000 \text{ mL}} 55.00 \text{ mL} = 0.0165 \text{ mol}$$

Based on the stoichiometry of the problem, and on the moles of acid and base, the acid is now the limiting reagent.

	$HNO_2 +$	$NaOH \rightarrow$	$Na^+ +$	$NO_2^- + H_2O$
init.	0.0150	0.0165 mol	0	0
react.	−0.0150	−0.0150	+0.0150	+0.0150
final	0.0000	0.0015	—	0.0150

The strong base will control the pH.

$$[OH^-] = 0.0015 \text{ mol}/0.155 \text{ L} = 9.7 \times 10^{-3} \; M$$

The stoichiometry part of the problem is finished.
Since this is now a solution of a strong base, it is now a simple pOH/pH problem.

$$pOH = -\log 9.7 \times 10^{-3} = 2.01$$

$$pH = 14.00 - pOH = 14.00 - 2.01 = 11.99$$

f. 75.00 mL. Since both an acid and a base are present (and they are not conjugates), this must be a stoichiometry problem. Stoichiometry requires a balanced chemical equation and moles.

$$HNO_2 + NaOH \rightarrow Na^+ + NO_2^- + H_2O$$

$$\text{Base: } \frac{0.300 \text{ mol}}{1,000 \text{ mL}} 75.00 \text{ ML} = 0.0225 \text{ mol}$$

Based on the stoichiometry of the problem, and on the moles of acid and base, the acid is now the limiting reagent.

	HNO_2 +	$NaOH \rightarrow$	Na^+ +	$NO_2^- + H_2O$
init.	0.0150	0.0225 mol	0	0
react.	-0.0150	-0.0150	$+0.0150$	$+0.0150$
final	0.0000	0.0075	—	0.0150

The strong base will control the pH.

$$[OH^-] = 0.0075 \text{ mol}/0.175 \text{ L} = 4.3 \times 10^{-2} \; M$$

The stoichiometry part of the problem is finished.
Since this is now a solution of a strong base, it is now a simple pOH/pH problem.

$$pOH = -\log 4.3 \times 10^{-2} = 1.37$$

$$pH = 14.00 - pOH = 14.00 - 1.37 = 12.63$$

Solubility Equilibria

Many salts are soluble in water, but some are only slightly soluble. These salts, when placed in water, quickly reach their solubility limit and the ions establish an equilibrium system with the undissolved solid. For example, $PbSO_4$, when dissolved in water, establishes the following equilibrium:

$$PbSO_4(s) \rightleftharpoons Pb^{2+}(aq) + SO_4^{2-}(aq)$$

The equilibrium constant expression for systems of slightly soluble salts is called the **solubility product constant**, K_{sp}. It is the product of the ionic concentrations, each one raised to the power of the coefficient in the balanced chemical equation. It contains no denominator since the concentration of a solid is, by convention, 1 and does not appear in the equilibrium constant expressions. (Some textbooks will say that the concentrations of solids, liquids, and solvents are included in the equilibrium constant.) The K_{sp} expression for the $PbSO_4$ system would be:

$$K_{sp} = [Pb^{2+}][SO_4^{2-}]$$

For this particular salt, the numerical value of K_{sp} is 1.6×10^{-8} at 25°C. Note that the Pb^{2+} and SO_4^{2-} ions are formed in equal amounts, so the right-hand side of the equation could be represented as $[x]^2$. If the numerical value of the solubility product constant is known, then the concentration of the ions can be determined. And if one of the ion concentrations can be determined, then K_{sp} can be calculated.

For example, the K_{sp} of magnesium fluoride in water is 8×10^{-8}. How many grams of magnesium fluoride will dissolve in 0.250 L of water?

$$MgF_2(s) \rightleftharpoons Mg^{2+}(aq) + 2F^-(aq)$$
$$K_{sp} = [Mg^{2+}][F^-]^2 = 8 \times 10^{-8}$$
$$= (x)(2x)^2 = 4x^3 = 8 \times 10^{-8}$$
$$x = 3 \times 10^{-3} = [Mg^{2+}]$$
$$\frac{(3 \times 10^{-3} \text{ mol } Mg^{2+})}{(L)}(0.250 \text{ L})\frac{(1 \text{ mol } MgF_2)(62.3 \text{g } MgF_2)}{(1 \text{ mol } Mg^{2+})(1 \text{ mol } MgF_2)}$$
$$= 0.05 \text{ g}$$

If a slightly soluble salt solution is at equilibrium and a solution containing one of the ions involved in the equilibrium is added, the solubility of the slightly soluble salt is decreased. For example, let's again consider the $PbSO_4$ equilibrium:

$$PbSO_4(s) \rightleftharpoons Pb^{2+}(aq) + SO_4^{2-}(aq)$$

Suppose a solution of Na_2SO_4 is added to this equilibrium system. The additional sulfate ion will disrupt the equilibrium, by Le Châtelier's principle, and shift it to the left, decreasing the solubility. The same would be true if you tried to dissolve $PbSO_4$ in a solution of Na_2SO_4 instead of pure water—the solubility would be lower. This application of Le Châtelier's principle to equilibrium systems of slightly soluble salts is called the **common-ion effect**. Calculations like the ones above involving finding concentrations and K_{sp} can still be done, but the concentration of the additional common ion will have to be inserted into the solubility product constant expression. Sometimes, if K_{sp} is very small and the common ion concentration is large, the concentration of the common ion can simply be approximated by the concentration of the ion added.

For example, calculate the silver ion concentration in each of the following solutions:

a. $Ag_2CrO_4(s)$ + water
b. $Ag_2CrO_4(s)$ + 1.00 M Na_2CrO_4

$K_{sp} = 1.9 \times 10^{-12}$

a. $Ag_2CrO_4(s) \rightleftharpoons 2Ag^+(aq) + CrO_4^{2-}(aq)$

$\quad\quad\quad\quad\quad\quad 2x \quad\quad x$

$K_{sp} = (2x)^2(x) = 1.9 \times 10^{-12} = 4x^3$

$x = 7.8 \times 10^{-5}$
$[Ag^+] = 2x = 1.6 \times 10^{-4}$ M

b. $1.00\ M\ Na_2CrO_4 \rightarrow 1.00\ M\ CrO_4^{2-}$ (common ion)

$$Ag_2CrO_4(s) \rightleftharpoons 2Ag^+(aq) + CrO_4^{2-}(aq)$$
$$\ 2x \qquad 1.00 + x$$

$$K_{sp} = (2x)^2(1.00 + x) = 1.9 \times 10^{-12} = 4x^2 \text{ (neglect } x)$$

$$x = 6.9 \times 10^{-6}\ M$$

$$[Ag^+] = 2x = 1.4 \times 10^{-6}\ M$$

Knowing the value of the solubility product constant can also allow us to predict whether a precipitate will form if two solutions, each containing an ion component of a slightly soluble salt, are mixed. The **ion-product**, sometimes represented as Q (same form as the solubility product constant), is calculated taking into consideration the mixing of the volumes of the two solutions, and this ion-product is compared to K_{sp}. If it is greater than K_{sp}, precipitation will occur until the ion concentrations have been reduced to the solubility level.

If 10.0 mL of a 0.100 M $BaCl_2$ solution is added to 40.0 mL of a 0.0250 M Na_2SO_4 solution, will $BaSO_4$ precipitate? K_{sp} for $BaSO_4 = 1.1 \times 10^{-10}$.

To answer this question, the concentrations of the barium ion and the sulfate ion *before* precipitation must be used. These may be determined simply from $M_{dil} = M_{con}\ V_{con}/V_{dil}$.

For Ba^{2+}: $M_{dil} = (0.100\ M)(10.0\ mL)/(10.0 + 40.0\ mL) = 0.0200\ M$

For SO_4^{2-}: $M_{dil} = (0.0250\ M)(40.0\ mL)/(50.0\ mL) = 0.0200\ M$

Entering these values into the following relation produces:

$$Q = [Ba^{2+}][SO_4^{2-}] = (0.0200)(0.0200) = 0.000400$$

Since Q is greater than K_{sp}, precipitation will occur.

Other Equilibria

Other types of equilibria can be treated in much the same way as the ones discussed above. For example, there is an equilibrium constant associated with the formation of complex ions. This equilibrium constant is called the **formation constant, K_f**. $Zn(H_2O)_4^{2+}$ reacts with ammonia to form the $Zn(NH_3)_4^{2+}$ complex ion according to the following equation:

$$Zn(H_2O)_4^{2+}(aq) + 4NH_3(aq) \rightleftharpoons Zn(NH_3)_4^{2+}(aq) + 4H_2O(l)$$

The K_f of $Zn(NH_3)_4^{2+}(aq)$ is 7.8×10^8, indicating that the equilibrium lies to the right.

Experiments

Equilibrium experiments such as 10, 11, and 13 in Chapter 19 (Experimental Investigations), directly or indirectly involve filling a table like the following:

Reactants and Products
Initial amount
Change
Equilibrium amount

The initial amounts—concentrations or pressures—are normally zero for the products, and a measured or calculated value for the reactants. Once equilibrium has been established, the amount of at least one of the substances is determined. Based on the change in this one substance and the stoichiometry, the amounts of the other materials may be calculated.

Measurements may include the pressure, the mass (to be converted to moles), the volume (to be used in calculations), and the pH (to be converted into either the hydrogen ion or hydroxide ion concentration). Some experiments measure the color intensity (with a spectrophotometer), which may be converted to a concentration.

Do not make the mistake of "measuring" a change. Changes are never measured; they are always calculated.

Common Mistakes to Avoid

1. Be sure to check the units and significant figures of your final answer.
2. When writing equilibrium constant expressions, use products over reactants. Each concentration is raised to the power of the coefficient in the balanced chemical equation.
3. In converting from K_c to K_p be sure to use the ideal gas constant, R, whose units are consistent with the units of the partial pressures of the gases.
4. Remember, in working Le Châtelier problems, pressure effects are important only for gases that are involved in the equilibrium.
5. Be sure, when working weak-base problems, to use K_b and not K_a.
6. In titration problems, make sure you compensate for dilution when mixing two solutions together.
7. A K_a expression must have $[H^+]$ in the numerator, and a K_b expression must have $[OH^-]$ in the numerator.

❯ Review Questions

Use these questions to review the content of this chapter and practice for the AP Chemistry exam. First are 22 multiple-choice questions similar to what you will encounter in Section I of the AP Chemistry exam. Following those is a long free-response question like the ones in Section II of the exam. To make these questions an even more authentic practice for the actual exam, time yourself following the instructions provided.

Multiple-Choice Questions

Answer the following questions in 30 minutes. You may not use a calculator. You may use the periodic table and the equation sheet at the back of this book.

1. A 0.1 molar solution of acetic acid (CH_3COOH) has a pH of about:

   (A) 1
   (B) 3
   (C) 7
   (D) 10

2.

Acid	K_a, acid dissociation constant
H_3PO_4	7.2×10^{-3}
$H_2PO_4^-$	6.3×10^{-8}
HPO_4^{2-}	4.2×10^{-13}

Using the given information, choose the best answer for preparing a pH = 8 buffer.

   (A) $K_2HPO_4 + KH_2PO_4$
   (B) H_3PO_4
   (C) $K_2HPO_4 + K_3PO_4$
   (D) K_3PO_4

Use the following information for questions 3–4.

Ionization Constants:

HCOOH	$K_a = 1.8 \times 10^{-4}$
CH_3NH_2	$K_b = 4.4 \times 10^{-4}$
H_3PO_2	$K_{a1} = 3 \times 10^{-2}$
	$K_{a2} = 1.7 \times 10^{-7}$

3. What is a solution with an initial KCOOH concentration of 1 M, and an initial K_2HPO_2 concentration of 1 M?

    (A) a solution with a pH > 7, which is a buffer
    (B) a solution with a pH < 7, which is not a buffer
    (C) a solution with a pH < 7, which is a buffer
    (D) a solution with a pH > 7, which is not a buffer

4. What is a solution with an initial H_3PO_2 concentration of 1 M and an initial KH_2PO_2 concentration of 1 M?

    (A) a solution with a pH > 7, which is a buffer
    (B) a solution with a pH < 7, which is not a buffer
    (C) a solution with a pH < 7, which is a buffer
    (D) a solution with a pH > 7, which is not a buffer

5. A solution of a weak base is titrated with a solution of a standard strong acid. The progress of the titration is followed with a pH meter. Which of the following observations would occur?

    (A) The pH of the solution gradually decreases throughout the experiment.
    (B) Initially the pH of the solution drops slowly, and then it drops much more rapidly.
    (C) At the equivalence point, the pH is 7.
    (D) After the equivalence point, the pH becomes constant because this is the buffer region.

6. What is the ionization constant, K_a, for a weak monoprotic acid if a 0.30 molar solution has a pH of 4.0?

    (A) 3.3×10^{-8}
    (B) 4.7×10^{-2}
    (C) 1.7×10^{-6}
    (D) 3.0×10^{-4}

7. Phenol, C_6H_5OH, has $K_a = 1.0 \times 10^{-10}$. What is the pH of a 0.010 M solution of phenol?

    (A) between 3 and 7
    (B) 10
    (C) 2
    (D) between 7 and 10

8. You are given equimolar solutions of each of the following. Which has the lowest pH?

    (A) NH_4Cl
    (B) NaCl
    (C) K_3PO_4
    (D) Na_2CO_3

9. When sodium nitrite dissolves in water:

    (A) The solution is acidic because of hydrolysis of the sodium ion.
    (B) The solution is basic because of hydrolysis of the NO_2^- ion.
    (C) The solution is basic because of hydrolysis of the sodium ion.
    (D) The solution is acidic because of hydrolysis of the NO_2^- ion.

10. Which of the following solutions has a pH nearest 7?

    (A) 1 M $H_2C_2O_4$ (oxalic acid) and 1 M KHC_2O_4 (potassium hydrogen oxalate)
    (B) 1 M KNO_3 (potassium nitrate) and 1 M HNO_3 (nitric acid)
    (C) 1 M NH_3 (ammonia) and 1 M NH_4NO_3 (ammonium nitrate)
    (D) 1 M CH_3NH_2 (methylamine) and 1 M $HC_2H_3O_2$ (acetic acid)

11. Determine the OH^-(aq) concentration in 1.0 M aniline ($C_6H_5NH_2$) solution. (The K_b for aniline is 4.0×10^{-10}.)

    (A) 2.0×10^{-5} M
    (B) 4.0×10^{-10} M
    (C) 3.0×10^{-6} M
    (D) 5.0×10^{-7} M

12. A student wishes to reduce the zinc ion concentration in a saturated zinc iodate solution to 1×10^{-6} M. How many moles of solid KIO_3 must be added to 1.00 L of solution? [K_{sp} $Zn(IO_3)_2 = 4 \times 10^{-6}$ at 25°C]

    (A) 1 mol
    (B) 0.5 mol
    (C) 2 mol
    (D) 4 mol

13. At constant temperature, a change in volume will NOT affect the moles of substances present in which of the following?

(A) $H_2(g) + I_2(g) \rightleftarrows 2\,HI(g)$
(B) $CO(g) + Cl_2(g) \rightleftarrows COCl_2(g)$
(C) $PCl_5(g) \rightleftarrows PCl_3(g) + Cl_2(g)$
(D) $N_2(g) + 3\,H_2(g) \rightleftarrows 2\,NH_3(g)$

14. The equilibrium constant for the hydrolysis of $C_2O_4^{2-}$ is best represented by which of the following?

(A) $K = [OH^-][C_2O_4^{2-}]/[HC_2O_4^-]$
(B) $K = [H_3O^+][C_2O_4^{2-}]/[HC_2O_4^-]$
(C) $K = [HC_2O_4^-][OH^-]/[C_2O_4^{2-}]$
(D) $K = [C_2O_4^{2-}]/[HC_2O_4^-][OH^-]$

15. $ZnS(s) + 2H^+(aq) \rightleftarrows Zn^{2+}(aq) + H_2S(aq)$

What is the equilibrium constant for the above reaction? The successive acid dissociation constants for H_2S are 9.5×10^{-8} (K_{a1}) and 1×10^{-19} (K_{a2}). The K_{sp}, the solubility product constant, for ZnS equals 1.6×10^{-24}.

(A) $1.6 \times 10^{-24}/9.5 \times 10^{-8}$
(B) $1 \times 10^{-79}/1.6 \times 10^{-24}$
(C) $1.6 \times 10^{-24}/9.5 \times 10^{-27}$
(D) $9.5 \times 10^{-8}/1.6 \times 10^{-24}$

16. $C(s) + H_2O(g) \rightleftarrows CO(g) + H_2O(g)$ endothermic

An equilibrium mixture of the reactants is placed in a sealed container at 150°C. The amount of the products may be increased by which of the following changes?

(A) decreasing the volume of the container
(B) raising the temperature of the container and increasing the volume of the container
(C) lowering the temperature of the container
(D) adding 1 mol of C(s) to the container

17. $CH_4(g) + CO_2(g) \rightleftarrows 2\,CO(g) + 2\,H_2(g)$

A 1.00 L flask is filled with 0.30 mol of CH_4 and 0.40 mol of CO_2, and allowed to come to equilibrium. At equilibrium, there are 0.20 mol of CO in the flask. What is the value of K_c, the equilibrium constant, for the reaction?

(A) 1.2
(B) 0.027
(C) 0.30
(D) 0.060

18. $NO_2(g) \rightleftarrows 2\,NO(g) + O_2(g)$

The above materials were sealed in a flask and allowed to come to equilibrium at a certain temperature. A small quantity of $O_2(g)$ was added to the flask, and the mixture was allowed to return to equilibrium at the same temperature. Which of the following has increased over its original equilibrium value?

(A) the quantity of $NO_2(g)$ present
(B) the quantity of $NO(g)$ present
(C) the equilibrium constant, K, increases
(D) the rate of the reaction

19. $2CH_4(g) + O_2(g) \rightleftarrows 2CO(g) + 4H_2(g) \quad \Delta H < 0$

In order to increase the value of the equilibrium constant, K, which of the following changes must be made to the above equilibrium?

(A) increase the temperature
(B) increase the volume
(C) decrease the temperature
(D) add CO(g)

20. The addition of nitric acid increases the solubility of which of the following compounds?

(A) KCl(s)
(B) $Pb(CN)_2(s)$
(C) $Cu(NO_3)_2(s)$
(D) $NH_4NO_3(s)$

21. At constant temperature, a change in the volume of the system will NOT affect the moles of the substances present in which of the following?

(A) $C(s) + H_2O(g) \leftrightarrows H_2(g) + CO(g)$
(B) $3\,O_2(g) \leftrightarrows 2\,O_3(g)$
(C) $Xe(g) + 2\,F_2(g) \leftrightarrows XeF_4(g)$
(D) $6\,CO_2(g) + 6\,H_2O(l) \leftrightarrows 6\,O_2(g) + C_6H_{12}O_6(aq)$

22. Which of the following is the strongest Brønsted-Lowry acid?

(A) HBrO
(B) $HBrO_3$
(C) $HBrO_2$
(D) $HBrO_4$

Answers and Explanations for the Multiple-Choice Questions

1. **B**—An acid, any acid, will give a pH below 7; thus, answers C and D are eliminated. A 0.1 molar solution of a strong acid would have a pH of 1. Acetic acid is not a strong acid, and this eliminates answer A.

2. **A**—The K nearest 10^{-8} will give a pH near 8. The answer must involve the $H_2PO_4^-$ ion.

3. **D**—The two substances are not a conjugate acid–base pair, so this is not a buffer. Both compounds are salts of a strong base and a weak acid; such salts are basic (pH > 7).

4. **C**—The two substances constitute a conjugate acid–base pair, so this is a buffer. The pH should be near $-\log K_{a1}$. This is about 2 (acid).

5. **B**—Any time an acid is added, the pH will drop. The reaction of the weak base with the acid produces the conjugate acid of the weak base. The combination of the weak base and its conjugate is a buffer, so the pH will not change very much until all the base is consumed. After all the base has reacted, the pH will drop much more rapidly. The equivalence point of a weak base–strong acid titration is always below 7 (only strong base–strong acid titrations will give a pH of 7 at the equivalence point). The value of pOH is equal to pK_b halfway to the equivalence point.

6. **A**—If pH = 4.0, then $[H^+] = 1 \times 10^{-4} = [A^-]$, and $[HA] = 0.30 - 1 \times 10^{-4}$. The generic K_a is $[H^+][A^-]/[HA]$, and when the values are entered into this equation: $(1 \times 10^{-4})^2/0.30 = 3.3 \times 10^{-8}$. Since you can estimate the answer, no actual calculations are necessary.

7. **A**—This is an acid-dissociation constant, thus the solution must be acidic (pH < 7). The pH of a 0.010 M strong acid would be 2.0. This is not a strong acid, so the pH must be above 2.

8. **A**—A is the salt of a strong acid and a weak base; it is acidic. B is a salt of a strong acid and a strong base; they are neutral. C and D are salts of a weak acid and a strong base; they are basic. The lowest pH would be the acidic choice.

9. **B**—Sodium nitrite is a salt of a weak acid and a strong base. Ions from strong bases, Na^+ in this case, do not undergo hydrolysis, and do not affect the pH. Ions from weak acids, NO_2^- in this case, undergo hydrolysis to produce basic solutions.

10. **D**—The weak acid and the weak base partially cancel each other to give a nearly neutral solution.

11. **A**—The equilibrium constant expression is: $K_b = 4.0 \times 10^{-10} = [OH^-][C_6H_5NH_3^+]/[C_6H_5NH_2]$. This expression becomes: $(x)(x)/(1.0 - x) = 4.0 \times 10^{-10}$, which simplifies to: $x^2/1.0 = 4.0 \times 10^{-10}$. Taking the square root of each side gives: $x = 2.0 \times 10^{-5} = [OH^-]$. Since you can estimate the answer, no actual calculations are necessary.

12. **C**—The solubility-product constant expression is: $K_{sp} = [Zn^{2+}][IO_3^-]^2 = 4 \times 10^{-6}$. This may be rearranged to: $[IO_3^-]^2 = 4 \times 10^{-6}/[Zn^{2+}]$. Inserting the desired zinc ion concentration gives: $[IO_3^-]^2 = 4 \times 10^{-6}/(1 \times 10^{-6}) = 4$. Taking the square root of each side leaves a desired IO_3^- concentration of 2 M. Two moles of KIO_3 must be added to 1.00 L of solution to produce this concentration. Since you can estimate the answer, no actual calculations are necessary.

13. **A**—When dealing with gaseous equilibriums, volume changes are important when there is a difference in the total number of moles of gas on opposite sides of the equilibrium arrow. All the answers, except A, have differing numbers of moles of gas on opposite sides of the equilibrium arrow.

14. **C**—Hydrolysis of any ion begins with the interaction of that ion with water. Thus, both the ion and water must be on the left side of the equilibrium arrow, and hence in the denominator of the equilibrium-constant expression (water, as all solvents, will be left out of the expression). The oxalate ion is the conjugate base of a weak acid. As a base it will produce OH^- in solution along with the conjugate acid ($HC_2O_4^-$) of the base. The equilibrium reaction is: $C_2O_4^{2-}(aq) + H_2O(l) \rightleftharpoons OH^-(aq) + HC_2O_4^-(aq)$.

15. **C**—The equilibrium given is actually the sum of the following three equilibriums:

$$ZnS(s) \rightleftarrows Zn^{2+}(aq) + S^{2-}(aq)$$
$$K_{sp} = 1.6 \times 10^{-24}$$

$$S^{2-}(aq) + H^+(aq) \rightleftarrows HS^-(aq)$$
$$K = 1/K_{a2} = 1/1 \times 10^{-19}$$

$$HS^-(aq) + H^+(aq) \rightleftarrows H_2S(aq)$$
$$K' = 1/K_{a1} = 1/9.5 \times 10^{-8}$$

Summing these equations means you need to multiply the equilibrium constants:

$$K_{sum} = K_{sp}KK' = K_{sp}/K_{a2}K_{a1}$$
$$= 1.6 \times 10^{-24}/[(1 \times 10^{-19})(9.5 \times 10^{-8})]$$

16. **B**—The addition or removal of some solid, as long as some remains present, will not change the equilibrium. An increase in volume will cause the equilibrium to shift toward the side with more moles of gas (right). Raising the temperature of an endothermic process will shift the equilibrium to the right. Any shift to the right will increase the amounts of the products.

17. **B**—Using the following table:

	[CH₄]	[CO₂]	[CO]	[H₂]
Initial	0.30	0.40	0	0
Change	−x	−x	+2x	+2x
Equilibrium	0.30 − x	0.40 − x	2x	2x

The presence of 0.20 mol of CO (0.20 *M*) at equilibrium means that $2x = 0.20$ and that $x = 0.10$. Using this value for *x*, the bottom line of the table becomes:

	[CH₄]	[CO₂]	[CO]	[H₂]
Equilibrium	0.20	0.30	0.20	0.20

The equilibrium expression is: $K = [CO]^2[H_2]^2/[CH_4][CO_2]$. Entering the equilibrium values into the equilibrium expression gives: $K = (0.20)^2(0.20)^2/(0.20)(0.30)$

18. **A**—The addition of a product will cause the equilibrium to shift to the left. The amounts of all the reactants will increase, and the amounts of all the products will decrease (the O_2 will not go below its earlier equilibrium value since excess was added). The value of *K* is constant, unless the temperature is changed. The rates of the forward and reverse reactions are equal at equilibrium.

19. **C**—The only way to change the value of *K* is to change the temperature. For an exothermic process ($\Delta H < 0$), *K* is increased by a decrease in temperature.

20. **B**—Nitric acid, being an acid, will react with a base. In addition to obvious bases containing OH^-, the salts of weak acids are also bases. All of the anions, except CN^-, are from strong acids.

21. **D**—As long as there are equal numbers of moles of gas on each side of the equilibrium arrow, then volume or pressure changes will not affect the equilibrium. The presence of solids, liquids, or aqueous phases does not make any difference as long as some of the phase is present.

22. **D**—Perbromic acid, $HBrO_4$, is expected to be the strongest acid in this group because the greater number of oxygen atoms pulls more electron density from the hydrogen atom making it easier to be lost as a hydrogen ion.

Free-Response Question

You have 15 minutes to answer the following long question. You may use a calculator and the tables in the back of the book.

Question 1

An aqueous solution is prepared that is initially 0.100 M in CdI_4^{2-}. After equilibrium is established, the solution is found to be 0.013 M in Cd^{2+}. The products of the equilibrium are $Cd^{2+}(aq)$ and $I^-(aq)$.

(a) Derive the expression for the dissociation equilibrium constant, K_d, for the equilibrium and determine the value of the constant.

(b) What will be the cadmium ion concentration arising when 0.400 mol of KI is added to 1.00 L of the solution in part **a**?

(c) A solution is prepared by mixing 0.500 L of the solution from part **b** and 0.500 L of 2.0×10^{-5} M NaOH. Will cadmium hydroxide, $Cd(OH)_2$, precipitate? The K_{sp} for cadmium hydroxide is 2.2×10^{-14}.

(d) When the initial solution is heated, the cadmium ion concentration increases. Is the equilibrium an exothermic or an endothermic process? Explain how you arrived at your conclusion.

Answer and Explanation for the Free-Response Question

(a) $K_d = [Cd^{2+}][I^-]^4/[CdI_4^{2-}]$

> Give yourself 1 point for this expression.
> Using the following table:

	CdI_4^{2-} (aq)	Cd^{2+} (aq)	I^- (aq)
Initial	0.100 M	0	0
Change	$-x$	$+x$	$+4x$
Equilibrium	$0.100 - x$	x	$4x$

> The value of $[Cd^{2+}]$ is given (= 0.013), and this is x. This changes the last line of the table to

	CdI_4^{2-} (aq)	Cd^{2+} (aq)	I^- (aq)
Equilibrium	$0.100 - x = 0.087$	$x = 0.013$	$4x = 0.052$

> Entering these values into the K_d expression gives: $(0.013)(0.052)^4/(0.087) = 1.1 \times 10^{-6}$.
> Give yourself 1 point for this answer. You can also get 1 point if you correctly put your values into the wrong equation.

(b) The table in part **a** changes to the following:

	CdI_4^{2-} (aq)	Cd^{2+} (aq)	I^- (aq)
Initial	0.100 M	0	0.400
Change	$-x$	$+x$	$+4x$
Equilibrium	$0.100 - x$	x	$0.400 + 4x$

$$K_d = [Cd^{2+}][I^-]^4/[CdI_4^{2-}] = 1.1 \times 10^{-6} = (x)(0.400 + 4x)^4/(0.100 - x)$$
$$= (x)(0.400)^4/(0.100)$$
$$x = 4.3 \times 10^{-6} M = [Cd^{2+}]$$

> Give yourself 1 point for the correct setup and 1 point for the correct answer. If you got the wrong value for K in part **a**, you can still get one or both points for using it correctly.

(c) The equilibrium is $Cd(OH)_2 \rightleftarrows Cd^{2+}(aq) + 2\ OH^-(aq)$

The dilution reduces both the Cd^{2+} and OH^- concentration by a factor of 2. This gives:

$$[Cd^{2+}] = 4.3 \times 10^{-6}/2 = 2.2 \times 10^{-6} \text{ and } [OH^-] = 2.0 \times 10^{-5}/2 = 1.0 \times 10^{-5}$$

The reaction quotient is $Q = [Cd^{2+}][OH^-]^2 = (2.2 \times 10^{-6})(1.0 \times 10^{-5})^2 = 2.2 \times 10^{-16}$. This value is less than the K_{sp}, so no precipitate will form.

Give yourself 1 point for a correct calculation, and another point for the correct conclusion. If you correctly use a wrong $[Cd^{2+}]$ you calculated in part **b**, you can still get both points.

(d) Since the cadmium ion concentration increases, the equilibrium must shift to the right. Endothermic processes shift to the right when they are heated. This is in accordance with Le Châtelier's principle.

Give yourself 1 point for endothermic. Give yourself 1 point for mentioning Le Châtelier's principle.

Your score is based on a total of 8 points. Subtract 1 point if any answer has an incorrect number of significant figures.

❯ Rapid Review

- A chemical equilibrium is established when two exactly opposite reactions occur in the same container at the same time and with the same rates of reaction.

- At equilibrium the concentrations of the chemical species become constant, but not necessarily equal.

- For the reaction $aA + bB \rightleftarrows cC + dD$, the equilibrium constant expression would be:

  $K_c = \dfrac{[C]^c[D]^d}{[A]^a[B]^b}$. Know how to apply this equation.

- Le Châtelier's principle says that if an equilibrium system is stressed, it will reestablish equilibrium by shifting the reactions involved. A change in concentration of a species will cause the equilibrium to shift to reverse that change. A change in pressure or temperature will cause the equilibrium to shift to reverse that change.

- Strong acids completely dissociate in water, whereas weak acids only partially dissociate.

- Weak acids and bases establish an equilibrium system.

- Under the Brønsted–Lowry acid–base theory, acids are proton (H^+) donors and bases are proton acceptors.

- Conjugate acid–base pairs differ only in a single H^+; the one that has the extra H^+ is the acid.

- The equilibrium for a weak acid is described by K_a, the acid dissociation constant.

  It has the form: $K_a = \dfrac{[H^+][A^-]}{[HA]}$. Know how to apply this equation.

- Most times the equilibrium concentration of the weak acid, [HA], can be approximated by the initial molarity of the weak acid.

- Knowing K_a and the initial concentration of the weak acid allows the calculation of the [H^+].

- Water is an amphoteric substance, acting either as an acid or a base.

- The product of the [H^+] and [OH^-] in a solution or in pure water is a constant, K_w, called the water dissociation constant, 1.0×10^{-14}. $K_w = [H^+][OH^-] = 1.0 \times 10^{-14}$ at 25°C. Know how to apply this equation.

- The pH is a measure of the acidity of a solution. $pH = -\log[H^+]$. Know how to apply this equation and estimate the pH from the [H^+].

- On the pH scale 7 is neutral; pH > 7 is basic; and pH < 7 is acidic.

- $pH + pOH = pK_w = 14.00$. Know how to apply this equation.

- K_b is the ionization constant for a weak base. $K_b = \dfrac{[HB^+][OH^-]}{[HB]}$. Know how to apply this equation.

- $K_a \times K_b = K_w$ for conjugate acid–base pairs. Know how to apply this equation.

- Buffers are solutions that resist a change in pH by neutralizing either an added acid or an added base.

- The Henderson–Hasselbalch equation allows the calculation of the pH of a buffer solution: $pH = pK_a + \log\dfrac{[A^-]}{[HA]}$. Know how to apply this equation.

- The buffer capacity is a quantitative measure of the ability of a buffer to resist a change in pH. The more concentrated the acid–base components of the buffer, the higher its buffer capacity.

- A titration is a laboratory technique to determine the concentration of an acid or base solution.

- An acid–base indicator is used in a titration and changes color in the presence of an acid or base.

- The equivalence point or endpoint of a titration is the point at which an equivalent amount of acid or base has been added to the base or acid being neutralized.

- Know how to determine the pH at any point of an acid–base titration.

- The solubility product constant, K_{sp}, is the equilibrium constant expression for sparingly soluble salts. It is the product of the ionic concentration of the ions, each raised to the power of the coefficient of the balanced chemical equation.

- Know how to apply ion-products and K_{sp} values to predict precipitation.

- Formation constants describe complex ion equilibria.

CHAPTER 16

Electrochemistry

IN THIS CHAPTER

Summary: Electrochemistry is the study of chemical reactions that produce electricity, and chemical reactions that take place because electricity is supplied. Electrochemical reactions may be of many types. Electroplating is an electrochemical process. So are the electrolysis of water, the production of aluminum metal, and the production and storage of electricity in batteries. All these processes involve the transfer of electrons and redox reactions.

Keywords and Equations

A table of half-reactions is given in the exam booklet and in the back of this book.

I = current (amperes)
$E°$ = standard reduction potential
$G°$ = standard free energy
Faraday's constant, F = 96,500 coulombs per mole of electrons
Gas constant, R = 8.31 volt coulomb mol^{-1} K^{-1}

q = charge (coulombs)
K = equilibrium constant

$$I = \frac{q}{t} \qquad \log K = \frac{nE°}{0.0592} \qquad \Delta G° = -nFE°$$

$$E_{cell} = E°_{cell} - \left(\frac{RT}{nF}\right) \ln Q = E°_{cell} - \left(\frac{0.0592}{n}\right) \log Q \text{ at } 25°C$$

$$Q = \frac{[C]^c [D]^d}{[A]^a [B]^b} \quad \text{where } aA + bB \rightarrow cC + dD$$

Redox Reactions

Electrochemical reactions involve redox reactions. In the chapter on Reactions and Periodicity, we discussed redox reactions, but here is a brief review: *Redox* is a term that stands for reduction and oxidation. Reduction is the gain of electrons, and oxidation is the loss of electrons. For example, suppose a piece of zinc metal is placed in a solution containing Cu^{2+}. Very quickly, a reddish solid forms on the surface of the zinc metal. That substance is copper metal. At the molecular level, the zinc metal is losing electrons to form Zn^{2+} and Cu^{2+} is gaining electrons to form copper metal. These two processes can be shown as:

$$Zn(s) \rightarrow Zn^{2+}(aq) + 2e^- \qquad \text{(oxidation)}$$

$$Cu^{2+}(aq) + 2e^- \rightarrow Cu(s) \qquad \text{(reduction)}$$

The electrons that are being lost by the zinc metal are the same electrons that are being gained by the cupric ion. The zinc metal is being oxidized, and the cupric cation is being reduced.

Something must cause the oxidation (taking of the electrons), and that substance is called the oxidizing agent (the reactant being reduced). In the example above, the oxidizing agent is Cu^{2+}. The reactant undergoing oxidation is called the reducing agent, because it is furnishing the electrons used in the reduction half-reaction. Zinc metal is the reducing agent above. The two half-reactions, oxidation and reduction, can be added together to give you the overall redox reaction. The electrons must cancel—that is, there must be the same number of electrons lost as electrons gained:

$$Zn(s) + Cu^{2+}(aq) + 2e^- \rightarrow Zn^{2+}(aq) + 2e^- + Cu(s) \qquad \text{or}$$

$$Zn(s) + Cu^{2+}(aq) \rightarrow Zn^{2+}(aq) + Cu(s)$$

In these redox reactions, like the electrochemical reactions we will show you, there is a simultaneous loss and gain of electrons. In the oxidation reaction (commonly called a half-reaction) electrons are being lost, but in the reduction half-reaction those very same electrons are being gained. So, in redox reactions electrons are being exchanged as reactants are being converted into products. This electron exchange may be direct, as when copper metal plates out on a piece of zinc, or it may be indirect, as in an electrochemical cell (battery). In this chapter, we will show you both processes and the calculations associated with each.

The balancing of redox reactions is beginning to appear on the AP exam, so we have included the half-reaction method of balancing redox reactions in the appendixes, just in case you are having trouble with the technique in your chemistry class.

The definitions for oxidation and reduction given above are the most common and the most useful ones. A couple of others might also be useful: Oxidation is the gain of oxygen or loss of hydrogen and involves an increase in oxidation number. Reduction is the gain of hydrogen or loss of oxygen and involves a decrease in oxidation number.

Electrochemical Cells

In the example above, the electron transfer was direct; that is, the electrons were exchanged directly from the zinc metal to the cupric ions. But such a direct electron transfer doesn't allow for any useful work to be done by the electrons. Therefore, in order to use these electrons, indirect electron transfer must be done. The two half-reactions are physically separated and connected by a wire. The electrons that are lost in the oxidation half-reaction are allowed to flow through the wire to get to the reduction half-reaction. While those

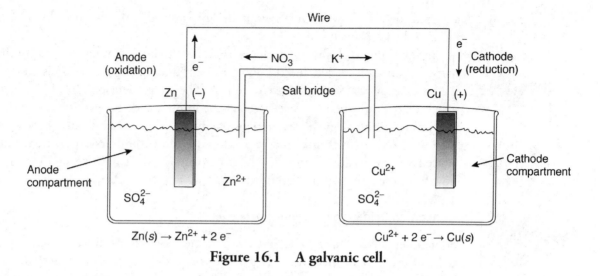

Figure 16.1   A galvanic cell.

electrons are flowing through the wire they can do useful work, like powering a calculator or a pacemaker. **Electrochemical cells** use indirect electron transfer to produce electricity by a redox reaction, or they use electricity to produce a desired redox reaction.

Galvanic (Voltaic) Cells

Galvanic (voltaic) cells produce electricity by using a redox reaction. Let's take that zinc/copper redox reaction that we studied before (the direct electron transfer reaction) and make it a galvanic cell by separating the oxidation and reduction half-reactions. (See Figure 16.1.)

Instead of one container, as before, two will be used. A piece of zinc metal will be placed in one, a piece of copper metal in another. A solution of aqueous zinc sulfate will be added to the beaker containing the zinc electrode and an aqueous solution of copper(II) sulfate will be added to the beaker containing the copper metal. The zinc and copper metals will form the **electrodes** of the cell, the solid portion of the cell that conducts the electrons involved in the redox reaction. The solutions in which the electrodes are immersed are called the **electrode compartments**. The electrodes are connected by a wire and . . . nothing happens. If the redox reactions were to proceed, the beaker containing the zinc metal would build up a positive charge due to the zinc cations being produced in the oxidation half-reaction. The beaker containing the copper would build up a negative charge due to the loss of the copper(II) ions. The solutions (compartments) must maintain electrical neutrality. To accomplish this, a salt bridge will be used. A **salt bridge** is often an inverted U-tube that holds a gel containing a concentrated electrolyte solution, such as KNO_3 in this example. Any electrolyte could be used as long as it does not interfere with the redox reaction. The anions in the salt bridge will migrate through the gel into the beaker containing the zinc metal, and the salt-bridge cations will migrate in the opposite direction. In this way, electrical neutrality is maintained. In electrical terms, the circuit has been completed and the redox reaction can occur. The zinc electrode is being oxidized in one beaker, and the copper(II) ions in the other beaker are being reduced to copper metal. The same redox reaction is happening in this indirect electron transfer as happened in the direct one:

$$Zn(s) + Cu^{2+}(aq) \rightarrow Zn^{2+}(aq) + Cu(s)$$

The difference is that the electrons are now flowing through a wire from the oxidation half-reaction to the reduction half-reaction. And electrons flowing through a wire is electricity, which can do work. If a voltmeter was connected to the wire connecting the two electrodes, a current of 1.10 V would be measured. This galvanic cell shown in Figure 16.1 is commonly called a Daniell cell.

In the Daniell cell shown in Figure 16.1, note that the compartment with the oxidation half-reaction is on the left and the compartment undergoing reduction is on the right. This is a convention that you will have to follow. The AP graders look for this. The electrode at which oxidation is taking place is called the **anode**, and the electrolyte solution in which it is immersed is called the **anode compartment**. The electrode at which reduction takes place is called the **cathode**, and its solution is the **cathode compartment**. The anode is labeled with a negative sign (−), while the cathode has a positive sign (+). The electrons flow from the anode to the cathode.

Remember: Oxidation is an anode process.

Sometimes the half-reaction(s) involved in the cell lack a solid conductive part to act as the electrode, so an **inert (inactive) electrode**, a solid conducting electrode that does not take part in the redox reaction, is used. Graphite and platinum are commonly used as inert electrodes.

Note: The electrode must be a conductor onto which a wire may be attached. It can never be an ion in solution.

Cell Notation

Cell notation is a shorthand notation representing a galvanic cell. To write the cell notation in Figure 16.1:

1. Write the chemical formula of the anode: $\mathbf{Zn(s)}$
2. Draw a single vertical line to represent the phase boundary between the solid anode and the solution: $\mathbf{Zn(s)|}$
3. Write the reactive part of the anode compartment with its initial concentration (if known) in parentheses (assume $1M$ in this case): $\mathbf{Zn(s)|Zn^{2+}(1\,M)}$
4. Draw a double vertical line to represent the salt bridge connecting the two electrode compartments: $\mathbf{Zn(s)|Zn^{2+}(1\,M)||}$
5. Write the reactive part of the cathode compartment with its initial concentration (if known) shown in parentheses: $\mathbf{Zn(s)|Zn^{2+}(1\,M)||Cu^{2+}(1\,M)}$
6. Draw a single vertical line representing the phase boundary between the solution and the solid cathode: $\mathbf{Zn(s)|Zn^{2+}(1\,M)||Cu^{2+}(1\,M)|}$
7. Finally, write the chemical formula of the cathode: $\mathbf{Zn(s)|Zn^{2+}(1M)||Cu^{2+}(1\,M)|Cu(s)}$

If an inert electrode is used because one or both redox half-reactions do not have a suitable conducting electrode material associated with the reaction, the inert electrode is shown with its phase boundary. If the electrode components are in the same phase, they are separated by commas; if not, a vertical phase boundary line. For example, consider the following redox reaction:

$$Ag^+(aq) + Fe^{2+}(aq) \rightarrow Fe^{3+}(aq) + Ag(s)$$

The oxidation of the ferrous ion to ferric doesn't involve a suitable electrode material, so an inert electrode, such as platinum, would be used. The cell notation would then be:

$$Pt(s)|Fe^{2+}(aq), Fe^{3+}(aq)||Ag^+(aq)|Ag(s)$$

Cell Potential

In the discussion of the Daniell cell, we indicated that this cell produces 1.10 volts. This voltage is really the difference in potential between the two half-cells. There are half-cell potentials associated with all half-cells. A list of all possible combinations of half-cells would be tremendously long. Therefore, a way of combining desired half-cells has been developed. The cell potential (really the half-cell potentials) depends on concentration and temperature, but initially we'll simply look at the half-cell potentials at the standard temperature of 298 K (25°C) and all components in their standard states (1 M concentration of all solutions, 1 atmosphere pressure for any gases, and pure solid electrodes). All the half-cell potentials are tabulated as the reduction potentials, that is, the potentials associated with the reduction reaction. The hydrogen half-reaction has been defined as the standard and has been given a value of exactly 0.00 V. All the other half-reactions have been measured relative to it, some positive and some negative. The table of **standard reduction potentials** provided on the AP exam is shown in Table 16.1, on the next page.

Here are some things to be aware of in looking at this table:

- All reactions are shown in terms of the reduction reaction relative to the standard hydrogen electrode.
- The more positive the value of the voltage associated with the half-reaction ($E°$), the more readily the reaction occurs.
- The strength of the oxidizing agent increases as the value becomes more positive, and the strength of the reducing agent increases as the value becomes more negative.

This table of standard reduction potentials can be used to write the overall cell reaction and to calculate the **standard cell potential ($E°$)**, the potential (voltage) associated with the cell at standard conditions. There are a few things to remember when using these standard reduction potentials to generate the cell reaction and cell potential:

1. The standard cell potential for a galvanic cell is a positive value, $E° > 0$.

2. Because one half-reaction must involve oxidation, one of the half-reactions shown in the table of reduction potentials must be reversed to indicate the oxidation. If the half-reaction is reversed, the sign of the standard reduction potential must be reversed. However, this is not necessary to calculate the standard cell potential.

3. Because oxidation occurs at the anode and reduction at the cathode, the standard cell potential can be calculated from the standard reduction potentials of the two half-reactions involved in the overall reaction by using the equation:

$$E°_{cell} = E°_{cathode} - E°_{anode} > 0$$

But remember, both $E°_{cathode}$ and $E°_{anode}$ are shown as reduction potentials, used directly from the table without reversing.

Once the standard cell potential has been calculated, the reaction can be written by reversing the half-reaction associated with the anode and adding the half-reactions together, using appropriate multipliers if needed to ensure that the numbers of electrons lost and gained are equal.

Suppose a galvanic cell was to be constructed utilizing the following two half-reactions taken from Table 16.1:

$$Ni^{2+}(aq) \rightarrow Ni(s) \qquad E° = -0.25V$$
$$Ag^{+}(aq) \rightarrow Ag(s) \qquad E° = 0.80V$$

Table 16.1 Standard Reduction Potentials in Aqueous Solution at 25°C

HALF-REACTION			$E°$(V)
$Li^+ + e^-$	$\rightarrow$	$Li(s)$	-3.05
$Cs^+ + e^-$	$\rightarrow$	$Cs(s)$	-2.92
$K^+ + e^-$	$\rightarrow$	$K(s)$	-2.92
$Rb^+ + e^-$	$\rightarrow$	$Rb(s)$	-2.92
$Ba^{2+} + 2\,e^-$	$\rightarrow$	$Ba(s)$	-2.90
$Sr^{2+} + 2\,e^-$	$\rightarrow$	$Sr(s)$	-2.89
$Ca^{2+} + 2\,e^-$	$\rightarrow$	$Ca(s)$	-2.87
$Na^+ + e^-$	$\rightarrow$	$Na(s)$	-2.71
$Mg^{2+} + 2\,e^-$	$\rightarrow$	$Mg(s)$	-2.37
$Be^{2+} + 2\,e^-$	$\rightarrow$	$Be(s)$	-1.70
$Al^{3+} + 3\,e^-$	$\rightarrow$	$Al(s)$	-1.66
$Mn^{2+} + 2\,e^-$	$\rightarrow$	$Mn(s)$	-1.18
$Zn^{2+} + 2\,e^-$	$\rightarrow$	$Zn(s)$	-0.76
$Cr^{3+} + 3\,e^-$	$\rightarrow$	$Cr(s)$	-0.74
$Fe^{2+} + 2\,e^-$	$\rightarrow$	$Fe(s)$	-0.44
$Cr^{3+} + e^-$	$\rightarrow$	Cr^{2+}	-0.41
$Cd^{2+} + 2\,e^-$	$\rightarrow$	$Cd(s)$	-0.40
$Tl^+ + e^-$	$\rightarrow$	$Tl(s)$	-0.34
$Co^{2+} + 2\,e^-$	$\rightarrow$	$Co(s)$	-0.28
$Ni^{2+} + 2\,e^-$	$\rightarrow$	$Ni(s)$	-0.25
$Sn^{2+} + 2\,e^-$	$\rightarrow$	$Sn(s)$	-0.14
$Pb^{2+} + 2\,e^-$	$\rightarrow$	$Pb(s)$	-0.13
$2\,H^+ + 2\,e^-$	$\rightarrow$	$H_2(g)$	0.00
$S(s) + 2\,H^+ + 2\,e^-$	$\rightarrow$	$H_2S(g)$	0.14
$Sn^{4+} + 2\,e^-$	$\rightarrow$	Sn^{2+}	0.15
$Cu^{2+} + e^-$	$\rightarrow$	Cu^+	0.15
$Cu^{2+} + 2\,e^-$	$\rightarrow$	$Cu(s)$	0.34
$Cu^+ + e^-$	$\rightarrow$	$Cu(s)$	0.52
$I_2(s) + 2\,e^-$	$\rightarrow$	$2I^-$	0.53
$Fe^{3+} + e^-$	$\rightarrow$	Fe^{2+}	0.77
$Hg_2^{2+} + 2\,e^-$	$\rightarrow$	$2\,Hg(l)$	0.79
$Ag^+ + e^-$	$\rightarrow$	$Ag(s)$	0.80
$Hg^{2+} + 2\,e^-$	$\rightarrow$	$Hg(l)$	0.85
$2\,Hg^{2+} + 2\,e^-$	$\rightarrow$	Hg_2^{2+}	0.92
$Br_2(l) + 2\,e^-$	$\rightarrow$	$2Br^-$	1.07
$O_2(g) + 4\,H^+ + 4\,e^-$	$\rightarrow$	$2\,H_2O(l)$	1.23
$Cl_2(g) + 2\,e^-$	$\rightarrow$	$2Cl^-$	1.36
$Au^{3+} + 3\,e^-$	$\rightarrow$	$Au(s)$	1.50
$Co^{3+} + e^-$	$\rightarrow$	Co^{2+}	1.82
$F_2(g) + 2\,e^-$	$\rightarrow$	$2F^-$	2.87

First, the cell voltage can be calculated using:

$$E°_{cell} = E°_{cathode} - E°_{anode} > 0$$

Since the cell potential must be positive (a galvanic cell), there is only one arrangement of −0.25 and 0.80 volts than can result in a positive value:

$$E°_{cell} = 0.80 \text{ V} - (-0.25 \text{ V}) = 1.05 \text{ V}$$

This means that the Ni electrode is the anode and must be involved in oxidation, so its reduction half-reaction must be reversed, changing the sign of the standard half-cell potential, and added to the silver half-reaction. **Note that the silver half-reaction must be multiplied by 2 to equalize electron loss and gain, but the half-cell potential remains the same:**

$$Ni(s) \rightarrow Ni^{2+}(aq) + 2e^- \qquad\qquad E° = 0.25 \text{ V}$$
$$2 \times (Ag^+(aq) + e^- \rightarrow Ag(s)) \qquad\qquad E° = 0.80 \text{ V}$$
$$\overline{Ni(s) + 2Ag^+(aq) \rightarrow Ni^{2+}(aq) + 2Ag(s) \qquad E°_{cell} = 1.05 \text{ V}}$$

Note that the same cell potential is obtained as using: $E°_{cell} = E°_{cathode} - E°_{anode} > 0$.

If, for example, you are given the cell notation, you could use this method to determine the cell potential. In this case, the cell notation would be: $Ni \,|\, Ni^{2+} \,||\, Ag^+ \,|\, Ag\,|$.

Electrolytic Cells

Electrolytic cells use electricity from an external source to produce a desired redox reaction. Electroplating and the recharging of an automobile battery are examples of electrolytic cells.

Figure 16.2, on the next page, shows a comparison of a galvanic cell and an electrolytic cell for the Sn/Cu system. On the left-hand side of Figure 16.2, the galvanic cell is shown for this system. Note that this reaction produces 0.48 V. But what if we wanted the reverse reaction to occur, the nonspontaneous reaction? This can be accomplished by applying a voltage in excess of 0.48 V from an external electrical source. This is shown on the right-hand side of Figure 16.2. In this electrolytic cell, electricity is being used to produce the nonspontaneous redox reaction.

Quantitative Aspects of Electrochemistry

One of the most widely used applications of electrolytic cells is in **electrolysis**, the decomposition of a compound. Water may be decomposed into hydrogen and oxygen. Aluminum oxide may be electrolyzed to produce aluminum metal. In these situations, several questions may be asked: *How long* will it take; *how much* can be produced; *what current* must be used? Given any two of these quantities, the third may be calculated. To answer these questions, the balanced half-reaction must be known. Then the following relationships can be applied:

1 Faraday = 96,500 coulombs per mole of electrons

(F = 96,500 C/mol e⁻ or 96,500 J/V mol)

1 ampere = 1 coulomb/second (A = C/s)

Knowing the amperage and how long it is being applied (seconds), the coulombs can be calculated. Then the coulombs can be converted into moles of electrons, and the moles of electrons can be related to the moles (and then grams) of material being electrolyzed through the balanced half-reaction.

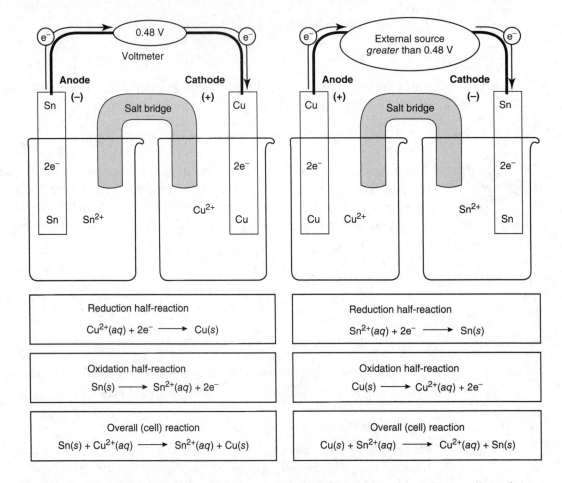

Figure 16.2   Comparison of a galvanic cell (left) and an electrolytic cell (right).

For example, if liquid titanium(IV) chloride (acidified with HCl) is electrolyzed by a current of 1.000 amp for 2.000 h, how many grams of titanium will be produced?

Answer:

$$TiCl_4(l) \rightarrow Ti(s) + 2Cl_2(g) \text{ (not necessary)}$$

$$Ti^{4+} + 4e^- \rightarrow Ti \text{ (necessary)}$$

$$(2.000 \text{ h})\left(\frac{3,600 \text{ s}}{\text{h}}\right)\left(\frac{1.000 \text{ C}}{\text{s}}\right)\left(\frac{1 \text{ mole } e^-}{96,485 \text{ C}}\right)\left(\frac{1 \text{ mole Ti}}{4 \text{ mole } e^-}\right)\left(\frac{47.90 \text{ g Ti}}{\text{mol Ti}}\right)$$
$$= 0.8936 \text{ g Ti}$$

Calculation of $E°_{cell}$ also allows for the calculation of two other useful quantities—the Gibbs free energy ($\Delta G°$) and the equilibrium constant (K).

The Gibbs free energy is the best single thermodynamic indicator of whether a reaction will be spontaneous (review the Thermodynamics chapter). The Gibbs free energy for a reaction can be calculated from the $E°$ of the reaction using the following equation:

$$\Delta G° = -nFE°_{cell}$$

where F is Faraday's constant of 96,500 C/mol e^- = 96,500 J/V mol.

If the redox reaction is at equilibrium, $E° = 0$, the equilibrium constant may be calculated by:

$$E°_{cell} = \frac{0.0592\,V}{n} \log K \quad \text{or} \quad \log K = \frac{nE°_{cell}}{0.0592\,V}$$

Let's apply these relationships. Determine $\Delta G°$ and K for the following reaction:

$$Ni(s) + 2Ag^+(aq) \rightarrow Ni^{2+}(aq) + Ag(s) \quad E°_{cell} = 1.05\,V$$

Answer:

For this reaction, two electrons are transferred from the Ni to the Ag. Thus, n is 2 for this reaction. The value of F (96,500 J/V mol) is given on the exam, so you will not need to memorize it.

The first answer is:

$$\Delta G° = -nFE°_{cell} = -2(96,500 \text{ J/V mol})(1.05\,V) = -2.03 \times 10^5 \text{ J/mol}$$

The second answer is:

$$\log K = \frac{nE°_{cell}}{0.0592\ V} = \frac{2(1.05\ V)}{0.0592\ V} = 35.5$$

This gives a K of about 10^{35} (actually $K = 3 \times 10^{35}$). In many cases, the approximate value will be all you need for the AP exam.

Nernst Equation

Thus far, all of our calculations have been based on the standard cell potential or standard half-cell potentials—that is, the standard state conditions that were defined previously. However, many times the cell is not at standard conditions—commonly the concentrations are not 1 M. The actual cell potential, E_{cell}, can be calculated by the use of the **Nernst equation**:

$$E_{cell} = E°_{cell} - \left(\frac{RT}{nF}\right) \ln Q = E°_{cell} - \left(\frac{0.0592}{n}\right) \log Q \text{ at } 25°C$$

where R is the ideal gas constant, T is the Kelvin temperature, n is the number of electrons transferred, F is Faraday's constant, and Q is the reaction quotient discussed in the Equilibrium chapter. The second form, involving $\log Q$, is the more useful form. If one knows the cell reaction, the concentrations of ions, and $E°_{cell}$, then the actual cell potential can be calculated. Another useful application of the Nernst equation is in calculating the concentration of one of the reactants from cell-potential measurements. Knowing the actual cell potential and $E°_{cell}$ allows calculation of Q, the reaction quotient. Knowing Q and all but one of the concentrations allows the calculation of the unknown concentration. Another application of the Nernst equation is in concentration cells. A **concentration cell** is an electrochemical cell in which the same chemical species is used in both cell compartments, but differing in concentration. Because the half-reactions are the same, $E°_{cell} = 0.00$ V. Simply substituting the appropriate concentrations into the reaction quotient allows calculation of the actual cell potential.

When using the Nernst equation on a cell reaction in which the overall reaction is not supplied, only the half-reactions and concentrations, there are two equivalent methods to work the problem. The first way is to write the overall redox reaction based upon $E°$ values, and then apply the Nernst equation. If E_{cell} turns out to be negative, it indicates that the reaction is not a spontaneous one (an electrolytic cell), or that the reaction is written backwards if it supposed to be a galvanic cell. If it is supposed to be a galvanic cell, all you need to do is reverse the overall reaction and change the sign on E_{cell} to positive. The other method involves using the Nernst equation with the individual half-reactions, then combining them depending on whether or not it is a galvanic cell. The only disadvantage to the second method is that you must use the Nernst equation twice. Either method should lead you to the correct answer.

Let's practice. Calculate the potential of a half-cell containing 0.10 M $K_2Cr_2O_7$(aq), 0.20 M Cr^{3+}(aq), and 1.0×10^{-4} M H^+(aq).

Answer:

The following half-reaction is given on the AP exam:

$$Cr_2O_7^{2-}(aq) + 14H^+(aq) + 6e^- \rightarrow 2Cr^{3+}(aq) + 7H_2O(l) \quad E° = 1.33\,V$$

$$E = E° - \frac{0.0592}{n}\ \log\frac{[Cr^{3+}]^2}{[Cr_2O_7^{2-}][H^+]^{14}} \quad (\text{ignore } H_2O)$$

$$= 1.33\ V - \frac{0.0592}{6}\log\frac{[.20]^2}{[.10][1.0\times10^{-4}]^{14}}$$

$$= 0.78\,V$$

Experiments

Electrochemical experiments are normally concerned with standard cell voltages. Measurements of the cell potential are essential and require a voltmeter (potentiometer). These measurements may be taken from different combinations of half-cells, or from measurements before and after changes of some aspect of the cell were made.

Using measurements of different half-cell combinations, a set of "standard" reduction potentials may be constructed. This set will be similar to a table of standard reduction potentials. The solutions used in the half-cells must be of known concentration. These solutions are produced by weighing reagents and diluting to volume. The measurements will require a balance and a volumetric flask. It is also possible to produce known concentrations by diluting solutions. This method requires a pipette and a volumetric flask. Review Chapter 13 on Solutions and Colligative Properties for solution techniques.

Common Mistakes to Avoid

1. Be sure your units cancel to give the unit wanted in your final answer.
2. Be sure to round your answer off to the correct number of significant figures.
3. Remember that oxidation is the loss of electrons and reduction the gain, and that in redox reactions the same number of electrons is lost and gained.
4. When diagramming an electrochemical cell, be sure the electrons go from anode to cathode.
5. Be sure that for a galvanic cell, the cell potential is greater than 0.
6. In cell notation, be sure to write anode, anode compartment, salt bridge, cathode compartment, cathode in this specific order.
7. When using a multiplier to equalize electron loss and gain in reduction half-cell potentials, **do not** use the multiplier on the voltage of the half-cell.

› Review Questions

Use these questions to review the content of this chapter and practice for the AP Chemistry exam. First are 14 multiple-choice questions similar to what you will encounter in Section I of the AP Chemistry exam. Following those is a long free-response question like the ones in Section II of the exam. To make these questions an even more authentic practice for the actual exam, time yourself following the instructions provided.

Multiple-Choice Questions

Answer the following questions in 20 minutes. You may not use a calculator. You may use the periodic table and the equation sheet at the back of this book.

Choose one of the following for questions 1 and 2.

(A) There is no change in the voltage.
(B) The voltage becomes zero.
(C) The voltage increases.
(D) The voltage decreases, but stays positive.

The following reaction takes place in a voltaic cell:

$$Zn(s) + Cu^{2+}(1\ M) \rightarrow Cu(s) + Zn^{2+}(1\ M)$$

The cell has a voltage that is measured and found to be +1.10 V.

1. What happens to the cell voltage when the copper electrode is made smaller?

2. What happens to the cell voltage when the salt bridge is filled with deionized water instead of 1 M KNO_3?

3. $MnO_4^-(aq) + H^+(aq) + C_2O_4^{2-}(aq) \rightarrow Mn^{2+}(aq) + H_2O(l) + CO_2(g)$

What is the coefficient of H^+ when the above reaction is balanced?

(A) 16
(B) 2
(C) 8
(D) 5

4. $S_2O_3^{2-}(aq) + OH^-(aq) \rightarrow SO_4^{2-}(aq) + H_2O(l) + e^-$

After the above half-reaction is balanced, which of the following are the respective coefficients of OH^- and SO_4^{2-} in the balanced half-reaction?

(A) 8 and 3
(B) 6 and 2
(C) 10 and 2
(D) 5 and 2

5. How many moles of Pt may be deposited on the cathode when 0.80 F of electricity is passed through a 1.0 M solution of Pt^{4+}?

(A) 1.0 mol
(B) 0.60 mol
(C) 0.20 mol
(D) 0.80 mol

6. $Cr_2O_7^{2-}(aq) + 14\ H^+(aq) + 3\ S^{2-}(aq) \rightarrow 2\ Cr^{3+}(aq) + 3\ S(s) + 7\ H_2O(l)$

For the above reaction, pick the true statement from the following.

(A) The S^{2-} is reduced by $Cr_2O_7^{2-}$.
(B) The oxidation number of chromium changes from +7 to +3.
(C) The oxidation number of sulfur remains –2.
(D) The S^{2-} is oxidized by $Cr_2O_7^{2-}$.

7. $H^+(aq) + NO_3^-(aq) + e^- \rightarrow NO(g) + H_2O(g)$

What is the coefficient for water when the above half-reaction is balanced?

(A) 3
(B) 4
(C) 2
(D) 1

8. $Co^{2+} + 2\ e^- \rightarrow Co\ E° = -0.28\ V$

$Cd^{2+} + 2\ e^- \rightarrow Cd\ E° = -0.40\ V$

Given the above standard reduction potentials, estimate the approximate value of the equilibrium constant for the following reaction:

$$Cd + Co^{2+} \rightarrow Cd^{2+} + Co$$

(A) 10^{-4}
(B) 10^{-2}
(C) 10^4
(D) 10^{16}

9. A sample of silver is to be purified by electrorefining. This will separate the silver from an impurity of gold. The impure silver is made into an electrode. Which of the following is the best way to set up the electrolytic cell?

   (A) an impure silver cathode and an inert anode
   (B) an impure silver cathode and a pure gold anode
   (C) a pure silver cathode with an impure silver anode
   (D) a pure gold cathode with an impure silver anode

10. $2 \, Fe^{3+} + Zn \rightarrow Zn^{2+} + 2 \, Fe^{2+}$

    The reaction shown above was used in an electrolytic cell. The voltage measured for the cell was not equal to the calculated $E°$ for the cell. Which of the following could cause this discrepancy?

    (A) The anion in the anode compartment was chloride instead of nitrate as in the cathode compartment.
    (B) One or more of the ion concentrations was not 1 M.
    (C) Both of the solutions were at 25°C instead of 0°C.
    (D) The solution in the salt bridge was Na_2SO_4 instead of KNO_3.

11. How many grams of mercury could be produced by electrolyzing a 1.0 M $Hg(NO_3)_2$ solution with a current of 2.00 A for 3.00 h?

    (A) 22.4 g
    (B) 201 g
    (C) 11.2 g
    (D) 44.8 g

12. An electrolysis cell was constructed with two platinum electrodes in a 1.00 M aqueous solution of KCl. An odorless gas evolves from one electrode, and a gas with a distinctive odor evolves from the other electrode. Choose the correct statement from the following list.

    (A) The gas with the distinctive odor was evolved at the anode.
    (B) The odorless gas was oxygen.
    (C) The gas with the distinctive odor was evolved at the cathode.
    (D) The odorless gas was evolved at the anode.

13. $2 \, BrO_3^-(aq) + 12 \, H^+(aq) + 10 \, e^- \rightarrow Br_2(aq) + 6 \, H_2O(l)$

    Which of the following statements is correct for the above reaction?

    (A) The BrO_3^- undergoes oxidation at the anode.
    (B) Br goes from a –1 oxidation to a 0 oxidation state.
    (C) Br_2 is oxidized at the anode.
    (D) The BrO_3^- undergoes reduction at the cathode.

14. $2 \, M(s) + 3 \, Zn^{2+}(aq) \rightarrow$
    $2 \, M^{3+}(aq) + 3 \, Zn^{2+}(aq)$ $\qquad E° = 0.90$ V
    $Zn^{2+}(aq) + 2e^- \rightarrow Zn(s)$ $\qquad E° = -0.76$ V

    Using the above information, determine the standard reduction potential for the following reaction:

    $$M^{3+}(aq) + 3 \, e^- \rightarrow M(s)$$

    (A) 0.90 V
    (B) –1.66 V
    (C) 0.00 V
    (D) –0.62 V

Answers and Explanations for the Multiple-Choice Questions

1. A—The size of the electrode is not important.

2. B—The salt bridge serves as an ion source to maintain charge neutrality. Deionized water would not be an ion source, so the cell could not operate.

3. A—The balanced equation is:

$$2\ MnO_4^-(aq) + 16\ H^+(aq) + C_2O_4^{2-}(aq) \rightarrow$$
$$2\ Mn^{2+}(aq) + 8\ H_2O(l) + 10\ CO_2(g)$$

4. C—The balanced equation is:

$$S_2O_3^{2-}(aq) + 10\ OH^-(aq) \rightarrow$$
$$2\ SO_4^{2-}(aq) + 5\ H_2O(l) + 8\ e^-$$

5. C—It takes 4 mol of electrons ($4\ F$) to change the platinum ions to platinum metal. The calculation would be: $(0.80\ F)\ (1\ mol\ Pt/4\ F) = 0.20\ mol\ Pt$.

6. D—The dichromate ion oxidizes the sulfide ion to elemental sulfur, as the sulfide ion reduces the dichromate ion to the chromium(III) ion. Chromium goes from +6 to +3, while sulfur goes from –2 to 0. The hydrogen remains at +1, so it is neither oxidized nor reduced.

7. C—The balanced chemical equation is:

$$4\ H^+(aq) + NO_3^-(aq) + 3\ e^- \rightarrow$$
$$NO(g) + 2\ H_2O(l)$$

8. C—Using the equation:

$$\log K = \frac{nE^\circ}{0.0592} = \frac{2(0.12)}{0.0592} = 4.05$$

You should realize that the $\log K = 4$ gives $K = 10^4$. The actual value is $K = 1.1 \times 10^4$.

9. C—The impure silver must be oxidized so it will go into solution. Oxidation occurs at the anode. Reduction is required to convert the silver ions to pure silver. Reduction occurs at the cathode. The cathode must be pure silver; otherwise, it could be contaminated with the cathode material.

10. B—If the voltage was not equal to E°, then the cell was not standard. Standard cells have 1 M concentrations and operate at 25°C with a partial pressure of each gas equal to 1 atm. No gases are involved in this reaction, so the cell must be operating at a different temperature or a different concentration (or both).

11. A—

$$\left(\frac{2.00\,C}{s}\right)\left(\frac{3,600\,s}{h}\right)(3.00\,h)\left(\frac{1F}{96,500\,C}\right)\times$$
$$\left(\frac{1\,mol\,Hg}{2\,F}\right)\left(\frac{200.6\,g\,Hg}{1\,mol\,Hg}\right)$$

You can estimate the answer by replacing 96,500 with 100,000 and 200.6 with 200.

12. A—The gases produced are hydrogen (at the cathode) and chlorine (at the anode). Hydrogen is odorless, while chlorine has a distinctive odor.

13. D—The bromate ion, BrO_3^-, is gaining electrons, so it is being reduced. Reduction always occurs at the cathode.

14. B—The half-reactions giving the overall reaction must be:

$$3\ [Zn^{2+}(aq) + 2\ e^- \rightarrow Zn(s)] \qquad E^\circ = -0.76\,V$$
$$2\ [M(s) \rightarrow M^{3+}(aq) + 3\ e^-] \qquad E^\circ = ?$$
$$2\ M(s) + 3\ Zn^{2+}(aq) \rightarrow$$
$$2\ M^{3+}(aq) + 2\ Zn(s) \qquad E^\circ = 0.90\,V$$

Thus, $-0.76 + ? = 0.90$, giving $? = 1.66\,V$. The half-reaction under consideration is the reverse of the one used in this combination, so the sign of the calculated voltage must be reversed. Do not make the mistake of multiplying the voltages when the half-reactions were multiplied to equalize the electrons.

Free-Response Question

You have 15 minutes to answer the following long question. You may use a calculator and the tables in the back of the book.

Question 1

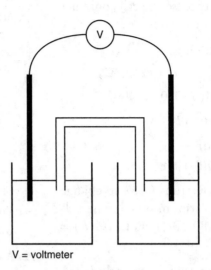

V = voltmeter

The above galvanic cell is constructed with a cobalt electrode in a 1.0 M Co(NO$_3$)$_2$ solution in the left compartment and a silver electrode in a 1.0 M AgNO$_3$ in the right compartment. The salt bridge contains a KNO$_3$ solution. The cell voltage is positive.

(a) What is the balanced net ionic equation for the reaction, and what is the cell potential?

$$Co^{2+} + 2\,e^- \rightarrow Co \qquad E° = -0.28\,V$$
$$Ag^+ + 1e^- \rightarrow Ag \qquad E° = +0.80\,V$$

(b) Which electrode is the anode? Justify your answer.

(c) If some solid Co(NO$_3$)$_2$ is added to the cobalt compartment, what will happen to the voltage? Justify your answer.

(d) If the cell operates until equilibrium is established, what will the potential be? Justify your answer.

Answer and Explanation for the Free-Response Question

(a) The cell reaction is:

$$Co(s) + 2\;Ag^+(aq) \rightarrow Co^{2+}(aq) + 2\;Ag(s)$$

Give yourself 1 point if you got this correct. The physical states are not necessary. The calculation of the cell potential may be done in different ways. Here is one method:

$$Co \rightarrow Co^{2+} + 2\;e^- \qquad\qquad E° = +0.28\,V$$
$$2(Ag^+ + 1\;e^- \rightarrow Ag) \qquad\qquad E° = +0.80\,V$$
$$Co(s) + 2\;Ag^+(aq) \rightarrow Co^{2+}(aq) + 2\;Ag(s) \qquad\qquad E° = +1.08\,V$$

Give yourself 1 point for the correct answer regardless of the method used. The most common mistake is to multiply the silver voltage by 2. You do not get the point for an answer of 1 V.

(b) The cobalt is the anode.
   You get 1 point for this statement.
   The reason Co is the anode is because the Co is oxidized.
   You get 1 point for this statement or if you state that the Co loses electrons.

(c) The voltage would decrease. The excess Co^{2+}, from the $Co(NO_3)_2$, would impede the reactions from proceeding as written.
   Give yourself 1 point for saying decrease. Give yourself 1 point for the explanation.

(d) At equilibrium the cell voltage would be 0 V.
   This is worth 1 point.
   At equilibrium no work is done, so the potential must be zero.
   Or give yourself 1 point for this answer.

There are a total of 7 points possible on this question.

› Rapid Review

- In redox reactions, electrons are lost and gained. Oxidation is the loss of electrons, and reduction is the gain of electrons.

- The same number of electrons is lost and gained in redox reactions.

- Galvanic (voltaic) cells produce electricity through the use of a redox reaction.

- The anode is the electrode at which the oxidation half-reaction takes place. The anode compartment is the solution in which the anode is immersed.

- The cathode is the electrode at which reduction takes place, and the cathode compartment is the solution in which the cathode is immersed.

- A salt bridge is used in an electrochemical cell to maintain electrical neutrality in the cell compartments.

- Be able to diagram an electrochemical cell.

- The cell notation is a shorthand way of representing a cell. It has the form:

   anode|anode compartment||cathode compartment|cathode

- Standard reduction potentials are used to calculate the cell potential under standard conditions. All half-reactions are shown in the reduction form.

- For a galvanic cell $E°_{cell} > 0$.

- $E°_{cell} = E°_{cathode} - E°_{anode} > 0$. Know how to use this equation to calculate $E°_{cell}$.

- Electrolytic cells use an external source of electricity to produce a desired redox reaction.

- Review how to diagram an electrolytic cell.

- The following relationships can be used to calculate quantitative changes that occur in an electrochemical cell, especially an electrolytic one: 1 F = 96,500 C per mole of electron (F = 96,500 C/mol e$^-$ = 96,500 J/V mol) and 1 amp = 1 C/s (A = C/s).

- The standard cell potential can be used to calculate the Gibbs free energy for the reaction: $\Delta G° = -nFE°_{cell}$. Know how to use this equation.

- The standard cell potential can also be used to calculate the equilibrium constant for a reaction: $\log K = \dfrac{nE°_{cell}}{0.0592\ \text{V}}$. Know how to use this equation.

Nuclear Chemistry

IN THIS CHAPTER

Summary: Radioactivity, the spontaneous decay of an unstable isotope to a more stable one, was first discovered by Henri Becquerel in 1896. Marie Curie and her husband expanded on his work and developed most of the concepts that are used today.

   Throughout this book, you have been studying traditional chemistry and chemical reactions. This has involved the transfer or sharing of electrons from the electron clouds, especially the valence electrons. Little has been said up to this point regarding the nucleus. Now we are going to shift our attention to nuclear reactions and, for the most part, ignore the electron clouds.

Keywords and Equations

No specific nuclear equations are provided, but review first-order equations in the Kinetics chapter.

Nuclear Reactions

Balancing Nuclear Reactions

Most nuclear reactions involve breaking apart the nucleus into two or more different elements or subatomic particles. If all but one of the particles is known, the unknown particle can be determined by balancing the nuclear equation. When chemical equations are balanced, coefficients are added to ensure that there are the same number of each type of atom on both sides of the reaction arrow. To balance nuclear equations, we ensure that there is the same sum of both mass numbers and atomic numbers on both the left and right of the reaction arrow. Recall that a specific isotope of an element can be represented by the following symbolization:

$$_Z^A X$$

In this symbolization A is the mass number (sum of protons and neutrons), Z is the atomic number (number of protons), and X is the element symbol (from the periodic table). In balancing nuclear reactions, make sure the sum of all A values on the left of the arrow equals the sum of all A values to the right of the arrow. The same will be true of the sums of the Z values. Knowing that these sums must be equal allows one to predict the mass and atomic number of an unknown particle if all the others are known.

Consider the **transmutation**—creation of one element from another—of Cl-35. This isotope of chlorine is bombarded by a neutron and H-1 is created, along with an isotope of a different element. First, a partial nuclear equation is written:

$$_{17}^{35}Cl + _0^1n \rightarrow _1^1H + _y^x?$$

The sum of the mass numbers on the left of the equation is $36 = (35 + 1)$ and on the right is $1 + x$. The mass number of the unknown isotope must be 35. The sum of the atomic numbers on the left is $17 = (17 + 0)$, and $1 + y$ on the right. The atomic number of the unknown must then be 16. This atomic number identifies the element as sulfur, so a complete nuclear equation can be written:

$$_{17}^{35}Cl + _0^1n \rightarrow _1^1H + _{16}^{35}S$$

Sulfur-35 does not occur in nature; it is an artificially produced isotope.

Natural Radioactive Decay Modes

Three common types of radioactive decay are observed in nature, and two others are occasionally observed.

Alpha Emission

An alpha particle is a helium nucleus with two protons and two neutrons. It is represented as: $_2^4He$ or α. As this particle is expelled from the nucleus of the radioisotope that is undergoing decay, it has no electrons and thus has a 2+ charge. However, it quickly acquires two electrons from its surroundings to form the neutral atom. Most commonly, the alpha particle is shown as the neutral particle and not the cation.

Radon-222 undergoes alpha decay according to the following equation:

$$_{86}^{222}Rn \rightarrow _{84}^{218}Po + _2^4He$$

Notice that in going from Rn-222 to Po-218, the atomic number has decreased by 2 and the mass number by 4.

Beta Emission

A beta particle is an electron and can be represented as either $_{-1}^0\beta$ or $_{-1}^0e$. This electron comes from the nucleus, *not* the electron cloud, and results from the conversion of a neutron into a proton and an electron: $_0^1n \rightarrow _1^1p + _{-1}^0e$.

Nickel-63 will undergo beta decay according to the following equation:

$$^{63}_{28}\text{Ni} \rightarrow {}^{63}_{29}\text{Cu} + {}^{0}_{-1}\text{e}.$$

Notice that the atomic number has increased by 1 in going from Ni-63 to Cu-63, but the mass number has remained unchanged.

Gamma Emission

Gamma emission is the giving off of high-energy, short-wavelength photons similar to X-rays. This radiation is commonly represented as γ. Gamma emission commonly accompanies most other types of radioactive decay, but is often not shown in the balanced nuclear equation because it has neither appreciable mass nor charge.

Alpha, beta, and gamma emissions are the most common types of natural decay mode, but positron emission and electron capture are also observed occasionally.

Positron Emission

A positron is essentially an electron that has a positive charge instead of a negative one. It is represented as $^{0}_{1}\beta$ or $^{0}_{1}\text{e}$. Positron emission results from the conversion of a proton to a neutron and a positron: $^{1}_{+1}\text{p} \rightarrow {}^{1}_{0}\text{n} + {}^{0}_{+1}\text{e}$. It is observed in the decay of some natural radioactive isotopes, such as K-40: $^{40}_{19}\text{K} \rightarrow {}^{40}_{18}\text{Ar} + {}^{0}_{+1}\text{e}$.

Electron Capture

The four decay modes described above all involve the emission or giving off a particle; electron capture is the capturing of an electron from the energy level closest to the nucleus (1s) by a proton in the nucleus. This creates a neutron: $^{0}_{-1}\text{e} + {}^{1}_{1}\text{p} \rightarrow {}^{1}_{0}\text{n}$. Electron capture leaves a vacancy in the 1s energy level, and an electron from a higher energy level drops down to fill this vacancy. A cascading effect occurs as the electrons shift downward and, as they do so, energy is released. This energy falls in the X-ray part of the electromagnetic spectrum. These X-rays give scientists a clue that electron capture has taken place.

Polonium-204 undergoes electron capture: $^{204}_{84}\text{Po} + {}^{0}_{-1}\text{e} \rightarrow {}^{204}_{83}\text{Bi} + \text{X-rays}$. Notice that the atomic number has decreased by 1, but the mass number has remained the same. Remember that electron capture is the only decay mode that involves adding a particle to the left side of the reaction arrow.

Nuclear Stability

Predicting whether a particular isotope is stable and what type of decay mode it might undergo can be tricky. All isotopes containing 84 or more protons are unstable and will undergo nuclear decay. For these large, massive isotopes, alpha decay is observed most commonly. Alpha decay gets rid of four units of mass and two units of charge, thus helping to relieve the repulsive stress found in these nuclei. For other isotopes, with atomic numbers less than 84, stability is best predicted by the use of the neutron-to-proton (n/p) ratio.

If one plots the number of neutrons versus the number of protons for the known stable isotopes, the nuclear belt of stability is formed. At the low end of this belt of stability (Z < 20), the n/p ratio is 1. At the high end (Z ≈ 80), the n/p ratio is about 1.5. One can then use the n/p ratio of the isotope under question to predict whether or not it will be stable. If it is unstable, the isotope will utilize a decay mode that will bring it back onto the belt of stability.

For example, consider Ne-18. It has 10 p and 8 n, giving an n/p ratio of 0.8. That is less than 1, so the isotope is unstable. This isotope is neutron-poor, meaning it doesn't have enough neutrons (or has too many protons) to be stable. Decay modes that increase the number of neutrons, decrease the number of protons, or both would be favored. Both positron emission and electron capture accomplish this by converting a proton into a neutron. As a general rule, positron emission occurs with lighter isotopes and electron capture with heavier isotopes.

Isotopes that are neutron-rich, that have too many neutrons or not enough protons, lie above the belt of stability and tend to undergo beta emission because that decay mode converts a neutron into a proton.

A particular isotope may undergo a series of nuclear decays until finally a stable isotope is formed. For example, radioactive U-238 decays to stable Pb-206 in 14 steps, a majority of which are alpha emissions, as one might predict.

Nuclear Decay Calculations

A radioactive isotope may be unstable, but it is impossible to predict when a certain atom will decay. However, if a statistically large enough sample is examined, some trends become obvious. The radioactive decay follows first-order kinetics (see Chapter 14 on Kinetics for a more in-depth discussion of first-order reactions and equations). If the number of radioactive atoms in a sample is monitored, it can be determined that it takes a certain amount of time for half the sample to decay; it takes the same amount of time for half the remaining sample to decay; and so on. The amount of time it takes for half the sample to decay is called the half-life of the isotope and is given the symbol $t_{1/2}$. The table below shows the percentage of radioactive isotope remaining versus half-life.

HALF-LIFE, $t_{1/2}$	PERCENT RADIOACTIVE ISOTOPE REMAINING
0	100
1	50
2	25
3	12.5
4	6.25
5	3.12
6	1.56
7	0.78
8	0.39
9	0.19
10	0.09

As a general rule, the amount of radioactivity at the end of 10 half-lives drops below the level of detection and the sample is said to be "safe."

Half-lives may be very short, 4.2×10^{-6} seconds for Po-213, or very long, 4.5×10^{9} years for U-238. The long half-lives of some waste products is a major problem with nuclear fission reactors. Remember, it takes 10 half-lives for the sample to be safe.

If only multiples of half-lives are considered, the calculations are very straightforward. For example, I-131 is used in the treatment of thyroid cancer and has a $t_{1/2}$ of 8 days. How long would it take to decay to 25% of its original amount? Looking at the chart, you see that 25% decay would occur at two half-lives or 16 days. However, since radioactive decay is not a linear process, you cannot use the chart to predict how much would still be radioactive at the end of 12 days or at some time (or amount) that is not associated with a multiple of a half-life. To solve these types of problems, one must use the mathematical relationships associated with first-order kinetics that were presented in the Kinetics chapter. In general, two equations are used:

$$(1) \ln [A]_t - \ln [A]_o = -kt$$

$$(2) \, t_{1/2} = \ln 2/k$$

In these equations, the ln is the natural logarithm; A_t is the amount of isotope radioactive at some time t; A_o is the amount initially radioactive; and k is the rate constant for the decay. If you know initial and final amounts and are looking for the half-life, you would use equation (1) to solve for the rate constant and then use equation (2) to solve for $t_{1/2}$.

For example: What is the half-life of a radioisotope that takes 15 min to decay to 90% of its original activity?

First use equation (1) to determine k, then use the value of k in equation (2) to determine the half-life:

Using equation (1): $\ln 90/100 = -k(15 \text{ min})$
$$-0.1054 = -k(15 \text{ min})$$
$$7.02 \times 10^{-3} \text{ min}^{-1} = k$$

Now equation (2): $t_{1/2} = \ln 2/7.02 \times 10^{-3} \text{ min}^{-1}$
$$t_{1/2} = 0.693/7.02 \times 10^{-3} \text{ min}^{-1}$$
$$t_{1/2} = 98.7 \text{ min}$$

If one knows the half-life and amount remaining radioactive, equation (2) can be used to calculate the rate constant k and equation (1) can then be used to solve for the time. This is the basis of C-14 dating, which is used to determine the age of objects that were once alive.

For example, suppose a wooden tool is discovered and its C-14 activity is determined to have decreased to 65% of the original. How old is the object?

The half-life of C-14 is 5,730 yr. Substituting this into equation (2):

$$5,730 \text{ yr} = \ln 2/k$$
$$5,730 \text{ yr} = 0.693/k$$
$$k = 1.21 \times 10^{-4} \text{ yr}^{-1}$$

Substituting this rate constant into equation (1):

$$\ln 65/100 = -(1.21 \times 10^{-4} \text{ yr}^{-1})t$$
$$-0.4308 = -(1.21 \times 10^{-4} \text{ yr}^{-1})t$$
$$t = 3,600 \text{ yr}$$

Mass–Energy Relationships

Whenever a nuclear decay or reaction takes place, energy is released. This energy may be in the form of heat and light, gamma radiation, or kinetic energy of the expelled particle and recoil of the remaining particle. This energy results from the conversion of a very small amount of matter into energy. (Remember that in nuclear reactions there is no conservation of matter, as in ordinary chemical reactions.) The amount of energy that is produced can be calculated by using Einstein's equation $E = mc^2$, where E is the energy produced, m is the mass converted into energy (the mass defect), and c is the speed of light. The amount of matter that is converted into energy is normally very small, but when it is multiplied by the speed of light (a very large number) squared, the amount of energy produced is very large.

For example: When 1 mol of U-238 decays to Th-234, 5×10^{-6} kg of matter is converted to energy (the mass defect). To calculate the amount of energy released:

$$E = mc^2$$
$$E = (5 \times 10^{-6}\,\text{kg})(3.00 \times 10^8\,\text{m/s})^2$$
$$E = 5 \times 10^{11}\,\text{kg} \times \text{m}^2/\text{s}^2 = 5 \times 10^{11}\,\text{J}$$

If the mass is in kilograms, the answer will be in joules.

Common Mistakes to Avoid

1. Make sure your answer is reasonable. Don't just write down the answer from your calculator.
2. Make sure your units cancel in your calculations, leaving the unit you want.
3. Make sure that in alpha, beta, gamma, and positron emissions the particle being emitted is on the right-hand side of the reaction arrow. In electron capture, the electron should be on the left side of the arrow.
4. In half-life problems, don't omit the minus sign. Watch your units.
5. In half-life problems, be sure to use the amount of isotope still radioactive as N_t and not the amount decayed.

› Review Questions

Use these questions to review the content of this chapter and practice for the AP Chemistry exam. Below are 6 multiple-choice questions similar to what you will encounter in Section I of the AP Chemistry exam. To make these questions an even more authentic practice for the actual exam, time yourself following the instructions provided.

Multiple-Choice Questions

Answer the following questions in 10 minutes. You may not use a calculator. You may use the periodic table and the equation sheet at the back of this book.

1. When $^{226}_{88}\text{Ra}$ decays, it emits 2 α particles, then a β particle, followed by an α particle. The resulting nucleus is:
   (A) $^{212}_{83}\text{Bi}$
   (B) $^{222}_{86}\text{Rn}$
   (C) $^{214}_{82}\text{Pb}$
   (D) $^{214}_{83}\text{Bi}$

2. The formation of $^{230}_{90}\text{Th}$ from $^{234}_{92}\text{U}$ occurs by:
   (A) electron capture
   (B) α decay
   (C) β decay
   (D) positron decay

3. Which of the following lists the types of radiation in the correct order of increasing penetrating power?
   (A) α, γ, β
   (B) β, α, γ
   (C) α, β, γ
   (D) β, γ, α

4. Which of the following statements is correct concerning β particles?

(A) They are electrons, with a mass number of zero and a charge of −1.

(B) They have a mass number of zero, a charge of −1, and are less penetrating than α particles.

(C) They are electrons with a charge of +1 and are less penetrating than α particles.

(D) They have a mass number of zero and a charge of +1.

5. An atom of $^{238}_{92}U$ undergoes radioactive decay by α emission. What is the product nuclide?

(A) $^{230}_{90}Th$

(B) $^{234}_{90}Th$

(C) $^{230}_{92}U$

(D) $^{230}_{91}Pa$

6. If 75% of a sample of pure $^{3}_{1}H$ decays in 24.6 years, what is the half-life of $^{3}_{1}H$?

(A) 24.6 yr

(B) 18.4 yr

(C) 12.3 yr

(D) 6.15 yr

Answers and Explanations for the Multiple-Choice Questions

1. **D**—The mass should be 226 − (4 + 4 + 0 + 4) = 214. The atomic number should be 88 − (2 + 2 − 1 + 2) = 83.

2. **B**—Mass difference = 234 − 230 = 4, and atomic number difference = 92 − 90 = 2. These correspond to an α particle.

3. **C**—Alpha particles are the least penetrating, and gamma rays are the most penetrating.

4. **A**—In nuclear reactions, the mass of a β particle is treated as 0, with a charge of −1. Electrons and β particles are the same thing.

5. **B**—Mass number = 238 − 4 = 234, and atomic number = 92 − 2 = 90.

6. **C**—After one half-life, 50% would remain. After another half-life this would be reduced by one-half to 25%. The total amount decayed is 75%. Thus, 24.6 years must be two half-lives of 12.3 years each.

› Rapid Review

- Know the five naturally occurring decay modes:

  1. Alpha emission, in which a helium nucleus, ^4_2He, is emitted from the nucleus.
  2. Beta emission, in which an electron, $^0_{-1}\text{e}$, is emitted from the nucleus. This is due to the conversion of a neutron into a proton plus the beta particle.
  3. Gamma emission, in which high-energy electromagnetic radiation is emitted from the nucleus. This commonly accompanies the other types of radioactive decay. It is due to the conversion of a small amount of matter into energy.
  4. Positron emission, in which a positron, $^0_{+1}\text{e}$, a particle having the same mass as an electron but a positive charge, is emitted from the nucleus. This is due to a proton converting into a neutron and the positron.
  5. Electron capture, in which an inner-shell electron is captured by a proton in the nucleus with the formation of a neutron. X-rays are emitted as the electrons cascade down to fill the vacancy in the lower energy level.

- Know that nuclear stability is best related to the neutron-to-proton ratio (n/p), which starts at about 1/1 for light isotopes and ends at about 1.5/1 for heavier isotopes with atomic numbers up to 83. All isotopes of atomic number greater than 84 are unstable and will commonly undergo alpha decay. Below atomic number 84, neutron-poor isotopes will probably undergo positron emission or electron capture, while neutron-rich isotopes will probably undergo beta emission.

- Know that the half-life, $t_{1/2}$, of a radioactive isotope is the amount of time it takes for one-half of the sample to decay. Know how to use the appropriate equations to calculate amounts of an isotope remaining at any given time, or use similar data to calculate the half-life of an isotope.

- Know how to use Einstein's equation $E = mc^2$ to calculate the amount of energy produced from a mass defect (the amount of matter that was converted into energy).

CHAPTER 18

Organic Chemistry

SPECIAL NOTE

Although organic chemistry is not specifically tested on the AP Chemistry exam, an overview of the subject will help you recognize and understand organic structures that appear in relation to other topics on the exam. In addition, this material is taught by some high school and college teachers. This is an enrichment chapter that should be considered a bonus chapter to this book.

IN THIS CHAPTER

Summary: Organic chemistry is the study of the chemistry of carbon. Almost all the compounds containing carbon are classified as organic compounds. Only a few—for example, carbonates and cyanides—are classified as inorganic. It used to be thought that all organic compounds had to be produced by living organisms, but this idea was proven wrong in 1828 when German chemist Friedrich Wöhler produced the first organic compound from inorganic starting materials. Since that time, chemists have synthesized many organic compounds found in nature and have also made many never found naturally. It is carbon's characteristic of bonding strongly to itself and to other elements in long, complex chains and rings that gives carbon the ability to form the many diverse and complex compounds needed to support life.

Keywords and Equations

No keywords or equations specific to this chapter are listed on the AP exam.

Alkanes

Alkanes are members of a family of organic compounds called hydrocarbons, compounds of carbon and hydrogen. These hydrocarbons are the simplest of organic compounds, but are extremely important to our society as fuels and raw materials for chemical industries. We heat our homes and run our automobiles through the combustion (burning) of these hydrocarbons. Paints, plastics, and pharmaceuticals are often made from hydrocarbons. **Alkanes** are hydrocarbons that contain only single covalent bonds within their molecules. They are called saturated hydrocarbons because they are bonded to the maximum number of other atoms. These alkanes may be straight-chained hydrocarbons, in which the carbons are sequentially bonded; branched hydrocarbons, in which another hydrocarbon group is bonded to the hydrocarbon "backbone"; or they may be cyclic, in which the hydrocarbon is composed entirely or partially of a ring system. The straight-chained and branched alkanes have the general formula of C_nH_{2n+2}, whereas the cyclic alkanes have the general formula of C_nH_{2n}. The n stands for the number of carbon atoms in the compound. The first 10 straight-chained alkanes are shown in Table 18.1.

There can be many more carbon units in a chain than are shown in Table 18.1, but these are enough to allow us to study alkane nomenclature—the naming of alkanes.

Alkane Nomenclature

The naming of alkanes is based on choosing the longest carbon chain in the structural formula, then naming the hydrocarbon branches while indicating onto which carbon that branch is attached. Here are the specific rules for naming simple alkanes:

1. Find the continuous carbon chain in the compound that contains the most carbon atoms. This will provide the base name of the alkane.

2. This base name will be modified by adding the names of the branches (substituent groups) in front of the base name. Alkane branches are named by taking the name of the alkane that contains the same number of carbon atoms, dropping the *-ane* ending and adding *-yl*. Methane becomes methyl, propane becomes propyl, etc. If there is more than one branch, list them alphabetically.

Table 18.1   The First Ten Straight-Chained Alkanes

NAME	MOLECULAR FORMULA	STRUCTURAL FORMULA
methane	CH_4	CH_4
ethane	C_2H_6	CH_3-CH_3
propane	C_3H_8	$CH_3-CH_2-CH_3$
butane	C_4H_{10}	$CH_3-CH_2-CH_2-CH_3$
pentane	C_5H_{12}	$CH_3-CH_2-CH_2-CH_2-CH_3$
hexane	C_6H_{14}	$CH_3-CH_2-CH_2-CH_2-CH_2-CH_3$
heptane	C_7H_{16}	$CH_3-CH_2-CH_2-CH_2-CH_2-CH_2-CH_3$
octane	C_8H_{18}	$CH_3-CH_2-CH_2-CH_2-CH_2-CH_2-CH_2-CH_3$
nonane	C_9H_{20}	$CH_3-CH_2-CH_2-CH_2-CH_2-CH_2-CH_2-CH_2-CH_3$
decane	$C_{10}H_{22}$	$CH_3-CH_2-CH_2-CH_2-CH_2-CH_2-CH_2-CH_2-CH_2-CH_3$

3. The position where a particular substituent is attached to the chain is indicated by a location number. These numbers are assigned by consecutively numbering the carbons of the base hydrocarbon, starting at one end of the hydrocarbon chain. Choose the end that will result in the lowest sum of location numbers for the substituent groups. Place this location number in front of the substituent name and separate it from the name by a hyphen (for example, 2-methyl).

4. Place the substituent names with their location numbers in front of the base name of the alkane in alphabetical order. If there are identical substituents (two methyl groups, for example), give the location numbers of each, separated by commas using the common Greek prefixes (di-, tri-, tetra-, etc.) to indicate the number of identical substituent groups (i.e., 2,3-dimethyl). These Greek prefixes are not considered in the alphabetical arrangement.

5. The last substituent group becomes a part of the base name as a prefix.

Studying Figures 18.1 and 18.2 may help you learn the naming of substituted alkanes.

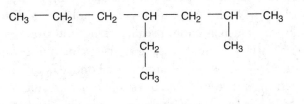

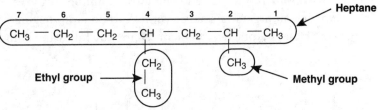

4-ethyl-2-methylheptane

Figure 18.1   Naming an alkane.

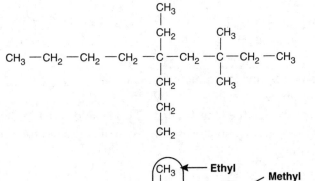

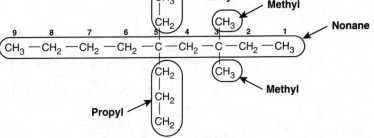

5-ethyl-3,3-dimethyl-5-propylnonane

Figure 18.2   Naming of another alkane.

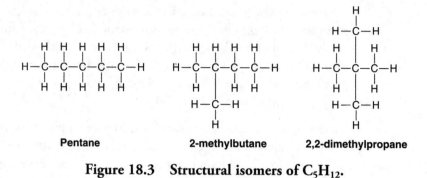

Pentane   2-methylbutane   2,2-dimethylpropane

Figure 18.3 Structural isomers of C$_5$H$_{12}$.

Structural Isomerism

Compounds that have the same molecular formulas but different structural formulas are called isomers. With hydrocarbons, this applies to a different arrangement of the carbon atoms. Isomers such as these are called **structural isomers**. Figure 18.3 shows the structural isomers of C$_5$H$_{12}$. Note that there are the same number of carbons and hydrogens in each structure. Only the way the carbons are bonded is different.

In writing structural isomers, or any other organic compounds, remember that **carbon forms four bonds**. One of the most common mistakes that a chemistry student makes is writing an organic structure with a carbon atom having fewer or more than four bonds.

Here is a practice problem. Name the following compound:

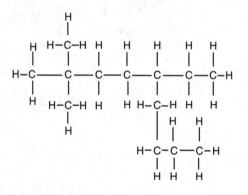

Answer: 5-ethyl-2,2-dimethylnonane
Solution:

First, pick the longest chain. This is bold-faced in the diagram below. The carbons are attached by single bonds, so this is an alkane. Because the longest chain has nine carbons, it is a nonane.

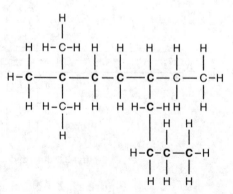

Next, the longest chain should be numbered from one end to the other with the lowest number(s) going to the branches. For the preceding example the numbering of the chain (bold-face carbon atoms) would be:

$$1 \quad 2 \quad 3 \quad 4 \quad 5$$
$$6$$
$$7 \quad 8 \quad 9$$

Once these numbers have been assigned, do not alter them later.

All carbon atoms that are not part of the nine-atom main chain are branches. Branches have -*yl* endings. It may help you to circle the carbon atoms belonging in the branches. In the above example, there are three branches. Two consist of only one carbon and are called methyl groups. The remaining branch has two carbons, so it is an ethyl group. The branches are arranged alphabetically. If there is more than one of a particular type, use a prefix (*di*-, *tri*-, *tetra*-, etc.). The two methyl groups are designated dimethyl. The position of each branch is indicated with a number already determined for the main chain. Each branch must get its own number, even if it is identical to one already used.

In the above example this gives: 5-ethyl-2,2-dimethylnonane

a. ethyl before methyl (alphabetical—prefixes are ignored)
b. two methyl groups = dimethyl
c. three branches = three numbers

Numbers are separated from other numbers by commas, and numbers are separated from letters by a hyphen.

Another type of isomerism is optical isomerism. These molecules are capable of rotating light to either the left or right and are said to be optically active. The presence of an asymmetric or chiral carbon (a carbon atom with four different groups attached to it) will make a compound optically active.

Common Functional Groups

If chemistry students had to learn the properties of each of the millions of organic compounds, they would face an impossible task. Luckily, chemists find that having certain arrangements of atoms in an organic molecule causes those molecules to react in a similar fashion. For example, methyl alcohol, CH_3-OH, and ethyl alcohol, CH_3-CH_2-OH, undergo the same types of reactions. The $-OH$ group is the reactive part of these types of molecule. These reactive groups are called functional groups. Instead of learning the properties of individual molecules, one can simply learn the properties of functional groups.

In our study of the simple hydrocarbons, there are only two functional groups. One is a carbon-to-carbon double bond. Hydrocarbons that contain a carbon-to-carbon double bond are called alkenes. Naming alkenes is very similar to naming alkanes. The major difference is that the carbon base has an -*ene* ending instead of the -*ane* ending. The carbon backbone of the base hydrocarbon is numbered so the position of the double bond has the lowest location number.

The other hydrocarbon functional group is a carbon-to-carbon triple bond. Hydrocarbons that contain a triple bond are called alkynes. Alkynes use the -*yne* ending on the base hydrocarbon. The presence of a double or triple bond make these hydrocarbons unsaturated.

The introduction of other atoms (N, O, Cl, etc.) to organic compounds gives rise to many other functional groups. The major functional groups are shown in Table 18.2, on the next page.

Table 18.2   Common Functional Groups

FUNCTIONAL GROUP	COMPOUND TYPE	SUFFIX OR PREFIX OF NAME	EXAMPLE	SYSTEMATIC NAME (COMMON NAME)
C=C (alkene structure)	alkene	-ene	H₂C=CH₂ (ethene structure)	ethene (ethylene)
—C≡C—	alkyne	-yne	H—C≡C—H	ethyne (acetylene)
—C—Ö—H (alcohol structure)	alcohol	-ol	H—C—Ö—H (methanol structure)	methanol (methyl alcohol)
—C—Ẍ: (X=halogen)	haloalkane	halo-	H—C—Cl̈: (chloromethane structure)	chloromethane (methyl chloride)
—C—N̈— (amine structure)	amine	-amine	H—C—C—N̈—H (ethylamine structure)	ethylamine
—C—H (aldehyde structure with :O:)	aldehyde	-al	H—C—C—H (ethanal structure)	ethanal (acetaldehyde)
—C—C—C— (ketone structure with :O:)	ketone	-one	H—C—C—C—H (propanone structure)	propanone (acetone)
—C—Ö—H (carboxylic acid structure with :O:) (acetic acid)	carboxylic acid	-oic acid	H—C—C—Ö—H (ethanoic acid structure)	ethanoic acid
—C—Ö—C— (ester structure with :O:)	ester	-oate	H—C—C—Ö—C—H (methyl ethanoate structure)	methyl ethanoate (methyl acetate)
—C—N̈— (amide structure with :O:)	amide	-amide	H—C—C—N̈—H (ethanamide structure)	ethanamide (acetamide)

Macromolecules

As we mentioned in the introduction to this chapter, carbon has the ability to bond to itself in long and complex chains. These large molecules, called **macromolecules**, may have molecular masses in the millions. They are large, complex molecules, but most are composed of repeating units called **monomers**. Figure 18.4 shows two macromolecules, cellulose and nylon, and indicates their repeating units.

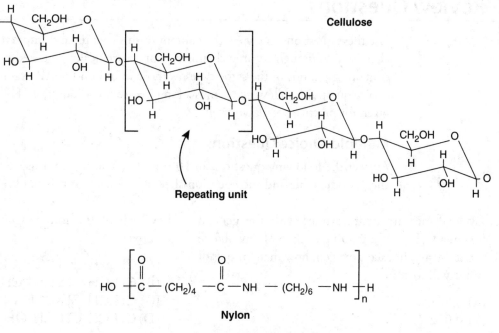

Cellulose

Repeating unit

Nylon

Figure 18.4   Two macromolecules.

Macromolecules are found in nature. Cellulose, wool, starch, and DNA are but a few of the macromolecules that occur naturally. Carbon's ability to form these large, complex molecules is necessary to provide the diversity of compounds needed to make up a tree or a human being. But many of the useful macromolecules that we use every day are created in the lab and industrial complex by chemists. Nylon, rayon, polyethylene, and polyvinyl chloride are all synthetic macromolecules. They differ by which repeating units (monomers) are joined together in the polymerization process. Our society has grown to depend on these plastics, these synthetic fabrics. The complexity of carbon compounds is reflected in the complexity of our modern society.

Experiments

Any experiment would probably apply the concepts of organic chemistry in a synthesis situation.

Common Mistakes to Avoid

1. When writing organic formulas, make sure that every carbon has four bonds.
2. When naming alkanes, make sure to number the carbon chain so the sum of all location numbers is as small as possible.

3. When naming branched alkanes, be sure to consider the branches when finding the longest carbon chain. The longest chain isn't always the one in which the carbon atoms all lie in a horizontal line.

4. In naming identical substituents on the longest carbon chain, be sure to use repeating location numbers, separated by commas (2,2-dimethyl).

5. **Be sure that every carbon has four bonds!**

› Review Questions

Use these questions to review the content of this chapter and improve your understanding of chemistry. Although organic chemistry won't specifically be tested on the exam, this section contains questions of the same types as those found on the AP exam. First are five multiple-choice questions; following them is a long free-response question. Follow the time limitations given for practice pacing yourself.

Multiple-Choice Questions

Answer the following questions in 10 minutes. You may not use a calculator. You may use the periodic table and the equation sheet at the back of this book.

1. Cycloalkanes are hydrocarbons with the general formula C_nH_{2n}. If a 0.500 g sample of any alkene is combusted in excess oxygen, how many moles of water will form?

   (A) 0.50
   (B) 0.072
   (C) 0.036
   (D) 1.0

2.
$$CH_3-\overset{\overset{\displaystyle OH}{|}}{CH}-CH_2-CH_3$$

   The organic compound shown above would be classified as:

   (A) an organic base
   (B) an ether
   (C) an alcohol
   (D) an aldehyde

3.
$$HO-\overset{\overset{\displaystyle O}{||}}{C}-CH_2-CH_3$$

   The above compound would be classified as:

   (A) an aldehyde
   (B) a ketone
   (C) an ester
   (D) a carboxylic acid

4. Which of the following compounds is optically active?

   (A) $CH_3CHClCH_2CH_2CH_3$
   (B) $CH_3CH{=}CHCH_2CH_3$
   (C) $CH_3CH_2CHClCH_2CH_3$
   (D) $CH_3CH_2CH_2CH_2OH$

5. A carboxylic acid may be represented as:

   (A) ROH
   (B) RCHO
   (C) R-O-R
   (D) RCOOH

Answers and Explanations for the Multiple-Choice Questions

1. **C**—The general formula, C_nH_{2n}, means that 1 mol of H_2O will form per mole of empirical formula unit, regardless of the value of n. The moles of water formed are the mass of the alkene divided by the empirical formula mass. (0.500 g alkene) (1 mol alkene/14 g alkene)(1 mol H_2O/mol alkene) = 0.036 mol.

2. **C**—Organic bases are, in general, amines (contain N). An ether would have an oxygen single-bonded to two carbons (R groups). An aldehyde has oxygen double-bonded to a carbon at the end of a chain. Aldehydes (RCHO) and alcohols (ROH) are often confused because of the similarity in their general formulas. Ketones have oxygen double-bonded to a carbon not at the end of a chain.

3. **D**—Based on classification of organic compounds.

4. **A**—Redrawing the structures may help you to recognize the correct answer. An optical isomer must be a carbon atom with four *different* groups attached to it. For A, the groups on the second carbon are: CH_3—, H, Cl, and —$CH_2CH_2CH_3$. Answer C is misleading. It is similar to A, but two of the groups, the —CH_2CH_3 groups, are the same.

5. **D**—A = alcohol, B = aldehyde, C = ether

Free-Response Question

You have 20 minutes to answer the following question. You may use a calculator and the tables in the back of the book.

Question 1

The alkane hexane, C_6H_{14}, has a molecular mass of 86.17 g mol^{-1}.

(a) Like all hydrocarbons, hexane will burn. Write a balanced chemical equation for the complete combustion of hexane. This reaction produces gaseous carbon dioxide, CO_2, and water vapor, H_2O.

(b) The complete combustion of 10.0 g of hexane produces 487 kJ. What is the molar heat of combustion (ΔH) of hexane?

(c) Determine the pressure exerted by the carbon dioxide formed when 5.00 g of hexane is combusted. Assume the carbon dioxide is dry and stored in a 20.0 L container at 27°C.

(d) Hexane, like most alkanes, may exist in different isomeric forms. The structural formula of one of these isomers is pictured below. Draw the structural formula of any two other isomers of hexane. Make sure all carbon atoms and hydrogen atoms are shown.

Answer and Explanation for the Free-Response Question

Note that, while organic chemistry is not an AP topic, all of the materials in these questions depend upon basic AP chemistry knowledge, which is why this chapter can be valuable.

(a) $2\ C_6H_{14} + 19\ O_2 \rightarrow 12\ CO_2 + 14\ H_2O$

   Give yourself 2 points for the answer shown above, or for the coefficients: 1, 9/2, 6, and 7. Give yourself 1 point if you have one or more, not all, of the elements balanced.

(b) $(-487 \text{ kJ}/10.0 \text{ g hexane})(86.17 \text{ g hexane/mol hexane}) = -4.20 \times 10^3 \text{ kJ/mol}$

Give yourself 2 points for the above setup and correct answer (this requires a negative sign in the answer). If the setup is partially correct, give yourself 1 point.

(c) The ideal gas equation should be rearranged to the form $P = nRT/V$.

$$\text{Moles} = n = (5.00 \text{ g } C_6H_{14})\left(\frac{1 \text{ mol } C_6H_{14}}{86.17 \text{ g } C_6H_{14}}\right)\left(\frac{12 \text{ mol } CO_2}{2 \text{ mol } C_6H_{14}}\right) = 0.3481 \text{ mol } CO_2$$

This answer has an extra significant figure. The mole ratio should match the one given in your balanced equation. You will not be penalized again for an incorrectly balanced equation.

You will lose a point if you do not include a hexane-to-CO_2 conversion.
$R = 0.08206 \text{ L atm mol}^{-1} \text{ K}^{-1}$ (This value is in your test booklet.)

$$T = 27°C + 273 = 300.0 \text{ K}$$

In this case, there is no penalty if you forget to use the Kelvin temperature.

$$V = 20.0 \text{ L}$$

$$P = (0.3481 \text{ mol } CO_2)(0.08206 \text{ L atm mol}^{-1} \text{ K}^{-1})(300.0 \text{ K})/(20.0 \text{ L}) = 0.429 \text{ atm}$$

Give yourself 2 points for the correct setup and answer. Give yourself 1 point if you did everything correctly, except the mole ratio or the Kelvin conversion.

(d) You may need to redraw one or more of your answers to match the answers shown below.

Give yourself 1 point for each correct answer, with a 2-point maximum. There are no bonus points for additional answers.

These compounds are 2-methylpentane, 3-methylpentane, 2,2-dimethylbutane, and 2,3-dimethylbutane, respectively. These four, along with the original *n*-hexane, are the only isomers. If you think you have another isomer, you have simply redrawn one of these. Try naming your answer and see if it matches one of these names.

Total your points. The maximum is 8 points. Subtract one point if all your answers do not have the correct number of significant figures.

› Rapid Review

- Organic chemistry is the chemistry of carbon and its compounds.

- Hydrocarbons are organic compounds of just carbon and hydrogen atoms.

- Alkanes are hydrocarbons in which there are only single bonds.

- Alkanes are named in a very systematic way. Review the rules for naming alkanes.

- Isomers are compounds that have the same molecular formulas but different structural formulas. Review the writing of the various structural isomers of alkanes. **Make sure that each carbon atom has four bonds.**

- A functional group is a group of atoms that is the reactive part of the molecule. Review the general functional groups.

- Macromolecules are large molecules that may have molecular masses in the millions. Macromolecules are generally composed of repeating units called monomers.

CHAPTER 19

Experimental Investigations

IN THIS CHAPTER

Summary: The free-response portion of the AP exam will contain a question concerning an experiment, and there may also be a few multiple-choice questions on one or more of these experiments. This chapter reviews the basic experiments that the AP Exam Committee believes to be important. You should look over all of the experiments in this chapter and pay particular attention to any experiments you did not perform. In some cases, you may find, after reading the description, that you did a similar experiment. Not every AP class does every experiment, but any of these experiments may appear on the AP exam.

The free-response questions on recent exams have been concerned with the equipment, measurements, and calculations required. In some cases, sources of error are considered. To answer the question completely, you will need an understanding of the chemical concepts involved.

To discuss an experiment, you must be familiar with the equipment needed. In the keywords section at the beginning of this chapter is a complete list of equipment for the experiments (see also Figure 19.1). Make sure you are familiar with each item. You may know an item by a different name, or you may need to talk to your teacher to get additional information concerning an item.

In some cases, the exam question will request a list of the equipment needed, while in other cases you will get a list from which to choose the items you need. Certain items appear in many experiments. These include the analytical balance, beakers, support stands, pipets, test tubes, and Erlenmeyer flasks. Burets, graduated cylinders, clamps, desiccators, drying ovens, pH meters, volumetric flasks, and thermometers are also commonly used. If you are not sure what equipment to choose, these serve as good guesses. Most of the remaining equipment appears in three or fewer experiments.

You will need to know the basic measurements required for the experiment. For example, you may need to measure the initial and final temperatures. Do not make the mistake of saying you measure the change in temperature. You *calculate* the change in temperature from your measured initial and final temperatures. You do not need to give a lot of detail when listing the required measurements, but you need to be very specific in what you *measure*. Many students have lost exam points for not clearly distinguishing between measured and calculated values.

The basic calculations fall into two categories. Simple calculations, such as the change in temperature or the change in volume, are the easiest to forget. Simple calculations may also include mass-to-mole conversions. The other calculations normally involve entering values into one of the equations given at the beginning of the previous chapters of this book.

Keywords and Equations

Pay particular attention to the specific keywords and equations in the chapters associated with the individual experiments.

$A = abc$ (A = absorbance; a = molar absorbtivity; b = path length; c = concentration)

analytical balance	filter crucibles	rubber tubing
barometer	and adapters	spectrophotometer
beaker(s)	filter flasks	stirrer
buret	forceps	stopwatch
burner	funnel	support stand
calorimeter	graduated cylinder	test-tube rack
capillary tubes	hot plate	test tube(s)
centrifuge	ice	thermometer
clamp	ion exchange resin	tongs
crucible and cover	or silica gel	triangle crucible support
cuvettes	Meker burner	voltmeter
desiccator	mortar and pestle	volumetric flask
drying oven	pH meter	wash bottle
electrodes	pipet	watch glass
Erlenmeyer flask	power supply (battery)	water bath
evaporating dish	Pt or Ni test wire	wire gauze

Experiment 1: Spectroscopy

Synopsis

Specific experiments that are performed in this investigation are an introduction to the field of spectroscopy. They are designed to demonstrate the relationship between the amount of light absorbed by some solutions and their concentrations. Light of a specific wavelength is passed through both the solvent and a sample. The amount of light transmitted by the solvent is subtracted from the amount of light transmitted by the sample. If you made a

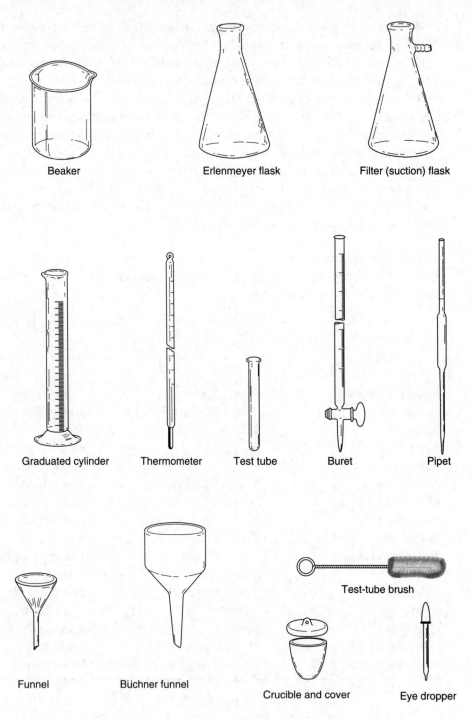

Figure 19.1 Common laboratory equipment.

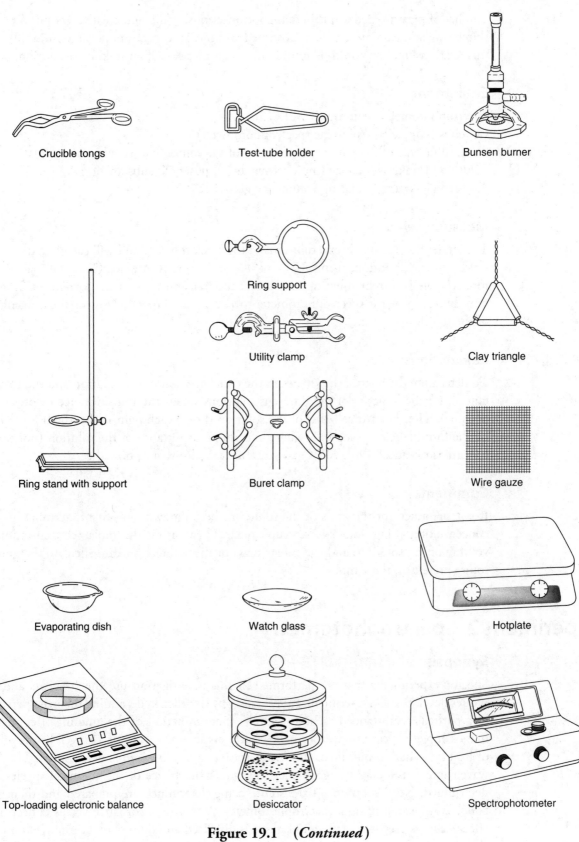

Crucible tongs

Test-tube holder

Bunsen burner

Ring support

Utility clamp

Clay triangle

Ring stand with support

Buret clamp

Wire gauze

Evaporating dish

Watch glass

Hotplate

Top-loading electronic balance

Desiccator

Spectrophotometer

Figure 19.1 (*Continued*)

number of measurements at different concentrations, you could create a graphical relationship between the amount of light absorbed and the concentration of the solution. By using this relationship, you could determine the concentration of an unknown solution.

Equipment

Spectrophotometer (commonly SPEC 20)
Cuvettes (sample tubes for the spectrophotometer)
Stock solutions (of known concentrations) of the solute (commonly some dye)
Solution of unknown concentration (may be a household substance)
Assorted glassware, including volumetric glassware

Measurements

The student will make several dilutions of the stock solution and will calculate the concentration of each dilution (using $M_1V_1 = M_2V_2$). The transmittance (%T) will be measured for each solution (remembering to subtract the transmittance of the solvent—this may be done by adjusting the spectrophotometer to 100% T and then measuring the transmittance of the solution).

Calculations

To determine the relationship between the concentration of the solution and the transmittance, plot the molarity of the different solutions versus the transmittance (expressed as a decimal). The absorbance (Abs) of the solution (how much light is absorbed) is calculated by the formula Abs = −log (T), where T is the transmittance of the solution (not the percent transmittance). On a SPEC 20 you can read absorbance directly.

Comments

If you are asked for the mass of the solute in the unknown, you first determine its molar concentration using your spectroscopy data. Then, using the molar concentration, the volume of the solution, and the molar mass of the solute, you can calculate the grams of solute present in the sample.

Experiment 2: Spectrophotometry

Synopsis

Specific experiments that are performed in this investigation use the concepts and techniques developed in Experiment 1: Spectroscopy in order to determine the mass percentage of a particular substance in a solid sample. Determination of the amount of copper in a brass sample is a common experiment that is used in this category as well as the amount of iron in a vitamin pill. First, the "best" wavelength to be used is determined. The "best" wavelength is the one that gives the maximum absorbance of the chemical species being determined. Next, solutions of the solute being determined are prepared and their absorbance is measured using a spectrophotometer. A plot of absorbance versus concentration (Beer's law) is prepared. The solid sample is dissolved and diluted to a certain volume. The absorbance of a portion of this sample is measured and its concentration is determined using the graph. From this information the mass of the substance can be found. Using this mass information and the mass of the sample allows you to calculate the mass percentage of the substance in the sample.

Equipment

Spectrophotometer (commonly SPEC 20)
Cuvettes (sample tubes for the spectrophotometer)
Stock solution (known concentration) of the solute
Sample to be analyzed
Assorted glassware, including volumetric glassware

Measurements

The student will make several dilutions of the stock solution (solution of known concentration of the substance being determined) and will calculate the concentration of each dilution (using $M_1V_1 = M_2V_2$). The absorbance of one of the stock solutions is measured at a number of wavelengths (generally 400–700 nm in 10- to 20-nanometer increments) using a spectrophotometer. The data of absorbance versus wavelength is plotted, and the wavelength that gives the maximum absorbance is chosen to be used for the rest of the experiment. The absorbance of each of the dilutions is measured. A plot of absorbance versus concentration (Beer's law plot) is prepared either by hand or using a spreadsheet. The solid sample is dissolved (if it is copper, this will require the use of nitric acid) and diluted to a certain volume. The concentration of that solution is determined using the Beer's law plot. Using the concentration of the solution and the solution's volume, you can calculate the moles and then grams of the substance. Using the initial mass of the sample, you can finally calculate the mass percentage of the substance in the sample.

Calculations

You can determine the concentrations of the diluted stock solution by using the dilution equation ($M_1V_1 = M_2V_2$). The mass percentage is calculated by:

$$(\text{grams substance/grams sample}) \times 100\%.$$

Comments

If you are doing a brass analysis for percentage of copper, you will dissolve the brass in concentrated nitric acid. Be extremely careful. The nitric acid is corrosive and the NO gas that is produced is toxic. On the AP exam be sure to stress safety if you are describing this process.

Experiment 3: Gravimetric Analysis

Synopsis

Specific experiments that are performed in this investigation use determination of the mass of a specific substance in a sample by precipitation, drying, and weighing. A common experiment done in this category is determination of the hardness of a water sample. The hardness of a water sample is related to the amounts of calcium, magnesium, and iron ions in solution. These ions may be precipitated as the carbonate salts. For simplicity's sake, hard-water samples are commonly prepared with only one of these ions, generally calcium. The carbonate salt is precipitated, separated from the solution by suction filtration, and dried in a drying oven. The mass of the dry salt is determined, and the water sample hardness is calculated as mg calcium carbonate per liter of water sample.

Equipment

Various salt solutions of known concentration
Analytical balance
Drying oven
Suction filtration apparatus
Büchner funnel
Filter paper
Aspirator
Ring stands
Assorted glassware, including volumetric glassware

Measurements

The student will make several measurements in gravimetric analysis, especially mass and volume determinations.

Calculations

If a water hardness analysis is being done, the grams of calcium carbonate per milliliter of water sample are initially calculated. This value is then converted to milligrams of calcium carbonate per liter of water sample (hardness) using appropriate conversions.

Comments

All measurements must be done accurately, especially the mass and volume measurements.

Experiment 4: Titration

Synopsis

In the titration procedure, the concentration of an acid is determined by adding small quantities at a time of a base of known concentration until the point at which the moles of base equal the moles of acid present (the equivalence point). It is possible to do a titration by adding small amounts of a solution of a known concentration of acid to determine the concentration of a base solution. Many times this neutralization point cannot be determined unaided, so an indicator or a pH meter is used. The point at which a color change happens with the indicator or an abrupt change in pH occurs with the pH meter is called the endpoint of the titration. Knowing the volume of the unknown acid, the concentration of the base, and the number of milliliters it took to reach the endpoint allows you to calculate the concentration of the unknown acid. The concentration of an unknown base can be determined by titration with an acid of known concentration (Figure 19.2).

Equipment

Burets
Erlenmeyer flasks
Pipets
Acid-base indicators
pH meter
Base or acid solution of known concentration
Assorted glassware

Measurements

You will be placing a required volume of the unknown acid (or base) solution into the Erlenmeyer flask with a pipet. The buret will be filled with the base (or acid) solution. Be

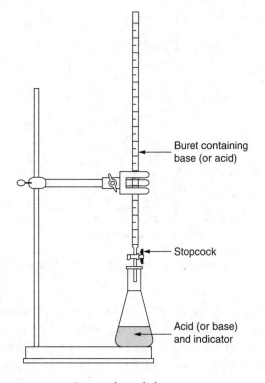

Figure 19.2   General acid–base titration setup.

sure to record your initial volume. You will add small amounts of base drop by drop until the indicator changes color. Record the final volume. The final volume reading minus the initial volume reading is the volume of base added.

Calculations

The calculation of the concentration of the base is essentially a stoichiometry reaction. Most of the time you will be able to generalize the process using the equation:

$$H^+ + OH^- \rightarrow H_2O.$$

From the molarity of the base and the volume used, you can calculate the moles of base (OH^-). Because of the 1:1 stoichiometry that also will be the moles of acid. Dividing that by the liters of acid solution pipetted into the flask gives the acid's molarity.

Comments

This type of titration can be performed with a pH meter without an indicator. The pH readings will be plotted against the volume. The endpoint is the point of inflection of the curve. A titration, either with an indicator or a pH meter, can be used to determine the acid content of household substances such as fruit juices or sodas.

Experiment 5: Chromatography

Synopsis

Many times the components (solutes) in a solution cannot be separated by simple physical means. This is especially true of polar solutes because of their interactions. One method that is commonly used is chromatography (Figure 19.3). A very small amount of the solution is spotted onto a strip of filter paper or chromatography paper and allowed to dry. The strip is placed vertically into a jar containing a small amount of solvent. As the solvent

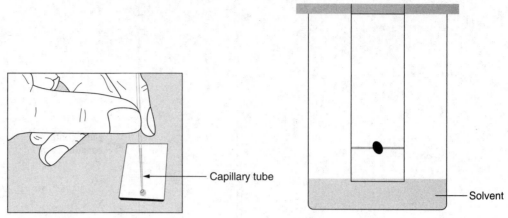

(a) Spotting the Chromatography Paper

Capillary tube

(b) Chromatography Development Jar

Solvent

Figure 19.3   Basic procedure for a paper chromatography experiment.

is drawn up the strip by capillary action, it dissolves the sample. The various solutes have different affinities to the paper and to the solvent and can thus be separated as the solvent moves up the strip. Choice of the solvent is critical and can be related to its polarity; however, the choice sometimes must be done by trial and error.

Equipment

Filter paper or chromatography paper
Chromatography jar
Various solvents
Metric rules
Sample to be analyzed
Assorted glassware

Measurements

The student will make measurements of the distance that each component travels and the distance that the solvent traveled.

Calculations

The calculations involve determining the R_f value for each component. The R_f value is the distance the component travels divided by the distance the solvent traveled. Substances that interact strongly with the paper do not travel very far (low R_f values), while those that interact strongly with the solvent travel much farther (high R_f values).

Comments

Chromatography is a very powerful separation technique.

Experiment 6: Determination of the Type of Bonding in Solid Samples

Synopsis

In this type of experiment, the student is given a set of bottles that contain solids of various types of bonding—ionic, covalent, or metallic. The student uses various physical and chemical tests to determine the bonding type. These tests might include melting point, conductivity, solubility, etc. along with observations of physical properties such as luster and hardness.

Equipment

Assorted solids—ionic, covalent, metals
Assorted solvents—polar and nonpolar
Conductivity tester
pH paper
Thermometer
Assorted glassware

Measurements

A number of measurements and observations may be made:

Luster: Metals tend to have a metallic luster; solid nonmetals often have a dull luster.
Melting point: Ionic solids and metals have high melting points; covalent compounds have lower melting points.
Solubility: Ionic compounds and polar covalent solids are generally soluble in water; metals and nonpolar covalent solids are generally insoluble or very slightly soluble in water.
Conductivity: Aqueous solutions of ionic compounds are conductors; aqueous solutions of most polar covalent compounds are nonconductors.

Calculations

There are generally no calculations associated with this experiment.

Comments

Many other tests could be used: pH of the aqueous solutions, solubility on organic solvents, and so on.

Experiment 7: Stoichiometry

Synopsis

In this experiment, you are asked to verify the results of an experiment by checking both the stoichiometric calculations and the procedure. You will be asked to determine the percent by mass of substances such as sodium bicarbonate in a mixture. You will do this by making use of the unique properties of the components in this mixture.

Equipment

Bunsen burners and strikers
Digital balances
Ring stands and rings
Ceramic triangles
Crucibles and lids
Assorted glassware, including volumetric glassware

Measurements

A weighed sample mixture of sodium bicarbonate and sodium carbonate is heated to constant mass. The sodium bicarbonate decomposes to sodium carbonate, carbon dioxide (gas), and water vapor: $2\ NaHCO_3(s) \rightarrow Na_2CO_3(s) + H_2O(g) + CO_2(g)$. The loss of mass is the loss in mass of $CO_2 + H_2O$. Examining the equation for the decomposition reaction, you can see that there is a 1:1 ratio of moles of water and carbon dioxide.

Calculations

If you let z = moles CO_2 = moles H_2O, then the total grams of mass lost can be shown as the sum of the moles of each (which will be the same) times the molar mass of each substance:

$$\text{Mass lost (grams)} = (z \times 18.02 \text{ g } H_2O/\text{mole}) + (z \times 44.01 \text{g } CO_2/\text{mole}).$$

You can then solve for z, the number of moles. As you can see from the balanced equation, the moles of $NaHCO_3$ solid that decomposed is $2z$. The mass of $NaHCO_3$ that decomposed will be:

$$2z \times 84.02 \text{g } NaHCO_3/\text{mole}.$$

The percent of $NaHCO_3$ in the mixture will be the mass of the sodium bicarbonate divided by the mass of the mixture sample times 100%:

$$(\text{grams } NaHCO_3/\text{grams mixture}) \times 100\%.$$

Comments

In order to increase the precision (and hopefully the accuracy) of the determination, several runs should be made and an average taken. This same procedure may be applied to many other reactions and mixtures. These samples could also be analyzed by a titration procedure.

Experiment 8: Redox Titration

Synopsis

In this experiment, the concentration of a substance will be determined by using a redox titration. The titrant will need to be standardized before it can be used in the titration. Commonly, the redox titration involves the titration of hydrogen peroxide (H_2O_2) with potassium permanganate ($KMnO_4$), with the goal of analyzing the commercial hydrogen peroxide that can be found in a pharmacy. The $KMnO_4$ solution can be standardized against a $Fe(NH_4)_2(SO_4)_2 \cdot 6H_2O$ solution. You will prepare a standard (known concentration) solution of the $Fe(NH_4)_2(SO_4)_2 \cdot 6H_2O$, a sulfuric acid solution, and a solution of potassium permanganate. The redox half-reactions involved in the standardization are:

$$Fe^{2+}(aq) \rightarrow Fe^{3+}(aq) + 1\ e^- \text{ and}$$

$$MnO_4^-(aq) + 8\ H^+(aq) + 5\ e^- \rightarrow Mn^{2+}(aq) + 4\ H_2O(l),$$

giving an overall redox reaction of:

$$5\ Fe^{2+}(aq) + MnO_4^-(aq) + 8\ H^+(aq) \rightarrow 5\ Fe^{3+}(aq) + Mn^{2+}(aq) + 4\ H_2O(l)$$

The half-reactions involved in the titration of the hydrogen peroxide are:

$$H_2O_2(aq) \rightarrow O_2(g) + 2\ H^+(aq) + 2\ e^- \text{ and}$$

$$MnO_4^-(aq) + 8\ H^+(aq) + 5\ e^- \rightarrow Mn^{2+}(aq) + 4\ H_2O(l),$$

giving the overall redox-reaction:

$$5\ H_2O_2(aq) + 2\ MnO_4^-(aq) + 6\ H^+(aq) \rightarrow 2\ Mn^{2+}(aq) + 8\ H_2O(l) + 5\ O_2(g).$$

Equipment

Buret
Ring stand and clamps
Pipets of assorted volumes
Pipet bulbs
Assorted glassware, including volumetric glassware

Measurements

You will be making mass measurements of the $Fe(NH_4)_2(SO_4)_2 \cdot 6H_2O$ and the $KMnO_4$ and many volume measurements of the pipets, volumetric flasks, and the buret.

Calculations

For the standardization: from the number of grams of $Fe(NH_4)_2(SO_4)_2 \cdot 6H_2O$ used, you can calculate the moles of Fe^{2+} used. Knowing this, you can determine the moles MnO_4^- used from the stoichiometry in the overall reaction (1 MnO_4^- : 5 Fe^{2+}) and then its molarity.

For the peroxide titration: from the buret volume and the molarity of the $KMnO_4$ solution, you can calculate the moles used in the titration, and applying the overall reaction stoichiometry you can get the moles of hydrogen peroxide (5 H_2O_2 : 2 MnO_4^-). From the moles, you can get grams and finally mass percent (assuming the mass of the peroxide solution is 1.00 g/mL).

Comments

Be very careful in making your measurements. The same general procedure can be applied to a number of other systems.

Experiment 9: Chemical and Physical Changes

Synopsis

Commonly this experiment involves separating the components of a mixture by using the chemical and physical properties of the mixture components. This is the basis of the analysis of commercially available samples such as over-the-counter acetaminophen- or aspirin-based pain relievers. The binder (many times sucrose), aspirin, and acetaminophen can be separated by the difference in their solubility in water and organic solvents, their acidity, and the difference in the way they react with hydrochloric acid and sodium bicarbonate solutions.

Equipment

Büchner funnels
Vacuum filtration apparatus
Separatory funnel
Hot plate or drying oven
Assorted glassware

Measurements

You will be making mass measurements of the sample, and every time a component is separated as a solid, it is dried and the mass determined.

Calculations

The overall percent recovery for the sample would be the sum of the masses of all the recovered components divided by the initial mass of the sample:

(sum of the grams of all recovered components/grams of sample) × 100%.

The percentage of each component can be calculated by dividing the mass of a component by the total mass of all recovered components:

(grams of component/sum of the grams of all recovered components) × 100%.

Comments

Be very careful in making your measurements. The same general procedure can be applied to a number of other systems.

Be especially careful when handling the acid solutions and organic solvents. Be sure to vent the separatory funnel before opening it.

Experiment 10: Kinetics

Synopsis

In this experiment, some of the factors involved in the speed of a chemical reaction will be explored. Commonly this experiment focuses on the decomposition of calcium carbonate—limestone, $CaCO_3$(s), and hydrochloric acid, HCl(aq). Pieces of calcium carbonate of different sizes (to test how the speed of reaction varies with surface area) and HCl solutions of different concentrations will be available. The temperature of the reaction mixture can be varied by using an ice bath or heating the mixture. In order to measure the speed of the reaction, the carbon dioxide gas product can be collected in a syringe, or a gas pressure probe can be used to monitor the production of the CO_2(g) as a function of time. The mass of sample consumed (or the decrease in the total mass of the reaction flask) versus time can also be used as an indication of the speed of reaction.

Equipment

Balance
Hotplate
Syringes
Stopwatch
Assorted glassware
Magnetic stirrer and stir bar
Gas pressure probe and data collection device

Measurements

Measurements include the initial and final mass of the calcium carbonate sample, the volume of gas evolved, and time measurements.

Calculations

Calculations commonly involve determining the mass of sample consumed (lost) as a function of time. The results of the mass versus time measurements are commonly plotted.

Comments

When plotting the data, the time is commonly the horizontal axis, while the mass lost or mL of gas produced is the vertical axis.

Be especially careful when handling the hydrochloric acid.

Experiment 11: Rate Laws

Synopsis

In this experiment, you will determine the rate law for a specific chemical reaction. Commonly the reaction involved is the reaction of crystal violet (CV) with sodium hydroxide (NaOH). The progress of the reaction is followed with a spectrophotometer or colorimeter. You will initially create a Beer's law calibration curve by measuring the absorbance of solutions of crystal violet of varying concentrations. Then you will use the same spectrophotometer to follow the change in concentration of crystal violet as it reacts with NaOH as a function of time:

$$CV^+(aq) + OH^-(aq) \rightarrow CVOH(aq).$$

The rate expression for this reaction would be:

$$\text{rate} = k \, [CV^+]^x [OH^-]^y.$$

If we use a large stoichiometric excess of NaOH, then the rate equation becomes

$$\text{rate} = k^* \, [CV^+]^x$$

since there is so much hydroxide ion present that its concentration essentially becomes constant.

Equipment

Spectrophotometer (commonly SPEC 20)
Cuvettes (sample tubes for the spectrophotometer)
Pipettes and bulbs
Assorted glassware, including volumetric glassware

Measurements

You will be making measurements of absorbance and time. Be sure to use a blank containing only water and NaOH but no crystal violet.

Calculations

You will be making different concentrations of the stock crystal violet solution by dilution, so that you will use the dilution equation: $M_1 V_1 = M_2 V_2$. You will be making three graphs: (1) concentration versus time (straight line indicates zero order with respect to CV [$x = 0$ in rate expression]); (2) ln(concentration) versus time (straight line indicates first order with respect to CV [$x = 1$ in rate expression]) and (3) 1/concentration versus time (straight line indicates second order with respect to CV [$x = 2$ in rate expression]).

Comments

Be especially careful when handling the sodium hydroxide solution.

Experiment 12: Calorimetry

Synopsis

In this experiment, you will be measuring the heat produced during the dissolving of various ionic substances in water with the goal of determining which of the salts is most efficient (with respect to cost) in generating heat. Substances to test might include anhydrous calcium chloride ($CaCl_2$), anhydrous sodium carbonate (Na_2CO_3), anhydrous ammonium nitrate (NH_4NO_3), anhydrous sodium acetate ($NaC_2H_3O_2$), and similar salts. You will calculate the change in enthalpy of dissolution in kJ/mol (ΔH_{soln}) by using a coffee-cup calorimeter (see Figure 9.1 in Chapter 9, Thermodynamics). You may be using a magnetic stirrer instead of the stirring wire shown in the figure.

Equipment

Thermometers or temperature probes
Polystyrene cups
Magnetic stirrers and stir bars
Assorted glassware

Measurements

You will be making measurements of the initial and final temperatures of the solutions formed by adding a certain mass of solute to a measured amount of water. The ΔT is the final temperature minus the initial temperature. The value of ΔT is a calculated number and not a measured number.

Calculations

You may be given or may have to calculate the calorimeter constant, C, for your calorimeter—the heat absorbed by the calorimeter per degree of temperature change. The energy of solution formation (q_{rxn}) is calculated by multiplying the mass times the specific heat of the solution (given) times the change in temperature ($q_{rxn} = mc\Delta T$) and the energy of solution (q_{soln}) is calculated by: $q_{soln} = -(q_{rxn} + C\Delta T)$. The enthalpy of dissolution (ΔH_{soln}) is calculated by dividing the q_{soln} (in kJ) by the number of moles of salt used.

Comments

Be especially careful with the ammonium nitrate—it is a strong oxidizer.

Experiment 13: Chemical Equilibrium—Le Châtelier's Principle

Synopsis

Experiments that fall into this category examine systems that are at equilibrium and what happens when that equilibrium is disturbed. Many times this involves having a small tray of reagents and testing an equilibrium system by mixing selected reagents and making observations. You may change concentrations (adding more reagent) or change the temperature of the solutions. This may involve an acid–base equilibrium or complex ion equilibriums. Reactions will be given, and you should be able to describe the stress that you imposed and how the system reacted to that stress.

Equipment

Test tubes
Stirring rods
Spatula
Assorted glassware

Measurements

This experiment involves no measurements, only estimations of volumes and masses.

Calculations

This experiment involves no calculations.

Comments

Be very careful when working with concentrated ammonia and hydrochloric acid. Always wear goggles, gloves, and an apron, and keep these reagents in the hood.

Experiment 14: Acid–Base Titrations

Synopsis

Experiments that fall into this category are acid–base titrations involving weak acids or weak bases. Many times the course of the titration is followed by a pH meter and the equivalence point is determined graphically. This allows you to determine not only the concentration of the weak acid or base but also its pK_a or pK_b. Both monoprotic and polyprotic acids may be examined. From an examination of the specific reaction involving a weak acid or base, you should be able to determine whether the solution at the equivalence point will be acidic or basic.

Equipment

Stirring rods
pH meters or pH probes
Buret
Assorted glassware

Measurements

You will be making pH measurements and plotting them against volume of titrant added. In many cases, you will titrate various acids (strong and weak) with a NaOH solution of known concentration. The equivalence point for such a titration is the point at which a dramatic increase in pH occurs; this is called the point of inflection of the curve. The pH at the volume corresponding to half the equivalence point volume is the pK_a of the acid. The same is true of bases, except the pH will be decreasing during the titration. A polyprotic acid or base will give you two points of inflection, and two pKs and Ks may be calculated.

Calculations

The K_a of the acid can be calculated by the equation $K_a = 10^{-pK_a}$. If the K_b of a weak base is to be determined, use $K_b = 10^{-pK_b}$.

Comments

Be extremely careful when working with the acids and bases and wear all of your personal protective equipment, especially your goggles. When making dilutions, always add the acid (or base) to water, NOT water to acid.

Experiment 15: Buffer pH

Synopsis

A buffer is a substance that resists a change in pH when an acid or base is added to it. It is normally a mixture of a weak acid and its conjugate base. Experiments in this category involve examining the properties of buffers and household substances that are buffers. This will involve titrating a substance with an acid or base while following the course of the titration with a pH meter, plotting the pH versus mL of titrant added, and determining the equivalence point graphically. At any point before the equivalence point, you have a buffer present. Common household substances may be tested for their buffer ability. The curve of pH versus mL of a substance that has some buffering ability rises sharply initially and then levels off much more than a titration of a substance that is not a buffer. You can use this to determine whether an unknown solution exhibits any buffering capability.

Equipment

pH meter
Burets and clamps
Magnetic stirrer
Assorted glassware

Measurements

You will be making measurements of volume and pH for a wide variety of substances. The point in a titration involving a buffer that corresponds to halfway to the equivalence point is called the point of maximum buffering.

Calculations

The K_a of the acid can be calculated by the equation $K_a = 10^{-pK_a}$. If the K_b of a weak base is to be determined, then use $K_b = 10^{-pK_b}$.

Comments

Be careful in handling the acid and base solutions.

Experiment 16: The Capacity of a Buffer

Synopsis

Experiments in this category are designed to explore the capacity of a buffer, which is the amount of acid or base that can be neutralized by the buffer. You can determine this by using different amounts of the conjugate acid and base components or by changing the concentration of each by the same amount. Normally, the higher the concentration of the conjugate acid and base in the buffer, the more moles of added base or acid can be neutralized and thus the higher the buffer capacity. You will also be asked to create a buffer of a specific pH.

Equipment

Balance
Burets and clamps
Assorted glassware

Measurements

You will be making measurements of volume and pH for a wide variety of substances. You will be making graphs of pH versus mL of titrant added.

Calculations

You can calculate the initial pH of a conjugate acid/base buffer by using the following equations:

$$[H^+] = K_a \, [\text{weak acid}]/[\text{conjugate base}]; \text{ then } pH = -\log [H^+].$$

If you want a buffer of a certain pH, then put in the K_a of the weak acid you want to use and the $[H^+]$ desired and solve for the ratio of acid to base. If you have a choice of several acid/base systems, then choose the one whose pK_a is closest to the desired pH.

Comments

Be extremely careful when working with the acids and bases and wear all of your personal protective equipment, especially your goggles. When making dilutions, always add the acid (or base) to water, NOT water to acid.

› Common Mistakes to Avoid

1. You *measure* initial and final values, but *calculate* the change.
2. You use an analytical balance to weigh the mass (grams), but not the moles.

› Review Questions

Below you will find a long free-response question like the ones in Section II of the exam. Use this question to review the content of this chapter and practice for the AP Chemistry exam. To make this an even more authentic practice for the actual exam, time yourself following the instructions provided.

Free-Response Question

You have 15 minutes to answer the following question. You may use a calculator and the tables in the back of the book.

Question 1

A sample of a solid, weak monoprotic acid, HA, is supplied, along with solid sodium hydroxide, NaOH, a phenolphthalein solution, and primary standard potassium hydrogen phthalate (KHP).

(a) Describe how a standardized sodium hydroxide solution may be prepared for the titration.
(b) Sketch a graph of pH versus volume of base added for the titration.
(c) Sketch the titration curve if the unknown acid was really a diprotic acid.
(d) Describe the steps to determine K_a for HA.
(e) What factor determines which indicator should be chosen for this titration?

Answer and Explanation for the Free-Response Question

(a) A sample of sodium hydroxide is weighed and dissolved in deionized water to give a solution of the approximate concentration desired. (Alternatively, a concentrated NaOH solution could be diluted.)

1. Samples of dried KHP are weighed into flasks and dissolved in deionized water.

2. A few drops of the appropriate acid–base indicator (phenolphthalein) are added to each sample.

3. A buret is rinsed with a little of the NaOH solution; then the buret is filled with NaOH solution.

4. Take an initial buret reading.

5. NaOH solution is titrated into the KHP samples until the first permanent pink color.

6. Take the final buret reading.

7. Using the molar mass of KHP, determine the moles of KHP present. This is equal to the moles of NaOH.

8. The difference in the buret readings is the volume of NaOH solution added (convert this to liters).

9. The molarity of the NaOH solution is the moles of NaOH divided by the liters of NaOH solution added.

10. (Repeat the procedure for each sample.)

Give yourself 2 points for this entire list, if the items are in order. If three or more items are in the wrong order or missing, you get only 1 point. You get 0 points for three or fewer items.

(b)

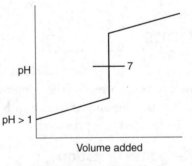

Equivalence point at pH < 7

You get 1 point for this graph. You get an additional point for noting that the equivalence point is greater than 7.

(c)

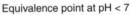

You get 1 point for this graph. You must show two steps.

(d) There are several related ways to do this problem. One method is to split the sample into two portions. Titrate one portion to the equivalence point. Add the titrated sample to the untitrated sample, and add a volume of deionized water equal to the volume of NaOH solution added. The pH of this mixture is equal to the pK_a of the acid (this corresponds to a half-titrated sample).

You get 1 point for anything concerning a half-titrated sample and an additional point for pH = pK_a.

(e) The pH at the equivalence point must be close to the pK_a of the indicator.

You get 1 point for this answer.

There are a total of 8 points possible.

〉 Rapid Review

Reviewing the experiments should include looking at the synopsis, apparatus, calculations, and comments, as well as the appropriate concept chapters, if needed.

- Pay particular attention to any experiment you did not perform.

- Be familiar with the equipment used in each experiment.

- Know the basic measurements required in each experiment.

- Know what values are measured and which are calculated.

- Pay attention to significant figures.

- Balances are used to measure the mass of a substance, not the moles.

STEP 5

Build Your Test-Taking Confidence

AP Chemistry Practice Exam 1
AP Chemistry Practice Exam 2

AP Chemistry Practice Exam 1—Multiple Choice

ANSWER SHEET

1 Ⓐ Ⓑ Ⓒ Ⓓ	21 Ⓐ Ⓑ Ⓒ Ⓓ	41 Ⓐ Ⓑ Ⓒ Ⓓ
2 Ⓐ Ⓑ Ⓒ Ⓓ	22 Ⓐ Ⓑ Ⓒ Ⓓ	42 Ⓐ Ⓑ Ⓒ Ⓓ
3 Ⓐ Ⓑ Ⓒ Ⓓ	23 Ⓐ Ⓑ Ⓒ Ⓓ	43 Ⓐ Ⓑ Ⓒ Ⓓ
4 Ⓐ Ⓑ Ⓒ Ⓓ	24 Ⓐ Ⓑ Ⓒ Ⓓ	44 Ⓐ Ⓑ Ⓒ Ⓓ
5 Ⓐ Ⓑ Ⓒ Ⓓ	25 Ⓐ Ⓑ Ⓒ Ⓓ	45 Ⓐ Ⓑ Ⓒ Ⓓ
6 Ⓐ Ⓑ Ⓒ Ⓓ	26 Ⓐ Ⓑ Ⓒ Ⓓ	46 Ⓐ Ⓑ Ⓒ Ⓓ
7 Ⓐ Ⓑ Ⓒ Ⓓ	27 Ⓐ Ⓑ Ⓒ Ⓓ	47 Ⓐ Ⓑ Ⓒ Ⓓ
8 Ⓐ Ⓑ Ⓒ Ⓓ	28 Ⓐ Ⓑ Ⓒ Ⓓ	48 Ⓐ Ⓑ Ⓒ Ⓓ
9 Ⓐ Ⓑ Ⓒ Ⓓ	29 Ⓐ Ⓑ Ⓒ Ⓓ	49 Ⓐ Ⓑ Ⓒ Ⓓ
10 Ⓐ Ⓑ Ⓒ Ⓓ	30 Ⓐ Ⓑ Ⓒ Ⓓ	50 Ⓐ Ⓑ Ⓒ Ⓓ
11 Ⓐ Ⓑ Ⓒ Ⓓ	31 Ⓐ Ⓑ Ⓒ Ⓓ	51 Ⓐ Ⓑ Ⓒ Ⓓ
12 Ⓐ Ⓑ Ⓒ Ⓓ	32 Ⓐ Ⓑ Ⓒ Ⓓ	52 Ⓐ Ⓑ Ⓒ Ⓓ
13 Ⓐ Ⓑ Ⓒ Ⓓ	33 Ⓐ Ⓑ Ⓒ Ⓓ	53 Ⓐ Ⓑ Ⓒ Ⓓ
14 Ⓐ Ⓑ Ⓒ Ⓓ	34 Ⓐ Ⓑ Ⓒ Ⓓ	54 Ⓐ Ⓑ Ⓒ Ⓓ
15 Ⓐ Ⓑ Ⓒ Ⓓ	35 Ⓐ Ⓑ Ⓒ Ⓓ	55 Ⓐ Ⓑ Ⓒ Ⓓ
16 Ⓐ Ⓑ Ⓒ Ⓓ	36 Ⓐ Ⓑ Ⓒ Ⓓ	56 Ⓐ Ⓑ Ⓒ Ⓓ
17 Ⓐ Ⓑ Ⓒ Ⓓ	37 Ⓐ Ⓑ Ⓒ Ⓓ	57 Ⓐ Ⓑ Ⓒ Ⓓ
18 Ⓐ Ⓑ Ⓒ Ⓓ	38 Ⓐ Ⓑ Ⓒ Ⓓ	58 Ⓐ Ⓑ Ⓒ Ⓓ
19 Ⓐ Ⓑ Ⓒ Ⓓ	39 Ⓐ Ⓑ Ⓒ Ⓓ	59 Ⓐ Ⓑ Ⓒ Ⓓ
20 Ⓐ Ⓑ Ⓒ Ⓓ	40 Ⓐ Ⓑ Ⓒ Ⓓ	60 Ⓐ Ⓑ Ⓒ Ⓓ

The AP exam is a timed exam; keep this in mind as you prepare. When taking the various tests presented in this book, you should follow the AP exam rules as closely as possible. Anyone can improve his or her score by using notes, books, or an unlimited time. You will have none of these on the AP exam, so resist the temptation to use them on practice exams. Carefully time yourself, do not use other materials, and use a calculator only when expressly allowed to do so. After you have finished an exam, you may use other sources to go over questions you missed or skipped. We have seen many students get into trouble because the first time they attempted a test under "test conditions" was on the test itself.

AP Chemistry Practice Exam 1, Section I (Multiple Choice)

Time—1 hour and 30 minutes
NO CALCULATOR MAY BE USED WITH SECTION I

Answer the following questions in the time allowed. You may use the periodic table in the back of the book.

Use the following information to answer questions 1–7.

Sodium azide, NaN_3, is a component of automobile airbags. It is useful because it quickly decomposes to generate a large volume of nitrogen gas. The balanced chemical equation for the reaction is:

$$2\ NaN_3(s) \rightarrow 2\ Na(s) + 3\ N_2(g)$$

There are additional components in the airbag to react with the elemental sodium formed.

Sodium azide is an unstable compound; therefore, it is often necessary to analyze samples as a check of its purity. A chemist is attempting to develop a new analytical, which employs the following reaction:

$$NaN_3(aq) + Na_2S(aq) + 3\ H_2O(l) \rightarrow N_2(g) + NH_3(g) + S(s) + 3\ NaOH(aq)$$

The chemist weighed a small flask both with and without a sample of sodium azide and recorded the masses. Next, she connected the flask to the system shown below.

The flask in the middle and the rubber tubing leading to the beaker were completely filled with dilute acid, and then the clamp was removed. Excess sodium sulfide solution was added to the flask containing the sample. The liquid level in the second flask dropped as the generated nitrogen gas displaced the water into the beaker. The system was left intact until gas generation ceased. After the system returned to room temperature, the beaker was raised until the water in the beaker was at the same level as in the second flask. When the

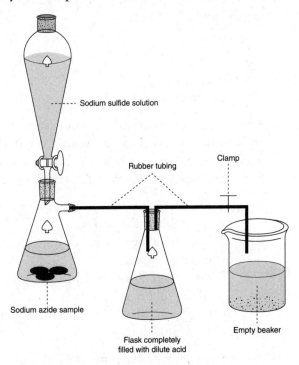

liquid levels were the same, the clamp was replaced to prevent further transfer. The chemist completed the following data table in her lab book.

Mass of empty flask	175.245 g
Mass of flask plus sodium azide	176.604 g
Volume of displaced water	315 mL
Barometric pressure	748.2 torr
Room temperature	27.0°C
Vapor pressure of water at 27.0°C	27.0 torr (assumed to be equal to that of dilute acid)

GO ON TO THE NEXT PAGE

1. What type of reaction generated the nitrogen gas?

   (A) Oxidation-reduction
   (B) Combination
   (C) Decomposition
   (D) Combustion

2. Why must the liquid in the flask be dilute acid?

   (A) Dilute acid is necessary to neutralize the sodium hydroxide formed.
   (B) Dilute acid removes ammonia from the gas leaving the nitrogen behind.
   (C) Dilute acid causes the reaction to go to completion.
   (D) Dilute acid is easier to handle than many other liquids.

3. What is the partial pressure of the hydrogen gas in the flask?

   (A) 775.2 torr
   (B) 748.2 torr
   (C) 760.0 torr
   (D) 721.2 torr

4. After the system returned to room temperature an adjustment was made by raising the beaker until the liquid level in both the beaker and the flask were the same. Why was this step necessary?

   (A) To remove excess water from the rubber tubing and into the beaker
   (B) To equilibrate the pressure in the flask with the external pressure
   (C) To make sure all of the hydrogen gas was out of the rubber tubing
   (D) To make sure there was no contamination by the hydrochloric acid

5. Approximately, how many moles of nitrogen gas formed?

   (A) 0.1 moles
   (B) 0.02 moles
   (C) 0.005 moles
   (D) 0.01 moles

6. If the sample were pure sodium azide, approximately how many moles of nitrogen gas would form?

   (A) 0.04 moles
   (B) 0.002 moles
   (C) 0.02 moles
   (D) 0.2 moles

7. Would it be possible to use this experimental setup to study a reaction that produced gaseous sulfur dioxide, SO_2? If not, why?

   (A) No, because some of the sulfur dioxide gas would dissolve in the acid.
   (B) No, because sulfur dioxide reacts with acids to produce solid sulfur.
   (C) No, because sulfur dioxide is only a gas at very high temperatures.
   (D) Yes, this apparatus could be used.

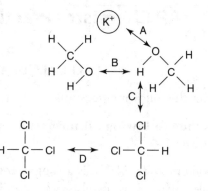

8. Which of the labeled arrows in the diagram above represents the strongest intermolecular force of the four indicated?

   (A) Arrow **A**
   (B) Arrow **B**
   (C) Arrow **C**
   (D) Arrow **D**

9. If about 88% of a sample of pure ^{131}I decays in 24 days, what is the approximate half-life of ^{131}I?

   (A) 24 days
   (B) 16 days
   (C) 8 days
   (D) 90 days

GO ON TO THE NEXT PAGE

Use the following information for questions 10–12.

Acid	K_a, Acid Dissociation Constant
HIO_3	1.7×10^{-1}
HIO_4	2.8×10^{-2}
HNO_2	4.5×10^{-4}
HCN	6.2×10^{-10}

10. A buffered solution with a pH near 5 is needed for an experiment. Using the above information, which of the combinations would be the best choice to prepare the buffer?

(A) $HIO_3 + KIO_3$
(B) $HCN + KCN$ *pKa*
(C) $HNO_2 + KNO_2$
(D) $HIO_4 + NaIO_4$

11. A student wishes to measure the pH of a 0.10 M solution of the sodium salt of each of the acids in the table. These salts are $NaIO_3$, $NaIO_4$, $NaNO_2$, and $NaCN$, respectively. Which of the four salt solutions will have the highest pH?

(A) $NaIO_3$
(B) $NaIO_4$ *hydrolysis of conj base.*
(C) $NaNO_2$
(D) $NaCN$

12. Which of the acids in the table would be the easiest to titrate with a weak base like ammonia ($K_b = 1.8 \times 10^{-5}$)?

(A) HIO_3
(B) HIO_4
(C) HNO_2
(D) HCN

Use the following information to answer questions 13–17.

pH versus volume of titrant added

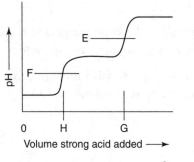

$$H_2C_6O_6 \quad K_{a1} = 8.0 \times 10^{-5} \quad K_{a2} = 1.6 \times 10^{-12}$$

Ascorbic acid (vitamin C), $H_2C_6O_6$, is a diprotic acid used as a dietary supplement. As with all dietary supplements, it is important to analyze samples for purity. The vitamin C may be extracted from natural sources or synthesized. The extraction vitamin C may contain additional extracted ingredients to which some people are allergic. Synthetic vitamin C may contain other forms of the vitamin; however, modern synthetic methods do not generate this contaminate. The above titration curve is an idealized graph for a diprotic acid. On this graph, E and F represent the pH at the endpoints with the possibility that E may shift slightly and one or the other may not be present. H is the volume of base required to titrate the first hydrogen ion and G is the quantity of base necessary to titrate both hydrogen ions. G is twice H.

13. What is the approximate pH at ½ H?

(A) 7
(B) 5
(C) 2
(D) Impossible to predict

14. If G were not twice H, what would this indicate?

(A) There is a contaminant that is either an acid or a base.
(B) The other form of vitamin C is present.
(C) The vitamin C was extracted from a plant.
(D) The vitamin C is synthetic.

15. Which of the following bases would be the best choice for the titration?

(A) $Al(OH)_3$
(B) Na_2CO_3
(C) NH_3
(D) KOH

16. In the titration of a sample of vitamin C, what is the approximate value of F?

(A) < 7
(B) > 7
(C) = 7
(D) Unknown

GO ON TO THE NEXT PAGE

17. While the titration of a diprotic acid to produce a curve similar to the idealized one above is useful in many analyses, ascorbic acid is not a good candidate for this type of analysis. Why?

(A) K_{a2} and K_{a1} are too close together.
(B) Ascorbic acid may occur in more than one form.
(C) Ascorbic acid is not soluble in water.
(D) K_{a2} for ascorbic acid is too small.

18. Which of the following CANNOT behave as both a Brønsted base and a Brønsted acid?

(A) $H_2PO_4^{2-}$
(B) CO_3^{2-}
(C) HSO_3^-
(D) HCO_3^-

19. A student mixes 50.0 mL of 0.10 M potassium chromate, K_2CrO_4, solution with 50.0 mL of 0.10 M $AgNO_3$. A red precipitate of silver chromate forms and the concentration of the silver ion becomes very small. Which of the following correctly places the concentrations of the remaining ions in order of decreasing concentration?

(A) $[K^+] > [CrO_4^{2-}] > [NO_3^-]$
(B) $[CrO_4^{2-}] > [NO_3^-] > [K^+]$
(C) $[K^+] > [NO_3^-] > [CrO_4^{2-}]$
(D) $[NO_3^-] > [K^+] > [CrO_4^{2-}]$

20. There are a number of experiments for the determination of the molecular mass of a gas. One method begins by heating a solid or liquid in a flask to produce a gaseous product. The gas passes through a tube and displaces water in an inverted, water-filled bottle. The mass of the starting material is measured, along with the volume of the displaced water and the temperature of the system. The pressure in the inverted water-filled bottle is equal to the external pressure. Once the barometric pressure has been recorded, what other information is needed to finish the experiment?

(A) The heat of formation of the gas
(B) The density of the water
(C) The mass of the displaced water
(D) The vapor pressure of the water

$H_2(g) + 1/2\ O_2(g) \rightarrow H_2O(l)$　　$\Delta H° = -300$ kJ

$C(s) + O_2(g) \rightarrow CO_2(g)$　　$\Delta H° = -400$ kJ

$C_2H_2(g) + 5/2\ O_2(g) \rightarrow$
　　$H_2O(l) + 2\ CO_2(g)$　　$\Delta H° = -1300$ kJ

21. Using the information given above, calculate the enthalpy change for the following reaction:

$$2\ C(s) + H_2(g) \rightarrow C_2H_2(g)$$

(A) 200 kJ
(B) −200 kJ
(C) 500 kJ
(D) −500 kJ

22. Cerium(III) sulfate, $Ce_2(SO_4)_2$, is less soluble in hot water than it is in cold. Which of the following conclusions may be related to this?

(A) The heat of solution of cerium(III) sulfate is exothermic.
(B) The hydration energies of cerium ions and sulfate ions are very low.
(C) The heat of solution for cerium(III) sulfate is endothermic.
(D) The solution is not an ideal solution.

Use the information on the containers in the following diagram to answer questions 23-25.

A	B	C	D
He	CH₄	O₂	SO₂
250 K	250 K	250 K	250 K
1.0 mole	1.0 mole	1.0 mole	1.0 mole
1.0 L	1.0 L	1.0 L	1.0 L

(The table above: A contains He, B contains CH_4, C contains O_2, D contains SO_2; each at 250 K, 1.0 mole, 1.0 L.)

Approximate molar masses:

He = 4 g mol^{-1}, CH_4 = 16 g mol^{-1},
O_2 = 32 g mol^{-1}, SO_2 = 64 g mol^{-1}

23. Under the conditions indicated, in which of the gas sample is the average velocity of the molecules half that of methane, CH_4?

(A) He
(B) CH_4
(C) SO_2
(D) They are all at the same temperature; therefore, they have the same average velocity.

24. Which of the four gases will probably show the least deviation from ideal behavior?

(A) He
(B) CH_4
(C) O_2
(D) SO_2

GO ON TO THE NEXT PAGE

25. If one of the containers sprang a small leak, which of the following would change?

   (A) Moles, temperature, and pressure
   (B) Moles and pressure
   (C) Temperature and pressure
   (D) Moles and temperature

26. The specific rate constant, k, for a certain first-order reaction is 86 h^{-1}. What mass of a 0.0500 g sample of starting material will remain after 58 s?

   (A) 0.0500 g
   (B) 0.0250 g
   (C) 0.0125 g
   (D) 0.00625 g

Use the information on the containers in the following diagram to answer questions 27–31 concerning the following equilibrium:

$$CO(g) + 2 H_2(g) \leftrightarrows CH_3OH(g)$$

A	B	C	D
CO H₂	CH₃OH	CO H₂ CH₃OH Not equilibrium	CO H₂ CH₃OH Equilibrium

27. Container A initially contains 0.60 mole of H_2 and 0.60 mole of CO and is allowed to come to equilibrium. At equilibrium, there are 0.40 mole of CO in the flask. What is the value of K_c, the equilibrium constant, for the reaction?

   (A) 0.40
   (B) 2.5
   (C) 0.080
   (D) 12

28. A 1.00-mole sample of CH_3OH is placed in container B and the system is allowed to go to equilibrium. What can be said about the relative rates of reaction with respect to the various components?

   (A) The rate of CO formation is numerically equal to the rate of CH_3OH loss.
   (B) The rate of H_2 formation is numerically equal to the rate of CH_3OH loss.
   (C) The rate of $H_2(g)$ formation is half the rate of $CO(g)$ formation.
   (D) The rate of $H_2(g)$ formation is equal to the rate of $CO(g)$ formation.

29. The mixture in container D is in equilibrium. Which of the following is true?

   (A) The rate of the forward and reverse reactions is equal to zero.
   (B) The rate of the forward reaction is equal to the rate of the reverse reaction.
   (C) The pressure in the system is increasing.
   (D) The pressure in the system is decreasing.

30. The mixture in container A goes to equilibrium. If the initial moles of $H_2(g)$ is twice the initial moles of $CO(g)$, which of the following is true?

   (A) Both reactants are limiting; therefore, the reaction will continue until there are zero moles of each remaining.
   (B) The total pressure of the system decreases until the system reaches equilibrium.
   (C) The total pressure of the system increases until the system equals equilibrium.
   (D) No reaction occurs until a catalyst is added.

31. As the mixture in container B approaches equilibrium, the partial pressure of CH_3OH gas decreases by 1.5 atm. What is the net change in the total pressure of the system?

   (A) +1.5 atm
   (B) +3.0 atm
   (C) −1.5 atm
   (D) −3.0 atm

Use the information on standard reduction potentials in the following table to answer questions 32–36.

	$E°$ (V)
$F_2(g) + 2 e^- \rightarrow 2 F^-(aq)$	+2.87
$Ag^+(aq) + 1 e^- \rightarrow Ag(s)$	+0.80
$O_2(g) + 2 H_2O(l) + 4 e^- \rightarrow$ $4 OH^-(aq)$	+0.40
$AgCl(s) + 1 e^- \rightarrow Ag(s) + Cl^-(aq)$	+0.22
$Pb^{2+}(aq) + 2 e^- \rightarrow Pb(s)$	−0.13
$NO_2^-(aq) + 5 H_2O(l) + 6 e^- \rightarrow$ $NH_3(aq) + 7 OH^-(aq)$	−0.15
$2 H_2O(l) + 2 e^- \rightarrow H_2(g) + 2 OH^-(aq)$	−0.83
$Cr^{2+}(aq) + 2 e^- \rightarrow Cr(s)$	−0.91
$Al^{3+}(aq) + 3 e^- \rightarrow Al(s)$	−1.66
$Rb^+(aq) + 1 e^- \rightarrow Rb(s)$	−2.93

GO ON TO THE NEXT PAGE

32. A student constructs an electrolysis cell with two inert electrodes in an aqueous solution that is 1.0 M in rubidium nitrite, $RbNO_2$, and 1.0 M in rubidium hydroxide, RbOH. As the cell operates, an odorless gas evolves from one electrode and a gas with a distinctive odor evolves from the other electrode. Choose the correct statement from the following list.

    (A) The odorless gas is oxygen.
    (B) The odorless gas is the result of reduction.
    (C) The gas with the distinctive odor is the result of oxidation.
    (D) The odorless gas evolves at the negative electrode.

33. There is a galvanic cell involving a lead, Pb, electrode in a 1.0 M lead(II) nitrate, $Pb(NO_3)_2$, solution and a chromium, Cr, electrode in a 1.0 M chromium(II) sulfate, $CrSO_4$, solution. What is the cell potential?

    (A) +0.78 V
    (B) −0.78 V
    (C) +1.04 V
    (D) 0.00 V

34. A student attempted to prepare an electrolysis cell to produce aluminum metal (Al) from an aqueous solution of aluminum chloride, $AlCl_3$, using a 6.0 V battery. The cathode compartment of the electrolysis contained 1.0 M aluminum chloride. The student was unsuccessful. Why was the student unable to produce aluminum metal?

    (A) The voltage from the battery was insufficient to force the reaction to occur.
    (B) Reduction of chloride ion occurred in preference to reduction of calcium ion.
    (C) Calcium chloride solutions do not conduct electricity.
    (D) Reduction of water occurred in preference to reduction of calcium ion.

35. Which of the substances in the table would be capable of reducing the aluminum ions in solid aluminum fluoride, AlF_3, to aluminum metal? Assume the cell potentials in the table also apply to the solid state.

    (A) Cr(s)
    (B) Rb(s)
    (C) $F_2(g)$
    (D) None

36. A student constructs a galvanic cell that has a chromium, Cr, electrode in a compartment containing a 1.0 M chromium(II) nitrate, $Cr(NO_3)_2$, solution and a silver, Ag, electrode in a compartment containing 1.0 M silver nitrate, $AgNO_3$, solution. A salt bridge containing a 1.0 M potassium chloride, KCl, solution connects the two compartments. When the student measures the cell potential, the value is far from the ideal predicted value. What is the cause of this discrepancy?

    (A) The initial concentrations should have been lower than 1.0 M.
    (B) The initial concentrations should have been higher than 1.0 M.
    (C) The potassium chloride in the salt bridge interfered with the reaction.
    (D) The student did not allow the cell to come to equilibrium.

Use the information on the acids in the following diagram to answer questions 37–38.

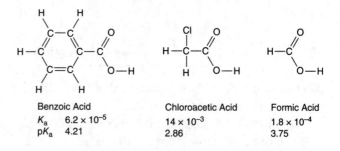

Benzoic Acid	Chloroacetic Acid	Formic Acid
K_a 6.2×10^{-5}	14×10^{-3}	1.8×10^{-4}
pK_a 4.21	2.86	3.75

37. Sample solutions of each of the three acids were titrated with 0.10 M sodium hydroxide, NaOH. Each of the acid solutions had a concentration of 0.10 M. Which of the acid titrations had the highest pH at the endpoint?

    (A) Formic acid
    (B) Benzoic acid
    (C) Chloroacetic acid
    (D) They all had a pH of 7 at the endpoint.

GO ON TO THE NEXT PAGE

38. A student prepares three buffer solutions. Each solution is 1.0 M in one of the acids in the table and 1.0 M in its corresponding sodium salt. Which of the solutions has the greatest buffer capacity with respect to added NaOH and why?

(A) The benzoic acid buffer because it is the strongest acid.
(B) The chloroacetic acid buffer because it is the strongest acid.
(C) The formic acid buffer because it donate both of its hydrogen atoms.
(D) All are the same.

39. Hypochlorous acid is an unstable compound, and one of the decomposition products is chlorine gas, Cl_2. The decomposition of the acid lowers its concentration over time. What effect will the decomposition of one-fourth of the acid have on the agreement between the endpoint of the titration and the equivalence point during a titration with standard sodium hydroxide?

(A) The endpoint would still remain near the ideal equivalence point.
(B) The endpoint would be after the ideal equivalence point.
(C) The endpoint would be before the ideal equivalence point.
(D) It is impossible to determine.

40. Three 25.00 mL samples of approximately 0.10 M phenol, C_6H_5OH, $K_a = 1.0 \times 10^{-10}$ were removed from a container and placed in separate 250 mL beakers. The samples were titrated with standard potassium hydroxide, KOH, solution. Cresol red was the acid-base indicator used in the titration. The samples required 31.75, 32.38, and 41.75 mL to reach the endpoint. Which of the following might explain why one of the samples required significantly more base to reach the endpoint?

(A) The indicator was added too late.
(B) The wrong indicator was used.
(C) There was a base contaminating the unclean beaker.
(D) There was an acid contaminating the unclean beaker.

41. During the study of the reaction A → 2B, a chemist constructs several graphs. The graph of [A] versus time and the graph of ln [A] versus time both give a curved line; however, the graph of 1/[A] versus time and gives a straight line. This implies the rate law is

(A) Rate $= k[A]$
(B) Rate $= k[A]^2$
(C) Rate $= k[A]^0$
(D) Rate $= k[A]^{-1}$

42. The photoelectron spectrum of carbon has three equally sized peaks. What peak is at the lowest energy?

(A) The 1s peak has the lowest energy.
(B) The 2s peak has the lowest energy.
(C) The 2p peak has the lowest energy.
(D) The 1p peak has the lowest energy.

COMPOUND	FORMULA	MOLAR MASS (g mol^{-1})	BOILING POINT (°C)
Ethyl methyl ether	$C_2H_5\text{-}O\text{-}CH_3$	60.10	10.8
Ethyl methyl amine	$C_2H_5NH\text{-}CH_3$	59.11	36.7
Propylamine	$C_3H_7NH_2$	59.11	47.8
Trimethyl amine	$N(CH_3)_3$	59.11	2.9

43. According to the data in the table above, which of the compounds has the strongest intermolecular forces?
(A) Propylamine
(B) Ethyl methyl ether
(C) Trimethyl amine
(D) Ethyl methyl amine

GO ON TO THE NEXT PAGE

Use the following information to answer questions 44-45.

METAL	ION	IONIC RADIUS (pm) (CUBIC ENVIRONMENT)	MELTING POINT OF OXIDE (°C)
Sodium	Na^+	132	1275 (sublimes)
Cadmium	Cd^{2+}	124	1500
Lanthanum	La^{3+}	130	2256

44. Each of the ions in the table form stable oxides (Na_2O, CdO, and La_2O_3). Lanthanum oxide, La_2O_3, has a melting point significantly higher than that of the other oxides. Which of the following is the best explanation of why this is true?

(A) Lanthanum is a lanthanide element and the melting points of these elements are always high.

(B) There is more oxygen in the formula La_2O_3 than in the other formulas.

(C) Lanthanum had the highest charge; therefore, it has the highest lattice energy.

(D) Alkali metals like sodium and transition metals like cadmium tend to have low melting points.

45. The lithium ion, Li^+, is smaller than the sodium ion. How does the melting point of lithium oxide, Li_2O, compare to that of sodium oxide?

(A) It is higher because smaller ions have a higher lattice energy.

(B) It is the same because the charges are the same.

(C) It is lower because smaller ions have a smaller lattice energy.

(D) It is impossible to predict because there is insufficient information in the problem.

46. During the investigation of a chemical reaction by a chemistry student, she was able to determine that the reaction was nonspontaneous at 1 atm and 298 K. However, she learned that cooling the system with dry ice (−78°C) caused the reaction to become spontaneous. Which of the following combinations must apply to this reaction?

(A) $\Delta H < 0$, $\Delta S < 0$, and $\Delta G = 0$

(B) $\Delta H > 0$, $\Delta S < 0$, and $\Delta G > 0$

(C) $\Delta H < 0$, $\Delta S < 0$, and $\Delta G > 0$

(D) $\Delta H > 0$, $\Delta S > 0$, and $\Delta G > 0$

47. What is the ionization constant, K_a, for a weak monoprotic acid if a 0.060 molar solution has a pH of 2.0?

(A) 2.0×10^{-3}

(B) 2.0×10^{-1}

(C) 1.7×10^{-1}

(D) 5.0×10^{-3}

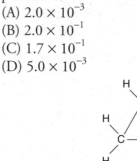

48. Cyclopropane, pictured above, is a relatively unstable compound. As seen in the diagram, the carbon atoms form the corners of an equilateral triangle and each carbon atom has two hydrogen atoms attached to complete an octet of electrons around the carbon atoms. Based upon this structure, why is cyclopropane a relatively unstable compound?

(A) Hydrocarbon compounds are relatively unstable in general.

(B) Compounds that have identical atoms bonded to each other are relatively unstable.

(C) The bonds do not match the angles.

(D) There is no resonance to stabilize the compound.

49. A chemist has a 500 mL beaker with a small amount of mercury(II) oxide, HgO, on the bottom. Mercury(II) is insoluble in water but will dissolve in strong acid. She adds 250 mL of water and begins adding 1.0 M hydrochloric acid. She continues adding acid until the solid just dissolves. She then tests the solution and finds that it is nonconducting. Which of the following best represents the result for the solution just as the last of the solid dissolves?

(A)

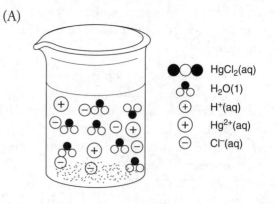

GO ON TO THE NEXT PAGE

(B)

(C)

(D)

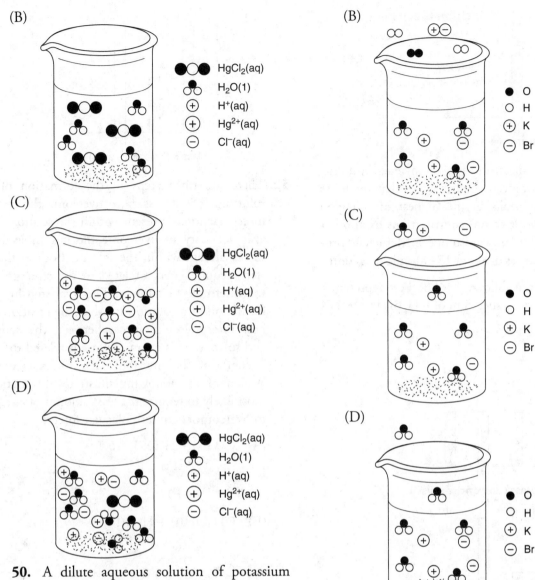

(B)

(C)

(D)

50. A dilute aqueous solution of potassium bromide, KBr, is heated to the boiling point. Which of the following best represents this system?

(A)

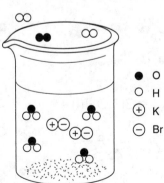

The average distribution of bromine isotopes on Earth is in the following table:

ISOTOPE	PERCENT ABUNDANCE
^{79}Br	50.7%
^{81}Br	49.3%

The highest mass peaks in the mass spectrum of methyl bromide, CH_3Br, are at 94 and 96 atomic mass units (there are smaller peaks corresponding to the small quantities of the less common isotopes of carbon and hydrogen). The spectrum plot below is of this region.

GO ON TO THE NEXT PAGE

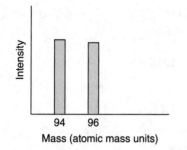

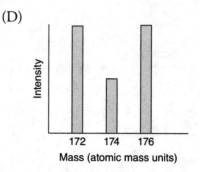

(D)

The mass spectrum for methylene bromide, CH_2Br_2, is more complicated in that there are three main peaks in the highest mass region (again ignoring minor contributions from other carbon and hydrogen isotopes). Methylene bromide has a mass of about 174 atomic mass units.

51. Which of the following is the best representation of the mass spectrum of CH_2Br_2 in the 174 region?

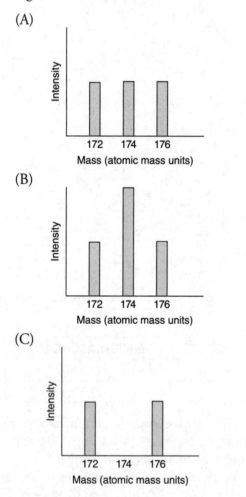

(A)

(B)

(C)

52. There are three steps in the formation of a solution. It is necessary to overcome the intermolecular forces present within the solute. It is also necessary to overcome the intermolecular forces present within the solvent. Both of these steps require energy related to the strength of the intermolecular forces. The final step in the formation of a solution involves the creation of new intermolecular forces between the solute and solvent. This energy release is related to the strength of the intermolecular forces created. Which of the following illustrates a situation most likely to require the least amount of energy to overcome the intermolecular forces?

(A) $CaO(s) + H_2O(l)$

(B) $CH_3OH(l) + H_2O(l)$

(C) $CCl_4(l) + Cl_2(g)$

(D) $CCl_4(l) + CH_3OH(l)$

GO ON TO THE NEXT PAGE

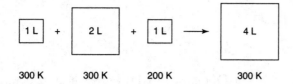

300 K   300 K   200 K   300 K

53. The contents in the three containers on the left in the diagram above are transferred to the container on the right. The volumes of the original containers are exactly the values indicated. The pressure in the first three containers is 1.0 atm. What is the pressure in the container on the right?

(A) 3.0 atm
(B) 4.0 atm
(C) 1.1 atm
(D) 0.50 atm

$$\ddot{O}{=}C{=}\ddot{O} \qquad \ddot{O}{=}C{=}\ddot{S}$$

54. The diagram above shows the structure of molecules of CS_2 and COS. The boiling point of COS is 223 K, and the boiling point of CS_2 is 319 K. Which of the following is the best explanation of why the boiling point of CS_2 is higher?

(A) The molar mass of CS_2 is greater.
(B) COS has weaker covalent bonds than CS_2.
(C) Only CS_2 can form intermolecular dipole-dipole forces.
(D) COS has stronger intermolecular forces because it is polar and CS_2 is not.

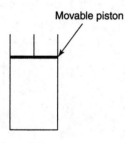

Movable piston

$$CO(g) + Cl_2(g) \rightleftarrows COCl_2(g) \qquad \Delta H = -109 \text{ kJ}$$

55. The above equilibrium is established in a closed system with a movable piston. After establishing equilibrium, the piston is rapidly moved up (pressure change). Which of the following graphs best illustrates the rate of the reverse reaction as the system returns to equilibrium?

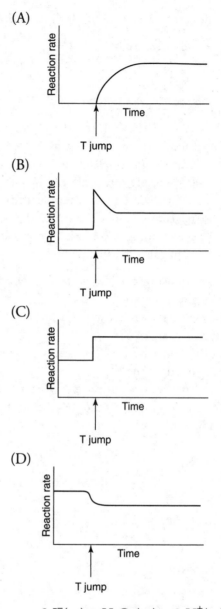

(A)

(B)

(C)

(D)

$$2\,I^-(aq) + H_2O_2(aq) + 2\,H^+(aq) \rightarrow I_2(aq) + 2\,H_2O(l)$$

The proposed mechanism for the above reaction is as follows:

Step 1: $H_2O_2(aq) + I^-(aq) \rightarrow$
    $HOI(aq) + OH^-(aq)$ (slow) k_1

Step 2: $HOI(aq) + I^-(aq) \rightarrow$
    $I_2(aq) + OH^-(aq)$ (fast) k_2

Step 3: $2\,OH^-(aq) + 2\,H^+(aq) \rightarrow$
    $2\,H_2O(l)$ (fast) k_3

GO ON TO THE NEXT PAGE

56. What is the rate law expression for this reaction?

(A) Rate = $k[H_2O_2][I^-]$
(B) Rate = $k[HOI][I^-]$
(C) Rate = $k[H_2O_2]$
(D) Rate = $\dfrac{[I_2]}{[I^-]^2[H^+]^2[H_2O_2]}$

57. A 30.00 g sample of metal (X) was heated to 100.00°C. This sample was clamped in contact with a 40.00 g sample of a different metal (Y) originally at 25.00°C. The final temperature of the two metals was 37.30°C, and no heat was lost to the surroundings. What is one possible conclusion from this experiment?

(A) The heat lost by the X was greater than the heat gained by the Y.
(B) The heat lost by the X was equal to the heat gained by the Y.
(C) The heat lost by the X was less than the heat gained by the Y.
(D) The final temperature was incorrectly determined, as it should be the average (62.50°C).

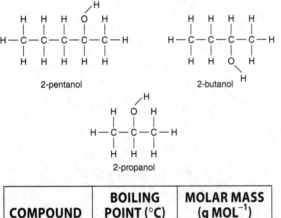

COMPOUND	BOILING POINT (°C)	MOLAR MASS (g MOL⁻¹)
2-pentanol	118.9	88.15
2-butanol	99.5	74.14
2-propanol	82.4	60.11

58. Which of the following best explains why the boiling point of 2-propanol is lower than the other two compounds in the diagram and table above?

(A) Larger molecules get tangled and cannot escape each other.
(B) It has weaker hydrogen bonds.
(C) It is the lightest of the three.
(D) It is a more symmetrical molecule.

59. The Dumas method is a procedure for determining the molar mass of a gas. In this procedure the mass of a gas is divided by the moles of gas determined from the ideal gas equation ($n = PV/RT$). The molar masses of some compounds, such as acetic acid, illustrated above, show significant deviations from the "correct" values. Why does the presence of dimers as illustrated make it unlikely to obtain an accurate molar mass of acids, such as acetic acid?

(A) Acetic acid, like all acids, will lose a hydrogen ion, so the molar mass is that of the acetate ion, which is less than that of acetic acid.
(B) Acetic acid is a liquid at room temperature, and its boiling point is too high to get accurate results.
(C) Acids are too reactive to give accurate results.
(D) The presence of strong intermolecular forces (hydrogen bonding) makes the gas nonideal; therefore the ideal gas law is not applicable.

60. In which of the following groups are the species listed correctly in order of increasing ionization energy?

(A) Sr, Ca, Ba
(B) Se, Tc, Ba
(C) Mn, Fe, Ni
(D) Cl, Br, I

STOP: End of AP Chemistry Practice Exam 1, Section I (Multiple Choice).

> # Answers and Explanations for Exam 1, Section 1 (Multiple Choice)

1. **A**—The reaction is an oxidation-reduction reaction since the sulfide ion undergoes oxidation to elemental sulfur and the azide ion undergoes reduction.

2. **B**—It is necessary to remove the ammonia from the gas; otherwise the part of the volume generated would be due to the ammonia. Since ammonia is a base, it will react with the acid.

3. **D**—The pressure inside the flask is the sum of the partial pressures. Therefore, the pressure of hydrogen gas is the total pressure (748.2 torr) minus the vapor pressure of water (27.0 torr). The leveling of the water in the beaker and flask adjusted the pressure in the flask to the external (barometric) pressure.

4. **B**—When the two liquid levels are the same then the pressures must be equal. In this case, both pressures are equal to the barometric pressure.

5. **D**—The ideal gas equation ($PV = nRT$) gives the moles of hydrogen gas formed.

$$\text{Moles H}_2 = n = \frac{PV}{RT}$$

$$= \frac{(721.2 \text{ torr}/760 \text{ torr})(0.315 \text{ L})}{(0.0821 \text{ L atm mol}^{-1} \text{ K}^{-1})(300.2 \text{ K})}$$

$$= 0.0121 \text{ moles H}_2$$

It is easier to calculate the answer by simple rounding as:

$$= \frac{(1 \text{ atm})(0.3 \text{ L})}{(0.08 \text{ L atm mol}^{-1} \text{ K}^{-1})(300 \text{ K})} \approx$$

$$\frac{(1)}{(0.1)}\left(\frac{0.3}{300}\right) = \left(\frac{0.3}{30.0}\right) = 0.01 \text{ moles}$$

6. **C**—The moles of nitrogen gas formed equal the moles of sodium azide reacting (see the balanced chemical equation). If the sample were pure sodium azide, the mass of sodium azide would be (176.604 − 175.245) g = 1.359 g sample (= NaN_3). The moles of sodium azide are the

mass of sodium azide divided by its molar mass (65.0 g mol^{-1}).

$$\text{Moles N}_2 = \text{moles NaN}_3 = \frac{1.359 \text{ g}}{65.0 \text{ g mol}^{-1}} \approx$$

$$\frac{1.359}{65} \approx \frac{1.3}{5(13)} \approx \frac{0.13}{5} \approx 0.026$$

Due to rounding, the actual answer must be a little smaller (0.0209 moles).

7. **A**—Sulfur dioxide gas is soluble in water and, while less soluble in dilute acid, some would still dissolve to give a smaller volume.

8. **A**—This represents an ion-dipole force, which is stronger than a hydrogen bond (B), a dipole-dipole force (C), or a London dispersion force (D).

9. **C**—After one half-life, 50% would remain. Another half-life would reduce this by one-half to 25% and a third half-life would reduce the remaining material by 12.5%. Thus, three half-lives = (50 + 25 + 12.5)% = 87.5% decayed. The total amount decayed is 88%. For this reason, 24 days years must be three half-lives of about 8 days each.

10. **C**—The best choice to prepare the buffer is the one where the pK_a is closest to the desired pH. It is possible to estimate the pK_a for an acid (without a calculator) by taking the negative of the exponent for the different K_a values. This gives 1 for HIO_3, 2 for HIO_4, 4 for HNO_2, and 10 for HCN. The HNO_2 has the value closest to the desired pH. It would not be a good choice since the pK_a is so far from the pH; however, it is the best choice.

11. **D**—This is due to hydrolysis of the conjugate base of the acid (IO_3^-, IO_4^-, NO_2^-, and CN^-). The smaller the K_a of the acid, the greater the K_b of the conjugate base. A larger K_b means a stronger base.

12. **A**—In order to get good results when titrating a weak base, it is important to use as strong an acid as possible to get a sharp endpoint. HIO_3 is the strongest acid in the table.

13. **B**—The position ½ H is halfway to the first equivalence point. The pH at the halfway point is equal to pK_a. The value of K_{a1} is 8.0×10^{-5}, which gives an approximate pK_a of 5 (actual 4.1).

14. **A**—To reach H, it is necessary to convert all the ascorbic acid to the hydrogen ascorbate ion, which means the moles of hydrogen ascorbate ion formed must equal the moles of ascorbic acid originally present. The moles of hydrogen ascorbate ion formed would require the same number of moles of base as that required to convert the ascorbic acid to hydrogen ascorbate. Equal moles would mean equal volumes added.

15. **D**—In any acid-base titration, it is always easier to use a strong base (and a strong acid). Potassium hydroxide, KOH, is the only strong base among the choices.

16. **B**—The titration of a weak acid with a strong base always has an equivalence point above 7.

17. **D**—Since K_{a2} is $K_{a2} = 1.6 \times 10^{-12}$, the pH at the equivalence point would be greater than 12, which is too high for a simple titration.

18. **B**—All can behave as Brønsted bases (accept a hydrogen ion). Only B cannot behave as an acid (donate a hydrogen ion).

19. **C**—Initially, doubling the volume will result in halving the concentrations. Next, consider the reaction. The balanced equation is: K_2CrO_4(aq) + 2 $AgNO_3$(aq) → Ag_2CrO_4(s) + 2 KNO_3(aq). The silver ion is the limiting reagent, so very little remains in solution (due to its K_{sp}). The precipitation of silver chromate reduces the chromate concentration from 0.050 *M*. The nitrate does not change (soluble) remaining 0.050 *M*. Since two potassium ions (soluble) are formed per potassium chromate, after mixing the potas-

sium ion concentration was 0.10 *M* and does not change (soluble).

20. **D**—To determine the molar mass of the gas it is necessary to know the mass of the gas (measured) and the moles of the gas. The ideal gas equation is necessary to determine the number of moles of gas present. To use the equation, it is necessary to know the temperature (measured), volume (measured = volume of displaced water), and pressure of the gas. The pressure of the gas is equal to the barometric pressure minus the vapor pressure of water. Water, whenever present, will contribute its vapor pressure.

21. **A**—

[H_2(g) + 1/2 O_2(g) → H_2O(l)]	(−300 kJ)
2[C(s) + O_2(g) → CO_2(g)]	2(−400 kJ)
−[H_2O(l) + 2 CO_2(g) →	
C_2H_2(g) + 5/2 O_2(g)]	−(−1300 kJ)
2 C(s) + H_2(g) → C_2H_2(g)	200 kJ

22. **A**—Since the compound is less soluble in hot water, the solution process must be exothermic. Exothermic processes shift toward the starting materials (solid cerium(III) sulfate) when heated.

23. **C**—The gases are all at the same temperature; therefore their average kinetic energies are the same. Since kinetic energy is equal to ½ mv^2, ½ $m_1v_1^2$ = ½ $m_2v_2^2$, the subscripts refer to two different gases. Setting m_1 = 16 g mol^{-1} and v_2 = ½ v_1 gives: ½ $16v_1^2$ = ½ m_2(½ v_1)^2; this leads to: $16v_1^2 = m_2$(1/4 v_1^2). Rearranging and cancelling v_1 yields m_2 = 4(16) = 64 g mol^{-1}.

24. **A**—The smaller the molecule and the less polar (more nonpolar) the gas is, the smaller the deviation from ideal gas behavior.

25. **A**—Escaping gas would decrease the number of moles. Less gas remaining in the container would mean less pressure. The faster moving gas molecules would escape faster, lower the average velocity of those remaining in the container. A lower average velocity means a lower temperature.

26. C—It is necessary to use the half-life relationship for first-order kinetics. This relationship is $t_{1/2} = 0.693/k$, and $t_{1/2} = (0.693/86\ h^{-1})(3600\ s/h) = 29\ s$. To save time on the exam you can approximate this equation as $t_{1/2} = (0.7/90)(3600)$. Dividing 3600 by 90 gives 40, and 40 times 0.7 is equal to 28. If the half-life is ≈ 28 s, then the time (58 s) is equivalent to about two half-lives, so one-fourth of the sample should remain.

27. D—The loss of 0.20 mol of CO means that 0.40 mol of H_2 reacted (leaving 0.20 mol) and 0.20 mol of CH_3OH formed. Dividing all the moles by the volume gives the molarity, and:

$$K_c = (0.20)/(0.40)(0.20)^2 = (0.10)/(0.20)(0.20)^2 = 0.10/(0.20 \times 0.04) = 0.10/0.008 = 12$$

28. A—Based upon the stoichiometry of the reaction, $H_2(g)$ will form twice as fast as $CH_3OH(g)$ disappears. The numerical values are the same; however, the rates have opposite signs.

29. B—At equilibrium, there is no net change because the forward and reverse reactions are going at the same rate.

30. B—As the reaction approaches equilibrium, there is a net decrease in the number of moles of gas present. A decrease in the number of moles of gas will lead to a decrease in pressure

31. B—The loss of 1.5 atm of $CH_3OH(g)$, based on stoichiometry leads to the formation of 1.5 atm of $CO(g)$ and 3.0 atm of $H_2(g)$; therefore, the net change is $(-1.5 + 1.5 + 3.0)$ atm = 3.0 atm.

32. A—Oxygen (odorless) evolves at the anode (positive) and ammonia (distinctive odor) evolves at the cathode (negative). From the choices given, the only gas with a distinctive odor that could form is ammonia, NH_3. For this reason, the nitrite ion half-reaction must be the cathode reaction. The anode half-reaction must be the reverse of one of the reactions in the table. The only one of the half-reactions given that generates an odorless gas is the one involving oxygen, O_2.

33. A—The lead electrode is the cathode (−0.13 V), and the chromium electrode is the anode (reverse sign, +0.91 V). Cell voltage = (−0.13 + 0.91) V = +0.78 V. The standard voltage of a galvanic cell is always positive.

34. D—It is necessary to consider all possible half-reactions that might occur during electrolysis. Of the half-reactions listed, only the reduction of water and the reduction of aluminum ions are applicable to this experiment. For any electrolysis, the half-reaction requiring the least amount of energy will take place. So, while it is possible to reduce both water and the aluminum ion, the reduction potential for water is lower (requiring less energy), so water will reduce in preference to aluminum ion.

35. B—In order for substance A to reduce substance B, substance A must be a stronger reducing agent than substance B. Aluminum is a strong reducing agent as indicated by the large negative potential in the table (−1.66 V). The only substance in the table that has a more negative potential is rubidium, Rb (−2.93 V).

36. C—Silver appears twice in the list of half-reactions, once in the simple reduction of silver ions and once in the reduction of silver chloride, AgCl. The AgCl half-reaction clearly shows that this compound is a solid. This solid will form as the silver ion in the silver nitrate solution reacts with chloride ion from the potassium chloride in the salt bridge. The formation of solid silver chloride will alter the concentration of the silver ion, which leads to a change in the cell potential.

37. B—The weakest acid (smallest K_a) will have the highest pH at the endpoint.

38. D—The buffer capacity only depends on the number of moles present. All three solutions have the same number of moles.

39. C—Less acid would require less than the ideal amount of base to reach the endpoint. Therefore, the endpoint would occur too soon.

40. D—An acid contaminant was present and it would be necessary to add additional base to titrate this acid in addition to the phenol.

41. B—Since only the plot of 1/[A] versus time yielded a straight line, this implies that the reaction is second-order in A.

42. C—The electron configuration of carbon in $1s^2 2s^2 sp^2$. The removal of the last electron (2p) requires the least amount of energy.

43. **A**—The compound with the highest boiling point has the strongest intermolecular forces. This is only valid if the molar masses are similar.

44. **C**—The melting points of ionic materials depend upon the lattice energy. The higher the lattice energy, the higher the melting point is. Lattice energies depend upon the sizes of the ions and the magnitude of the charge. All three metal ions are approximately the same size; therefore, the size factor is minimal. This leaves the magnitude of the charge, and lanthanum, with the largest charge, should have the highest lattice energy.

45. **A**—The lattice energy depends upon both the charge and the size of the ions involved. The greater the charge is, the greater the lattice energy will be (higher melting point). There is an inverse relationship between the lattice energy and the size of the ion. Therefore, the smaller the ion is, the greater the lattice energy will be (higher melting point).

46. **C**—If the reaction is nonspontaneous at 1 atm and 298 K, then $\Delta G > 0$. For this reaction to become spontaneous at a lower temperature the reaction must be impeded by entropy (entropy was negative). The enthalpy must be negative or the reaction could never be spontaneous.

47. **A**—Enter the information into the K_a expression. A pH of 2.0 means that $[H^+] = 10^{-2.0}$ M or 1.0×10^{-2}. $K_a = [H^+][A^-]/[HA]$; $[H^+] = [A^-] = 1.0 \times 10^{-2}$ $[HA] = 0.060 - 1.0 \times 10^{-2} = 0.05$; therefore, $K_a = (1.0 \times 10^{-2})/0.050 = 0.002 = 2 \times 10^{-3}$.

48. **C**—A carbon atom with four single bonds should be tetrahedral. Tetrahedral atoms have an ideal bond angle of 109.5°. However, the carbon atoms in cyclopropane are at the corners of an equilateral triangle, where the ideal angle is 60°. The discrepancy between the two ideal bond angles leads to the relative instability of cyclopropane.

49. **B**—The reaction is:

$$HgO(s) + 2\ HCl(aq) \rightarrow HgCl_2(aq) + H_2O(l)$$

When the last of the solid dissolves, we are at the stoichiometric point indicated by this reaction. No HgO remains and the chemist stopped adding HCl at this point, so there is no excess HCl present. The $HgCl_2$ must be soluble because there is no solid remaining in the beaker. Since the resultant solution is nonconducting, there must be no electrolytes present; therefore, the products must be molecular species. The best answer should show only water molecules and $HgCl_2$ molecules.

50. **D**—This answer shows the potassium ions and bromide ions as separate ions in solution, which is a property of strong electrolytes. The water molecules are present in both the liquid and gas states. Other diagrams incorrectly show water dissociating, potassium bromide ion pairs, and potassium bromide vaporizing.

51. **B**—There are two bromine isotopes with equal abundances, which is why there are two nearly equally intense peaks in the mass spectrum of CH_3Br. One of the peaks corresponds to $CH_3{}^{79}Br$ and the other corresponds to $CH_3{}^{81}Br$. The separation between the peaks is two mass units because the isotopic masses differ by two units. In the case of CH_2Br_2, the possible combinations and masses are $CH_2{}^{79}Br^{79}Br$ (172), $CH_2{}^{79}Br^{81}Br$ (174), $CH_2{}^{81}Br^{79}Br$ (174), and $CH_2{}^{81}Br^{81}Br$ (176). The four possible combinations are equally probably since the abundances of the two bromine isotopes are nearly equal. If they all had different masses, the mass spectrum would consist of four equally intense peaks. However, two of the combinations have the same mass, which results in the 174 peak being twice as intense as the other two peaks.

52. **C**—In diagram A, the forces to overcome are ionic bonding (lattice energy) and hydrogen bonding. In diagram B, the forces to overcome are hydrogen bonding for both the solvent and the solute. In diagram C, the forces to overcome are London dispersion forces in both cases; however, since the chlorine is a gas, the London dispersion forces have already been overcome. In diagram D, the forces to overcome are London dispersion forces and hydrogen bonding. Since London dispersion forces are normally weaker than the other intermolecular forces, answer C requires the least amount of energy.

53. C—There are several ways of solving this problem. One way is to determine the moles present in the original containers, which must be the same as in the final container. In each case, moles = $n = PV/RT$. Numbering the containers from left to right as 1, 2, 3, and 4 gives:

$$n_4 = n_1 + n_2 + n_3$$

$$= \left(\frac{(1.0 \text{ atm})(1 \text{ L})}{\left(0.0821\dfrac{\text{L}\cdot\text{atm}}{\text{mol}\cdot\text{K}}\right)(300 \text{ K})} \right) +$$

$$\left(\frac{(1.0 \text{ atm})(2 \text{ L})}{\left(0.0821\dfrac{\text{L}\cdot\text{atm}}{\text{mol}\cdot\text{K}}\right)(300 \text{ K})} \right) +$$

$$\left(\frac{(1.0 \text{ atm})(1 \text{ L})}{\left(0.0821\dfrac{\text{L}\cdot\text{atm}}{\text{mol}\cdot\text{K}}\right)(200 \text{ K})} \right)$$

$$= \left(\frac{1}{(0.0821)(300)} \right) + \left(\frac{2}{(0.0821)(300)} \right) +$$

$$\left(\frac{1}{(0.0821)(200)} \right)$$

$$= \left(\frac{3}{(0.0821)(300)} \right) + \left(\frac{1}{(0.0821)(200)} \right)$$

$$= \left(\frac{1}{(0.0821)(100)} \right) + \left(\frac{1}{(0.0821)(200)} \right)$$

$$= \left(\frac{1}{(0.0821)} \right)\left(\frac{1}{100} + \frac{1}{200} \right) \text{mol}$$

$$P_4 = n_4 RT/V =$$

$$\frac{\left(\left(\dfrac{1}{(0.0821)} \right)\left(\dfrac{1}{100} + \dfrac{1}{200} \right) \text{mol}\right)\left(0.0821\dfrac{\text{L}\cdot\text{atm}}{\text{mol}\cdot\text{K}}\right)(300 \text{ K})}{4 \text{ } L} =$$

$$\frac{\left(\left(\dfrac{1}{100} + \dfrac{1}{200} \right) \text{mol}\right)(\text{atm})(300)}{4} =$$

$$(0.010 + 0.0050) \text{ atm } (75.0) = 1.1 \text{ atm}$$

On the exam, it is not necessary to write out all these steps. Take shortcuts.

54. A—Stronger intermolecular forces lead to higher boiling points. Even though COS has dipole-dipole forces, which are usually stronger than the London dispersion forces present in CS_2, the greater molar mass of CS_2 leads to a London dispersion force contribution that is sufficient to compensate for the general trend of dipole-dipole forces being stronger than London dispersion forces. This is why comparisons should only be made between molecules of similar molecular masses.

55. B—At equilibrium the reverse reaction is going at a steady rate (equal to that of the forward reaction and not equal to 0). A sudden decrease in pressure will cause the rate of the reverse reaction to increase to generate more gas to increase the pressure. It will eventually slow and become constant again.

56. A—Only the slow step in a mechanism leads to the rate law. There is one H_2O_2 and one I^- in the slow step; therefore, one of each of these will be in the rate law.

57. B—This must be true according to the Law of Conservation of Energy (First Law of Thermodynamics). Answers A and C violate the Law of Conservation of Energy. For the final temperature to be the average, the metals would need to have equal masses and equal specific heats. The masses given in the problem are clearly different, and it is extremely unlikely that two different metals would have the same specific heat.

58. C—All three compounds are capable of hydrogen bonding; therefore, this cannot be the cause of difference. In general, all other things being equal, it takes less energy to move a lighter molecule from the liquid state to the gaseous state.

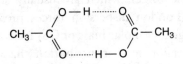

59. D—Strong hydrogen bonds hold two molecules of acetic acid together. Ideal gases have no intermolecular forces. Therefore, the ideal gas law used in experiment is invalid.

60. C—Increasing ionization energy applies to an element higher in a column on the periodic table, or in a position further to the left in a period on the periodic table. Note, this type of explanation is unacceptable on the Free Response portion of the AP Exam, where your explanation would require information on radii and effective nuclear charges.

› AP Chemistry Practice Exam 1, Section II (Free Response)

Time—1 hour and 45 minutes

Answer the following questions in the time allowed. You may use a calculator and the resources at the back of the book. Write the answers on separate sheets of paper.

Compound	K_{sp}
$AgIO_3$	3.0×10^{-8}
$Ba(IO_3)_2$	1.5×10^{-9}
$Cu(IO_3)_2$	7.4×10^{-8}
$La(IO_3)_3$	6.2×10^{-12}
$Ni(IO_3)_2$	1.4×10^{-8}
$Zn(IO_3)_2$	2.0×10^{-8}

Question 1

Use the K_{sp} data given above to answer the following questions.

A chemist is investing the chemistry of metal iodate compounds. Some of her data are in the K_{sp} table given above. In addition to this information, she knows that sodium iodate, $NaIO_3$, is soluble in water and that iodic acid, HIO_3, has $K_a = 0.16$ at 25°C.

(a) (i) Write a balanced chemical equation for the dissolution equilibrium of nickel(II) iodate, $Ni(IO_3)_2$, in water.

  (ii) Write the K_{sp} relationship for the dissolution equilibrium of nickel(II) iodate.

  (iii) What is the concentration of iodate ions in a saturated solution of nickel(II) iodate?

(b) What is the solubility of copper(II) iodate, $Cu(IO_3)_2$, in a 0.10 M copper(II) nitrate, $Cu(NO_3)_2$, solution?

(c) (i) How does the solubility of silver iodate, $AgIO_3$, in 1.0 M nitric acid compare to its solubility in pure water?

  (ii) Explain your answer to part c(i).

(d) Which of the following will produce a higher iodate ion concentration in solution, barium iodate, $Ba(IO_3)_2$, or lanthanum iodate, $La(IO_3)_3$? What is the iodate ion concentration for each of these two compounds?

(e) Write a balanced net ionic equation for the addition of a sodium iodate solution to a zinc nitrate, $Zn(NO_3)_2$ solution. Recall that sodium nitrate, $NaNO_3$, is very soluble in water.

GO ON TO THE NEXT PAGE

Question 2

Selenous acid, H_2SeO_3, reacts with hydrogen peroxide, H_2O_2, in acid solution according to the following equation:

$$H_2SeO_3(aq) + H_2O_2(aq) \rightarrow HSeO_4^-(aq) + H^+(aq) + H_2O(l)$$

The following information was obtained in a series of reactions:

EXPERIMENT	INITIAL CONCENTRATIONS (MOLARITIES)			RATE OF DISAPPEARANCE OF H_2SeO_3 ($M\ S^{-1}$)
	$[H_2SeO_3]$	$[H_2O_2]$	$[H^+]$	
1	0.100	0.100	0.100	7.4×10^{-8}
2	0.200	0.100	0.100	2.9×10^{-7}
3	0.100	0.200	0.100	1.5×10^{-7}
4	0.100	0.100	0.200	3.7×10^{-8}

(a) Determine the order of the reaction for H_2SeO_3, H_2O_2, and H^+. Justify your answers.

(b) Write the rate law for the reaction.

(c) Determine the value of the rate constant including units.

(d) (i) Is H_2O_2 acting as an oxidizing or as a reducing agent?
   (ii) What is the oxidation state of oxygen in H_2O_2?
   (iii) Write the balanced half-reaction for H_2O_2 in this reaction.

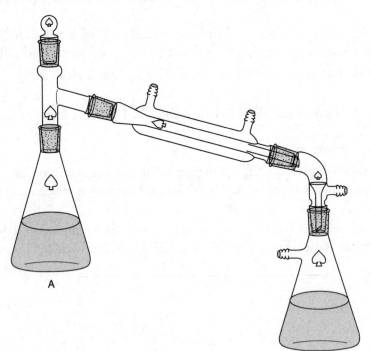

A

B

GO ON TO THE NEXT PAGE

Question 3

A student wishes to analyze a sample of ammonium sulfate, $(NH_4)_2SO_4$, contaminated with sodium sulfate, Na_2SO_4. She constructs the apparatus shown above to carry out this analysis. She weighs 1.002 grams of sample into flask A and dissolves the solid in 50 mL of water. Then she adds 50.00 mL of 0.4000 M hydrochloric acid, HCl, to flask B. In the next step, she quickly adds an excess of concentrated sodium hydroxide, NaOH, solution to flask A and quickly seals the system. She then heats flask A to boiling and distills over about 25 mL of water to flask B; during this process all the ammonia, NH_3, generated in flask A transfers to flask B. After the distillation is complete, she disassembles the apparatus and adds a small amount of methyl red indicator to flask B and titrates the solution in flask B with standard sodium hydroxide solution. The titration requires 35.25 mL of 0.1600 M sodium hydroxide solution to reach the endpoint.

The reactions are:

(1) $(NH_4)_2SO_4(aq) + 2\ NaOH(aq) \rightarrow Na_2SO_4(aq) + 2\ NH_3(aq) + 2\ H_2O(l)$
(2) $NH_3(aq) + HCl(aq) \rightarrow NH_4Cl(aq)$
(3) $NaOH(aq) + HCl(aq) \rightarrow NaCl(aq) + H_2O(l)$

The first equation is for a weak acid ($pK_a\ NH_4^+ = 9.25$)/strong base reaction. The second equation is for a weak base/strong acid reaction. The third equation is for a strong base/strong acid reaction.
Information on indicators:

	pH Range	pK_a	Color Change
Methyl red	4.2–6.2	5.0	Red → Yellow
Phenolphthalein	8.2–10.0	9.3	Colorless → Pink

(a) (i) Calculate the moles of hydrochloric acid originally in flask B.
   (ii) Calculate the moles of hydrochloric acid reacting with the sodium hydroxide solution.
   (iii) Calculate the moles of ammonia that reacted with the hydrochloric acid.

(b) (i) Calculate the mass of ammonium sulfate in the sample. (Molar mass of ammonium sulfate = 132.139 g.)
   (ii) Calculate the percent ammonium sulfate in the sample.

(c) (i) Strong acid strong base titrations commonly use phenolphthalein as an indicator. Give a good reason why the student chose to use methyl red instead.
   (ii) A second student used phenolphthalein in place of methyl red and got significantly different results. Was the second student's percent higher or lower than the student using methyl red? What was the cause of this discrepancy?

(d) In the box below, sketch the Lewis electron-dot structure of ammonium chloride.

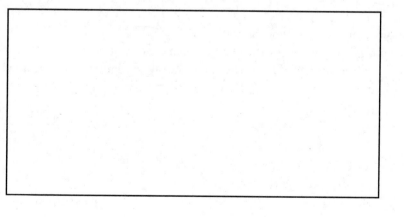

Question 4

The following equipment is available for the determination of the molar mass of an unknown solid mono-protic acid, HA. Assume the unknown acid is a weak acid.

analytical balance	thermometer	beaker(s)	support stand and clamp
stoppers	glass tubing	hot plate	pipette(s)
test tube(s)	stopwatch	wire gauze	flask(s)
buret	pH meter		graduated cylinder

In addition to this equipment there is standardized hydrochloric acid, HCl, solution and unstandardized sodium hydroxide, NaOH, solution available and a suitable acid-base indicator such as phenolphthalein.

(a) Which of the above equipment is necessary for this experiment?

(b) Describe how the above equipment may be used to calculate the molar mass of the unknown solid.

(c) How would you calculate the K_a of the unknown acid?

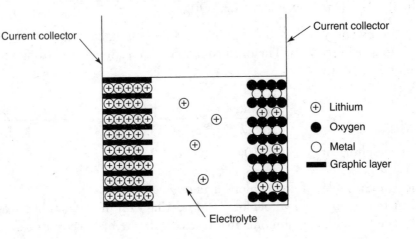

Question 5

The above schematic is one form of a lithium ion battery. The negative electrode (on the left) consists of graphite with lithium ions trapped between carbon layers. The positive electrode (on the right) is a layered metal oxide that allows lithium ions to enter the solid. The electrolyte is a lithium salt dissolved in an organic solvent. The negative electrode has the approximate composition LiC_6, and the positive electrode can reach a composition of $LiCoO_2$ in a fully discharged battery. The half-reactions are:

$$x LiC_6(s) \rightarrow x Li^+ + x e^- + x C_6$$

$$Li_{1-x}CoO_2 + x Li^+ + x e^- \rightarrow LiCoO_2$$

(a) What is the balanced net ionic equation for the reaction?

(b) Why is it necessary to use an organic solvent for the electrolyte and not water?

(c) What is the oxidation state of cobalt in $LiCoO_2$? Write the electron configuration for this cobalt ion in the ground state.

GO ON TO THE NEXT PAGE

Question 6

Acetylene, C_2H_2, will react with a limited amount of bromine vapor, Br_2, to form 1,2-dibromoethene, $C_2H_2Br_2$. The product of the reaction is contaminated with unreacted acetylene and 1,1,2,2-tetrabromo-ethane, $C_2H_2Br_4$. The key reactions are:

$$C_2H_2(g) + Br_2(g) \rightarrow C_2H_2Br_2(g)$$

$$C_2H_2(g) + 2\ Br_2(g) \rightarrow C_2H_2Br_4(g)$$

(a) The left box below shows the Lewis electron-dot diagram for acetylene. The box on the right has an incomplete Lewis electron-dot diagram for 1,2-dibromoethene. Complete the diagram on the right by adding all the electron pairs.

(b) In the box below, draw the complete Lewis electron-dot structure for 1,1,2,2-tetrabromoethane.

(c) Arrange the compounds C_2H_2, $C_2H_2Br_2$, and $C_2H_2Br_4$ in order of decreasing H–C–C bond angle. Why did you place these compounds in the order you predicted? Your explanation should include approximate bond angles.

Question 7

A student in Denver, Colorado, used the following reaction to generate oxygen gas in a gas generator:

$$2\ KClO_3(s) \rightarrow 2\ KCl(s) + 3\ O_2(g)$$

The gas generator was connected by a tube to an inverted flask, filled with water, in a water bath. The gas displaced all the water. The volume of the sample was 500.0 mL at 26°C, and the pressure in the room was 626 mm Hg. The vapor pressure of water at 26°C is 25 mm Hg.

A second student conducted a similar experiment under identical conditions beginning with the following reaction:

$$Mg_3N_2(s) + 6\ H_2O(l) \rightarrow 3\ Mg(OH)_2(s) + 2\ NH_3(g)$$

The second student's results were dramatically different from those of the first student (not as good), indicating that there was something drastically different.

(a) How many grams of oxygen are in the flask? Show all calculations.

(b) How many hydrogen atoms are in the flask after it is filled with oxygen?

(c) Why is the most likely reason why the second student did not get good results? Explain your reasoning.

STOP: End of AP Chemistry Practice Exam 1, Section II (Free Response).

❯ Answers and Explanations for Exam 1, Section II (Free Response)

Question 1

(a) (i) $Ni(IO_3)_2(s) \leftrightarrows Ni^{2+}(aq) + 2\,IO_3^-(aq)$

You get 1 point for this answer. The equilibrium arrow and the ionic charges must be present.

(ii) $K_{sp} = [Ni^{2+}]\,[IO_3^-]^2$

You get 1 point for this answer. The charges must be present and the iodate ion concentration must be squared.

(iii) $K_{sp} = [Ni^{2+}]\,[IO_3^-]^2 = 1.4 \times 10^{-8}$

Setting $[Ni^{2+}] = x$ and $[IO_3^-] = 2x$ and inserting into the mass-action expression gives:

$$(x)\,(2x)^2 = 4x^3 = 1.4 \times 10^{-8}.$$

Solving for x gives $x = 1.5 \times 10^{-3}$, and $[IO_3^-] = 2x = 3.0 \times 10^{-3}\ M$.

You get 1 point for the correct $[IO_3^-]$.

(b) Copper(II) nitrate is soluble in water (obviously because you are given a solution), which separates into copper(II) ions and nitrate ions. The copper(II) ion concentration is $0.10\ M$ and it is a common ion affecting the equilibrium.

$$K_{sp} = [Cu^{2+}]\,[IO_3^-]^2 = 7.4 \times 10^{-8}$$

Setting $[Cu^{2+}] = 0.10 + x$ and $[IO_3^-] = 2x$ and inserting into the mass-action expression gives:
$(0.10 + x)\,(2x)^2 = 7.4 \times 10^{-8}$. Assuming x is much smaller than 0.10 allows a simplification of the calculation to $(0.10)\,(2x)^2 = 0.4\,x^2 = 7.4 \times 10^{-8}$.

Solving for x gives $x = 4.3 \times 10^{-4}\ M$, which leads to $[IO_3^-] = 2x = 8.6 \times 10^{-4}\ M$.

You get 1 point for the correct $[IO_3^-]$.

(c) (i) Silver iodate is more soluble in nitric acid than in pure water.

You get 1 point for this answer.

(ii) Iodic acid is a weak acid ($K_a = 0.16$); therefore, according to Le Châtelier's principle, the solubility equilibrium will be displaced to the right as iodate ion combines with hydrogen ions from the nitric acid to form unionized iodic acid. The reactions are: $AgIO_3(s) \leftrightarrows Ag^+(aq) + IO_3^-(aq)$ and $H^+(aq) + IO_3^-(aq) \rightarrow HIO_3(aq)$

You get 1 point for this answer.

(d) If the two compounds have the same stoichiometry, the larger K_{sp} would generate the higher iodate ion concentration. However, this is not the case, so it is necessary to calculate the iodate ion concentration for each.

$$K_{sp} = [Ba^{2+}]\,[IO_3^-]^2 = 1.5 \times 10^{-9}$$

Setting $[Ba^{2+}] = x$ and $[IO_3^-] = 2x$, and inserting into the mass-action expression gives:

$$(x)\,(2x)^2 = 4x^3 = 1.5 \times 10^{-9}.$$

Solving for x gives $x = 7.2 \times 10^{-4}$, and $[IO_3^-] = 2x = 1.4 \times 10^{-3}\ M$.

$$K_{sp} = [La^{3+}]\,[IO_3^-]^3 = 6.2 \times 10^{-12}$$

Setting $[La^{3+}] = x$ and $[IO_3^-] = 3x$, and inserting into the mass-action expression gives:

$$(x)\,(3x)^3 = 27x^4 = 6.2 \times 10^{-12}.$$

Solving for x gives $x = 6.9 \times 10^{-4}$, and $[IO_3^-] = 3x = 2.0 \times 10^{-3}\ M$.

You get 1 point for doing the calculations and showing $La(IO_3)_3$ is more soluble and 1 additional point for the correct answers.

(e) It is easier to begin with the balanced molecular equation:

$$2\ NaIO_3(aq) + Zn(NO_3)_2(aq) \rightarrow Zn(IO_3)_2(s) + 2\ NaNO_3(aq)$$

Converting the molecular equation to a complete ionic equation:

$$2\ Na^+(aq) + 2\ NO_3^-(aq) + Zn^{2+}(aq) + 2\ NO_3^-(aq) \rightarrow Zn(IO_3)_2(s) + 2\ Na^+(aq) + 2\ NO_3^-(aq)$$

The ionic compounds $NaIO_3$ and $Zn(IO_3)_2$ should be separated into their ions since you are supplied with solutions and the sodium nitrate is also shown in the ionic form since you are told it is soluble in water. There is a K_{sp} for $Zn(IO_3)_2$ given in the table; therefore, it does not separate into ions.

Removing the spectator ions (Na^+ and NO_3^-) from the complete ionic equation leaves the net ionic equation:

$$Zn^{2+}(aq) + 2\ IO_3^-(aq) \rightarrow Zn(IO_3)_2(s)$$

You get 1 point for this answer.

Total your points for the different parts. There is a maximum of 10 points possible. Subtract one point if all answers did not have the correct number of significant figures.

Question 2

(a) The order for H_2SeO_3 is 2. The order for H_2O_2 is 1. The order for H^+ is –1.

If you get all three of these correct, you get 1 point.

Comparing experiments 2 and 1 (placing the larger over the smaller makes the calculations a little easier): The concentration of H_2SeO_3 is doubled, and the rate is quadrupled; $\dfrac{2.9 \times 10^{-7}}{7.4 \times 10^{-8}} \approx 4$. This leads to H_2SeO_3 having an order of 2.

You get 1 point for this reasoning.

Comparing experiments 3 and 1: The concentration of H_2O_2 is doubled, and the rate is doubled; $\dfrac{1.5 \times 10^{-7}}{7.4 \times 10^{-8}} \approx 2$. This leads to H_2O_2 having an order of 1.

You get 1 point for this reasoning.

Comparing experiments 4 and 1: The concentration of H^+ is doubled, and the rate is halved; $\dfrac{3.7 \times 10^{-8}}{7.4 \times 10^{-8}} \approx 0.5 = 2^{-1}$. This leads to H^+ having an order of –1.

You get 1 point for this reasoning.

(b) Rate $= k[H_2SeO_3]^2[H_2O_2][H^+]^{-1}$

This answer is worth 1 point. You will still get 1 point if you use incorrect orders from part (a).

(c) Rearrange the rate law to: $k = \dfrac{\text{Rate}}{[H_2SeO_3]^2[H_2O_2][H^+]^{-1}} = \dfrac{7.4 \times 10^{-8} \; M \; s^{-1}}{[0.100 \; M]^2 \; [0.100 \; M] \; [0.100 \; M]^{-1}} =$
$7.4 \times 10^{-6} \; M^{-1} \; s^{-1}$

This example uses the values from experiment 1. You could use any of the four experiments.

You get 1 point for calculating the value of k. You get 1 additional point for the correct units.

(d) (i) H_2O_2 is acting as an oxidizing agent.

You get 1 point for this answer.

(ii) The oxidation state of oxygen in −1.

You get 1 point for this answer.

(iii) $H_2O_2(aq) + 2 \; H^+(aq) + 2 \; e^- \rightarrow 2 \; H_2O(l)$

You get 1 point for this answer.

Total your points for the different parts. There are 10 possible points. Subtract 1 point if you did not report the correct number of significant figures (2) in part (c).

Question 3

(a) (i) 50.00 mL 0.4000 M HCl

$\left(\dfrac{0.4000 \; \text{mol HCl}}{L}\right)(50.00 \; \text{mL})\left(\dfrac{1 \; L}{1000 \; \text{mL}}\right) = 0.02000 \; \text{mol HCl}$ (4 significant figures)

You get 1 point for this answer.

(ii) $HCl(aq) + NaOH(aq) \rightarrow NaCl(aq) + H_2O(l)$

35.25 mL 0.1600 M NaOH

$\left(\dfrac{0.1600 \; \text{mol NaOH}}{L}\right)(35.25 \; \text{mL})\left(\dfrac{1 \; L}{1000 \; \text{mL}}\right)\left(\dfrac{1 \; \text{mol HCl}}{1 \; \text{mol NaOH}}\right) = 0.005640 \; \text{mol HCl}$ (4 significant figures)

You get 1 point for this answer.

(iii) $NH_3(aq) + HCl(aq) \rightarrow NH_4Cl(aq)$

$(0.02000 - 0.005640) \; \text{mol HCl}\left(\dfrac{1 \; \text{mol NH}_3}{1 \; \text{mol HCl}}\right) = 0.01436 \; \text{mol NH}_3$ (4 significant figures)

You get 1 point for this answer. If you miscalculated either of the preceding two answers but use your results correctly in this step, you still earn this point.

(b) (i) $(0.01436 \; \text{mol NH}_3)\left(\dfrac{1 \; \text{mol (NH}_4)_2SO_4}{2 \; \text{mol NH}_3}\right)\left(\dfrac{132.139 \; \text{g (NH}_4)_2SO_4}{1 \; \text{mol (NH}_4)_2SO_4}\right) = 0.9488 \; \text{g} \; (NH_4)_2SO_4$

(4 significant figures)

You get 1 point for this answer.

(ii) $\dfrac{0.9488 \; \text{g (NH}_4)_2SO_4}{1.002 \; \text{g sample}} \times 100\% = 94.69 \; \% \; (NH_4)_2SO_4$ (4 significant figures)

You get 1 point for this answer. If you got the wrong result for (b)(i), but used it correctly here, you still get the point.

(c) (i) The sodium hydroxide solution will react with not only the hydrochloric acid (reaction 3) but also the ammonium ion (reaction 1). The methyl red endpoint is below where the ammonium ion begins to react; therefore, it is a better measure of the amount of HCl reacting than phenolphthalein, which has an endpoint after at least some of the ammonium ion has reacted.

You get 1 point for this answer.

(ii) The percent will be lower. It will be necessary to use more sodium hydroxide solution to reach the endpoint, making it appear that less ammonia reacted with the HCl. If there were less ammonia, then the percentage would be lower.

You get 1 point for predicting the percent will be lower and 1 point for the explanation.

(d)

You get 1 point for having an octet on the nitrogen and an octet on the chlorine with no additional electrons shown.

You get 1 point for showing an ionic structure with no hint of a covalent bond between the ammonium ion and the chloride ion. The brackets are not essential but are present only as an aid to stress that these are ions with no covalent (electron-sharing).

Total your points. There is a maximum of 10 possible points. Subtract 1 point if any of your answers does not have the correct number of significant figures.

Question 4

(a) Analytical balance, buret, pipette, support stand and clamp, beakers or flask

You must have these five items to get 1 point.

(b) 1. It is necessary to standardize the sodium hydroxide solution.

(i) Pipette a known volume of the standardized hydrochloric acid into a beaker or flask (record the volume).

(ii) Add a small quantity of indicator to the acid.

(iii) Fill the buret with sodium hydroxide solution and take and record the initial volume.

(iv) Carefully add sodium hydroxide solution from the buret until the indicator indicates the endpoint.

(v) Record the final volume of sodium hydroxide solution in the buret.

(vi) The difference in the initial volume and final volume from the buret gives the quantity of sodium hydroxide solution added.

(vii) Use the recorded data and the concentration of the standard acid to determine the concentration of the sodium hydroxide solution.

The above steps are worth 1 point.

2. It is possible to determine the molar mass of the unknown acid using the standard sodium hydroxide solution.

(i) Weigh and record the mass of a sample of the unknown acid on an analytical balance.

(ii) Dissolve the unknown in a small quantity of DI water.

(iii) Fill the buret with sodium hydroxide solution and record the initial volume.

(iv) Carefully add sodium hydroxide solution from the buret until the indicator indicates the endpoint.

(v) Record the final volume of sodium hydroxide solution in the buret.

(vi) The difference in the initial volume and final volume from the buret gives the quantity of sodium hydroxide solution added.

(vii) Use the recorded data and the concentration of the sodium hydroxide solution to determine the moles of acid.

(viii) The mass of the acid divided by the moles of acid gives the molar mass of the acid.

The above steps are worth 1 point.

(c) (i) Weigh a small quantity of unknown acid into a beaker and add sufficient water to dissolve the solid.

(ii) Using the mass of the acid and the molar mass calculated above determine the volume of standard sodium hydroxide solution necessary to neutralize one-half of the acid in the beaker.

(iii) Fill the buret with sodium hydroxide solution and record the initial volume.

(iv) Carefully add sodium hydroxide solution from the buret until the calculated volume has been added.

(v) Measure the pH of the half-titrated solution with the pH meter provided.

(vi) The pH of the half-titrated solution is equal to the pK_a of the acid and $K_a = 10^{-pK}$.

The above steps are worth 1 point.

Total your points. There are 4 possible points.

Question 5

(a) Regardless of the value of x, it is the same in each half-reaction; therefore it is only necessary to add the two half-reactions together.

$$xLiC_6(s) \rightarrow xLi^+ + xe^- + xC_6$$
$$Li_{1-x}CoO_2 + xLi^+ + xe^- \rightarrow LiCoO_2$$
$$Li_{1-x}CoO_2 + xLiC_6(s) \rightarrow LiCoO_2 + xC_6$$

You get 1 point for the correct equation.

(b) Lithium metal will react with water.

You get 1 point for this explanation.

(c) The oxidation state of cobalt is +3. This is determined by assuming the oxidation states of lithium and oxygen are +1 and –2, respectively. This leads to Li + Co + 2 (O) = 0 or (+1) + Co + 2 (–2) = 0. The ground state electron configuration of Co^{3+} is $1s^2 2s^2 2p^6 3s^2 3p^6 3d^6$ or $[Ar]3d^6$.

You get 1 point for the correct oxidation state of cobalt and 1 point for the correct electron configuration. If you did not get the correct oxidation state, you can still get the second point if you give the correct electron configuration of the ion predicted to be present. Note that no reasonable ion will have any 4s electrons present.

Total your points; there are 4 points possible.

Question 6

(a)

You get 1 point for the correct Lewis structure.

(b)

You get 1 point for the correct Lewis structure.

(c) The order is $C_2H_2 > C_2H_2Br_2 > C_2H_2Br_4$.

The structure of acetylene shown in the problem indicates a linear molecule with a HCC bond angle of 180°. The correct Lewis electron-dot diagram for $C_2H_2Br_2$ indicates a trigonal planar arrangement about each carbon atom with a HCC bond angle of 120°. The correct Lewis electron-dot diagram for $C_2H_2Br_4$ indicates a tetrahedral arrangement about each carbon atom with a HCC bond angle of 109°.

You get 1 point if you list the compounds in the correct order, and you get 1 point for a correct explanation including the bond angles.

Total your points for the problem. There is a maximum of 4 possible points.

Question 7

(a) P_{total} = 626 mm Hg

P_{oxygen} = 626 − 25 = 601 mm Hg

P = 601 mm Hg/760 mm Hg = 0.791 atm (The 760 mm Hg = 1 atm is in the exam booklet and in the back of this book.)

V = 500.0 mL = 0.5000 L

T = 26°C = 299 K

R = 0.0821 L atm mol^{-1} K^{-1} (given in the exam booklet and in the back of this book)

$n = PV/RT$ (Rearranged from $PV = nRT$, which is in exam booklet and in the back of this book.)

= (0.791 atm × 0.5000 L)/(0.0821 L atm mol^{-1} K^{-1} × 299 K)

= 0.0161 mol O_2 (32.0 g O_2/mol O_2) = 0.516 g O_2 (3 significant figures)

Give yourself 1 point for the correct answer (no deduction for rounding differently). You must include ALL parts of the calculation (including "="). There is no deduction for combining steps. You cannot get this point if you did not subtract the vapor pressure of water from the total pressure.

(b) The hydrogen atoms are in the water molecules present in the flask; therefore it is necessary to calculate the mole of water present, convert to moles of hydrogen atoms, and use Avogadro's number to convert from moles to the number of atoms.

P_{water} = 25 mm Hg/760 mm Hg = 0.033 atm. T and V are the same as in (a).

$n = PV/RT$ = (0.033 atm × 0.5000 L)/(0.0821 L atm mol^{-1} K^{-1} × 299 K)

= 6.7 × 10^{-4} mol H_2O

Number of H atoms = $(6.7 \times 10^{-4} \text{ mol } H_2O)\left(\dfrac{2 \text{ mol H}}{1 \text{ mol } H_2O}\right)\left(\dfrac{6.022 \times 10^{23} \text{ H atoms}}{1 \text{ mol H}}\right)$ = 8.1 × 10^{20} H atoms

Give yourself 1 point for the correct answer (no deduction for rounding variations).

(c) Unlike oxygen gas, ammonia gas is very soluble in water because it, like water, is capable of hydrogen bonding. The formation of hydrogen between water molecules and ammonia molecules enhances the solubility of ammonia in water. Oxygen, on the other hand, is nonpolar and is only weakly attracted to water, giving oxygen a much lower solubility.

Give yourself 1 point for indicating the problem is the solubility of ammonia in water. Give yourself 1 additional point for the explanation if you invoke hydrogen bonding.

Total your points for this question. There are 4 points possible. Deduct 1 point if you reported the wrong number of significant figures in any answer.

AP Chemistry Practice Exam 2—Multiple Choice

ANSWER SHEET

1 Ⓐ Ⓑ Ⓒ Ⓓ   21 Ⓐ Ⓑ Ⓒ Ⓓ   41 Ⓐ Ⓑ Ⓒ Ⓓ
2 Ⓐ Ⓑ Ⓒ Ⓓ   22 Ⓐ Ⓑ Ⓒ Ⓓ   42 Ⓐ Ⓑ Ⓒ Ⓓ
3 Ⓐ Ⓑ Ⓒ Ⓓ   23 Ⓐ Ⓑ Ⓒ Ⓓ   43 Ⓐ Ⓑ Ⓒ Ⓓ
4 Ⓐ Ⓑ Ⓒ Ⓓ   24 Ⓐ Ⓑ Ⓒ Ⓓ   44 Ⓐ Ⓑ Ⓒ Ⓓ
5 Ⓐ Ⓑ Ⓒ Ⓓ   25 Ⓐ Ⓑ Ⓒ Ⓓ   45 Ⓐ Ⓑ Ⓒ Ⓓ
6 Ⓐ Ⓑ Ⓒ Ⓓ   26 Ⓐ Ⓑ Ⓒ Ⓓ   46 Ⓐ Ⓑ Ⓒ Ⓓ
7 Ⓐ Ⓑ Ⓒ Ⓓ   27 Ⓐ Ⓑ Ⓒ Ⓓ   47 Ⓐ Ⓑ Ⓒ Ⓓ
8 Ⓐ Ⓑ Ⓒ Ⓓ   28 Ⓐ Ⓑ Ⓒ Ⓓ   48 Ⓐ Ⓑ Ⓒ Ⓓ
9 Ⓐ Ⓑ Ⓒ Ⓓ   29 Ⓐ Ⓑ Ⓒ Ⓓ   49 Ⓐ Ⓑ Ⓒ Ⓓ
10 Ⓐ Ⓑ Ⓒ Ⓓ   30 Ⓐ Ⓑ Ⓒ Ⓓ   50 Ⓐ Ⓑ Ⓒ Ⓓ
11 Ⓐ Ⓑ Ⓒ Ⓓ   31 Ⓐ Ⓑ Ⓒ Ⓓ   51 Ⓐ Ⓑ Ⓒ Ⓓ
12 Ⓐ Ⓑ Ⓒ Ⓓ   32 Ⓐ Ⓑ Ⓒ Ⓓ   52 Ⓐ Ⓑ Ⓒ Ⓓ
13 Ⓐ Ⓑ Ⓒ Ⓓ   33 Ⓐ Ⓑ Ⓒ Ⓓ   53 Ⓐ Ⓑ Ⓒ Ⓓ
14 Ⓐ Ⓑ Ⓒ Ⓓ   34 Ⓐ Ⓑ Ⓒ Ⓓ   54 Ⓐ Ⓑ Ⓒ Ⓓ
15 Ⓐ Ⓑ Ⓒ Ⓓ   35 Ⓐ Ⓑ Ⓒ Ⓓ   55 Ⓐ Ⓑ Ⓒ Ⓓ
16 Ⓐ Ⓑ Ⓒ Ⓓ   36 Ⓐ Ⓑ Ⓒ Ⓓ   56 Ⓐ Ⓑ Ⓒ Ⓓ
17 Ⓐ Ⓑ Ⓒ Ⓓ   37 Ⓐ Ⓑ Ⓒ Ⓓ   57 Ⓐ Ⓑ Ⓒ Ⓓ
18 Ⓐ Ⓑ Ⓒ Ⓓ   38 Ⓐ Ⓑ Ⓒ Ⓓ   58 Ⓐ Ⓑ Ⓒ Ⓓ
19 Ⓐ Ⓑ Ⓒ Ⓓ   39 Ⓐ Ⓑ Ⓒ Ⓓ   59 Ⓐ Ⓑ Ⓒ Ⓓ
20 Ⓐ Ⓑ Ⓒ Ⓓ   40 Ⓐ Ⓑ Ⓒ Ⓓ   60 Ⓐ Ⓑ Ⓒ Ⓓ

The AP exam is a timed exam; keep this in mind as you prepare. When taking the various tests presented in this book, you should follow the AP exam rules as closely as possible. Anyone can improve his or her score by using notes, books, or an unlimited time. You will have none of these on the AP exam, so resist the temptation to use them on practice exams. Carefully time yourself, do not use other materials, and use a calculator only when expressly allowed to do so. After you have finished an exam, you may use other sources to go over questions you missed or skipped. We have seen many students get into trouble because the first time they attempted a test under "test conditions" was on the test itself.

AP Chemistry Practice Exam 2, Section I (Multiple Choice)

Time—1 hour and 30 minutes
NO CALCULATOR MAY BE USED WITH SECTION I

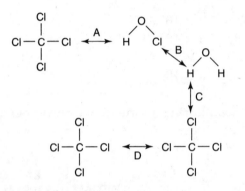

1. Which of the labeled arrows in the diagram above represents the strongest intermolecular force?

   (A) A
   (B) B
   (C) C
   (D) D

The following information applies to questions 2–5.

A student builds a galvanic cell to take advantage of the following reaction:

$$Zn(s) + 2\,AgNO_3(1\ M) \rightarrow 2\,Ag(s) + Zn(NO_3)_2(1\ M)$$

The cell's voltage is measured and found to be +1.56 volts.

2. What happens to the voltage when a small amount of silver nitrate is added to the silver compartment?

   (A) There is no change in the voltage.
   (B) The voltage becomes zero.
   (C) The voltage increases.
   (D) The voltage decreases, but stays positive.

3. What happens to the cell voltage when the student replaces the $Zn(NO_3)_2$ solution with 1 M $ZnCl_2$?

   (A) There is no change in the voltage.
   (B) The voltage becomes zero.
   (C) The voltage increases.
   (D) The voltage decreases, but stays positive.

4. If the standard reduction potential of silver is 0.80 V, what is the standard reduction potential of zinc?

   (A) +0.76 V
   (B) −0.76 V
   (C) −0.04 V
   (D) +0.04 V

5. What happens to the cell voltage after the cell has reached equilibrium?

   (A) There is no change in the voltage.
   (B) The voltage becomes zero.
   (C) The voltage increases.
   (D) The voltage decreases, but stays positive.

GO ON TO THE NEXT PAGE

Use the following information to answer questions 6–9.

Many metal salts crystallize from solution in the form of a hydrate. If the formula of the anhydrous salt is A_aX_x, then the generic formula of the hydrated form would be $A_aX_x \cdot xH_2O$. A student conducts an experiment to determine the formula of a metal oxide by collecting the following data:

Mass of crucible	53.120 g
Mass of crucible plus hydrated salt	58.677 g
Mass of crucible plus anhydrous salt	57.857 g
Molar mass of anhydrous salt	208.232 g mol^{-1}

The hydrated salt is finely powdered to ensure complete water loss to produce the anhydrous salt.

6. How many grams of water were in the hydrate?

(A) 5.557 g
(B) 4.737 g
(C) 0.987 g
(D) 0.820 g

7. What is the approximate percent water in the hydrated salt?

(A) 14%
(B) 86%
(C) 50%
(D) 28%

8. The student did not have time to finish the experiment during the lab period and was forced to store the anhydrous salt and crucible in his lab drawer until the next day. At the beginning of the next lab period the student weighed the anhydrous salt and beaker. After calculating the percent water in the sample, the student found that the percentage was lower than predicted. Assuming all weighing were done correctly, what might be the cause of the lower than expected percentage?

(A) The sample dried further overnight.
(B) The student performed one or more weighings before the crucible had cooled to room temperature.
(C) The sample absorbed water from the air overnight.
(D) The sample decomposed to another salt.

9. In another experiment on a different metal hydrate a student found that the salt was 62.9% water. In this case, the molar mass of the anhydrous salt was 106 g mol^{-1}. Which of the following general formulas gives the correct value of x?

(A) $A_aX_x \cdot 5H_2O$
(B) $A_aX_x \cdot 10H_2O$
(C) $A_aX_x \cdot 2H_2O$
(D) $A_aX_x \cdot 6H_2O$

10. For the following reaction, $2\ NO(g) + O_2(g) \rightarrow 2\ NO_2(g)$, the rate law is: Rate $= k[NO]^2[O_2]$. In one experiment, the rate of appearance of NO_2 was determined to be $0.0138\ M\,s^{-1}$ when $[NO] = 0.0125\ M$ and $[O_2] = 0.0125\ M$. What was the value of the rate constant?

(A) $7.1 \times 10^3\ M^2\,s^{-1}$
(B) $7.1 \times 10^3\ M\,s^{-1}$
(C) $7.1 \times 10^3\ M^{-2}\,s^{-1}$
(D) 7.1×10^3

Use the following information to answer questions 11–12.

EXPERIMENT	INITIAL [H$^+$] (*M*)	INITIAL [CN$_2$H$_4$O] (*M*)	INITIAL RATE OF DISAPPEARANCE OF CN$_2$H$_4$O (*M* s^{-1})
1	0.100	0.200	8.6×10^{-5}
2	0.200	0.100	4.3×10^{-5}
3	0.200	0.200	8.6×10^{-5}

11. The table above gives the initial concentrations and rate for three experiments involving the decomposition of urea, CN_2H_4O. The reaction is $H^+(aq) + 2\ H_2O(l) + CN_2H_4O(aq) \rightarrow 2\ NH_4^+(aq) + HCO_3^-(aq)$. What is the rate law for this reaction?

(A) Rate $= k[CN_2H_4O]$
(B) Rate $= k[CN_2H_4O]^2[H^+]^2$
(C) Rate $= k[H^+]$
(D) Rate $= k[CN_2H_4O]^2[H^+]$

12. The chemical equation for the reaction described in table indicates that there are three reactants (H^+, H_2O, and CN_2H_4O); however, only two reactants appear in the data table. Why is there no column in the table for the third reactant?

    (A) The H_2O behaves as a catalyst.
    (B) The H_2O is not a reactant; it is the solvent.
    (C) The H_2O concentration does not change.
    (D) It is only possible to deal with two reactants.

13. Oxalic acid, $H_2C_2O_4$, is a useful chemical for rust removal. A student prepared five oxalic acid samples by dissolving 0.9000 grams of oxalic acid in 100.00 mL of water and pipetting 10.00 mL samples of this solution into five separate beakers. Each of the samples was diluted with deionized water, and an appropriate indicator was added as an indicator. The samples were then titrated with standard 0.05000 M sodium hydroxide, NaOH, until the appearance of a permanent color change of the indicator indicated the endpoint of the titration. The following volumes were obtained. Molar mass of $H_2C_2O_4$ = 90.04 g mol^{-1}.

	VOLUME OF STANDARD NaOH
Sample 1	39.68 mL
Sample 2	40.27 mL
Sample 3	40.54 mL
Sample 4	39.66 mL
Sample 5	39.74 mL

The student calculated a concentration of approximately 0.20 M in each case. This is not the correct value. What is the most likely mistake that the student made?

    (A) The student used the total sample volume of the acid instead of the pipetted sample volume.
    (B) The student did not use the correct mole ratio in the calculation.
    (C) The student did not use the correct indicator.
    (D) The student contaminated the samples during preparation.

14. $Co^{2+} + 2\,e^- \rightarrow Co$ $E° = -0.28$ V
    $Zn^{2+} + 2\,e^- \rightarrow Zn$ $E° = -0.76$ V

Given the above standard reduction potentials, estimate the approximate value of the $\Delta G°$ for the following reaction:

$$Zn + Co^{2+} \rightarrow Zn^{2+} + Co$$

    (A) -4.6×10^4 J mol^{-1}
    (B) -9.3×10^4 J mol^{-1}
    (C) $+9.3 \times 10^4$ J mol^{-1}
    (D) $+4.6 \times 10^4$ J mol^{-1}

Use the following information to answer questions 15–19.

pH versus volume of titrant added

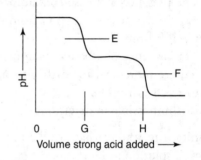

The diagram above represents the idealized titration curve for the reaction of pure sodium carbonate, Na_2CO_3, with a strong acid such as hydrochloric acid, HCl. E and F represent the pH at the endpoints corresponding to the formation of HCO_3^- and H_2CO_3, respectively. G and H correspond to the quantity of acid required to reach the endpoints.

15. A trial run used a sample of pure sodium carbonate. How does the volume of acid necessary to reach G from 0 compare to the volume of acid necessary to get from G to H?

    (A) They are the same.
    (B) It takes more to reach point G.
    (C) It takes more to get from G to H.
    (D) It is impossible to determine.

16. The analysis of a sample contaminated with NaHCO₃ gave slightly different results. How does the volume of acid necessary to reach G from 0 compare to the volume of acid necessary to get from G to H for the second sample?

    (A) It takes more to get from G to H.
    (B) It takes more to reach point G.
    (C) They are the same.
    (D) It is impossible to determine.

17. How could a student determine if there was a strong acid or a strong base contaminant in the original sample?

    (A) The presence of an acid contaminant would require less acid to reach H from G than to reach G from 0.
    (B) The presence of a base contaminant would require less acid to reach G from 0 than to reach F from G.
    (C) The presence of a base contaminant would require more acid to reach G from 0 than to reach F from G.
    (D) It is impossible to determine.

18. In addition to water, what are the predominant species in solution at F?

    (A) Na_2CO_3 and HCl
    (B) Na^+, Cl^-, and H_2CO_3
    (C) HCO_3^- and H^+
    (D) Na^+, Cl^-, H^+, and CO_3^{2-}

19. At what point on the graph for the titration of pure sodium carbonate is the pH = pK_{a2} for carbonic acid?

    (A) At point G
    (B) Halfway between the start and point G
    (C) At point H
    (D) Halfway between points G and H

20. Three steel containers hold gas samples. The containers are all the same size and at the same temperature. One container has 4.0 g of helium, another has 28.0 g of nitrogen, and the third has 44.0 g of carbon dioxide. Pick the FALSE statement from the following list:

    (A) The densities increase in the order helium < nitrogen < carbon dioxide.
    (B) The number of molecules in all the containers is the same.

(C) The pressure in all three containers is the same.
(D) The average speed of all the molecules is the same.

21. When potassium perchlorate, $KClO_4$, dissolves in water, the temperature of the resultant solution is lower than the initial temperature of the components. Which of the following conclusions may be related to this?

    (A) This is a spontaneous process because it is exothermic.
    (B) This is a spontaneous process because of an entropy increase.
    (C) This is a spontaneous process because of an entropy decrease.
    (D) This is a spontaneous process because it is exothermic.

22. The graph shows the variation of boiling point with Group number for the hydrogen compounds of the four lightest members of Group 15 on the periodic table (NH_3, PH_3, AsH_3 and SbH_3).

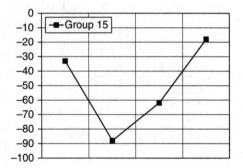

What is the reason that the lightest member of Group 15 does not follow the trend of the other members, which show that the boiling point decreases with decreasing atomic mass of the Group 15 element?

    (A) Ionic bonds
    (B) Hybrid orbitals
    (C) Resonance structures
    (D) Hydrogen bonding

GO ON TO THE NEXT PAGE

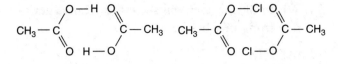

23. A dimer consists of two closely associated molecules. In the gas phase, acetic acid tends to form dimers as illustrated on the left in the above diagram. Acetyl chloride, on the right in the above diagram, is not very efficient in forming dimers. Why is acetic acid better able to form dimers than acetyl chloride?

(A) The molecular mass of acetyl chloride is higher than that of acetic acid making it harder for the acetyl chloride to form dimers.

(B) It is easier to form a covalent bond between acetic acid molecules than between acetyl chloride molecules.

(C) Acetic acid can form strong hydrogen bonds but acetyl chloride can only form weaker dipole-dipole attractions.

(D) Acetic acid is an acidic compound but acetyl chloride is a neutral compound.

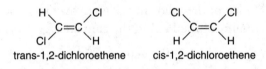

trans-1,2-dichloroethene   cis-1,2-dichloroethene

24. Two compounds with the formula $C_2H_2Cl_2$ appear in the above diagram. These two compounds are isomers. The molecules are planar and have the approximate structures shown in the diagram. The boiling point of trans-1, 2-dichloroethene is 47.5°C and the boiling point of cis-1,2-dichloroethene is 60.3°C. Which of the following best explains why cis-1,2-dichloroethene has a higher boiling point than its isomer, trans-1, 2-dichloroethene?

(A) The higher boiling isomer is more polar than the other isomer.

(B) The higher boiling isomer is better able to form hydrogen bonds than the other isomer.

(C) The higher boiling isomer has a greater molar mass.

(D) The higher boiling isomer has greater London dispersion forces than the other isomer.

Use the information on the following proposed mechanism to answer questions 25–27.

Step 1: $N_2O_5(g) \rightarrow NO_3(g) + NO_2(g)$ Slow

Step 2: $NO_3(g) \rightarrow NO(g) + O_2(g)$ Fast

Step 3: $NO(g) + N_2O_5(g) \rightarrow$
         $N_2O_4(g) + NO_2(g)$ Fast

Step 4: $N_2O_4(g) \leftrightarrows 2\ NO_2(g)$ Fast

25. The above represents a proposed mechanism for the gaseous dinitrogen pentoxide, N_2O_5. What are the overall products of the reaction?

(A) $N_2O_4(g) + O_2(g)$
(B) $2\ NO_2(g) + O_2(g)$
(C) $N_2O_4(g) + NO_2(g) + O_2(g)$
(D) $4\ NO_2(g) + O_2(g)$

26. Choose the energy profile that best describes this mechanism.

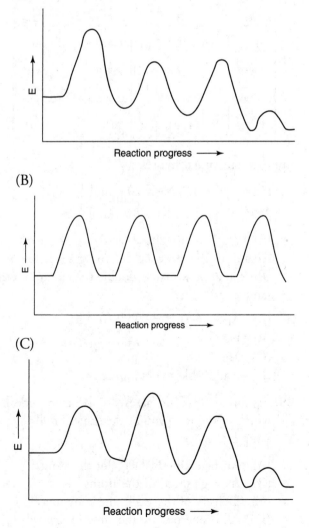

(A)

(B)

(C)

GO ON TO THE NEXT PAGE

(D)

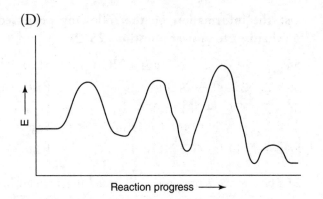

27. What is the rate law for the reaction?

(A) Rate = $k[N_2O_5]^2$
(B) $k = [N_2O_5]$
(C) Rate = $k[N_2O_5]$
(D) $k = \dfrac{[NO_2]^4[O_2]}{[N_2O_5]^2}$

Use the information on the containers in the following diagram to answer questions 28–30.

A	B	C	D
He	Ne	Ar	Kr
298 K	298 K	298 K	298 K
0.5 mole	0.5 mole	0.5 mole	0.5 mole
10.0 L	10.0 L	10.0 L	10.0 L

Approximate molar masses:

He = 4 g mol^{-1}, Ne = 20 g mol^{-1},
Ar = 40 g mol^{-1}, Kr = 84 g mol^{-1}

28. If a sample of Kr effuses at a rate of 35 mL per second at 298 K, which of the gases below will effuse at approximately double the rate under the same conditions?

(A) Ar
(B) He
(C) Ne
(D) Impossible to determine

29. Assuming all four gases are behaving ideally, which of the following is the same for all the gas samples?

(A) Average kinetic energy of the atoms
(B) Average speed of the atoms
(C) Density of the gas in the container
(D) All properties are the same for gases behaving ideally

30. Which of the gases will show the greatest deviation from ideal behavior?

(A) He
(B) Ne
(C) Ar
(D) Kr

Use the information on the containers in the following diagram to answer questions 31–34 concerning the following equilibrium.

$$2\ Cl_2(g) + 2\ H_2O(g) \leftrightarrows 4\ HCl(g) + O_2(g)$$

$$\Delta H = +100\ kJ$$

A	B	C	D
Cl$_2$	HCl	Cl$_2$	Cl$_2$
H$_2$O	O$_2$	H$_2$O	H$_2$O
		HCl	HCl
		O$_2$	O$_2$
		Not equilibrium	Equilibrium

31. An equilibrium mixture (container D) is at 75°C. Which of the following changes may increase the amount of the HCl in the container?

(A) Increasing the volume of the container
(B) Decreasing the volume of the container
(C) Lowering the temperature of the container
(D) Adding 1 mole of He(g) to the container

32. Containers A, B, and C are not at equilibrium. If each container begins with equal amounts of the indicated substances present at the same temperature, which of the three will reach equilibrium first?

(A) A because producing products from reactants is faster than the reverse.
(B) B because producing reactants from products is faster than the reverse.
(C) C because there are both reactants and products already in the container.
(D) It is impossible to determine which will reach equilibrium first.

GO ON TO THE NEXT PAGE

33. If the initial partial pressure of Cl_2 in container A is 1.0 atm and the initial partial pressure of H_2O is also 1.0 atm, what will be the pressure at equilibrium?

(A) > 2.0 atm
(B) = 2.0 atm
(C) < 2.0 atm
(D) Impossible to determine

34. If the moles of HCl in container B are equal to five times the O_2 present, what can be said about the moles of O_2 present at equilibrium?

(A) It will be zero because it is the limiting reagent
(B) It will remain the same
(C) It will be increase
(D) It is impossible to determine

Use the following information on the bases in the following diagram to answer questions 35–37.

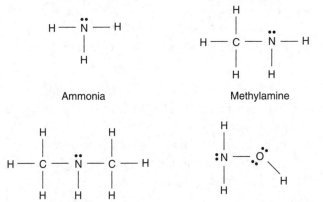

Ammonia

Methylamine

Dimethylamine

Hydroxylamine

Ammonia is only present as a reference. Questions 35–37 only refer to the other three bases.

pH of a 1.0 *M* solution

Ammonia	11.6
Methylamine	12.9
Dimethylamine	12.5
Hydroxylamine	10.0

35. Solutions of methylamine, dimethylamine, and hydroxylamine are titrated. The base concentrations were 0.1000 *M*, and 0.1000 *M* hydrochloric acid, HCl, was used for the titrations. Which of the three bases will yield the highest pH at the equivalence point?

(A) Hydroxylamine
(B) Methylamine
(C) Dimethylamine
(D) The concentrations of all the bases were the same; therefore, the pH at the equivalence point will be the same.

36. All the bases in the diagram behave as Brønsted-Lowry bases in the same way; in each case, they accept a hydrogen ion to the same atom. How is this acceptance of a hydrogen ion accomplished?

(A) A hydrogen ion attaches to the lone pair on the nitrogen atom.
(B) The hydroxide ion reacts with the hydrogen ion to form water.
(C) The hydrogen ion forms a hydrogen bond to the base.
(D) The hydrogen ion combines with a hydrogen atom from the base to form H_2 gas.

37. Which of the following explains why the pH of a hydroxylamine solution is lower than any of the other solutions?

(A) The –OH is capable of donating a hydrogen ion, which will lower the pH.
(B) The presence of carbon makes the bases less stable.
(C) The presence of the very electronegative oxygen inhibits the nitrogen atom from donating its electron pair.
(D) There is insufficient information to explain this observation.

38. Oxidation of which of the following substances will yield a stronger acid?

(A) HNO_2
(B) HNO_3
(C) H_2SO_4
(D) H_3PO_4

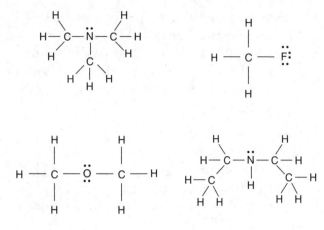

39. Which of the compounds in the above diagram is capable of participating in hydrogen bonding?

(A) C_3H_9N
(B) CH_3F
(C) C_2H_6O
(D) $C_4H_{11}N$

40. Choose the reaction expected to have the greatest decrease in entropy.

(A) $C(s) + CO_2(g) \rightarrow 2\ CO(g)$
(B) $2\ Na(s) + O_2(g) \rightarrow Na_2O_2(s)$
(C) $CH_4(g) + 2\ O_2(g) \rightarrow CO_2(g) + 2\ H_2O(g)$
(D) $2\ NI_3(s) \rightarrow 3\ I_2(s) + N_2(g)$

41. A certain reaction is nonspontaneous under standard conditions, but becomes spontaneous at higher temperatures. What conclusions may be drawn under standard conditions?

(A) $\Delta H < 0$, $\Delta S < 0$, and $\Delta G = 0$
(B) $\Delta H > 0$, $\Delta S < 0$, and $\Delta G > 0$
(C) $\Delta H < 0$, $\Delta S < 0$, and $\Delta G > 0$
(D) $\Delta H > 0$, $\Delta S > 0$, and $\Delta G > 0$

42. Which of the following is the correct order of increasing acid strength?

(A) $H_2SeO_3 < H_2SO_3 < HClO < HBrO$
(B) $HClO < H_2SeO_3 < HBrO < H_2SO_3$
(C) $HBrO < HClO < H_2SeO_3 < H_2SO_3$
(D) $H_2SO_3 < H_2SeO_3 < HClO < HBrO$

Use the following information on the bases in the following table to answer questions 43–44.

A large number of compounds adopt the sodium chloride structure. The following table contains some examples of the compounds in this group with their respective melting points and the sum of the cation-anion radii.

COMPOUND	FORMULA	MELTING POINT (°C)	SUM OF IONIC RADII (PM)
Sodium Chloride	NaCl	801	283
Sodium Fluoride	NaF	996	235
Calcium Oxide	CaO	2898	240
Strontium Oxide	SrO	2531	258
Barium Oxide	BaO	1972	275

43. Why are the melting points of the alkaline earth oxides (CaO, SrO, and BaO) so much higher than those of the other two compounds in the table?

(A) Smaller ions have lower lattice energy.
(B) Smaller ionic charges lead to higher lattice energy.
(C) Larger ions have higher lattice energy.
(D) Higher ionic charges lead to higher lattice energy.

44. Why do the melting points of the alkaline metal oxides decrease in the order CaO > SrO > BaO?

(A) Larger ions have higher lattice energies, which leads to lower melting points.
(B) Smaller ions have lower lattice energies, which leads to higher melting points.
(C) Larger ions have lower lattice energies, which leads to lower melting points.
(D) Smaller ions have a greater affinity for oxygen, which leads to a higher melting point.

GO ON TO THE NEXT PAGE

45. Joseph Priestly discovered oxygen gas by the decomposition of solid mercury(II) oxide, HgO, to oxygen gas, O_2, and liquid mercury metal, Hg. How many moles of oxygen gas will form when 4.32 g of solid mercury(II) oxide decomposes? The formula mass of mercury(II) oxide is 216 g mol^{-1}.

(A) 0.100 mol
(B) 0.0100 mol
(C) 0.0200 mol
(D) 0.0150 mol

COMPOUND	FORMULA	MOLAR MASS (g mol^{-1})	MELTING POINT (°C)
Carbon tetrafluoride	CF_4	88	−184
Carbon tetrachloride	CCl_4	154	−23
Carbon tetrabromide	CBr_4	332	92
Carbon tetraiodide	CI_4	520	171

46. According to the data in the table above, which of the following best explains the trend in increasing melting points?

(A) All the molecules are nonpolar and, for such molecules, intermolecular forces increase with increasing molar mass.
(B) All the molecules are polar and, for such molecules, intermolecular forces increase with increasing molar mass.
(C) The molecules with the lower melting points are nonpolar and the molecules with the higher molar masses are polar.
(D) The sequence is a coincidence since all the molecules have the same intermolecular forces.

47. Determine the H$^+$(aq) concentration in 1.0 M phenol, C_6H_5OH, solution. (The K_a for phenol is 1×10^{-10}.)

(A) $1 \times 10^{-10}\ M$
(B) $1 \times 10^{-9}\ M$
(C) $1 \times 10^{-3}\ M$
(D) $1 \times 10^{-5}\ M$

Diazene   Triazene

Tetrazene

48. Ammonia is the best-known nitrogen-hydrogen compound; however, there are a number of other nitrogen-hydrogen compounds, three of which are in the above diagram. Which of these has the longest average N-N bond length?

(A) N_2H_2
(B) N_3H_3
(C) N_4H_4
(D) They are all the same.

49. The above equilibrium was established in a 1.00 L container at a certain temperature. Once the system came to equilibrium, it was found that the following amounts of materials were present in the container:

$(NH_4)_2CO_3$ = 8.00 moles, NH_3 = 4.00 moles,

CO_2 = 2.00 moles, and H_2O = 2.00 moles.

Determine the value of K_c at this temperature.

(A) 8.00
(B) 64.0
(C) 4.00
(D) 32.0

50. A solution of a weak base is titrated with a solution of a standard strong acid. The progress of the titration is followed with a pH meter. Which of the following observations would occur?

(A) Initially, the pH slowly decreases, then there is a rapid decrease to give a pH below 7 at the equivalence point.
(B) The pH of the solution gradually decreases throughout the experiment, and the pH at the equivalence point is below 7.
(C) Initially, the pH slowly decreases, then there is a rapid decrease to give a pH equal to 7 at the equivalence point.
(D) Initially, the pH quickly decrease, then there is a gradual decrease to the equivalence point where the pOH equals the pK_b of the base.

GO ON TO THE NEXT PAGE

51. A student mixes 100.0 mL of a 0.10 M hydrofluoric acid, HF, solution with 50.0 mL of a 0.10 M potassium hydroxide, KOH, solution. The K_a for hydrofluoric acid is 6.8×10^{-4}. Which of the diagrams below best represents the species, other than H_2O, in the solution after the acid reacts with the base?

(A)

(B)

(C)

(D)

52. Which of the following best represents the result for the reaction of 50.0 mL of a 0.20 M barium hydroxide, $Ba(OH)_2$, solution with 50.0 mL of a 0.10 M sulfuric acid, H_2SO_4, solution to form a precipitate of $BaSO_4$?

(A)

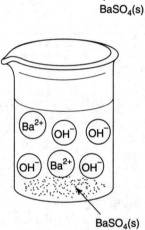

$BaSO_4(s)$

(B)

$BaSO_4(s)$

(C)

$BaSO_4(s)$

(D)

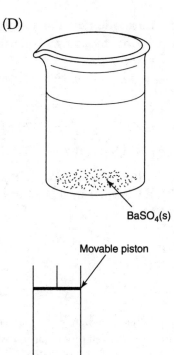

BaSO₄(s)

Movable piston

53. The container in the above diagram had an initial volume of 10.0 L. The container was heated until the temperature was double the original temperature. After heating, the pressure was measured and the piston moved down until the pressure was four times the original value. What was the final volume of the container?

(A) 10.0 L
(B) 1.25 L
(C) 5.00 L
(D) 20.0 L

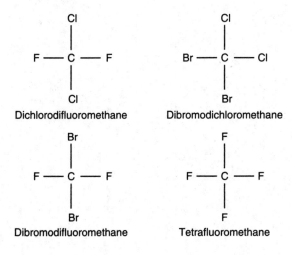

COMPOUND	BOILING POINT (°C)	MOLAR MASS (g mol⁻¹)
Dichlorodifluoromethane	−30	121
Dibromodichloromethane	150	243
Dibromodifluoromethane	23	210
Tetrafluoromethane	−128	88

54. The diagram above shows the structure of molecules of CCl_4 and CBr_4, and the above table gives the boiling points and molar masses of the compounds. Which of the compounds is nonpolar?

(A) Dichlorodifluoromethane
(B) Dibromodichloromethane
(C) Dibromodifluoromethane
(D) Tetrafluoromethane

$$2\ SO_2(g) + O_2(g) \rightleftarrows 2\ SO_3(g)$$

55. The reaction above is allowed to continue until equilibrium is established. After equilibrium is established a catalyst is added to the system. How does the rate of the forward reaction compare to the rate of the reverse reaction after the addition of the catalyst?

(A) The forward rate is faster than the reverse rate.
(B) The forward and reverse rates are the same.
(C) The reverse rate is faster than the forward rate.
(D) There is insufficient information to determine the relative rates.

A reaction has the following suggested mechanism:

1. $NH_3(aq) + OCl^-(aq) \rightarrow NH_2Cl(aq) + OH^-(aq)$
2. $NH_3(aq) + NH_2Cl(aq) \rightarrow Cl^-(aq) + N_2H_5^+(aq)$
3. $OH^-(aq) + N_2H_5^+(aq) \rightarrow N_2H_4(aq) + H_2O(l)$

56. Referring to the above mechanism, which of the following would support the suggested mechanism?

(A) Heating increases the rate of the reaction.
(B) Spectroscopy shows that $N_2H_5^+(aq)$ is present in trace amounts.
(C) The rate constant does not change with temperature.
(D) The first step is the rate-determining step.

GO ON TO THE NEXT PAGE

57. Determine the final temperature, in °C, of a sample of helium gas. The sample initially occupied a volume of 5.00 L at 127°C and 875 mm Hg. The sample was heated, at constant pressure, until it occupied a volume of 10.00 L.

    (A) 454°C
    (B) 527°C
    (C) 45°C
    (D) 181°C

58. A solution contains 2.00 mole of acetic acid, CH_3COOH, and 1.00 mole of calcium acetate, $Ca(CH_3COO)_2$. The solution is able to resist the addition of a small amount of strong acid or strong base with only minor changes in the pH of the solution. Larger quantities of strong acid or strong base can cause a significant change in pH. How many moles of nitric acid, HNO_3, may be added before the pH begins to change significantly?

    (A) 0.500 mole
    (B) 1.00 mole
    (C) 2.00 mole
    (D) 3.00 mole

Use the following information in the following thermochemical equations to answer questions 59–60.

$$C_2H_5OH(l) + 3\ O_2(g) \rightarrow$$
$$2\ CO_2(g) + 3\ H_2O(l) \qquad \Delta H = -1370\ kJ$$
$$2\ H_2(g) + O_2(g) \rightarrow 2\ H_2O(l) \qquad \Delta H = -570\ kJ$$
$$2\ H_2(g) + O_2(g) \rightarrow 2\ H_2O(g) \qquad \Delta H = -480\ kJ$$

59. Determine ΔH for the combustion of ethanol, C_2H_5OH, if $H_2O(g)$ formed in the above reaction instead of $H_2O(l)$.

    (A) +1280 kJ
    (B) −1280 kJ
    (C) +1100 kJ
    (D) −1100 kJ

60. What is the energy change when 72.0 g of water vapor decomposes to the elements at constant pressure? The molar mass of H_2O is 18.0 g mol^{-1}.

    (A) −1144 kJ
    (B) −572 kJ
    (C) +960 kJ
    (D) +1144 kJ

STOP: End of AP Chemistry Practice Exam 2, Section I (Multiple Choice).

》 Answers and Explanations for Exam 2, Section 1 (Multiple Choice)

1. **B**—This is a dipole-dipole force, which is stronger than a dipole-induced dipole (A and C) or a London dispersion force (D).

2. **C**—This will increase the concentration of Ag^+, causing a shift to the right, which will lead to an increase in the cell voltage.

3. **A**—The zinc ion concentration remains the same (1 M); therefore, the voltage will remain the same. The identity of the anion associated with the zinc is not important unless the compound is not soluble. Zinc chloride must be soluble; otherwise the student could not make a 1 M solution.

4. **B**—The cell voltage (1.56 V) is the sum of the standard reduction potential for silver (0.80 V) and the reverse of the standard reduction potential for zinc. Therefore, (1.56 − 0.80) V = 0.76 V = the reverse of the standard reduction potential for zinc. Reversing the value gives −0.76 V as the standard reduction potential for zinc.

5. **B**—As the cell begins to run, the voltage decreases until the system reaches equilibrium where the voltage is zero.

6. **D**—The mass of water is the difference in the masses of the hydrated salt and the anhydrous salt. In this case, (mass of crucible plus hydrated salt) − (mass of crucible plus anhydrous salt) = 58.677 g − 57.857 g = 0.820 g. This assumes the weight of the crucible is constant.

7. **A**—The percent water is 100% times the grams of water divided by the mass of the hydrated salt. The mass of water is:

   (mass of crucible plus hydrated salt) − (mass of crucible plus anhydrous salt) = (58.677 − 57.857) g = 0.820 g water.

   The mass of the hydrated salt is:

   (mass of crucible plus hydrated salt) − (mass of crucible) = (58.677 − 53.120) g = 5.557 g hydrated salt.

Finally, percent water $= \dfrac{0.820 \text{ g } H_2O}{5.557 \text{ g}}$ (100%) = 14.8%. The simplified calculation would be:

Percent water $\approx \dfrac{0.8 \text{ g } H_2O}{5.6 \text{ g}}$ (100%) $\approx \dfrac{1}{7}$ (100%)

$\approx 14\%$

8. **C**—Leaving the sample overnight in the lab drawer would cause the sample to be no longer anhydrous. The mass of the "anhydrous" salt would now be higher indicating a smaller amount of water loss, which would lead to a lower percentage of water in the sample.

9. **B**—It is necessary to determine the empirical formula of the compound. If the sample is 63% water, then it is 37% anhydrous salt. Assuming 100 grams of compound, the masses of water and anhydrous salt are 63 g and 37 g, respectively. Converting each of these to moles gives:

Moles anhydrous salt = (37 g anhydrous salt) × $\left(\dfrac{1 \text{ mole anhydrous salt}}{106 \text{ g anhydrous salt}} \right) = 0.35$ mole anhydrous salt

Moles water = (63 g H_2O) $\left(\dfrac{1 \text{ mole } H_2O}{18.0 \text{ g } H_2O} \right) =$ 3.5 mole H_2O

Since there are ten times as many moles of water as moles of the anhydrous salt, the formula must be $A_aX_x \bullet 10H_2O$.

10. **C**—No calculations are necessary as this is the only answer with the correct units.

11. **A**—Comparing experiments 1 and 3 shows that changing the hydrogen ion concentration has no effect upon the rate; therefore the reaction is zero order in hydrogen ion. Comparing experiments 2 and 3 shows that doubling the urea concentration doubles the rate; therefore, the reaction is first order with respect to urea.

12. **C**—The reaction is taking place in aqueous solution. For this reason, there is no significant change in the H_2O concentration. It is not possible to determine the effect of a reactant if the concentration does not change.

13. **B**—The first step is to calculate the true concentration of the sample to see how the student results compare. The balanced chemical equation is $H_2C_2O_4(aq) + 2\ NaOH(aq) \rightarrow Na_2C_2O_4(aq) + 2\ H_2O(l)$

    All the volumes are similar; therefore, it is possible to use any one of them and calculate an approximate molarity using rounded numbers for simplicity.

    $M\ H_2C_2O_4 \approx (40\ mL\ NaOH) \times$

    $$\left(\frac{0.050\ mol\ NaOH}{1000\ mL}\right)\left(\frac{1\ mol\ H_2C_2O_4}{2\ mol\ NaOH}\right)\left(\frac{1}{10\ mL}\right) \times$$

    $$\left(\frac{1000\ mL}{L}\right) \approx 0.1\ M$$

    The calculated value should be about half what the student reported. This indicates that the student did not include the 1:2 mole ratio relating the acid to the base or that the student incorrectly used a relationship such as $M_1V_1 = M_2V_2$.

14. **B**—The relationship is: $\Delta G = -nFE°$ (given on the exam)

    The number of electrons transferred = 2 = n

    $F = 96,500$ coulombs mol^{-1} and volt = 1 joule coulomb^{-1} (both given on the exam), these two relationships lead to $F = 96,500$ J V^{-1} mol^{-1}.

    $E° = (0.76 - 0.28)$ V = 0.48 V

    Entering this information in the equation gives $\Delta G = -(2)(96,500$ J V^{-1} $mol^{-1})(0.48$ V$) \approx$

    $-(2)(100,000)(0.50) \approx -100,000$ J mol^{-1} (actual value = -9.26×10^4 J mol^{-1})

15. **A**—At point G, all the CO_3^{2-} has been converted to HCO_3^- and the moles of HCO_3^- will equal the moles of CO_3^{2-} originally present. It will require an equal volume of acid to titrate an equal number of moles of HCO_3^- as required for the CO_3^{2-}. For pure sodium carbonate, F will always be 2G.

16. **A**—At point G, all the CO_3^{2-} has been converted to HCO_3^- and the moles of HCO_3^- will equal the moles of CO_3^{2-} originally present plus the quantity of HCO_3^- originally present. It will require a greater volume of acid to titrate a greater number of moles of HCO_3^- as required for the CO_3^{2-}.

17. **C**—It would be necessary to titrate the strong base and the CO_3^{2-} to reach G. However, it is only necessary to titrate the HCO_3^- to reach H, which means less acid is necessary.

18. **B**—At G the CO_3^{2-} is now HCO_3^-, so no CO_3^{2-} remains. The Na^+ did not react, so it is still present as ions. The Cl^- is from the HCl and remains as separate ions in solution. After G, the H^+ from the acid begins to convert HCO_3^- to form H_2CO_3, which is complete at point F leaving no HCO_3^- in the solution. Other than water, all species are strong electrolytes and exist as ions in solution. The H_2CO_3 will be decomposing to H_2O and $CO_2(g)$.

19. **D**—The pH will equal the pK_{a2} when the concentration of HCO_3^- equals the concentration of H_2CO_3. This occurs when one-half of the HCO_3^- has been converted to H_2CO_3.

20. **D**—The average kinetic energy, not the average speed, is the same if the temperatures are the same. Each container has one mole of gas, which means that at the same volume and temperature they will have the same pressure. The greater the molar mass, divided by a constant volume, the greater the density. One mole of gas will have Avogadro's number of molecules.

21. **B**—The decrease in temperature indicates that the system absorbed heat, meaning that this is an endothermic process. For an endothermic process to be spontaneous, the entropy must increase.

22. **D**—Hydrogen bonding may occur when hydrogen is attached directly to N, O, or F.

23. **C**—The two molecules are hydrogen bonded together. Hydrogen bonding is a relatively strong intermolecular force. Acetyl chloride cannot exhibit anything stronger than dipole-dipole forces, which are, in general, weaker than hydrogen bonds.

24. A—The higher boiling isomer is more polar than the other isomer because the two very electronegative chlorine atoms are on one side, which leads to their polar bonds working together. When the chlorine atoms are on opposite sides, their polar bonds work against each other.

25. D—Add the equations together and cancel any species that appear on both sides (intermediates).

26. A—The first step in the mechanism is the slow (rate-determining) step. It is the slowest because it has the highest activation energy. For the first step to be the slow step, the first peak must be the highest.

27. C—The rate law always considers the slowest step in a mechanism. There is one molecule of N_2O_5 as the reactant in the slow step; therefore, the rate law will only use the concentration of this reactant raised to a power equal to the number of molecules in the slow step.

28. C—Use Graham's law; a molecule with one-fourth the molar mass will diffuse at double the rate. Neon is the nearest to one-fourth the molar mass of krypton.

29. A—This is a consequence of kinetic molecular theory. The average kinetic energy depends only on the absolute temperature.

30. D—Heavier nonpolar species exhibit greater London dispersion forces, and stronger attractive forces lead to greater deviation from ideal behavior under a given set of conditions.

31. A—An increase in volume will cause an equilibrium to shift toward the side with more gas. There are four gas molecules on the left side and five gas molecules on the right side; therefore, an increase in volume will result in a shift to the right, which increases the amount of HCl (and O_2). B will have the opposite effect. Cooling an endothermic equilibrium will cause a shift to the left, which will decrease the amount of HCl. D will yield no change because helium is not part of the equilibrium.

32. D—The amount of time necessary is a kinetics problem. There is not kinetic data presented to make the determination possible.

33. A—The ICE table for this equilibrium is:

Cl_2	H_2O	HCl	O_2
1.0 atm	1.0 atm	0	0
$-2x$	$-2x$	$+4x$	$+x$
$1.0 - 2x$	$1.0 - 2x$	$+4x$	$+x$

From the equilibrium line on the table, the equilibrium pressure should be:

$$(1.0 - 2x) + (1.0 - 2x) + (+4x) + (+x) = 2.0 + x$$

Therefore, the equilibrium pressure will be greater than 2.0 atm by an amount equal to x.

34. D—To determine the amount, it would be necessary to know the value of the equilibrium constant. A cannot be correct because it is not possible for the amount of any of the materials to be zero at equilibrium. B and C cannot be correct because at least some of the O_2 would be converted to Cl_2 and H_2O leading to a decrease in the amount.

35. B—The pH of a 1.0 M methylamine solution is the highest; therefore, it is the strongest of the bases. For this reason, the pH at the equivalence point of the methylamine titration will be the highest.

36. A—As in ammonia, all these compounds behave as Brønsted–Lowry bases by accepting a hydrogen ion. The reaction involves the hydrogen ion attaching to the lone pair on the nitrogen atoms.

37. C—These are all bases because the nitrogen atom is capable of reacting with a hydrogen ion by donating its lone pair to the hydrogen ion. The oxygen atom pulls electron density away from the nitrogen atom causing the nitrogen atom to attract the lone pair more strongly making it less able to donate the pair to a hydrogen ion.

38. A—Only A can undergo oxidation, as there are higher oxidation states of nitrogen. For example, HNO_3 is the most likely oxidation product and, unlike HNO_2, it is a strong acid.

39. D—Hydrogen bonding is possible when hydrogen is attached to N, O, and F. D is the only compound in the diagram where this is true. The simple presence of hydrogen and N, O, or F is insufficient.

40. B—In general, gases have much higher entropy than either liquids or solids. For this reason, the predictions depends primarily upon which reaction results in the greatest decrease in the number of moles of gas. A and D both result in an increase in the number of moles of gas, so there is an increase in entropy. C shows no change in the number of moles of gas; therefore, the change in entropy will be small.

41. D—The relationship, given on the equations page of the exam is $\Delta G = \Delta H - T\Delta S$. Nonspontaneous under standard conditions means: $\Delta G > 0$. To become spontaneous, ΔG must be less than zero. Increasing the temperature will change the $T\Delta S$ term (entropy). If ΔH is greater than zero and ΔS is also greater than zero, the combination will be positive as long as the ΔH is greater than $T\Delta S$. As the temperature increases, $T\Delta S$ will eventually become larger than ΔH, making the process spontaneous.

42. C—In general, the more oxygen atoms present not attached to hydrogen atoms, the stronger the oxyacid. If two oxyacids have the same number of oxygen atoms not attached to hydrogen atoms, the acid with the more electronegative central atom is the stronger acid. The number of oxygen atoms without hydrogen atoms attached are $HClO = 0$, $HBrO = 0$, $H_2SeO_3 = 1$, and $H_2SO_3 = 1$. The electronegativities increase in the order $Se < S$ and $Br < Cl$.

43. D—The melting points of ionic compounds increase with increasing lattice energy. Lattice energy increases with increasing ionic charge and with decreasing sum of ionic radii. It is apparent from comparing NaF to CaO that charge is more important than small changes in radii. The charges are Na^+, Ca^{2+}, Sr^{2+}, Ba^{2+}, F^-, Cl^-, and O^{2-}.

44. C—The melting points of ionic compounds increase with increasing lattice energy. Lattice energy increases with increasing ionic charge and with decreasing sum of ionic radii. The oxide ion radius is a constant, while the metal radii decrease in the order $Ba^{2+} > Sr^{2+} > Ca^{2+}$. The decrease in metal radii is due to the smaller ions having fewer electron shells.

45. B—The balanced chemical equation is:
$$2\ HgO(s) \rightarrow 2\ Hg(l) + O_2(g)$$

The calculation is:

$$(4.32\ g\ HgO)\left(\frac{1\ mol\ HgO}{216\ g\ HgO}\right)\left(\frac{1\ mole\ O_2}{2\ mole\ HgO}\right) =$$

$$(4.32)\left(\frac{1}{216}\right)\left(\frac{1\ mole\ O_2}{2}\right) = (2.16)\left(\frac{1}{216}\right) \times$$

$$\left(\frac{1\ mole\ O_2}{1}\right) = 0.0100\ mole\ O_2$$

46. A—The substance with the highest melting point has the strongest intermolecular forces. All four molecules are nonpolar; therefore, the intermolecular forces are London dispersion forces. In general, London dispersion forces, for molecules with similar structures, London dispersion forces increase with increasing molar mass.

47. D—Since phenol has a K_a values given, it is a weak acid; as such, the equilibrium expression is:

$$C_6H_5OH(aq) \leftrightarrows H^+(aq) + C_6H_5O^-(aq)$$

Use the K_a expression:

$$K_a = \frac{[H^+][CB]}{[CV]} = 1 \times 10^{-10} = \frac{[x][x]}{[1.0]}$$

This leads to:

$$[H^+] = (1.0 \times 1 \times 10^{-10})^{1/2} = (1 \times 10^{-10})^{1/2} = 1 \times 10^{-5}\ M$$

48. C—The higher the average number of bonds between the nitrogen atoms, the shorter the bond is. For diazene there are two bonds, for triazene the average is 1.5 bonds, and for tetrazene the average is 1.33 bonds. The length of the average bond length increases in the order $2 < 1.5 < 1.33$.

49. D—The carbon is a solid and the water is a liquid; therefore, neither of these will be in the calculation. Since the volume of the container is 1.00 L, the molarities of the other two substances are 4.00 M NH_3 and 2.00 M CO_2.

$$K_c = [NH_3]^2\ [CO_2] = (4.00)^2\ (2.00) = 32.0$$

50. **A**—Strong acids and strong bases have pH = 7 at the equivalence point. The presence of a weak base with a strong acid lowers this value.

51. **C**—The reaction is:

$$HF(aq) + KOH(aq) \rightarrow KF(aq) + H_2O(l)$$

The potassium hydroxide is the limiting reagent, and all of the hydroxide ions from the base combine with one-half of the hydrogen ions produced from the acid. The potassium fluoride is a strong electrolyte and is present in solution as fluoride ions and potassium ions. The hydrofluoric acid is a weak acid, as indicated by the K_a, and it will partially ionize in solution to form hydrogen ions and fluoride ions with the remaining acid being undissociated.

52. **B**—The reaction is $Ba(OH)_2(aq) + H_2SO_4(aq) \rightarrow BaSO_4(s) + 2\ H_2O(l)$

There are 0.010 moles of barium hydroxide and 0.0050 moles of sulfuric acid. The barium hydroxide is in excess and the sulfuric acid is limiting. All the sulfate ions combine with barium ions to form the $BaSO_4$ precipitate with the excess barium ions remaining in solution. All the hydrogen ions from the acid react with the hydroxide ions from the base to produce water and leave the excess hydroxide ions in solution.

53. **C**—There are several ways of solving this problem. One way is to use the combined gas equation $(P_1V_1)/T_1 = (P_2V_2)/T_2$. In this problem, $V_1 = 10.0$ L, $T_2 = 2\ T_1$, and $P_2 = 4\ P_1$. Rearranging the combined gas equation and entering the values gives:

$$V_2 = (V_1)\left(\frac{T_2}{T_1}\right)\left(\frac{P_1}{P_2}\right) = (10.0\ \text{L})\left(\frac{2\ T_1}{T_1}\right)\left(\frac{P_1}{4\ P_1}\right)$$
$$= 5.00\ \text{L}$$

54. **D**—Tetrafluoromethane is the only nonpolar molecule in the diagram. All the other compounds are polar.

55. **B**—The catalyst will increase the rate of both the forward and reverse reactions. The rates will still remain the same, as the presence of a catalyst does not alter the position of the equilibrium, just the time necessary to reach equilibrium.

56. **B**—The presence of $N_2H_5^+(aq)$ supports this mechanism because the detection of an intermediate supports the mechanism. None of the other choices support or refute the overall mechanism.

57. **B**—It is necessary to convert the temperature to kelvin and back again.

$$T_2 = (V_2T_1)/V_1 = [(10.00\ \text{L} \times (127 + 273)\ \text{K})/(5.00\ \text{L})] - 273 = 527°C$$

Simplified by $(10.00/5.0) = 2.00$; therefore, $400\ K \times 2 = 800 - 273 = 527°C$.

58. **C**—The original solution is a buffer, which will resist changes in pH until all the acetic acid or acetate ions are reacted. The reaction of nitric acid with the acetate ion is $HNO_3(aq) + CH_3COO^-(aq) \rightarrow CH_3COOH(aq) + NO_3^-(aq)$

One mole releases 2.00 mole of acetate ion into the solution. As long as any of the acetate ion remains, the solution will have some buffering ability and the pH will remain about the same. Once sufficient nitric acid has been added to react with all the acetate ion, it is possible to drastically lower the pH by adding more acid. The reaction will require 2.00 moles of nitric acid to completely react with the acetate ion.

59. **D**—Using Hess's law:

$$C_2H_5OH(l) + 3\ O_2(g) \rightarrow$$
$$2\ CO_2(g) + 3\ H_2O(l) \qquad \Delta H = -1370\ \text{kJ}$$
$$3[2\ H_2O(l) \rightarrow$$
$$2\ H_2(g) + O_2(g)] \qquad \Delta H = 3(+570\ \text{kJ})$$
$$3[2\ H_2(g) + O_2(g) \rightarrow$$
$$2\ H_2O(g)] \qquad \Delta H = 3(-480\ \text{kJ})$$
$$\Delta H = -1100\ \text{kJ}$$

It is possible to simplify the problem by determining the heat of vaporization of water ($H_2O(l) \rightarrow H_2O(g)$), which is 90 kJ.

60. **C**—The decomposition of water vapor is the reverse of the last reaction shown; therefore, the enthalpy change is positive instead of negative. The amount of water decomposing is 4.00 mole, which is double the amount of water in the reaction. Double the water will require double the energy.

› AP Chemistry Practice Exam 2, Section II (Free Response)

Time—1 hour and 45 minutes

Answer the following questions in the time allowed. You may use a calculator and the resources at the back of the book. Write the answers on separate sheets of paper.

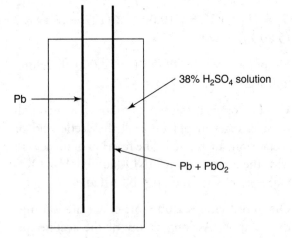

Question 1

A simplified diagram of one cell of a lead-acid battery as used in most automobiles is shown above. The half-reactions are:

$$PbO_2(s) + HSO_4^-(aq) + 3\ H^+(aq) + 2\ e^- \rightarrow PbSO_4(s) + 2\ H_2O(l)$$

$$Pb(s) + HSO_4^-(aq) \rightarrow PbSO_4(aq) + H^+(aq) + 2\ e^-$$

The standard cell potential is +2.04 V at 25°C. Initially the electrode on the left is pure lead, and the electrode on the right is pure lead coated with lead(IV) oxide.

(a) The standard reduction potential for the PbO_2 half-reaction is 1.68 V.
  (i) Write the overall reaction for the lead-acid battery.
  (ii) Calculate the value of the standard reduction potential for the Pb half-reaction.
(b) A student constructs a brand-new cell and it is fully charged.
  (i) Calculate the initial value of $\Delta G°$ for the cell.
  (ii) Calculate the value of K for the cell.
  (iii) The cell is allowed to operate until it reaches equilibrium. What is the value of $\Delta G°$ for the cell at equilibrium?
(c) In an automobile, the water from the electrolyte evaporates. Explain how will this affect the cell potential.
(d) Why is the PbO_2 electrode made of Pb coated with PbO_2 and not pure PbO_2?

GO ON TO THE NEXT PAGE

Question 2

$$2 \text{ NO(g)} + \text{Cl}_2\text{(g)} \rightarrow 2 \text{ NOCl(g)}$$

Thermodynamic values related to the above reaction are given in the table below.

SUBSTANCE	ΔH_F° (kJ/mol)	S° (J/mol K)	BONDS	BOND ENERGIES (kJ/mol)
NO(g)	90	210	N–O	170
Cl$_2$(g)	0	220	N=O	610
NOCl(g)	50	260	Cl–Cl	240
			N–Cl	200

(a) Determine the enthalpy change for the above reaction.
(b) Assuming that the NO bond in NOCl is a double bond, estimate the NO bond energy in NO.
(c) Does the NO bond energy in NO agree with any of the values in the table? What is there about the electronic structure of NO that might be the cause of this observation?
(d) Calculate the entropy change for the reaction.
(e) Is this reaction spontaneous or nonspontaneous at 25°C? Justify your prediction.

Question 3

$$5 \text{ Fe}^{2+}\text{(aq)} + \text{MnO}_4^-\text{(aq)} + 8 \text{ H}^+\text{(aq)} \rightarrow \text{Mn}^{2+}\text{(aq)} + 5 \text{ Fe}^{3+}\text{(aq)} + 4 \text{ H}_2\text{O(l)}$$

The above reaction is to be used in the analysis of a sample containing iron metal. A sample is dissolved in acid and the iron reduced to iron(II) ions with a little solid zinc. Excess zinc is filtered from the solution and a titration with standard potassium permanganate is performed immediately before air has had time to oxidize any of the iron(II) ions. The presence of a permanent pink color of excess permanganate ion indicates the endpoint of the titration.

(a) It is possible to standardize the potassium permanganate solution using solid iron(II) ammonium sulfate hexahydrate, Fe(NH$_4$)$_2$(SO$_4$)$_2 \cdot$6H$_2$O. You are given a potassium permanganate solution. Outline the general experimental procedure (not the calculations) for standardizing this solution.
(b) Show how to calculate the concentration of the potassium permanganate solution.
(c) Show how to calculate the percent iron in an unknown.
(d) If some of the excess zinc was not filtered from the solution, would the reported percentage of iron in the sample be higher, lower, or the same as when the zinc is removed? Explain.
(e) Standardization with iron(II) ammonium sulfate hexahydrate has the advantage of employing the same reaction as in the iron determination. However, there is a problem with using this compound to standardize the potassium permanganate. What might this problem be?
(f) Give the electron configuration of iron(II) ions, Fe^{2+}.

Question 4

$$\text{Ca(CN)}_2\text{(s)} + \text{H}_2\text{SO}_4\text{(aq)} + 2 \text{ H}_2\text{O(l)} \rightarrow 2 \text{ HCN(g)} + \text{CaSO}_4 \cdot 2\text{H}_2\text{O(s)}$$

It is possible to generate HCN gas by the above reaction. The gas is extremely toxic and great care is necessary when using this compound or related cyanides in any form.

(a) Calculate the number of moles of HCN present in 1.00 L of this gas at 273 K and 1.00 atm.
(b) What volume of HCN gas would the reaction of 1.00 g of Ca(CN)$_2$ with excess H$_2$SO$_4$ form? The volume is measured at 298 K and 1.00 atm. The molar mass of Ca(CN)$_2$ is 92.1 g mol^{-1}.

GO ON TO THE NEXT PAGE

(c) The reaction in (b) went to completion; however, the volume of gas generated was lower than expected. Explain why the volume was low.

(d) In the box below, draw the Lewis electron-dot structure for HCN.

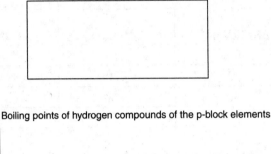

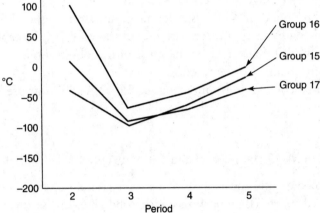

Boiling points of hydrogen compounds of the p-block elements

Question 5

Answer each of the following with respect to the plot of the boiling points of the hydrogen compounds in the above graph. Group 15 is the nitrogen family, Group 16 is the oxygen family, and Group 17 is the halogen family.

(a) On the above plot draw a line to indicate the boiling points of the hydrogen compounds in Group 14 (carbon family).

(b) What is the cause of the upward turn in the three lines shown on the graph?

(c) Where would the compound LiH appear on this graph, and why would it appear in this position?

Question 6

Five beakers (A–E) are on a countertop. Each contains 200 mL of a 0.10 M solution. Beaker A contains $SrCl_2$; beaker B contains NH_4Cl; beaker C contains CH_3CH_2OH; beaker D contains $Na_2C_2O_4$; and beaker E contains $Ni(NO_3)_2$.

(a) Which beaker has the lowest pH and why?

(b) Which solution is most likely to be colored?

(c) Which solution is basic?

(d) Which solution has the lowest electrical conductivity and why?

COMPOUND	FORMULA	K_{SP}
Silver sulfate	Ag_2SO_4	1.6×10^{-5}
Barium Sulfate	$BaSO_4$	1.1×10^{-10}
Calcium sulfate	$CaSO_4$	9.1×10^{-6}
Strontium sulfate	$SrSO_4$	3.2×10^{-7}

Question 7

The solubility product constants for some insoluble sulfates are given in the table above.

(a) Write a balanced chemical equation for the dissolution equilibrium of silver sulfate, Ag_2SO_4, in water.

(b) A sodium sulfate solution is slowly titrated into a solution that is 0.10 M in $Ba(NO_3)_2$ and 0.10 M in $Sr(NO_3)_2$.

    (i) Show, with calculations, which salt will precipitate first, the barium salt or the strontium salt.

    (ii) If the titration is continued, eventually the second salt will begin to precipitate. What is the concentration of the other ion (Ba^{2+} or Sr^{2+}) remaining in solution when the second salt begins to precipitate?

(c) Show, with calculations, which of the solids in the table is the most soluble.

STOP: End of AP Chemistry Practice Exam 2, Section II (Free Response).

❯ Answers and Explanations for Exam 2, Section II (Free Response)

Question 1

(a) (i) $PbO_2(s) + 2\ HSO_4^-(aq) + 2\ H^+(aq) + Pb(s) \rightarrow 2\ PbSO_4(aq) + 2\ H_2O(l)$

You get 1 point for this answer.

(ii) $PbO_2(s) + HSO_4^-(aq) + 3\ H^+(aq) + 2\ e^- \rightarrow PbSO_4(s) + 2\ H_2O(l)$ 1.68 V

$Pb(s) + HSO_4^-(aq) \rightarrow PbSO_4(aq) + H^+(aq) + 2\ e^-$? V

$PbO_2(s) + 2\ HSO_4^-(aq) + 2\ H^+(aq) + Pb(s) \rightarrow 2\ PbSO_4(aq) + 2\ H_2O(l)$ 2.04 V

If the cell voltage is 2.04 V then the two half-reaction voltages must add to this. Therefore, 2.04 V = (1.68 + ?) V making the voltage for the second half-reaction equal to 0.36 V. This is the voltage for the oxidation half-reaction; to change this to a standard reduction potential it is necessary to reverse the half-reaction, which means it is necessary to reverse the sign on the voltage. Thus, the standard reduction potential for the second half-reaction is −0.36 V.

You get 1 point for calculating 0.36 V and 1 point for changing the sign to a negative value.

(b) It is necessary to use two of the equations provided on the exam to answer this problem. (If you already know the equations, it will save you the time necessary to look them up).

(i) The exam (and the appendixes at the back of this book) provides the equation $\Delta G° = -nFE°$ plus the values of the Faraday constant, $F = 96,485$ coulombs per mole of electrons, and 1 volt = $\dfrac{1\ \text{joule}}{1\ \text{coulomb}}$. For this problem, $n = 2$ moles of electrons and $E° = + 2.04$ V. Entering the values into the given equation: $\Delta G° = -nFE° = -(2\ \text{mol electrons})\left(\dfrac{96.485\ \text{coul}}{\text{mol electrons}}\right)(2.04\ \text{V})\left(\dfrac{\text{J}}{(\text{V})(\text{coul})}\right)$ $= 393659 = 3.94 \times 10^5$ J or 394 kJ.

Give yourself 1 point for the correct setup of the equation including the conversion and 1 more point for the correct answer.

(ii) It is possible to get the answer by two different means by using the equations given on the test (in the back of this book). The values of the constants are also here. The important equations are $\Delta G° = -nFE°$ and $\Delta G° = -RT \ln K$. It is possible to combine these equations to $\ln K = \dfrac{nFE°}{RT}$. The first equation was used in part b(ii), and it is acceptable to use the answer from there and go directly to the second equation without recalculating the result. Using the third equation gives: $\ln K = \dfrac{nFE°}{RT}$

$$= \dfrac{(2\ \text{mol electrons})\left(\dfrac{96.485\ \text{coul}}{\text{mol electrons}}\right)(2.04\ \text{V})\left(\dfrac{\text{J}}{(\text{V})(\text{coul})}\right)}{\left(\dfrac{8.314\ \text{J}}{\text{mol K}}\right)(298\ \text{K})} = 159 \text{ (which is the same answer you}$$

get from using the answer to (b)(ii) and the second equation. Finally, if $\ln K = 159$, then $K = e^{159}$.

Give yourself 1 point for the correct setup of the equation, including the conversion, and 1 more point for the correct answer.

(iii) At equilibrium $\Delta G°$ is always 0.

Give yourself 1 point for this answer.

(c) As the water evaporates, the concentration of sulfuric acid will increase, which leads to an increase in the hydrogen ion concentration. An increase in the hydrogen ion concentration will promote the PbO_2 half-reaction more than it will change the Pb half-reaction. The result is a shift toward the left, which will increase the voltage.

Give yourself 1 point for this answer.

(d) It is necessary to have a conductor present for the transfer of electrons. Lead(IV) oxide is an ionic compound, which does not conduct electricity. Lead is a metal, which does conduct electricity.

Give yourself 1 point for this answer. Subtract 1 point if any of the answers has the wrong number of significant figures.

Total your points for the various parts. There are 10 possible points.

Question 2

(a) $\Delta H_{rxn}° = [2(50)] - [2(90) + 1(0)] = -80$ kJ

The answer with appropriate units is worth 1 point. You do not need to get the exact answer, but your answer should round to this one.

(b) The answer from part (a) equals the bonds broken minus the bonds formed.

$[(2 \text{ NO}) + (\text{Cl--Cl})] - 2 [(\text{N=O}) + (\text{NCl})] = -80$ kJ

$[(2 \text{ NO}) + (240)] - 2 [(610) + (200)] = -80$ kJ

$\text{NO} = 650$ kJ

The setup (broken – formed) is worth 1 point, and the answer is worth 1 point. You do not need to get the exact answer, but your answer should round to this one. If your answer from (a) was wrong, but you use it correctly in this part, you still get your setup and answer points.

(c) The value is higher than the value given for an N=O bond. The NO molecule has an odd number of electrons and this will alter its bonding.

You get 1 point for the correct observation, and 1 point for any explanation involving an odd number of electrons. If you got the wrong answer for part (b), you can still get 1 or 2 points if you used the answer correctly on this part.

(d) $\Delta S_{rxn}° = [2(260)] - [2(210) + 1(220)] = -120$ J/K

The setup (products – reactants) is worth 1 point, and the answer is worth 1 point. You do not need to get the exact answer, but your answer should round to this one.

(e) It is necessary to calculate the free-energy change.

$\Delta G_{rxn}° = \Delta H_{rxn}° - T\Delta S_{rxn}° = -80$ kJ $- (298$ K$)(1$ kJ/1000 J$)(-120$ J/K$) = -44$ kJ

The negative value means the reaction is spontaneous.

You get 1 point for the prediction that the reaction is spontaneous. The setup (plugging into the equation) is worth 1 point if you remember to change the temperature to kelvin and the joule-to-kilojoule conversion (or vice versa for an answer in J). An additional 1 point comes from the answer. If you got the wrong value in either part (a) or (b), but used it correctly, you will still get the point for the answer. The free-energy equation is part of the material supplied in the exam booklet.

Total your points for the different parts. There is a maximum of 10 points possible. Subtract 1 point if all your answers do not have the correct number of significant figures.

Question 3

(a) 1. Samples of iron(II) ammonium sulfate hexahydrate are weighed into beakers, and deionized water is added to dissolve each of the samples.

   2. A buret is rinsed with the potassium permanganate solution and then filled.

   3. The potassium permanganate solution is titrated into the iron(II) standard until a permanent pink color from the permanganate solution appears.

   4. Repeat these steps with the other samples.

   Listing these will get you 2 points. Missing one or more of these will get you 1 point. Other items are not necessary and will not change the scoring.

(b) [(Mass of $Fe(NH_4)_2(SO_4)_2 \cdot 6H_2O$)/(Molar mass of $Fe(NH_4)_2(SO_4)_2 \cdot 6H_2O$)] × (1 mol MnO_4^-/5 mol Fe^{2+})/(Volume of potassium permanganate solution)

   You get 2 point for this complete answer. You get 1 point if a step is missing and 0 points if two or more steps are missing.

(c) (Volume permanganate solution) × (Concentration permanganate solution) × (5 mol Fe/1 mol MnO_4^-) × (Molar mass of iron) = grams iron

   You get 1 point for this answer.

   Percent iron = (grams iron/grams sample) × 100%

   You get 1 point for this answer.

(d) The percent iron would be higher.

   You get 1 point for this answer.

   The titration would require more potassium permanganate solution to reach the endpoint because it would be necessary to titrate not only the iron but also the zinc.

   You get 1 point for this answer or by saying the zinc would reduce some of the iron back to iron(II), which would require it to be re-titrated.

(e) As noted in the initial comments for this question, air oxidizes iron(II) ions. For this reason, the iron(II) ions in iron(II) ammonium sulfate hexahydrate might undergo air oxidation before being used to standardize the potassium permanganate.

   This answer or simply stating that the compound is unstable is worth 1 point.

(f) The electron configuration may be written as [Ar] $3d^6$ or $1s^2 2s^2 2p^6 3s^2 3p^6 3d^6$. Recall that for the transition metals the s-electrons, in this case $4s^2$, are the first electrons lost in oxidation.

   This answer is worth 1 point.

Total your points for the various parts. There are 10 possible points.

Question 4

(a) The Ideal Gas Equation is one way of calculating the number of moles, *n*, of a gas.

$$\text{Moles} = n = \frac{PV}{RT} = \frac{(1.00\ \text{atm})(1.00\ \text{L})}{(0.0821\ \text{L atm mol}^{-1}\text{K}^{-1})(273\ \text{K})} = 0.0446\ \text{mol HCN (three significant figures)}$$

As an alternative, if you recognize the 273 K and 1.00 atm is STP, you can use the molar volume of a gas at STP to calculate the number of moles.

$$\text{Moles} = n = (1.00\ \text{L})\left(\frac{1\ \text{mol}}{22.4\ \text{L}}\right) = 0.0446\ \text{mol HCN (three significant figures)}$$

This answer is worth 1 point.

(b) Again it is possible to use the Ideal Gas Equation to solve for the volume, *V*, of a gas.

$$\text{Volume} = V = \frac{nRT}{P} =$$

$$\frac{\left[(1.00\ \text{g Ca(CN)}_2)\left(\frac{1\ \text{mol Ca(CN)}_2}{92.1\ \text{g Ca(CN)}_2}\right)\left(\frac{2\ \text{mol HCN}}{1\ \text{mol Ca(CN)}_2}\right)\right](0.0821\ \text{L atm mol}^{-1}\text{K}^{-1})(298\ \text{K})}{(1.00\ \text{atm})} =$$

0.531 L (three significant figures)

This answer is worth 1 point. Unlike part (a) you cannot use the molar volume of a gas because the conditions are not STP.

(c) Based upon its structure, HCN is polar and, therefore, must be soluble in water. For this reason, some will not be in the gas phase but in the solution, which means the volume of the gas will be less than expected.

This answer, including the explanation, is worth 1 point.

(d)

There must be a single bond between the hydrogen atom and the carbon atom and a triple bond between the carbon atom and the nitrogen atom. The lone pair on the nitrogen atom can be anywhere as long as it is obvious that it is only associated with the nitrogen atom. Both the carbon and the nitrogen atoms have an octet of electrons. This answer is worth 1 point.

Total your points for each part. There are 4 possible points. Subtract 1 point if all reported answers did not have the correct number of significant figures.

Question 5

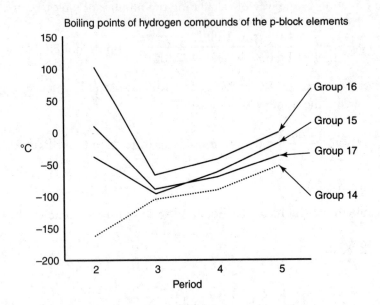

Boiling points of hydrogen compounds of the p-block elements

(a) The Group 14 line is the dotted line. The dotted line should always be below the other lines because the hydrogen compounds of the Group 14 elements are all nonpolar, while all the other hydrogen compounds on the graph are polar. The dotted line should not go up at the end because CH_4 is the only Period 2 hydrogen compound on the graph that is not capable of hydrogen bonding.

Give yourself 1 point if your line remains below all the other lines. Give yourself a second point if your line does not move up at the left end.

(b) The Period 2 compounds on the graph are, from top to bottom, H_2O, HF, NH_3, and CH_4. The first three of these compounds are the only compounds plotted that are capable of hydrogen bonding. Hydrogen bonding in stronger than any of the other intermolecular forces present in the compounds on the graph, which means their boiling points should be higher than those of compounds without hydrogen bonding.

Give yourself 1 point for this explanation.

(c) Li is a Period 2 element; therefore, it would appear on the left side of the graph and it would have a much higher boiling point than the other compounds because it is an ionic compound and ionic compounds, because of their high lattice energies, have very high boiling points.

You get 1 point if you give the correct approximate position and mention ionic bonding.

A total of 4 points is possible.

Question 6

The compounds are supplied as solutions; therefore, they must be soluble. This means any argument stating that one or more of the original substances is not soluble in water is invalid.

(a) The lowest pH will be for the solution containing an acid. Beaker B has the lowest pH. The NH_4^+ ion is the conjugate acid of a weak base, and as an acid (weak), it will lower the pH. There are no other acids present.

You get 1 point for choosing B with the correct explanation.

(b) Beaker E, because transition metal ions are often colored in solution.

You get 1 point for the correct choice.

(c) Solution D—solution D contains the conjugate base, $C_2O_4^{2-}$, of a weak acid. The conjugate bases of weak acids undergo hydrolysis to produce basic solutions.

You get 1 point for the correct choice.

(d) Solution C contains a nonelectrolyte; therefore, it does not conduct. All the remaining solutions contain electrolytes, which are conductors.

You get 1 point for choosing solution C with the explanation.

Total your points for the different parts. There are 4 possible points.

Question 7

(a) $Ag_2SO_4(s) \leftrightharpoons 2\,Ag^+(aq) + SO_4^{2-}(aq)$

You get 1 point for this equation.

(b) (i) Since the stoichiometries of $SrSO_4$ and $BaSO_4$ are the same, the one with the lower K_{sp} will precipitate first ($BaSO_4$). However, the problem states that it is necessary to show this with calculations.

Since the stoichiometries are the same, it is possible to use the generic equation and generic mass action expression with $M^{2+} = Ba^{2+}$ or Sr^{2+}.

$$MSO_4(s) \leftrightharpoons 2\,M^{2+}(aq) + SO_4^{2-}(aq) \qquad K_{sp} = [M^{2+}]\,[SO_4^{2-}]$$

Since both metals have the same concentration, it is only necessary to determine which requires the lower sulfate ion concentration. This is done as:

$$[SO_4^{2-}] = \frac{K_{sp}}{[M^{2+}]} = \frac{K_{sp}}{[0.10]}$$

For $BaSO_4 = 1.1 \times 10^{-9}$ M SO_4^{2-} and for $SrSO_4 = 3.2 \times 10^{-6}$ M SO_4^{2-}

You get 1 point for determining that the sulfate ion concentration shows that $BaSO_4$ will precipitate first.

(ii) From part (i), the second ion (Sr^{2+}) begins to precipitate at 3.2×10^{-6} M SO_4^{2-}. Using this value with the $BaSO_4$ K_{sp} allows the calculation of the barium ion concentration when the $SrSO_4$ first begins to precipitate. This calculation is:

$$[Ba^{2+}] = \frac{K_{sp}}{[SO_4^{2-}]} = \frac{1.1 \times 10^{-10}}{3.2 \times 10^{-6}} = 3.4 \times 10^{-5} \ M \ Ba^{2+}$$

You get 1 point for this answer. You also get 1 point if you if you did this calculation correctly but made the wrong prediction in part (i)

(c) For the compounds with the same stoichiometry ($BaSO_4$, $CaSO_4$, and $SrSO_4$) the one with the largest K_{sp} is the most soluble; therefore, it is only necessary to compare the solubilities of Ag_2SO_4 and $CaSO_4$.

For $CaSO_4$

$$K_{sp} = [Ca^{2+}] \ [SO_4^{2-}] = 9.1 \times 10^{-6} \text{ and } [Ca^{2+}] = [SO_4^{2-}] = x$$
$$K_{sp} = x^2 = 9.1 \times 10^{-6} \text{ so } x = 3.0 \times 10^{-3} \ M$$

For Ag_2SO_4

$$K_{sp} = [Ag^+] \ [SO_4^{2-}] = 1.6 \times 10^{-5} \text{ and } [Ag^+] = 2 \ [SO_4^{2-}], \ [Ag^+] = 2x \text{ and } [SO_4^{2-}] = x$$
$$K_{sp} = (2x)^2(x) = 4x^3 = 1.6 \times 10^{-5} \text{ so } x = 1.6 \times 10^{-2} \ M$$

The value for x from Ag_2SO_4 is larger; therefore it is more soluble.

Give yourself 1 point for this answer.

There is a total of 4 points possible. Subtract 1 point if any answer has the wrong number of significant figures.

5 Minutes to a 5

180 Activities and Questions in

5 Minutes a Day

INTRODUCTION

Welcome to *5 Minutes to a 5 – AP Chemistry*. We are very happy that you are using our book to help guide your study with the goal of a 5 on the AP Chemistry Exam (henceforth known as The Exam). This special section is another tool for you to use in achieving your goal. One of the secrets in doing well in your chemistry class is spending a certain amount of time each day studying chemistry. The same is true of The Exam. In this special section we have included 180 questions to be done in conjunction with the *5 Steps* book. We designed the questions to be done one per day; each should, on the average, take 5 minutes to complete. A few may take a little longer, a few a little less. There are some thought-provoking questions, some appropriate chemistry problems, some at-home labs to do, and some YouTube videos for you to watch. They are keyed to the *5 Steps* chapters with a few thrown is as review, so that you are constantly reinforcing your knowledge. There are also some that are marked with the chapter reference, but with an Experimental reference as well. The Experimental reference refers to Chapter 19, our chapter devoted to experimental techniques. These questions and problems are designed to review and hone your experimental skills.

The first 160+ questions should take you up to The Exam. We do realize that there is life after The Exam, so the last several questions are a bit more general and a bit more lighthearted in nature. Consider the first 160+ questions, labs, and videos as mental warm-up exercises, stretching your mind and getting you prepared for each day of chemistry and studying for The Exam. The last several exercises are cool-down exercises, a way of rewarding your hard work and high scores. Remember: Working on these questions for 5 minutes a day is much more effective than binging by doing a week's worth at one sitting. May the force be with you!

Check off each activity as it is completed.

1.	❏	46.	❏	91.	❏	136.	❏
2.	❏	47.	❏	92.	❏	137.	❏
3.	❏	48.	❏	93.	❏	138.	❏
4.	❏	49.	❏	94.	❏	139.	❏
5.	❏	50.	❏	95.	❏	140.	❏
6.	❏	51.	❏	96.	❏	141.	❏
7.	❏	52.	❏	97.	❏	142.	❏
8.	❏	53.	❏	98.	❏	143.	❏
9.	❏	54.	❏	99.	❏	144.	❏
10.	❏	55.	❏	100.	❏	145.	❏
11.	❏	56.	❏	101.	❏	146.	❏
12.	❏	57.	❏	102.	❏	147.	❏
13.	❏	58.	❏	103.	❏	148.	❏
14.	❏	59.	❏	104.	❏	149.	❏
15.	❏	60.	❏	105.	❏	150.	❏
16.	❏	61.	❏	106.	❏	151.	❏
17.	❏	62.	❏	107.	❏	152.	❏
18.	❏	63.	❏	108.	❏	153.	❏
19.	❏	64.	❏	109.	❏	154.	❏
20.	❏	65.	❏	110.	❏	155.	❏
21.	❏	66.	❏	111.	❏	156.	❏
22.	❏	67.	❏	112.	❏	157.	❏
23.	❏	68.	❏	113.	❏	158.	❏
24.	❏	69.	❏	114.	❏	159.	❏
25.	❏	70.	❏	115.	❏	160.	❏
26.	❏	71.	❏	116.	❏	161.	❏
27.	❏	72.	❏	117.	❏	162.	❏
28.	❏	73.	❏	118.	❏	163.	❏
29.	❏	74.	❏	119.	❏	164.	❏
30.	❏	75.	❏	120.	❏	165.	❏
31.	❏	76.	❏	121.	❏	166.	❏
32.	❏	77.	❏	122.	❏	167.	❏
33.	❏	78.	❏	123.	❏	168.	❏
34.	❏	79.	❏	124.	❏	169.	❏
35.	❏	80.	❏	125.	❏	170.	❏
36.	❏	81.	❏	126.	❏	171.	❏
37.	❏	82.	❏	127.	❏	172.	❏
38.	❏	83.	❏	128.	❏	173.	❏
39.	❏	84.	❏	129.	❏	174.	❏
40.	❏	85.	❏	130.	❏	175.	❏
41.	❏	86.	❏	131.	❏	176.	❏
42.	❏	87.	❏	132.	❏	177.	❏
43.	❏	88.	❏	133.	❏	178.	❏
44.	❏	89.	❏	134.	❏	179.	❏
45.	❏	90.	❏	135.	❏	180.	❏

Day 1

CHAPTER 5 – BASICS

The scientific method is a useful process that many scientists follow in their research and in problem solving. However, many great scientific discoveries were made through serendipity: an accidental discovery, especially in science. The discovery of the following products has been attributed to serendipity: Teflon®, Post-It Notes®, the microwave oven, and Rogaine® (minoxidil). Choose one or more of these products and conduct an Internet search on its discovery. What characteristics did the scientist(s) who were involved have that enabled them to make the discovery?

Day 2

Sometimes in the development of a model or theory, a scientist or a group of scientists might develop competing theories to explain a set of observations. In order to decide between two or more competing models/theories, the scientists sometimes invoke the concept of Occam's razor to reach a decision. One description of Occam's razor uses the following analogy: "If you hear hoof beats, think horses not zebras." Research Occam's razor and explain when this analogy is valid and when it is not valid.

Day 3

If you have ever wondered about a career in chemical engineering, check out these two YouTube videos:

https://www.youtube.com/watch?v=_UXwbxM8YfI

https://www.youtube.com/watch?v=k-7B_YfHWXQ

If you like both chemistry and biology, check out this YouTube video on being a bio-chemist (and a connection to sports medicine):

https://www.youtube.com/watch?v=pZbIYAFUGD8

Day 4

An adult human mouth can hold about a deciliter of water. How many water molecules is this?

Day 5

The toxicity of a chemical is reported as the LD_{50}. This is the dosage of the drug that kills 50% of the test subjects (usually mice) within a week. The LD_{50} for aspirin is 1.50 g/kg of body weight. The typical low-dose (baby) aspirin contains 81 mg of aspirin. How many baby aspirins would a 22-pound child have to ingest to reach the LD_{50} for aspirin?

(a) The following are some electron configurations reported by four students. One of these electron configurations is not possible. Which one?

A. $1s^2 2s^3 2p^3$

B. $1s^2 2s^2 2p^6 3s^2 3p^6 4s^2 3d^{10} 4p^6$

C. $1s^2 2s^2 2p^6 3s^2 3p^6 3d^3$

D. $1s^2 2s^2 2p^5$

(b) Which of the following is the electron configuration of a noble gas?

E. $1s^2 2s^2 2p^6 3s^2 3p^6 4s^2 3d^{10} 4p^5$

F. $1s^2 2s^2 2p^6 3s^2 3p^6$

G. $1s^2 2s^2 2p^6 3s^2 3p^6 3d^3$

H. $1s^2 2s^2 2p^6 3s^2 3p^6 3d^8 4s^2$

(c) The ground-state electron configuration of Co^{2+} is which of the following?

I. $1s^2 2s^2 2p^6 3s^2 3p^6 3d^5 4s^2$

J. $1s^2 2s^2 2p^6 3s^2 3p^6 3d^7$

K. $1s^2 2s^2 2p^6 3s^2 3p^6 3d^7 4s^2$

L. $1s^2 2s^2 2p^6 3s^2 3p^6 3d^9 4s^2$

Day 7

Within any period, why do the atomic radii decrease with increasing atomic number?

Day 8

Read the story *Omnilingual* by H. Beam Piper, and comment on its applicability to the importance of the periodic table to science. (This story is available online as an eBook through Project Gutenberg.)

Complete the following table:

NaBr _____ Silicon disulfide _____

N_2O_4 _____ Carbon tetrabromide _____

Li_2O _____ Barium nitride _____

CaO _____ Sulfur trioxide _____

K_2S _____ Magnesium fluoride _____

Day 10

The names of certain compounds and ions may be very similar. Give the correct formula for each compound in the following pairs

(a) ammonium ion and ammonia

(b) hydrochloric acid and chloric acid

(c) lithium nitride and lithium nitrite

(d) manganese(II) oxide and manganese(III) oxide

(e) manganese(II) oxide and magnesium oxide

(f) potassium nitrate and potassium nitrite

(g) tungsten(IV) oxide and tungsten(VI) oxide

(h) iodic acid and periodic acid

(i) ammonium hydrogen phosphate and ammonium dihydrogen phosphate

(j) calcium sulfite and calcium bisulfite

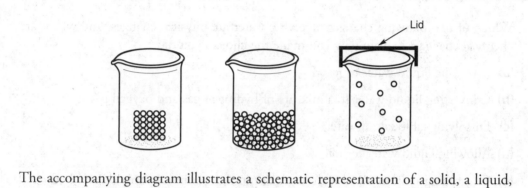

The accompanying diagram illustrates a schematic representation of a solid, a liquid, and a gas. The circles represent atoms. Based on these representations, what can be said about the shape and volume of these three phases?

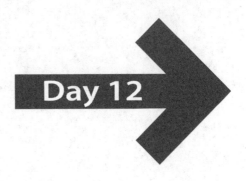

Which of the following changes involving water are physical changes, and which are chemical changes? Explain why you made the choices you did.

(a) Changing liquid water to ice

(b) Converting liquid water to a mixture of hydrogen gas and oxygen gas

(c) Dissolving table salt in water

(d) Allowing liquid water to boil

(e) Combining sodium metal with water to produce sodium hydroxide and hydrogen gas

Day 13

CHAPTER 6 – REACTIONS AND REACTIVITY

(a) Ammonia can be produced by the reaction of nitrogen gas that is isolated from the atmosphere and hydrogen gas that is produced from natural gas. Write the balanced chemical equation for this process.

(b) Urea is a fertilizer that is produced from ammonia and carbon dioxide according to the following unbalanced equation:

$$NH_3(g) + CO_2(g) \rightarrow NH_2CONH_2(aq) + H_2O(l)$$

Balance this equation.

(c) Nitrous oxide may be produced by reacting urea with sulfuric and nitric acids according to the following unbalanced reaction:

$$(NH_2)_2CO + HNO_3 + H_2SO_4 \rightarrow N_2O + CO_2 + (NH_4)_2SO_4 + H_2O$$

Balance this equation.

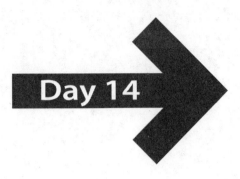

As part of a laboratory practicum a student is given three test tubes, each containing a small amount of a white crystalline substance. The first task is to determine whether each of the substances is an ionic or a covalent compound. Describe how you might make this determination and what laboratory apparatus you might use.

5 Minutes to a 5

Day 15

Water is sometimes called the "universal solvent." Explain why this label is justified, and indicate what structural property of water is responsible.

Which of the following best represents the balanced net ionic equation for the reaction of silver carbonate with concentrated hydrochloric acid? Silver ions have a 1+ charge. In this reaction, all silver compounds are insoluble. Explain why you chose the one you did.

A. $2\,AgCO_3 + 4\,H^+ + Cl^- \rightarrow Ag_2Cl + 2\,CO_2 + 2\,H_2O$

B. $Ag_2CO_3 + 2\,H^+ + 2\,Cl^- \rightarrow 2\,AgCl + CO_2 + H_2O$

C. $AgCO_3 + 2\,H^+ \rightarrow Ag^+ + CO_2 + H_2O$

D. $Ag_2CO_3 + 4\,Cl^- \rightarrow 2\,AgCl_2 + CO_3^{2-}$

A student has 25.00 mL of 0.1000 *M* acetic acid and 25.00 mL of 0.1000 *M* hydro-chloric acid. He wishes to titrate each of these samples with a sodium hydroxide solu-tion. He reasons that it will take more base to titrate the hydrochloric acid because it is a strong electrolyte, meaning that all the hydrogen ions are dissociated and can react. Acetic acid is a weak acid so some of the hydrogen ions are not dissociated, which means they cannot react. Do you agree with this student? Explain why or why not.

A student writes the following chemical equation:

$$2\,AgNO_3(aq) + Mg(s) \rightarrow Mg(NO_3)_2(aq) + 2\,Ag(s)$$

She then goes on the state that the silver, Ag, is a spectator ion. What is wrong with her statement?

Day 19

The reaction between magnesium metal and sulfur to form magnesium sulfide may be classified as a combination reaction, but it also may be classified as a redox reaction. Write the two balanced half-reactions for the formation of magnesium sulfide and label them as oxidation or reduction. Then write the balanced redox reaction.

A titration utilizing potassium dichromate may be used to determine the amount of iron in an ore. The half-reactions involved in the titration are shown below:

$$6\ e^- + Cr_2O_7^{2-} + 14\ H^+ \rightarrow 2\ Cr^{3+} + 7\ H_2O$$

$$Fe^{2+} \rightarrow Fe^{3+} + e^-$$

1.2802 grams of an ore sample are dissolved and all the iron is reduced to Fe^{2+}. It required 31.95 mL of 0.01525 M $K_2Cr_2O_7$ to titrate the sample.

Using the half-reactions, determine the balanced net ionic equation for the titration. Calculate the percent iron in the ore.

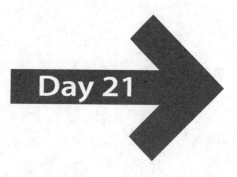

Day 21

Aluminum metal will react with the strong hydrohalic acids (HCl, HBr, and HI) to produce hydrogen gas and an aqueous aluminum halide ($AlCl_3$, $AlBr_3$, or AlI_3) solution. How many molecular equations are necessary to describe these three reactions? How many net ionic equations are necessary to describe these three reactions?

A student is investigating double-displacement reactions. She takes 100.0 mL of a 0.1 M hydrochloric acid solution and mixes it with 50.0 mL of a 0.1 M sodium carbonate solution. Write the balanced molecular equation for this double-displacement reaction. The student also notices that bubbles form in the solution and a clear solution results. Write a balanced chemical equation for the reaction that produces the gas. Then write a balanced chemical equation for the overall reaction.

While the student in the previous question (the one studying double-displacement reactions) is working, a friend of hers happens by and they discuss the reaction. Her friend says, "That reaction isn't a double-displacement reaction; it's an acid-base reaction!" Which student is correct and why? What type of reaction is the formation of the gas?

___CH$_4$(g) + ___O$_2$(g) → ___CO$_2$(g) + ___H$_2$O(l)   (Unbalanced)

How many moles of O$_2$ will react with 1.00 mole of CH$_4$ according to the above reaction?

LP gas (or liquid propane, C_3H_8, gas) burns in oxygen, O_2, gas according to the following equation:

$$C_3H_8(g) + 5\ O_2(g) \rightarrow 3\ CO_2(g) + 4\ H_2O(l)$$

Describe this reaction on a molecular level, a molar level, and a mass level.

There are several environmental issues associated with the smelting of ores. One of these issues involves sulfur compounds. Many metal ores are found as sulfides, such as PbS. As these ores undergo the smelting process, the first step is the reaction of the ore with oxygen. A common product of this reaction is sulfur dioxide, a toxic gas. The sulfur dioxide can then react with more oxygen gas to produce sulfur trioxide, another toxic oxide of sulfur. If the sulfur trioxide is allowed to enter the atmosphere, it can react with the water vapor in the atmosphere to produce sulfuric acid, which can fall to Earth as acid rain. Write balanced chemical equations for the combination (addition) reactions that produce sulfur trioxide and sulfuric acid.

5 Minutes to a 5

Day 27

A common way of generating small amounts of oxygen gas in the laboratory is to heat either solid potassium chlorate or mercury(II) oxide. Write a balanced equation for each of these two decomposition reactions. What are the potential problems associated with each method?

CHAPTER 7 – STOICHIOMETRY

Why does 6:02 a.m. on October 23 signal what is commonly referred to as Mole Day? Why is this not true of 6:02 p.m. on October 23?

The atomic mass of copper, Cu, is 63.546 amu. Natural copper consists of two isotopes, copper-63 and copper-65. The mass of a copper-63 atom is 62.9296 amu, and the mass of a copper-65 atom is 64.9278 amu. Determine the percent abundance of each isotope.

Determine the percent composition of glucose, $C_6H_{12}O_6$. The formula mass of glucose is 180.158 amu.

A 1.778-g sample of an unknown solid was burned in oxygen, and 2.842 g of CO_2, 0.2609 g of H_2O, and 0.4056 g of N_2 were produced. The compound contained C, H, N, and O. Determine its empirical formula.

Day 32

In the previous problem, it was also determined that the formula weight (FW) of the unknown was about 740 g/mole. Determine the molecular formula of the unknown.

Write the ionization of nitric acid, first without showing the water solvent and then using it. Then write the dissociation of sodium hydroxide. Why is it incorrect to show the hydroxide ion in combination with water, as you did with the hydrogen ion?

A student is studying the reaction between hydrogen and oxygen gases to produce water. The student places 50.0 grams of hydrogen gas and an excess of oxygen gas into a reaction vessel, seals the container, and ignites the mixture. What are the maximum grams of water that can be formed? How many grams of oxygen were consumed?

5 Minutes to a 5

A scientist is investigating the combustion reaction of acetone, C_3H_6O, with oxygen gas to produce carbon dioxide and water vapor. She mixes 300.0 grams of acetone with 600.0 grams of oxygen gas, seals the reaction container, and ignites the mixture. What is the maximum number of grams of carbon dioxide that can be formed? If she isolated only 300.0 grams of carbon dioxide, what would be the percent yield for the process?

One common method of analyzing a sample (such as fertilizer) for the amount of potassium is to dissolve a known mass of the sample in water and then treat it with an excess of a sodium tetraphenylborate ($NaB(C_6H_5)_4$) solution. The potassium will precipitate as potassium tetraphenylborate ($KB(C_6H_5)_4$). This is somewhat unusual because a vast majority of potassium salts are soluble. The potassium tetraphenylborate is then collected by filtration, dried, and weighed. Below are the results of such an analysis:

Mass of sample	4.2580 g
Mass of potassium tetraphenylborate collected	3.1215 g

Using this data, calculate the % K in the sample.

A chemistry teacher needs 10.0 liters of a solution that is approximately 0.5 molar in chloride ion for a class laboratory experiment. She has only solid magnesium chloride to use as a source of chloride ions. She asks you to prepare this solution. Describe what you need to do to prepare the solution. Include any appropriate calculations.

Day 38

Check out the following YouTube videos for a glimpse at what it is like to be chemist:

https://www.youtube.com/watch?v=L7GAx9b8HAQ

https://www.youtube.com/watch?v=s3N8qrdqzI8

Day 39

For a humorous look at lab safety (and zombies) check out

https://www.youtube.com/watch?v=S6WARqVdWrE

CHAPTER 8 – GASES

Many times, in labs dealing with gases, the atmospheric pressure is needed. If a barometer is not available, how can you find out the current barometric pressure in your location?

Day 41

The Kinetic Molecular Theory (KMT) works well under most conditions, but it does have limitations. What are the limitations of the KMT?

Day 42

Fill in the blank in each of the columns below with I (increases), D (decreases), or C (constant). The potential changes apply to a sample of gas.

	Condition 1	Condition 2	Condition 3	Condition 4	Condition 5
Moles	__(a)__	constant	constant	constant	constant
Volume	constant	__(b)__	constant	constant	increases
Temperature	constant	decreases	__(c)__	increases	constant
Pressure	increases	constant	increases	__(d)__	__(e)__

A lab section of students was determining the molar mass of an unknown gas by Graham's Law. They found that oxygen gas effused at a rate of 26.45 mL/min, whereas the unknown gas, under the same conditions, effused at a rate of 18.70 mL/min.

After the students completed their calculations and compared their answers, they noted that some students had an answer of 32.01 g/mole and others had an answer of 64.02 g/mole. Which group was correct and what common error probably accounted for the difference?

A sample of a gas occupies 11.5 L at a temperature of 25°C. What Celsius temperature is necessary to adjust the volume of the gas to 12.0 L?

Day 45

A 2.00-mole sample of hydrogen gas is placed in a sealed container. The gas is at a pressure of 1.00 atm at 25°C. What is the volume of the container?

Day 46

Part 1: A hydrocarbon is a compound containing only carbon and hydrogen. A 1.50-L container held 3.4 g of the unknown hydrocarbon at 37°C and 1.00 atm. Determine the molar mass of the hydrocarbon.

5 Minutes to a 5

Part 2: A chemistry student analyzed a sample of the unknown hydrocarbon gas from Part 1 and found that it contained 82.66% carbon and 17.34% hydrogen. What was the molecular formula of the hydrocarbon?

The reaction below is one method of preparing small amounts of nitrogen gas. How many grams of NH_2Cl would be necessary to produce 12.3 L of N_2 over water at 31°C and a total pressure of 795 mmHg? (The vapor pressure of water at 31°C is 32 torr.)

$$2 \, NH_2Cl(s) + N_2H_4(aq) \rightarrow 2 \, NH_4Cl(aq) + N_2(g)$$

Day 49

A chemist places a 2.50-mole sample of chlorine gas (Cl_2) into a 1.00-L steel container at 25°C. He calculates the pressure exerted by the gas to be 61.2 atm. However, when he measures the pressure of the gas, he finds it to be 31 atm. Was the discrepancy due to an error in his calculations or to some other factor? Justify your answer.

Day 50

Check out these two YouTube videos on Graham's Law:

> https://www.youtube.com/watch?v=I2klwb-V1HQ (large tube demo)

If one calculates molar masses using the data from the video, there is an error related to the procedure. What in the procedure would cause the error?

> https://www.youtube.com/watch?v=nqaNyvLKYdo

Are there any other factors that might cause the effect demonstrated? What could be done to control some of the other variables?

CHAPTER 9 – THERMODYNAMICS

A student places a thermometer in a beaker of water and measures the temperature. Next she adds some ice and, after five minutes, measures the temperature again. Explain whether she observed an exothermic or an endothermic change relative to the water.

A cook places two pans of water on a stove and turns the heat on high. One pan contains 1.5 L of water, and the other contains 3.0 L of water.

(a) If both pans are heated at the same rate, which will boil first? Does this observation indicate that heat is an intensive property or an extensive property?

(b) If the water in the pan with less water is boiling at 100°C, what is the temperature of boiling water in the other pan? Does this observation indicate that the boiling point is an intensive property or an extensive property?

Day 53

Discuss how a person driving from Los Angeles, California, to Atlanta, Georgia, is analogous to Hess's Law.

$$\text{N}_2(g) + 3\,\text{H}_2(g) \rightarrow 2\,\text{NH}_3(g) \qquad \Delta H° = -93 \text{ kJ/mol}$$

Given the above thermochemical equation, it is possible to determine the heat of reaction for the reverse reaction simply by changing the sign of $\Delta H°$. Why is this possible?

Hydrogen gas burns in oxygen gas according to the following reaction:

$$2\ H_2(g) + O_2(g) \rightarrow 2\ H_2O(l) \qquad \Delta H = -572\ kJ$$

What is the energy change when 2.00 moles of water decompose to the elements at constant pressure?

A 25.00-g sample of lead metal was heated to 75.00°C. This sample was clamped in contact with a 37.00-g sample of magnesium metal at 15.00°C. The specific heat of lead metal is 0.127 J/g °C, and the specific heat of magnesium metal is 1.024 J/g °C. Assuming no heat is lost to the surroundings, what was the final temperature of the two metals?

Day 57

Consider these three thermochemical equations:

(1) $2 H_2(g) + O_2(g) \rightarrow 2 H_2O(l)$ $\Delta H° = -571.6$ kJ

(2) $N_2O_5(g) + H_2O(l) \rightarrow 2 HNO_3(l)$ $\Delta H° = -76.6$ kJ

(3) $N_2(g) + 3 O_2(g) + H_2(g) \rightarrow 2 HNO_3(l)$ $\Delta H° = -348.2$ kJ

Determine $\Delta H°$ for the following reaction:

(4) $2 N_2(g) + 5 O_2(g) \rightarrow 2 N_2O_5(g)$

Watch the following YouTube video on determining the number of Calories in a nacho cheese Dorito by using "bomb calorimetry." What are some sources of experimental error in this experiment? Outline the measurements and calculations that one would have to do in determining the number of Calories in this chip.

https://www.youtube.com/watch?v=Ip8Nppmm11k

Day 59

For a discussion of the laws of thermodynamics, see the following YouTube video:

https://www.youtube.com/watch?v=8N1BxHgsoOw

According to the Second Law of Thermodynamics, a spontaneous process must be accompanied by a positive entropy change. How can water spontaneously freeze in a freezer when the entropy change of the water is negative?

Day 61

For a good discussion of entropy, see the following YouTube video:

https://www.youtube.com/watch?v=ZsY4WcQOrfk

Day 62

If going from the liquid state to the solid state is accompanied by a negative entropy change, explain, in terms of the Second Law of Thermodynamics, why water freezes.

A chemist is studying a new chemical reaction. She finds that the reaction is nonspontaneous under standard conditions but becomes spontaneous when the temperature is lowered. What conclusion can she draw about the reaction under standard conditions? Explain her reasoning.

A. $\Delta H < 0$, $\Delta S < 0$, and $\Delta G = 0$

B. $\Delta H > 0$, $\Delta S < 0$, and $\Delta G > 0$

C. $\Delta H < 0$, $\Delta S < 0$, and $\Delta G > 0$

D. $\Delta H > 0$, $\Delta S > 0$, and $\Delta G > 0$

Using the information in the following table, calculate $\Delta G°$ at 298 K for the reaction below. Then calculate the value of ΔG when the partial pressures are CH_3OH = 0.00180 atm, O_2 = 0.200 atm, CO = 0.00187 atm, and H_2O = 0.000375 atm.

$$CH_3OH(g) + O_2(g) \rightarrow CO(g) + 2\ H_2O(g)$$

	$\Delta G_F°$ (kJ/mol)
$CH_3OH(l)$	−166.2
$CH_3OH(g)$	−161.9
$CO(g)$	−137.2
$H_2O(l)$	−237.2
$H_2O(g)$	−228.6
$O_2(g)$	0.0

The Haber process is an industrial method for preparing ammonia. This process involves the combination of nitrogen gas with hydrogen gas. The reaction is

$$N_2(g) + 3 H_2(g) \rightarrow 2 NH_3(g)$$

Industrially, the Haber process operates at high pressure and at high temperatures in the presence of a catalyst. Determine the value of ΔG at the temperature of 300.0 K, given that the partial pressure of nitrogen is 33.3 atm, the partial pressure of hydrogen is 100.0 atm, and the partial pressure of ammonia is 67.7 atm. Assume $\Delta G° = -33.4$ kJ/mol.

Day 66

For a good discussion of how we can use Gibbs free energy to predict spontaneity, see the following YouTube video:

https://www.youtube.com/watch?v=huKBuShAa1w

↑ 5 Minutes to a 5

Day 67

CHAPTER 10 – SPECTROSCOPY, LIGHT, AND ELECTRONS

For a good overview of light, check out the following YouTube video:

https://www.youtube.com/watch?v=rLNM8zI4Q_M

What questions did this video raise in your mind? Write them down and ask your teacher.

Day 68

For a good overview of waves, check out the following YouTube video:

https://www.youtube.com/watch?v=RnllmggF8rw

Day 69

Check out the following YouTube video on atomic spectra:

https://www.youtube.com/watch?v=hO2m94rxpkM

Why does each element have many different spectra? Are the spectra shown emission spectra or absorbance spectra? What is the difference between absorbance and emission spectra?

Day 70

Helium was first discovered on the sun during a solar eclipse (1868). How could scientists determine that they had discovered a new element without having a sample to study?

Day 71

We are all familiar with reactions that give off heat. Included are the combustion reactions that enable us to cook our food, enjoy a nice campfire, and so on. But some reactions give off light. The scientific term for this is *chemiluminescence*. Peruse the YouTube videos on this topic and get illuminated!

Quantum mechanics identifies four quantum numbers (n, l, m_l, and m_s). Decide which of these quantum numbers applies in each of the following cases.

(a) The shape of the orbital the electron occupies.

(b) The energy of an electron on an atom.

(c) The size of the orbital the electron occupies.

(d) How the electron orbital is oriented in space.

(e) In which direction the electron is spinning.

How many sets of the four quantum numbers are possible to electrons in the 2p sub-shell of a helium atom?

At one time, the electrons were thought to move in orbits inside the atom in a manner analogous to planets orbiting the sun. What is wrong with this idea?

Day 75

Check out the following YouTube video on the shapes of orbitals:

https://www.youtube.com/watch?v=U7dEmdJnJMU

Find the error in the labeling of an orbital.

Day 76

How does the energy of the 4s orbital change from hydrogen to uranium?

Check out the following YouTube video for some practice in interpreting PES spectra:

https://www.youtube.com/watch?v=NRIqXeY1R_I

How could PES be used in identifying an unknown element?

A chemistry class performs an experiment to determine the formula of a hydrate. The general formula for a hydrate is Salt•xH_2O. Each student takes a crucible and lid and heats them with a Bunsen burner until they glow red. The crucible and lid are allowed to cool to room temperature and weighed. The heating/weighing procedure is repeated until the mass of the crucible plus lid is constant. At that point a few grams of a hydrated salt are added to the crucible, and the mass of the crucible plus lid plus hydrate is determined. The crucible, lid, and contents are first gently heated to drive away the water and then heated to a higher temperature to complete the process and yield the anhydrous salt. The crucible and contents are allowed to cool to room temperature and weighed. The heating/weighing of the sample is repeated until the mass is constant. One student reported the following data:

Mass of crucible plus lid	15.973 g
Mass of crucible, lid, and hydrate	20.603 g
Mass of crucible, lid, and anhydrous salt	17.693 g

Answer the following questions based on this data.

(a) What was the mass of water in the hydrate?

(b) How many moles of water were in the hydrate? (The molar mass of water is 18.015 g mol^{-1}.)

(c) How many moles of anhydrous salt were in the hydrate? (The molar mass of the anhydrous salt is 105.989 g mol^{-1}.)

(d) The general formula of a hydrate is Salt•xH_2O. What is the value of x?

(e) If the salt is Na_2CO_3, what are the name and formula of the hydrated salt?

CHAPTER 11 – BONDING

(a) Using Lewis structures, write balanced chemical equations illustrating the first and second electron affinities of sulfur.

(b) Using Lewis structures, write balanced chemical equations illustrating the first and second ionization energies of calcium.

(c) Based on these equations, comment on the third electron affinity of sulfur and the third ionization energy of calcium.

Which element can never obey the octet rule in any compound it forms? Explain your reasoning.

In the formation of an odd-electron molecule, such as NO_2, which atom is the most likely not to have an octet?

You are beginning to draw a Lewis structure for a compound. You come up with two different arrangements for the atoms. Give two factors that may help you decide which of the two arrangements is more likely.

Day 83

Write a balanced chemical equation for each of the following reactions. Use Lewis symbols for the reactants and products. Begin with individual atoms of the elements involved, and end with the appropriate compound.

(a) Chlorine atoms react with fluorine atoms to produce ClF_3.

(b) Aluminum atoms react with fluorine atoms to produce AlF_3.

Compound	Lattice Energy (kJ mol⁻¹)	Ion	Ionic Radius (pm)	Ion	Ionic Radius (pm)
NaF	900	F^-	119	Na^+	116
KF	800	O^{2-}	126	K^+	152
CaO	3600			Ca^{2+}	114
BaO	3200			Ba^{2+}	149
MgO	3900			Mg^{2+}	86

The lattice energy table above lists values for five compounds with the same structure. The lattice energy is the energy holding the structure together. The table also lists the ionic radii of the ions present in these ionic compounds. Based on this information, answer the following questions.

(a) Compare the compounds NaF and KF or CaO and BaO, and postulate why one of the compounds in each of these pairs has a higher lattice energy than the other.

(b) Compare the compounds NaF and CaO or KF and BaO, and postulate why one of the compound in each of these pairs has a higher lattice energy than the other.

(c) Which fundamental law of nature accounts for the observations in parts (a) and (b)?

(d) The compound CaS adopts the same structure as the other compounds in the lattice energy table. Predict how the lattice energy of CaS will compare to that of CaO, and justify your answer.

(e) Another compound that adopts the same structure as the other compounds in the lattice energy table is CrN. The ions in CrN are similar in size to the ions in MgO. Predict how the lattice energy of CrN will compare to that of MgO, and justify your answer.

5 Minutes to a 5

Day 85

The compounds BF_3, NF_3, and ClF_3 have very different structures. Why?

Explain why the ClF$_3$ molecule is polar and the BF$_3$ molecule is not polar. Use Lewis (electron-dot) structures in your answer.

Day 87

Are there any circumstances in which a molecule with the formula AX could be nonpolar?

Usually, a compound consisting of a metal and a nonmetal is ionic; however, there are exceptions. An ionic bond forms when the electronegativity difference between two atoms is 1.8 or greater. Using this criterion, is the bond between the metal beryllium (Be) and the nonmetal iodine (I) ionic, covalent, or polar covalent? What about the bond between gold (Au) and iodine (I)?

There are three compounds with the general formula $C_2H_2F_2$. Two of the compounds are polar and one is nonpolar. Draw the structures and label them as polar or nonpolar.

Acetic acid, CH_3COOH, is a covalently bonded molecule. What hybridizations do the carbon atoms utilize in acetic acid?

Day 91

For a discussion of common mistakes that students make in determining the shape of molecules, see the following YouTube video:

https://www.youtube.com/watch?v=8Tl_bDWCAmo

For a great discussion of paramagnetism and diamagnetism, see the following YouTube video:

https://www.youtube.com/watch?v=u36QpPvEh2c

Why is liquid oxygen paramagnetic?

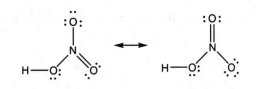

The accompanying figure shows two resonance forms of nitric acid. It is possible to use either of these structures and a table of bond energies to determine the standard heat of formation of nitric acid from the elements. How would the value determined by this method compare to the experimentally accepted value? Explain your answer.

Resonance structures are necessary to describe the bonding in which of the following? Explain your choice.

A. H_2S

B. BrF_3

C. HNO_3

D. SiH_4

The Haber process is used industrially to synthesize ammonia from the elements. The reaction is

$$N_2(g) + 3\ H_2(g) \rightarrow 2\ NH_3(g)$$

The standard enthalpy of formation of ammonia is -46.1 kJ mol^{-1}. Calculate the standard enthalpy of formation for the above reaction using bond energies, and compare your results to the standard enthalpy of formation reported. Use bond energies from the following table in your calculation.

Bond	Average Bond Energy (kJ mol^{-1})
H:H	436.4
H:N	393
N:N	159
N::N	418
N:::N	941.4

Day 96

CHAPTER 12 – SOLIDS, LIQUIDS, AND INTERMOLECULAR FORCES

A student wants to prepare 100.0 mL of a 50.0% (by volume) solution of an ethyl alcohol. She measures out 50.0 mL of water into a 100.0-mL volumetric flask, adds 50.0 mL of pure ethyl alcohol, and mixes. However, she notices that the liquid level is well below the 100.0-mL mark, about a 4-mL difference. Thinking that she has made a measuring error, she repeats the procedure but gets the same results. Explain why 50.0 mL + 50.0 mL does not equal 100.0 mL.

→ 5 Minutes to a 5

The hydrogen bonding that takes place in water is a strong interaction (intermolecular force). You can gain an appreciation of the strength of this force by a couple of simple activities. First, clean a penny (or any small coin). See how many drops of water you can place on the coin without the water overflowing. Next, fill a small cup with water until it overflows. You now have a full cup of water. Count how many paperclips you can add to this full cup before the cup overflows again.

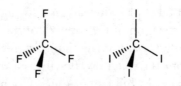

The two structures above show tetrahedral molecules CF_4 and CI_4. The reported boiling point of CF_4 is 145 K, and the reported boiling point of CI_4 is 408 K. What is the best explanation of why the boiling point of CI_4 so much higher than that of CF_4?

Which of the following molecules has hydrogen bonding as the strongest intermolecular force present?

A. CH_3OH

B. CH_3F

C. CH_4

D. $N(CH_3)_3$

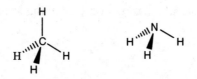

The above diagram shows the structures of methane, CH_4, and ammonia, NH_3. Methane is tetrahedral, and ammonia is trigonal pyramidal. The boiling point of methane is 112 K, and the boiling point of ammonia is 250 K. What is the best explanation of why the boiling point of ammonia is so much higher than that of methane?

Day 101

A chemist places a sample of a liquid into an open container and heats the liquid until it begins to boil. What is a way to increase the boiling point of the liquid?

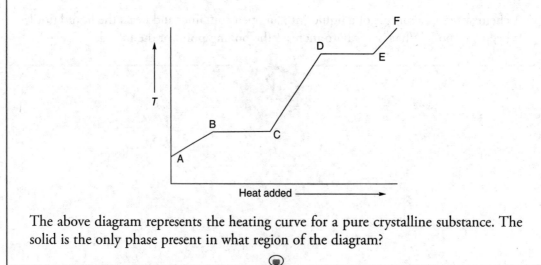

The above diagram represents the heating curve for a pure crystalline substance. The solid is the only phase present in what region of the diagram?

CHAPTER 13 – SOLUTIONS AND COLLIGATIVE PROPERTIES

Your chemistry teacher always told you that when you were diluting concentrated acid, you should carefully and slowly add the acid to the water. Why not add the water to the acid?

A student dissolves 3.224 g of sodium sulfate decahydrate ($Na_2SO_4 \cdot 10\ H_2O$) in enough water to make 750.0 mL of solution. Calculate the molarity of the sodium ion.

A chemistry student prepares a saturated aqueous solution of lithium bromide, LiBr. After she measures the electrical conductivity of the solution, she heats the solution to boiling. Which of the following best represents the behavior of this solution as it boils? Explain your choice.

The following symbols represent the various species that may be present:

● O   ○ H   ⊕ Li⁺   ⊖ Br⁻

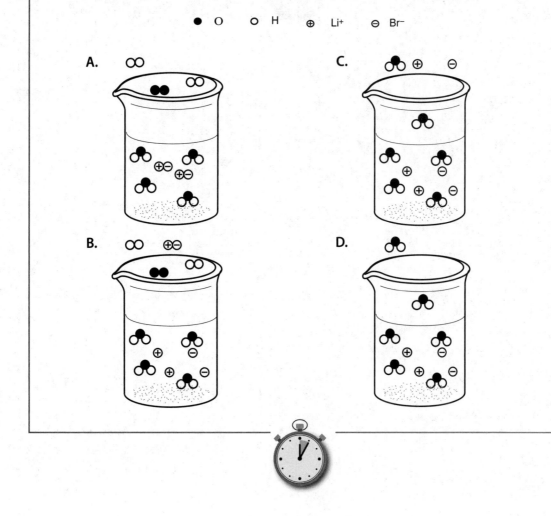

Day 106

What is the best method for isolating pure potassium phosphate, K_3PO_4, from a saturated aqueous solution of potassium phosphate?

For a discussion of colloids, see the following YouTube video:

https://www.youtube.com/watch?v=Yo07oWNJgAA

For a discussion of some applications of colloids, see the following YouTube video:

https://www.youtube.com/watch?v=s3yWnM2Y-rw

Day 108

For a discussion of hypertonic and hypotonic solutions related to red blood cells, view the following YouTube video:

https://www.youtube.com/watch?v=7-QJ-UUX0iY

Fish survive because of the presence of oxygen gas dissolved in water. Which of the following sets of conditions would result in the highest concentration of dissolved oxygen gas?

A. Temperature of water = 25°C; partial pressure of oxygen gas = 0.10 atm

B. Temperature of water = 35°C; partial pressure of oxygen gas = 0.050 atm

C. Temperature of water = 25°C; partial pressure of oxygen gas = 0.20 atm

D. Temperature of water = 45°C; partial pressure of oxygen gas = 0.20 atm

CHAPTER 14 – KINETICS

$$H_2O_2(aq) + 2\ Fe^{2+}(aq) + 2\ H^+(aq) \rightarrow 2\ Fe^{3+}(aq) + 2\ H_2O(g)$$

A chemist was studying the above reaction. She found that when she doubled the concentration of H^+(aq), there was no change in the rate of the reaction. What does this indicate about the mechanism of the reaction?

Experiment	Initial [H₂] (M)	Initial [NO] (M)	Initial Rate of Formation of N₂O (M s⁻¹)
1	0.200	0.200	2.24×10^6
2	0.400	0.200	4.48×10^6
3	0.200	0.400	8.96×10^6

The table above gives the initial concentrations and rates for three experiments examining the following reaction:

$$H_2(g) + 2\ NO(g) \rightarrow N_2O(g) + H_2O(g).$$

What is the rate law for this reaction?

Day 112

A method for modeling the process of chemical reactions is called collision theory. Describe the basic concepts of collision theory.

Step 1: $2 \, NO_2(g) \rightarrow N_2(g) + 2 \, O_2(g)$

Step 2: $2 \, CO(g) + O_2(g) \rightarrow 2 \, CO_2(g)$

Step 3: $N_2(g) + O_2(g) \rightarrow 2 \, NO(g)$

The above series of steps represents a proposed mechanism for the reaction of NO_2 with CO. Which of the following best represents the energy profile for this reaction?

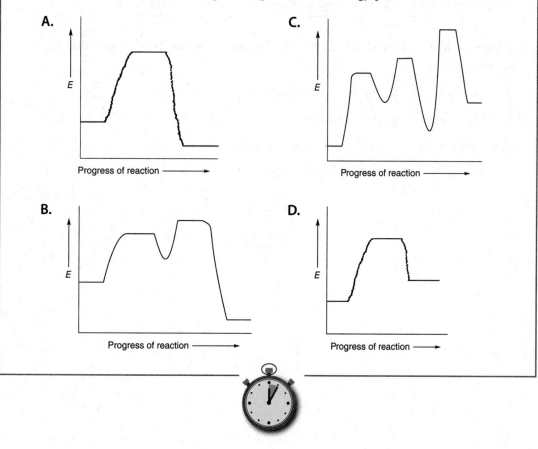

Day 114

The following mechanism is proposed for the reaction

$$CO(g) + Cl_2(g) \leftrightharpoons COCl_2(g) \qquad \Delta H = -109 \text{ kJ}$$

Step 1: $Cl_2(g) \leftrightharpoons 2\,Cl(g)$	(fast) k_1 and k_{-1}
Step 2: $Cl(g) + CH_4(g) \rightarrow HCl(g) + CH_3(g)$	(slow) k_2
Step 3: $Cl(g) + CH_3(g) \rightarrow CH_3Cl(g)$	(fast) k_3

Which of the following observations would support the suggested mechanism for the above reaction?

A. The rate of the reaction increases when the system is heated.

B. CH_3 is detected spectroscopically.

C. Changing the temperature does not change the rate constant.

D. The reaction does not reach equilibrium.

The reaction $2 \, ClO_2(aq) + 2 \, OH^-(aq) \rightarrow ClO_3^-(aq) + ClO_2^-(aq) + H_2O(l)$ has the rate law Rate $= k[ClO_2]^2[OH^-]$. The following is the proposed mechanism for this reaction:

Step 1: $ClO_2 + ClO_2 \rightarrow Cl_2O_4$

Step 2: $Cl_2O_4 + OH^- \rightarrow ClO_3^- + HClO_2$

Step 3: $HClO_2 + OH^- \rightarrow ClO_2^- + H_2O$

Which step is the rate-determining step?

Most chemistry students are familiar with the reaction of the alkali metals with water. The reaction involving lithium is tame, the reaction with sodium is a little more violent, and the reaction with potassium is even more violent. But what about adding rubidium and cesium to water? Check out the following YouTube video for a look at what happens when you add Rb and Cs to water:

https://www.youtube.com/watch?v=m55kgyApYrY

Then check out this film clip from 1947, where the Army is disposing of drums of sodium metal in a lake:

https://www.youtube.com/watch?v=HY7mTCMvpEM

Day 117

Botulinum toxin A is one of the most toxic substances in the world. It has an LD_{50} of 3.0×10^{-8} mg/kg of body weight. The average adult has a weight of 70 kg. If a 1.0-gram sample of botulinum toxin A were released in the United States, how many adults would be exposed to the LD_{50} dosage? Would they all die?

CHAPTER 15 – EQUILIBRIUM

Your teacher asks, "How do you know a system is in equilibrium?" Two of your fellow students respond with the following answers. Discuss whether or not each answer is correct.

Student 1: "The system is in equilibrium when the reaction stops."

Student 2: "The system is in equilibrium when the concentrations are the same."

Day 119

Sketch a diagram indicating what happens to the concentrations of the reactants and the products as a system approaches equilibrium. Indicate where the system reaches equilibrium.

Day 120

For a good discussion of factors affecting the equilibrium state, see the following YouTube video:

https://www.youtube.com/watch?v=g5wNg_dKsYY

$$N_2O_4(g) \leftrightharpoons 2\,NO_2(g)$$

The above equilibrium is established in a sealed container at 150°C. The reaction is endothermic as written. Which of the following changes may increase the amount of NO_2 in the container? Explain your choice.

A. Decreasing the temperature of the container

B. Raising the temperature of the container

C. Adding 1 mole of $Ar(g)$ to the container

D. Decreasing the volume of the container

Day 122

At constant temperature, a change in volume will NOT affect the moles of substances present at equilibrium in which of the following reactions?

A. $2 \, NO_2(g) \leftrightarrows 2 \, NO(g) + O_2(g)$

B. $H_2(g) + Cl_2(g) \leftrightarrows 2 \, HCl(g)$

C. $BrF_5(g) \leftrightarrows BrF_3(g) + F_2(g)$

D. $CaCO_3(s) \leftrightarrows CaO(s) + CO_2(g)$

Indicate which of the following is the K_p expression for this equilibrium:

$$C(s) + H_2O(g) \leftrightharpoons CO(g) + H_2(g)$$

A. $K_p = \dfrac{[CO][H_2]}{[H_2O]}$

B. $K_p = \dfrac{[CO][H_2]}{[C][H_2O]}$

C. $K_p = \dfrac{P_{CO}P_{H_2}}{P_{H_2O}}$

D. $K_p = \dfrac{P_{CO}P_{H_2}}{P_C P_{H_2O}}$

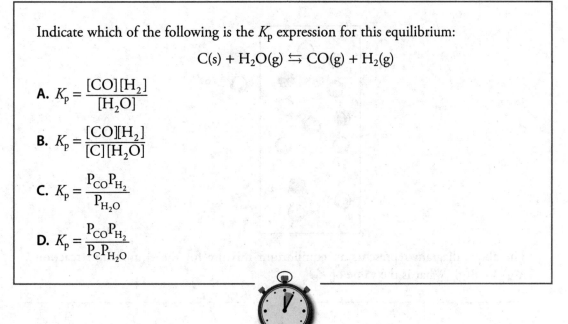

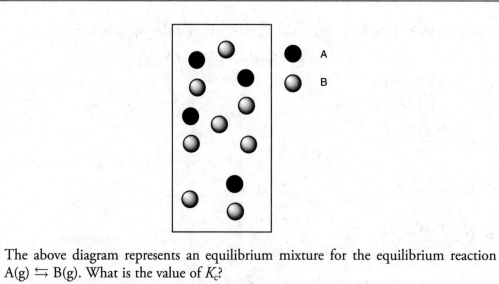

The above diagram represents an equilibrium mixture for the equilibrium reaction A(g) $\leftrightarrows$ B(g). What is the value of K_c?

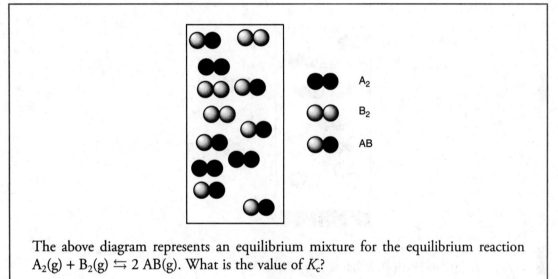

The above diagram represents an equilibrium mixture for the equilibrium reaction $A_2(g) + B_2(g) \leftrightarrows 2 AB(g)$. What is the value of K_c?

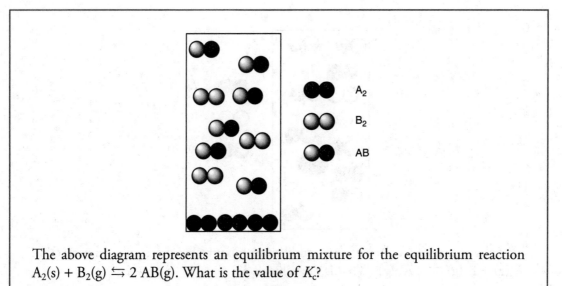

The above diagram represents an equilibrium mixture for the equilibrium reaction $A_2(s) + B_2(g) \rightleftharpoons 2\,AB(g)$. What is the value of K_c?

What will happen to the value of K as the temperature increases? Assume ΔG is also increasing.

A. K will decrease.

B. K will increase.

C. K will approach 1.

D. K is a constant and will not change.

Examine the following equilibrium problems. In each case, either give a means of simplification or state why the equilibrium problem is very difficult.

(a) $COCl_2(g) \leftrightharpoons CO(g) + Cl_2(g)$ has $K_c = 2.19 \times 10^{-10}$ at 100°C.

The initial concentration of phosgene, $COCl_2$, is 0.100 M, and the other two gases are initially 0 M.

(b) $BrF_3(g) + F_2(g) \leftrightharpoons BrF_5(g)$ has $K_c = 8.6 \times 10^{35}$ at 25°C.

The initial concentration of bromine pentafluoride is 0.250 M, and the other gases are initially 0 M.

(c) $2\ NOCl(g) \leftrightharpoons 2\ NO(g) + Cl_2(g)$ has $K_c = 1.6 \times 10^{-5}$ at 35°C.

All three gases have an initial concentration of 0.333 M.

(d) $NH_4HS(s) \leftrightharpoons NH_3(g) + H_2S(g)$ has $K_c = 1.2 \times 10^{-4}$ at 25°C.

Initially, there is 1.00 gram of NH_4HS in a 5.00-L container, and none of the other materials is present.

The addition of each of the following substances to water results in either an acidic or a basic solution. In each case, predict whether the solution will be acidic or basic, and write a balanced chemical equation(s) to support your prediction.

(a) $HC_2H_3O_2(l)$

(b) $NH_3(g)$

(c) $Na_2O(s)$

(d) $Cl_2O_7(l)$

(e) $NH_4Cl(s)$

(f) $KNO_2(s)$

The three most commonly used acid-base theories are the Arrhenius theory, the Brønsted-Lowry theory, and the Lewis theory. Define an acid and a base according to each of these three theories, and then use each of the theories to discuss the following acid-base reaction:

$$HCl(aq) + NH_3(aq) \rightarrow NH_4Cl(aq)$$

One of the salts of benzoic acid, $HC_7H_5O_2$, is sodium benzoate. This salt is a useful food preservative. A chemist at a food manufacturer obtains what she believes is a contaminated sample of benzoic acid. She prepares a 0.12 M solution of the acid and determines the acidity and the concentration of benzoate ion. She finds that $[H^+] = 4.0 \times 10^{-3}$ M and $[C_7H_5O_2^-] = 1.0 \times 10^{-5}$ M. Benzoic acid has $K_a = 6.5 \times 10^{-5}$ for the equilibrium shown below. Determine the value of ΔG of the solution.

$$HC_7H_5O_2(aq) \leftrightharpoons H^+(aq) + C_7H_5O_2^-(aq)$$

A sodium hydroxide solution has a pH of 12.00. Calculate the hydroxide ion concentration of this solution by two different methods.

A student prepares a 1.0×10^{-3} M solution of hydrochloric acid, HCl, which he labels solution A. He prepares solution B by adding 1.00 mL of solution A to a 100-mL volumetric flask containing some water, and then he fills the flask to the mark. He next prepares solution C by adding 1.00 mL of solution B and diluting it in another 100-mL volumetric flask. Finally, he prepares solution D via a similar dilution using solution C and another 100-mL volumetric flask. Finally, he calculates the following pH values for the solutions.

Solution	pH
A	3.0
B	5.0
C	7.0
D	9.0

Do you agree or disagree with his calculated results? Explain why you agree or disagree.

The K_a value for the compound phenol, C_6H_5OH, is 1.0×10^{-10}. A solution is prepared by dissolving 0.94 grams of phenol (0.010 moles) in 100.00 mL of water to produce a 0.10 M solution of phenol. What is the pH of this 0.10 M solution of phenol?

A. The pH is between 3 and 7.

B. The pH is about 10.

C. The pH is about 1.

D. The pH is between 7 and 10.

Which of the following is closest to the pH of a 0.10 M solution of formic acid, HCOOH? Explain your reason for making the choice you did.

A. 1

B. 3

C. 7

D. 10

A chemistry student is asked to determine the pH of a 1.00×10^{-8} M HNO$_3$ solution. He reasons that because HNO$_3$ is a strong acid, he can determine the pH as follows:

$$pH = -\log [H^+] = -\log (1.00 \times 10^{-8}) = 8$$

What mistake did the student make?

Citric acid, $H_3C_6H_5O_7$, is a triprotic acid from lemons and other citrus fruits. As a triprotic acid, it has three K_a values: K_{a1}, K_{a2}, and K_{a3}. The values of the equilibrium constants are $K_{a1} = 7.4 \times 10^{-4}$, $K_{a2} = 1.8 \times 10^{-5}$, and $K_{a3} = 4.0 \times 10^{-7}$. Determine the pH of a 0.100 M solution of citric acid. What assumptions, if any, can be made?

A chemist has equimolar solutions of each of the following substances. Which has the lowest pH? Explain your choice.

A. NH_4Cl

B. KCl

C. Na_3PO_4

D. K_2CO_3

Which of the following statements is true when sodium hypochlorite, NaClO, dissolves in water?

A. The solution is acidic because of hydrolysis of the sodium ion.

B. The solution is basic because of hydrolysis of the ClO^- ion.

C. The solution is basic because of hydrolysis of the sodium ion.

D. The solution is acidic because of hydrolysis of the ClO^- ion.

Acetic acid has the structural formula pictured below. It is a weak monoprotic acid. (A monoprotic acid has only one acidic hydrogen atom.) The formula is often written as $HC_2H_3O_2$ or CH_3COOH. Examine the structure of acetic acid, and predict which of the four hydrogen atoms in acetic acid is the only acidic hydrogen atom. Then discuss which of the two ways of writing the formula is more indicative of the structure.

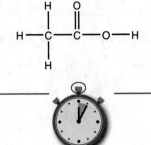

Chlorine forms the four oxyacids illustrated below. An oxyacid is an acid that contains hydrogen, oxygen, and another element. Rank the four acids in order of increasing strength, and explain your ranking.

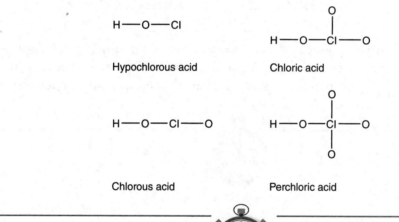

Acid	K_a, Acid Dissociation Constant
H_3PO_4	7.2×10^{-3}
$H_2PO_4^-$	6.3×10^{-8}
HPO_4^{2-}	4.2×10^{-13}

A chemist has some phosphoric acid, H_3PO_4; some potassium dihydrogen phosphate, KH_2PO_4; and some potassium hydrogen phosphate, K_2HPO_4. She wishes to prepare a pH = 8 buffer. Which two of these compounds are the best combination for preparing the buffer?

5 Minutes to a 5

Day 143

A chemist needs to prepare a buffer solution for a laboratory experiment. She determines that for the buffer to have the appropriate pH, she should use acetic acid, $HC_2H_3O_2$, as one of the components. For the second component of the buffer, her only choices are HCl, NaOH, and NaCl. What should she do to prepare a buffer solution where there is 1.00 mole of acetic acid present and an equal number of moles of the other component in 10.0 L of buffer?

A student is assigned the task of determining the concentration of citric acid in a lemon juice sample by titration. Citric acid is a triprotic acid.

(a) List the equipment and reagents needed.

(b) Outline the procedure and calculations.

Day 145

A student titrates a solution of an unknown weak base with a solution of a standard strong acid (0.1002 M HCl). The student follows the progress of the titration by plotting the readings from a pH meter to give a titration curve. Which of the following observations will the student make?

A. The addition of the acid causes the pH of the solution to gradually decrease during the experiment.

B. At first, the pH of the solution decreases slowly, and then there is a rapid decrease.

C. The endpoint of the titration occurs at a pH of 7.

D. After passing the endpoint, the pH becomes relatively constant because this is the buffer region.

Which of the following best indicates the titration curve for a titration involving the addition of standard hydrochloric acid, HCl, from a buret to a sodium carbonate solution? The reaction is as follows:

$$2\,HCl(aq) + Na_2CO_3(aq) \rightarrow 2\,NaCl(aq) + H_2O(l) + CO_2(g)$$

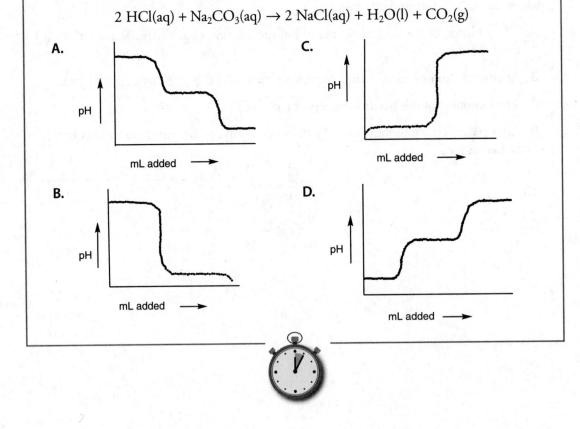

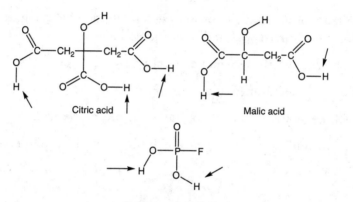

The arrows point to the acidic hydrogen atoms.

Acid	pH of a 1.0 *M* solution
Citric acid	1.56
Malic acid	2.23
Fluorophosphoric acid	0.28

During a chemistry laboratory experiment, solutions of each of the acids in the above diagram are titrated. The acid concentrations were 0.1000 *M*, and 0.1000 *M* sodium hydroxide, NaOH, was used for the titrations. Two of the acids required the same quantity of NaOH. Which two acids required the same volume of base for the titration?

A. Citric acid and malic acid.

B. Malic acid and fluorophosphoric acid.

C. Fluorophosphoric acid and citric acid.

D. The concentrations of all the acids were the same; therefore, all the acids required the same quantity of base.

5 Minutes to a 5

An indictor indicates the endpoint of an acid-base titration by changing color. Which of the following determines what indicator should be used?

A. The indicator should change color at a pH > 7.

B. The indicator should change color near pH = 7.

C. The pK_a of the indicator should be close to the pK_a of the acid.

D. The pK_a of the indicator should be close to the pH at the equivalence point.

The addition of hydrochloric acid increases the solubility of which of the following compounds?

A. KBr(s)

B. $Cd(CN)_2(s)$

C. $Mg(ClO_4)_2(s)$

D. $NH_4NO_3(s)$

The three compounds calcium carbonate, $CaCO_3$; silver chloride, AgCl; and lead(II) chloride, $PbCl_2$, are insoluble in water. It is possible to compare the solubilities of calcium carbonate and silver chloride directly by using their K_{sp} values. However, it is not possible to compare the solubility of lead(II) chloride to that of either of the other two compounds by directly comparing its K_{sp} value to theirs. Why is this the case?

Day 151

The K_{sp} of chromium(III) hydroxide, $Cr(OH)_3$, is 6.3×10^{-31}. The K_{sp} of chromium(II) hydroxide, $Cr(OH)_2$, is 1.0×10^{-17}. Explain why the K_{sp} for $Cr(OH)_3$ is smaller.

Write the solubility product, K_{sp}, chemical equation, and mass action expression for the addition of calcium arsenate, $Ca_3(AsO_4)_2$, to water. The K_{sp} of $Ca_3(AsO_4)_2$ is 6.8×10^{-19}. Ignore any other equilibria that might be present.

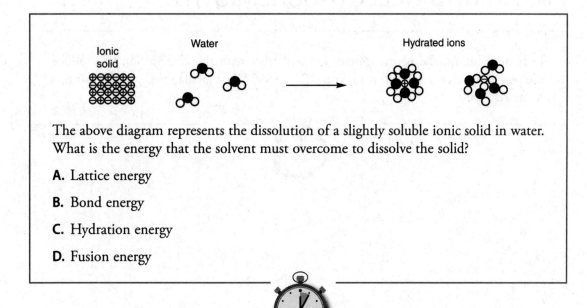

The above diagram represents the dissolution of a slightly soluble ionic solid in water. What is the energy that the solvent must overcome to dissolve the solid?

A. Lattice energy

B. Bond energy

C. Hydration energy

D. Fusion energy

Day 154

CHAPTER 16 – ELECTROCHEMISTRY

In basic solution, the permanganate ion will react with the chlorite ion to produce the perchlorate ion and solid manganese(IV) oxide. Write a balanced equation for this redox reaction.

Day 155

For an overview of electrochemical cells, view the following YouTube video:

https://www.youtube.com/watch?v=IV4IUsholjg

A chemist prepared a standard electrochemical cell and found that the voltage was 0.794 V. After constructing the cell, the chemist was interrupted and left for about 30 minutes. The cell was operating while the chemist was gone. Upon her return, the chemist checked the voltage and found that it had changed. Was the cell voltage higher or lower than it was at first? Explain why the voltage changed.

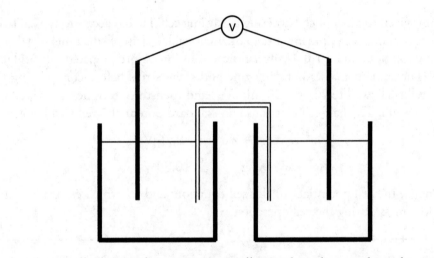

In the above cell, the anode reaction typically involves the metal anode undergoing oxidation to release ions into solution (for example, $Zn(s) \rightarrow Zn^{2+}(aq) + 2\ e^-$), and the cathode reaction typically involves ions in solution undergoing reduction to plate a metal onto the cathode (for example, $Cu^{2+}(aq) + 2\ e^- \rightarrow Cu(s)$). Give two reasons why the above cell will not work for the following redox reaction. One reason will apply to the anode compartment, and one will apply to the cathode compartment.

$$I_2(s) + 2\ Fe^{2+}(aq) \rightarrow 2\ I^-(aq) + 2\ Fe^{3+}(aq)$$

A student is given the task of constructing a galvanic cell. He has access to typical laboratory electrochemical equipment, a strip of zinc metal, a strip of silver metal, a 1.0 M zinc nitrate solution, and a 1.0 M silver nitrate solution. A pre-prepared salt bridge is available. The student masses both the zinc and silver strips before constructing the cell. The cell is allowed to run for 30 minutes, and then the electrodes are wiped dry and massed again. The half-cell reactions and standard potentials are listed below:

$$Zn^{2+} + 2\,e^- \rightarrow Zn \qquad -0.76\ V$$

$$Ag^+ + e^- \rightarrow Ag \qquad +0.80\ V$$

Determine (a) the cell potential; (b) the cell equation; and (c) which electrode, Zn or Ag, will lose mass during the cell operation.

A chemistry student attempts to prepare an electrolysis cell to produce potassium metal, K, from an aqueous solution of potassium chloride, KCl, using a 12.0-V automobile battery. The student was unsuccessful in producing any potassium. Why was he unable to produce potassium metal?

$$Ni^{2+} + 2\ e^- \rightarrow Ni(s) \qquad E° = -0.25\ V$$

$$Pb^{2+} + 2\ e^- \rightarrow Pb(s) \qquad E° = -0.13\ V$$

A chemist constructs an electrochemical cell to employ the two half-reactions above. Her goal is to isolate nickel metal from a nickel(II) chloride, $NiCl_2$, solution through a reaction with a lead(II) nitrate, $Pb(NO_3)_2$, solution. Is she constructing a galvanic cell or an electrolysis cell? Justify your answer.

Silicon that is to be used in the production of computer chips is produced by reacting purified silicon tetrachloride with hydrogen gas. The other product of the reaction is a gas that turns moist litmus paper red. Write the redox reaction for the process.

Day 162

A chemistry student constructs a voltaic cell to examine the following reaction:

$$Cd(s) + 2\,Ag^+(1\,M) \rightarrow 2\,Ag(s) + Cd^{2+}(1\,M)$$

The student found the cell voltage to be +1.20 volts. The student then accidently spills some deionized water into the cadmium compartment. What does the student find upon remeasuring the voltage after the accident?

A. The voltage does not change.

B. The voltage drops to zero.

C. The voltage increases.

D. The voltage decreases but stays above zero.

$$2\ \text{I}^-(aq) + 2\ \text{Fe}^{3+}(aq) \rightarrow \text{I}_2(s) + 2\ \text{Fe}^{2+}(aq)$$

A student constructed a voltaic cell to investigate the reaction shown above. When she measured the cell voltage, she found that her result was not equal to her calculated $E°$ for the cell. Which of the following might be the reason why her measured cell voltage was not the same as the standard cell voltage?

A. The cell was operated at 25°C instead of 0°C.

B. The anode and cathode were different sizes.

C. The cation in the anode compartment was potassium instead of sodium.

D. One or more of the ion concentrations were not 1 M.

A student is asked to construct an electrochemical (galvanic) cell. She is supplied with the appropriate equipment to construct a cell, including a pre-prepared salt bridge. However, the only chemicals she is given are a package of thin strips of copper metal and a 0.20 *M* copper(I) chloride solution. Describe how she could construct a galvanic cell and how she would go about calculating the cell voltage.

One type of rechargeable battery is the nickel-cadmium (NiCad) battery. The following half-reactions are important to the operation of this battery:

$$Cd(OH)_2(s) + 2e^- \rightarrow Cd(s) + 2\ OH^-(aq) \qquad E° = -0.76\ V$$

$$NiO_2(s) + 2\ H_2O(l) + 2e^- \rightarrow Ni(OH)_2(s) + 2\ OH^-(aq) \qquad E° = +0.49\ V$$

(a) Write a balanced redox equation for the discharging of a NiCad battery, and determine the standard cell potential.

(b) Write a balanced redox equation for the recharging of a NiCad battery.

(c) Calculate the $\Delta G°$ for discharging a NiCad battery.

(d) What are the values of ΔG and of E when a NiCad battery entirely discharges?

Day 166

POST – AP EXAM ENRICHMENT

How about a little chemistry trivia?

(a) Which element is found in the human body in the largest number of atoms? _____. In the greatest mass? _____.

(b) Which metal is most abundant in Earth's crust? _____.

(c) The most common element in the universe is _____.

(d) Which element is found in nature as a yellow solid but turns red when it melts? _____.

(e) Which metal is a liquid at room temperature (an easy one)? _____. Which element has such a low melting point that it will melt in your hand?

Now for a little chemistry fun at home (but don't forget your safety goggles). Let's make a polymer: Mix 15 mL of white glue with 15 mL of water. Then stir in 10 mL of a saturated borax solution. (Borax is a laundry booster and can be found in the grocery store with the laundry detergents. Add some of the solid borax to about a cup of water and mix well. If all the borax dissolves, add some more. Keep doing this until no more will dissolve, and you now have a saturated borax solution.) After mixing in the borax well, take the resulting substance (let's call it "Gluep") and knead it. Examine the properties of this substance. What type of polymer is this?

Back to our home lab: Get a box of corn starch from the pantry (but leave enough to make gravy later), put a cup of it into a metal or glass pie pan, and start adding water, just a little at a time. Mix the water and corn starch well. You should eventually get to a point where you can slap the corn starch mixture with your hand and not splash corn starch and water all over yourself and the kitchen. You have created a non-Newtonian substance. Examine its properties. Grab a handful and squeeze, then release. See if you can cut it with a knife. Put it into a balloon or rubber glove, tie it off and try squeezing. After experimenting, see if you can define the term *non-Newtonian substance* in your own words, and then look it up on the Internet.

Day 169

You are stranded on a desert island. Several cans of soda wash ashore, but most of the label has been worn off by the surf. You are reasonably sure the soda is a Coke® product from the little bit of remaining label, but is it regular Coke® or Diet Coke®? You are highly allergic to the artificial sweetener in Diet Coke®. Without tasting them, or even opening the cans, how can you determine whether the cans contain Coke® or Diet Coke®?

Are you aware of the dangers of dihydrogen monoxide (also known as hydroxyl acid)? It is a colorless, tasteless, and odorless liquid that causes the death of many people every year, normally by inhalation. It is the major component in acid rain and is classified as a greenhouse gas. The solid form is also dangerous, causing skin damage. Go online and learn more about this dangerous compound. There are petitions to ban dihydrogen monoxide in the United States. Evaluate the arguments for banning it. If you think banning it is a good idea, maybe you could start a petition at your school.

5 Minutes to a 5

Most concentrated acid solutions are stored in glass containers, but one of the few exceptions is hydrofluoric acid. Why is concentrated HF(aq) stored in plastic containers? What commercial process makes use of this property?

Here is another "try this at home" experiment: Take an empty soda can and put about 10 mL of water into it. Place it on a hot plate and heat until steam is coming out of the opening. Using tongs, quickly pick up the can, invert it, and place the open end of the can into shallow water in a pan. Describe what happens and explain why it happens.

The next time you are eating tacos at your favorite fast-food Mexican restaurant, pick up an extra packet of hot sauce. When you get home, find an empty 1- or 2-liter plastic bottle, put the unopened packet inside, and fill the bottle totally full of water. Screw the lid on tightly. Squeeze the bottle and make observations. Release and make more observations. Explain your results. What gas law are you demonstrating?

Day 174

One occasionally hears it said that Coke® contains cocaine. Do an Internet search on the formulation for Coke® and find out whether this claim is true.

Day 175

What do an orchestra and a cologne have in common?

Day 176

The lithium ion battery has many applications in consumer electronics, such as cell phones. During 2015–2016 there were a number of reports about these batteries causing fires. Research the reports of fires being caused by lithium ion batteries. (You might want to include "Samsung" among your search terms.) Do you think these batteries should be banned on commercial airline flights?

Almost everyone has witnessed someone inhaling helium and then speaking with a high, squeaky voice. This happens because helium's density is about one-sixth the density of air, so the sound waves travel much faster. But what happens when you breathe a gas that is denser than air? Do a YouTube video search on sulfur hexafluoride, and watch some of the videos associated with breathing SF_6. How do you get this gas out of your lungs?

Day 178

Have you ever wondered how, in the old days of the railroads, the road crews welded railroad tracks together? They used a redox reaction called the thermite reaction, in which rust (Fe_2O_3) is mixed with powdered aluminum metal and heated. Go on YouTube and view a couple of videos on the "thermite reaction." (One thing you will learn is why this experiment is not usually done in a high school lab.) Write the balanced equation for the thermite reaction. Then do another YouTube search on the "thermite reaction and railroad tracks" and learn about welding with thermite.

5 Minutes to a 5

Day 179

The technological wonders we see around us were once just an idea in some scientist's mind. It seems like almost every day a new material is made that can be used to solve some vexing problem. For an overview of some of these recent advances, check out the following YouTube video:

https://www.youtube.com/watch?v=az6oYcd-SfU

Day 180

Many chemistry teachers say very little about the rare-earth elements. For a neat little discussion, check out the following YouTube video:

https://www.youtube.com/watch?v=QiQoMDZGCs4

Day 181

Here are three bonus activities for the summer when you are bored and are starting to think about school again.

One of the statements I have often heard is that hot water freezes faster than cold water. That never really made sense to me. For a pretty good discussion of this phenomenon, watch the following YouTube video:

https://www.youtube.com/watch?v=UjIdzcxSe3g&list=PL245B82FF8F8ECAC2&index=25

The study of chemistry is interesting and fascinating, but chemistry can be dangerous. For a description of five of the world's most dangerous chemicals, check out the following YouTube video:

https://www.youtube.com/watch?v=ckSoDW2-wrc

Day 183

We just had to throw in the periodic table song:

https://www.youtube.com/watch?v=VgVQKCcfwnU

Here are the lyrics:

https://www.youtube.com/watch?v=1cqauZq4uYM

And this version is for you karaoke fanatics:

https://www.youtube.com/watch?v=bjQ3xZ3HKpI

Answers

Day 1

All of the scientists involved in these discoveries were well trained in their field, were very observant, and had keen, questioning minds. They were also able to think "outside the box." Check out the following video on serendipity:

https://www.youtube.com/watch?v=0WmZNGzhGHo

Day 2

Occam's razor says that if you have two or more competing explanations with no real way of distinguishing between them, choose the one that makes the fewest assumptions (that is, choose the simplest explanation). Thus, if you are on a Texas plain and you hear hoof beats, the simplest explanation is that horses are nearby. You don't have to make the assumption that zebras escaped from the zoo. But if you are in Africa, then the simplest explanation is that there are zebras nearby. The following videos offer some insight into the validity of Occam's razor:

https://www.youtube.com/watch?v=t0prjgMykU0

https://www.youtube.com/watch?v=KQeR0tZgjBY

Day 4

In order to do this conversion, make use of the density of water: 1.0 g/mL.

$$\frac{1.0 \text{ dL}}{1} \times \frac{0.1 \text{L}}{1 \text{ dL}} \times \frac{1{,}000 \text{ mL}}{\text{L}} \times \frac{1.0 \text{ g}}{1 \text{ mL}} \times \frac{1 \text{ mole water}}{18.0 \text{ g}} \times \frac{6.02 \times 10^{23} \text{ molecules}}{1 \text{ mole}}$$

$$= 3.3 \times 10^{24} \text{ molecules of water}$$

Day 5

$$\frac{1.50 \text{ g aspirin}}{\text{kg body weight}} \times \frac{1 \text{ kg}}{2.2 \text{ lb}} \times \frac{22 \text{ lb}}{1} \times \frac{1{,}000 \text{ mg}}{\text{g}} \times \frac{1 \text{ tablet}}{81 \text{ mg}} = 190 \text{ tablets}$$

This would amount to ingesting at least a couple of bottles, but unfortunately, small children have done worse things. A greater danger would be Reye's syndrome, a rare reaction to aspirin involving symptoms such as confusion, nausea, and even death.

Day 6

(a) **A**—A $2s^3$ configuration is not possible because s-orbitals cannot accommodate more than two electrons.

(b) **F**—The noble gases, except helium, are ns^2np^6. In this case, $n = 3$, and the gas is argon, Ar.

(c) **K**—The electron configuration for cobalt is $1s^2 2s^2 2p^6 3s^2 3p^6 3d^7 4s^2$. To produce a cobalt(II) ion, the two 4s electrons are removed first.

Day 7

Within a period, all the electrons enter the same outer shell. If no other changes were occurring, the atoms would all be the same size. However, moving toward the right in any period, the number of protons in the nucleus increases. This leads to an increase in the effective nuclear charge, which results in a greater attraction of the electrons to the nucleus. This greater attraction pulls the electrons in, to yield a smaller atom.

Day 8

The story points to the fact that the periodic table is universal.

Day 9

NaBr	sodium bromide	Silicon disulfide	SiS_2
N_2O_4	dinitrogen tetroxide	Carbon tetrabromide	CBr_4
Li_2O	lithium oxide	Barium nitride	Ba_3N_2
CaO	calcium oxide	Sulfur trioxide	SO_3
K_2S	potassium sulfide	Magnesium fluoride	MgF_2

Answers

Day 10

(a) ammonium ion, NH_4^+, and ammonia, NH_3

(b) hydrochloric acid, HCl, and chloric acid, $HClO_3$

(c) lithium nitride, Li_3N, and lithium nitrite, $LiNO_2$

(d) manganese(II) oxide, MnO, and manganese(III) oxide, Mn_2O_3

(e) manganese(II) oxide, MnO, and magnesium oxide, MgO

(f) potassium nitrate, KNO_3, and potassium nitrite, KNO_2

(g) tungsten(IV) oxide, WO_2, and tungsten(VI) oxide, WO_3

(h) iodic acid, HIO_3, and periodic acid, HIO_4

(i) ammonium hydrogen phosphate, $(NH_4)_2HPO_4$, and ammonium dihydrogen phosphate, $NH_4H_2PO_4$

(j) calcium sulfite, $CaSO_3$, and calcium bisulfite, $Ca(HSO_3)_2$

Note that although the AP test does not specifically test nomenclature, you are expected to know the nomenclature when you are working the problems. Basically, nomenclature is considered prior knowledge, and all prior knowledge is testable on the exam.

Day 11

The leftmost diagram (solid) illustrates a phase with a definite shape. In the other two diagrams (liquid and gas), the phase alters its shape to match that of the container. In the left two diagrams, the circles are in contact, with minimal space between the circles, which indicates the volume is relatively constant. In the case of the rightmost diagram (gas) there is a significant amount of space between the circles. It is easy to push these circles closer together, and hence the volume is variable.

Day 12

(a) Water can exist as a solid (ice), as a liquid, or as a gas (steam). It has the same composition in all cases; therefore, interconversions among these three phases are physical changes and not chemical changes.

(b) The conversion to the elements (hydrogen and oxygen) is the result of a chemical change.

(c) This is a physical change, which is easily reversible by allowing the water to evaporate, leaving the salt behind.

(d) Water can exist as a solid (ice), as a liquid, or as a gas (steam). It has the same composition in all cases; therefore, interconversions among these three phases are physical changes and not chemical changes.

(e) This is a chemical change because one set of chemicals (water and sodium) becomes a different set of chemicals (sodium hydroxide and hydrogen).

Day 13

(a) Haber process: $N_2(g) + 3\ H_2(g) \rightarrow 3\ NH_3(g)$

(b) Urea production: $2\ NH_3(g) + CO_2(g) \rightarrow NH_2CONH_2(aq) + H_2O(l)$

(c) N_2O production: $2\ (NH_2)_2CO + 2\ HNO_3 + H_2SO_4 \rightarrow 2\ N_2O + 2\ CO_2 + (NH_4)_2SO_4 + 2\ H_2O$

Day 14

One can use the melting point of substances to get some idea about their bonding. Ionic compounds tend to have higher melting points than covalent compounds. You would use an evaporating dish, a burner, and a thermometer or temperature probe. The problem with this procedure is that it will require a fairly large sample size in order to determine the melting point, and you were told that there was only a small amount of each sample.

   Another method of analysis is to determine whether the substances are electrolytes. This would require dissolving a small amount of each sample in water and then testing the solution with a conductivity apparatus. A simple, effective conductivity apparatus may be made from a 9-volt battery, a 100-ohm resistor, and an LED. If the LED lights, then the solution is conducting electricity and that substance is an electrolyte. Ionic compounds, even many of those that are only sparingly soluble, will produce enough ions to light the LED. Most molecular compounds will not produce ions in solution and thus will be nonelectrolytes.

Day 15

The general rule of solubility is that "like dissolves like." Water is a polar solvent, so it will dissolve polar solutes, such as ionic compounds and those molecular substances that have a polar part of the molecule. This includes acids, alcohols, and sugars. The polar nature of water is due to there being two O–H polar bonds and to the bent geometry of the water molecule. The oxygen end of the molecule is partial negative, and the hydrogen end is partial positive. Thus the molecule itself is polar.

Day 16

B—The question states that in this reaction all silver compounds are insoluble, which means that Ag^+ is not a possible product. Silver carbonate is insoluble, and its formula should be written as Ag_2CO_3. Hydrochloric acid is a strong acid, so it should be written as separate H^+ and Cl^- ions. Silver chloride, AgCl, is insoluble, and carbonic acid, H_2CO_3, quickly decomposes to CO_2 and H_2O.

Day 17

The student is incorrect. It will take the same amount of base to react with each of the acids because they have the same number of moles of acid. Although it is true that there are fewer dissociated hydrogen ions in the acetic acid solution, more will be released as the first hydrogen ions are titrated until all the acid hydrogen ions react.

Day 18

For an ion to be a spectator ion, it must be present on both sides of the reaction arrow in the same form. The silver is present as Ag^+ on the left and as Ag on the right. These are similar, but the fact that one is an ion and the other is not means that the silver is not a spectator.

Day 19

Magnesium is a metal and tends to lose two electrons:

$$Mg(s) \rightarrow Mg^{2+}(s) + 2\ e^- \qquad \text{oxidation (loss of electrons)}$$

Sulfur is found in nature as S_8. It is a nonmetal and tends to gain two electrons:

$$S_8(s) + 16\ e^- \rightarrow 8\ S^{2-}(s) \qquad \text{reduction (gain of electrons)}$$

Equalize electron loss and electron gain:

$$8 \times (Mg \rightarrow Mg^{2+}(s) + 2\ e^-)$$

$$S_8(s) + 16\ e^- \rightarrow 8\ S^{2-}(s)$$

Add the half-reactions and cancel electrons:

$$8\ Mg(s) + S_8(s) + \cancel{16\ e^-} \rightarrow 8\ Mg^{2+}(s) + \cancel{16\ e^-} + 8\ S^{2-}(s)$$

Simplify:

$$8\ Mg(s) + S_8(s) \rightarrow 8\ MgS(s)$$

Day 20

Equalize electron loss and gain:

$$6e^- + Cr_2O_7^{2-} + 14\ H^+ \rightarrow 2\ Cr^{3+} + 7\ H_2O$$

$$6 \times (Fe^{2+} \rightarrow Fe^{3+} + e^-)$$

Add the half-reactions and cancel electrons:

$$\cancel{6e^-} + Cr_2O_7^{2-} + 14\ H^+ + 6\ Fe^{2+} \rightarrow 2\ Cr^{3+} + 7\ H_2O + 6\ Fe^{3+} + \cancel{6e^-}$$

This means that there is a 1:6 mole ratio between dichromate and iron. Now apply the reaction stoichiometry:

$$\frac{0.01525\ \text{mole}\ Cr_2O_7^{2-}}{L} \times \frac{0.03195\ L}{1} \times \frac{6\ \text{moles}\ Fe^{2+}}{1\ \text{mole}\ Cr_2O_7^{2-}} \times \frac{1\ \text{mole}\ Fe}{1\ \text{mole}\ Fe^{2+}} \times \frac{55.845\ \text{g}\ Fe}{1\ \text{mole}\ Fe}$$

$$= 0.1633\ \text{g}\ Fe$$

To get the % iron in the sample, divide the mass of iron by the mass of the sample; then multiply by 100%:

$$\frac{0.1633\ \text{g}\ Fe}{1.2802\ \text{g}\ \text{sample}} \times 100\% = 12.75\%$$

Day 21

Three molecular equations are necessary:

$$2\ Al(s) + 6\ HCl(aq) \rightarrow 2\ AlCl_3(aq) + 3\ H_2(g)$$

$$2\ Al(s) + 6\ HBr(aq) \rightarrow 2\ AlBr_3(aq) + 3\ H_2(g)$$

$$2\ Al(s) + 6\ HI(aq) \rightarrow 2\ AlI_3(aq) + 3\ H_2(g)$$

The one and only net ionic equation is

$$2\ Al(s) + 6\ H^+(aq) \rightarrow 2\ Al^{3+}(aq) + 3\ H_2(g)$$

Day 22

The products of the double-displacement reaction between hydrochloric acid and sodium carbonate are aqueous carbonic acid and aqueous sodium chloride:

$$2\ HCl(aq) + Na_2CO_3(aq) \rightarrow H_2CO_3(aq) + 2\ NaCl(aq)$$

(Hydrogen and sodium have switched places.)

Carbonic acid is unstable and decomposes to carbon dioxide gas and water:

$$H_2CO_3(aq) \rightarrow CO_2(g) + H_2O(l)$$

Substituting the carbon dioxide and water for the carbonic acid gives the overall reaction:

$$2\ HCl(aq) + Na_2CO_3(aq) \rightarrow CO_2(g) + H_2O(l) + 2\ NaCl(aq)$$

Day 23

Both students are correct. The reaction is a double-displacement reaction because the hydrogen and sodium ions have displaced each other. However, the second student is also correct in that HCl is acting as an H^+ donor, and the carbonate ion is acting as an H^+ acceptor; therefore, the reaction may also be classified as an acid-base reaction. Remember: The same reaction may be classified in several different ways.

The formation of the carbon dioxide gas is a decomposition reaction because carbonic acid is decomposing to carbon dioxide gas and water.

Day 24

The balanced chemical equation is $CH_4(g) + 2\ O_2(g) \rightarrow CO_2(g) + 2\ H_2O(l)$.

According to the balanced chemical equation, 2.00 moles of O_2 are necessary to react with 1.00 mole of CH_4.

Day 25

Molecular: One molecule of C_3H_8 reacts with five molecules of O_2 to produce three molecules of CO_2 plus four molecules of H_2O.

Molar: One mole of C_3H_8 reacts with five moles of O_2 to produce three moles of CO_2 plus four moles of H_2O.

Mass: 44 grams of C_3H_8 reacts with 5×32 grams of O_2 to produce 3×44 grams of CO_2 plus 4×18 grams of H_2O.

Day 26

Formation of $SO_3(g)$:

$$2\ SO_2(g) + O_2(g) \rightarrow 2\ SO_3(g)$$

Formation of $H_2SO_4(aq)$:

$$SO_3(g) + H_2O(l) \rightarrow H_2SO_4(l)$$

Day 27

$$2\ KClO_3(s) \rightarrow 2\ KCl(s) + 3\ O_2(g)$$

$$2\ HgO(s) \rightarrow 2\ Hg(l) + O_2(g)$$

Potassium chlorate is explosive when heated in contact with organic material, so special care must be taken to ensure that no contamination occurs during heating it. It does have the advantage that the reaction produces three moles of oxygen for two moles of potassium chlorate. whereas mercury(II) oxide produces only one mole of oxygen for every two moles of reactant.

   The mercuric oxide decomposition produces liquid mercury metal that has a significant vapor pressure. Therefore, the oxygen gas that is produced will be contaminated with toxic mercury vapors.

Day 28

If you arrange 6:02 a.m. on October 23 by just the numbers (remember that October is the tenth month), you get 6:02 10 23, which is basically the same as Avogadro's number, 6.02×10^{23}. That doesn't work for the p.m. time, because in military time 6.02 a.m. would be 6:02, but 6:02 p.m. would be 18:02, ruining the relationship—and the joke!

Day 29

The best solution to this problem is to set up two equations with two unknowns.

The two unknowns are:

$x\%$ = percentage of copper-63, $y\%$ = percentage of copper-65.

The two equations are:

1. $x\% + y\% = 100\%$

   (The total of all isotopes must be exactly 100%.)

2. $(62.9296\ \text{amu})\left(\dfrac{x\%}{100\%}\right) + (64.9278\ \text{amu})\left(\dfrac{y\%}{100\%}\right) = 63.546\ \text{amu}$

   (This is the general method for determining the atomic mass of any element.)

Simplifying the equations by factoring out the 100% gives:

1. $x + y = 1$ (This 1 is an exact number.)

2. $(62.9296 \text{ amu})(x) + (64.9278 \text{ amu})(y) = 63.546 \text{ amu}$

Solving equation (1) for x gives $x = 1 - y$

Then substitute for x in (2): $(62.9296 \text{ amu})(1 - y) + (64.9278 \text{ amu})(y) = 63.546 \text{ amu}$

Multiplying gives $62.9296 \text{ amu} - (62.9296 \text{ amu})y + (64.9278 \text{ amu})(y) = 63.546 \text{ amu}$

Rearranging: $[(64.9278 - 62.9296) \text{ amu}]y = (63.546 - 62.9296) \text{ amu}$

Then:

$$y = [(63.546 - 62.9296) \text{ amu}] / [(64.9278 - 62.9296) \text{ amu}] = \left(\frac{0.6164 \text{ amu}}{1.9982 \text{ amu}} \right) =$$

$0.3084776 = 0.308$

From earlier:

$$x = 1 - y = 1 - 0.3084776 = 0.6915224 = 0.692$$

These two answers are decimal answers. To convert the answers to percentage answers, multiply the decimal values by 100%:

$$x = (0.3084776)(100\%) = \mathbf{30.8\%} \ ^{65}\mathbf{Cu} \text{ (Correct significant figures)}$$
$$y = (0.6915224)(100\%) = \mathbf{69.2\%} \ ^{63}\mathbf{Cu} \text{ (Correct significant figures)}$$

Day 30

There are three elements present; therefore, three calculations are necessary, one for each element:

$$\% \ C = \frac{(6 \text{ C atoms})\left(\dfrac{12.011 \text{ amu}}{\text{C atom}} \right)}{180.158 \text{ amu}} \times 100\% = 40.002\%$$

$$\% \ H = \frac{(12 \text{ H atoms})\left(\dfrac{1.00794 \text{ amu}}{\text{H atom}} \right)}{180.158 \text{ amu}} \times 100\% = 6.71370\%$$

$$\% \ O = \frac{(6 \text{ O atoms})\left(\dfrac{15.9994 \text{ amu}}{\text{O atom}} \right)}{180.158 \text{ amu}} \times 100\% = 53.2846\%$$

Total = 100.001%

The total should be 100% (apart from variations due to rounding). This provides a good means to check for correctness in the calculations.

Day 31

To get the empirical formula, it is necessary to determine the moles of each of the elements present. We will begin with the oxygen. The burning added an unknown amount of oxygen; therefore, it is necessary to determine the mass of oxygen in the original sample.

$$\text{Mass of O} = \text{g unknown} - \text{g C} - \text{g H} - \text{g N}$$

(You need the mass of carbon and the mass of hydrogen because the mass of nitrogen is given.)

$$\text{Moles of carbon} = \left(2.842 \text{ g CO}_2\right)\left(\frac{1 \text{ mole CO}_2}{44.009 \text{ g CO}_2}\right)\left(\frac{1 \text{ mole C}}{1 \text{ mole CO}_2}\right) = 0.06458 \text{ mole C}$$

$$\text{Mass of carbon} = \left(0.06458 \text{ mole C}\right)\left(\frac{12.011 \text{ g C}}{1 \text{ mole C}}\right) = 0.7756 \text{ g C}$$

$$\text{Moles of hydrogen} = \left(0.2609 \text{ g H}_2\text{O}\right)\left(\frac{1 \text{ mole H}_2\text{O}}{18.015 \text{ g H}_2\text{O}}\right)\left(\frac{2 \text{ moles H}}{1 \text{ mole H}_2\text{O}}\right)$$

$$= 0.02896 \text{ mole H}$$

$$\text{Mass of hydrogen} = \left(0.02896 \text{ mole H}\right)\left(\frac{1.00794 \text{ g H}}{1 \text{ mole H}}\right) = 0.02920 \text{ g H}$$

Mass of O = 1.778 g – 0.7756 g – 0.02920 g – 0.4056 g = 0.5676 g O

Now that we have the mass of oxygen, we can determine the moles of nitrogen and oxygen.

$$\text{Moles of nitrogen} = \left(0.4056 \text{ g N}_2\right)\left(\frac{1 \text{ mole N}_2}{28.014 \text{ g N}_2}\right)\left(\frac{2 \text{ moles N}}{1 \text{ mole N}_2}\right) = 0.02896 \text{ mole N}$$

$$\text{Moles of O} = \left(0.5676 \text{ g O}\right)\left(\frac{1 \text{ mole O}}{15.999 \text{ g O}}\right) = 0.03548 \text{ mole O}$$

To get the empirical formula, it is necessary to divide the moles of each element by the smallest number of moles present. In this case, the smallest number of moles present is that of hydrogen (or nitrogen).

$$\text{Carbon} = \frac{0.06458 \text{ mole C}}{0.02896 \text{ mole}} = 2.230$$

$$\text{Hydrogen} = \frac{0.02896 \text{ mole H}}{0.02896 \text{ mole}} = 1.000$$

$$\text{Nitrogen} = \frac{0.02896 \text{ mole N}}{0.02896 \text{ mole}} = 1.000$$

$$\text{Oxygen} = \frac{0.03548 \text{ mole O}}{0.02896 \text{ mole}} = 1.225$$

The values for carbon and oxygen are not close enough (within about 0.1) to a whole number to round; therefore, it will be necessary to multiply all values by the smallest common factor to get a whole number. In this case, the smallest common factor is 4. Multiplying by 4 gives

$$C = 4 (2.230) = 8.920 \approx 9$$

$$H = 4 (1.000) = 4.000 = 4$$

$$N = 4 (1.000) = 4.000 = 4$$

$$O = 4 (1.225) = 4.900 \approx 5$$

These values give the empirical formula $C_9H_4N_4O_5$.

Note that if you had used only two significant figures (or if you had rounded sloppily), you might have obtained the following incorrect results:

$$C = 5 (2.2) = 11$$

$$H = 4 (1.0) = 5.0$$

$$N = 5 (1.0) = 5.0$$

$$O = 5 (1.2) = 6.0$$

This would have led to the incorrect empirical formula $C_{11}H_5N_5O_6$.

Day 32

The molar mass of this formula (248 g/mol for $C_9H_4N_4O_5$) is about one-third of the given molar mass ($\approx$740 g/mol); therefore, the empirical formula must be multiplied by 3 to give $C_{27}H_{12}N_{12}O_{15}$. The molar mass of $C_{27}H_{12}N_{12}O_{15}$ is 744 g/mol, which is close to 740. Note that if you had used only two significant figures (or if you had rounded sloppily), you might have obtained the incorrect empirical formula $C_{11}H_5N_5O_6$, which does not lead to a simple conversion to a compound with a molar mass near 740.

Day 33

Nitric acid is a strong acid and completely ionizes in water. The second equation shows the formation of the hydronium ion, H_3O^+. This happens because the hydrogen ion is very small, which gives it a very high charge density; it easily attracts a water molecule and holds it tight to form the hydronium ion. In fact, it may attract other water molecules that solvate the hydronium ion. However, these additional water molecules are not bound as tightly as the first one, so we normally just show the hydronium ion.

$$HNO_3(aq) \rightarrow H^+(aq) + NO_3^-(aq)$$

$$HNO_3(aq) + H_2O(l) \rightarrow H_3O^+(aq) + NO_3^-(aq)$$

Sodium hydroxide dissociates into ions when dissolved in water. These ions are much larger than the hydrogen ion and have a much smaller charge density; they do not attract water molecules or solvate to any great extent.

$$NaOH(s) \rightarrow Na^+(aq) + OH^-(aq)$$

Day 34

The first step is to write the balanced chemical equation (remembering that both hydrogen and oxygen are diatomic gases):

$$2\ H_2(g) + O_2(g) \rightarrow 2\ H_2O(g)$$

Then apply the reaction stoichiometry:

$$\frac{50.0\text{ g H}_2}{1} \times \frac{1\text{ mole H}_2}{2.0158\text{ g H}_2} \times \frac{2\text{ moles H}_2O}{2\text{ moles H}_2} \times \frac{18.0148\text{ g H}_2O}{1\text{ mole H}_2O} = 447\text{ g H}_2O$$

There are two possible ways of calculating the amount of oxygen consumed. The quick way is to figure that all of the hydrogen (50.0 g) was converted to water, so that of the 447 g water, 50.0 g is hydrogen. The amount of oxygen is therefore the difference in the mass of the water and the mass of the hydrogen: 447 g water – 50.0 g hydrogen = 397 g oxygen. The problem with this method is that if you make a mistake in calculating the grams of water that will be formed, the amount of oxygen consumed will also be incorrect. A safer (but longer) method is to start with the original data and calculate the grams of oxygen that reacts with the 50.0 grams of hydrogen:

$$\frac{50.0\text{ g H}_2}{1} \times \frac{1\text{ mole H}_2}{2.0158\text{ g H}_2} \times \frac{1\text{ mole O}_2}{2\text{ mole H}_2} \times \frac{31.998\text{ g O}_2}{1\text{ mole O}_2} = 397\text{ g H}_2O$$

Day 35

The first thing to do is to write the reaction and balance it:

$$C_3H_6O(l) + 4\ O_2(g) \rightarrow 3\ CO_2(g) + 3\ H_2O(g)$$

Since we are given masses of the two reactants, this is a limiting reactant problem. There are a variety of methods for determining the limiting reactant. I will use the process of calculating the mole-to-coefficient ratio for both reactants, and the one with the smallest mole-to-coefficient ratio is the limiting reactant.

For C_3H_6O:

$$\frac{300.0\text{ g acetone}}{1} \times \frac{1\text{ mole acetone}}{58.0794\text{ g}} = 5.1653\text{ moles} \div \text{coefficient of }1 = 5.1653$$

For O_2:

$$\frac{600.0\text{ g oxygen}}{1} \times \frac{1\text{ mole oxygen}}{31.998\text{ g}} = 18.750\text{ moles} \div \text{coefficient of }4 = 4.6875\ \ \text{LR}$$

Since oxygen has the smallest mole-to-coefficient ratio, it is the limiting reactant, and we then base the stoichiometric calculations on it:

$$\frac{600.0\text{ g O}_2}{1} \times \frac{1\text{ mole O}_2}{31.998} \times \frac{3\text{ moles CO}_2}{4\text{ moles O}_2} \times \frac{43.999\text{ g CO}_2}{1\text{ mole CO}_2} = 618.8\text{ g CO}_2$$

[theoretical yield]

The 300.0 g of CO_2 that was isolated is the actual yield.

$$\% \text{ Yield} = \frac{\text{actual yield}}{\text{theoretical yield}} \times 100\% = \frac{300.0 \text{ g}}{618.8 \text{ g}} \times 100\% = 48.48\%$$

Day 36

Take the mass of the potassium tetraphenylborate, convert it to moles, and use the mole ratio between potassium and the potassium tetraphenylborate; then covert the moles of potassium to grams. Finally, take the number of grams of potassium, divide it by the mass of the sample, and multiply the product by 100% to give the percent potassium in the sample.

$$\frac{3.1215 \text{ g KB}(C_6H_5)_4}{1} \times \frac{1 \text{ mole } KB(C_6H_5)_4}{358.3249 \text{ g}} \times \frac{1 \text{ mole K}}{1 \text{ mole } KB(C_6H_5)_4}$$

$$\times \frac{39.0989 \text{ g K}}{1 \text{ mole K}} = 0.3406 \text{ g K}$$

$$\frac{0.3406 \text{ g K}}{4.2580 \text{ g sample}} \times 100\% = 7.999\%$$

Day 37

First, it is necessary to gather together the appropriate materials. This will include a container that will hold approximately 10 liters, the magnesium chloride, a large beaker to weigh the magnesium chloride into, and a balance to weigh the solid.

In order to know how much magnesium chloride you will need, you must calculate the mass of solid necessary:

$$\text{Mass MgCl}_2 = \left(\frac{0.5 \text{ mole Cl}^-}{L}\right)(10.0 \text{ L})\left(\frac{1 \text{ mole MgCl}_2}{2 \text{ moles Cl}^-}\right)\left(\frac{95.21 \text{ g MgCl}_2}{1 \text{ mole MgCl}_2}\right)$$

$$= 238 \text{ g MgCl}_2$$

Next, you will need to place a 250-mL or larger beaker on a balance and tare it. Then carefully add about 238 grams of magnesium chloride to the balance. (Since you require only an approximate molarity, this does not need to be exactly 238.0000 grams.) (If your balance does not have the capacity to handle the masses of the magnesium chloride and the beaker, you may need to weigh the solid in batches.)

Now add the magnesium chloride to the large container (approximately 10 liters), add 1 to 2 liters of water, and stir. After most, if not all, of the solid has dissolved, add, while stirring, 8 to 9 more liters of water to reach a total of approximately 10 liters.

Finally, clean all equipment, appropriately label the solution, and dispose of any waste as directed by your teacher.

You should know the nomenclature for this problem, and how to do mole calculations like the one in this problem, before taking AP Chemistry. If you do not, or if you feel weak on this material, you should review.

Day 40

One quick way is to run a Google search on your computer, tablet, or smartphone. You should be able to find the current barometric pressure from the Weather Channel or a local airport website.

Day 41

The KMT works well in situations of low to moderate pressure (a low to moderate concentration of gas particles minimizes the attractive forces between the gas molecules and makes the volume of the particles insignificant) and moderate to high temperatures (to keep the speed of the particles high in order to help minimize attractive forces between the gas particles).

Day 42

As long as one value changes, at least one other value must change. It is possible to ignore all constant terms.

(a) I—If the moles are increasing, the additional material will require an increase in the pressure.

(b) D—A decrease in temperature will decrease the kinetic energy of the gas particles, which will result in a decrease in the volume.

(c) I—Increasing the pressure increases the temperature because at higher temperatures, the greater kinetic energy of the particles causes the particles to "push" harder on the sides of the container.

(d) I—Increasing the temperature indicates an increase in pressure. This is for the same reason given in part (c).

(e) D—An increase in volume requires a decrease in pressure because the gas particles will not "hit" the walls of the container as often.

Day 43

Use Graham's Law: $\dfrac{\text{Rate A}}{\text{Rate B}} = \sqrt{\dfrac{\text{M B}}{\text{M A}}}$ Assume B is the unknown gas.

$$\frac{26.45 \text{ g/mL}}{18.70 \text{ g/mL}} = \sqrt{\frac{\text{M B}}{32.00 \text{ g/mol}}}$$

If the students incorrectly assumed that the formula of oxygen gas was O (16.00 g/mol) instead of O_2 (32.00 g/mol), they will get 32.01 g/mol instead of the correct 64.02 g/mol.

Make sure that your answer has the correct number of significant figures.

You should already know that oxygen is one of the diatomic elements.

If you had trouble with this problem, you might wish to review Chapter 8.

Day 44

Collect and label the information from the problem

$P_1 = \underline{}$ $\qquad\qquad$ $P_2 = \underline{}$
$V_1 = 11.5$ L $\qquad\qquad$ $V_2 = 12.0$ L
$T_1 = 25°C = 298$ K $\qquad$ $T_2 = ?$ °C

Based on the available information, it is possible to use Charles's law: $\dfrac{V_1}{T_1} = \dfrac{V_2}{T_2}$
The equation rearranges to: $T_2 = \dfrac{V_2 \, T_1}{V_1}$

Enter the appropriate values into the equation and cancel; then convert to °C:

$$T_2 = \frac{(12.0 \ \cancel{\text{L}}) \, (298 \text{ K})}{(11.5 \ \cancel{\text{L}})} = 311 \text{ K}$$

$$T_2 = (311 - 273)°C = \mathbf{38°C}$$

Do not make the mistake of leaving the temperature in degrees Celsius just because the starting and ending temperatures are in degrees Celsius.

Day 45

It is tempting to use the relationship 22.4 L/mole to determine the volume of the gas to get 44.8 L. However, this will not give the correct answer because 22.4 applies only at standard temperature and pressure, and this sample is not at STP. For this reason, it is necessary to use the ideal gas equation to calculate the volume.

$$V = \frac{nRT}{P} = \frac{(2.00 \ \cancel{\text{moles}}) \left(\dfrac{0.0821 \text{ L} \bullet \cancel{\text{atm}}}{\cancel{\text{mole}} \bullet \cancel{\text{K}}} \right) (298 \ \cancel{\text{K}})}{1.00 \ \cancel{\text{atm}}} = 48.9 \text{ L}$$

Day 46

Begin by organizing the data from the problem:

Mass = 3.4 g

$P = 1.00$ atm

$V = 1.50$ L

$T = 37°C = 310.$ K

Molar mass = ?

In order to determine the molar mass, we will need to know the mass and the number of moles present. The mass (3.4 g) is given; therefore, the next step is to determine the moles from the ideal gas equation rearranged to this form: $n = \dfrac{PV}{RT}$.

Enter the appropriate values into the equation and cancel:

$$n = \frac{(1.00 \ \cancel{\text{atm}})(1.50 \ \cancel{\text{L}})}{\left(\dfrac{0.0821 \ \cancel{\text{L}} \bullet \cancel{\text{atm}}}{\text{mole} \bullet \cancel{\text{K}}} \right)(310. \ \cancel{\text{K}})} = 0.05894 \text{ mole (unrounded)}$$

We can finish determining the molar mass by taking the mass given (3.4 g) and dividing by the calculated moles (0.05894 mole):

$$\text{Molar mass} = \left(\frac{3.4 \text{ g}}{0.05894 \text{ mole}}\right) = 58 \text{ g/mol}$$

Day 47

In order to determine the molecular formula, it is necessary begin by calculating the empirical formula, which requires us to determine the moles of each element present in the compound. In order to determine the moles of each element, it is necessary to know the mass and molar mass of each element. The problem gives percentages; we will need to convert the values to mass. Since percentage is an intensive quantity, we can choose any sample mass. The simplest sample mass is 100 g (exactly). Using this mass, the numerical values of the percentages (82.66 and 17.34) are the same as the numerical values of the masses (82.66 and 17.34) in grams. Converting the masses to moles yields

$$\text{Mole C} = (82.66 \text{ g C})\left(\frac{1 \text{ mole C}}{12.011 \text{ g C}}\right) = 6.882 \text{ moles C}$$

$$\text{Mole H} = (17.34 \text{ g H})\left(\frac{1 \text{ mole H}}{1.0079 \text{ g H}}\right) = 17.20 \text{ moles H}$$

The next step is to divide each mole value by the lower value (6.88202):

$$C = \left(\frac{6.882 \text{ moles C}}{6.882}\right) = 1 \text{ C}$$

$$H = \left(\frac{17.20 \text{ moles H}}{6.882}\right) = 2.500 \text{ H}$$

The values for the empirical formulas must be whole numbers (or close to whole numbers). Since the value for hydrogen is not close, it is necessary to apply a conversion. We will simply need to multiply the hydrogen value by 2, and we get a whole number (5). If we multiply the hydrogen by 2, we must multiple all values by 2. This gives C = 2 and H = 5, which makes the empirical formula C_2H_5. The relationship between the empirical and molecular formulas must be a simple one. We need to compare the molar mass of the empirical formula (29.062 g/mol) to the molar mass determined in Part 1 (58 g/mol). The calculated molecular molar mass is twice the empirical molar mass, which means that the molecular formula is twice the empirical formula, or C_4H_{10}.

Day 48

Begin by transferring the given information to the balanced chemical equation.

$$2 \text{ NH}_2\text{Cl(s)} + \text{N}_2\text{H}_4\text{(aq)} \rightarrow 2 \text{ NH}_4\text{Cl(aq)} + \text{N}_2\text{(g)}$$

$$? \text{ g} \qquad\qquad 12.3 \text{ L}$$

$$31°C$$

$$P_{\text{Total}} = 795 \text{ torr}$$

$$P_{\text{H}_2\text{O}} = 31.824 \text{ torr}$$

Answers ↑

It is necessary to use Dalton's law to determine the partial pressure of dry nitrogen gas.

$$P_{Total} = P_{Dry} + P_{H_2O}$$

Rearranging this equation gives

$$P_{Dry} = P_{Total} - P_{H_2O}$$

Using the values from the problem and the vapor pressure table gives

$$P_{Dry} = 795 \text{ torr} - 32 \text{ torr} = 763 \text{ torr}$$

We now have the following information to enter into the ideal gas equation:

$$P = 763 \text{ torr}$$

$$V = 12.3 \text{ L}$$

$$T = 31°C = 304 \text{ K}$$

$$R = \frac{0.0821 \text{ L} \bullet \text{atm}}{\text{mole} \bullet \text{K}}$$

$$\text{Mass} = ? \text{ g NH}_2\text{Cl}$$

This is a stoichiometry problem, which means that moles are the key. Based on the given information, we will need to rearrange the ideal gas equation to find moles: $n = \dfrac{PV}{RT}$

Entering the appropriate values into the equation and canceling units wherever possible, we find that

$$n = \frac{(763 \text{ torr})(12.3 \text{ L})}{\left(\dfrac{0.0821 \text{ L} \bullet \text{atm}}{\text{mole} \bullet \text{K}}\right)(304 \text{ K})}$$

It is obvious that an additional conversion is necessary. Adding the appropriate pressure conversion (1 atm = 760 torr) gives

$$n = \frac{(763 \text{ torr})(12.3 \text{ L})}{\left(\dfrac{0.0821 \text{ L} \bullet \text{atm}}{\text{mole} \bullet \text{K}}\right)(304 \text{ K})}\left(\frac{1 \text{ atm}}{760 \text{ torr}}\right)$$

This is the number of moles of dry nitrogen gas. In order to convert to the substance of interest (NH_2Cl), we need to add a mole ratio:

$$n = \frac{(763 \text{ torr})(12.3 \text{ L})}{\left(\dfrac{0.0821 \text{ L} \bullet \text{atm}}{\text{mole} \bullet \text{K}}\right)(304 \text{ K})}\left(\frac{1 \text{ atm}}{760 \text{ torr}}\right)\left(\frac{2 \text{ moles NH}_2\text{Cl}}{1 \text{ mole N}_2}\right)$$

Finally, it is necessary to use the molar mass of NH_2Cl:

$$\text{Mass} = \frac{(763 \text{ torr})(12.3 \text{ L})}{\left(\dfrac{0.0821 \text{ L} \bullet \text{atm}}{\text{mole} \bullet \text{K}}\right)(304 \text{ K})}\left(\frac{1 \text{ atm}}{760 \text{ torr}}\right)\left(\frac{2 \text{ moles NH}_2\text{Cl}}{1 \text{ mole N}_2}\right)\left(\frac{51.476 \text{ g NH}_2\text{Cl}}{1 \text{ mole NH}_2\text{Cl}}\right)$$

$$= 50.93709 = \textbf{50.9 g NH}_2\textbf{Cl}$$

Day 49

First, check the calculations by using the ideal gas equation.

$P = ?$

$V = 1.00 \text{ L}$

$n = 2.50 \text{ mole}$

$T = 25°C = 298 \text{ K}$

$R = \dfrac{0.0821 \text{ L} \bullet \text{atm}}{\text{mole} \bullet \text{K}}$

Rearrange the ideal gas equation to: $P = \dfrac{nRT}{V}$

Enter the appropriate values into the equation and cancel:

$$P = \frac{(2.50 \text{ moles})\left(\dfrac{0.0821 \text{ L} \bullet \text{atm}}{\text{mole} \bullet \text{K}}\right)(298 \text{ K})}{(1.00 \text{ L})} = \textbf{61.2 atm}$$

Therefore, his calculations were correct, and the discrepancy must lie elsewhere. The calculated pressure is very high, and very few (if any) gases behave ideally under these conditions. The problem is that the ideal gas equation was used for a non-ideal gas.

Day 50

In the large tube demonstration, the chemist places one of the cotton balls in the tube, and a few seconds later he places the other cotton ball in the other end. The first gas has a head start on the second gas. It would have been better if there had been two chemists, and they had placed the cotton balls in the ends of the tube at the same time.

In the balloon demonstration, the moisture (or saliva) from blowing up the balloon might have had a minor effect. It would have been better if the balloon had been filled with nitrogen gas from a tank. Are the balloons exactly the same size, and do they have the same amount of elasticity?

Day 51

The temperature after five minutes is lower than the first reading. This means the water has lost heat. If water loses heat, the process must be exothermic.

Day 52

(a) The smaller pan will boil first, which indicates that heat is an extensive property (that is, it depends on the amount of water in the pan).

(b) The two pans are boiling at the same temperature, which indicates that boiling point is an intensive property (that is, it does not depend on the amount of water in the pan).

Day 53

According the Hess's Law, no matter what reaction pathway is chosen, the energy change will always be the same. This is analogous to the fact that no matter what road is chosen, the driver will finish in Atlanta, Georgia.

Day 54

This is possible because of the Law of Conservation of Energy. If the reaction releases 93 kJ/mol to get from the reactants to the products, it must require the same amount of energy to get back to the beginning.

Day 55

The decomposition of water is the reverse of the reaction shown; therefore, the enthalpy change is positive instead of negative (+572 kJ). The amount of water decomposing is 2.00 moles, which is the same amount of water in the reaction; therefore, the answer is +572 kJ.

Day 56

The hot piece of metal (lead) will lose heat to the cold piece of metal (magnesium). Since no heat is lost to the surroundings, the energy gained by the magnesium must be identical to the heat lost by the lead. Using the relationship heat = $q = Cm\Delta T$ for the two metals and setting the two equal to each other gives

$$-\left[\left(\frac{0.127\ J}{g\ ^\circ C}\right)(25.00\ g)(T_f - 75.00)\,^\circ C\right] = +\left[\left(\frac{1.024\ J}{g\ ^\circ C}\right)(37.00\ g)(T_f - 15.00)\,^\circ C\right]$$

Significant figures are underlined.

$- [(3.175\ J)\ (T_f - 75.00)] = + [(37.888\ J)\ (T_f - 15.00)]$

$- [3.175\ T_f - 238.125] = + [37.888\ T_f - 568.32]$

$238.125 + 568.32 = (37.888 + 3.175)\ T_f$

$806.445 = (41.063)\ T_f$

$T_f = 806.445/41.063 = 19.6392 = \mathbf{19.6\,^\circ C}$

A common error is to simply average the two temperatures (45.00°C).

Day 57

The answer is $\mathbf{\Delta H^\circ = 28.4\ kJ}$, to the correct number of significant figures.

This problem involves using Hess's law to combine the given thermochemical equations to produce the desired thermochemical equation. Examining the first component of equation (4), the $N_2(g)$, we see that it is in equation (3); however, the coefficients do not match, so we will need to multiply equation (3), including the energy, by 2:

$$2\ N_2(g) + 6\ O_2(g) + 2\ H_2(g) \rightarrow 4\ HNO_3(l) \qquad \Delta H^\circ = 2(-348.2\ kJ)$$

This takes care of the $N_2(g)$, but it generates more $O_2(g)$ than needed. The excess $O_2(g)$ will have to be adjusted later.

Skipping to the $N_2O_5(g)$, this compound appears on the reactant side of equation (2) with the wrong coefficient. It will be necessary to multiply equation (2) by 2 and to reverse the result (including the sign on the enthalpy change) to give the following equation:

$$4\ HNO_3(l) \rightarrow 2\ N_2O_5(g) + 2\ H_2O(l) \qquad \Delta H° = -2(-76.6\ kJ)$$

Finally, to compensate for the excess $O_2(g)$, it will be necessary to include equation (1) as is. We now have the following combination of equations:

$$2\ N_2(g) + 6\ O_2(g) + 2\ H_2(g) \rightarrow 4\ HNO_3(l) \qquad \Delta H° = 2(-348.2\ kJ)$$
$$4\ HNO_3(l) \rightarrow 2\ N_2O_5(g) + 2\ H_2O(l) \qquad \Delta H° = -2(-76.6\ kJ)$$
$$2\ H_2O(l) \rightarrow 2\ H_2(g) + O_2(g) \qquad \Delta H° = -(-571.6\ kJ)$$

It is now possible to cancel any components that appear on each side of the reaction arrow. For example, there are two moles of $H_2O(l)$ on opposite sides of the reaction arrow, so it is possible to cancel these. (Note that if either of these were $H_2O(g)$, they would not cancel.) In a similar manner, the $H_2(g)$ on each side will cancel. The four moles of $HNO_3(l)$ will also cancel. Finally, one mole of $O_2(g)$ will cancel from each side. Here are the results of these cancellations:

$$2\ N_2(g) + 5\ 6\ O_2(g) + 2\ H_2(g) \rightarrow 4\ HNO_3(l) \qquad \Delta H° = 2(-348.2\ kJ)$$
$$4\ HNO_3(l) \rightarrow 2\ N_2O_5(g) + 2\ H_2O(l) \qquad \Delta H° = -2(-76.6\ kJ)$$
$$2\ H_2O(l) \rightarrow 2\ H_2(g) + O_2(g) \qquad \Delta H° = -(-571.6\ kJ)$$

Adding the components that have not been canceled and the enthalpy changes gives the desired equation (4):

$$2\ N_2(g) + 5\ O_2(g) \rightarrow 2\ N_2O_5(g) \qquad \mathbf{\Delta H° = 28.4\ kJ}$$

If the result of combining the equations is not an EXACT match to equation (4), there has been an error. A common mistake in multiplying an equation by a value is to skip one or more components.

Day 58

In the Dorito experiment, the can containing the water was not kept over the flame, and the distance between the can and the flame was changed. Both of these conditions led to the loss of a significant amount of heat. The change in temperature of the aluminum can probably was not figured into the calculations and was another source of error.

You would need the mass of the Dorito, the mass of the water ([mass of can + water] – [mass of can]) and the temperature change in degrees Celsius (final temperature – initial temperature). You would also need the specific heat of water (1 cal/g °C). Assuming the heat (calories) lost by the Dorito equals the heat gained by the water, then

Heat gained by the water = mass of water (g) × temperature change (°C)
  × specific heat of water (1 cal/g °C) = calories of heat lost by the Dorito.

You could divide this value by the grams of Dorito to get the cal/g. However, don't forget that the Calorie (the nutritional kind) is really a kilocalorie (kcal). You would have to divide your answer by 1,000 to convert from cal to kcal. If you looked on the package, you could determine the number of grams per serving and therefore the number of Calories per serving. Comparing your answer with the value on the package might give you an idea of the amount of error in the experiment.

Day 60

The entropy change in the surroundings is positive, and the total entropy change of the system is positive.

Day 62

Energy must leave the system (water) for the water to freeze. This energy enters the surroundings, causing the entropy of the surroundings to increase. As long as the increase in the entropy of the surroundings is greater than the decrease in the entropy of the system, the total entropy change will be positive, making the process spontaneous.

Day 63

C—For the reaction to become spontaneous when the temperature was lowered means that entropy impeded the reaction (entropy was negative). The enthalpy must be negative. Nonspontaneous under standard conditions means $\Delta G > 0$.

Day 64

First, calculate $\Delta G°$ for the reaction, paying attention to the states of the reactants and products.

$$CH_3OH(g) + O_2(g) \rightarrow CO(g) + 2\ H_2O(g)$$

$$-161.9 \qquad 0 \qquad -137.2 \qquad -228.6\ \text{kJ/mol}$$

$$\Delta G = [-137.2 + 2(-228.6)] - [-161.9 + 0] = -432.5\ \text{kJ/mol}$$

The partial pressures given in the problem indicate that the system is not under standard conditions (the pressures are not one atmosphere). Therefore, it is necessary to adjust the value to account for nonstandard conditions:

$$\Delta G = \Delta G° + RT \ln Q = \Delta G° + RT \ln \frac{P_{CO}\ P_{H_2O}^2}{P_{CH_3OH}\ P_{O_2}}$$

$$\Delta G = -432.5\ \text{kJ/mol} + (8.314\ \text{J/mol K}) \left(\frac{\text{k}}{10^3}\right) (298\ \text{K}) \ln \frac{(0.00187)\ (0.000375)^2}{(0.00180)\ (0.200)}$$

$$\Delta G = -432.5\ \text{kJ/mol} + (-35.00705\ \text{kJ/mol}) = -467.50705\ \text{kJ/mol} = -467.5\ \text{kJ/mol}$$

Day 65

$$\Delta G = \Delta G° + RT \ln Q = \Delta G° + RT \ln \frac{[NH_3]^2}{[N_2][H_2]^3}$$

$$\Delta G = -33.4 \text{ kJ/mol} + (8.314 \text{ J/mol K})\left(\frac{k}{1000}\right)(300.0 \text{ K}) \ln \frac{[67.7]^2}{[33.3][100.0]^3}$$

$$= -55.57567 = -55.6 \text{ kJ/mol}$$

Day 69

All elements have unique spectra because they have differing separations of the energy levels due to differences in effective nuclear charge. In addition, in hydrogen and helium the transitions are due to s-electrons, whereas in nitrogen the transitions are due to both s- and p-electrons. This is emission spectroscopy. What we see is the result of energy being emitted as an electron drops from a higher energy state to a lower one (s or p levels). If we were measuring the energy being absorbed (the movement of an electron from a lower to a higher energy state), it would be an absorbance spectrum.

Day 70

Helium was discovered by examining the spectra from the sun. This spectrum did not match any that was known at the time. Twenty years later helium was discovered on Earth in a sample of uranium ore. The names of four elements (rubidium, cesium, indium, and thallium) refer to bright lines in their spectra: red for rubidium, sky blue for cesium, indigo for indium, and green for thallium. All of these elements were discovered by observing their spectra.

Day 71

Now you should have a good idea what is going on inside a glow stick, but did you find out about how fireflies produce their light? This process is called bioluminescence.

Day 72

(a) The shape of the orbital depends on the angular momentum quantum number, l.

(b) The principal quantum number, n, designates the energy level and, therefore, the energy of the electron.

(c) The principal quantum number, n, designates the energy level and, therefore, the size of the orbital.

(d) The magnetic quantum number, m_l, refers to the orientation of the orbital.

(e) The spin quantum number, m_s, indicates in which direction the electron is spinning.

Day 73

The p-subshell always has six possible combinations, which is no different in this case. The fact that a ground-state helium atom does not have electrons in the 2p subshell is irrelevant. The orbitals are there, and in a helium atom in an excited state, at least some of those orbitals may be occupied.

Day 74

If electrons were particles, this approach might work. However, electrons have wave properties and, unlike planets, are subject to the Heisenberg uncertainty principle.

Day 75

At about 32 seconds into the video, a p-orbital is mislabeled as a d-orbital.

Day 76

The energy of the 4s-orbital is lower in uranium than in hydrogen because the effective nuclear charge has increased.

Day 77

PES can be used to identify the number of electrons present in an atom and the number of electrons in a particular shell/subshell.

Day 78

(a) The mass of water in the hydrate is simply the mass of the crucible + lid + original sample minus the mass of the crucible + lid + sample after heating:

$$20.603 \text{ g} - 17.693 \text{ g} = 2.920 \text{ g } H_2O$$

(b) It is necessary to use the answer from part (a) and the molar mass of water:

$$(2.920 \text{ g } H_2O)\left(\frac{1 \text{ mole } H_2O}{18.015 \text{ g } H_2O}\right) = 0.1621 \text{ mole } H_2O$$

(c) In this case, you need to determine the mass of the anhydrous salt first. To obtain this mass, simply take the final mass and subtract the mass of the crucible and lid. Once you have the mass of anhydrous salt, convert the mass to moles using the molar mass given.

(17.693 g salt plus crucible and lid) – (15.973 g crucible and lid) = 1.720 g anhydrous salt

$$(1.720 \text{ g anhydrous salt})\left(\frac{1 \text{ mole salt}}{105.989 \text{ g salt}}\right) = 0.01623 \text{ mole salt}$$

(d) The value of x is determined from the mole ratio of water to anhydrous salt:

$$\frac{0.1621 \text{ mole } H_2O}{0.01623 \text{ mole anhydrous salt}} = 9.988 \rightarrow 10$$

(e) The name and formula of the hydrated salt

come from your answer to part (e) and the general rules of nomenclature:

Sodium carbonate decahydrate, $Na_2CO_3 \cdot 10 \text{ } H_2O$

Day 79

(a) First electron affinity:

$$S(g) + e^- \rightarrow S^-(g)$$

$$:\!\overset{\cdot\cdot}{\underset{\cdot\cdot}{S}}\!\cdot \quad + \quad \cdot \quad \longrightarrow \quad :\!\overset{\cdot\cdot}{\underset{\cdot\cdot}{S}}\!\cdot^-$$

Second electron affinity:

$$S^-(g) + e^- \rightarrow S^{2-}(g)$$

$$:\!\overset{\cdot\cdot}{\underset{\cdot\cdot}{S}}\!\cdot^- \quad + \quad \cdot \quad \longrightarrow \quad :\!\overset{\cdot\cdot}{\underset{\cdot\cdot}{S}}\!:^{2-}$$

(b) First ionization energy:

$$Ca(g) \rightarrow Ca^+(g) + e^-$$

$$Ca\cdot \quad \longrightarrow \quad Ca\cdot^+ + \cdot$$

Second ionization energy:

$$Ca^+(g) \rightarrow Ca^{2+}(g) + e^-$$

$$Ca\cdot^+ \quad \longrightarrow \quad Ca^{2+} + \cdot$$

(c) The third electron affinity of sulfur and the third ionization energy of calcium would be difficult processes to achieve. After the second electron affinity of sulfur, the outer shell (s and p orbitals) is full; there is no easy way to add another electron. After the second ionization energy of calcium, there are no more electrons in the valence shell to remove. To achieve the third ionization would necessitate the removal of a core electron. The removal of core electrons is very difficult compared to the removal of a valence electron.

Day 80

Hydrogen can never obey the octet rule. Hydrogen has only the 1s orbital to use in bonding. The 1s orbital fills with two electrons, and there is no room for any more electrons. (This applies to helium also, but helium does not form any stable compounds.) For this reason, structures like X–H–X never form in simple compounds.

Day 81

This molecule has 17 electrons to use. Since there are an odd number of electrons, at least one atom will have an unpaired electron (not an octet). The nitrogen atom is the most likely not to have an octet, because it is the least electronegative atom of the three present.

Day 82

Complete both Lewis structures and see which gives the more stable structure with respect to completed octets and number of bonds. Second, assign formal charges to all atoms in each Lewis structure and see which structure gives the more reasonable distribution of formal charges.

Day 83

(a) The reaction of one nonmetal with another leads to the formation of a molecule held together with covalent bonds:

$$\cdot \ddot{\text{Cl}}: \quad + \quad 3\; \cdot \ddot{\text{F}}: \quad \longrightarrow \quad :\ddot{\text{F}}\!-\!\overset{\displaystyle \ddot{\text{Cl}}}{\underset{\displaystyle :\ddot{\text{F}}:}{|}}\!-\!\ddot{\text{F}}:$$

(b) The reaction of a metal with a nonmetal leads to the formation of ions and a compound containing ionic bonds:

$$\cdot \overset{\cdot}{\underset{\cdot}{\text{Al}}} \cdot \quad + \quad 3\; \cdot \ddot{\text{F}}: \quad \longrightarrow \quad \text{Al}^{3+} \quad + \quad 3 \quad :\ddot{\text{F}}:^{-}$$

Day 84

(a) In both pairs the compound with the higher lattice energy contains the cation (Na^+ or Ca^{2+}) with the smaller radius. All other factors (anion and charges) are the same. Therefore, lattice energy is inversely proportional to the ionic radius.

(b) In both pairs the compound containing ions with higher charges has the higher lattice energy. In these pairs, the radii of the cations are similar and probably do not lead to a significant change in the lattice energy. Therefore, lattice energy is directly proportional to charge.

(c) The observations recorded in parts (a) and (b) are explained by Coulomb's Law.

(d) The lattice energy of CaS will be lower than that of CaO. Sulfur is lower on the periodic table than oxygen; therefore, the sulfide ion will be larger than the oxide ion because the sulfide ion has an additional electron shell. The conclusion from part (a) is that there is an inverse relationship between the lattice energy and the ionic radius. For this reason, the larger sulfide ion will lead to a lower lattice energy.

(e) The lattice energy of CrN will be larger than that of MgO. Because the ions are similar in size, the key factor must be the charges on the ions. Based on its position on the periodic table, the nitride ion should be N^{3-}, which means the chromium ion must be Cr^{3+}. Since the ions in CrN have higher charges than those in MgO (Mg^{2+} and O^{2-}), the lattice energy will be higher as predicted in part (b).

Day 85

The Lewis structures have different numbers of electron pairs surrounding the central atoms. Boron has no lone pairs, nitrogen has one, and chlorine has two lone pairs. The differing numbers of electrons surrounding the central atoms mean that, according to valence-shell electron-pair repulsion (VSEPR) theory, the molecules will have different structures.

Day 86

The Lewis structures are

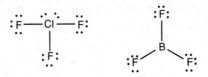

Chlorine trifluoride, ClF_3, is a T-shaped molecule. T-shaped molecules are polar. Boron trifluoride, BF_3, is trigonal planar. In general, trigonal planar molecules are nonpolar.

Day 87

In general, a molecule with the general formula would be polar. There is a slight chance that two elements with the same electronegativity could form a molecule, but in most cases two different elements have different electronegativity. However, if both electronegativity values were the same, the molecule would be nonpolar.

Day 88

The electronegativity of beryllium is 1.5 and the electronegativity of iodine is 2.5, which gives 1.0 as the electronegativity difference. An electronegativity difference of 1.0 makes the bond polar covalent. The electronegativity of gold is 2.4 and the electronegativity of iodine is 2.5, which gives 0.1 as the electronegativity difference. An electronegativity difference of 0.1 makes the bond covalent.

Day 89

The structures are

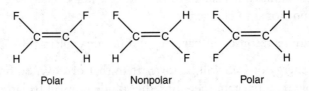

The carbon–carbon and the carbon–hydrogen bonds exhibit minimum polarity. The fluorine atoms are the most electronegative atoms present, and therefore the carbon–fluorine bonds are polar covalent. If the carbon–fluorine bonds point in opposite directions, as they do in the center structure, the polarities cancel to produce a nonpolar molecule. In the other two cases, the two carbon–fluorine bonds pull together to some degree to produce a polar molecule.

Day 90

Draw the Lewis structure as shown below. The carbon on the left in the structure has sp^3 hybridization, and the other carbon atom has sp^2 hybridization.

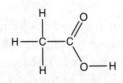

Day 92

Liquid O_2 is paramagnetic because it has unpaired electrons in its bonding structure.

Day 93

Nitric acid is more stable than predicted from the bond energies. Resonance makes substances more stable, and because there is resonance present in nitric acid, the compound is more stable than bond energies would predict. This difference would be greater than the difference usually observed in a typical prediction.

Day 94

C—All the other answers involve species containing only single bonds. Substances without double or triple bonds seldom need resonance structures.

Day 95

To use bond energies to calculate the enthalpy of a reaction, it is necessary to know what bonds are present. This is done by drawing the appropriate Lewis structures:

$$:N \equiv N: \qquad H-H \qquad H-\overset{\displaystyle ..}{\underset{\displaystyle |}{N}}-H$$
$$\qquad\qquad\qquad\qquad\qquad\qquad\qquad\qquad H$$

Using these Lewis structures and the table given, we find that

$$[941.4 \text{ kJ} + 3\,(436.4 \text{ kJ})] - [2(3(393 \text{ kJ}))] = -107.4 = -107 \text{ kJ}$$

The energy calculated should be twice the heat of formation for ammonia; therefore, the standard enthalpy of ammonia from this calculation is -53.5 kJ mol^{-1}. The apparent error is the result of using average bond energies for the bonds. Some, or all, the bonds in the calculation show some deviation from the average.

Day 96

The water molecules are hydrogen bonded to each other in a rather open framework. Adding ethyl alcohol disrupts this open arrangement. The –OH end of the ethyl alcohol can also hydrogen bond to the water molecules. The result is that the water/alcohol mixture is more closely packed than the water itself, causing the volume difference.

Day 97

My students are able to stack approximately 20 drops of water on the penny. Did you notice how the convex surface of the water magnified the engraving on the coin? They were also able to add 50–70 paperclips to a full six-ounce cup of water.

Day 98

Stronger intermolecular forces lead to higher boiling points. Both molecules are nonpolar; therefore, the key intermolecular force is London dispersion. CI_4 has more electrons than CF_4 does, so it has stronger intermolecular forces.

Day 99

A—Hydrogen bonding requires the presence of a hydrogen atom bonded to a nitrogen, oxygen, or fluorine atom. In CH_3OH, the last hydrogen in the formula is bonded to the oxygen. In CH_3F, all the hydrogen atoms are bonded to the carbon atom and none to the fluorine. There is no N, O, or F in CH_4 to form hydrogen bonds. In $N(CH_3)_3$, the nitrogen atom is bonded only to the carbon atoms and not to any of the hydrogen atoms. It may help to draw the Lewis structure of any molecule that you are unsure about.

Day 100

Methane and ammonia are similar in size and mass. The boiling points of such molecules depend on the strength of the intermolecular forces. The stronger the intermolecular forces, the higher the boiling point. In the case of ammonia, the main intermolecular force is hydrogen bonding, whereas methane has only London dispersion forces. Hydrogen bonding is a stronger intermolecular force than London dispersion forces; therefore, ammonia has a higher boiling point.

Day 101

Neither the size of the container nor the number of moles will make any difference. Decreasing the pressure over the liquid will lower the boiling point. If the container is sealed, the pressure inside the container will increase, which will increase the boiling point.

Day 102

Only the solid is present from point A to point B. The solid begins to melt at B and finishes melting at C. Once the solid begins to melt, both solid and liquid are present.

Day 103

The mixing of a concentrated acid, such as sulfuric acid, with water is a highly exothermic process. A great deal of heat is evolved. If you were adding a small amount of water to the acid, enough heat could be given off to instantly vaporize the water and cause splattering of the hot acid solution. Adding the acid to the water allows the bulk of the water to absorb the heat, especially with stirring, and no spattering should occur.

Day 104

$$\left(\frac{3.224 \text{ g Na}_2\text{SO}_4 \cdot 10\text{H}_2\text{O}}{750.0 \text{ mL}}\right)\left(\frac{1000 \text{ mL}}{1 \text{ L}}\right)\left(\frac{1 \text{ mole Na}_2\text{SO}_4 \cdot 10\text{H}_2\text{O}}{322.4 \text{ g Na}_2\text{SO}_4 \cdot 10\text{H}_2\text{O}}\right)$$

$$\times\left(\frac{2 \text{ moles Na}^+}{1 \text{ mole Na}_2\text{SO}_4 \cdot 10\text{H}_2\text{O}}\right) = 0.02667 \text{ } M \text{ Na+}$$

The significant figures must be correct.

A common error is not to include the 10 H_2O when calculating the molar mass.

If you have trouble solving this problem, you might wish to review Chapter 13.

Day 105

D—This shows the lithium ions and bromide ions as separate ions in solution, which is a property of strong electrolytes. The water molecules are present in both the liquid and gas states, which occurs at the boiling point of any aqueous solution. Answer A is incorrect because it shows undissociated LiBr molecules and the dissociation of water molecules to produce H_2 and O_2 molecules. The problems with choice B are the dissociation of water to H_2 and O_2 and the vaporization of LiBr. Answer C correctly shows the vaporization of water molecules to give water vapor but incorrectly shows the vaporization of lithium ions and bromide ions.

Day 106

Evaporation of the solution will separate the volatile water from the nonvolatile potassium phosphate. It is not possible to separate the components of a solution by titration or filtration. The electrolysis of the solution would produce hydrogen and oxygen gas.

Day 109

C—The solubility of a gas is increased by increasing the partial pressure of the gas and by lowering the temperature. For these reasons, it is best to pick the answer with the lowest temperature and the highest partial pressure of oxygen.

Day 110

Changing the concentration of any substance involved in the rate-determining step will change the rate of the reaction. Hydrogen ions are necessary to balance chemical equations; therefore, H^+ cannot be a spectator ion. If H^+ is not a spectator ion, it must appear in the mechanism. A catalyst will change the rate of a reaction, so H^+ cannot be a catalyst. In addition, the reaction consumes H^+, so it cannot be a catalyst for a second reason. Because H^+ does not affect the rate, the reaction is zero order with respect to this ion.

Day 111

The doubling of the hydrogen concentration in experiments 1 and 2 led to a doubling of the rate; the reaction is first order with respect to hydrogen. The doubling of the NO concentration in experiments 2 and 3 led to a quadrupling (2^2) of the rate; the reaction is second order with respect to nitrogen oxide. The reaction is first order in H_2 and second order in NO. Therefore, the rate law is Rate = $k[NO]^2[H_2]$.

Day 112

Collision theory states that a chemical reaction can occur when all the following conditions are met:

1. There is a collision between two reacting particles.

2. The collision must occur at a reactive site with the particles in the correct orientation.

3. The collision must transfer enough energy to provide the activation energy for the reaction.

A collision that exhibits all three of these characteristics is an effective collision.

Day 113

C—The mechanism has three steps; therefore, the energy profile must have three peaks (transition states). Each peak corresponds to one of the steps in the mechanism.

Day 114

B—CH_3 is an intermediate in the mechanism. The detection of an intermediate supports a mechanism. In general, the rates of all reactions increase when the system is heated. Rate constants change when the temperature changes. The reaction will eventually reach equilibrium regardless of the mechanism.

Day 115

The rate law for Step 2 would appear to be Rate = $k[Cl_2O_4][OH^-]$; however, Cl_2O_4 is a reaction intermediate and should not appear in the rate law. The term representing the intermediate, $[Cl_2O_4]$, should be replaced with the reactants used to prepare it (Step 1). Therefore, it is necessary to replace $[Cl_2O_4]$ with $[ClO_2]^2$, which changes the rate law to Rate = $k[ClO_2]^2[OH^-]$.

Day 116

In the first video, you can really see how much more reactive these elements are than the first three members of the alkali metal family. Reactivity is one measure of the activity of a substance. The reactivity is related to how far the valence electrons are from the nucleus. In lithium the valence electrons are tightly bound, but in Rb and Cs the valence electrons are much farther from the nucleus and thus much easier to remove (low ionization energy) in chemical reactions. This equates to a much more reactive substance.

Day 117

$$\frac{1.0 \text{ g toxin}}{1} \times \frac{1,000 \text{ mg}}{1 \text{ g}} \times \frac{1 \text{ kg body weight}}{3.0 \times 10^{-8} \text{ mg toxin}} \times \frac{1 \text{ adult}}{70 \text{ kg}} = 4.8 \times 10^8 \text{ adults}$$

The LD_{50} (lethal dosage 50%) implies that only half of the adults would die.

Day 118

The response from Student 1 is incorrect because an equilibrium is a dynamic process. In a dynamic process, nothing ever stops. The reaction *appears* to stop because the forward and reverse reactions are going at equal rates, so the concentrations "stop" changing.

The response from Student 2 is also incorrect in nearly all cases. There is a special case that may occur when $K = 1$, where the concentrations might be equal, but this is not generally true. What the student meant was that the concentration of each component remains the same, not, as implied, that the concentrations of all the components are the same.

Day 119

The sketch will look something like this:

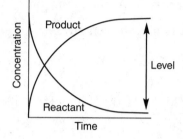

The point where the two curves level off is where the system has reached equilibrium.

Day 121

B—Increasing the temperature of an endothermic equilibrium will increase the amount of product, which eliminates answer A. Adding Ar yields no change, because it is not part of the equilibrium, which eliminates answer C. Decreasing the volume will cause the equilibrium to shift to the left, thus decreasing the amount of NO_2 and eliminating answer D.

Day 122

B—In dealing with equilibria, volume changes are important when there is a difference in the total number of moles of gas on opposite sides of the equilibrium arrow. In answers A and C there are different numbers of moles of gas on opposite sides of the equilibrium arrow. Ignore the solids in part D.

Day 123

C—The question asks for a K_p expression, which means it is necessary to use partial pressures, P, rather than molarities, [ ]. This eliminates choices A and B. Solids do not appear in equilibrium expressions, which eliminates choice D.

Day 124

The mass action expression is $K_c = \dfrac{[B]}{[A]}$. Counting the spheres in the diagram and entering the number into the mass action expression gives $K_c = \dfrac{[8]}{[4]} = 2$.

Day 125

The mass action expression is $K_c = \dfrac{[AB]^2}{[A_2][B_2]}$. Counting the spheres in the diagram and entering the number into the mass action expression gives $K_c = \dfrac{[6]^2}{[3][3]} = 4$.

Day 126

The mass action expression is $K_c = \dfrac{[AB]^2}{[B_2]}$. Note that A_2 is a solid and should not appear in the mass action expression. Counting the spheres in the diagram and entering the number into the mass action expression gives $K_c = \dfrac{[6]^2}{[3]} = 12$.

Day 127

A—Recall that $\Delta G = -RT \ln K$. As the value of ΔG increases, the value of K will decrease.

Day 128

(a) $COCl_2(g) \leftrightarrows CO(g) + Cl_2(g)$ has $K_c = 2.19 \times 10^{-10}$ at 100°C.

The value of K_c is very low, so it is possible to simplify the term for $[COCl_2]$ in the equilibrium expression by setting $[0.100 - x] \approx [0.100]$.

(b) $BrF_3(g) + F_2(g) \leftrightarrows BrF_5(g)$ has $K_c = 8.6 \times 10^{35}$ at 25°C.

The value of K_c is very high, so it is possible to simplify the term for $[BrF_5]$ in the equilibrium expression by setting $[0.250 - x] \approx [0.250]$.

(c) $2\,NOCl(g) \leftrightarrows 2\,NO(g) + Cl_2(g)$ has $K_c = 1.6 \times 10^{-5}$ at 35°C.

This is a cubic equation (it will have an x^3 term). Cubic equations cannot be solved by simple means.

(d) $NH_4HS(s) \leftrightarrows NH_3(g) + H_2S(g)$ has $K_c = 1.2 \times 10^{-4}$ at 25°C.

This is a heterogeneous equilibrium. The solid NH_4HS will not appear in the equilibrium expression.

Day 129

(a) Acidic: $HC_2H_3O_2(l) \leftrightarrows H^+(aq) + C_2H_3O_2^-(aq)$

Acetic acid is a weak acid and generates $H^+(aq)$; therefore, the solution is acidic.

(b) Basic: $NH_3(g) + H_2O(l) \leftrightarrows NH_4^+(aq) + OH^-(aq)$

Ammonia is a weak base that reacts with water to generate $OH^-(aq)$. The formation of $OH^-(aq)$ means that the solution is basic.

(c) Basic: $Na_2O(s) + H_2O(l) \rightarrow 2\,Na^+(aq) + 2\,OH^-(aq)$

Sodium oxide is a base anhydride, which means that it will react with water to form a base (sodium hydroxide in this case). The formation of $OH^-(aq)$ means that the solution is basic. Most metal oxides are base anhydrides unless they are too insoluble.

(d) Acidic: $Cl_2O_7(l) + H_2O(l) \rightarrow 2\,H^+(aq) + 2\,ClO_4^-(aq)$

Dichlorine heptoxide is an acid anhydride, which means that it will react with water to form an acid (perchloric acid in this case). The formation of $H^+(aq)$ means that the solution is acidic. Most nonmetal oxides are acid anhydrides.

(e) Acidic: $NH_4Cl(s) \rightarrow NH_4^+(aq) + Cl^-(aq)$

$NH_4^+(aq) \leftrightarrows NH_3(aq) + H^+(aq)$

Ammonium chloride is a soluble salt that dissociates in solution, as indicated by the first equation. The ammonium ion formed is the conjugate acid of a weak base, and since it is an acid, it will generate hydrogen ions in solution. The formation of $H^+(aq)$ means that the solution is acidic. Salts formed from the reaction of a weak base with a strong acid produce acidic solutions.

(f) Basic: $KNO_2(s) \rightarrow K^+(aq) + NO_2^-(aq)$

$NO_2^-(aq) + H_2O(l) \leftrightarrows HNO_2(aq) + OH^-(aq)$

Potassium nitrite is a soluble salt that dissociates in solution, as indicated by the first equation. The nitrite ion formed is the conjugate base of a weak acid, and since it is a base, it will generate hydroxide ions in solution. The formation of $OH^-(aq)$ means that the solution is basic. Salts formed from the reaction of a weak acid with a strong base produce basic solutions.

Day 130

According to the Arrhenius acid-base theory, an acid increases the hydrogen ion concentration in the solution, and a base increases the hydroxide ion concentration in the solution. In the example, HCl is the acid because it increases the hydrogen ion concentration by dissociation:

$$HCl(aq) \rightarrow H^+(aq) + Cl^-(aq)$$

The NH_3 is a base because it increases the hydroxide ion concentration through the following equilibrium:

$$NH_3(aq) + H_2O(l) \leftrightarrows NH_4^+(aq) + OH^-(aq)$$

The Brønsted-Lowry theory defines an acid as a substance that donates a hydrogen ion to the base, and it defines a base as a substance that accepts a hydrogen ion from the acid. In the example equation, the HCl is an acid because it donates a hydrogen ion to the NH_3, and the NH_3 is a base because it accepts a hydrogen ion from the HCl.

In Lewis acid-base theory, electron pairs are the key. A Lewis acid is a substance that accepts an electron pair from a Lewis base, and a Lewis base is a substance that donates an electron pair to a Lewis acid. In the equation shown in the example, this is best illustrated by the following diagram:

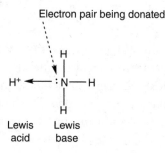

Day 131

$$\Delta G° = -RT \ln K \quad K_a = 6.5 \times 10^{-5}$$

$$\Delta G° = -(8.314 \text{ J/mol K})(298 \text{ K}) \ln (6.5 \times 10^{-5}) = 23886.577 = 2.4 \times 10^4 \text{ J/mol}$$

$$\Delta G = \Delta G° + RT \ln Q = \Delta G° + RT \ln \frac{[H^+][C_7H_5O_2^-]}{[HC_7H_5O_2]}$$

$$= 23886.577 \text{ J/mol} + (8.314 \text{ J/mol K})(298 \text{ K}) \ln \frac{[4.0 \times 10^{-3}][1.0 \times 10^{-5}]}{[0.12]}$$

$$= -1.3 \times 10^4 \text{ J/mol}$$

Day 132

One method is to convert the pH to the hydrogen ion concentration and to use K_w to convert from the hydrogen ion concentration to the hydroxide ion concentration:

$$[H^+] = 10^{-pH} = 10^{-12.00} = 1.0 \times 10^{-12} \text{ M H}^+(aq)$$

$$K_w = [H^+][OH^-] = 1.0 \times 10^{-14}$$

$$[OH^-] = \frac{K_w}{[H^+]} = \frac{1.00 \times 10^{-14}}{1.0 \times 10^{-2}} = 1.0 \times 10^{-2} \text{ M OH}^-(aq)$$

Another method is to convert the pH to a pOH and then use the pOH to determine the concentration:

$$pOH = pK_w - pH = 14.000 - 12.00 = 2.00$$

$$[OH^-] = 10^{-pOH} = 10^{-2.00} = 1.0 \times 10^{-2} \text{ M OH}^-(aq)$$

Both methods yield the same concentration.

Day 133

The concentrations of HCl (from $M_iV_i = M_fV_f$) are as follows:

$$A = 1.0 \times 10^{-3} \text{ M}$$

$$B = 1.0 \times 10^{-5} \text{ M}$$

$$C = 1.0 \times 10^{-7} \text{ M}$$

$$D = 1.0 \times 10^{-9} \text{ M}$$

Using these values and pH = $-\log [H^+]$ does give these values for any strong acid with these concentrations. However, a strong acid can never give a pH of 7 or 9, no matter how dilute the solution is. Acids always give an acidic solution (pH < 7). He overlooked the fact that water also contributes hydrogen ions. The hydrogen ion contribution from water is normally too small to be significant, but it becomes significant in very dilute acid or base solutions.

Day 134

A—Phenol has a K_a, which is an acid-dissociation constant; therefore, phenol is an acid. Since phenol is an acid, the solution must be acidic (pH < 7). Answers B and D refer to a basic solution and therefore can be eliminated. A 0.10 M strong acid solution would have 1.0 for its pH. Phenol is not a strong acid, so the pH must be above 1, which eliminates answer C.

Day 135

B—The presence of an acid, any acid, will always yield a pH below 7. Since the pH must be below 7, neither C nor D can be correct. A 0.10 M solution of a strong acid would have a pH of 1. Formic acid is not a strong acid, so the pH of a formic acid solution must be greater than 1.

Day 136

A pH of 8 is basic. It is not possible to prepare a basic solution by adding an acid (of any concentration) to water. The student neglected the autoionization of water.

Day 137

Beginning with K_{a1}:

$$K_{a1} = \frac{[H^+][H_2C_6H_5O_7^-]}{[H_3C_6H_5O_7]} = 7.4 \times 10^{-4} = \frac{x^2}{0.100 - x} \rightarrow x = 0.0086023 = 0.0086\ M$$

$[H_3C_6H_5O_7] = 0.100 - x = (0.100 - 0.0086023)\ M = 0.0913977 = 0.091\ M\ H_3C_6H_5O_7$

Using K_{a2}:

$$K_{a2} = \frac{[H^+][HC_6H_5O_7^{2-}]}{[H_2C_6H_5O_7^-]} = 1.8 \times 10^{-5} = \frac{(0.0086023 + x)(x)}{0.0086023 - x} \rightarrow x = 1.8 \times 10^{-5}\ M$$

$[H_2C_6H_5O_7^-] = 0.0086023 - x = (0.0086023 - 1.8 \times 10^{-5})\ M = 0.0085843$
$\qquad\qquad = 0.0086\ M\ H_2C_6H_5O_7^-$

$[H^+] = 0.0086023 + x = (0.0086023 + 1.8 \times 10^{-5})\ M = 0.0086203 = 0.0086\ M\ H^+$

Since there was no significant change due to K_{a2}, it is possible to assume that K_{a3} can be ignored. In retrospect, K_{a2} could have been ignored.

Finally, pH = $-\log[H^+] = -\log(0.0086203) = 2.064 = 2.10$.

Day 138

A—A is the salt of a strong acid, HCl, and a weak base, NH_3; it is acidic (pH < 7). B is a salt of a strong acid, HCl, and a strong base, KOH; they will give a neutral solution (pH = 7). C and D are salts of weak acids (H_3PO_4 and H_2CO_3) and strong bases (NaOH and KOH); they are basic (pH > 7). The lowest pH would be the acidic choice.

Day 139

B—Sodium nitrite is a salt of a weak acid and a strong base. Ions from strong bases, Na^+ in this case, do not undergo hydrolysis and do not affect the pH. Ions from weak acids, ClO^- in this case, undergo hydrolysis to produce basic solutions.

Day 140

The hydrogen atom attached to the oxygen atom is unique; therefore, it must be the one acidic hydrogen atom. Writing the formula as CH_3COOH is a better representation of the structure than the alternative, which emphasizes only that one of the hydrogen atoms (the one in front) is unique.

Day 141

From weakest acid to strongest acid, the sequence is

hypochlorous acid < chlorous acid < chloric acid < perchloric acid.

The H–O–Cl portion is identical in all the acids; therefore, the variation in strength must depend on something else. In this group, the something else is the number of additional oxygen atoms attached to the chlorine atom. The number of additional oxygen atoms ranges from zero to three. Oxygen is a very electronegative element and, for this reason, pulls electrons toward itself. This shift in electrons is transmitted to the least electronegative element present, which in this case is the hydrogen atom. As the hydrogen atom loses more electron density, the H–O bond becomes more polar and easier to ionize. The easier it is to ionize, the stronger the acid. The "ease" of ionization increases with the number of additional oxygen atoms present.

Day 142

The K_a nearest 10^{-8} will give a pH near 8. The second K_a is for the equilibrium $H_2PO_4^-(aq) \leftrightharpoons H^+(aq) + HPO_4^{2-}(aq)$, which involves $H_2PO_4^-$ (from KH_2PO_4) and HPO_4^{2-} (from K_2HPO_4).

Day 143

If one component of the solution is to be acetic acid, then the other component must be the acetate ion. For this reason, she needs an acetate salt such as sodium acetate. Since her choices do not include sodium acetate, she must make it. It is possible to produce sodium acetate by the reaction of acetic acid with sodium hydroxide. In order to produce the solution, she needs to add a solution containing 2.00 moles of acetic acid to a solution containing 1.00 mole of sodium hydroxide. The sodium hydroxide will react with 1.00 mole of the acetic acid to produce 1.00 mole of sodium acetate, will leave 1.00 mole of acetic acid unreacted and will dilute the solution to 10.0 L. Thus, she will have 10.0 L of a buffer solution containing 1.00 mole of acetic acid and 1.00 mole of the second component (sodium acetate).

Day 144

(a) The necessary equipment/reagents are as follows:

A flask into which you would put the sample

Standard base solution

A buret into which you would put the base

An appropriate acid-base indicator

A volumetric pipet to measure the lemon juice

A ring stand with a buret clamp

(b) Procedure:

Use the volumetric pipet to add a sample of lemon juice to the flask.

Add a few drops of indicator to the sample.

Charge (rinse) the buret (including the tip) with a few milliliters of standard base, and then drain.

Fill the buret with standard base and record the initial volume.

Add standard base from the buret to the sample until the indicator changes color.

Wait a minimum of 30 seconds; if the color does not change back, take a final buret reading.

Calculations:

Subtract the initial buret reading from the final buret reading to get the volume of standard base:

$$\frac{\text{Volume of base} \times \text{concentration of base} \times \text{mole ratio}}{\text{Volume of lemon juice (L)}}$$

A common error is to forget the mole ratio.

Another common error is to use the relation $M_1V_1 = M_2V_2$ in the calculation. If you do, your answer will be off by a factor of 3 because this relation does not include a mole ratio.

If you had trouble with this question, you might want to review Chapters 7, 15, and 19.

Day 145

B—The reaction of the weak base with the strong acid will produce the conjugate acid of the weak base. Until all the weak base has reacted, the solution contains unreacted weak base and the conjugate acid that has formed. This is a buffer solution, which will slowly decrease in pH until all the weak acid has reacted. Once all the weak base has reacted, the pH will decrease rapidly through the endpoint (eliminating A). The endpoint of a weak base–strong acid titration is always below 7, eliminating C (only strong base–strong acid titrations will give a pH of 7 at the endpoint). After the endpoint, the solution contains the conjugate acid of the weak base and the excess strong acid; this combination is not a buffer (eliminating D).

Day 146

A—The titration is an acid-base titration with HCl being the acid and Na_2CO_3 being the base. The question says that the acid is being added to the base; therefore, the initial pH (due to the base) must be high, which eliminates answers C and D. The reaction has two equivalence points (breaks), which eliminates choice B. The equivalence points are for

$$HCl(aq) + Na_2CO_3(aq) \rightarrow NaHCO_3(aq) + NaCl(aq)$$

$$HCl(aq) + NaHCO_3(aq) \rightarrow NaCl(aq) + H_2O(l) + CO_2(g)$$

Day 147

B—Malic and fluorophosphoric acids are both diprotic acids (that is, they have two acidic hydrogen atoms); therefore, they will require the same amount of base. Citric acid is a triprotic acid (it has three acidic hydrogen atoms), which will require 50% more base.

Day 148

D—The pK_a ($= -\log K_a$) should be near the pH at the equivalence point.

Day 149

B—Hydrochloric acid, being an acid, will react with a base. In addition to obvious bases containing OH^-, the salts of weak acids are also bases. All of the anions, except CN^-, are from strong acids (HBr, $HClO_4$, and HNO_3).

Day 150

It is possible to compare the solubilities of calcium carbonate and silver chloride because their stoichiometries both lead to $K_{sp} = (x)(x) = x^2$. The stoichiometry of lead(II) chloride is different, leading to a different representation as $K_{sp} = (x)(2x)^2 = 4\,x^3$.

Day 151

The higher the charge on the cation (+3 versus +2), the less soluble a substance, because there is a greater attraction between the ions (higher lattice energy).

Day 152

The chemical equation is $Ca_3(AsO_4)_2(s) \leftrightharpoons 3\ Ca^{2+}(aq) + 2\ AsO_4^{3-}(aq)$.

The mass action expression is $K_{sp} = [Ca^{2+}]^3\ [AsO_4^{3-}]^2$.

Common errors are showing water in the chemical equation and placing $Ca_3(AsO_4)_2$ in the denominator of the mass action expression. Water appears only as "(aq)" and $Ca_3(AsO_4)_2$ is a solid, which should never be included.

Day 153

A—The energy holding a solid together is the lattice energy. Therefore, it is necessary to overcome this energy to separate the ions in the solid. The bond energy would be important if this were covalent. The hydration energy is only important after the ions are separated from the solid. The fusion energy would be important if the solid were melting and not dissolving.

Day 154

$MnO_4^-(aq) + ClO_2^-(aq) \rightarrow ClO_4^-(aq) + MnO_2(s)$

$MnO_4^-(aq) \rightarrow MnO_2(s)$

$ClO_2^-(aq) \rightarrow ClO_4^-(aq)$

$4 (3 e^- + 2 H_2O(l) + MnO_4^-(aq) \rightarrow MnO_2(s) + 4 OH^-(aq))$

$3 (4 OH^-(aq) + ClO_2^-(aq) \rightarrow ClO_4^-(aq) + 2 H_2O(l) + 4 e^-)$

$3 ClO_2^-(aq) + 2 H_2O(l) + 4 MnO_4^-(aq) \rightarrow 4 MnO_2(s) + 4 OH^-(aq) + 3 ClO_4^-(aq)$

If you have trouble balancing this redox equation, you should probably refer to the appendix titled "Balancing Redox Equations Using the Ion-Electron Method." In addition, although naming compounds is not an AP topic, it is assumed that you know basic nomenclature, such as that in this problem, before you begin AP Chemistry.

Day 156

As the cell begins to run, it moves away from being a standard cell, which leads to a decrease in the cell voltage.

Day 157

The reaction in the anode compartment is

$$Fe^{2+}(aq) \rightarrow Fe^{3+}(aq) + 1 e^-.$$

Since none of the components is a conducting solid (metal), some other substance will need to serve as the anode. A platinum anode would be an acceptable choice because platinum is very unreactive.

The reaction in the cathode compartment is

$$I_2(s) + 2 e^- \rightarrow 2 I^-(aq).$$

There is a solid here, but it is a nonmetal (iodine). Nonmetals typically do not conduct electricity, so the iodine cannot serve as the cathode. The solid iodine would need to be in contact with a metal cathode to allow electron transfer. A platinum cathode would be an acceptable choice because platinum is very unreactive.

Day 158

(a) The cell voltage may be determined by $E_{cathode} - E_{anode} > 0$. Therefore, the cell potential is $0.80 - (-0.76) = 1.56$ volts.

(b) The zinc electrode must be the anode since the –0.76 is the anode position in the equation. Oxidation (loss of electrons) takes place at the anode, so the actual half-cell equation involving the zinc electrode would be $Zn \rightarrow Zn^{2+} + 2\ e^-$. Combining that half-cell with the silver half-reaction (and remembering to equalize electron loss with electron gain) yields $Zn + 2\ Ag^+ \rightarrow Zn^{2+} + 2\ Ag$ for the overall cell reaction (electrons canceled).

(c) Looking at the overall cell reaction reveals that the zinc electrode will be reacting to produce zinc cations. Therefore, the zinc electrode will decrease in mass.

Day 159

It is possible to reduce both water and the potassium ion; however, the reduction potential for water is less, so water will be reduced in preference to the potassium ion.

Day 160

She is constructing an electrolysis cell. To isolate nickel metal, it is necessary to use the nickel half-reaction (reduction) and the reverse of the lead half-reaction (oxidation). (It is always necessary to have both an oxidation and a reduction.) Reversing the lead half-reaction reverses the sign on $E°$. The cell potential is the sum of the two half-reaction potentials (+0.13 V and –0.25 V), and because the sum of the voltages is negative, this must be an electrolysis cell (nonspontaneous). If the sum of the half-reaction voltages were positive, this would be a galvanic cell.

Day 161

Reactants: $SiCl_4$ and H_2; products: Si and HCl (an acidic gas)

The overall reaction: $SiCl_4(l) + 2\ H_2(g) \rightarrow Si(s) + 4\ HCl(g)$

Day 162

C—This will lower the concentration of Cd^{2+}, causing a shift to the right, which will result in a voltage increase.

Day 163

D—The discrepancy means the cell must be nonstandard. A nonstandard cell is one that operates at some temperature other than 25°C, operates at a pressure not equal to 1 atmosphere, or has one or more concentrations that are not 1 M.

Day 164

The student would have to construct a concentration cell. The Nernst equation tells us that the half-cell potential depends on the concentration of the solution in which the electrode is immersed. Therefore, she could use a portion of the 0.20 M CuCl solution as one electrode and dilute another portion of the solution. Using the Nernst equation enables her to calculate the potential of each half-cell; combining them so that the resultant cell potential is positive enables her to calculate the actual cell potential.

Day 165

(a) It is necessary to combine the two half-reactions to generate the cell reaction. In order to combine these half-reactions, one of them must be reversed to convert it from a reduction to an oxidation. A battery spontaneously generates electricity; therefore, it is a voltaic cell and must have a positive voltage. The only way to reverse one half-reaction, and to have the combination sum to a positive number, is to reverse the cadmium equation. The result is

$$Cd(s) + 2\ OH^-(aq) \rightarrow Cd(OH)_2(s) + 2e^- \qquad E° = +0.76\ V$$
$$NiO_2(s) + 2\ H_2O(l) + 2e^- \rightarrow Ni(OH)_2(s) + 2\ OH^-(aq) \qquad E° = +0.49\ V$$
$$\overline{NiO_2(s) + 2\ H_2O(l) + Cd(s) \rightarrow Ni(OH)_2(s) + Cd(OH)_2(s) \qquad E° = +1.25\ V}$$

(b) Recharging is the reverse of discharging, so all that is necessary is to reverse the equation:

$$Ni(OH)_2(s) + Cd(OH)_2(s) \rightarrow NiO_2(s) + 2\ H_2O(l) + Cd(s)$$

(c) The value of $\Delta G°$ uses the equation $\Delta G° = -nFE°$, where n is the number of electrons transferred (here 2), F is the Faraday constant (96500 J/N mol), and $E°$ is the standard cell potential.

$$\Delta G° = -nFE° = -(2)\ (96500\ J/V\ mol)\ (1.25\ V) = -2.41 \times 10^5\ J/mol.$$

(d) Once the battery is completely discharged, it is "dead." A dead battery generates no voltage ($E = 0$); therefore, ΔG is also 0.

Day 166

(a) Hydrogen is present in the greatest number of atoms, but oxygen is present in the greatest mass.

(b) Aluminum is the most abundant metal in Earth's crust; however, an argument can be made for silicon because it is a semi-metal. (If you guessed hydrogen or oxygen, remember that they are nonmetals.)

(c) Hydrogen is the most abundant. There is more hydrogen than all the other elements combined.

(d) Yellow sulfur melts to produce a red viscous liquid.

(e) Mercury is a liquid at room temperature, and gallium will melt in your hand. (Cesium will also melt in your hand, but the metal is too reactive to risk touching.)

Day 167

The white glue is a solution of long polymer strands; the borax cross-links the polymer strands and creates a new polymer that has new properties that resemble the properties of Silly Putty®. Try pulling it quick and hard, and it should make a clean break. However, if you pull gently, it will easily stretch. You have made a cross-linked polymer.

Day 168

A non-Newtonian substance is one whose viscosity (resistance to flow) varies with pressure. It flows easily when poured from the pie pan (low viscosity) but behaves more like a solid when a strong force is applied over a short time frame (high viscosity). Another substance that behaves in this fashion is ketchup.

Day 169

Regular Coke® contains a lot of sugar and weighs several grams more than the artificially sweetened variety. Since the volumes of the cans are the same but the mass differs, the density of the regular Coke® is greater than that of the diet variety. You could therefore put the cans in pure water, and the Diet Coke® cans should float while the regular Coke® cans should sink. You must use pure water, not sea water. The sea water would provide enough extra buoyancy for the regular Coke® to float also.

Day 170

The IUPAC (International Union of Pure and Applied Chemistry) name for dihydrogen monoxide is water, H_2O. Water does kill many people every year, and the solid form, ice, does cause damage to skin. But it is absolutely necessary for life on Earth. Banning water is not a good idea (but it is a good way to get people interested in chemical nomenclature).

Day 171

Concentrated HF(aq) reacts with silicon dioxide (glass) to produce gaseous and water-soluble fluoride products. It would quickly destroy a glass container, so it must be stored in plastic containers. This reactivity toward glass has been known since the 17th century and is used in commercial glass etching.

Day 172

If this is done rapidly enough, the can quickly collapses, and when it is lifted, 15–20 mL of water will drain out. Explanation: As the can is heated, the small amount of water inside vaporizes, replacing the air with steam. When the can is inverted into the water, the steam condenses back into a microscopic drop of water. Since the opening is sealed off by the water, the condensing of the water vapor creates a partial vacuum. The atmospheric pressure is much greater than the pressure now inside the can, and two things happen simultaneously: The can is crushed inward by the greater atmospheric pressure, and the greater pressure forces water up into the can. There are videos of a tanker car being crushed by air pressure in a similar fashion.

Day 173

As you squeeze the bottle, the packet should sink to the bottom of the bottle. Releasing the pressure should cause the packet to rise to the top. The packet contains a small amount of air. Water is not very compressible, so when you squeeze the bottle, the force is transmitted through the water to the packet. The increased pressure compresses the confined air within the packet. The volume of the packet is now smaller, but its mass is the same. Therefore, the packet's density is greater and exceeds the density of water,

Answers

so it sinks. When you release the pressure, the air in the packet expands, decreasing the density of the packet to a value less than water's density, and the packet rises to the top. You have made a Cartesian Diver. Plenty of other examples of Cartesian Divers can be found on YouTube. The gas law that this demonstrates is Boyle's Law, the pressure/volume relationship (with amount and temperature constant). Good luck getting the hot sauce packet out of the bottle.

Day 174

The original recipe for Coke® did contain cocaine, but that recipe was modified in 1900 to include a process that removed the cocaine.

Day 175

Both depend on notes. The orchestra plays notes, and a cologne is composed of volatile chemicals that react with the nose in three distinct phases, which perfumers refer to as notes:

1. The top note impacts the nose first and makes the initial impression. Chemicals of the first note are more volatile than chemicals of the other notes. An example is phenylacetaldehyde, the aroma of lilacs.

2. The middle note is next and is the most noticeable. The compound 2-phenylethyl alcohol gives the middle note of the aroma of roses.

3. The end note is the longest-lasting aroma of the cologne. It gives the cologne its lingering aroma. Civetone, the aroma of musk, is an example of an end note.

Day 176

Lithium ion batteries have been implicated in the fires on at least three cargo aircraft, including a UPS cargo plane. Transport of large numbers of these batteries is clearly a problem, but what about passenger flights? Read and reach your own conclusions.

Day 177

Breathing sulfur hexafluoride gives you a very deep voice because the density of this gas is much greater than the density of air. To get it out of your lungs, you have to stand on your head and breathe out. This allows the gas to be exhaled.

Day 178

Thermite reaction: $Fe_2O_3(s) + 2\ Al(s) \rightarrow 2\ Fe(l) + Al_2O_3(s)$

Day 179

I think some of these new materials hold a lot of promise. See if you can come up with another use for one of the new materials the video highlighted.

Day 180

Did you catch how international politics could affect our supplies of critical rare earth elements?

Day 181

Did you find it a bit unsettling that there are simple things like this that scientists are unsure about? Welcome to science!

Day 182

Certainly makes you want to avoid chemicals containing fluorine, doesn't it?

Day 183

We just had to throw in the Periodic Table song:

https://www.youtube.com/watch?v=VgVQKCcfwnU

Here are the lyrics:

https://www.youtube.com/watch?v=1cqauZq4uYM

And here's a version for you Karaoke fanatics:

https://www.youtube.com/watch?v=bjQ3xZ3HKpI

Appendixes

SI Prefixes

PREFIX	ABBREVIATION	MEANING
pico-	p	0.000000000001 or 10^{-12}
nano-	n	0.000000001 or 10^{-9}
micro-	μ	0.000001 or 10^{-6}
milli-	m	0.001 or 10^{-3}
centi-	c	0.01 or 10^{-2}
deci-	d	0.1 or 10^{-1}
deka-	da	10 or 10^{1}
hecto-	h	100 or 10^{2}
kilo	k	1,000 or 10^{3}
Mega-	M	1,000,000 or 10^{6}
Giga-	G	1,000,000,000 or 10^{9}
Tera-	T	1,000,000,000,000 or 10^{12}

SI Base Units and SI/English Conversions

Length

The base unit for length in the SI system is the *meter*.

1 kilometer (km) = 0.62 mile (mi)
1 mile (mi) = 1.61 kilometers (km)
1 yard (yd) = 0.914 meters (m)
1 inch (in) = 2.54 centimeters (cm)

Mass

The base unit for mass in the SI system is the *kilogram* (kg).

1 pound (lb) = 454 grams (g)
1 metric ton (t) = 10^{3} kg

Volume

The unit for volume in the SI system is the *cubic meter* (m^{3}).

1 dm^{3} = 1 liter (L) = 1.057 quarts (qt)
1 milliliter (mL) = 1 cubic centimeter (cm^{3})
1 quart (qt) = 0.946 liters (L)
1 fluid ounce (fl oz) = 29.6 milliliters (mL)
1 gallon (gal) = 3.78 liters (L)

Temperature

The base unit for temperature in the SI system is *kelvin* (K).

Celsius to Fahrenheit: $°F = (9/5)°C + 32$
Fahrenheit to Celsius: $°C = (5/9)(°F - 32)$
Celsius to kelvin: $K = °C + 273.15$

Pressure

The unit for pressure in the SI system is the *pascal* (Pa).

1 millimeter of mercury (mm Hg) = 1 torr
$1 \text{ Pa} = 1 \text{ N/m}^2 = 1 \text{ kg/m s}^2$
$1 \text{ atm} = 1.01325 \times 10^5 \text{ Pa} = 760 \text{ torr}$
$1 \text{ bar} = 1 \times 10^5 \text{ Pa}$

Energy

The unit for energy in the SI system is the *joule* (J).

$1 \text{ J} = 1 \text{ kg m}^2/\text{s}^2 = 1$ coulomb volt
1 calorie (cal) = 4.184 joules (J)
1 food Calorie (Cal) = 1 kilocalorie (kcal) = 4,184 joules (J)
1 British thermal unit (BTU) = 252 calories (cal) = 1,053 joules (J)

BALANCING REDOX EQUATIONS USING THE ION-ELECTRON METHOD

The following steps may be used to balance oxidation–reduction (redox) equations by the ion-electron (half-reaction) method. While other methods may be successful, none is as consistently successful as this particular method. The half-reactions used in this process will also be necessary when considering other electrochemical phenomena; thus, the usefulness of half-reactions goes beyond balancing redox equations.

The basic idea of this method is to split a "complicated" equation into two parts called half-reactions. These simpler parts are then balanced separately, and recombined to produce a balanced overall equation. The splitting is done so that one of the half-reactions deals only with the oxidation portion of the redox process, whereas the other deals only with the reduction portion. What ties the two halves together is the fact that the total electrons lost by the oxidation process MUST equal the total gained by the reduction process (step 6).

It is very important that you follow each of the steps listed below completely, in order; do not try to take any shortcuts. There are many modifications of this method. For example, a modification allows you to balance all the reactions as if they were in acidic solution followed by a step, when necessary, to convert to a basic solution. Switching to a modification before you completely understand this method very often leads to confusion, and an incorrect result.

1. Assign Oxidation Numbers and Begin the Half-Reactions, One for Oxidation and One for Reduction

Beginning with the following example (phases are omitted for simplicity):

$$CH_3OH + Cr_2O_7^{2-} + H^+ \rightarrow HCOOH + Cr^{3+} + H_2O$$

(For many reactions, the substance oxidized and the substance reduced will be obvious, so this step may be simplified. However, to be safe, at least do a partial check to confirm your predictions. Note: One substance may be both oxidized and reduced; do not let this situation surprise you—it is called disproportionation.)

Review the rules for assigning oxidation numbers if necessary, in the Basics chapter. These numbers are only used in this step. Do not force them into step 5.

Start the half-reactions with the entire molecules or ions from the net ionic form of the reaction. Do not go back to the molecular form of the reaction or just pull out atoms from their respective molecules or ions. Thus from the example above, the initial half-reactions should be:

$$CH_3OH \rightarrow HCOOH$$

$$Cr_2O_7^{2-} \rightarrow Cr^{3+}$$

The carbon is oxidized (C^{2-} to C^{2+}) and the chromium is reduced (Cr^{6+} to Cr^{3+}). Check to make sure you get the same oxidation numbers for the carbon and the chromium (hydrogen and oxygen are +1 and −2 respectively).

2. Balance All Atoms Except Oxygen and Hydrogen

(In many reactions this will have been done in step 1; because of this many people forget to check this step. This is a very common reason why people get the wrong result.)

In the above example, carbon (C) and chromium (Cr) are the elements to be considered. The carbon is balanced, so no change is required in the first half-reaction. The chromium needs to be balanced, and so the second half-reaction becomes:

$$Cr_2O_7^{2-} \rightarrow 2\ Cr^{3+}$$

Note: To carry out the next two steps correctly, it is necessary to know if the solution is acidic or basic. A basic solution is one that you are specifically told is basic, or one that contains a base of OH^- anywhere within the reaction. Assume that all other solutions are acidic (even if no acid is present).

3. Balance Oxygen Atoms

a. In Acidic Solutions Add 1 H₂O/O to the Side Needing Oxygen

b. In Basic Solutions Add 2 OH⁻ for Every Oxygen Needed on the Oxygen-Deficient Side, Plus 1 H₂O/O on the Opposite Side

Do not forget that two things (OH^- and H_2O) must be added in a basic solution. Also these must be added to opposite sides.

Example acid:

acid: $$Cr_2O_7^{2-} \rightarrow 2\ Cr^{3+}$$

becomes: $$Cr_2O_7^{2-} \rightarrow >2\ Cr^{3+} + 7\ H_2O$$

Example base:

base: $$Cr_2O_7^{2-} \rightarrow 2\ CrO_2^-$$

becomes: $$3\ H_2O + Cr_2O_7^{2-} \rightarrow 2\ CrO_2^- + 6\ OH^-$$

4. Balance Hydrogen Atoms

a. In Acidic Solutions Add H⁺(aq)

b. In Basic Solutions Add 1 H₂O/H Needed, Plus 1 OH⁻/H on the Opposite Side

Again, do not forget that two things must be added in basic solutions (OH^- and H_2O). In this case, they are still added to opposite sides, but with a different ratio.

Example acid:

acid: $$Cr_2O_7^{2-} \rightarrow 2\ Cr^{3+} + 7\ H_2O$$

becomes: $$14\ H^+(aq) + Cr_2O_7^{2-} \rightarrow 2\ Cr^{3+} + 7\ H_2O$$

Example base:

base: $$6\ OH^- + C_2H_5OH \rightarrow 2\ CO_2 + 3\ H_2O$$

becomes: $$6\ OH^- + 6\ OH^- + C_2H_5OH \rightarrow 2\ CO_2 + 3\ H_2O + 6\ H_2O$$

If the basic step is done correctly, the oxygens should remain balanced. This may be used as a check at this point.

5. Balance Charges by Adding Electrons

The electrons must appear on opposite sides of the two half-reactions. They will appear on the left for the reduction, and on the right for the oxidation. Once added, make sure you check to verify that the total charge on each side is the same. Not being careful on this step is a major cause of incorrect answers. Do not forget to use both the coefficients and the overall charges on the ions (not the oxidation numbers from step 1).

Examples:

acid: $$6\ e^- + 14\ H^+(aq) + Cr_2O_7^{2-} \rightarrow 2\ Cr^{3+} + 7\ H_2O$$

base: $$6\ OH^- + 6\ OH^- + C_2H_5OH \rightarrow 2\ CO_2 + 3\ H_2O + 6\ H_2O + 12\ e^-$$

6. Adjust the Half-Reactions So That They Both Have the Same Number of Electrons

(Find the lowest common multiple, and multiply each of the half-reactions by the appropriate factor to achieve this value. This is the key step, as the number of electrons lost MUST equal the number gained.)

Example:

Lowest common multiple = 12

$$3 \times (H_2O + CH_3OH \rightarrow HCOOH + 4\ H^+(aq) + 4\ e^-)$$
$$2 \times (6\ e^- + 14\ H^+(aq) + Cr_2O_7^{2-} \rightarrow 2\ Cr^{3+} + 7\ H_2O)$$

giving:

$$3\ H_2O + 3\ CH_3OH \rightarrow 3\ HCOOH + 12\ H^+(aq) + 12\ e^-$$
$$12\ e^- + 28\ H^+(aq) + 2\ Cr_2O_7^{2-} \rightarrow 4\ Cr^{3+} + 14\ H_2O$$

7. Add the Half-Reactions and Cancel

(The electrons must cancel.)

Example (from step 6):

$$12\ e^- + 3\ H_2O + 3\ CH_3OH + 28\ H^+(aq) + 2\ Cr_2O_7^{2-}$$
$$\rightarrow 4\ Cr^{3+} + 14\ H_2O + 3\ HCOOH + 12\ H^+(aq) + 12\ e^-$$

becomes:

$$3\ CH_3OH + 16\ H^+(aq) + 2\ Cr_2O_7^{2-} \rightarrow 4\ Cr^{3+} + 11\ H_2O$$
$$+ 3\ HCOOH$$

8. Check to See If All Atoms Balance and That the Total Charge on Each Side Is the Same

This step will let you know whether you have done everything correctly.

If all the atoms and charges do not balance, you have made a mistake. Look over your work. If you have made an obvious mistake, then you should correct it. If the mistake is not obvious, it may take less time to start over from the beginning. The most common mistakes are made in steps 2 and 5, or step 3 in a basic solution.

Make sure you learn to apply each of the preceding steps. Look over the individual examples and make sure you understand them separately. Then make sure you learn the order of these steps. Finally, balance redox reactions; this will take a lot of practice. Make sure that you reach the point of being able to consistently balance equations without looking at the rules.

COMMON IONS

Ions Usually with One Oxidation State

Li^+	lithium ion	N^{3-}	nitride ion
Na^+	sodium ion	O^{2-}	oxide ion
K^+	potassium ion	S^{2-}	sulfide ion
Mg^{2+}	magnesium ion	F^-	fluoride ion
Ca^{2+}	calcium ion	Cl^-	chloride ion
Sr^{2+}	strontium ion	Br^-	bromide ion
Ba^{2+}	barium ion	I^-	iodide ion
Ag^+	silver ion		
Zn^{2+}	zinc ion		
Cd^{2+}	cadmium ion		
Al^{3+}	aluminum ion		

Cations with More than One Oxidation State

	+1		**+2**
Cu^+	copper(I) ion or cuprous ion	Cu^{2+}	copper(II) ion or cupric ion
Hg_2^{2+}	mercury(I) ion or mercurous ion	Hg^{2+}	mercury(II) ion or mercuric ion

	+2		**+3**
Fe^{2+}	iron(II) ion or ferrous ion	Fe^{3+}	iron(III) ion or ferric ion
Cr^{2+}	chromium(II) ion or chromous ion	Cr^{3+}	chromium(III) ion or chromic ion
Mn^{2+}	manganese(II) ion or manganous ion	Mn^{3+}	manganese(III) ion or manganic ion
Co^{2+}	cobalt(II) ion or cobaltous ion	Co^{3+}	cobalt(III) ion or cobaltic ion

	+2		**+4**
Sn^{2+}	tin(II) ion or stannous ion	Sn^{4+}	tin(IV) ion or stannic ion
Pb^{2+}	lead(II) ion or plumbous ion	Pb^{4+}	lead(IV) ion or plumbic ion

Polyatomic Ions and Acids

Formula	Name	Ion	Ion name
H_2SO_4	sulfuric acid	SO_4^{2-}	sulfate ion
H_2SO_3	sulfurous acid	SO_3^{2-}	sulfite ion
HNO_3	nitric acid	NO_3^-	nitrate ion
HNO_2	nitrous acid	NO_2^-	nitrite ion

Formula	Name	Ion	Ion name
H_3PO_4	phosphoric acid	PO_4^{3-}	phosphate ion
H_2CO_3	carbonic acid	CO_3^{2-}	carbonate ion
$HMnO_4$	permanganic acid	MnO_4^-	permanganate ion
HCN	hydrocyanic acid	CN^-	cyanide ion
$HOCN$	cyanic acid	OCN^-	cyanate ion
$HSCN$	thiocyanic acid	SCN^-	thiocyanate ion
$HC_2H_3O_2$	acetic acid	$C_2H_3O_2^-$	acetate ion
$H_2C_2O_4$	oxalic acid	$C_2O_4^{2-}$	oxalate ion
H_2CrO_4	chromic acid	CrO_4^{2-}	chromate ion
$H_2Cr_2O_7$	dichromic acid	$Cr_2O_7^{2-}$	dichromate ion
$H_2S_2O_3$	thiosulfuric acid	$S_2O_3^{2-}$	thiosulfate ion
H_3AsO_4	arsenic acid	AsO_4^{3-}	arsenate ion
H_3AsO_3	arsenous acid	AsO_3^{3-}	arsenite ion

Oxyhalogen Acids

Formula	Oxy name	Ion	Ion name
$HClO$	hypochlorous acid	ClO^-	hypochlorite ion
$HClO_2$	chlorous acid	ClO_2^-	chlorite ion
$HClO_3$	chloric acid	ClO_3^-	chlorate ion
$HClO_4$	perchloric acid	ClO_4^-	perchlorate ion

Br or I can be substituted for chlorine Cl. F may form hypofluorous acid and the hypofluorite ion.

Other Ions

Ion	Ion name
O_2^{2-}	peroxide ion
OH^-	hydroxide ion
HSO_4^-	bisulfate ion; hydrogen sulfate ion
NH_4^+	ammonium ion
O_2^-	superoxide ion
HCO_3^-	bicarbonate ion; hydrogen carbonate ion
HPO_4^{2-}	hydrogen phosphate ion
$H_2PO_4^-$	dihydrogen phosphate ion

Ligands

Ligand	Formula (abbreviation)	Ligand name
Bromide ion	Br^-	bromo
Carbonate ion	CO_3^{2-}	carbonato
Chloride ion	Cl^-	chloro

Ligand	Formula (abbreviation)	Ligand name
Cyanide ion	CN^-	cyano
Fluoride ion	F^-	fluoro
Hydride ion	H^-	hydrido
Hydroxide ion	OH^-	hydroxo
Iodide ion	I^-	iodo
Nitrite ion	NO_2^-	nitrito
Oxalate ion	$C_2O_4^{2-}$	oxalato
Sulfide ion	S^{2-}	thio
Thiocyanate ion	SCN^-	thiocyanato
Ammonia	NH_3	ammine
Ethylenediamine	en	ethylenediamine
Water	H_2O	aqua

Colors of Common Ions in Aqueous Solution

Most common ions are colorless in solution; however, some have distinctive colors. These colors have appeared in questions on the AP exam.

Fe^{2+} and Fe^{3+}	various colors
Cu^{2+}	blue to green
Cr^{2+}	blue
Cr^{3+}	green or violet
Mn^{2+}	faint pink
Ni^{2+}	green
Co^{2+}	pink
MnO_4^-	dark purple
CrO_4^{2-}	yellow
$Cr_2O_7^{2-}$	orange

BIBLIOGRAPHY

Brown, Theodore L., H. Eugene Le May, Jr., and Bruce E. Bursten. 2011. *Chemistry: The Central Science*, 12th ed. Upper Saddle Creek, NJ: Prentice Hall.

Cates, Charles R., Richard H. Langley, and John T. Moore. 2003. *Introductory Chemical Practice*: *A Quantitative Approach*, 6th ed. San Francisco, CA: Burgess Publishing.

Goldberg, David E. 2006. *Fundamentals of Chemistry*, 5th ed. New York: McGraw-Hill Education.

Hostage, David, and Martin Fossett. 2005. *Laboratory Investigations: AP Chemistry*, Saddle Brook, NJ: Peoples Publishing Group.

Moore, John T. 2011. *Chemistry for Dummies*. Hoboken, NJ: Wiley Publishing, Inc.

Moore, John T. 2010. *Chemistry Essentials for Dummies*. Hoboken, NJ: Wiley Publishing, Inc.

Moore, John T., and Richard Langley. 2007. *Chemistry for the Utterly Confused*. New York: McGraw-Hill Education.

Russo, Steve, and Mike Silver. 2010. *Introductory Chemistry*, 4th ed. Upper Saddle Creek, NJ: Prentice Hall.

Silberberg, Martin S. 2011. *Chemistry: The Molecular Nature of Matter and Change*, 6th ed. New York: McGraw-Hill Education.

Zumdahl, Steven S., and Susan A. Zumdahl. 2013. *Chemistry*, 9th ed. Belmont, CA: Brooks Cole.

WEBSITES

Here is a list of websites that contain information and links that you might find useful in your preparation for the AP Chemistry exam:

www.chemistry.about.com
www.webelements.com
www.collegeboard.com/student/testing/ap/sub_chem.html?chem
www.chemistrygeek.com/ap.htm
www.rsc.org/

absolute zero Absolute zero is 0 K and is the point at which all molecular motion ceases.

acid dissociation constant (K_a) The acid dissociation constant is the equilibrium constant associated with a weak acid dissociation in water.

acidic A solution whose pH is *less* than 7.00 is said to be acidic.

acids Acids are proton (H^+) donors.

activation energy Activation energy is the minimum amount of energy that must be supplied to initiate a chemical reaction.

activity series for metals The activity series lists metals in order of decreasing ease of oxidation.

actual yield The actual yield is the amount of product that is actually formed in a chemical reaction.

alkali metals Alkali metals are in Group 1 on the periodic table.

alkaline earth metals Alkaline earth metals are in Group 2 on the periodic table.

alkanes Alkanes are hydrocarbons that contain only single covalent bonds within the molecule.

alkenes Alkenes are hydrocarbons that contain a carbon-to-carbon double bond.

alkynes Alkynes are hydrocarbons that contain a carbon-to-carbon triple bond.

alpha particle An alpha particle is essentially a helium nucleus with two protons and two neutrons.

amorphous solids Amorphous solids are solids that lack extensive ordering of the particles.

amphoteric Amphoteric substances will act as either an acid or a base, depending on whether the other species is a base on an acid.

amplitude Amplitude is the height of a wave and is related to the intensity (or brightness for visible light) of the wave.

amu An amu is ½ the mass of a carbon atom that contains 6 protons and 6 neutrons (C-12).

angular momentum quantum number (*l*) The angular momentum quantum number is the quantum number that describes the shape of the orbital.

anions Anions are negatively charged ions.

anode The electrode at which oxidation is taking place is called the anode.

anode compartment The anode compartment is the electrolyte solution in which the anode is immersed.

aqueous solution An aqueous solution is a solution in which water is the solvent.

atomic number (*Z*) The atomic number of an element is the number of protons in the nucleus.

atomic orbital The atomic orbital is the region of space in which it is most likely to find a specific electron in an atom.

atomic solids In atomic solids, individual atoms are held in place by London forces.

Aufbau principle The Aufbau principle states that the electrons in an atom fill the lowest energy levels first.

Avogadro's law Avogadro's law states that there is a direct relationship between the volume and the number of moles of gas.

Avogadro's number Avogadro's number is the number of particles (atoms or molecules or ions) in a mole and is numerically equal to 6.022×10^{23} particles.

barometer A barometer is an instrument for measuring atmospheric pressure.

base dissociation constant, K_b The base dissociation constant is the equilibrium constant associated with the dissociation of a weak base in water.

bases Bases are defined as proton (H^+) acceptors.

basic A solution whose pH is *greater* than 7.00 is called basic.

beta particle A beta particle is an electron.

bimolecular reactions Bimolecular reactions are chemical reactions that involve the collision of two chemical species.

binary compounds Binary compounds are compounds that consist of only two elements.

body-centered unit cell A body-centered unit cell has particles located at the corners of a cube and in the center of the cube.

boiling The process of going from the liquid state to the gaseous state is called boiling.

boiling point The boiling point (b.p.) is the temperature at which a liquid boils.

bond order The bond order relates the bonding and antibonding electrons in the molecular orbital theory (# electrons in bonding MOs – # electrons in antibonding MOs)/2.

Boyle's law Boyle's law states that there is an inverse relationship between the volume and pressure of a gas, if the temperature and amount are kept constant.

buffer capacity The buffer capacity is the ability of the buffer to resist a change in pH.

buffers Buffers are solutions that resist a change in pH when an acid or base is added to them.

calorie The calorie is the amount of energy needed to raise the temperature of 1 gram of water 1°C.

calorimetry Calorimetry is the laboratory technique used to measure the heat released or absorbed during a chemical or physical change.

capillary action Capillary action is the spontaneous rising of a liquid through a narrow tube against the force of gravity.

catalyst A catalyst is a substance that speeds up the reaction rate and is (at least theoretically) recoverable at the end of the reaction in an unchanged form.

cathode The cathode is the electrode in an electrochemical cell at which reduction takes place.

cathode compartment The cathode compartment is the electrolyte solution in which the cathode is immersed.

cations Cations are positively charged ions.

cell notation Cell notation is a shorthand notation for representing a galvanic cell.

Charles's law Charles's law states that there is a direct relationship between the volume and temperature of a gas, if the pressure and amount are kept constant.

chemical equilibrium A chemical equilibrium has been reached when two exactly opposite reactions are occurring at the same place, at the same time, and with the same rates of reaction.

colligative properties Colligative properties are solution properties that are simply dependent upon the *number* of solute particles, and not the type of solute.

colloids Colloids are homogeneous mixtures in which solute diameters fall in between solutions and suspensions.

combination reactions Combination reactions are reactions in which two or more reactants (elements or compounds) combine to form one product.

combined gas equation The combined gas equation relates the pressure, temperature, and volume of a gas, assuming the amount is held constant.

combustion reactions Combustion reactions are redox reactions in which the chemical species rapidly combines with oxygen and usually emits heat and light.

common-ion effect The common-ion effect is an application of Le Châtelier's principle to equilibrium systems of slightly soluble salts.

complex A complex is composed of a central atom, normally a metal, surrounded by atoms or groups of atoms called ligands.

compounds Compounds are pure substances that have a fixed proportion of elements.

concentrated Concentrated is a qualitative way of describing a solution that has a relatively large amount of solute in comparison to the solvent.

concentration Concentration is a measure of the amount of solute dissolved in the solvent.

concentration cell A concentration cell is an electrochemical cell in which the same chemical species are used in both cell compartments, but differ in concentration.

conjugate acid–base pair This is an acid–base pair that differs by only a single H^+.

continuous spectrum A continuous spectrum is a spectrum of light much like the rainbow.

coordinate covalent bonds Coordinate covalent bonds are covalent bonds in which one of the atoms furnishes both of the electrons for the bond.

coordination compounds Coordination compounds are a type of complex in which a metal atom is surrounded by ligands.

coordination number Coordination number is the number of ligands that can covalently bond to the metal ion in the complex ion.

covalent bonding In covalent bonding, one or more electron pairs are shared between two atoms.

crisscross rule The crisscross rule can be used to help determine the formula of an ionic compound.

critical point The critical point of a substance is the point on the phase diagram beyond which the gas and liquid phases are indistinguishable from each other.

crystal lattice The crystal lattice is a three-dimensional structure that crystalline solids occupy.

crystalline solids Crystalline solids display a very regular ordering of the particles (atoms, molecules, or ions) in a three-dimensional structure called the crystal lattice.

Dalton's law Dalton's law states that in a mixture of gases (A + B + C . . .) the total pressure is simply the sum of the partial pressures (the pressures associated with each individual gas).

decomposition reactions Decomposition reactions are reactions in which a compound breaks down into two or more simpler substances.

diamagnetism Diamagnetism is the repulsion of a molecule from a magnetic field due to the presence of all electrons in pairs.

dilute Dilute is a qualitative term that refers to a solution that has a relatively small amount of solute in comparison to the amount of solvent.

dimensional analysis Dimensional analysis, sometimes called the factor label method, is a method for generating a correct setup for a mathematical problem.

dipole–dipole intermolecular force Dipole–dipole intermolecular forces occur between polar molecules.

double displacement (replacement) or metathesis reaction A double displacement (replacement) or metathesis reaction is a chemical reaction where at least one insoluble product is formed from the mixing of two solutions.

effective nuclear charge The overall attraction that an electron experiences is called the effective nuclear charge. This is less than the actual nuclear charge, because other electrons interfere with the attraction of the protons for the electron being considered.

electrochemical cells Electrochemical cells use indirect electron transfer to produce electricity by a redox reaction, or they use electricity to produce a desired redox reaction.

electrochemistry Electrochemistry is the study of chemical reactions that produce electricity and chemical reactions that take place because electricity is supplied.

electrode The electrode is that solid part of the electrochemical cell that conducts the electrons that are involved in the redox reaction.

electrode compartment The solutions in which the electrodes are immersed are called the electrode compartments.

electrolysis Electrolysis is a reaction in which electricity is used to decompose a compound.

electrolyte An electrolyte is a substance that, when dissolved in solution or melted, conducts an electrical current.

electrolytic cells Electrolytic cells use electricity from an external source to produce a desired redox reaction.

electromagnetic spectrum The electromagnetic spectrum is radiant energy, composed of gamma rays, X-rays, ultraviolet light, visible light, etc.

electron affinity The electron affinity is the energy change that results from adding an electron to an atom or ion.

electron capture Electron capture is a radioactive decay mode that involves the capturing of an electron from the energy level closest to the nucleus (1s) by a proton in the nucleus.

electron cloud The electron cloud is a volume of space in which the probability of finding the electron is high.

electronegativity The electronegativity (EN) is a measure of the attractive force that an atom exerts on a bonding pair of electrons.

electronic configuration The electronic configuration is a condensed way of representing the pattern of electrons in an atom.

elementary step Elementary steps are the individual reactions in the reaction mechanism or pathway.

empirical formula The empirical formula is a chemical formula that tells us which elements are present in the compound and the simplest whole-number ratio of elements.

endothermic Endothermic reactions absorb energy from their surroundings.

endpoint The endpoint of a titration is the point signaled by the indication that an equivalent amount of base has been added to the acid sample, or vice versa.

enthalpy The enthalpy change, ΔH, is the heat gained or lost by the system during constant pressure conditions.

entropy Entropy (S) is a measure of the disorder of a system.

equilibrium constant The quantity calculated when the equilibrium concentrations of the chemical species are substituted into the reaction quotient.

equivalence point The equivalence point is that point in the titration where the moles of H^+ in the acid solution have been exactly neutralized with the same number of moles of OH^-.

excited state An excited state of an atom is an energy state of higher energy.

exothermic An exothermic reaction releases energy (heat) to its surroundings.

face-centered unit cell The face-centered unit cell has particles at the corners and one in the center of each face of the cube, but not in the center of the cube.

First Law of Thermodynamics The First Law of Thermodynamics states that the total energy of the universe is constant.

formation constant The formation constant is the equilibrium constant for the formation of a complex ion from a metal ion and ligands.

frequency The frequency, ν, is defined as the number of waves that pass a point per second.

functional group Functional groups are reactive groups on a compound that react in a characteristic way no matter what the rest of the molecule consists of.

galvanic (voltaic) cells Galvanic (voltaic) cells are electrochemical cells that produce electricity by a redox reaction.

gamma emission Gamma emission is a radioactive decay process in which high-energy, short-wavelength photons that are similar to X-rays are given off.

gas A gas is a state of matter that has neither definite shape nor volume.

Gay-Lussac's law Gay-Lussac's law describes the direct relationship between the pressure of a gas and its Kelvin temperature, if the volume and amount are held constant.

Gibbs free energy The Gibbs free energy (G) is a thermodynamic function that combines the enthalpy, entropy, and temperature. ΔG is the best indicator of whether or not a reaction will be spontaneous.

Graham's law Graham's law says that the speed of gas diffusion (mixing of gases due to their kinetic energy) or effusion (movement of a gas through a tiny opening) is inversely proportional to the square root of the gases' molecular mass.

ground state The ground state of an atom is the lowest energy state that the electron can occupy.

groups Groups (families) are the vertical columns on the periodic table.

half-life The half-life, $t_{1/2}$, is the amount of time that it takes for a reactant concentration to decrease to one-half its initial concentration.

halogens Halogens are in Group 17 on the periodic table.

heat capacity Heat capacity is the quantity of heat needed to change the temperature by 1 K.

heat of vaporization The heat of vaporization is the heat needed to transform a liquid into a gas.

Henderson–Hasselbalch equation The Henderson–Hasselbalch equation can be used to calculate the pH of a buffer.

Henry's law The solubility of a gas will increase with increasing partial pressure of the gas.

Hess's law Hess's law states that if a reaction occurs in a series of steps, then the enthalpy change for the overall reaction is simply the sum of the enthalpy changes of the individual steps.

heterogeneous catalyst A heterogeneous catalyst is a catalyst that is in a different phase or state of matter from the reactants.

homogeneous catalyst A homogeneous catalyst is a catalyst that is in the same phase or state of matter as the reactants.

Hund's rule Hund's rule states that electrons are added to the orbitals, half filling them all before any pairing occurs.

hybrid orbitals Hybrid orbitals are atomic orbitals formed as a result of the mixing of the atomic orbitals of the atoms involved in a covalent bond.

hydrocarbons Hydrocarbons are organic compounds containing only carbon and hydrogen.

hydrogen bonding Hydrogen bonding is a specific type of dipole–dipole attraction in which a hydrogen atom is polar-covalently bonded to one of the following extremely electronegative elements: O, N, or F.

ideal gas An ideal gas is a gas that obeys the five postulates of the Kinetic Molecular Theory of Gases.

ideal gas equation The ideal gas equation relates the temperature, volume, pressure, and amount of a gas, and has the mathematical form of $PV = nRT$.

indicators Indicators are substances that change their color during a titration to indicate the endpoint.

inert (inactive) electrode An inert (inactive) electrode is a solid conducting electrode in an electrochemical cell that does not take part in the redox reaction.

inner transition elements The inner transition elements are the two horizontal groups that have been pulled out of the main body of the periodic table.

integrated rate law The integrated rate law relates the change in the concentration of reactants or products over time.

intermediates Intermediates are chemical species that are produced and consumed during the reaction, but that do not appear in the overall reaction.

intermolecular forces Intermolecular forces are attractive or repulsive forces between molecules caused by partial charges.

ion–dipole intermolecular force Ion–dipole intermolecular forces are attractive forces that occur between ions and polar molecules.

ion-induced dipole intermolecular forces Ion-induced dipole intermolecular forces are attractive forces that occur between an ion and a nonpolar molecule.

ion-product The ion-product has the same form as the solubility product constant, but represents a system that is not at equilibrium.

ionic bond Ionic bonds result from some metal losing electrons to form cations and some nonmetal gaining those electrons to form an anion.

ionic equation The ionic equation shows the soluble reactants and products in the form of ions.

ionic solids Ionic solids have their lattices composed of ions held together by the attraction of opposite charges of the ions.

ionization energy The ionization energy (IE) is the energy needed to completely remove an electron from an atom in the vapor state.

isoelectronic Isoelectronic means having the same electronic configuration.

isomers Isomers are compounds that have the same molecular formulas but different structural formulas.

isotopes Isotopes are atoms of the same element (same number of protons) that have differing numbers of neutrons.

joule (J) The joule is the SI unit of energy.

kinetic energy Kinetic energy is energy of motion.

Kinetic Molecular Theory The Kinetic Molecular Theory attempts to represent the properties of gases by modeling the gas particles themselves at the microscopic level.

kinetics Kinetics is the study of the speed of reactions.

Law of Conservation of Matter The Law of Conservation of Matter says that, in ordinary chemical reactions, matter is neither created nor destroyed.

Le Châtelier's principle Le Châtelier's principle states that if a chemical system at equilibrium is stressed (disturbed), it will reestablish equilibrium by shifting of the reactions involved.

Lewis electron-dot structure The Lewis electron-dot structure is a structural formula that represents the element and its valence electrons.

limiting reactant The limiting reactant is the reactant that is used up first in a chemical reaction.

line spectrum A line spectrum is a series of fine lines of colors representing wavelengths of photons that are characteristic of a particular element.

liquid A liquid is a state of matter that has a definite volume but no definite shape.

macromolecules Macromolecules are extremely large molecules.

magnetic quantum number (m_l) The magnetic quantum number describes the orientation of the orbital around the nucleus.

main-group elements Main-group elements are the groups on the periodic table that are labeled 1–2 and 13–18.

manometer A manometer is an instrument used to measure the gas pressure inside a container.

mass number The mass number is the sum of the protons and neutrons in an atom.

mass percent The mass percentage of a solution is the mass of the solute divided by the mass of the solution and then multiplied by 100% to get percentage.

mass-volume percent The mass-volume percent of a solution is the mass of the solute divided by the volume of the solution and then multiplied by 100% to yield percentage.

mechanism The mechanism is the sequence of steps that a reaction undergoes in going from reactants to products.

melting point The temperature at which a solid converts into the liquid state is called the melting point (m.p.) of the solid.

metallic bonding In metallic bonding the electrons of the atoms are delocalized and are free to move throughout the entire solid.

metallic solids Metallic solids have metal atoms occupying the crystal lattice and held together by metallic bonding.

metalloids Metalloids are a group of elements that have properties of both metals and nonmetals.

metals Metals are normally solids (mercury being an exception), shiny, and good conductors of heat and electricity. They can be hammered into thin sheets (malleable) and extruded into wires (ductile). Chemically, metals tend to lose electrons in reactions.

metathesis reaction In a metathesis reaction two substances exchange bonding partners.

molality (*m*) Molality is defined as the moles of solute per kilogram of solvent.

molar heat capacity The molar heat capacity (*C*) is the amount of heat needed to change the temperature of 1 mole of a substance by 1 K.

molar mass The mass in grams of 1 mole of a substance.

molarity (*M*) or sometimes [ ] Molarity is a concentration term that represents the moles of solute per liters of solution.

mole The mole (mol) is defined as the amount of a substance that contains the same number of particles as atoms in exactly 12 g of carbon-12.

molecular equation The molecular equation is an equation in which both the reactants and products are shown in the undissociated form.

molecular formula The molecular (actual) formula shows which elements are in the compound and the actual number of atoms of each element.

molecular orbital theory The molecular orbital (MO) theory of covalent bonding proposes that atomic orbitals combine to form molecular orbitals that encompass the entire molecule.

molecular solids Molecular solids have their lattices composed of molecules held in place by London forces, dipole–dipole forces, and hydrogen bonding.

molecule A molecule is a covalently bonded compound.

monomers Macromolecules are composed of repeating units, called monomers.

Nernst equation The Nernst equation allows the calculation of the cell potential of a galvanic cell that is not at standard conditions.

net ionic equation The net ionic equation is written by dropping out the spectator ions and showing only those chemical species that are involved in the chemical reaction.

network covalent solids Network covalent solids have covalent bonds joining the atoms together in an extremely large crystal lattice.

neutral Neutral is 7.00 on the pH scale.

neutralization reactions Neutralization reactions are acid–base reactions in which an acid reacts with a base to give a salt and usually water.

noble gases Noble gases are in Group 18 on the periodic table. They are very unreactive owing to their filled valence shell.

nonelectrolytes Nonelectrolytes are substances that do not conduct electricity when dissolved in water or melted.

nonmetals Nonmetals have properties that are generally the opposite of metals. Some are gases, are poor conductors of heat and electricity, are neither malleable nor ductile, and tend to gain or share electrons in their chemical reactions.

nonpolar covalent bond In a nonpolar covalent bond the electrons are shared equally by the two atoms involved in the bond.

nuclear belt of stability The nuclear belt of stability is a plot of the number of neutrons versus the number of protons for the known stable isotopes.

nucleus The nucleus is a dense core of positive charge at the center of the atom that contains most of the mass of the atom.

octet rule The octet rule states that during chemical reactions, atoms lose, gain, or share electrons in order to achieve a filled valence shell, to complete their octet.

orbital An orbital or wave function is a quantum mechanical mathematical description of the location of electrons. The electrons in a particular subshell are distributed among these volumes of space of equal energies.

order of reaction The order of reaction is the exponent in the rate equation that indicates what effect a change in concentration of that particular reactant species will have on the reaction rate.

organic chemistry Organic chemistry is the study of the chemistry of carbon.

osmosis Osmosis is the passing of solvent molecules through a semipermeable membrane.

osmotic pressure The osmotic pressure is the amount of pressure that must be exerted on a solution in order to prevent osmosis of solvent molecules through a semipermeable membrane.

oxidation Oxidation is the loss of electrons.

oxidation numbers Oxidation numbers are bookkeeping numbers that allow chemists to do things like balance redox equations.

oxidizing agent The oxidizing agent is the reactant being reduced.

paramagnetism Paramagnetism is the attraction of a molecule to a magnetic field and is due to unpaired electrons.

pascal The pascal is the SI unit of pressure.

percent yield The percent yield (% yield) is the actual yield divided by the theoretical yield, with the result multiplied by 100.

periods Periods are the horizontal rows on the periodic table that have consecutive atomic numbers.

phase changes Phase changes are changes of state.

phase diagram A phase diagram is a graph representing the relationship of the states of matter of a substance to temperature and pressure.

pi (π) bonds Pi bonds result from the overlap of atomic orbitals on both sides of a line connecting two atomic nuclei.

polar covalent bonds Polar covalent bonds are covalent bonds in which there is an unequal sharing of the bonding pair of electrons.

polyprotic acids Polyprotic acids are acids that can donate more than one proton.

potential energy Potential energy is stored energy.

positron A positron is essentially an electron that has a positive charge instead of a negative one.

precipitate A precipitate is an insoluble product that forms in a solution; the formation of a solid from ions in solution.

precipitation reactions Precipitation reactions are reactions that involve the formation of an insoluble compound, a precipitate, from the mixing of two soluble compounds.

pressure Pressure is the force exerted per unit of surface area.

principal quantum number (n) The principal quantum number describes the size of the orbital and relative distance from the nucleus.

proof The proof of an aqueous ethyl alcohol solution is twice the volume percent.

quantized Quantized means that there could be only certain distinct energies associated with a state of the atom.

quantum numbers Quantum numbers are used to describe each electron within an atom corresponding to the orbital size, shape, and orientation in space.

radioactivity Radioactivity is the spontaneous decay of an unstable isotope to a more stable one.

rate constant (k) The rate constant is a proportionality constant that appears in the rate law and relates the concentration of reactants to the speed of reaction.

rate-determining step The rate-determining step is the slowest one of the reaction steps and controls the rate of the overall reaction.

rate equation The rate equation relates the speed of reaction to the concentration of reactants and has the form: Rate $= k[A]^m[B]^n$. . . . where k is the rate constant and m and n are the orders of reaction with respect to that specific reactant.

reactants The starting materials in a chemical reaction, which get converted into different substances called products.

reaction intermediate A reaction intermediate is a substance that is formed but then consumed during the reaction mechanism.

reaction mechanism The reaction mechanism is the sequence of individual reactions that occur in an overall reaction in going from reactants to products.

reaction quotient The reaction quotient, Q, is the numerical value that results when non-equilibrium concentrations are inserted into the equilibrium expression. When the system reaches equilibrium, the reaction quotient becomes the equilibrium constant.

reactive site The reactive site of a molecule is the place at which the reaction takes place.

redox reactions Redox reactions are chemical reactions in which electrons are lost and gained.

reducing agent The reactant undergoing oxidation in a redox reaction is called the reducing agent.

reduction Reduction is the gain of electrons in a redox reaction.

resonance Resonance is a way of describing a molecular structure that cannot be represented by a single Lewis structure. Several different Lewis structures are used, each differing only by the position of electron pairs.

reverse osmosis Reverse osmosis takes place when the pressure on the solution side exceeds the osmotic pressure and solvent molecules are forced back through the semipermeable membrane into the solvent side.

root mean square speed The average velocity of the gas particles is called the root mean square speed.

salt bridge A salt bridge is often an inverted U-tube that contains a gel containing a concentrated electrolyte solution, used in an electrochemical cell to maintain electrical neutrality in the cell compartments.

saturated hydrocarbons Saturated hydrocarbons are hydrocarbons that are single bonded to the maximum number of other atoms.

saturated solution A solution in which one has dissolved the maximum amount of solute per given amount of solvent at a given temperature is called a saturated solution.

Second Law of Thermodynamics The Second Law of Thermodynamics states that all processes that occur spontaneously move in the direction of an increase in entropy of the universe (system + surroundings).

semipermeable membrane A semipermeable membrane is a thin porous film that allows the passage of solvent molecules but not solute particles.

shells The electrons in an atom are located in various energy levels or shells that are located at different distances from the nucleus.

SI system The system of units used in science is the SI system (Système International), which is related to the metric system.

sigma (σ) bonds Sigma bonds have the orbital overlap on a line drawn between the two nuclei.

simple cubic unit cell The simple cubic unit cell has particles located at the corners of a simple cube.

single displacement (replacement) reactions Single displacement reactions are reactions in which atoms of an element replace the atoms of another element in a compound.

solid A solid is a state of matter that has both a definite shape and a definite volume.

solubility product constant (K_{sp}) The solubility product constant is the equilibrium constant associated with sparingly soluble salts and is the product of the ionic concentrations, each one raised to the power of the coefficient in the balanced chemical equation.

solute The solute is the component of the solution that is present in smallest amount.

solution A solution is defined as a homogeneous mixture composed of solvent and one or more solutes.

solvation Solvation is the forming of a layer of bound solvent molecules around a solute.

solvent The solvent is that component of a solution that is present in largest amount.

specific heat capacity (or specific heat) (c) The specific heat capacity is the quantity of heat needed to raise the temperature of 1 g of the substance by 1 K.

spectator ions Spectator ions are ions that are not actually involved in the chemical reaction taking place, but simply maintain electrical neutrality.

speed of light (c) The speed of light is the speed at which all electromagnetic radiation travels in a vacuum, 3.0×10^8 m/s.

spin quantum number (m_s) The spin quantum number indicates the direction the electron is spinning.

standard cell potential ($E°$) The standard cell potential is the potential (voltage) associated with an electrochemical cell at standard conditions.

standard enthalpy of formation The standard enthalpy of formation of a compound ($\Delta H_f°$) is the change in enthalpy when 1 mol of the compound is formed from its elements and when all substances are in their standard states.

standard molar entropies ($S°$) Standard molar enthalpies of elements and compounds are the entropies associated with 1 mole of a substance in its standard state.

standard reduction potentials The standard reduction potential is the voltage associated with a half-reaction shown in the form of reduction.

state function A state function is a function that doesn't depend on the pathway, only the initial and final states.

stoichiometry Stoichiometry is the calculation of the amount (mass, moles, particles) of one substance in the chemical reaction through the use of another.

strong acid A strong acid is an acid that ionizes completely in solution.

strong base A strong base is a base that ionizes completely in solution.

strong electrolytes Strong electrolytes completely ionize or dissociate in solution.

structural isomers Structural isomers are compounds that have the same molecular formula but differ in how the atoms are attached to each other.

sublimation Sublimation is going directly from the solid state to the gaseous state without ever having become a liquid.

subshells Within the shells, the electrons are grouped in subshells of slightly different energies.

supersaturated solution A supersaturated solution has more than the maximum amount of solute dissolved in the solvent at a given temperature.

surface tension Surface tension is the amount of force that is required to break through the molecular layer at the surface of a liquid.

surroundings The surroundings is a thermodynamic term meaning the part of the universe that is not the system that is being studied.

suspension A heterogeneous mixture in which the particles are large (in excess of 1,000 nm).

system The system is a thermodynamics term meaning the part of the universe that we are studying.

ternary compounds Ternary compounds are those containing three (or more) elements.

theoretical yield The theoretical yield is the maximum amount of product that can be formed.

thermochemistry Thermochemistry is the part of thermodynamics dealing with the changes in heat that take place during chemical processes, for example, ΔH_{fusion}.

thermodynamics Thermodynamics is the study of energy and its transformations.

titrant The titrant is that solution in a titration that has a known concentration.

titration A titration is a laboratory procedure in which a solution of known concentration is used to determine the concentration of an unknown solution.

transition elements Groups 3–12 on the periodic table are called the transition elements.

transmutation Transmutation is a nuclear reaction that results in the creation of one element from another one.

triple point The triple point of a substance is the combination of temperature and pressure on a phase diagram at which all three states of matter can exist in equilibrium.

Tyndall effect The Tyndall effect is exhibited when a light is shone through a colloid and is visible, owing to the reflection of the light off the larger colloid particles.

unimolecular reactions Unimolecular reactions are reactions in which a single chemical species decomposes or rearranges.

unit cells Unit cells are the repeating units in a crystal lattice.

unsaturated Unsaturated organic compounds have carbons that do not have the maximum number of bonds to other atoms; there is at least one carbon-to-carbon double or triple bond present.

unsaturated solution An unsaturated solution has less than the maximum amount of solute dissolved in a given amount of solvent.

valence bond theory The valence bond theory describes covalent bonding as the overlap of atomic orbitals to form a new kind of orbital, a hybrid orbital.

valence electrons Valence electrons are the electrons in the outermost energy level (outermost shell). Valence electrons are normally considered to be only the s and p electrons in the outermost energy level.

van der Waals equation The van der Waals equation is an equation that is a modification of the ideal gas equation to compensate for the behavior of real gases.

van't Hoff factor (*i*) The van't Hoff factor is the ratio of moles of solute particles formed to moles of solute dissolved in solution.

vapor pressure The pressure exerted by the gaseous molecules that are at equilibrium with a liquid in a closed container.

viscosity Viscosity is the resistance to flow of a liquid.

volume percent The volume percent of the solution is the volume of the solute divided by the volume of the solution and then multiplied by 100% to generate the percentage.

VSEPR theory The VSEPR (valence-shell electron-pair repulsion) theory says that the electron pairs around a central atom will try to get as far as possible from each other in order to minimize the repulsive forces. This theory is used to predict molecular geometry.

water dissociation constant (K_w) The water dissociation constant is the equilibrium constant associated with the ionization of pure water.

wave function The wave function is a mathematical description of the electron's motion.

wavelength (λ) A wavelength is the distance between two identical points on a wave.

weak acid A weak acid is an acid that only partially ionizes in solution.

weak base A weak base is a base that only partially ionizes in solution.

weak electrolytes Weak electrolytes only partially ionize or dissociate in solution.

AVOIDING "STUPID" MISTAKES ON THE FREE-RESPONSE SECTION

We (the authors) have been grading the free-response part of the AP Chemistry exam for quite a while. Between the two of us, we have nearly 20 years of grading experience—that's more than 100,000 exams! Over the years, we have seen quite a number of careless mistakes made by students. These mistakes resulted from not being careful rather than not being prepared for the exam. Here are some practical tips to avoid the most common careless errors.

- **Don't forget to state the units of measurement.** Many students would have gotten more credit if they had shown the units, both in the calculations and in the final answer. The units help you stay on the right track and help the grader determine if (or where) you went wrong.
- **Use the formula given.** If the exam gives you a chemical formula, don't use a different formula in your answer. In general, do not alter anything given to you on the exam. For example, we have seen $Ba(NO_3)_2$ become $Ba(NO_2)_2$.
- **Be careful with the math.** We have seen many errors involving the simplest math such as 12 mL + 3 mL = 0.042 L (rather than 0.015 L).
- **Don't confuse molarity and moles.** The units M and [ ] are identical (molarity) and are completely different from moles.
- **Show your work for conversions.** For example, if you are changing grams to moles and make a simple mistake, showing your work (labeled) may get you partial credit.
- **Don't argue with the test.** This is an argument you cannot win. For example, if the question asks for calculations, you are unlikely to get full credit without any calculations even if you have the right answer. It won't help to write that you feel the calculations are unnecessary.
- **Be careful in applying gas laws.** Gas laws can be very useful. However, they should *never* be used when there is not a gas in the problem. Having a volume included in the question information doesn't necessarily mean you are dealing with a gas.
- **Be careful making comparisons.** We have seen many students incorrectly say that 10^{-8} is smaller than 10^{-12} and actually write $10^{-8} < 10^{-12}$. We have even seen students write the relationship correctly ($10^{-8} > 10^{-12}$) but still state that 10^{-8} is smaller.
- **Be careful using 22.4 L/mol.** You will probably not need to use this on the exam. But if you do want to use this value, you *must* have a gas and this gas *must* be at 0°C (273 K) and 1 atm (STP). If you forget the values for STP, they can be found on the exam. We have seen quite a few students incorrectly use this value at 298 K.
- **There are no trick questions on the exam.** If you think you have found a trick question, you need to reevaluate your thinking and reread the question.
- **Don't confuse solutions and precipitates in solution.** They are different phases and are not interchangeable. The color of one is not necessarily the color of the other.
- **Be careful describing reactions.** If the problem gives you, for example, a sodium nitrate solution, part of your answer describing a reaction cannot be "the sodium nitrate dissolves." You already have a solution, so the process of dissolving happened before you got to the problem. Furthermore, dissolving should not be treated as a reaction.
- **Be careful using positive and negative charges.** In the following equation, each reactant and product is wrong: $NH_4 + NO_3 \rightarrow NH_4^+ NO_3^-$, and will not substitute for the

correct $NH_4^+ + NO_3^- \rightarrow NH_4NO_3$. Remember, ionic equations, of any type, have ions (with charges) on one or both sides of the reaction arrow.

- **Don't do a calculator dump** (write down every number displayed by your calculator). For example, your final answer will not be 3.27584827 g.
- **Keep in mind the meaning of "observe."** If the problem asks about observation, tell what you would actually observe (see, hear, or smell). You will *not* see a compound separating into ions; usually you will *not* see the excess reagent, and you will *not* see the atoms forming bonds. In contrast, you might observe a compound dissolving.
- **Remember a solvent is usually not a reactant.** Therefore, changing the grams of solvent to moles is probably wrong. (However, you will need to know the moles of solvent if you are looking for a mole fraction.)
- **Think before creating mole ratios.** Since the solvent is not a reactant, a mole ratio relating the solvent to anything else in the problem is most likely wrong. We have seen many students change the grams of water to moles and then use these moles in a mole ratio to relate to some other substance in the problem.
- **Don't go off on a tangent.** Stay focused on answering the original question.
- **Double-check the numbers you use.** We have seen many cases where the problem gave a number like 2.75×10^{-18}, and the student worked the problem with 2.75×10^{-8}. If you show your work, it will be obvious to the grader that you miscopied the value and you might pick up some points; otherwise, you just have a wrong answer.
- **Remember that sometimes not all of the information given is needed to solve the problem.** For example, in the equilibrium problem, many times the temperature is given but it is not actually part of the calculations.
- **Only round your final answer.** Don't round off the results of intermediate calculations; only use rounding after you've gotten your final answer.
- **Be careful in reading graphs.** Especially take care in reading the scales. We have seen students write down that 0.5 is between 1.0 and 2.0.
- **Don't confuse intermolecular and intramolecular forces.** These are two different concepts and are not interchangeable.

In addition to avoiding the careless mistakes mentioned above, here are some easy ways to help improve your score on the free-response questions:

- **Show your work.** In most cases, no work, no credit.
- **Use the space provided for answers.** It helps you and the grader if you answer the question in the space provided instead of crowding the answers between the questions. You will have more than enough room on the following page(s). It also helps to label the parts (a, b, etc.) and to answer the parts in order.
- **Make sure your answer can be easily read.** It will really help the grader—and your score—if you write legibly, in a normal size (not too small, please), and use a pencil or pen that writes dark enough to be easily read.
- **Don't use periodic trends and general rules as explanations.** General rules such as "like dissolves like" are never explanations. They may help you in answering the multiple-choice part of the exam, but will be of little benefit by themselves in the free-response section.
- **Don't confuse "define" and "describe."** They are two different processes. If you are asked to describe or explain, simply giving a definition will earn you very few points.
- **Use only standard abbreviations.** Your instructor may understand your abbreviations, but the grader may not. If you want to use abbreviations in a response, be sure to define them.
- **Don't ramble.** Normally an explanation or justification can be done in five sentences or less. Your answers should be clear, concise, and to the point.

Keywords and Equations: For Use with Free-Response Questions Only

Basics

T = temperature	n = moles	m = mass	P = pressure
V = volume	D = density	v = velocity	M = molar mass
KE = kinetic energy	t = time		

Boltzmann's constant, $k = 1.38 \times 10^{-23}$ J K^{-1}
electron charge $= -1.602 \times 10^{-19}$ coulombs
1 electron volt per atom = 96.5 kJ mol^{-1}
Avogadro's number $= 6.022 \times 10^{23}$ mol^{-1}
K = °C + 273 $D = m/V$

Gases

u_{rms} = root mean square speed
r = rate of effusion
STP = 0.000° C and 1.000 atm
$PV = nRT$
$(P + n^2 a/V^2)(V - nb) = nRT$
$P_A = P_{total} \times X_A$, where X_A = moles A/total moles
$P_{total} = P_A + P_B + P_C + \ldots$
$P_1 V_1 / T_1 = P_2 V_2 / T_2$

$$u_{rms} = \sqrt{3kT/m} = \sqrt{3RT/M}$$

KE per molecule $= \frac{1}{2} mv^2$

KE per mol $= \frac{3}{2} RT$

$$r_1/r_2 = \sqrt{M_2/M_1}$$

1 atm = 760 mm Hg
     = 760 torr
Gas constant, R = 8.31 J mol^{-1} K^{-1}
            = 0.0821 L atm mol^{-1} K^{-1}
            = 8.31 volt coulomb mol^{-1} K^{-1}
            = 62.36 L torr mol^{-1} K^{-1}

Thermodynamics

$S°$ = standard entropy	$H°$ = standard enthalpy
$G°$ = standard free energy	q = heat
c = specific heat capacity	C_p = molar heat capacity at constant pressure

$\Delta S° = \Sigma\, S°$ products $- \Sigma\, S°$ reactants
$\Delta H° = \Sigma\, \Delta H_f°$ products $- \Sigma\, \Delta H_f°$ reactants
$\Delta G° = \Sigma\, \Delta G_f°$ products $- \Sigma\, \Delta G_f°$ reactants

$$\Delta G^\circ = \Delta H^\circ - T\Delta S^\circ$$
$$\quad = -RT \ln K = -2.303\, RT \log K$$
$$\quad = -nFE^\circ$$
$$\Delta G = \Delta G^\circ + RT \ln Q = \Delta G^\circ + 2.303\, RT \log Q$$
$$q = mc\Delta T$$
$$C_p = \Delta H / \Delta T$$

Light and Electrons

E = energy	v = frequency	λ = wavelength
p = momentum	v = velocity	n = principal quantum number
m = mass	$E = hv$	$c = \lambda v$

$$E_n = (-2.178 \times 10^{-18}/n^2)\text{J}$$
Speed of light, $c = 3.0 \times 10^8\ \text{ms}^{-1}$
Planck's constant, $h = 6.63 \times 10^{-34}\ \text{Js}$

Solutions

Molarity, M = moles solute per liter solution

Kinetics

$$\ln[A]_t - \ln[A]_o = -kt$$

$$\frac{1}{[A]_t} - \frac{1}{[A]_o} = kt$$

$$\ln k = \frac{-E_a}{R}\left(\frac{1}{T}\right) + \ln A$$

E_a = activation energy
k = rate constant
A = frequency factor
$t_{1/2} = 0.693/k$

Electrochemistry

I = current (amperes)	q = charge (coulombs)
E° = standard reduction potential	K = equilibrium constant

Faraday's constant, $F = 96{,}500$ coulombs per mole of electrons

$$I = q/t \quad \log K = \frac{nE^\circ}{0.0592}$$

Equilibrium

Q = reaction quotient

$$Q = \frac{[C]^c[D]^d}{[A]^a[B]^b}, \text{ where } aA + bB \rightleftharpoons cC + dD$$

equilibrium constants:

K_a (weak acid)	K_b (weak base)	K_w (water)
K_p (gas pressure)	K_c (molar concentrations)	

$$K_a = \frac{[H^+][A^-]}{[HA]} \quad K_b = \frac{[OH^-][HB^+]}{[B]} \quad K_p = \frac{(P_c)^c(P_d)^d}{(P_a)^a(P_b)^b}$$

$K_w = [OH^-][H^+] = 1.0 \times 10^{-14} = K_a \times K_b$ at 25°C

$pH = -\log [H^+]$, $pOH = -\log [OH^-]$

$14 = pH + pOH$

$$pH = pK_a + \log \frac{[A^-]}{[HA]}$$

$$pOH = pK_b + \log \frac{[HB^+]}{[B]}$$

$pK_a = -\log K_a$, $pK_b = -\log K_b$

$K_p = K_c(RT)^{\Delta n}$, where Δn = moles product gas − moles reactant gas

Experimental

Beer's Law: $A = abc$ (A = absorbance; a = molar absorbtivity; b = path length; c = concentration)

Periodic Table of the Elements

May be used with all questions.

The periodic table

Key:

| Atomic number |
| Symbol |
| Atomic weight (mean relative mass) |

1	2		3	4	5	6	7	8	9	10	11	12	13	14	15	16	17	18
1 **H** 1.008																		2 **He** 4.002602(2)
3 **Li** 6.94	4 **Be** 9.012182(3)												5 **B** 10.81	6 **C** 12.011	7 **N** 14.007	8 **O** 15.999	9 **F** 18.9984032(5)	10 **Ne** 20.1797(6)
11 **Na** 22.9897692B(2)	12 **Mg** 24.3050(6)												13 **Al** 26.9815386(2)	14 **Si** 28.085	15 **P** 30.973762(2)	16 **S** 32.06	17 **Cl** 35.45	18 **Ar** 39.948(1)
19 **K** 39.0983(1)	20 **Ca** 40.078(4)		21 **Sc** 44.955912(6)	22 **Ti** 47.867(1)	23 **V** 50.9415(1)	24 **Cr** 51.9961(6)	25 **Mn** 54.938045(5)	26 **Fe** 55.845(2)	27 **Co** 58.933195(5)	28 **Ni** 58.6934(4)	29 **Cu** 63.546(3)	30 **Zn** 65.38(2)	31 **Ga** 69.723(1)	32 **Ge** 72.63(1)	33 **As** 74.92160(2)	34 **Se** 78.96(3)	35 **Br** 79.904(1)	36 **Kr** 83.798(2)
37 **Rb** 85.4678(3)	38 **Sr** 87.62(1)		39 **Y** 88.90585(2)	40 **Zr** 91.224(2)	41 **Nb** 92.90638(2)	42 **Mo** 95.96(2)	43 **Tc** [97.91]	44 **Ru** 101.07(2)	45 **Rh** 102.90550(2)	46 **Pd** 106.42(1)	47 **Ag** 107.8682(2)	48 **Cd** 112.411(8)	49 **In** 114.818(3)	50 **Sn** 118.710(7)	51 **Sb** 121.760(1)	52 **Te** 127.60(3)	53 **I** 126.90447(3)	54 **Xe** 131.293(6)
55 **Cs** 132.9054519(2)	56 **Ba** 137.327(7)	57-70 *	71 **Lu** 174.9668(1)	72 **Hf** 178.49(2)	73 **Ta** 180.94788(2)	74 **W** 183.84(1)	75 **Re** 186.207(1)	76 **Os** 190.23(3)	77 **Ir** 192.217(3)	78 **Pt** 195.084(9)	79 **Au** 196.966569(4)	80 **Hg** 200.59(2)	81 **Tl** 204.38	82 **Pb** 207.2(1)	83 **Bi** 208.98040(1)	84 **Po** [209]	85 **At** [210]	86 **Rn** [222]
87 **Fr** [223.02]	88 **Ra** [226.03]	89-102 **	103 **Lr** [262.11]	104 **Rf** [265.12]	105 **Db** [268.13]	106 **Sg** [271.13]	107 **Bh** [270]	108 **Hs** [277.15]	109 **Mt** [276.15]	110 **Ds** [281.16]	111 **Rg** [280.16]	112 **Cn** [285.17]	113 **Nh** [284.18]	114 **Fl** [289.19]	115 **Mc** [288.19]	116 **Lv** [293]	117 **Ts** [294]	118 **Og** [294]

*lanthanoids

57 **La** 138.90547(7)	58 **Ce** 140.116(1)	59 **Pr** 140.90765(2)	60 **Nd** 144.242(3)	61 **Pm** [144.91]	62 **Sm** 150.36(2)	63 **Eu** 151.964(1)	64 **Gd** 157.25(3)	65 **Tb** 158.92535(2)	66 **Dy** 162.500(1)	67 **Ho** 164.93032(2)	68 **Er** 167.259(3)	69 **Tm** 168.93421(2)	70 **Yb** 173.054(5)

**actinoids

89 **Ac** [227.03]	90 **Th** 232.03806(2)	91 **Pa** 231.03588(2)	92 **U** 238.02891(3)	93 **Np** [237.05]	94 **Pu** [244.06]	95 **Am** [243.06]	96 **Cm** [247.07]	97 **Bk** [247.07]	98 **Cf** [251.08]	99 **Es** [252.08]	100 **Fm** [257.10]	101 **Md** [258.10]	102 **No** [259.10]